Principles of Community Property

Principles of
Community Property

SECOND EDITION

by

WILLIAM Q. DE FUNIAK, LL.B., LL.M., Jur. D.
OF THE CALIFORNIA AND KENTUCKY BARS

and

MICHAEL J. VAUGHN, J.D., LL.M.
OF THE TEXAS BAR

THE UNIVERSITY OF ARIZONA PRESS
Tucson, Arizona

About the Authors . . .

WILLIAM QUINBY DE FUNIAK has been recognized as the foremost authority on the American community property system since publication of the first edition of *Principles of Community Property* in 1943. His other contributions to this field include *Cases and Materials on Community Property* (two editions) and many articles, courtroom consultations, and lectures.

Books he has authored attest to de Funiak's diversification in other areas of law: *American Notaries Manual, Handbook of Modern Equity, Cyclopedia of Federal Procedure* (1943–44, 1951–52, co-author), *Municipal Corporations* (co-author), and three co-authored publications dealing with pleading and practice in Wisconsin, Illinois, and Michigan.

For years a legal editor, de Funiak joined the law faculty at the University of San Francisco in 1941. Upon leaving he taught at the University of the Pacific. He has been a visiting professor at the University of Arizona, the University of California, the University of London, and the University of Edinburgh. He holds an LL.B. and a Jur.D. from the University of Virginia and an LL.M. from the University of San Francisco.

MICHAEL J. VAUGHN, a partner in a private law firm in Waco, Texas, has specialized in Texas community property law. His writings include a book, *Appellate Advocacy in Texas,* and various articles. He received an A.B. from Baylor University in 1964 and while earning his J.D. from that university was editor of the *Baylor Law Review.* He received an LL.M. from Yale in 1967 and taught at Baylor before going into private practice in 1971.

THE UNIVERSITY OF ARIZONA PRESS

Copyright © 1971
The Arizona Board of Regents
All Rights Reserved
Manufactured in the U.S.A.

I.S.B.N.-0-8165-0264-1
L.C. No. 72-101099

Foreword

There seems to exist today a popular opinion that the world began, at the very latest, on the day before yesterday. If this opinion be valid, then the study of history is, of course, irrelevant. To those of us who do not share this opinion, it is a comfort to find legal scholars reiterating their position that an understanding of present legal principles must start with the source of those principles. In this second edition of *Principles of Community Property*, authors de Funiak and Vaughn take such a position and then set out to prove it.

Reading this volume, a modern American wife blessed with a domicile in a community property state is delighted to discover an abiding sisterhood with the Visigoth woman who stood and worked and fought shoulder to shoulder with her man, a sisterhood in fact as well as in law. Like her ancient prototype, the wife in community property states who shares equally in the work of establishing and maintaining a marriage shares equally in the acquisitions of that marriage. This is the basic principle of the community property system, a system based on elemental fairness and justice. It is a system which accords to the husband-wife relationship the status, not of master-servant, but of co-equal partners in marriage.

The authors of this work are not only exponents of the principles of the system; they are unabashedly proponents of those principles. In the 1940s, Professor de Funiak first called for recognition of the fact that the

v

twentieth century American wife is not a toy of the idle rich nor is she simply unpaid domestic help; she is a person, co-equal with her husband in contributions to the marriage. Today, there is agitation in some common-law states for the enactment of legislation which would compel a husband to pay a part of his income to his wife as a salary for the housekeeping, cooking, nursing, chauffeuring and the like which she does for her family. It is submitted that this proposal stigmatizes the marital relation as that of employer-employee. It is suggested that the appropriate solution is the enactment of legislation to adopt the community property system. As our authors point out, some of our states have acquired the system by adoption.

Since the first appearance of Professor de Funiak's work, Congress has extended some of the benefits of the community property system to husbands and wives who live in states which do not enjoy the system. The "joint" income tax return allows treatment of income of spouses, whether earned by only one or by both in unequal pro-portions, as "community" income for tax purposes. The "marital deduction" is designed to subtract from the estate of a deceased spouse up to one-half of the assets devised to the surviving spouse, a subtraction which approximates the partition of the community estate on the death of a spouse in community property states.

Principles of Community Property deals not only with legal principles but also with philosophical principles. The philosophy may be said to consider that the func-tions of husbands and wives are complementary, rather than competitive. A marriage is regarded as a total which is larger than the sum of its parts.

Finally, the authors establish that a scholarly treatise need not be dull. For its scholarship, this book should be required reading for lawyers and judges; for its lively charm, it is fascinating reading for everyone.

MARGARET H. AMSLER
Professor of Law
Baylor Law School

CONTENTS

CONTENTS

IV. ESTABLISHMENT OF COMMUNITY PROPERTY SYSTEM
IN THE UNITED STATES

V. INITIATION AND EXISTENCE
OF MARITAL COMMUNITY

VI. COMMUNITY AND SEPARATE PROPERTY

A. INITIAL CONSIDERATIONS

B. TIME, METHOD AND TYPE OF ACQUISITION

C. RIGHTS OF ACTION, AND DAMAGES OR COMPENSATION, FOR INJURIES

CONTENTS

CONTENTS

X. DISSOLUTION OF MARITAL COMMUNITY

A. IN GENERAL

B. DEATH OF SPOUSE

PREFACE

The system of community property as developed in the law of Spain is, with some modifications, today the law in several of our American states. To understand it fully it is as necessary to draw upon the original body of that law and the commentaries thereon by the Spanish jurisconsults, as it is necessary to have available the older English and American decisions which define and set forth the principles which constitute the basis of marital property laws in others of our states; these laws and commentaries are to the Spanish law what the court decisions are to the English and American common law.

Judges and lawyers faced with the task of interpreting and deciding questions concerning marital community of property have not had available the material which would aid in and permit of such interpretation. Moreover, they frequently have been handicapped in their own mental processes by trying to apply to such interpretation a legal training in the intricacies of the common law, which is entirely foreign to the law of community property. Just as it is necessary to have an understanding of the principles of the common law to arrive at a decision of problems concerning marital property and rights in those American states which follow the common law, so it is necessary to understand at their source those principles of the Spanish law which govern and from which spring the marital community of property in our states in which that system is established.

The failure to have access to appropriate source material, the consequent unfamiliarity with the basic principles of the community property system, the influence of judges' common-law training; all these have frequently resulted in erroneous, indeed sometimes startling, interpretations by some of our courts.

This work discusses in detail the Spanish laws relating to community property, the commentaries of leading Spanish jurisconsults, and other pertinent material, thus placing in the hands of the user material heretofore available only in old and rare volumes or in scarce, privately printed editions, i.e., in works not ordinarily obtainable by the judge or lawyer.

Response to the 1943 edition of *Principles of Community Property* was so gratifying and inquiries as to the possibility of further treatment of the subject so numerous, that we have felt it incumbent upon ourselves to prepare this revised and enlarged edition of the book. The background material in Volume 2 of the original work remains valid and largely unchanged, so we have cited it as reference but felt it unnecessary to re-issue that material. The reader can easily refer to it in the original edition, and it is in this volume that the Spanish source material is unfolded.

Principles of Community Property is the product of study and research, not only on our part, but on the part of many others, without whose efforts the end product would not have been possible. We have received so much valuable help and advice on the present volume that it is difficult to list the names of all those to whom we are indebted. We would be remiss, however, if we did not especially acknowledge the valuable aid and comments of Judge Jack Marks of Arizona; of Dean Emeritus John Lyons, Dean Charles Ares, Professor Jack J. Rappeport, Professor Charles Smith, and Professor Thomas J. Tormey, law librarian, all of the University of Arizona College of Law; of Dean Angus McSwain, Jr., Professor Loy Simpkins, and Miss Della Geyer, law librarian, all of Baylor University School of Law; of Professor W. J. Brockelbank of the University of Idaho College of Law and of Professor Robert W. Clark, formerly of the University of New Mexico School of Law and later of the University of Arizona College of Law. We are also grateful for the valuable work by Gayle Albritton and Fred J. Horner III, research assistants at Baylor University School of Law.

In the original 1943 edition, there also were many people whose efforts contributed to make this work possible. Foremost among them was Mr. Lloyd M. Robbins of the San Francisco bar. Mr. Robbins had for many years immersed himself in the study of this subject, had been counsel in many important cases involving community property problems, had spent several years in Spain and England in pursuit of knowledge and in the acquisition of scarce and valuable books on the subject, and had himself prepared and published translations of the Spanish laws and of the commentaries of the most cited Spanish jurisconsults. The vast amount of material gathered by him, his fund of knowledge on the subject, and his encouragement and assistance have been so great as to be almost inestimable, and it was due primarily to him that the original book was made possible. No mere acknowledgment could do justice to his aid and encouragement or adequately express appreciation therefor. We also are greatly indebted to Miss Lillian Roark of San Francisco, who gave without stint the results of her research upon the Spanish jurisconsults, as well as providing invaluable translations of ancient Spanish laws; to Miss Marguerite Doran, librarian of the University of San Francisco Law Library, who lightened the work in many ways and especially by her aid in the preparation of the table of statutes of the American community property states in Appendix V of Volume 2; to Miss Mabel R. Gillis, librarian of the California State Library at Sacramento, who so kindly allowed use of the magnificent Robbins collection of community property material; to Mr. Owens, librarian of the San Francisco Law Library, and his assistants, who cheerfully gave access to the resources of that excellent library; to Dean Edward A. Hogan, Jr., of the University of San Francisco School of Law, whose helpfulness and whose critical consideration of the original Chapter XI furthered the work; to Mr. Joseph Rock, S.J., of the University of San Francisco, whose scholarly aid in preparing certain translations from the Latin proved extremely valuable; to the American Bar Association, which allowed use of the excellent translations by Samuel Parsons Scott published by it; and to many others whose efforts are equally highly appreciated. At pertinent points throughout this work we have attempted to instance, more specifically, the nature of the aid given and the reliance upon it.

For the present volume, we owe thanks to Marshall Townsend and his staff at the University of Arizona Press for their aid and understanding which helped bring this book into being. Finally, we certainly would be remiss if we did not pay tribute to the encouragement and understanding of our respective wives.

WILLIAM Q. DE FUNIAK
MICHAEL J. VAUGHN

CHAPTER I

INTRODUCTION

§ 1.   In general.

Community of property between husband and wife is that system whereby the property which the husband and wife have is common property, that is, it belongs to both by halves. There are varying forms of this marital community of property system, ranging from the general community, of which the Roman-Dutch law is an example, in which all the property of the spouses owned by each at the time of the marriage, as well as all that acquired after marriage, becomes a part of the community property; to the community only of acquests and gains during the continuance of the marriage.[1] It is this latter or ganancial system and which came to this country from Spain which prevails in several of our American states,[2] specifically, in Arizona, California, Idaho, Louisiana, Nevada, New Mexico, Texas and Washington.[3] It includes

---

[1] See Brissaud, History of French Private Law, pp. 793-861; Huebner, History of Germanic Private Law, pp. 639-656; Lee, Introduction to Roman-Dutch Law, pp. 65, 66.

Roman-Dutch law in Netherlands and South Africa, see post, § 16.

In the countries recognizing a system of community of ownership between husband and wife "fall the co-partnership in acquisitions recognized in Spain and southwest France, the co-ownership of movables and acquisitions recognized in France in the *pays du droit coutumier* and in some parts of Germany, and the

co-ownership in all property recognized in other parts of Germany." Holdsworth, History of English Law, vol. 3, p. 522.

[2] *Bienes gananciales* in Spanish law is that property held in community by husband and wife, having been acquired or gained by them during the marriage.

Separate property held by a spouse was known in the Spanish law as *bienes proprios*.

[3] See post, Chap. IV. It also prevails in Puerto Rico, the Virgin Islands (from Denmark) and the Philippines.

1

the property earned or gained by onerous title by either during the union, as well as that given to both during the marital union. All property which they possess is presumed to be held and owned by them in common unless or until it is proved to be the separate property of one of them.[4] In respect of separate property each spouse is equally capable of owning separate property, and separate property owned by either before marriage continues to constitute separate property of that spouse during marriage. Likewise, property given to one spouse alone, during marriage, is the separate property of that spouse.[5] The community property system is marked by two essential characteristics: (1) the transmissibility of the wife's interests to her heirs, so that if the wife dies first, her heirs take the share to which she would have been entitled if she had survived; and (2) during the existence of the marital relationship the spouses are the joint owners, or partners, with respect to gains and losses.[6] This is not to say that the husband's interest is not also transmissible to his heirs if he dies first, but the point of the essential characteristic relating to the wife is that she is placed on a basis of equality with the husband as to her ownership and rights in the community property.[7] The essential characteristic as to the joint ownership or partnership in the acquests and gains is also particularly to be noticed. Not only are the spouses on the same plane of equality as to ownership but the matter of ownership is of primary importance, as compared with the English common law principle of giving primary importance to the technical matter of in whose name title appears.

Equality is the cardinal precept of the community property system. At the foundation of this concept is the principle that all wealth acquired by the joint efforts of the husband and wife shall be common property; the theory of the law being that, with respect to marital property acquisitions, the marriage is a community of which each spouse is a member, equally contributing by his or her industry to its

---

Temporary enactment of community property laws in Hawaii, Michigan, Nebraska, Oregon, Oklahoma and Pennsylvania, see discussion and statutes, § 53.1.

[4] See §§ 60, 61, as to presumptions.

[5] "Ganancial property (*bienes de ganancias*) is all that which is increased or multiplied during marriage. By multiplied, is understood all that is increased by onerous cause or title, and not that which is acquired by a lucrative one, as inheritance, donation, etc." Asso and Manuel, Institutes of the Civil Law of Spain, Book 1, Title VII, Cap. 5, § 1. See also post, Chap. VI.

That property acquired by husband and wife during marriage by labor or other valuable consideration is acquired by "onerous" title, while that acquired by gift, succession, inheritance and the like is acquired by "lucrative" title. Escriche, Diccionario. See also post, § 62.

For further discussion and definition, see post, Chaps. VI, VII.

[6] Brissaud, History of French Private Law, p. 812. See also post, Chaps. VI, VII.

[7] In some of our American states, transmissibility of the share of either spouse has been altered by statute so that not infrequently the share of a deceased spouse goes to the survivor. See post, Chap. X, B.

prosperity, and possessing an equal right to succeed to the property after its dissolution.

A rational process of thought culminated in the decision that the wife should have equal property rights in property acquired during marriage. Community of property is the application of this thought, and the rubric itself is a shorthand rendition of the whole concept that the husband and wife are equals. Beginning then, with this overall premise of equality, the system was constructed around it, to present an integrated whole in which each segment, in its interaction with the remainder of the doctrine, would be operative.[8]

This community or ganancial system was brought into Spain by the Visigoths and in turn introduced on this continent in the territory acquired by Spain and has remained the law of many of our states carved from that former Spanish territory.[9] However, in other states carved from those former Spanish territories the community system has been abandoned and has been superseded by the common law, frequently because it was not understood and the material by which it might have been interpreted was not easily available to the early settlers. The foregoing matters, however, are more fully developed subsequently in this work.[10]

§ 2.   Antiquity and concept of community system in contradistinction to common law.

The community or ganancial system is of a far greater antiquity than the common law principles relating to marital rights in property. In fact, its antiquity is so great that it first obtained recognition in written form in 693 A.D., in Visigothic Spain, in the so-called Visigothic Code or Fuero Juzgo, centuries before the development and

---

[8] Vaughn, "The Policy of Community Property and Inter-Spousal Transactions," 19 *Baylor Law Review* 20 (1967).

[9] The system was continued in California, Louisiana, New Mexico, and Texas; but "adopted" in Arizona, Idaho, Nevada and Washington. By "adopted" is meant that the legislation recognizing community property came after a period when the common law was in force with respect to marital property acquisitions. In the case of Arizona, see Lyons, Development of Community Property Law in Arizona, (1955) 15 Arizona L. Rev. 512; Idaho, see Brockelbank, The Community Property Law of Idaho, 1962, pp. 14-18. Continuation, as in California and Texas, see, for example, Spreckels v. Spreckels, 116 Cal. 339, 48 p. 228, 36 L.R.A. 497, 58 Am. St. Rep. 170; and Burr v. Wilson, 18 Tex. 367 (1857), which declares that the Texas laws regulating marital property rights are but a continuation of the rules of Spanish jurisprudence on the same subject matter.

More fully as to the foregoing states, see post, Chap. IV.

In Oklahoma, it clearly was adopted in 1939, to the extent that the spouses had the option to elect to have their marital property governed by its provisions. More fully as to the foregoing state, see post, Chap. IV.

[10] See post, Chap. IV.

formation of the common law.[11] It is a concept of property that is entirely alien and foreign to that of common law as to the conjugal relationship and the marital rights in property,[12] although the community system itself can hardly be called a "foreign" institution.[13]

We are not here concerned with tracing the origin and development of the common law, but in its developed form in England and as it was inherited by many of our American states from England, it embodied the basic concept that in marriage the husband and wife were merged into one and, in effect, the husband was that "one." The wife was subject to the husband to the extent that she was only his mere shadow, or at most his alter ego. It is a concept which considers the wife as only another chattel or belonging of the husband. She is not recognized, perhaps through some element of male vanity or obtuseness, as an individual, as having a character, a mind, a personality of her own.[14] Whatever movables the wife has at the date of the marriage become the husband's and he is entitled to take possession and make his own any movables to which she becomes entitled during the marriage. Whatever realty the wife has at the time of the marriage, or to which she becomes entitled during marriage the husband has the administration thereof and is entitled to the usufructs thereof. The

---

[11] See Fuero Juzgo, Book 4, Title 2, Law 17. More fully as to the Fuero Juzgo, see post, § 24.

Historical outline of Visigothic and Spanish codes, see post, Chap. III.

The community system appeared in Sweden in the Law of West Goths, according to the Manuscript of Aeskil or Eskil, about 1200 A.D. See post, § 17.

[12] Ballinger, A Treatise on the Property Rights of Husband and Wife, Under the Community or Ganancial System, Sec. 253, Bancroft-Whitney Co. (1895); see also post, § 3.

Text quoted in Willcox v. Penn. Mut. L. Ins. Co., 357 Pa. 581, 55 A.2d 521, 174 A.L.R. 220, at 226.

[13] See Lobingier, History of the Conjugal Partnership, 63 Am. L. Rev. 250, 278-280. See also post, § 3; Chaps. II, IV.

[14] "The husband and wife are one person in law; that is, the very being or legal existence of the woman is suspended during the marriage, or at least is incorporated and consolidated into that of the husband, under whose protection, wing and cover she per-

forms everything." Cooley's Blackstone, 4th Ed., p. 387. See also Buckland & McNair, Roman Law and Common Law, pp. 31, 32.

In Pollock & Maitland, History of English Law, 2nd Ed., vol. 2, p. 406, the authors protest that the English common law does not treat the wife as a thing but as a person, and that the fundamental principle of the English common law is merely that the husband is the wife's "guardian." Since this at most is an assumption that a married woman is an incompetent or irresponsible person needing a guardian, it hardly constitutes a convincing apologia.

"The Common Law under its classical form, such as it appears in Blackstone, with that extreme logic which does not hesitate at the absurd, seems to organize the entire system of property between spouses as a function of the incapacity of the married woman. During the marriage the wife is nothing and has nothing. . . . Marriage is for the woman a sort of civil death." Brissaud, History of French Private Law, p. 783.

wife cannot alienate her land without the husband's concurrence. In other words she is practically without proprietary capacity.[15]

Under the community or ganancial system the wife retains her own personality as an individual and is an equal partner with the husband in the conjugal relationship.[16] Moreover, her property rights and her rights to enter into transactions with her husband as an equal have long represented in the community property system the advanced state that is only now being reached through statutory modifications in common law jurisdictions. This recognition of the wife as a person in her own right is one of the outstanding principles of the civil law and is one of those in which it diverges sharply from the common law.[17] To

[15] See Pollock & Maitland, History of English Law, 2nd Ed., vol. 2, pp. 403-408; Haskins, The Estate by the Marital Right, 97 U. of Pa. L. Rev. 345.

It may be noted, however, that now the various married women's property acts have changed much of the law relating to husband and wife and made obsolete much of the common law so that for most purposes husband and wife are no longer one person in law but separate persons. See Ramsay v. Margrett, [1894] 2 Q. B. 18; Kirkwood, Equality of Property Interests Between Husband and Wife, 8 Minn. Law Rev. 579, 580-583.

It has been argued that this strict common law concept was not held in this country even in the colonial period and that the legal position of woman and the married woman's proprietary capacity was always much superior to that of her English sister. Morris, Studies in the History of American Law, pp. 126-200. To the contrary, see Burge, Colonial and Foreign Laws, vol. 1, pp. 567-598.

[16] See post, Chaps. VII, VIII, especially.

In the homely language of a Florida judge: "Viewed solely as a matter of economy, the labor, pain and drudgery required of the mother in sustaining the home, giving birth to and rearing the children will often more than offset the contribution of the father to the family budget. There are no five or six day weeks in her cycle of duties, nor is she awarded extra pay for overtime. She is subject to call at all hours of the day and night and in nine cases of ten, where there comes a rift in the marital ties, she is awarded the custody of the minor children. This of course has reference to the mother who takes motherhood seriously, who knows the virtue in the catechism, castor oil, paregoric and hickory tea." Terrell, J., in Strauss v. Strauss, 148 Fla. 23, 3 So.2d 727. See also the language of the same judge in Merchant's Hostess Service v. Cain, 151 Fla. 253, 9 So.2d 373.

[17] See Buckland & McNair, Roman Law and Common Law; Daggett, Legal Essays on Family Law; Daggett, Civil-Law Concept of Wife's Position in the Family, 15 Ore. Law Rev. 291; Smithers, Matrimonial Property Rights Under Modern Spanish and American Law, 70 Univ. of Pa. Law Rev. 259.

"There is a marked distinction between the civil law and other systems of jurisprudence in the civil rights and capacities of the husband and wife. It does not recognize in the husband and wife that union of persons by which the rights of the wife were incorporated and consolidated during the coverture, with those of the husband. It does not, therefore, subject her to those disabilities which must have resulted from that union. The husband and wife are regarded as distinct persons, with separate rights, and capable of holding distinct and separate estates." Burge, Colonial and Foreign Laws, vol. 1, p. 263. To the

understand this divergence between the concepts of these two systems of law requires an analysis of underlying causes and operative factors which are more properly dealt with in the succeeding chapter, to which the reader is referred for the origin, and the reasons therefor, of the community property system.[18]

§ 3.   Misunderstanding of the community system.

Because the legal concept of the community property or ganancial system is so foreign to that of the common law, it is frequently very difficult for the judge or lawyer, trained and versed in the common law, to grasp and understand its principles. He usually makes the primary mistake of trying to understand it and interpret it by the principles and terminology of the common law; a most serious mistake, for those principles and terminology are not in the least applicable.[19] This is nowhere more evident than in the tendency to interpret the administration of the community property by the husband in terms of the control exercised by the husband at common law.[20] This inability properly to understand community of property has led, as has already been observed, to its abandonment at an early day in many of our states where it was through the logical course of events well established as the governing law.[21]

A too frequent and most unfortunate result of this inability to grasp and understand the principles of the law of community property seems to be the engendering of a strong resentment against it in the minds of many members of the legal profession, not to mention the minds of the public generally. It is sometimes difficult to put a finger on the exact reason for this resentment. It may sometimes arise because of the mistaken belief that the community property system substitutes

---

same effect, see Huebner, History of Germanic Private Law, p. 654.

"Husband and wife are not one under our laws. The existence of the wife is not merged in that of the husband. Most certainly is this true, so far as the rights of property are concerned. . . . They are co-equals in life; and at death the survivor, whether husband or wife, remains the head of the family." Woods v. Wheeler, 7 Tex. 19.

[18] See post, §§ 9-11.

[19] Chief Justice Stone of the United States Supreme Court said, while Attorney General of the United States, that the confusion in the decisions of the California courts with respect to community property undoubtedly arose "from the fact that the courts have been attempting, in their opinions, to apply the terminology of the common law to community property which embodies a legal concept wholly foreign to the common law and to which the terminology of the common law cannot be applied with accuracy and precision." 34 Op. Atty. Gen. 395.

The inutility and futility of the use of the common law to explain the features of the community property system has been referred to, time after time. See, e. g., Ballinger, Community Property, § 255; Nicholas, California Community Property, 14 Calif. State Bar Jour. 9.

[20] See post, Chaps. VII, XI.

[21] See also post, Chap. IV.

some sort of cold blooded partnership for marriage as a sacrament, that it substitutes a business relationship for what they consider a sacred relation between husband and wife.[22] It may sometimes arise from injured male vanity which resents anything recognizing woman as a person in her own right and which would seem to threaten or question male dominance of all conjugal affairs.[23] It may and frequently does arise where the community system comes in contact with the realm of income taxation,[24] for one finds many lawyers outraged at the community system to the point of absurdity.[25] One would almost suppose from the language of some of these lawyers that the community property system is a recent invention for the express purpose of aiding some residents of the country to escape "just taxes" and to throw "undue burdens" on residents of other than community property states.[26]

Actually, as has already been mentioned and as will be more fully developed in subsequent chapters, the community property system is one with its roots far back in the past, of a much more ancient lineage than that of any of the "common law" principles, is a development of democratic rather than aristocratic societies,[27] and was firmly established in eight of our states for generations before the advent of inheritance and income taxes.[28]

[22] Actually the marital partnership in the common earnings and gains is not a substitute for but something in addition to marriage as a sacrament (or status or whatever one views it as being). The marital partnership in the earnings and gains may be dissolved by agreement during the marriage without in any way affecting the subsistence of the marriage itself. See post, Chap. VII.

". . . matrimony is only the occasion for the partnership which the spouses have in the profits, and the cause of this partnership is the law which establishes it." Llamas y Molina, No. 14, to Nov. Rec. Law 8.

[23] This attitude of mind seems to take the form of assuming that the husband is entitled in full to the benefit of the wife's services in the marital relation, that she must fulfill the functions of cook, chambermaid, nurse, washwoman, etc., with no obligation on the husband to do more than supply her with food and clothing and other such necessaries, while he on his side is entitled in full to ownership of everything he earns. This puts the wife in the status, not of a partner with equal rights and responsi-

bilities, but of a combined domestic chattel and servant who must give all her services for "bed and board," an illuminating phrase in itself. In this respect see the language of Terrell, J., in Merchant's Hostess Service v. Cain, 151 Fla. 253, 9 So.2d 373: "The disability of coverture (i. e., at common law) was the product of a period in which man was smeared with the externals of a potential culture. The wife was little more than a chattel and was considered incapable of taking an education or following a career. All she was expected to thrill over was accouchement and the kitchen."

[24] Income tax, see post, Chap. XI, B.

[25] See, e. g., the article of Professor Lowndes in Tax Magazine, Jan. 1942; he feels that residents of community property states are demanding a "subsidy" from the federal government and that there is "outrageous" discrimination in their behalf.

[26] This is dealt with more fully, post, Chap. XI.

[27] See post, Chaps. II, III.

[28] See post, Chap. IV. Temporary establishment in some states for tax advantages, see post, § 53.1.

If there are any who object to the community property system on the ground that it is the development of a Latin rather than an Anglo-Saxon or Nordic race and thus has no place in our country, it need only be pointed out that actually it comes to us from its origin with the Visigoths, as Nordic a race as one could desire and blood-cousins to the Angles, Saxons, Jutes and Danes; and that forms of the community property system may be found in Scotland, Scandinavia, Switzerland and the Netherlands.[29] The community property system is as legitimately the law of some of our states as the common law principles of marital property are in others. If ours is a government of laws and not of men, as has so often been said, the community property laws of certain states are entitled to as much respect and consideration as any other laws and are as much entitled to the protection of the United States Constitution as are any other laws. They have been the law of some of our states for well over a hundred years and if they bring any advantages to those living under them, such advantages are legitimately theirs by virtue of law and they are entitled to be protected in them. Laws which have been in force in some of our states for generation after generation, which trace their source almost unchanged back through the centuries, must have continued to exist through such lengths of time because of their manifold excellences and are not lightly to be abrogated or tossed aside.[30]

§ 4.   Primary sources and basis of the community property law.

The origin, causes and extent of the community property system is traced in succeeding chapters. But it is important to point out immediately that the common law custom of relying upon precedent in the shape of prior judicial decisions does not obtain in the Spanish or civil law. Thus one does not look to court decisions to determine what was the community property law which was brought to this continent.[31] The governing principles are to be found in the Spanish

[29] In fact, not only is it widespread among countries of Latin culture and civilization, but among most of those countries described as Germanic or Teutonic in origin and of which England has been one of the very few to reject the idea of the community. See post, Chap. II; and see Lobingier, History of Conjugal Partnership, 63 Am. Law Rev. 250, 279-280, who listed as of that date (1929) 46 jurisdictions having the community system.

[30] "Louisiana, the only state in the group of eight which lays claims to civilian principles in toto, is relatively free from common law disaffections of the ideal of community property. In the other seven states, though the influence of common law ideas is strong, this one civilian trait has been handed down despite disavowals of civilian family ties in all other respects and clear adoption of the common law." Daggett, 2 La. Law Rev. 575.

[31] This matter of judicial precedent becomes yearly more difficult in this country with the yearly flood of thousands of cases and threatens to be broken down by its own bulk. The various Restatements of the Law represent an effort to establish statements of principles upon which dependence may be had and the courts have frequently turned to these statements of principles for guidance.

codes and in the commentaries of the Spanish jurisconsults. Those were the authorities presented to the courts of Spain to demonstrate what the law was and those were the authorities upon which those courts based their decisions. Accordingly, to determine the basic principles of the community property law which now exists in certain of our American states one looks to those codes and commentaries, just as the common law lawyer in our common law states looks to the old decisions of the English courts to determine the common law principles applicable in his question.[32] At an early date this was recognized by the courts of our community property states.[33]

[32] Commentaries of the eminent jurisconsults on the various Spanish codes were cited as authorities and only where those proved insufficient or there were doubts as to the proper interpretation of the law, then, according to Law 1 of the Laws of Toro (1505), the subject had to be referred to the King. Altamira, Historia de España, 3rd Ed., vol. 2, p. 515. See also Saul v. His Creditors, 5 Mart. N. S. (La.) 569, 16 Am. Dec. 212.

Jurisconsults, in the civil law, were ones so skilled in the law that not only did they have such knowledge of the laws and customs as to be able to advise, act and to secure a person in his dealings, but also their opinions if unanimous had the force of law. See Moore, Cyc. Law Dict.

Indeed, it has long been declared as a matter of policy in California that the "unwritten law . . . has no certain repository, but is collected from the reports of the decisions of the courts, *and the treatises of learned men.*" Cal. Code of Civ. Proc. § 1899. (Italics ours.)

[33] "This jurisprudence, or common law, in some nations, is found in the decrees of their courts; in others, it is furnished by private individuals, eminent for their learning and integrity, whose superior wisdom has enabled them to gain the proud distinction of legislating, as it were, for their country, and enforcing their legislation by the most noble of all means, that of reason alone. After a long series of years, it is sometimes difficult to say whether these opinions and judgments were originally the effect of principles previously existing in society, or whether they were the cause of the doctrines, which all men at last recognize. But whether the one or the other, when acquiesced in for ages, their force and effect can not be distinguished from statutory law. No civilized nation has been without such a system. . . . Spain, who was among the first of the European nations that reduced her laws into codes, and who carried that mode of legislation farther than any other people, early felt the necessity of a jurisprudence which would supply the defects and soften the asperities of her statutes. The opinions of her jurisconsults seem to have obtained an authority with her of which the history of no other country offers an example." Porter, J., in Saul v. His Creditors, 5 Mart. N. S. (La.) 569, 16 Am. Dec. 212.

"Our whole system by which the rights of property between husband and wife are regulated and determined is borrowed from the civil and Spanish law, and we must look to those sources for the reasons which induced its adoption and the rules and principles which govern its operation and effect." Cope, J., in Packard v. Arrellanes, 17 Cal. 531, 537 (1861).

And the Texas Supreme Court, in Routh v. Routh, 57 Tex. 596, declared that "the learned commentaries of civilians which have construed provisions of their own system of marital rights, unquestionably are to be considered with the highest respect in the construction, meaning and interpretation of such parts of our system as are borrowed from theirs."

The importance of those codes and commentaries cannot, therefore, be too strongly stressed. It is there that the basic principles of community property law will be found, subject of course to such modifications as have been made by our local legislatures to meet new conditions. Even the so-called "adoption" of the community property system by statute in some of our states merely has the effect of making the law of such states that law as set out in the codes and commentaries aforementioned. This is so, because one must then look to such codes and commentaries to determine what the community property law is which has been adopted.[34] Even in the case of the local statutory modifications, the original laws and commentaries of Spain should be looked to, in order that the modifications may be understood in the light of the whole law and find their place in the pattern of the whole picture. Too often the local courts interpret these modifications without an adequate knowledge of the whole law and its background.

The common-law lawyer will grasp the foregoing easily when an analogous situation is presented by way of illustration. For example, in many of our states statutes have been enacted which declare, usually with certain qualifications, that the common law of England shall henceforth be the rule of decision. Such a statute does not, of course, set out all such law which has been adopted. To determine such law in any given situation the judge or lawyer then has to resort to the English judicial decisions to determine what is the law or rule of decision that has been so adopted. And it will be recalled that penal or criminal statutes frequently prescribe a punishment for an offense without defining it further than giving it a name known to the common law, as "murder," "rape," "robbery," etc. In such case the common

[34] See, e.g., Bulgo v. Bulgo, 41 Hawaii 578, 581; In re Salvini's Estate, (Wash.) 397 P. 2d 811. That the statutes are simply declaratory of the law as it previously existed was early recognized by the courts of the community property states. Buchanan's Estate, 8 Cal. 507; Stiles v. Lord, 2 Ariz. 154, 11 P. 314; Ray v. Ray, 1 Idaho 566; Holyoke v. Jackson, 3 Wash. 235. Later decisions, see Nixon v. Brown, 46 Nev. 439, 214 P. 524; Laughlin v. Laughlin, 49 N.M. 20, 155 P.2d 1010; McDonald v. Senn, 53 N.M. 198, 204 P.2d 990, 10 A.L.R. 2d 966. And see Vallera v. Vallera, 21 Cal. 2d 681, 134 P.2d 761.

"Texas, with just a few other states of the Union, has adopted as the basis of its laws relating to estates held by husband and wife the principles of the civil law, and our statutory enactments are in a large measure declaratory of these principles. This is particularly true with reference to the laws relating to community property." Lee v. Lee, 112 Tex. 392, 247 S. W. 828.

"The jurisprudence of Spain came to us with her laws. We have no more power to reject the one than the other; the people of Louisiana have the same right to have their cases decided by that jurisprudence as the subjects of Spain have; except so far as the genius of our government, or our positive legislation has changed it, . . . and what is settled as law in Spain cannot be considered as unsettled here." Porter, J., in Saul v. His Creditors, 5 Mart. N. S. (La.) 569, 16 Am. Dec. 212.

law must be resorted to in order to determine the nature and elements of the offense.[35] Similarly, then, in our community property states, in which there has been a continuation of the Spanish community property system, to determine what is the community property law one must have resort to what is the Spanish or civil law equivalent of the judicial decisions which set forth the common law, that is, the Spanish codes and commentaries of the jurisconsults thereon. Just as later decisions in England and in America may modify to some extent the common law principles, enactments of our local legislatures have sometimes modified some features of the community property law. Nevertheless the law of origin in each case must be resorted to in order to determine the governing principles.

As a matter of fact, even in the common law, dependence upon authoritative writers was well recognized. In the words of Chief Justice Shaw of Massachusetts, the "judges are bound to resort to the best sources of instruction, such as the records of courts of justice, well-authenticated histories of trials, and books of reports, digests, and brief statements of such decisions, prepared by suitable persons, *and the treatises of sages of the profession, whose works have an established reputation for correctness.*" (Italics ours.)[36]

§ 5.   Failure to resort to the primary sources.

While it has not been uniformly true in our community property states, in some of them the absence and unavailability, in the early days of statehood, of the primary source material on which the community system is based, plus the tendency of the courts to attempt the interpretation and decision of community problems by the application of common law principles, has led to many glaringly inaccurate and erroneous decisions in the field of community property law.[37] What is more unfortunate is that many erroneous principles and many misconceptions have been allowed to stand even to the present day, both on the part of the courts and on the part of legal writers on the subject of the community. This results from the tendency of later judges and writers to depend merely upon the earlier opinions, rather than to have resort to the primary sources of the community law which are now more readily available than in early days and which would immediately demonstrate the errors of earlier judicial decisions. This dependence upon former opinions in itself results from the common law training of judges and writers, since under that system precedent as established by former opinions is all important. This tendency to follow the common law custom of relying on judicial precedents serves therefore to

[35] See Clark & Marshall, Treatise on Law of Crimes, 6th Ed., § 1.07.

[36] Commonwealth v. Chapman, 13 Metc. (Mass.) 68.

[37] See post, §§ 51, 62. And even in states where decisions are usually uniformly praiseworthy, an occasional misconception appears.

perpetuate much error.[38] It will frequently follow that even when the original codes and commentaries are presented to a court to demonstrate the error of earlier judicial decisions, the court will still be inclined to follow the previous judicial decisions because the judges are unable to realize that in relying upon former decisions they are allowing, even in that respect, common law principles to govern the application of community property principles. Since the principles of the community system are, in almost all respects, thoroughly and fully set forth and explained in the Spanish codes and in the commentaries of the jurisconsults, it is usually only necessary to consult such sources to determine the truth of most matters. The courts, as well as the legal writers and practitioners, should cultivate the habit of referring directly to that source material and where former decisions are found to be in conflict with it, those decisions should be discountenanced and ignored where clearly not based on express statutory authority.[39] They must erase from their minds all tendency to rely upon the common law custom of precedent as illustrated by prior judicial decisions. No consideration should be given prior decisions unless they in their turn adequately illustrate that they were rendered in full reliance upon the principles of the community system and not merely upon former judicial decisions.[40] Most of the legal treatises and encyclopedic articles, and particularly the latter, on the subject of community property are written in entire or almost entire reliance on judicial decisions and with no

[38] See, for example, McKay, Community Property, 2nd Ed., which continually tries to prove or illustrate its points by heavy reliance on common law authorities. In fact, in his Preface, Mr. McKay flatly states that his point of approach and interpretation is in the light of common law concepts.

[39] "The Bench and Bar in California generally have not been familiar with the Spanish and Mexican laws with respect to community property. It has been exceedingly difficult to procure copies of Mexican Statutes and sometimes impossible to procure the works of the most distinguished commentators on the Spanish Civil Code. And even when procured, it was equally difficult to obtain correct translations of such laws and of the works of such law writers. Add to this the fact that nearly all the Mexican orders, laws, decrees, etc., respecting California are still in manuscript, scattered through immense masses of unarranged archives, almost inaccessible, and known, even imperfectly, to scarcely half a dozen persons, and will it appear surprising that errors have been committed by our judiciary? *Must we persevere in these errors, no matter how great, or how much opposed to justice they may be, even after new lights, new authorities, and new laws are brought to our notice, proving these mistakes beyond a doubt? We cannot believe that any court would sustain such a doctrine respecting its decisions."* Baldwin, J., in which Field, C. J., concurred, in Hart v. Burnett, 15 Cal. 611. (Italics ours.)

[40] And most certainly should the lawyer and judge beware of pronouncements on the law of community property by courts of noncommunity property states which are usually full of the most egregious errors and misunderstandings. See for example the case of Commonwealth v. Terjen, 197 Va. 596, 90 S. E. 2d 801 (1956) and comments on it by de Funiak, "Commonwealth v. Terjen: Common Law Mutilates Community Property," 43 Va. L. Rev. 49 (1957).

knowledge of the sources and primary principles of the subject. Thus, their accomplishment is only to perpetuate much error and mislead the bench and bar. Frequently, their only claim to scholarliness is a heavy reliance upon Gustave Schmidt's *Civil Law of Spain and Mexico*. As excellent as that work is, it must be borne in mind that it presents merely the author's condensation of the original law and does not give such law in its original language or reproduce the full text of the commentaries of the jurisconsults.

§ 6.   Plan of treatment of this work.

This work is neither a digest nor an encyclopedic article. It will afford no satisfaction to the lawyer who is attempting, without discrimination, merely to compile a long list of cases. Here will not be found that too frequent text treatment of a legal subject: the thin string of text beaded with every case, good and bad, extant upon that subject.

The plan and purpose of this work is to present the principles of the law of community property as it actually existed in its fully developed form in Spain, the form, in other words, in which it came to this country and which is actually the law in this country in the community property states. And to present it freed and disencumbered of the many misconceptions and erroneous interpretations which have like barnacles attached to it. In subsequent chapters in which is discussed the community property law as it affects all aspects of the marital relationship and property, full cognizance is taken of the applicable Spanish code provisions and the commentaries thereon of the Spanish jurisconsults, which together provide the governing principles of the community property law as it has been continued in our community property states. Cognizance is also taken of the local statutory modifications which exist in many instances. The judicial decisions of our courts are discussed, analyzed, and, where believed necessary, criticized. No effort, as has already been intimated, is made to cover or include every case extant on the subject of community property. Many are merely cumulative or duplicative in nature and it would only unduly burden this work to attempt their inclusion. Others are so erroneous in their conception of community property principles that it is probable the very courts themselves would welcome their being consigned to limbo.[41] Nor is any effort made to cover every possible factual situation arising in the law of community property. Once the principles of the law of community property are understood, their application to whatever factual situation arises should be readily possible.

[41] Where cases are numerous and more or less in accord with each other, we have frequently deemed it sufficient to refer to sources whence they may be obtained, rather than burden the footnotes with long citations of cases.

The Spanish text of the several Spanish code provisions relating to the community, taken directly from the original sources, will be found in Volume 2 of the original edition of this work, in Appendix I, accompanied by careful and accurate translations made by experienced scholars. In Appendix III of that volume are set out in full the commentaries of Matienzo, Azevedo, Gutiérrez, and Llamas y Molina, as they relate to the community provisions of those codes. In addition, excerpts from the works of other jurisconsults are set out from time to time in the footnotes.[42] Additional appendices in that volume present further material of value, such as treaty and constitutional provisions. It is believed that the availability of such a wealth of original material should be of the greatest aid to the judge and lawyer, for much of it is material only to be found in widely scattered sources, and frequently only in books not easily obtainable by reason of their being out of print or extremely rare.

A bibliography of much of the source material of this work is also there, included for the benefit of those who are interested in going to this material themselves.

[42] Biographical matter concerning these commentators, see Appendix II, vol. 2, 1943 edition of this work.

CHAPTER II

ORIGIN AND EXTENT OF COMMUNITY PROPERTY SYSTEM

§ 7.   In general.

It is impossible to put one's finger on a certain period or time in history or on a certain tribe, race or nation and say that there is to be found the actual origin of the community property system. It may be found in existence in different periods of history among some tribe, race or nation, while a neighboring tribe, race or nation has entirely different customs, or laws concerning the wife's marital property rights.[1] Features of the community system may be discerned in the Code of Hammurabi,[2] in the law of ancient Egypt, where a kind of matrimonial community by contract existed,[3] and ancient Greece,[4] and in the

---

[1] See Pollock & Maitland, History of English Law, 2nd Ed., vol. 2, p. 399 et seq.

[2] See Lobingier, History of Conjugal Partnership, 14 Am. Bar Ass'n Jour. 211; ibid., 63 Am. Law Rev. 250, quoting pertinent parts of the Code.

[3] See Howe, Community of Acquests and Gains, 12 Yale Law Jour. 216; Lobingier, History of Conjugal Partnership, 63 Am. Law Rev. 250;

ibid., 14 Am. Bar Ass'n Jour. 211.

[4] See Lobingier, History of Conjugal Partnership, 63 Am. Law Rev. 250; ibid., 14 Am. Bar Ass'n Jour. 211; Roby, Twelve Tables of Gortyn, 2 Law Quart. Rev. 136. And see Glotz, Aegean Civilization, pp. 142-146.

Under the laws of Athens husband and wife were regarded as distinct persons with separate rights and capable of holding distinct and separate

Byzantine empire;[5] it existed among the ancient Germanic tribes[6] and evidently among the Celtic.[7]

Certainly, as will be seen, the existence of the community property system does not depend upon "civilization"; it results rather from economic causes.[8] Thus, it is not a system which is borrowed by one race or nation from another but rather has developed at various times and places from independent local causes, or upon being carried by settlers or conquerors from one part of the world to another has continued to exist in the place of its transplantation because the customs and habits of such settlers or conquerors and the local conditions have favored its continuance.[9] However, we are not primarily concerned here with a study of the community system as it has existed or does exist in varying forms throughout the world, but rather with the origin and development of the form of community which is now the law of certain of our American states. This, as we shall see, has come to us from the Visigoths by way of Spain.[10] Accordingly it is this existence and development of the community system among the Visigoths in Spain which is primarily in point in this work and no effort is made to trace with exactitude and thoroughness the various changes and developments in the community system among the other Germanic tribes themselves or in the countries in which they implanted the system upon conquering and occupying those countries. These changes and developments have been analyzed by many scholars and students

estates, the wife being placed on an even more independent status as to property rights than under the Roman law. See Ballinger, Community Property, p. 4 (citing Herrick, Attic Law, p. 44).

[5] See Brissaud, History of French Private Law, p. 822, n. 1.

[6] See post, §§ 8–11.1.

[7] Lobingier records that the community system has been ascribed a Celtic origin by some (Lobingier, History of Conjugal Partnership, 63 Am. Law Rev. 250; ibid., 14 Am. Bar Ass'n Jour. 211), and it seems to have existed among the ancient Celtic tribes as it did among the Germanic, since their customs and ways of life were similar. See post, § 11, n. 27.

In ancient Ireland it appears that in most respects women were, as to social rights and property, on a level with men. Husband and wife continued to own the respective shares they brought in at marriage. Natural increases during the marriage were joint property of which the wife owned a proportion based on the amount of property she brought into the marriage. All transactions affecting the joint property, such as buying and selling, had to be with the consent of both husband and wife. Moreover, women could institute legal proceedings on their own account. Joyce, Social History of Ancient Ireland, 2nd Ed., vol. 2, pp. 8–12.

[8] See post, §§ 11, 11.1.

[9] See Brissaud, History of French Private Law, p. 817; McKay, Community Property, 2nd Ed., p. 6.

It must be admitted that Scotland would appear to be an exception to this rule. See post, § 18. And note the case of Turkey which in 1926 adopted the Swiss Federal Civil Code. See Lobingier, History of Conjugal Partnership, 63 Am. Law Rev. 250; ibid., 14 Am. Bar Ass'n Jour. 211.

[10] See post, this chapter and Chaps. III, IV.

of the subject, many of whose books are cited throughout these first chapters.

§ 8.   Roman or Germanic origin of our community system.

Because the community system exists in some form or other in many of the present day countries which were at one time part of the Roman Empire and which have incorporated much of the Roman law into their systems of jurisprudence, early writers, frequently attributed a Roman origin to such community systems.[11] But while the Roman law concept of marriage and its effect on property relations is entirely alien to that of the common law,[12] aside from what seems nothing more than a suspicion that a *communio bonorum* might have existed during the very early period of Roman law,[13] there is absolutely nothing in the written Roman law concerning a marital community of property.[14] On the contrary, it is now unquestioned that the marital community system was brought into the Roman provinces by the various Germanic tribes[15] among whom the system existed in varying forms.[16] One of these Germanic tribes in particular, the Goths,

[11] See White, A New Collection of Laws, Charters and Local Ordinances of Great Britain, France and Spain, p. 60, n. 43, calling attention to the fact.

[12] "The common law conception of marriage, which makes the parties one person for many purposes of property law, is in sharp contrast with the Roman view, under which, apart from *manus*, the marriage produces no effect whatever on property relations." Buckland & McNair, Roman Law and Common Law, pp. 31, 32.

Effect of marriage on property relations, under Roman law, see also Leage, Private Roman Law, 2nd Ed., p. 103 et seq.

"After the Punic triumphs, the matrons of Rome aspired to the common benefits of a free and opulent republic; their wishes were gratified. . . . Of their private fortunes, they communicated (i. e., shared) the use, and secured the property; the estates of a wife could neither be alienated nor mortgaged by a prodigal husband." Gibbon, Decline and Fall of the Roman Empire, Milman's Ed., vol. 3, p. 687.

[13] See Burge, Colonial and Foreign Laws, vol. 1, pp. 263, 418; White, p. 60, n. 43.

Some of the jurisconsults, in discussing the widespread existence of the community property system, have referred to "the law of Romulus." See Matienzo, Gloss I, No. 3, to Nov. Rec. Law 1: "And to these we should add, says Covarruvias, the law of Romulus which ordains that a married woman, being joined to her husband by holy laws, is his partner in money and in all property and in holy things, according to Dionysius who is quoted by Antonius Garro on Dig. 1.2.2. (col. 8)."

[14] See Calisse, History of Italian Law, p. 571 et seq.; Fraser, Husband and Wife, 2nd Ed., p. 649; Matienzo, Gloss I, No. 2, to Nov. Rec. Law 1; Llamas y Molina, Nos. 4, 5, to Nov. Rec. Law 6, and No. 15 to Nov. Rec. Law 8.

[15] See Calisse, History of Italian Law; Dill, Roman Society in Gaul in the Merovingian Age.

[16] Huebner, History of Germanic Private Law, p. 621 et seq. And see the interesting discussion by Mayer, Some Aspects of the Historical Origin of Continental Community Property Law, 4 S. W. L. Jour. 1.

Sir Henry Maine, in discussing the concepts of property in ancient law, argues that rude as were the laws of

who harried the Roman empire from eastern Europe to western Europe and who settled as far north as Scandinavia,[17] had a form of the marital community. The Visigoths (West Goths) carried this system into southwest France, leaving traces of it there after their expulsion,[18] and into Spain where, as we shall see, it developed and became an integral part of the written law.[19]

§ 9.   Causes and reasons of origin and continuation of community system.

We have so far in this chapter, in considering the origin of the community property system, been concerned with the "where" rather than the "why." We come now to some consideration of the reasons and causes for the origin and continuation of the community property system, which involves as incident thereof the reasons why it failed to continue in some countries, with special reference to England.

§ 10.   — Culture versus barbarism.

Gibbons says, "Experience has proved that savages are the tyrants of the female sex, and that the condition of woman is usually softened by the refinement of social life."[20] Yet, paradoxically enough, our community system which recognizes the wife as a person and as an equal partner in the marriage stems from the customs of the Visigoths at an age when they could hardly be called refined.[21] The true explanation is that there is no yardstick in mere terms of culture and savagery which provides any measure of woman's status and her marital property

those Germanic tribes they were not rude enough to satisfy the theory of their purely barbarous origin and that a considerable element of debased Roman law must have filtered in among their customs even before they had conquered any portion of the Roman empire. Pollock's Maine, Ancient Laws, 4th American Ed., pp. 287, 288. This, however, enters into the realm of pure speculation and disregards the existence and results of natural economic causes which have brought about similar concepts among other primitive peoples having not the slightest connection or contact with the Roman law. Consider, for example, the Yassa Gengizcani, post, § 10.

[17] See Gibbon, Decline and Fall of the Roman Empire (Milman's Ed.), Chap. X; Calisse, History of Italian Law, p. 3 et seq.; Cambridge Ancient History, vol. 12.

The Goths themselves, in a written history in the sixth century, attributed their origin to Scandinavia and this origin was later maintained by the Swedish historian Geijer. It is believed, however, that they were one vast branch of the Indo-Teutonic race who spread at intervals over the face of Europe. Gibbon, ante.

Scott, however, in the Preface to his Visigothic Code, insists that the Goths are to be distinguished from the Germans or Teutons.

[18] See Brissaud, History of French Private Law, p. 809.

[19] See post, Chap. III.

[20] Gibbon, Decline and Fall of the Roman Empire, Milman's Ed., vol. 3, pp. 685, 686.

[21] See post, this chapter and Chap. III.

rights.[22] In some civilizations and periods considered refined and enlightened, woman's position is considerably superior to her position in other civilizations and periods considered equally refined and enlightened. Conversely, among primitive and crude peoples her position varied among those different peoples; mere lack of the so-called refining influences of culture and civilization has not necessarily been the factor deciding woman's sphere in the domestic life of her day and her rights in property.[23] So far as so-called refining influences are concerned in fixing the wife's status and position, it is a far cry indeed from the civilization of England with its common law, requiring the effacement of the married woman, to that of the rude peoples under the sway of the Mongol ruler, Genghis Khan. Consider the *Yassa Gengizcani* (Laws of Genghis Khan) which Petis de la Croix succeeded in collecting,[24] with its law relating to marriage which enjoined that "The women should attend to the care of the property, buying and selling at their pleasure. Men should occupy themselves only with hunting and war."[25] We are forced to conclude that the wife's condition in the life of her day is not a matter dependent upon the particular state of civilization of the time or period and that Gibbon's statement, if it has any validity at all, can only be true so far as it might relate to mere creature comforts.

§ 11.   — Economic causes.

The most logical explanation, that most largely borne out by the facts, is that the causes which make the wife the partner of the husband are economic in nature.[26] It is among those races or among those classes of society in which the wife works shoulder to shoulder with the husband to maintain and preserve the common home and possessions, in which she contributes labor rather than the mere "adornment" of her presence, that she is found to be the partner of her husband with an ownership in the acquests and gains of their common labor

---

[22] In Pollock & Maitland, History of English Law, vol. 2, p. 403, the authors protest against the generalization "that from the age of savagery until the present age every change in marital law has been favorable to the wife."

[23] Marc Lescarbot, a French lawyer, in his Novia Francia, 1606, speaks of the low position of women among the Canadian Indians of that day. Yet at the same time one may compare the opposite situation existing among the Iroquois Indian nations in New York as to communal life and the exalted position of the women in the council chamber. See Avery, History of United States, vol. 1, p. 355, referring to the women's veto power in the council.

[24] Petis de la Croix, Histoire du Grand Genghizcan, Paris, 1710.

[25] See Lamb, Genghis Khan, p. 204.

[26] See Brissaud, History of French Private Law, p. 817 et seq.; Huebner, History of Germanic Private Law, p. 630; McKay, Community Property, 2nd Ed., p. 6. And see Wissner v. Wissner, 338 U.S. 655, 70 S. Ct. 398, 94 L.Ed. 424.

and struggles. Thus, it may be noticed that among some migratory and nomadic peoples which led a hard and dangerous existence, the wife shared with her husband its dangers and vicissitudes, she was fully cognizant of the details of and shared in his daily life and labor, she lingered on the edge of the battlefields to succor him from or to help him to despoil his enemies, she was side by side with him on dangerous migrations, and took equal part in his councils; among such races the wife was fully recognized as an equal partner. Such a race was that of the Visigoths and indeed most of the Germanic tribes, including the Angles and Saxons, among all of whom the community property system was to be found in varying forms.[27] These Germanic tribes did not have a complex form of society, with gradation of classes and its accompanying privileged or landed aristocracy. Their society was essentially democratic in nature. Their kings and chiefs, in essence military leaders, were elected on the basis of ability and bravery. Matters affecting the common welfare of the tribe were decided upon in common meeting of the members of the tribe.[28] Of course, as these Germanic tribes settled in conquered territories, the complexion of their political and social life changed; particularly in Portugal, Spain and France, a landed and privileged aristocracy arose. But the community system continued to exist among, and owed its continued virility to, the merchants, the traders and small farmers. Even the serfs on the great feudal estates, who could not themselves own land, continued the community as to movables.[29]

[27] The presence of the women on the battlefield exhorting and encouraging the men was a common practice among the ancient Germans, as attested by a number of Roman historians, among them Caesar, Tacitus and Florus. It was also true of the ancient Britons, according to Tacitus. The latter writer adds that the German women were most highly regarded and their advice always sought and heard. Because of the high esteem in which the women were held, it was frequently the practice, according to both Tacitus and Suetonius, to demand their women as hostages, to insure the men observing their treaties. The foregoing facts seem to have been equally true of the ancient Celtic tribes as they emigrated across the Alps, according to Plutarch.

"The wives participating in the hardships, expeditions and combats of their husbands, it was believed that they should also participate in the prizes taken from the enemy." Gomez and Montalban, Elements of Civil and Penal Law of Spain, 4th Ed., vol. 1, p. 256.

"The Germanic idea of marriage, higher certainly than that of the Romans before Christianity had influenced their law, placed husband and wife in a relation of mixed rights and duties to one another. . . . The wife was also called upon to be a co-worker with her husband in the family interests, and a partner in his joys and misfortunes. Though legally subject to him, she was evidently in fact the companion of her husband, who in turn owed her the duties of protection and fidelity, which found a sanction in the law." Calisse, History of Italian Law, p. 570.

[28] See Tacitus, Germania.

[29] See Brissaud, History of French Private Law, pp. 817-822; Huebner, History of Germanic Private Law, p. 630.

In other words, the community system is most frequently found to exist and to continue to exist among the common masses of the people, those who do not own great worldly possessions, those who must labor from day to day to maintain themselves and their children, those among whom the husband and wife work equally together in one capacity or another. It will exist among one class, the common people, in countries having a class system or privileged class, or among the bulk of the people in those countries or races which are largely of one class, that is, essentially democratic countries or races.[30] Since the United States, is primarily of the latter type, the existence of the community system, even though found in only some of our states, is much more natural to our way of life, to our habits and customs, than is a system or concept of marital property rights coming to us from privileged and aristocratic classes, who, indeed, rarely cling to the community system.[31]

It is curious to note that the common people in some countries, such as France, have kept alive and maintained the community system to this day, bringing it through the period of dominance of an aristocratic class, while on the other hand in England the opposite has been true. While the community system was undoubtedly brought into England by the Angles and Saxons, the English law early rejected the idea of community. Pollock and Maitland doubt that this can be attributed to ethnic considerations, and lay the rejection to two causes. First, about the year 1200 the property law was cut in two and the whole province of succession to movables was placed under the jurisdiction of the tribunals of the church (and the canon law based on the Roman law could not find, of course, any "community" in the latter law). Secondly, said those authors, the community of goods is found among the "lower strata of society" and since in England "the law for the great becomes the law for all" and "the habits of the great folk are more important than the habits of the small," the upper classes in turning their faces against the community system effectively strangled its development in England, even among the masses of the people among whom,

---

[30] See Brissaud, History of French Private Law, pp. 817-822; Pollock & Maitland, History of English Law, 2nd Ed., pp. 402, 403.

"With regard to community of goods the law has regard to the industry and common labor of each spouse and to the burdens of partnership and community. . . . They adopt a false premise when they say that one of the spouses contributes nothing to such a partnership, neither money nor work. The wife can work and take care of and preserve the family property. . . . Frequently the poorer spouse by work and labor makes up the deficiency in his or her estate. . . . The principle in accordance with which it was enacted by royal law that profits should be shared between husband and wife . . . being the fact that while the one spouse supplies work and labor the other supplies money or other property, the fact of their undivided habit of life ordained by both natural and divine law, the fact of the mutual love between husband and wife which should be encouraged. . . ." Matienzo, Gloss I, Nos. 6, 8, 13, to Nov. Rec. Law 1.

[31] See Jacobs, "Marital Property," Encyclopedia of Social Sciences.

as in other countries, it would most naturally tend to continue and develop.[32] Certainly, it may be considered that the attitude of the Norman nobles who ruled England from the time of the conquest by William in 1066 was strongly determinative of the question. It is to be noted that the idea of the community was rejected in Normandy at much the same time it seems to have been rejected in England.[33] The feudal system, introduced into England by the Norman nobles, was hostile to and destroyed the equality between husband and wife in England,[34] just as it tended to elsewhere, at least among the nobles; for, as we have seen, it continued in other countries among the common people and this even in the face of the hostility of feudalism. Among the nobles, the wife, unless heiress of some fief, herself brought no property into the marriage,[35] and of course she contributed no labor to the marriage in the manner that wives of commoners did. Under the feudal system, accompanied as it was by the artificial institution of chivalry, the woman was not sought for wife as a helpmate so much as a beautiful possession to adorn and grace the manor and for whatever lands she might bring, and, very importantly, to provide heirs, preferably male. Incidentally, however flattering it may seem at the moment to women to be considered lovely and mysterious beings to be worshipped and eventually possessed, they will discover that such a system leads to their being considered just that — possessions, not conjugal partners.[36]

[32] See Pollock & Maitland, History of English Law, 2nd Ed., vol. 2, pp. 402, 403. To the same effect, Holdsworth, History of English Law, vol. 3, pp. 524, 525, who states that in the thirteenth century the English law took the turn which resulted in the rejection of any theory of community.

Holdsworth notes the possibility of communal or family ownership among the ancient Anglo-Saxons in England. And it seems, definitely, that in cases of divorce where the wife retained custody of the children she took half of the property. Holdsworth, History of English Law, vol. 2, pp. 90, 91. See Kahn-Freund, Matrimonial Property; Some Recent Developments, 22 Modern L. Rev. 16, discussing situation as to developments in English marital property law, including recent suggestions as to forms of community property or joint or common family assets.

[33] See Pollock & Maitland, History of English Law, 2nd Ed., vol. 2, p. 402.

"As soon as the wife is under the authority of her husband he can do as he wishes with her and with her property and her inheritance; she cannot be heard as long as she lives under him." Grand Coutumier de Normandie, ch. 100, quoted in Brissaud, History of French Private Law, p. 787.

[34] See Pollock & Maitland, History of English Law, 2nd Ed., vol. 2, p. 419.

Excellent and learned discussion of displacement of Anglo-Saxon law by Norman law and hostility of feudal system to woman's equality in property, see Buckstaff, 4 Annals of American Academy of Political and Social Science 233.

[35] See Brissaud, History of French Private Law, p. 819, who says that in France, however, the community system was in time extended to the nobility themselves.

[36] Much of the male criticism in this country (whether or not it is valid) directed at woman's struggle

Some may object that religious as well as economic causes must have aided in producing and developing the idea of the marriage as a conjugal partnership in which the spouses, by reason of sharing equally the burdens of the marriage, share equally the profits and gains. But if by "religion" particular reference is had to Christianity, it is clear that marital community of property developed among the Germanic tribes from economic causes, i.e., from their manner and custom of life, long prior to their inculcation with Christian doctrines.[37] It is true that religion has a strong influence in fixing, through its dogmas and views, the place of woman in the contemporary society, and this has been true of Christianity. But the views and sentiments concerning woman of the Christian church during the Middle Ages can scarcely be described as favorable to the view of woman as an equal partner in the conjugal relationship. The fact that marital community of property based upon the idea of a conjugal partnership survived unabated through that era was due to its own vigor and the continuance of economic causes favorable to its continuance among the common people. It has continued due to economic causes irrespective of whether the prevailing religion of a country has been Catholicism, Lutheranism or Calvinism.[38]

§ 11.1.   The policy of community property.

Most discussions of community property have been content only to describe the system; few have asked why it began and was continued to the present. But inquiry is necessary for a full understanding of community property. Any complexity in the system today originated from a failure to appreciate the policy that supported the genesis and continuation of community property, and with an actual understanding of this policy the concept of community can be fully carried out.

Three distinct levels of policy will be considered: the policy that produced the system originally, the policy that supported its utilization

for equal rights and full partnership in the conjugal relation is that while they demand such equal rights they do not at the same time wish to assume the accompanying responsibilities, but wish at one and the same time to have the equal rights and yet receive the deference and respect prescribed by "chivalry." Incidentally, some now anonymous male once described the modern woman's idea of "chivalry" as being that a man will run upstairs and get her handkerchief for her when she requests it, whereas, he pointed out, actually under the code of chivalry, to the gentleman or knight a woman's handkerchief was something to be worn on his helmet as a token and that he would have been highly insulted at the request to run upstairs and get it, since that was not a thing for a gentleman but for a lackey to do.

[37] And see Brissaud, History of French Private Law, p. 817; General Survey of Continental Legal History, p. 545.

[38] Witness its continued existence in countries having widely divergent religious faiths, such as Spain, the Netherlands, Scandinavia, as to which see post, this chapter and Chap. III.

in this country, and the policy that maintains the system now. It should be noted, however, that policy does not arise overnight; rather it develops from the needs and customs of a people throughout time.

The preceding section detailed the causes that originated community property, and set the stage for its expansion. Among the Visigothic tribes the wife worked shoulder to shoulder with her husband to build and keep the home and property. She participated in his battles, migrations, and councils of government. The activity of each spouse was directed toward making the marriage a "going concern," to providing food, shelter, and clothing for the family. This tangible evidence of the wife's work, coupled with the mutual rights and obligations that each spouse has to the comfort, affection, association, and assistance of the other — the mutual loyalty of the spouses, the mutual sharing of the burdens of the marriage — was the operative factor which created a community of goods between the husband and wife.[39]

In adopting the concept of a community of goods, the law was realistic. It had regard for the industry and common labor of each spouse and the burdens of the conjugal partnership and community of interest. With the feeling in mind that during marriage the time and attention of husband and wife should be directed toward furthering the goals — economic, moral, social — of the marriage, the community was instituted as the most suitable vehicle for accomplishing these goals.

Thus the policy of community property was to establish equality between husband and wife in the area of property rights in marital property acquisitions, in recognition of and to give effect to the fundamental equality between the spouses based on the separate identity of each spouse and the actual contribution that each made to the success of the marriage. Note the striking difference between this and the common law doctrine of the merger of the identity of the wife into that of the husband.[40]

The ganancial property system was introduced into the United States when the Spanish conquistadors settled New Spain; it continued unabated through the decline of Spanish authority and the period of

[39] "The causes which made the wife partner to the husband are of an economic, rather than a moral nature. It grew out of the natural impulse toward a suitable provision for the wife's support and the reaction against the husband's despotic power. The rights of the wife have their origin in the modification and limitation of the husband's power by custom, contract and law. The struggle has been against his power and the fruits of the struggle have been her rights." Sebree, Outlines of Community Property, 6 N.Y.U. Law Rev. 32 (1928).

[40] "[The civil law] does not recognize in the spouses that union of persons, by which the rights of the wife were incorporated and consolidated, during coverture, with those of her husband. It does not, therefore, subject her to those civil disabilities, which must have resulted from that union [at common law]. On the contrary, it regards the husband and wife as distinct persons, with separate rights and capable of holding distinct and separate estates." Ballinger, A Treatise on the Property Rights of Husband and Wife, Under the Community or Ganancial System, Sec. 4. Bancroft-Whitney Co. (1895).

Mexican rule, and as new governments were established when territory was purchased from Mexico, or won its independence by revolution, it was necessary to determine whether or not to continue the community property system. It is not surprising that Louisiana maintained the system, because it retained the entire civil law structure. But in the other seven states that have community property, it appears that this is their most substantial vestige of the civil law. Why they retained this form of ownership is not easily determined.[41]

More often than not, when the question arose, the established residents of the area, who had been operating under the system, favored its retention; whereas, the recent migrants from common law jurisdictions advocated its abolition. In California the major reasons argued in favor of community property were that it would encourage women to settle in the area and that the common law treatment of women as inferiors was a product of the dark ages. The opponents of the system were vehement in their opposition, contending that the doctrine of women's rights was "the doctrine of those mental hermaphrodites, Abby Folsom, Fanny Wright and the rest of that tribe."[42]

But these arguments did not strike the crucial issue. Community property was continued in the western states after the end of Spanish and Mexican domination primarily because the factors which originally produced it were closely approximated. The women worked side by side with their husbands to provide the necessities of life for the family. When the husband was away from home the wife was head of the household: she cared for the family, fed the livestock, tended the crops, managed the family business and in all ways participated with her husband as an equal worker attempting to see that their marital partnership prospered and succeeded. The system was accepted and continued among those who came from common law jurisdictions to protect the wife and secure to her that to which she was entitled.[43]

Even though the community property system was supported by valid, functional factors at the time of its inception and continuation — a belief in the equality of the spouses because of the actual contribution of each to the success of the marriage — if these no longer concur the system should be abolished. Contrarily, if these circumstances obtain

---

[41] "Undoubtedly the debates in the various legislatures at the time of the adoption of the statutes in question would throw light upon this question, but, unfortunately, these debates are not preserved. It might reasonably be expected that the courts in early decisions on community property problems would give us some information regarding the causes of its adoption, but no such cases have been found." Kirkwood, Historical Background of the Law of Community Property in the Pacific Coast States, 11 Wash. L. Rev. 1 (1936).

[42] Ibid.

[43] "It seems safe to assume that the adoption of the community system in all these western states was simply a reflection of the larger movement toward improvement in the property status of married women, its particular form being in large measure influenced by California legislation." Ibid.

now in states which do not have community property, consideration should be given to the adoption of this form of concurrent ownership of marital property acquisitions by husband and wife, because of the inherent unsuitability of the common law to achieve modern purposes.[44]

All the marital property systems in the United States at the time of this writing have one point in common — the discarding of the common law idea of the unity of the husband and wife in the person of the husband, which gave the husband all the wife's chattels, a life estate in all her lands, and virtual control of all her transactions, while she had to be content with a life estate in one-third of his lands.[45] But the adoption of the various married women's property acts was based on the common law, which was "so illogical and unjust as to be beyond the possibility of correction by mere tinkering."[46]

A major problem in those acts is that they were drafted with no fundamental objective in mind. The legislators assumed that it was necessary to bring the legal position of wives closer to that of their husbands, but in so doing they closed their eyes to the biological inequality.[47] The legislation simply gave married women the right to own, manage, and possess the property which they acquired during marriage, without more: this was markedly naive. It ignored the fact that during the time women were bearing and rearing children they have little opportunity to acquire property. And by virtue of the fact that the husband is freed from these duties, and has his abilities greatly enhanced by the benefits of the very home the making of which has occupied the energies of his wife, he is able to acquire more property as his own, to the exclusion of his wife. The changes in the basic common law made by the married women's property acts theoretically give a wife equal rights with her husband, but her function as homemaker seriously impairs her ability to take advantage of this opportunity. Even in common

---

[44] "The Common Law notion being fundamentally wrong and in accord with a more primitive state of society and designed for an age when the position of women entitled them to little education or recognition of any sort, cannot be readily adjusted to meet the social and economic changes of this era. When parts of the structure are torn away for replacements, the decayed condition of other timbers is only the more readily discernable. The Community Property System on the other hand being fundamentally sound needs only new decorations and a few modern additions to make it a perfect habitat for the husband and wife of today." Daggett, Community Property System of Louisiana, p. 1 (1931).

[45] Lobingier, "An Historical Introduction to Community Property Law," 8 National Univ. L. Rev. 45 (1928).

[46] Brockelbank, The Community Property Law of Idaho, Sec. 1.5 (1962).

[47] ". . . The bearing of children must be done by women and the rearing of children is in fact done by them. Twenty of the most productive years taken from the career of a woman plays the same kind of havoc with it economically that the same time would play if taken from the career of a man. Thus not only is the sexual function different, but this difference creates for women a whole new economic and social position." Ibid.

law states where the wife has an intestate share in her husband's property she is not so well off as in a community jurisdiction. Obviously the community share is greater, and the benefits in the community states are automatic, whereas she must take affirmative action to get that share to which she is entitled in such common law states.[48]

Even though there is general agreement to discard the strict common law system of marital property law, the question remains as to whether or not community of property between husband and wife is the best alternative. At this juncture in time, *it is,* because the community greatly surpasses other systems which fail to recognize the status of the wife as a partner in the family enterprise, in which each spouse fulfills a specialized but equal function.[49]

New factors bolster the historical basis of community property as increasing numbers of wives are engaged in remunerative employment. The female labor force in 1965 totaled almost twenty-six million, of which sixteen million were married. Furthermore, the female labor force accounts for 36.7% of the female population over fourteen, and of the lady workers 62.2% are married. Since personal earnings are community property under the ganancial system the contribution of these working women is apparent.[50] These figures relate only to the tangible, monetary contribution of the wife to the connubial partnership. The moral support, love, devotion, trust and sympathy that the wife extends the husband are of inestimable value in supporting his efforts and energies.

An article that appeared some thirty years ago propounded three criteria for evaluating the ganancial concept as a marital property system.[51] They are the following: (1) the individualistic standard, (2) convenience for the facilitation of business transactions, and (3) lack of complexity in operation.

Regarding the first criteria it was contended that the real controversy with respect to marital property systems was whether the family or the individuals comprising it are of greater importance. The author there accepted the idea that the individuals are primary, and then criti-

---

[48] ". . . But to see only these obvious differences is to ignore the more fundamental and far reaching ones. The law in the common law states fails to recognize the wife as a helpmate and partner engaged with the husband in the common enterprise of creating a family as well as a fortune, and refuses her the place of dignity to which she is entitled." Ibid.

[49] ". . . By comparison the law of the community property states puts the spouses in an association not only of the affairs of the heart, but also of the whole gamut of interests, both material and affectional, that are inherent in the establishment and maintenance of both the family and the family fortune. Ambition and affection are united." Ibid.

[50] U.S. Bureau of the Census, Statistical Abstract of the United States: 1966, 87th edition (Washington, D.C.; U.S. Gov. Printing Office, 1966), p. 227.

[51] Powell, Community Property — A Critique of Its Regulation of Intra-Family Relations, 11 Wash. L. Rev. 12 (1936).

cized the community system on the ground that it merged the individuals into the family with little concern for them. What he failed to realize is that one of the most important principles of the community system is the individuality of the husband and wife. It is antithetical to the common law notion of merger of spouses into the husband, which may have been individualistic, but, if so, the only individual involved was the husband. The wife was not accorded the status of a legal entity: rather she was almost a salable chattel dependent on the whim and caprice of her husband. The community system, on the other hand, merely operates within the framework of a marriage, or family, and recognizes that husband and wife are separate, legal individuals who are working on a common endeavor: it does not merge them at all. This is not to say that the system does not accord the family an important position, for it does. Its recognition that their energies are spent in making the marital enterprise a successful operation has the effect of benefiting the family, but this is incidental to the main purpose of the concept — the treatment of the spouses as equal partners.

The last two criteria in the article are well satisfied by the community in its true form; but when it is mixed with common law to form a hybrid jurisprudence, it is inconvenient and complex. This will be pointed out throughout the remainder of the book to show the error of mixing common law and community property.

Originally established to articulate this feeling of equality, and still resting on this foundation, community of property is frustrated when restraints are placed upon the interaction between husband and wife when they are not accorded the status of equals. The underlying drive of community is that each spouse is equal to the other — and the policy of the law, whether expressed in the custom of the Germanic tribes or the statutes of a modern state, is, or should be, to effectuate this equality. Any provision denying equality is inconsistent with community property — and a modern community property system that contains laws creating inequality can best be described as a bifurcated unity.

§ 12.   Effect and interrelationship of the dotal system.

Although a discussion of the dotal system is not strictly within the scope of this work, it would be improper to pass it by without notice. As it existed and does still exist among various races and peoples it has been most fully treated by dozens of experts and scholars in works which are readily available to the reader.[52] However, we refer to it briefly because it seems to have existed even among those peoples hav-

---

[52] Reference may be made to many of those works already cited, such as Buckland & McNair, Roman Law and Common Law; Burge, Colonial and Foreign Laws; Brissaud, History of French Private Law; Calisse, History of Italian Law; Huebner, History of Germanic Private Law; Pollock & Maitland, History of English Law. And see Kagan, The Nature of Dowry in Roman Law — Rights of Husband and Wife, 20 Tulane Law Rev. 557.

ing the community property system and because there is some indication that in some instances it was the precursor of or at least had some influence on the development of the community system. Thus, since the property or dowry brought into the marriage by the wife was a contribution to the conjugal relationship and helped to make possible future earnings or gains, this frequently in itself gave rise to the belief that the wife should share in such earnings or gains in the proportion that her contribution constituted a part of the whole marital property.[53] Eventually, perhaps because it was frequently difficult to evaluate exactly the extent or proportion of the whole which her contribution constituted and because her actual labor and services in the marital union were considered of equal importance with that of the husband, it came to pass that she was considered entitled to half of the earnings and gains.[54]

In addition to the foregoing we may note briefly the relation of the *dos* or dowry to the community in the Spanish law,[55] although the dotal system has not been retained, as has the community, in our American states[56] (except in the case of the former Territory of New

---

[53] "The right to *ganancias* (gains) is founded on the partnership or society which is supposed to exist between the husband and wife, because she bringing her fortune in *dote*, gift, and paraphernalia, and he his in the estates and property which he possesses, it is directed that gains which result from the joint employment of this mass of property or capital be equally divided between both partners." Asso and Mañuel, Institutes of Civil Law of Spain, Book I, Title VII, Cap. 5.

[54] See Joyce, Social History of Ancient Ireland, 2nd Ed., vol. 2, pp. 8-12; Brissaud, History of French Private Law, p. 818; Huebner, History of Germanic Private Law, p. 631.

It is to be noted that in Spain the Fuero Juzgo in 693 A.D. provided that the spouses' shares in the acquisitions and increases during marriage should be in proportion to the amount of property each brought to the marriage. See Law 17 of Book 4, Title 2. Subsequently, it was provided that the fruits or earnings should be common to both, regardless of whether one spouse's property exceeded that of the other. See

Novísima Recopilación, Book 10, Title 4, Law 3.

Caesar said, two thousand years ago, of the ancient Gauls: "Whatever sums of money the husbands have received in the name of dowry from their wives, making an estimate of it, they add the same amount out of their own estates. An account is kept of all this money conjointly, and the profits are laid by: whichever one of them shall survive, to that one the portion of both reverts together with the profits of the previous time." De Bello Gallico, Book vi, chap. xix. This is describable in common law terms as a sort of tenancy by entireties, rather than community of property, but it is noted here because it probably represents an incipient stage of community of property.

[55] See commentaries to Novísima Recopilación, Book 10, Title 3, Law 4.

[56] Revival of interest in and study of Roman jurisprudence, which contained the dotal system, influenced its development and retention in some countries alongside the community system, notably in Spain; and the same appears to have been true in Roman-Dutch law.

Mexico[57] and in Louisiana).[58] The property brought into the marriage as dowry did not become a part of the community, although its fruits were part of the community.[59] This, it will be noted, is in entire accord with the principle of the Spanish law of community as a community of acquests and gains only. Incidentally, it is not to be supposed that the Spanish law did not recognize the right of the spouses to hold separate property. This was known as *bienes proprios* as opposed to the *bienes gananciales* (community property). Also the wife's *paraphernalia* was her separate property. In fact, the dowry also was her separate property and had to be returned to her or to those entitled to it otherwise, upon the dissolution of the marriage.[60]

§ 13.   Extent of the community system stemming from the Germanic tribes.

The Germanic tribes in spreading over and subjugating most of western Europe carried their community system with them and left its imprint, with some exceptions, on most of that territory. That system survived through the centuries in some of those regions, in others it disappeared, dependent upon whether or not local conditions and manner of life favored its continuance and development.[61] It is found, however, in most of the countries of western Europe and in many parts of the world to which it was carried by settlers coming from western

---

[57] See Chavez v. McKnight (1857) 1 N. M. 153; Martinez v. Lucero, 1 N. M. 208; Ballinger, Community Property, pp. 24, 31.

[58] See La. Civ. Code, art. 2336 et seq.

Settling of dower has become practically obsolete in Louisiana. Daggett, Community Property System of Louisiana, p. 30.

[59] *Dote, arras,* marriage gift and *paraphernalia* are not gancial property or property subject to partition or division. Asso and Mañuel, Institutes of Civil Law of Spain, Book I, Title VII, Cap. 5, § 2.

Both the husband and wife might bring property into the marriage. That which was given by the husband to the wife by reason of the marriage was known as the *arras*. That contributed by the wife, the *dote,* comprised both the *bienes dotales* (dowry) and the *bienes paraphernales* (briefly, property brought to the marriage or ac-

quired afterwards which was not included in the dowry or added thereto). The *dote* which the wife gave was divided first into *profecticia* and *adventicia,* and secondly into necessary and voluntary. The latter two terms are self explanatory. *Profecticia* was that which the father or grandfather or other of the ascendants in the direct line gave of their own property to the husband. *Adventicia* was that which the wife herself gave, of what belonged to her, to her husband, or which her mother gave for her, or any other of her relations who were collaterals and not of the paternal line. See Asso and Mañuel, Institutes of Civil Law of Spain, Book I, Title VII, Cap. 1, § 1.

"Dower is the capital which the wife, or some one for her, gives the husband for the purpose of supporting the matrimonial expenses." Martínez v. Lucero, 1 N.M. 208.

[60] More fully, see post, § 112.

[61] See ante, §§ 9-11.

Europe.[62] Thus, after the Visigoths carried the system into southern France and into Spain,[63] from Spain it spread to the Spanish-American republics of South and Central America[64] and to a large part of North America.[65] It exists, of course, in the commonwealth of Puerto Rico and in the Philippine Republic.[66]

In the sections immediately following are treated some of those countries in which the community system exists. The treatment does not pretend to be complete or comprehensive, but is offered merely by way of illustration.

§ 14. — France; Quebec.

It has been remarked in the preceding section that the Visigoths carried the community system into southern France. However, in respect to southern France the Visigothic overlordship was overthrown at an early date, and their influence removed, so that, except for some traces of the community system left by them, the Roman law which did not recognize a community of property held sway.[67] France, indeed, formerly presented a somewhat puzzling picture. In some districts the community system existed, in others it did not, depending upon the various local *Coutumes* (Customs) of those districts. In those districts governed by the Roman or civil law, it did not exist. However, where it did not prevail, nevertheless the parties could usually by agreement adopt its provisions, except in Normandy. Somewhat generally it may be stated that the community system did not exist to any considerable extent in the south of France, while in the north of France it did, with the later exception of Normandy.[68] Whether the

[62] Lobingier, History of Conjugal Partnership, 63 Am. Law Rev. 250; ibid., 14 Am. Bar Ass'n Jour. 211, lists 46 jurisdictions having some form of the community property system.

It existed with much vigor in Germany throughout the centuries (see Huebner, History of Germanic Private Law), but probably was not in accord with the doctrines of the former National Socialist party in Germany, which relegated woman to mere child-bearing for the benefit of the state. Presently as to an intermediate statutory system, see Friedmann, Matrimonial Property Law, Toronto, 1955, Part III.

[63] See ante, § 8.

[64] See Walton, Civil Law of Spain and Spanish-America; Lobingier, History of Conjugal Partnership, 63 Am. Law Rev. 250, 280-281; ibid., 14 Am.

Bar Ass'n Jour. 211; Smithers, Matrimonial Property Rights Under Modern Spanish and American Law, 70 Univ. of Pa. Law Rev. 259, with special reference to Peru; Lobingier, "Modern Civil Law," 40 Corpus Juris.

Martindale-Hubbell Legal Directory, vol. 5, is recommended as a ready reference source for the law in brief of these countries.

[65] As to Mexico, see post, § 15; also Chap. IV. As to the United States, see post, Chap IV.

[66] See post, § 53.

[67] See Brissaud, History of French Private Law; Dill, Roman Society in Gaul in the Merovingian Age.

[68] Brissaud, History of French Private Law, pp. 807-811; Burge, Colonial and Foreign Laws, vol. 1, p. 332.

In the time of Pothier, four classes of community are noted: 1. In territory

Norsemen who conquered and occupied Normandy brought the community system with them or found it already existent there is immaterial at this point. What is interesting to note is that, although they carried the system into Sicily,[69] they themselves subsequently rejected the idea in Normandy, thus differing in that respect from the customs of the rest of northern France.[70] Indeed, not only was it declared by the custom of Normandy not to exist, it was not permitted to be introduced into a nuptial contract.[71]

However, marital community of property was introduced into all of France by the Code Napoleon, now the Code Civil, which provides that in the absence of any antenuptial contract or agreement as to the title or rights in after-acquired property, such property is to be held in community.[72]

French settlers brought the community property system to that part of Canada formerly known as Lower Canada and which now largely constitutes the Province of Quebec. This community system was derived from the *Coutume de Paris* (Custom of Paris), established in Canada by edict of the king of France in 1663,[73] and existed until 1866 when the French Civil Code was adopted in that province, which in turn continues the community system.[74] The French also introduced the community system, as part of the *Coutume de Paris,* into their

governed by customary law, especially the Custom of Paris, it resulted from the formal marriage contract, or from the silence of such contract, or from marriage without any contract. 2. In Brittany and Anjou it resulted from the silence of the parties if the marriage lasted for a year and a day. 3. In the country of *droit ecrit* (written law) it did not exist unless expressly provided for by prenuptial contract. 4. In Normandy it was not permitted at all, even by contract. See Howe, Community of Acquests and Gains, 12 Yale Law Jour. 216.

The custom of Burgundy provided for partnership between spouses in sharing acquisitions made by either of them during marriage. See Cassaneus, *Consuetudines Burgundiae* (Customs of Burgundy), much cited by Matienzo, Azevedo and Guiterrez in their Commentaries, as comparative law.

[69] Calisse, History of Italian Law, p. 581; Brissaud, History of French Private Law, p. 822, n. 7.

[70] Burge, Colonial and Foreign Laws, vol. 1, p. 332; Pollock & Maitland, History of English Law, 2nd Ed., vol. 2, p. 402. See also ante, § 11.

[71] Brissaud, History of French Private Law, p. 790; Burge, Colonial and Foreign Laws, vol. 1, p. 332.

"As soon as the wife is under the authority of her husband he can do as he wishes with her and with her property and her inheritance; she cannot be heard as long as she lives under him." Grand Coutumier de Normandie, ch. 100, quoted in Brissaud, History of French Private Law, p. 787.

[72] See Code Civil, §§ 1387-1539; Ancel, Matrimonial Property Law in France, in Part I of Friedmann, Matrimonial Property Law, Toronto, 1955.

This feature of French law is illustrated by an important English case in the field of Conflict of Laws which will be familiar to most American lawyers, i.e., De Nicols v. Curlier, [1900] App. Cas. 21.

[73] Langelier, Cours de Droit Civil, vol. 1, p. 52; Howe, Roman and Civil Law in America, 16 Harv. Law Rev. 342.

[74] See Lobingier, History of Conjugal Partnership, 63 Am. Law. Rev. 250; ibid., 14 Am. Bar Ass'n Jour. 211; Howe, Roman and Civil Law in America, 16 Harv. Law Rev. 342, 345;

province of Louisiana where it remained in effect until displaced in 1769 by the Spanish law of community.[75]

§ 15.   — Mexico.

Since some of our community property states were formerly part of the Republic of Mexico before becoming part of this country, it is important to notice that the community property law of Spain was introduced into Mexico while it was a Spanish colony and still remained the law of Mexico after Mexico achieved its independence from Spain. The laws of the Republic of Mexico left the community system of acquests and gains unchanged, so that the Spanish law of community still remained the law of those parts of the Mexican republic which later passed under our flag.[76] Although in 1871 the Mexican Civil Code was enacted, the community property system was virtually unaffected thereby and was continued in effect by that code and later amendments.[77]

§ 16.   — Netherlands; South Africa.

In ancient times, in what is now the Netherlands, Germanic customs were predominant but the Roman law began to make headway there in the late fifteenth century and had become firmly fixed under the Spanish rule. The admixture of the Roman law to these Germanic customs gave rise to the Roman-Dutch law, the name applied to the system of law in force in the Province of Holland during the existence

---

Turgeon, Quebec, in Part I of Friedmann, Matrimonial Property Law, Toronto, 1955. See also Beaulieu, Community of Property in Law of Quebec, 17 Can. B. R. 486; Baudoin v. Trudel, (Ont. Ct. of App.) [1937] 1 Dom. L. R. 216.

[75] See post, § 40.

[76] See Hall, Mexican Law; Schmidt, Civil Law of Spain and Mexico, chap. VI; Vance, Old Spanish Code of "Las Siete Partidas" in Mexico, 14 Am. Bar Ass'n Jour. 219; Vance, The Background of Hispanic-American Law.

"The marriage produces some legal effects which we proceed to explain. . . . The second, which is treated of entirely in title 9 of Book 5 of the Recopilación, or title 4 of Book 10 of the Novísima, and which was unknown to the Roman law, is the acquisition by both spouses by halves of what each of them gained during the

marriage; so that all the properties which the husband and wife may have, belong to both equally, excepting those which either of the two may prove belongs to him or her separately." Novísimo Sala Mexicano, sec. 2a, Title 4, No. 1.

[77] See García v. Estate of Contreras, Diario de Jurisprudencia, May-Aug. 1904, p. 667 et seq., by Superior Court of the Mexican Federal District, declaring: "The principles established regarding this subject (i.e., community of property between spouses) by the antique legislation are equal to those fixed by the legislation now in force." And see Wheeler's Compendium of Laws of Mexico, Rev. Ed.

A brief attempt at suspension of the community property system in Mexico by Venustiano Carranza, during the revolutionary period in the early part of the twentieth century, came to nothing.

of the Republic of the United Netherlands. It was this Roman-Dutch law which was carried to the East and West Indies and to South Africa by Dutch settlers. In the Netherlands it remained the law until 1809 when the Napoleonic Code was introduced, which in turn gave way to the modern codes of 1838, which now constitute the law of the Netherlands and of those colonial possessions still remaining under their flag.

By the Roman-Dutch law, in the absence of antenuptial contract to the contrary, the marriage created a community of goods between the parties. This community has been spoken of as statutory, not because it was introduced by statute but because its existence was recognized by numerous ancient statutes. It is a purely Germanic institution and owes nothing to Roman law, although it is to be noted that its continued existence would not in any way have been weakened during the Spanish rule over the Netherlands, since the Spanish themselves had the community system. The community consists of all property of the spouses at the time of the marriage as well as all after-acquired property, both real and personal, and is under the administration of the husband. It is subject both to antenuptial and postnuptial debts of both spouses.[78]

The codes now governing the Netherlands and their colonial possessions have made little if any change in the basic concept of community property.

The Roman-Dutch law, with its community property system, remained the law of South Africa, Ceylon and that part of Guiana (now British Guiana) which passed at various times into the possession of Great Britain, beginning in the late eighteenth century. While the English common law is said to have displaced the Roman-Dutch law in British Guiana and the community system was definitely abolished in Ceylon in 1876, the Roman-Dutch law with its community system has remained firmly entrenched as the law of the Republic of South Africa, in Rhodesia and in the territories mandated to the Republic of South Africa.[79]

---

[78] In Spain, the town of Albuquerque, under the Statute of Baylio, had a similar community of property in all that brought to the marriage by the spouses as well as in that acquired during the marriage. See Llamas y Molina, No. 19, to Nov. Rec. Law 6, Book 10, Title 4. See also Novísima Recopilación, Book 10, Title 4, Law 12.

[79] For the foregoing sketch of the Roman-Dutch law in the Netherlands and South Africa the author acknowledges a heavy debt to that excellent work of Lee, An Introduction to Roman-Dutch Law, p. 2 et seq., p. 65 et seq. See also Price, South Africa, in Part I of Friedmann, Matrimonial Property Law, Toronto, 1955; Burge, Colonial and Foreign Laws, vol. 1, pp. 276-280; Williams, Roman-Dutch Law, 19 Yale Law Jour. 156; Bisschop, Roman-Dutch Law in South Africa, 20 Law Quart. Rev. 41.

The various influences on the legal system of the Netherlands will be found competently discussed by van Hamel in the chapter on the Netherlands, in A General Survey of Continental Legal History, pp. 455-479.

§ 17.   —Scandinavia.

It has been said that the Scandinavian law shows that the community system took the place, by means of agreements, of a still older system analogous to that of unity of possessions.[80] However that may be, that the community system existed at an early date in Scandinavia is attested by the Icelandic sagas and recognized in the oldest sources of the Scandinavian law, the Icelandic Gragas and the Norwegian law of Gulathing of King Haakon.[81] And in Gotland (what is now southern Sweden) the Goths had a strongly developed community property system, for that is clearly indicated by the Law of the Westgoths, according to the Manuscript of Eskil, dating from about 1200 A.D. That law not only shows that the wife was the husband's free equal and might own property in her own name but contains a great number of provisions relating to community of property, including provisions as to purchases, increases and inheritances.[82]

At the present day, in Denmark and Norway, a community of goods obtains unless the parties by agreement or contract otherwise stipulate.[83] In Sweden, however, the tendency seems to be to give each spouse independent control of the property of that spouse owned at the time of marriage or acquired thereafter but with a special legal right in the property of the other which permits of a half share therein upon termination or dissolution of the marriage.[84]

§ 18.   —Scotland.

Scotland presents the only example, so far as the authors know, of an artificial transplantation of the community property system from one country to another. That is, instead of having arisen among the people of Scotland from natural economic causes or of having been brought into the country by settlers among whom it had arisen else-

[80] Brissaud, History of French Private Law, p. 819, n. 2.

[81] See Lobingier, History of the Conjugal Partnership, 63 Am. Law Rev. 250, quoting Olivecrona's L'Origine et Development de la Communaute des Biens entre Epoux. See also Brissaud, History of French Private Law, p. 819, n. 3; p. 822, n. 6.

[82] See Law of the Westgoths, according to the Manuscript of Eskil (Bergin's translation), pp. 8, 9, 15, 53, 54, 59, 66.

"The collections of ancient Swedish law manuscripts afford much enlightenment on the legal conditions of society at an age when the influence of the Christian dogmas had only in a mechanical and superficial manner affected the ancient legal conceptions and practices. The oldest among these is the 'Vestgöta-lag,' from the early 1200s." General Survey of Continental Legal History, p. 545. This work gives a brief but interesting survey of the ancient Scandinavian law-men and law-texts.

[83] Denmark, see article by Judge Pedersen in 28 Modern Law Review 137. Danish Virgin Islands, see post, § 53.

[84] As to the form of intermediate system set up by statute, see Malmström, Sweden, in Part II of Friedmann, Matrimonial Property Law, Toronto, 1955.

where from natural causes, it seems to have been brought to Scotland from continental Europe by Scottish lawyers who studied on the continent and who were enthusiastic about its principles. Their enthusiasm is, perhaps, understandable but the result has not been an entirely happy one since much disagreement has resulted as to the scope and effect of community principles.

Its introduction into Scotland is generally attributed to French influence in the sixteenth and seventeenth centuries,[85] during most of which period Scotland and France, animated by a common enmity toward England, were closely allied, and during which period Scottish lawyers studying in the French universities brought back many principles of French law.[86] While earlier Scottish writers, Lord Stair and Erskine, appear to have considered the *communio bonorum* in its true light, as an equal ownership of goods between married persons and with the administration in the husband, it appears that even so in Scotland the *communio* was of a limited character and did not extend to "heritable property" but was confined to "subjects of a temporary nature" not producing any yearly profit while they continued.[87] But a more recent writer, Fraser, has attacked the community of goods most strongly, asserting that it is alien to Scottish law and that as it exists in Scotland it is a fiction, a sham, a mere name.[88] Fraser correctly states that the community of property was not recognized by Roman law[89] and originated with the ancient Germans who introduced it into France and that among them it was in truth a full partnership, but he insists that the community existing in France and which was brought to Scotland was at that time entirely changed and was no longer the true community of property as it had originally existed and that the husband was the sole proprietor with only the right of the wife to half the goods at the husband's death; and he insists that always under the law of Scotland the husband has been

---

[85] Fraser, Husband and Wife According to Law of Scotland, 2nd Ed., vol. 1, pp. 651, 661.

[86] See Fraser, Husband and Wife According to Law of Scotland, 2nd Ed., vol. 1, pp. 648-678; Gibb, Legal Systems of Scotland and England, 53 Law Quart. Rev. 61; Jenks, Scottish Law, 12 Law Quart. Rev. 155.

On the other hand it has been stated that the Scots law, in its formative period in the sixteenth and seventeenth centuries, owes its greatest debt to the legal learning of the Netherlands. Lord Macmillan, Scots Law as a Comparative Study, 48 Law Quart. Rev. 477. This article represented, however, an address given at a legal convention in the Netherlands, and may have been colored to compliment the audience.

[87] Burge, Colonial and Foreign Laws, vol. 1, pp. 423, 424.

[88] Fraser, Husband and Wife According to Law of Scotland, 2nd Ed., Vol. 1, p. 648 et seq.
This view has also been intimated by English writers. Pollock & Maitland, History of English Law, 2nd Ed., vol. 2, pp. 400, 401.

[89] Generally as to Roman law in Scotland, see Stein, Influence of Roman Law on the Law of Scotland, (1963) Juridical Review 205.

the absolute owner and *dominus* of the property.[90] He criticizes Lord Stair for not attaching to his definition of community the qualification that the husband is the absolute owner of the marital property. Of course, if Lord Stair had attached such a qualification he would not have truly defined the community, since such a principle is foreign to the very spirit of the community.[91]

But whatever the situation might formerly have been in Scotland, the union of Scotland with England in 1707 seems to mark a turning point. It may be that English views laid a heavy hand on Scottish interpretations. After 1707 we find Scottish writers[92] and courts[93] declaring that communion of goods or community of property has no place in Scottish law. The result is that we must now recognize that

---

[90] Fraser, Husband and Wife According to Law of Scotland, 2nd Ed., vol. 1, pp. 650-656, 672.

"By the common law of Scotland, marriage transfers to the husband all the personal property of the wife at the time of the marriage, or which may accrue to her during its subsistence, with the exception of personal bonds bearing interest, and the *paraphernalia,* which are limited to her clothes, jewels and ornaments of dress. The wife remains proprietor of her lands or real estate; but the husband is entitled to the administration, and to the whole yearly rents and profits, during the marriage. It is commonly said that the property so acquired by the husband in right of his wife falls under the communion of goods, as if there was a common fund for behoof of both spouses; but, as the husband has the absolute power of use and disposal under the *jus mariti,* the goods nominally in communion are in reality his property." Mackenzie, Studies in Roman Law with Comparative Views of the Laws of France, England and Scotland, 5th Ed., p. 119.

Somewhat curiously, an English court in De Nicols v. Curlier, [1900] App. Cas. 21, in upholding the reality of the French community of property, discusses obiter the community in Scotland and relying upon Fraser describes the community in Scotland as a mere fiction, not to be compared with the reality of that of France. Yet Fraser attributes the fiction of the community in Scotland wholly to the

fact that it was a fiction in France from whence it was brought to Scotland.

[91] Burge declares that the husband has the sole right, called the *jus mariti,* of administering the community. Burge, Colonial and Foreign Laws, vol. 1, p. 424. Fraser declares that the mere right of administration or curatorial power of the husband is to be distinguished from the *jus mariti* which he defines as an ancient principle of Scottish law, being the right by which the husband acquires to himself absolutely the personalty of the wife. Fraser, Husband and Wife According to Law of Scotland, 2nd Ed., vol. 1, p. 676.

[92] See Fraser. More modernly, see Smith, A Short Commentary of the Law of Scotland (1962), pp. 344-351; Walker, The Scottish Legal System (1959), pp. 51, 52; Walton, Law of Husband and Wife According to Law of Scotland (3rd Ed., 1951), pp. 197, 198. And see the writings of Professor A. E. Anton of the University of Glasgow, especially, The Effect of Marriage upon Property in Scots Law, 19 Modern Law Rev. 653; and the Stair Society Introduction to Scottish Legal History.

[93] Fraser v. Walker, 10 M. 837 (1872); see also Shearer v. Christie, 5 D. 132 (1842); cf. Thomson v. Fraser, 9 M. 1069 (1871), where on divorce wife received one-half of goods in communion.

no community of property is existent in Scots law,[94] no matter how interesting it may be to the legal historian to trace its former existence in Scotland.

[94] See de Funiak, Community of Property in Scots Law, 10 S. D. Law Rev. 70; de Funiak, The Legal System of Scotland, 38 Tulane Law Rev. 91.

CHAPTER III

SPANISH LAWS
AND THEIR HISTORICAL BACKGROUND

§ 19.   Tables.

That the reader may more conveniently follow the discussion in this chapter, and in order to summarize the matter in brief, tables or lists of the Spanish codes, statutes and ordinances, and particularly of those containing community provisions, are presented here.[1] The dates of the publication or promulgation of some of the more ancient of the Spanish codes and compilations are difficult of exact ascertainment. Variations of a year or more frequently appear among the different authorities. The dates here given are those most uniformly agreed upon.

[1] In the preparation of this material, the authors are deeply indebted to Lloyd M. Robbins, Community Property Laws, pp. 7, 8; Lloyd M. Robbins and Bernardine M. Murphy, Laws of Community Property, pp. 5, 6; Lillian Roark, Translation of Biographies of Noted Spanish Commentators, p. 5; Gustavus Schmidt, Civil Law of Spain and Mexico, p. 102; A General Survey (Continental Legal History Series), Appendix A; Vance, 14 Am. Bar Ass'n Jour. 219; Llamas y Molina, Commentaries on the Laws of Toro; Alvarez, Institutes of Royal Law of Spain.

The Spanish codes, statutes and ordinances of chief interest are as follows:

Year	Title	Books	Titles	Vols.	Laws
693	Fuero Juzgo	12	55	1	559
992	Fuero Viejo	5	33	1	229
1255	Fuero Real	4	72	2	549
1263	Las Siete Partidas	7	182	4	2479
1310	Leyes del Estilo			1	252
1348	Ordenamiento de Alcalá		32	1	125
1490	Ordenamiento Real	8	115	2	1133
1505	Leyes de Toro			1	83
1567	Nueva Recopilación	9	214	2	3391
1680	Recopilación de Indias	9	218	3	6447
1805	Novísima Recopilación	12	330	4	4036

The laws respecting community property (*bienes gananciales*) are to be found in the following:

Year	Title	Laws
693	Fuero Juzgo	Book 4, Title 3, Law 17.[2]
1255	Fuero Real	Book 3, Title 3, Laws 1-3; Title 20, Law 14.
1263	Las Siete Partidas	Partida 4, Title 11, Law 24; and see Partida 3, Title 2, Law 5; Partida 7, Title 17, Law 15.
1310	Leyes del Estilo	Laws 203, 205, 207 (added in 1566), 223. And see Laws 206, 208.
1505	Leyes de Toro	Laws 14, 15, 16, 53, 60, 77, 78. And see Law 61.
1567	Nueva Recopilación	Book 5, Title 1, Law 4; Title 3, Laws 7-9; Title 9, Laws 1-11.
1805	Novísima Recopilación	Book 10, Title 3, Law 4; Title 4, Laws 1-13; Title 11, Laws 2, 3.

[2] Scott, in his translation of the Fuero Juzgo from the original Latin, gives this as Law 16 (see Scott, Visigothic Code), but the thirteenth century Castilian translation gives it as Law 17.

In connection with the table immediately preceding, the following parallel reference table will undoubtedly be found helpful:

Fuero Real A. D. 1255 Book III, Tit. 3	Leyes de Toro A. D. 1505	Nueva Recopilación A. D. 1567 Book V, Title 9	Novísima Recopilación, A. D. 1805 Book X, Tit. 4
1	—	2	1
2	—	3	2
3	—	4	3
—	—	1	4
—	—	5	5
—	14	6	6
—	15	—	7
—	16	7	8
—	53	8	—
—	60	9	9
—	77	10	10
—	78	11	11
—	—	—	12
—	—	—	13

In addition, it is to be noted that Law 14 of Book 3, Title 20 of the Fuero Real was carried forward as part of Law 207 of the Leyes del Estilo and promulgated in 1310; that Law 203 of the Leyes del Estilo, and promulgated in 1566, became Law 1 of Book 5, Title 9 of the Nueva Recopilación and was carried into the Novísima Recopilación as Law 4 of Book 10, Title 4; that Law 9, Title 3, Book 5 of the Nueva Recopilación was continued as Law 3, Book 10, Title 11 of the Novísima Recopilación; that Law 53 of the Leyes de Toro which became Law 8 of Book 5, Title 9 of the Nueva Recopilación was included in the Novísima Recopilación as Law 4 of Book 10, Title 3; that Law 15 of the Leyes de Toro, continued as Law 4 of Book 5, Title 1 of the Nueva Recopilación became Law 7 of Book 10, Title 4 of the Novísima Recopilación.

Most of these community property laws, with their translation and legislative history, are set out in full in Appendix I in Volume 2 of the 1943 edition of this work.

§ 20.   Periods of Spanish legal history.

Since our community property system comes to us by way of Spain and finds its expression in the successive codes and laws of that country, it becomes necessarily important that we consider those codes and laws and, briefly, their historical background. Of course, any detailed presentation of the history of Spain is out of the question but the history of a country cannot be ignored in following the development of its laws.

Altamira, the eminent Spanish historian, although criticizing the divisions as illogical, notes that most studies of Spanish law divided the subject into nine periods, comprising the primitive period, colonization by the Greeks and Phoenicians, Roman rule from approximately 200 B.C. to 400 A.D., Visigothic rule into the seventh century, Moorish rule and the early period of reconquest by the Christians, the completion of the reconquest up to the fifteenth century, and thereafter certain dynastic periods, ending with the constitutional period of the nineteenth century.[3] John T. Vance divides the subject into six periods: The pre-Roman period; the Roman period; the period of Visigothic rule; the period of reconquest; the period of renaissance and colonial expansion, characterized by the recopilaciónes and colonial legislation; and the constitutional period.[4] Schmidt considers the matter under four divisions, Spain under the Romans, under the Visigoths, under the Moors, and after the expulsion of the Moors.[5] Whatever the divisions, we are concerned chiefly with Spain from the inception of Visigothic rule up to the early part of the nineteenth century, and it is from this standpoint that the subject will be dealt with here.[6]

§ 21.   Pre-Roman period and Roman rule.

The early Iberian and Celtic inhabitants of Spain prior to the time of Roman rule have left little trace of their laws, which were probably mainly made up of unwritten customs. The Romans in the course of their six or more centuries of rule firmly impressed their own laws on the peninsula. While it is probably true that many customs of the early inhabitants survived and possibly tinged the Roman law in force, the absence of any community property system in the Roman law in Spain indicates that neither the original inhabitants nor the Romans (as far as we are aware) possessed any community system as part of their law.[7]

---

[3] Altamira, A General Survey (Continental Legal History Series), pp. 581, 582.

[4] See Vance, Background of Hispanic-American Law (1943), p. 27.

[5] Schmidt, Civil Law of Spain and Mexico, p. 10 et seq.; Vance, Background of Hispanic-American Law, 1943.

[6] The legal history of Spain is most excellently treated by Professor Rafael Altamira, both in his Historia de España, and in his contribution to A General Survey (Continental Legal History Series), Part VIII. Also by Gustavus Schmidt, Civil Law of Spain and Mexico; Lislet and Carleton, Introduction to their translation of Las Siete Partidas; Walton, Introduction to

his Civil Law of Spain and Spanish America; Lobingier, Las Siete Partidas and Its Predecessors, 1 Calif. Law Rev. 487; Loewy, Spanish Community of Acquests and Gains, 1 Calif. Law Rev. 32; Vance, Las Siete Partidas, 14 Am. Bar Ass'n Jour. 219; Alvarez, Institutes of Royal Law of Spain.

General history of Spain, see Bury, History of Later Roman Empire; Gibbon, Decline and Fall of Roman Empire; Cambridge Ancient History; Altamira, Historia de España, 3rd Ed.; etc.

[7] Roman law, see ante, § 8.

"Although there are some who have wished to discover the laws by which the first founders of Spain were gov-

The Roman rule and influence in Spain is, of course, well documented, but since it did not include the community system we need give it no more than the foregoing passing notice.

§ 22.   Visigothic rule — Its inception.

The Visigoths came into Spain originally as the allies, nominally at least, of Rome in order to oppose the Vandals and other Germanic tribes which had already invaded Spain. Undoubtedly the Romans considered Spain already lost to the empire and since the Visigoths themselves had become a source of trouble to Rome and were demanding lands, Spain was offered to them if they would conquer or evict the Vandals and others. The Visigoths accepted the offer and entered Spain in 415 A.D. and gradually brought the province under their rule.[8]

§ 23.   — Dual systems of law.

The impression sometimes prevails that the Roman empire suddenly collapsed and immediately and instantaneously was replaced by a dark period of barbarism. But just as Rome was not built in a day, it did not fall in one day. Its decline was gradual over the centuries. The Germanic tribes or nations which gradually conquered and occupied such a great portion of the Roman empire eventually became intramixed with the conquered populations. While imposing many of their own customs on the conquered, many of the customs of the latter lingered and the two diverse sets of customs were merged into one whole.[9]

For over two centuries of Visigothic rule, after their conquest of Spain, two systems of law appear to have existed side by side in that country. The Hispano-Romans continued to live under the Roman law, as modified by custom and to some extent, of course, as affected

---

erned before its invasion by the Carthaginians, yet it is necessary to confess that we have nothing certain upon this subject. The most probable appears that they had no laws written, and that they undoubtedly were governed by those of custom, and by arbitrary decrees founded in equity and justice. It is believed that the Carthaginians would begin at least by introducing theirs into the provinces which they ruled; but even this conjecture is not altogether fixed, if we consider the short time which their government lasted, which was a little more than two hundred years, during which they were agitated by continual wars." Alvarez, Institutes of Royal Law of Spain.

[8] See Bury, History of Later Roman Empire; Cambridge Ancient History; Gibbon, Decline and Fall of Roman Empire; etc.

[9] It has been remarked of Gaul, an illustrative case, that it must be considered that the invaders were dispersed over a vast new territory; their leader, no longer a mere military chief, became ruler of a wide territory still retaining the tradition of Roman administration, and in himself administering this new territory he was of necessity obliged to use the skill of lawyers and administrators trained in the Roman law and administration. Dill, Roman Society in Gaul in the Merovingian Age, p. 44.

by principles of Visigothic law; whereas the Visigothic conquerors lived under their own law and customs, which also governed relations between them and the Hispano-Romans.

In the time of King Euric (467-485), the first written code of the Visigothic laws was compiled. It appears to be largely a reduction to writing of the Germanic customs of the Visigoths.[10] This code applied in all cases between the Visigoths themselves and between them and the Hispano-Romans. Under Euric's son, Alaric, this dual or double system of laws was confirmed by the completion from various Roman sources of a code to govern the Hispano-Romans. This code, approved in 506 A.D., is usually known as the Breviary of Alaric or *Lex Romana Visigothorum*.[11]

Successive editions of Euric's code were made in the time of King Leovigild (568-586) and the latter's son Reccared (586-601), in which the Roman law is said to have had some influence.

§ 24.   —Fuero Juzgo.

The double system of law in the course of time began to disappear, however, and was supplanted by law common to all. A culmination of this merging came in the reign of Kindasvinth who framed a new code which in turn was improved by his son Reccesvinth (649-672), the entire text of whose code has come down to us. Known as the "Liber Iudiciorum" it later came to be known as the "Fori Iudicium" or "Forum Iudicum," or in the Castilian, the "Fuero Juzgo," that is, the Book of the Judges. It suffered some slight modifications and changes and in its more or less final form the publication of the Fuero Juzgo is attributed to the year 693 A.D.[12] In its original form it was in Latin[13] but in the thirteenth century, by order of Ferdinand III, it was rendered into Castilian.[14]

[10] Llamas y Molina, in his commentary No. 277 to Law 1 of the Leyes de Toro, attributes its publication to "about 469 A.D."

An ancient palimpsest has been discovered in Paris which is considered by many to be a copy of this code, but Altamira doubts whether it is not in fact a redaction of the later period of Reccared (586-601).

[11] This code is exhaustively discussed by Llamas y Molina, and by his annotator Caravantes, in the former's commentaries No. 277 et seq. to Law 1 of the Leyes de Toro. Its date of publication, according to Llamas y Molina, was 505 A.D.

"It antedated by some years the works of Justinian, and in this respect alone possesses considerable interest." Howe, Roman and Civil Law in America, 16 Harv. Law Rev. 342.

[12] Alvarez, in his Institutes, somewhat astonishingly refers to this code as having been "published in the 12th century in Latin." If by this he refers to its first publication or promulgation he is far out of accord with all other commentators. Vance has excellent discussion of this code in his Background of Hispanic-American Law, 1943.

[13] Samuel Parsons Scott, in the preface to his translation, entitled The Visigothic Code, terms it a monkish Latin, a barbarous jargon extremely difficult to translate.

[14] Scott, again in a critical frame

While the Fuero Juzgo was intended to represent purely Visigothic law and contained an express prohibition against the use or citing of the Roman law, imposing severe penalties therefor,[15] it was undoubtedly influenced to some degree by the Roman law, although the extent to which it was so influenced has been the subject of much disagreement. On the other hand it imposed many customs of Gothic or Germanic origin upon all the inhabitants of Spain, of which the community property system was one.[16] Indeed, while the Fuero Juzgo is of great importance as the earliest of the Germanic codes covering all fields of the law, it is of chief importance to us because it contains the first written recognition of the community property system.[17] That this provision as to community property represents a purely Visigothic custom, uninfluenced by Roman law, is readily apparent from the existence of the community which is shown in the Visigothic code in

of mind, terms this translation incorrect and unsatisfactory and as being the work of monkish translators. It is more probable, however, that these "monkish translators" of the thirteenth century were more familiar with the "monkish Latin" they were called upon to translate than would be a translator of this century. Moreover, we must consider that it was this Castilian translation that was looked to through the centuries as the law, whatever criticism may be made of it. See criticism of scholarly qualities of Scott's work by Vinogradoff, 27 Law Quarterly Review 373.

[15] Citing of Roman law or basing a judgment thereon was punished by heavy fine, and at a later date the punishment was increased to death, according to some writers. Llamas y Molina remarked, however, "From what has been said, it is evident that Oldrado and those who followed his opinion are mistaken in stating that there was a law in Spain which prohibited the use of the Roman under capital punishment; for the Decree of King Alaric, which established the penalty, did not direct it against those who invoked the Roman or other laws, but against the governors of the provinces who should employ, for the determination of litigation, other laws, Roman or not, than those contained in the new Code." See Commentary No. 278 to Law 1 of Leyes de Toro.

[16] See Judge Hamilton, Germanic and Moorish Elements of Spanish Civil Law, 30 Harv. Law Rev. 302. Scott declares the Fuero Juzgo consisted of laws from four different sources; those based on ancient Gothic customs, those adopted from Roman jurisprudence, acts of ecclesiastical councils, and edicts of the kings promulgated at various times. Scott, The Visigothic Code, Preface, xxix. See also Llamas y Molina, Commentaries to Law 1 of Leyes de Toro.

The Salic Law of the Franks in Gaul, for example, may be instanced as a picture of mingled Germanic and Roman law. See Dill, Roman Society in Gaul in the Merovingian Age, p. 44.

"The Germanic tribes were the first who adopted the idea of community of property between the spouses, it being the signal characteristic of all the legislation founded on the principles of Germanic law, while the notion of an absolute separation of the property of the husband and wife characterized the marriage of the Romans . . . and if it still exists in Spain and Portugal, notwithstanding the Roman base of legislation of these peoples, it is as a reminiscence of the Germanic tribes which invaded and conquered the Iberian Peninsula." Felipe Sanchez Roman, Estudios de Derecho Civil, 1898 Ed., vol. 1, p. 339 et seq.

[17] See Fuero Juzgo, Book 4, Title 2, Law 17. Scott, in his translation from the original Latin, gives this as

Sweden, the existence of the custom among the other Germanic tribes, and its entire absence from the Roman law.[18]

The Fuero Juzgo remained in force as a general code, excluding all others, in the whole of the Spanish kingdom, from the time of its publication until the invasion by the Moors in 711, and thereafter continued in force in the unconquered parts of Spain as well as in those parts gradually reconquered from the Moors. While the later centuries saw the enactment of new codes of laws, it was declared as late as 1788, by Royal Edict of June 15 of that year, that when the law of the Fuero Juzgo had not been abrogated by any other law it should be given consideration by the court, with less preference to the law of the Partidas.[19] Prior to that time it had been declared in 1505 by Law 1 of the Leyes de Toro that the Fuero Juzgo as well as the Fuero Real should be effective only if custom approved them, and the laws of the Partidas were more absolute and positive.[20] So far, however, as the Fuero Juzgo dealt with community property, there is little need to resort to it, for the later codes dealt at length and in more detail with the subject. It is interesting to notice that no change was made by later codes in the provision of the Fuero Juzgo that the spouses might by written contract stipulate some other arrangement of sharing than that provided by statute.[21]

§ 25.   Moorish rule and beginning of Christian reconquest.

In the early years of the eighth century the Moors, carrying the banner of Islam, swept into Spain from North Africa and subjugated the greater part of the peninsula. Only the mountainous regions in the extreme north remained unconquered, and from this vantage point the inhabitants, joined by those from other parts of Spain who had fled there, waged relentless war on the Moorish invaders. The grim tenacity and determination of these Spaniards who fought for nearly eight hundred years to expel the invaders presents a remarkable picture of courage. It was not, indeed, until the time of Columbus that the last Moorish stronghold was obliterated.

The reader will notice the use of the word "Spaniards" in the preceding paragraph. We have already seen that the dual system of law had disappeared even before the advent of the Moors. The long struggle against the Moors removed the last distinction between Visigoth and Hispano-Roman and welded the people into the Spanish nation. Accordingly, these distinguishing terms may now be dispensed with.

Moorish or Moslem law seems to have left little or no imprint

---

Law 16, while the thirteenth century Castilian translation is authority for it being Law 17.

[18] See ante, Chap. II.

[19] Partidas, see post, § 29.

[20] Llamas y Molina, Nos. 23, 24, to Nov. Rec. Law 7, Book 10, Title 4.

[21] See post, § 133.

upon Spain.[22] But the political situation engendered by the Moorish invasion did result in a new political and administrative law differing from the former Visigothic type. The unconquered part of the peninsula, due to geography and the exigencies of war and defense, became broken into small kingdoms or countries, whose fortunes rose and fell until eventually they again became merged into one whole. To retain the support of the several classes, the kings at various times granted certain privileges or concessions to the nobility, the clergy and the towns. These grants were in the form of *fueros.*

The term *fuero,* unfortunately, is one difficult of definition, since it has many meanings. It includes among its meanings that of a compilation or general code of laws, a charter granted to a city or town, and even usages and customs which have acquired in the course of time the force of unwritten law. However, both in Castile and Catalonia, the Fuero Juzgo continued to exist, although subject to a considerable modification and change over the centuries, and nullified in some particulars by local *fueros.* But where such local *fueros* did not regulate, the people followed either the Fuero Juzgo or the old customs and traditions. These latter, in considerable part of Visigothic origin, kept or again regained their old vigor because the centuries of war returned the people to a kind of life similar to the ancient Germanic type. Among these customs or laws which continued to exist, on what has been remarked by many legal historians as a truly national scale, was that of the community of property between spouses. Its widespread existence on a national scale, its general recognition by the people through all the vicissitudes of time and warfare and changed political conditions, is indication of its vigor and has been noted as a matter of course by the Spanish legal historians.[23]

---

[22] See footnote following.

The Moorish rule has been credited by many non-Spanish writers, however, as having left definite influences upon the manners and customs of the people of southern Spain. See, e.g., the works of Washington Irving; also W. Somerset Maugham's *Andalusia.* In view of the more than seven centuries of Moorish rule this is a reasonable assumption. Spanish writers insist that this was not true to any great extent as to legal influences. See Altamira, in the succeeding note. And see Judge Hamilton, Germanic and Moorish Elements of Spanish Civil Law, 30 Harv. Law Rev. 303; Vance, Background of Hispanic-American Law, 1943.

[23] Only in the customs of Cordova and in the law of Valencia and Majorca did a system of separate conjugal property exist for a period as an exception to the generally recognized community system. See Altamira, A General Survey, Part VIII, p. 605, who says that it has been supposed of Moorish introduction. In 1802, Don Carlos IV abolished such local custom in Cordova and decreed that the general law of partition of gains in marriages be extended to all that kingdom. This decree became Law 13 of Book 10, Title 4 of the Novísima Recopilación of 1805.

Matienzo remarks that anciently in Hispala community of property was not the custom. Matienzo, Gloss I, No. 65, to Nov. Rec. Law 1.

The town of Albuquerque was governed by the Statute of Baylio granted by its founder Sancho Tellez, son-in-

§ 26.   —Fuero Viejo.

The Fuero Viejo (old or ancient code), the publication of which is usually attributed to the year 992, is frequently listed among the Spanish codes or *fueros*. Even those writers who do not question its existence as a validly published code declare it far less comprehensive than its predecessor, the Fuero Juzgo, and assert that it was compiled mainly to define the prerogatives of the nobility, whose power was increasing.[24] Altamira, however, strongly doubts that it was even a legal code and believes that it was a compilation of the fifteenth century made on private initiative for private ends, and he declares that the privileges of the nobility are mainly to be sought in other sources.[25] This is also essentially the view of the late John T. Vance.[26] However that may be, the question is merely moot from our standpoint, since the code contains no community property provisions.

§ 27.   Moorish decline and the earlier codifications.

In the reign of Ferdinand (or Fernando) III, the Moors were expelled from the greater part of Spain; and while the wars between the Moors and Christians continued for over two centuries longer, Christian Spain had now won through the hardest part of its struggle. The way now clearly lay open as well for political unification as for compilation of the laws which would remove the confusion which had developed through the heaviest period of warfare. Unfortunately, the period of unification in the 1200's and 1300's itself presents a somewhat confused picture when attempted to be presented in brief form, because of the multitude of names of various compilations, some of which were never officially published or promulgated and others not for many years after their completion. In the case of codes officially published or promulgated it must be borne in mind that new provisions were frequently added over the years. These codes, in the main enacted for the kingdom of Castile, became the law of all Spain due to the eventual supremacy of Castile.

law of Sancho II of Portugal, according to which all property brought to the marriage as well as that acquired during the marriage was community property. Llamas y Molina, No. 19, to Nov. Rec. Law 6. The observance of this law was approved by Don Carlos III in 1778. See Novísima Recopilación, Book 10, Title 4, Law 12.

[24] See Schmidt, Civil Law of Spain and Mexico; Loewy, 1 Calif. Law Rev. 32, 35; Lislet and Carleton, Introduction to Las Siete Partidas.

Both Schmidt and Lislet and Carleton describe it as only adding to the existing confusion in the law and assert that in some parts of Spain the Fuero Juzgo was followed, in others the Fuero Viejo. See also Lobingier, 1 Calif. Law Rev. 490; Alvarez, Institutes of Royal Law of Spain.

[25] Altamira, A General Survey, Part VIII, p. 625.

[26] Vance, Background of Hispanic-American Law, 1943, p. 83, declaring it was not officially promulgated until 1356.

§ 28. — Fuero Real.

The preparation of a code intended to be in seven parts, called the "Septenario" was initiated in the reign of Ferdinand III and carried on through the reigns of Alfonso IX and Alfonso X and completed by the last named. This seems never to have been promulgated, however, but in 1254, or according to some writers in 1255, Alfonso X issued the Fuero Real, which was based on the Fuero Juzgo and preserved the general character of the Visigothic law as modified during the centuries in Castile and Leon. This code necessarily has great interest to us because it includes several provisions on community property[27] which continued to exist as the law and three of which were carried into the Neuva Recopilación of 1557 and the Novísima Recopilación of 1805, and one into the Leyes del Estilo, with very little change from their original form.[28]

§ 29. — Las Siete Partidas; Ordenamiento de Alcalá

In 1256, according to modern authors, also under the direction of Alfonso X, began the compilation of a new and larger work, apparently in scope or arrangement modeled after the Septenario, for it was divided into seven parts, and for that reason has come to be called Las Siete Partidas.[29] Completed according to some writers in 1263, according to others in 1265, it was based in large part upon the Fuero Juzgo and the Fuero Real, and there is considerable question as to whether it was intended to supersede or replace the latter code. It gained wide prestige and authority and seems to have had great influence with lawyers and students of the law.[30] Yet curiously enough it seems not to have been promulgated or officially sanctioned for many

---

[27] Fuero Real, Book 3, Title 3, Laws 1-3; Book 3, Title 20, Law 14.

[28] See Tables, ante, § 19.

[29] For excellent and scholarly discussions, see Lobingier, Las Siete Partidas and its Predecessors, 1 Calif. Law Rev. 487; Vance, Old Spanish Code of "Las Siete Partidas" in Mexico, 14 Am. Bar Ass'n Jour. 219; and particularly Llamas y Molina, Commentaries to Law 1 of Leyes de Toro.

"Our national authors have expressed themselves very diversely in regard to the Seven Partidas, which after the Code of Justinian is without doubt the most complete of those published in Europe. There is very little definite information concerning it, for nearly all that can be said with certainty as to its author and the time when it was commenced and terminated, we know from what King Alfonso himself, who was its author, has told us in the Prologue. That is merely that his father King Ferdinand thought of compiling these laws, and not having had time to do so, he charged his son with the mandate of the execution of this work, who in consequence began this immortal task on the Eve of the Feast of St. John the Baptist, 4 years and 23 days after the commencement of his reign. He says: 'And this book was commenced and begun to be compiled on the Eve of St. John the Baptist, 4 years and 23 days after the commencement of our reign, which began in the Era of the Incarnation in 1251, roman years, and 152 days more.' " Llamas y Molina, No. 16 to Law 1 of Toro.

[30] Altamira, Historia de España, 3rd Ed., vol. 2, p. 88 et seq.; Altamira, A General Survey, Part VIII, p. 262.

years, although there is strong indication that in many aspects it had gained the force of law. However, in the reign of Alfonso XI it was confirmed in the Cortes of Alcalá in 1348 by ordinance, known as the Ordenamiento de Alcalá, and was made obligatory on all points not contradictory of the Fuero Real, the municipal fueros and the privileges of the nobility. It will be noted in this respect that the community property provisions of the Fuero Real were thus not affected.[31]

Indeed the Partidas themselves contain little relating to community property other than Part 4, Tit. 11, Law 24, providing as to the law of the country where the spouses marry or their antenuptial contract is made as governing the partition of their earnings; Part 3, Tit. 2, Law 5, referring to rights of action between spouses and administration by the husband; and Part 7, Tit. 17, Law 15, providing as to the effect of the wife's adultery upon her right to the community property. There are, however, numerous provisions relating to marriage, dowry, donations, etc.

§ 30.   — Leyes del Estilo.

In 1310 appeared the Leyes del Estilo which related to the form of legal proceedings. This is worthy of our attention because § 203 thereof, which was promulgated and added to the Leyes del Estilo in 1566, provides that property of the husband and wife should be presumed common property until proved otherwise. This provision passed into the Nueva Recopilación as Law 1 of Book 5, Title 9; and later into the Novísima Recopilación as Law 4 of Book 10, Title 4. Likewise worthy of attention are §§ 205, 207 and 228, which relate to the liability of the community for the debts of husband and wife, and kindred matters. These sections, and particularly § 207, have their origin in Law 14 of Book 3, Title 20, of the Fuero Real, and in the main were further developed in the Nueva and Novísima Recopila-ciónes.[32] The obligatory legal force of these Leyes del Estilo was questioned by many of the commentators in view of provisions of the later Leyes de Toro and other codes, as to the order of authority of the

---

[31] Law 1, Title 28, of the Ordenamiento de Alcalá, is set out by Llamas y Molina in the forepart of his Commentaries on the Laws of Toro, and it declared in part: "Desiring therefore to find a suitable remedy for these conditions, we establish and ordain that the Statutes in question (i.e., the Partidas) can be observed in the matters in which they were employed.

"As the laws of our *fueros* (i.e., local or municipal laws) have not an absolute sanction, but are merely conditional and only effective if custom should approve them and observe them,

as Don Alfonso XI ordained, and was confirmed by Law of Toro No. 1, they produced no effect if not sanctioned by practice.

"The authority of the Leyes de Partida is more absolute and positive, and it is ordained that these should be kept and observed whether or not sanctioned by practice." Llamas y Molina, Nos. 23, 24, of commentaries to Nov. Rec. Law 7, Book 10, Title 4.

[32] See Tables ante, § 19.

Debts contracted by husband after marriage, see also Novísima Recopilación, Book 10, Title 11, Law 2.

various codes, and it was contended that the Leyes del Estilo were merely declaratory of the preceding Fuero Real, which with the Leyes de Toro and later compilations, was to be looked to for guidance.[33] The question is more or less immaterial so far as concerns the community property provisions in the Leyes del Estilo, for these provisions chiefly had their origin in the Fuero Real and were continued in the same or similar language of the Estilo in the Nueva and Novísima Recopilaciónes.

§ 31.   Final period of codification.

With the opening of the sixteenth century, we find the Moorish influence completely removed, the unification of Spain rapidly being completed, and the expansion of the nation as a great colonial power beginning. We also find the codes from the beginning of this period up to the early part of the nineteenth century giving full recognition to the community system which had continued to exist with full vigor, as has already been remarked. The community system still retains its full vigor in the modern Spanish codes, of course, but our interest in the Spanish codes does not extend beyond the early part of the nineteenth century when those Spanish territories in which the community system was in force became part of the United States.

§ 32.   —Leyes de Toro.

For a period of 150 years after the promulgation of Las Siete Partidas by the Ordenamiento de Alcalá in 1348, a struggle seems to have been carried on between proponents of the native law and proponents of the Roman law, the study of which had been pressed for some time and which law had considerably influenced the Partidas. Eventually, an effort was made to end the confusion and strife resulting therefrom by an Ordenamiento of the Cortes of Toledo in 1502, and first officially issued or promulgated in the Cortes of Toro in 1505 and known as the Leyes de Toro (Laws of Toro).[34] The principles of the Partidas were affirmed in part; on the other hand, principles ignored by it were affirmed by the Leyes de Toro, particularly the community system of acquests and gains. A number of important provisions relating to the community are contained in these Leyes de Toro; accordingly, for that reason it is of great interest to us, as is also the much older Fuero Real, which contains community provisions. The community provisions of these two codes were carried virtually intact into the Nueva Recopilación of 1567 and later into the Novísima Recopilación of 1805.[35]

[33] See Llamas y Molina, Commentaries, No. 259 et seq. to Law 1 of Toro. See also post, § 36.

[34] The Royal Ordinance of Queen Doña Juana for the publication of the Laws of Toro was issued on March 7, 1505. See Llamas y Molina, Prologue to Commentaries on Laws of Toro, and Royal Ordinance, set forth therein.

[35] See post, §§ 33, 34.

§ 33.   — Nueva Recopilación.

The Nueva Recopilación (New Compilation), promulgated in 1567, was a code which was furthered in the reign of Philip II. It was a compilation of the various past *"ordenamientos"* of the Cortes, of the royal orders, the laws of Toro and other laws which had been enacted since the laws of Toro. It contained, as stated in the preceding section, the community provisions of the Fuero Real and of the Leyes de Toro, as well as § 203 of the Leyes del Estilo which had been added to the Estilo in 1566.[36]

While the reputation and effect of this compilation of the laws has been questioned,[37] the fact is that it was the subject of interpretation and comment by many of the leading Spanish jurisconsults,[38] and new editions were continually issued during the sixteenth, seventeenth and eighteenth centuries, each successive edition including the statutes enacted since the date of the prior edition. Thse intervening statutes as published from time to time formed a supplement to the Recopilación (until incorporated in a new edition thereof) known as the "Autos Acordados."[39]

§ 34.   — Novísima Recopilación.

Eventually, of course, new editions of the Nueva Recopilación became insufficient to meet all needs and a new compilation was authorized which was published in 1805 under the name of the Novísima Recopilación de las Leyes de España (i.e., Latest Compilation of the Laws of Spain). This code or compilation retains intact the community property provisions carried into the previous compilation of 1567, and with the addition of two new provisions, local in nature, promulgated respectively in 1778 and 1802.[40]

§ 35.   — Recopilación de las Leyes de las Indias.

Some consideration of this compilation or code (i.e., Compilation of the Laws of the Indies, usually referred to as Recopilación de Indias)

---

[36] See ante, § 30.

[37] See Altamira, A General Survey, Part VIII, p. 662.

[38] A resurgence of activity in legal writing, thought and analysis seems a definite result of the reign of Philip II, surnamed by the Spaniards "the Great," in the second half of the sixteenth century. However, the view of Philip as great or not must depend upon the side one took, for as Hayes points out in his Political and Social History of Modern Europe, this was a period of struggle between England and Spain for commercial and maritime supremacy and prejudices ran high.

[39] The best known of the "Autos Acordados" seems to be that of 1745. Many American writers have seemed to believe that the term was confined only to the publication of that date, but see to the contrary, Altamira, Part VIII of A General Survey (Continental Legal History Series), p. 675; Alvarez, Institutes of Royal Law of Spain.

[40] Laws 12 and 13 respectively of Book 10, Title 4.

is necessary, since some misconception may exist as to its nature and effect. With the growth and extension of Spanish colonial possessions in the New World, a continually growing body of royal orders, decrees and laws for the government of these colonies came into being. Eventually it was considered advisable, and indeed necessary, to collect these scattered laws, orders and decrees. They were so collected and digested under the order of Philip IV in the same form as the Nueva Recopilación and were published in 1680.[41]

But while this compilation was expressly designed to apply to all the Spanish territories in the New World, it must be noted that it was exclusively administrative and political in nature. It contained no provision relating to the civil law, and indeed expressly provided that where it had no provisions on a subject the Nueva Recopilación, Partidas, and laws of Castile should govern. Upon the publication in 1805 of the Novísima Recopilación, the royal decree declaring this latter compilation in force and effect was addressed, among others, to the governors of the East and West Indies. And in 1807 a royal order was addressed, among others, to the governors of the East and West Indies which directed that a supplemental compilation of laws of 1805 and 1806 should be considered as forming part of the Novísima Recopilación and should have the same force and vigor as that compilation. Thus, it is clearly evidenced that the Novísima Recopilación, as in the case of the Nueva Recopilación before it, and in the same manner, was in force and effect in the colonies and possessions of Spain.

§ 36.   Summary of force and effect of Spanish codes.

Since the Recopilación de Indias, as discussed in the preceding section, had no provisions on the subject of the community and expressly provided that where it had no provisions on a subject, the Nueva Recopilación, Partidas and laws of Castile should govern, it naturally followed that the community provisions of that Recopilación became the law of the Spanish colonial possessions in North America, as well as such subsequent laws of Castile as the two provisions of 1778 and 1802, which with the other provisions of the Nueva Recopilación were carried into the Novísima Recopilación of 1805. The Novísima Recopilación thus represents the basic principles of the community property law which became and remained the law in the Spanish possessions in North America and has continued to remain the law in our community property states. The fact that the Louisiana territory became part of this country in 1803, two years before the publication of the Novísima Recopilación in 1805, becomes immaterial in the light

[41] The year 1661 has also been credited as the year of publication but most sources agree on the year 1680. It will be noted that from the standpoint of chronology this compilation comes prior to the Novísima Recopilación but it is here discussed after the latter compilation for purposes of convenience.

of the fact that the latter compilation merely carries forward laws already long in existence.

The foregoing is not to be considered as an assertion that only laws found in the Nueva and Novísima Recopilaciónes represented the community system of acquests and gains. The fact is that an unusual feature of Spanish legislation was that upon the promulgation of a new code, no effort was made to abrogate the old one. Accordingly, although the last in point of time was first in point of authority, all the codes had to be examined in order to ascertain the law. However, since the majority of the community property provisions were incorporated into the Nueva and later the Novísima Recopilación, the latter remains our chief source for determining the code provisions, although community property provisions not conflicting therewith which are in any other of the compilations, such as those provisions in the Fuero Real and probably as well those in the Leyes del Estilo, are equally valid, and should be referred to to determine the full meaning of the law of the community.[42]

It is also to be noted that since the community provisions of both Recopilaciónes are virtually the same, the commentaries of the Spanish jurisconsults on the provisions of the Nueva which are of such importance as authority are equally applicable to such provisions as they appear in the Novísima.

Elsewhere is discussed the extent to which the Spanish codes were in force and effect in the Americas and later supplied the basis of the codes of these various regions.[43]

---

[42] "The third law, title 1st, book 2nd, of the (Nueva) Recopilación of Castille, prescribing the manner in which the laws of that code, of Partidas and of other codes, are to be observed, declares that the first in order, are the laws of the Recopilación of Castille, and those that have been subsequently enacted; next the laws of the Fuero Real, and the municipal customs; and finally, the laws of Las Siete Partidas. This law does not speak of the Recopilación of the Indies, which was not compiled until long after the promulgation of the Recopilación of Castille.

"Murillo, an able Spanish law writer, speaking on that subject in his treatise entitled Cursus Juris Canonici Hispani et Indici, after having repeated what is said in law 3rd, title I, book 2, of the Recopilación of Castille; says that the laws of the Recopilación, of Toro, and the Partidas, ought to be enforced by judges, in all cases submitted to their decisions, even when it is alleged, that they have not been usually observed in the place. But that when the authority of the Fuero Real, and of the laws of Estilo is invoked, it is necessary to prove that they are conformable to the usages of the place, unless they be found in the Recopilación for then it is only necessary to plead them." Lislet & Carleton, Introduction, Las Siete Partidas.

The Fuero Real was said to have no force in itself except in so far as it was proved that it was observed by local custom. Matienzo, Gloss I, No. 16, to Nov. Rec. Law 1, Book 10, Title 4. Of course, where laws of the Fuero Real were continued in later compilations, their force was above that of local custom.

[43] See ante, Chap. II; post, Chap. IV.

CHAPTER IV

ESTABLISHMENT OF COMMUNITY PROPERTY SYSTEM IN THE UNITED STATES

§ 37.   In general.

While the community property law of our American states is the community property law of Spain established in the Spanish possessions of North America from which our community property states were formed, it is interesting to note that the French also brought the community property system to their colonies on this continent. While many of these French possessions passed ultimately under our flag, the French community system therein either was displaced by that of Spain or by the English common law. Thus, the Spanish law displaced the French law in the Louisiana territory, and although France later regained that territory from Spain, it was sold to us so soon after the French repossession that the Spanish law was still in force, as will be seen hereafter in the specific discussion of Louisiana.[1]

Accordingly, not only the Louisiana territory but also the Floridas, Texas, and the region acquired from Mexico in 1848 passed under

[1] See post, § 40.

our suzerainty with the Spanish law in effect.[2] In many of these various regions, particularly in those virtually uninhabited and in which the Americans of English descent settled, the community property system was displaced by the common law derived from England. Many of the courts of states carved from these regions seemed to feel that the former legal system of Spain was displaced merely by common consent or custom of the new settlers without any formal legislation. However, by accepted canons of international law, the community system would continue until formally superseded, and a regularly established legal system cannot be displaced merely by common consent and without formal legislation.[3] And the United States Supreme Court has declared that according to world usage, the laws of a territory or province ceded to the United States (except those laws political in character) remain in force until altered by the government of the United States or by the state government when such territory or province has been created a state.[4]

Any discussion becomes more or less immaterial at this late date, because in some of those states laws were eventually enacted which were so inconsistent with the community system, as by providing for dower, that they impliedly abrogated and superseded the community system. In others of the states the community system was, of course, abrogated by express legislation. But on the other hand, in much of those regions, particularly those more settled parts, the Spanish law of community was affirmed and continued to exist in the states created from those regions; specifically, in the states of Arizona, California, Idaho, Louisiana, Nevada, New Mexico, Texas and Washington. And in 1939 it was restored in Oklahoma, and in 1943 in Oregon, for temporary periods.[5]

Where the community system had not been abrogated it remained

[2] See Vance, Background of Hispanic-American Law, 1943.

[3] See Lobingier, 63 Am. Law Rev. 250, 272; ibid., 14 Am. Bar Ass'n Jour. 214, exhaustively citing the cases; see also White, vol. 1, p. xi.

English law has always recognized the difference between a colony or possession obtained by conquest or cession where there was an established system of law and an uninhabited or practically uninhabited territory discovered and settled by Englishmen. In the former the local system of laws remains in force until actually declared to be replaced by the law of England. Cooper v. Stewart (1889), 14 A. C. 286; Blankard v. Galdy (1693), 2 Salk. 411; Blackstone, I Comm. 107.

[4] American Ins. Co. v. Canter, 1 Pet. (U. S.) 511, 7 L. Ed. 242, per Marshall, C. J.; Mitchell v. United States, 9 Pet. (U. S.) 711, 9 L. Ed. 283, with particular reference to Florida.

The Supreme Court of Utah recognized this principle in First Nat. Bank v. Kinner (1873), 1 Utah 100, 106, but distorted it by resorting to the ingenious argument that the court could determine what law had been adopted by the common or tacit consent of the people even though the law-making power had not yet acted. So, in effect, the court arrogated to itself the powers of the legislative department.

[5] See specific treatments in the sections following.

in force with exactly the principles formulated by the community property law of Spain. It is important to notice this, for its continued existence would not be affected by statutes enacted, unless those statutes altered or modified those principles in some way. Therefore, unless altered, modified or repealed by statute, those principles still remain the law of our community property states. The existing statutes, in the main, however, are merely declaratory of the community property law of Spain, as has been recognized by the courts.[6] Where the existing Spanish or Spanish-Mexican law of community property in force was continued by virtue of constitutional provision, as it was in California, Nevada and Texas, the then existing principles of community property were necessarily continued in force and effect in those states and continue to be in force as part of the community property system in those states. It is true that the constitutional provisions do not set out all those principles in specific language. But to do so would have been, of course, extremely inconvenient, if not verging on the impossible in a document such as a constitution. It is obvious, however, that the constitutional provision providing for community of property must mean a community of property according to some system with established principles, and it is equally obvious that the system provided for was the continuation of the system already in force and effect in the respective states at that time: that is to say, the Spanish community property system.[7] It is even more obvious, although it seems largely forgotten, that the state legislatures cannot constitutionally abrogate the community property system so incorporated in the constitutional framework or alter the principles of such system, for to attempt such alteration tends to substitute a system not in accord with that provided for by the constitution. It is probable, indeed, that many of the present legislative enactments in these states are in fact unconstitutional and invalid.[8] The situation differs somewhat in those states in which the community property system was continued without

---

[6] See ante, Chap. I.

[7] "It is not expressly declared (in the state constitution) what right or title she shall possess in the common property, nor is common property defined; but at the time of the formation of the Constitution, it was a term of well-known signification in the laws then in force, and a right on the wife's part in property of that character was recognized by the Constitution." Dow v. Gould & Curry Silver Mining Co., 31 Cal. 630.

[8] In Texas, the unconstitutionality of occasional legislation has sometimes been declared by the courts. See, e.g.,

Arnold v. Leonard, 114 Tex. 535, 273 S.W. 799.

And in Nevada it seems to have been considered that it was the Spanish-Mexican community property law as administered in Mexico and under early statutes of California that was adopted in Nevada and that it is to those sources that the Nevada courts must look for solutions. See Nixon v. Brown, 46 Nev. 439, 214 P. 524. Similarly in New Mexico, see McDonald v. Senn, 53 N.M. 198, 204 P.2d 990, 10 A.L.R. 966.

Notice the action of the California Supreme Court, despite the constitu-

benefit of constitutional provision. It continues to exist, of course, so long as not abrogated by legislative enactment and exists unchanged in its principles except as specific legislation may have altered or amended those principles. It is doubtful that the so-called "comprehensive" statutes on community property enacted in some states have had the effect of abrogating principles not actually covered by such statutes. The principles are so many that even these "comprehensive" statutes nowhere near approach covering all of them. Unless, therefore, such "comprehensive" statutes expressly state that all previous existing law of community property is abrogated or repealed, and the new statute itself is to represent the whole law of the subject, it is more reasonable to construe that principles not touched on by the "comprehensive" statute are still effective. Indeed, some astonishing holes will be found to exist in the community property system if this construction is not followed. Undoubtedly, in states where community of property never existed or where it had been displaced by another system, statutes enacted which adopt or re-adopt a community property system and abrogate any conflicting system must be construed to present the complete law of the adopted system, at least to a degree. But even here, it will frequently be impossible to give full effect and interpretation to the enacted statutes unless basic principles of the system are considered and used to interpret, explain and fill in gaps in the statutes.[9]

§ 38. New France.

The French possessions on the North American continent originally comprised an enormous extent of territory. They included most of Canada, the region between the Alleghenies on the east and the Rockies on the west, the territory along the Mississippi River to the Gulf of Mexico and most of the gulf coastal regions from western Florida to Texas. This immense region was governed as two colonies, that of Canada and that of Louisiana. Canada, however, was explored and settled by the French long before Louisiana was. In fact it was from Canada that the explorations were begun of the Mississippi

---

tional provision for the continuation of the existing community property system, in declaring unconstitutional a legislative enactment merely declaratory of an important principle of the existing system to the effect that income from separate property was community property. See post, § 71. Since the existing system had been continued by the constitution, it is difficult to see by what authority the court could assume to hack off and toss aside one of the basic principles of that system.

[9] See post, §§ 43, 46. "The law in this state regarding the property rights of husband and wife is statutory, but was modeled after the civil law of Spain and Mexico and those laws will be looked to for definitions and interpretations." McDonald v. Senn, 53 N.M. 198, 204 P.2d 990, 10 A.L.R. 966. The same question has come up in regard to Arizona, California and Nevada. See post, §§ 50, 52, 53.

region which came to constitute Louisiana.[10] Both Canada and Louisiana derived their law from the Custom of Paris which, as we have seen, included the community property system.[11]

In 1763, by the Peace of Paris, at the close of the war known in our history as the French and Indian Wars and in Europe as the Seven Years War, France was compelled to cede part of these immense possessions to her victorious enemy, England, and the rest to her ally, Spain, in consideration of the losses sustained by the latter.[12] The town of New Orleans on the east side of the Mississippi and all of Louisiana on the west side of that river went to Spain. Canada and the French possessions around and south of the Great Lakes and east of the Mississippi went to England. Thus the Mississippi became the western boundary of the English North American possessions and the eastern boundary of the Spanish possessions. The latter continued to be known as Louisiana, although much of the territory formerly part of it, such as that now included in the present state of Illinois, was now definitely parted from Louisiana and placed under English rule.[13] However, it was this Louisiana as it thereafter existed which later, in the main, made up the territory this country acquired under the Louisiana Purchase. But before taking up more specifically the legal history of Louisiana, let us digress to trace the fate of the community property system in those French possessions which were ceded to England and later became part of our own country.

§ 39.   — Northwest Territory.

In the French possessions ceded to England, the French inhabitants were left by that country undisturbed as to their local laws and customs. This continued to be true after the American Revolution, as to the inhabitants of that part of the French possessions which still remained under the English crown, that is, Canada. The result has been that the Province of Quebec, which was created from that part of Canada most heavily inhabited by French people, still retains the community property system.[14]

However, there was a different result as to those former French possessions ceded to England and which England recognized as part of this country at the close of the American Revolution. This region, which was roughly that enclosed by the Great Lakes, the Alleghenies and the Ohio and Mississippi rivers, was but sparsely settled by the French, the most important settlement in size being those of Kaskaskia,

---

[10] Louisiana, see post, § 40 et seq.

[11] See ante, § 14; post, § 40.

[12] Spain was compelled to cede Florida to England. See post, § 44.

[13] See Avery, History of the United States, vol. 4, pp. 332, 333; White, vol. 1, p. 709 et seq., vol. 2, p. 508 et seq.

The cession was made in 1762 but the treaty was not finally confirmed by all the parties until 1763.

[14] See ante, Chap. II, § 14.

Cahokia and Vincennes, the first two of which were in what is now Illinois, the last named in what is now Indiana.[15] As the American settlers spread into this great region, mostly virgin, uninhabited country, they found that theoretically it was governed by a law with which they were unfamiliar and as to which there was little, if any, source material available. Without the means of learning any of the advantages of the existing law, their tendency was to introduce their own law.[16] Thus when the Ordinance of 1787 organized and established this region as the Northwest Territory, that ordinance put into force the common law derived from England. Certainly the provision therein as to the widow's right of dower is entirely inconsistent with any theory of community property which must accordingly be considered to have been abrogated.[17]

This view as to the common law has been taken by the Wisconsin Supreme Court, which declared that the English common law so far as it was applicable to local conditions was in force in that state, and that it was established as the law by the Ordinance of 1787 for the Northwest Territory and later expressly by the constitution of Wisconsin.[18] On the other hand, in Michigan the Custom of Paris was recognized as undoubtedly having been in force there, but it was expressly abrogated by the territorial legislature in 1810.[19] In any event, it is to be noticed that none of the states formed from the Northwest Territory — Ohio, Indiana, Michigan, Illinois and Wis-

[15] Charters for exclusive trading privileges in Louisiana granted by the King of France to Antoine Crozat and later to the Company of the West, and which established the Custom of Paris as the law of the colony, expressly included the Illinois country. More specifically as to these charters, see post, § 40.

[16] See Crane v. Reeder (1870) 21 Mich. 24, 4 Am. Rep. 430, wherein the court notes that the Michigan territorial legislature found it necessary in 1810 to abolish expressly the Custom of Paris and the English, French, Canadian, Northwest Territory and Indiana statutes which may have been in force "for the reason that they did not exist in any attainable form, and the people were liable to be ensnared by their ignorance."

[17] See the Ordinance of 1787 as to estates of those dying intestate with the injunction as to "saving in all cases to the widow of the intestate, her third part of the real estate for life, and one third of the personal estate."

[18] Coburn v. Harvey (1864) 18 Wis. 147. See also O'Ferrall v. Simplot (1857) 4 Iowa 399: "But the Ordinance of 1787, for the government of the Northwest Territory, made it [the common law] the law of that country; and that was extended over Wisconsin, and the laws of Wisconsin, over Iowa."

[19] Lorman v. Benson (1860) 8 Mich. 18, 25, where the court said, however: "Practically the common law has prevailed here, in ordinary matters, since our government took possession; and the country has grown up under it. . . . A custom which is as old as the American settlements, and which has been universally recognized by every department of government, has made it the law of the land, if not made so otherwise." While this is mere dictum, in view of the express legislative action, it is to be noticed that it is not in accord with canons of international law as recognized by the United States Supreme Court, ante, § 36.

"But we are bound to know, as a matter of legal history, that the law

consin — has retained the community property system originally established by the Custom of Paris.

§ 40. Louisiana Purchase.

While the Spaniards under De Soto had explored much of the Mississippi in the sixteenth century, no permanent settlements resulted therefrom. In the seventeenth century the French began their explorations of the region, pushing southward from the Great Lakes. In 1673, Joliet and Marquette, and in 1680, LaSalle, made explorations of the Mississippi and its tributaries; and in 1682 LaSalle journeyed all the way to the mouth of the Mississippi, taking possession of the country in the name of, and calling it Louisiana in honor of the French king Louis XIV.[20]

In 1699, the French first approached the Louisiana territory by way of the Gulf of Mexico and made their first settlement, building a fort on Biloxi Bay, in the present state of Mississippi, and which was the first capital of the colony. In 1702 the capital was moved to a settlement established on Mobile Bay, in the present state of Alabama, and finally in 1722 to New Orleans, the foundations of which city had been laid in 1718.[21]

In the colony of Louisiana the Custom of Paris was definitely established as the law in 1712 by the charter granting the exclusive right to trade in the colony to Antoine Crozat. When he surrendered his charter in 1717 and the same privileges were thereupon granted to the "Company of the West" (which later became the "Company of the West Indies"), its charter also established the Custom of Paris as the fundamental law of the colony.[22] The Custom of Paris remained

which governed this territory in civil matters, prior to the taking effect of the ordinance [of 1787], and when Jay's treaty was negotiated, was the French law, including the Custom of Paris, as modified by royal edicts." Crane v. Reeder (1870) 21 Mich. 24, 4 Am. Rep. 430.

Modern temporary enactment of a community property law, see post, § 53.1.

[20] See Avery, History of the United States, vol. 3, chap. 9; Howe, Roman and Civil Law in America, 16 Harv. Law Rev. 342.

[21] See Avery, History of the United States, vol. 3, chap. 22; White, vol. 2, pp. 645-656. Incidentally, the first permanent settlement on the Mississippi River south of Illinois was the present city of Natchez, Miss.

[22] Avery, History of the United States, vol. 3, pp. 319, 320; White,

vol. 1, pp. 624 et seq., 704-708, vol. 2, pp. 188-190; Kaskaskia v. McClure (1897) 163 Ill. 23, 47 N.E. 72.

"Our edicts, ordinances, and customs, and the usages of the mayoralty and shrievealty of Paris shall be observed for laws and customs in the said country of Louisiana." Extract from grant by King of France to Crozat, Sept. 24, 1712.

"XV. The judges established in all the said places shall be bound to administer justice according to the laws and statutes of the kingdom, and more particularly according to the common law of the provosty and viscounty of Paris, which shall be followed in all the contracts the inhabitants shall pass, and no other law shall be allowed to be introduced, to avoid confusion." Extract from grant by King of France to Company of the West, Aug. 1717.

the law of Louisiana until Spain took possession of the colony under the Peace of Paris.[23]

Although the treaty, known as the Peace of Paris, ceding Louisiana to Spain was confirmed in 1763, it was not until 1769 that Count Alexander O'Reilly arrived with Spanish forces and formally took possession of the colony for Spain.[24] In the same year he issued a proclamation which made the Spanish law the law of Louisiana.[25] Although some doubt was expressed later, particularly by President Jefferson, that this proclamation did nothing more than change the civil organization and judicial procedure and that the French law still remained in force,[26] that the Spanish law was introduced is shown conclusively by the proclamation itself and by the report to the King of Spain in 1772 by the Council and Chamber of the Indies on O'Reilly's acts and recommendations. The report, in part, declares

---

[23] See ante, § 38.

[24] A Spanish nobleman and captain-general with the arresting name of O'Reilly is worthy of more than a passing mention. Born about 1722 in Ireland as his name indicates, he entered the Spanish military service as a young man and served in the campaigns against the Austrians in Italy. Subsequently, in 1757 he served in the Austrian army against the Prussians, then in 1759 joined the French army. Invited to return to the Spanish army with the rank of colonel, he rose rapidly in that service, becoming major-general and governor of Havana, from whence he was sent to take possession of Louisiana. Thereafter, he was inspector general of infantry and governor of Madrid. As a foreigner he was the object of much jealousy, but nevertheless when in 1793 France declared war on Spain, despite his advanced years he was considered the only general capable of leading the armies. He died suddenly while on his way to take over the command, March 23, 1794. See Dictionary of National Biography, vol. 14.

[25] See Howe, Roman and Civil Law in America, 16 Harv. Law Rev. 342; Wigmore, Louisiana: The Story of Its Jurisprudence, 22 Am. Law Rev. 890.
"It was under these circumstances that O'Reilly issued a proclamation, changing the form of the government of Louisiana, abolishing the authority of the French laws, and substituting those of Spain in their stead. This proclamation which was accompanied by an ordinance, establishing the several branches of the new government of Louisiana, and defining their respective powers, appears to have been published on the 26th of November 1769. From the time of its promulgation until now, the French laws ceased to have any authority in this country, and all controversies were tried and decided conformably to the Spanish laws, by a tribunal, of which the governor was the only judge, though he was bound to take the advice of a lawyer (lettrado) appointed and commissioned to that effect, by the king of Spain, and called the Auditor of War. From all the judgments of the governor's tribunal, there was an appeal to the Royal Audience, sitting at Puerto Principe, in the island of Cuba, and presided by the capt. general of that Island." Lislet and Carleton, Introduction, Las Siete Partidas.

That the French conventional community (i.e., by marriage contract) continued to exist after the French legal community was displaced by the Spanish, see Childers v. Cutter, 16 Mo. 41, 42; Cutter v. Waddingham, 22 Mo. 206, 257. Conventional and legal community, see post, § 54.

[26] See White, vol. 2, pp. 692, 693; Cutter v. Waddingham (1855) 22 Mo. 252.

that "General O'Reilly, in his second statement, considers it necessary that the said province [Louisiana] should be subject to the same laws as the other dominions in America; that all the proceedings should be carried on in the Spanish language. . . . Your majesty approved these dispositions of O'Reilly and the Council, considering this as an evidence of the advantages to be derived," then recommended that the necessary decrees be issued.[27]

Because Spain by the secret treaty of St. Ildefonso in 1800 re-ceded Louisiana to France, which in turn sold it to the United States in 1803, it is quite commonly assumed that French law was re-established in Louisiana during this three-year interim. Such definitely was not the case. France did not actually take formal possession until about three weeks before turning the territory over to this country and in that brief period France made no change in the law of Louisiana.[28] Of course, whether the Spanish law or the Custom of Paris prevailed, in either event the community property system would have prevailed in the Louisiana territory when it became a part of this country, but accuracy as to which law governed is essential to our consideration. For when it is understood that the Spanish law of community governed in the Louisiana Purchase, it becomes at once apparent that the community system in the states created from the Louisiana Purchase is derived from the same source and is uniform with the community system prevailing in the other community property states.[29]

A brief review of the period will provide a proper explanation of the continuance of the Spanish law in the Louisiana Purchase. During the years of the American Revolution and especially in the years immediately following there was a steady emigration of Americans across the Alleghenies into what was then the western part of our country, that is, the region between the Alleghenies and the Mississippi River. Because the rivers in that day provided a ready means of transportation, the Mississippi and its tributaries were the scene of a flourishing trade. The settlers, in this western region particularly, developed a considerable trade down the Mississippi to New Orleans, which provided an outlet for the sale of their goods as well as the source of many necessary commodities. During this period New

[27] Report to King of Spain on Don A. O'Reilly's Statements, by Council and Chamber of the Indies, Feb. 27, 1772, set out in full in White, vol. 2, pp. 462-467.

"This publication [of O'Reilly's proclamation] followed from that moment by an uninterrupted observance of the Spanish law has been received as an introduction of the Spanish law in all its parts and must be considered as having repealed the laws formerly prevailing in Louisiana, whether they had continued in force by the tacit or express consent of the [French] government." Beard v. Poydras (1816) 4 Mart. (La.) 368. See also Saul v. His Creditors, 6 Mart. N.S. (La.) 569, 16 Am. Dec. 212; Cole's Widow v. His Executors, 7 Mart. N.S. (La.) 41, 18 Am. Dec. 241; and post, § 41.

[28] See post, this section.

[29] See post, § 41. And see Pugh, The Spanish Community of Gains in 1803, 30 La. Law Rev. 1 (1969).

Orleans and the mouth of the Mississippi were in Spanish hands, and satisfactory, or at least partially satisfactory, arrangements had been made with the Spanish authorities for such entry and trade. There was a fear, however, among our people that the mouth of the Mississippi might pass under the control of a strong nation which from enmity or otherwise might close New Orleans to American trade; and this fear was accompanied by a determination to take strong steps to prevent any such occurrence.

When France obtained a re-cession of Louisiana from Spain in 1800 by the Treaty of St. Ildefonso, the treaty was kept secret by France, both because of the American attitude and because of fear that England might seize the colony. Accordingly, France made no effort to take formal possession of Louisiana and it was left under the control of Spain. The royal order of the King of Spain in October, 1802, officially informing his officials in Louisiana of re-cession of the colony to France and directing them to put the authorized French representative in possession when he should arrive, concludes with the order that meanwhile "the ordinary judges may, together with established tribunals, continue to administer justice according to the laws, and customs in force in the colony."[30] This injunction was repeated in the official proclamation to the inhabitants of the colony by the Spanish governor informing them of the re-cession to France.[31]

Despite the precautions of France, news of the treaty leaked out and caused much disturbance of mind in the United States. President Jefferson referred openly to the necessity of war against France or alliance with England; and in his message to Congress in December, 1802, he spoke of the seriousness to this country of French suzerainty of Louisiana. Both the president and Congress seemed to be agreed that the proper solution of the problem was to attempt the purchase of New Orleans and the mouth of the Mississippi. Accordingly, both houses of Congress voted to appropriate two million dollars for such purchase, and the Senate confirmed Jefferson's appointment of Monroe as special envoy to France to negotiate for such a purchase. Thereupon, Monroe and Livingston, our minister to France, carried on the negotiations for the purchase of New Orleans, and no one was more thunderstruck than they when France offered to sell the entire province. With commendable vigor they assumed the responsibility of going beyond their instructions and contracted to purchase the entire province for seventeen million dollars. It is history, of course, that both the president and Congress approved their action and the purchase was consummated. The treaty between the two countries was ratified Oct. 1, 1803.[32] France then proceeded to take formal possession from Spain in order that it might in turn formally deliver possession to

[30] Royal order set out in White, vol. 2, pp. 190-192.
[31] Proclamation of May 18, 1803, set out in White, vol. 2, pp. 192-194.
[32] Avery, History of the United States, vol. 7, chap. 18.

this country, and it did formally receive possession from Spain on Nov. 30, 1803. Thereafter, on Dec. 20, 1803, France delivered possession of Louisiana to this country. During this brief period of occupation by the French, they made no alteration in the Spanish law which governed.[33] This fact that no change was made and that the Spanish law was in force and effect when the region became part of this country has been recognized by the states created from this region, as well by those which later abrogated the Spanish law,[34] as by those which retained it.[35]

§ 41.   — Territory of Orleans; State of Louisiana.

Congress organized the Louisiana Purchase into two territories, that south of the thirty-third parallel as the Territory of Orleans, that north of it as the District, then the Territory, of Louisiana.[36] The act of Congress provided that all laws in force in the Territory of Orleans at the commencement of the act, and not inconsistent with its provisions, should continue in force until altered, modified or repealed by the legislature.[37]

As early as 1807, the territorial legislature of Orleans, which in

[33] Lislet and Carleton, Introduction to Las Siete Partidas: "The return of Louisiana under the dominion of France, and its transfer to the United States, did not for a moment, weaken the Spanish laws in that province. The French, during the short continuation of their power, from the 30th November to the 20th December 1803, made no alteration in the jurisprudence of the country; and the government of of the United States, left the task of legislation to the people of Louisiana themselves, giving to them the right to make whatever changes they might deem necessary in the existing system of their laws, (see sect. 11, of the act to divide Louisiana into two territories, passed by Congress on the 26th of March 1804, and the fourth section of another act passed the 2nd of March, 1805, to provide for the government of the territory of Orleans. See likewise sect. 4 of the Schedule annexed to the constitution of this state.)"

"When the country was first ceded to Spain, she wisely preserved many of the French regulations, but by almost imperceptible degrees, these have disappeared; and now the prov-ince is governed entirely by the laws of Spain, and ordinances formed expressly for the colony; it is believed that no correct code can possibly be procured; excepting only a few ordinances promulgated and printed by order of General O'Reilly, respecting principally the laws of inheritance and rights of dower (i.e., dowry in the civil law)." Answers to Queries showing the condition of Louisiana in 1803, in answer to Mr. Jefferson, Query No. 16, set out in White, vol. 2, p. 690 et seq.

[34] See post, § 42.

[35] See post, §§ 41, 42.

[36] Act of March 26, 1804, of Eighth Congress, First Session; Act of March 2, 1805, and Act of March 3, 1805, Eighth Congress, Second Session. See also Avery, History of the United States, vol. 7, p. 342 et seq.; Lislet and Carleton, Introduction, Las Siete Partidas; Howe, Roman and Civil Law in America, 16 Harv. Law Rev. 342.

[37] Act of March 26, 1804, sec. 11, Eighth Congress, First Session. To same effect, Act of March 2, 1805, sec. 4, Eighth Congress, Second Session.

1812 was admitted to the Union as the state of Louisiana, recognizing that the ancient Spanish law secured to them by the acts of Congress needed to be made available, ordered a digest of those laws to be made. And later, in 1819, the legislature of the state of Louisiana authorized at its expense a translation of Las Siete Partidas, which it considered as having the force of law in Louisiana.[38] Many writers on the jurisprudence of Louisiana have stated that much of the French Code Napoleon — now the French Civil Code — was made use of in drafting a civil code in Louisiana in 1808 and that the Code Napoleon had a strong influential effect.[39] The assumption has thus appeared, in a number of the later cases of Louisiana and of the United States Supreme Court concerning Louisiana jurisprudence, that present community property principles as set forth in the Louisiana codes have their origin in the French law, and their interpretation and construction has frequently been attempted in the light of French commentaries on community property. On the other hand, it has been pointed out that at the time the civil code was formulated in Louisiana in 1808 the French Code Napoleon was not actually available.[40] Actually the code of 1808 served chiefly to modify, to meet changed conditions, those principles of the law familiar during the colonial period, and these principles were chiefly principles of Spanish law.[41] That the principles

---

[38] Lislet and Carleton, Introduction, Las Siete Partidas, published in 1820, in which the translators say, in part, "This work has been undertaken under the patronage of the legislature of Louisiana, which passed a law on the 3rd of March, 1819, authorizing it to be executed at the expense of the state. It contains a translation of all that portion of Las Siete Partidas which is considered as having the force of law in Louisiana. Those parts which relate to the Catholic faith, and to matters of criminal nature, having been repealed, are therefore entirely omitted."

"When the French colony, known as Louisiana, was ceded to Spain in 1760 (sic), the code known as the Partidas was introduced and became really a large part of the fundamental law of the vast domain. Portions of it were translated into French for the benefit of the inhabitants. Some of its provisions remained as a part of the law of the State of Louisiana, and are referred to in the earlier decisions of her Supreme Court." Howe, Roman and Civil Law in America, 16 Harv. Law Rev. 342.

And see Dart, Influence of Ancient Laws of Spain on Jurisprudence of Louisiana, 6 Tulane L. Rev. 83.

[39] See Wigmore, Louisiana: The Story of Its Jurisprudence, 22 Am. Law Rev. 890; Franklin, Spanish Law in Louisiana, 16 Tulane Law Rev. 319.

[40] Mr. Dart, in his Introduction to the Louisiana Civil Code (1932 Ed.), remarks that it is only "technically correct" to say that the Code of 1808 was a copy of the Code Napoleon.

[41] "However, the legislature of the territory of Orleans, as early as the year 1807, considering that the ancient laws secured to the inhabitants of Louisiana by the acts of Congress, were written in a foreign language, and contained in books difficult to be procured, ordered a digest of those to be made and prepared in the English and French languages, by two jurisconsults. This digest was adopted. by an act passed the 31st of March, 1808, but was not promulgated before the month of November of the same year, when printed copies of it were officially sent to all the tribunals of the territory of Orleans. This code.

of the Spanish law, including the Spanish principles of community property, continued to constitute the basis of the Louisiana law was recognized by the action of the legislature in 1807 and again in 1819, already referred to. Likewise, during and even after this period, it was recognized by the state supreme court that the Spanish law of community property, subject to any statutory modification, continued to be the law of Louisiana. And even statutory modifications were interpreted in the light of Spanish community property principles.[42] Certainly, it would not seem that positive influence from the French Code Napoleon could have become effective until the adoption of the Louisiana Civil Code of 1825. It is to be noticed that by Act No. 83 of 1828 there was an express repeal of all civil laws in force before the adoption of the code of 1825, excepting as to the provisions of the code of 1808 as it treated of the dissolution of marital communities.

In any event, the matter becomes one of academic interest only. To whatever extent the introduction of French civil code provisions, whether at an early or later date, may have influenced the Louisiana civil code, it is apparent from comparison that the Louisiana code provisions are also similar in most particulars to the Spanish principles of community property.[43] And whatever may be said of the French community property system prior to the Code Napoleon, that Code presents a

commonly known under the name of the Civil Code, has therefore become a part of our statute laws. But it is easy to perceive that a work of that nature, however excellent it may be, can only contain general rules and abstract maxims, still leaving many points doubtful in the application of the law; hence the necessity of going back to the original source, in order to obtain new and additional light. It was moreover perceived that the Civil Code did not contain many and important provisions of the Spanish laws still in force, nor any rules of judicial proceedings; that the statutes regulating these proceedings had proved insufficient; and that the Superior Court had in divers instances, and particularly in the case of Cottin v. Cottin, Martin's Rep. Vol. 5, p. 93, determined that the Spanish laws 'must be considered as untouched whenever the alterations and amendments introduced in the digest do not reach them; and that such parts of those laws only are repealed, as are either contrary to, or incompatible with the provisions of the code.' It thus appeared that a much greater portion of the Spanish laws remained in force than had been at first supposed. It was then doubtless the desire of the legislature to spread generally the knowledge of such of these laws as are not to be found in the Civil Code, or in the digest of our statutes, that induced them to make provisions for the printing of this translation. They felt the force and justice of that acknowledged rule of reason, that in order to inforce obedience to the laws, it is necessary that they should be fully understood by the people." Lislet and Carleton, Introduction to their translation of Las Siete Partidas, authorized by the Legislature.

42 Beard v. Poydras (1816) 4 Mart. (La.) 368; Saul v. His Creditors (1827) 6 Mart. N.S. (La.) 569, 16 Am. Dec. 212; Cole's Widow v. His Executors (1828) 7 Mart. N.S. (La.) 41, 18 Am. Dec. 241; Cottin v. Cottin, 5 Mart. O.S. (La.) 93.

43 See Daggett, Community Property System of Louisiana, p. 4: "The customary or unwritten law of Northern France was incorporated into the Code Napoleon upon which the

system which in such particulars as recognizing an immediate half interest in the wife follows closely the outlines of the Spanish system.[44]

The community property system has, of course, remained the law of Louisiana, and its interpretation by the Louisiana courts, particularly in the earlier cases, is extremely invaluable because of the fact that Louisiana has retained the civil law in almost all other respects so that its courts' interpretations are in the light of the civil law and not attempts to interpret marital property rights by applying common law principles.[45]

§ 42.   — Territory of Louisiana.

As stated in the preceding section, Congress organized the Louisiana Purchase into two territories, that of Orleans which later became the state of Louisiana, and the District, later the Territory, of Louisiana, which included all of that region north of the thirty-third parallel.[46] The latter territory was so great in extent and so unknown in large part that its boundaries were extremely vague to the westward and northwestward. However, a treaty between the United States and Spain in 1819 did much to clarify the boundaries between this territory and the possessions still remaining to Spain in the western part of the continent.[47]

The acts establishing first the District and then the Territory of Louisiana provided that the laws and regulations in force therein and not inconsistent with the provisions of the acts should continue in force until altered, modified or repealed by the legislature.[48] This, of

present Louisiana Civil Code was patterned. The community system, however, made its way to colonial Louisiana before the adoption of the first code in 1808 via the Custom of Paris and the laws of Spain." See also Howe, Roman and Civil Law in America, 16 Harv. Law Rev. 342; McKay, Community Property, 2nd Ed., p. 1032; Dart, Influence of Ancient Law of Spain, etc. 6 Tulane L. Rev. 83.

Present evidence of French influence derives from Code Napoleon. Pecquet v. Pecquet's Ex'r, 17 La. Ann. 204.

[44] See French Civil Code (Cachard, Rev. Ed.) § 1399 et seq.; De Nicols v. Curlier, [1900] App. Cas. 21.

[45] Formerly, the most thorough and exhaustive treatise on the present community property law of Louisiana was Daggett's Community Property System of Louisiana with Comparative Studies, Louisiana State Univ. Press, 1931. More recent discussions and outlines will be found in the annotated codes of the state. And see the helpful outline by Oppenheim in 21 Temple L. Quart. 235. Effect of 1944 enactments, see Daggett, 6 La. L. Rev. 1; Oppenheim, 19 Tulane L. Rev. 200.

[46] See Act of March 26, 1804, §§ 12-16, Eighth Congress, First Session; Act, March 1805, Eighth Congress, Second Session.

[47] Treaty provisions in part, see Appendix IV, vol. 2, 1943 edition of this work.

The Oregon Country as included in the Louisiana Purchase, see post, § 46.

[48] See Act of March 26, 1804, § 13, Eighth Congress, First Session; Act of March 3, 1805, § 9, Eighth Congress, Second Session. And see Howe, Law in the Louisiana Purchase, 14 Yale Law Jour. 77.

course, continued in effect the existing community property laws, but a territorial act of July 4, 1807, providing for a widow's right of dower has been considered by the Supreme Court of Missouri to have had the effect of displacing the community system.[49] However, other states formed from the Missouri Territory created in 1816 trace the displacement of the community system in the Missouri Territory, and thus in all states formed therefrom, to an act of the territorial legislature of Missouri in 1816 making the common law the rule of decision.[50] This seems to be the view of the courts of Arkansas[51] and of Iowa.[52]

As a matter of interest, we may notice that Montana by its Probate Practice Act, § § 551, 557 (Comp. Stats. 1888, § § 551, 557), enacted prior to its statehood in 1889, had two statutes relating to the disposition of community property upon dissolution of the marriage by the death of one of the spouses. These provisions were apparently taken from the California Civil Code, but whether adopted by some mistake is difficult to say.[53] In remarking upon one of these statutes the Montana Supreme Court said: "This species of property right, called 'community property,' is certainly not indigenous to this jurisdiction; and, as an exotic, it has not been transplanted with sufficient root to develop a form having definite attributes or symmetrical proportions."[54] It appears that the legislature had omitted from the Revised Statutes of 1879 the entire chapter on dower, and whether this coupled with the enactment of the community property statutes indicated an intention to adopt the community property system is a moot ques-

---

[49] Spanish community property law remained in effect in Missouri until territorial act of July 4, 1807, providing for dower, took effect. Riddick v. Walsh (1852) 15 Mo. 519, 534.

That the French conventional community still continued to exist in Missouri after French legal community was displaced by the Spanish, see Childers v. Cutter (1852) 16 Mo. 41, 42; Cutter v. Waddingham (1855) 22 Mo. 206, 257.

[50] It may be noted that this act of the Missouri territorial legislature making the common law the rule of decision did so insofar as the common law was not contrary to the laws of the territory. Geyer's Dig. 124, cited in Grande v. Foy (1831) Hemp. (Ark.) 105.

[51] Grande v. Foy (1831) Hemp. (Ark.) 105, which adds, however, "We are induced to believe, however, from the numerous common law phrases and terms in our statutes anterior to the passage of the law of

1816, that it [the common law] must have been adopted either by statutory provision or common consent at an earlier day. As far back as the year 1807, we find most of the common law actions mentioned in the acts of the legislature of [the Territory of] Louisiana."

[52] The Iowa court has argued that displacement by common consent or customs of new settlers without the necessity of formal legislation is valid but its argument seems unnecessary in the face of the fact that the court admits that Iowa was a part of Missouri territory when the common law was there substituted for the civil law, and that the laws of Wisconsin which were extended to Iowa had substituted the common law. O'Ferrall v. Simplot, 4 Iowa 399.

[53] See Ballard, Real Property, vol. 3, § 83.

[54] Chadwick v. Tatem, 9 Mont. 370, 23 P. 729.

tion, for the Supreme Court held that the chapter on dower was not expressly or impliedly repealed,[55] and of course its existence as well as subsequent statutory law on dower is inconsistent with the community property system.[56] It is true that recent statutes provide that a husband and wife may hold real or personal property together, jointly or *in common* and that their property rights are to be governed other than by the usual law,[57] but if thereby the holding of property in community is authorized, it seems not to be availed of at the time of this writing.

§ 43.   The Floridas.

Any discussion of the Floridas might be deemed unimportant on the ground that although the community system was in effect there under Spain and France, it is no longer in effect in those states formed wholly or partly from that territory. However, there are certain features which make that region worthy of notice in a work such as this.

Formerly, the name Florida was applied to two colonies, East Florida and West Florida, referred to collectively as the Floridas. At the time of the Peace of Paris in 1763, by which Spain ceded the Floridas to England, the boundaries of East and West Florida were as follows. East Florida was bounded on the west by the Apalachicola River and on the north by a line drawn from that part of such river where the Chattahoochee and Flint rivers meet, to the source of the St. Mary's River and along that river to the Atlantic. West Florida extended from the Apalachicola River to Lakes Pontchartrain and Maurepas and the Mississippi River and on the north was bounded by the thirty-first degree of latitude.[58]

Historically, Florida represents the earliest settled portion of our country. The Spaniards explored eastern Florida in the sixteenth century and in 1565 laid the foundations of St. Augustine, our oldest city. And in 1696 they founded Pensacola in western Florida. However, Spanish Florida remained chiefly a system of military posts to insure control of the Gulf of Mexico.[59] Much later, as mentioned previously in this chapter, the French settled along the gulf coast of southern Mississippi and Alabama and western Florida, and for a long period this section was part of the French colony of Louisiana.[60] Lying as it did between the chief French settlements on the Mississippi River

---

[55] Chadwick v. Tatem, 9 Mont. 370, 23 P. 729.

[56] See Mont. Rev. Codes 1935, ch. 8.

[57] Mont. Rev. Codes 1935, §§ 5789, 5803.

[58] See Proclamation of King of Great Britain, set out in White, vol. 2, pp. 292, 293.

The Perdido River represents the western boundary of the present state of Florida, but its northern boundary is still the thirty-first parallel and the rivers mentioned. Fla. Const., 1885, art. I.

[59] Avery, History of the United States, vol. 3, p. 327.

[60] See ante, § 38.

and the Spanish settlements in East Florida, it was long fought over by the two countries. Ultimately, it passed to Spain which governed it under the name of West Florida. In 1763, by the Peace of Paris, Spain ceded the Floridas to England. But shortly thereafter, in the general treaty of peace at the end of the American Revolution, England returned East and West Florida to Spain.

In 1803, when the United States purchased Louisiana, it claimed that much of West Florida was included in Louisiana and in 1812 it took forcible possession of much of this territory and put much pressure on the Spaniards in East Florida. Even at the time there were Americans who believed our claim unjustified and now, with the documents and information we have at our disposal, it would clearly appear so.[61] Any argument is now moot, however, for by treaty with Spain in 1819 we obtained title to both the Floridas.[62] All of East Florida and part of West Florida were incorporated into the present state of Florida, while the remainder of West Florida became part of the states of Alabama and Mississippi.[63]

It is thus immediately apparent that, as in the case of Louisiana, the Spanish community property system was in effect in the Floridas, and indeed it continued to be the law of the territory after it was ceded to the United States until expressly altered.[64] While the community system was superseded, the territorial legislature of Florida in 1824 expressly secured the property rights of husband and wife derived previous to the cession of Florida to the United States,[65] and the Florida courts have several times adjudicated the property rights of husband and wife arising under the Spanish community property law.[66]

The Florida state constitution of 1885, art. XI, contains express provisions relating to a married woman's separate property but contains nothing that would be foreign to the existence of a community property system. However, the legislation is definitely modeled after the English common law and the community system does not exist,[67] although as recently as 1941 it has approvingly been declared by the Florida Supreme Court that there is a perfectly sound basis for the community property rule that husband and wife share equally in

[61] See White, vol. 2, pp. 508-516.

[62] Treaty in part, see Appendix IV, C. in vol. 2 of 1943 edition of this work.

[63] That the community system existed at one time in what is now Alabama, see McVoy v. Hallett (1847) 11 Ala. 864, 867.

Western boundary of present state of Florida, see ante, n. 58.

[64] American Ins. Co. v. Canter, 1 Pet. (U.S.) 511, 7 L. Ed. 242, per Marshall, C. J.

[65] Pub. Act of Territory of Florida, p. 45, still preserved as Rev. Gen. Stat. 1920, § 3946.

As to establishment of English common law, see Hart v. Bostwick, 14 Fla. 16.

[66] McHardy v. McHardy's Ex'rs (1857) 7 Fla. 301; MaGee v. Doe (1861) 9 Fla. 382, 398; Commodore's Point Terminal Co. v. Hudnall (D.C. Fla. 1922) 283 Fed. 150, 183.

[67] See Fla. Rev. Gen. Stats. 1920.

all property accumulated during coverture and that it will apply that rule in Florida where the circumstances warrant.[68]

§ 44.   Texas.

The history of Texas represents one of the most interesting and adventurous chapters in the story of the development of our country. It is unfortunate that limitations of space and the scope of this work prevent more than the barest outline, since its history is one that can never be repeated too often. It must suffice to say, however, that permission from the Spanish government was originally obtained by Moses Austin in 1821 for Americans to settle in what later became the Mexican state of Coahuila and Texas. Upon his death shortly thereafter, his son, Stephen F. Austin, proceeded to carry out his plans, and in December, 1821, the first colonists arrived. However, in 1824, Mexico achieved its independence from Spain and proclaimed itself a republic. Austin then had to make the long difficult trip overland to Mexico City to obtain grant of approval of his plan from the new government. This he eventually succeeded in accomplishing after many hardships, difficulties and delays.[69]

During the years following many settlers arrived in Texas from the United States. Eventually, repeated difficulties with the Mexican government and what the colonists considered its unjust restrictions and impositions resulted in the Texas War for Independence which successfully culminated in the establishment of the Republic of Texas in 1836.[70]

It has already been remarked in a previous chapter that the Spanish laws, including the community property system, remained the basic law of Mexico after it achieved its independence from Spain.[71] These laws also continued for some time to constitute the laws of the Republic of Texas,[72] being confirmed by the Constitution of 1836,[73] until on Jan. 20, 1840, the Republic adopted the common law as the law of the Republic, but expressly retained the community property

---

[68] Strauss v. Strauss, 148 Fla. 23, 3 So.2d 727, per Terrell, J.

[69] See White, vol. 1, pp. 559-583.

[70] Texas Declaration of Independence. See also Amaya v. Stanolind Oil & Gas Co., (D.C. Tex.) 62 F. Supp. 181.

[71] See ante, § 15.

[72] Joseph M. White noted in his invaluable work in 1839 that the laws of Spain, "are the present laws of that young and rapidly increasing Republic." White, vol. 1, p. xi.

"The laws of Mexico, of force in Texas previous to the Texan Revolution, were the laws not of a foreign, but of an antecedent government, to which the Government of the United States, through the medium of the Republic of Texas, is the direct successor. Its laws are not deemed foreign laws, for as to that portion of our territory they are domestic laws; and we take judicial notice of them." United States v. Perot, (1879) 98 U.S. 428, 25 L. Ed. 251, per Bradley, J.

[73] Tex. Const. 1836, Schedule, § 1.

system as to "land and slaves."[74] In 1845, when Texas joined the Union as a state, its first state constitution expressly continued the community property system, but restored it to include all property,[75] and pursuant thereto, the legislature in 1848 provided that the community should include "all property acquired by either husband or wife during the marriage" but making the usual exclusions as to separate property owned before the marriage and property acquired during the marriage by either spouse by way of gift, descent or devise.[76] The community of property was again confirmed in the Constitution of 1876, and has continued to remain the law of the State of Texas to this day, with some statutory modifications necessary to meet modern conditions.[77]

§ 45.   The Oregon Country.

Whether the Oregon Country, so-called, from which the states of Idaho, Oregon and Washington were formed, was included in the Louisiana Purchase has been a matter of argument. There can be no doubt, however, that our claim to that region is primarily bottomed on the Louisiana Purchase and on the explorations of Lewis and Clark through the West and Northwest immediately after the Louisiana

[74] Gammell, Laws of Texas, vol. 2, pp. 177-180, §§ 3, 4; Paschal's Dig. art. 4641, n. 1048.

The title and provisions of this act show clearly the intention to maintain in reference to marital rights a radically different system from the common law otherwise adopted. Speer, Law of Marital Rights in Texas, 3rd Ed., § 335, citing Barkley v. Dumke, 99 Tex. 150, 87 S.W. 1147. And in Crim v. Austin, (Tex. Com. App.), 6 S.W.2d 348, it was said, "The common law is not, and never has been in force with respect to the marital rights in Texas. They are purely statutory." Similarly, see Edrington v. Mayfield, 5 Tex. 366.

[75] Tex. Const. 1845, art. VII, § 19.

[76] Tex. Laws 1848, ch. 79, §§ 2, 3. And see Speer, Law of Marital Rights in Texas, 3rd Ed., § 336.

[77] Tex. Const. 1876, art. XVI, § 15.

"Texas, with just a few other states of the Union, has adopted as the basis of its laws relating to estates held by husband and wife the principles of the civil law, and our statutory enactments are in large measure declaratory of these principles. This is particularly true with reference to the laws relating to community property." Lee v. Lee, 122 Tex. 392, 247 S.W. 828, whose pronouncement has the effect of discrediting statements of a contrary nature in Routh v. Routh, 57 Tex. 589 and others of like ilk.

Judge Speer refers to "the Spanish civil law, from which in a large degree has sprung our community system." Speer, Law of Marital Rights in Texas, 3rd Ed., § 334. Reference may be made to that work for a collection of the Texas cases on the subject of community property (as well as to the later edition by Oakes) and also to the same author's article, "Husband and Wife" in 23 Texas Jurisprudence. See also Simkins, Some Phases of Law of Community Property in Texas, 3 Tex. Law Rev. 363; Platt, Property Rights of Married Women, affording an excellent comparison between the Texas and the California law prior to 1885; McKnight, The Spanish Legacy to Texas Law, 3 American Jour. of Legal History 222 (1959).

Purchase. Later our title to the Oregon Country was clarified by treaty with England in 1846.[78] The treaty with Spain clearly shows that the boundaries of the Louisiana Purchase were considered to extend to the Pacific Ocean north of the present state of California which was then still part of the Spanish possessions.[79] But whether or not this region was part of the Louisiana Purchase, the circumstances surrounding its development warrant an independent treatment.

The Oregon Territory, including the present states of Idaho, Oregon and Washington, was organized by Congress in 1848,[80] but pending the action of Congress the settlers in that region organized a provisional government in 1843 and a year later provided that the statutes of the Iowa Territory passed in 1839, where not local in character and not incompatible with conditions and circumstances in Oregon, should be the law unless otherwise modified, and that the common law of England and principles of equity, not modified by the statutes of Iowa or of the local government and not incompatible with its principles "shall constitute a part of the law of this land."[81] Aside from any question of the validity of such action by the settlers prior to action by Congress, it will be noticed that the adoption of the Iowa statutes and the English common law to "constitute a part of the law of this land" is in itself so vague as to leave doubt as to what was meant to constitute the "whole" of the law.[82] In any event, after the organization of the territory by Congress in 1848, the territorial legislature by act of 1849 recognized dower, which was thus inconsistent with community of property; and the community property system has never been the law of the region constituting the present state of Oregon, either prior to statehood in 1859 or since statehood,[83] except for a brief period discussed later.[84]

---

[78] See Avery, History of the United States, vol. 7.

Dean Kirkwood states flatly, but without his reasons or authorities therefor, that the suggestion "that this territory was acquired by the United States as a part of the Louisiana Purchase . . . is now recognized as incorrect." Historical Background and Objective of Law of Community Property in Pacific Coast States, 11 Wash. Law Rev. 1.

[79] Treaty provisions in part, see Appendix IV, C, of vol. 2 of 1943 edition of this work.

[80] Act of August 18, 1848, Thirtieth Congress, First Session.

[81] Kirkwood, Historical Background and Objective of Law of Community Property in Pacific Coast States, 11 Wash. Law Rev. 1, citing Abbott, Real Property Statutes of Washington Territory, 1843–1899.

[82] Some of the confusion existing at this period is briefly described by Powell, Critique of Community Property, 11 Wash. Law Rev. 12, 17.

[83] Admitted as state by Act of February 11, 1859, Thirty-Fifth Congress, Second Session.

The only applicable provision of the Constitution of 1857 would seem to be art. XV, § 5: "The property and pecuniary rights of every married woman, at the time of marriage, or afterwards, acquired by gift, devise, or inheritance, shall not be subject to the debts or contracts of the husband, and laws shall be passed providing for the registration of the wife's separate property."

[84] See post, § 53.1.

§ 46.   — Idaho.

It has been remarked of Idaho that the community system apparently does not antedate the statutes of 1867,[85] which are declared to have been borrowed from California.[86] Since Idaho was part of the Oregon Territory until 1853, when part of it was included in the Washington Territory organized in that year and then the remainder of Idaho added to the Washington Territory in 1859 when Oregon was admitted as a state, it would seem clear that the common law which was in force in Oregon and at that time in Washington was also the law of Idaho.[87] In 1863 Idaho was organized as a separate territory[88] and the territorial legislature in 1864 expressly provided that the common law should continue to be the rule of decision.[89] Thus, it seems that 1867 definitely marks the recognition of the community property system in Idaho and it has consistently been the law of Idaho, and the state constitution, upon Idaho's admission as a state in 1890, providing that all laws in force in the territory should remain in force where not repugnant to the constitution until altered or repealed by the legislature,[90] in no way affected but rather confirmed the community system.[91]

§ 47.   — Washington.

Part of the Oregon Territory was in 1853 organized by Congress as the Washington Territory with the provision in the act of organization that the laws of the Oregon Territory should continue in force until repealed or amended.[92] However, it was stipulated that those laws which were continued in force were those enacted and passed in the Oregon Territory subsequent to September 1, 1848,[93] and this most definitely made inapplicable any attempted legislation of the provisional government of Oregon prior to that date, although the act of the territorial legislature of Oregon in 1849 in recognizing dower naturally remained effective.[94] In 1854 the territorial legislature of Washington

[85] Terr. Laws of Idaho, 1866–7, ch. 9.

[86] See Lobingier, History of Conjugal Partnership, 63 Am. Law Rev. 250, 277; ibid., 14 Am. Bar Ass'n Jour. 211; Brockelbank, The Community Property Law of Idaho, State Bar, 1962, ch. 1.

[87] Kirkwood, Historical Background and Objective of Law of Community Property in Pacific Coast States, 11 Wash. Law Rev. 1.

[88] Provision for temporary government of Territory of Idaho, Act of March 3, 1863, Thirty-Seventh Congress, Third Session.

[89] Terr. of Idaho Laws 1864, p. 527. And see Brockelbank, The Community Property Law of Idaho, State Bar, 1962.

[90] Idaho Const. 1890, art. XXI, § 2.

[91] For an excellent discussion of the community property law in Idaho, see Brockelbank, cited above.

[92] 10 U.S. Stat. at Large 172; Act of March 2, 1853, Thirty-Second Congress, Second Session.

[93] Section 12 of above cited act.

[94] See ante, § 46.

itself recognized dower and in 1856 repealed all the laws derived from Oregon and provided that the common law should be the rule of decision. Again in 1860 it recognized curtesy and in 1864 it expressly provided for dower and curtesy.[95] Thus, there is sound authority for the statement that Washington, like Idaho, never actually had the community property system until it was introduced by statute borrowed from California,[96] in this case in 1869.[97] However, while establishing the community property system in 1869, the territorial legislature strangely enough did not abolish dower and curtesy until 1871.[98] Indeed, the early legislators seem to have been infected with some fever of uncertainty, for in 1871 they substituted an entirely different piece of legislation, which has been described as a marital partnership property act,[99] but which was repealed in 1873 and the original act of 1869 substantially restored;[1] the restored act was modified in 1879,[2] and again in 1881, but this last enactment has remained in force since that time, substantially unchanged.[3]

The chief feature of the earlier acts, which that of 1881 changed, was that the community property law governed the property rights of the spouses unless by marriage settlements or postnuptial agreement it was provided otherwise. The effect of the enactment of 1881 was to make the community property system compulsory so that the parties could not by settlement or agreement reject it. However, it did not prohibit contracts relating to presently held property.[4]

When Washington was admitted as a state in 1889, the constitution provided that all laws in force in the Territory, not repugnant to the constitution, should remain in force until altered or repealed by

---

[95] See Kirkwood, Historical Background and Objective of Law of Community Property in Pacific Coast States, 11 Wash. Law Rev. 1, citing Abbott, Real Property Statutes of Washington Territory, 1843–1899.

[96] See Lobingier, 63 Am. Law Rev. 250, 278; ibid., 14 Am. Bar Ass'n Jour. 211; Hill, Early Washington Marital Property Statutes, 14 Wash. Law Rev. 118; Kirkwood, 11 Wash. Law Rev. 1.

[97] Laws of Washington Territory, 1869, p. 318 et seq.

[98] From the time of organization of the Territory of Washington the common law was followed as to marital property rights, and dower and curtesy were recognized until abolished by statute in 1871. Hill, Early Washington Marital Statutes, 14 Wash. Law Rev. 118.

[99] Laws of Washington Territory, 1871, p. 67 et seq.

[1] Laws of Washington Territory, 1873, pp. 450, 486.

[2] Laws of Washington Territory, 1879, p. 77 et seq.

[3] Wash. Code 1881, ch. 183.

[4] Hill, Early Washington Marital Property Statutes, 14 Wash. Law Rev. 118, 121, containing excellent discussion of these various statutes. And see Mechem, Progress of the Law in Washington Community Property, 7 Wash. Law Rev. 367; 8 Wash. Law Rev. 1.

"The manifest object of our community property system is to place the husband and wife on an equal footing as to their property rights, and perhaps the law should be so administered as to accord to each the same property rights on the death of the other." See Hall v. Hall, 41 Wash. 186, 83 P. 108.

the legislature.[5] It is perhaps unnecessary to add that there was nothing in the constitution which rendered the community property law repugnant thereto.

§ 48.   Territory ceded by Mexico under Treaty of Guadalupe Hidalgo.

Following the admission, in 1845, of the independent republic of Texas as a state in our federal union, this country assumed the burden of the boundary disputes existing between Texas and Mexico. In 1846 these disputes developed into war between the United States and Mexico which was not officially terminated until 1848 by the Treaty of Guadalupe Hidalgo. By that treaty the boundaries between the two countries were established, and in consideration of a payment of fifteen million dollars Mexico ceded to the United States the region which now comprises the states of Arizona, Nevada, California and Utah and, in part, the states of New Mexico, Colorado and Wyoming.[6] By Articles VIII and IX of that treaty it was expressly provided that citizens of the Mexican republic residing in those regions, whether electing to preserve their character as citizens of Mexico or electing to become citizens of the United States, should be protected in the property of every kind which they might possess.

By supplemental agreement in 1853, known as the Gadsden Purchase, an additional cession of territory was made to this country, constituting in the main the southern part of the present state of Arizona. In 1850, Texas ceded to the United States, in consideration of ten million dollars, a considerable part of the territory claimed by it. The major part of the territory so ceded was added to what is now the state of New Mexico.[7] From the three foregoing cessions of territory were formed in full the present states of Arizona, California,

[5] Wash. Const. 1889, art. XXVII, § 1.

[6] Notice that the treaty does not apply to Texas. See Amaya v. Stanolind Gas & Oil Co., (D.C. Tex.) 62 F. Supp. 181.

[7] "A claim has been advanced by the State of Texas to a very large portion of the most populous district of the territory commonly designated by the name of New Mexico. If the people of New Mexico had formed a plan of state government for that territory as ceded by the treaty of Guadalupe Hidalgo, and had been admitted by Congress as a state, our constitution would have afforded the means of obtaining an adjustment of the question of boundary with Texas by judicial decision. At present, however, no judicial tribunal has the power of deciding that question, and it remains for Congress to devise some mode for its adjustment. Meanwhile, I submit to Congress the question whether it would be expedient, before such adjustment, to establish a territorial government, which, by including the district so claimed, would practically decide the question adversely to the State of Texas, or, by excluding it, would decide it in her favor. In my opinion such a course would not be expedient, especially as the people of this territory still enjoy the benefit and protection of their municipal laws, originally derived from Mexico, and

Nevada, New Mexico and Utah. Of these five states only Utah failed to retain the community system which had been in effect in that region, probably because early Mormon religious practices were inimical to the idea of community of property between spouses.[8] The other four states, as will be more fully developed in the succeeding sections, have continued under the community property law.

§ 49.   — New Mexico.

New Mexico, which until 1863 also included the present state of Arizona,[9] recognized and continued the community property system just as did California, Louisiana and Texas. Upon occupation of that region by American forces in 1846, General Kearney, commanding the American army, issued the following order: "All laws heretofore in force in this territory, which are not repugnant to or inconsistent with the constitution of the United States, and the laws thereof, or the statute laws in force for the time being, shall be the rule of action and decision in this territory."[10] The Organic Act of 1850, establishing the Territory of New Mexico, while establishing a system of procedure according to the course of the common law, did not introduce the body of the common law but only provided the methods by which rights already existing, defined and limited by the existing civil law,

have a military force stationed there to protect them against the Indians." Message of President Zachary Taylor to House of Representatives, Jan. 21, 1850.

An Act proposing to the State of Texas the Establishment of her Northern and Western Boundaries, the Relinquishment by the said State of all Territory claimed by her exterior to said Boundaries, and of all her Claims upon the United States, and to establish a territorial Government for New Mexico, see Acts of Thirty-first Congress, First Session, Act of Sept. 9, 1850.

[8] See First Nat. Bank v. Kinner (1873) 1 Utah 100, in which the court stated that the civil law had been displaced by the common law by the common or tacit consent of the people of Utah and that the court had the power to determine that fact, although the law making power had not yet acted. See also Hilton v. Thatcher, 31 Utah 360.

[9] As to Arizona, see following section.

[10] Kearney's Code 1846, p. 82, "Laws" § 1. And see In re Chavez, 149 Fed. 73.

Recognition in President Taylor's message of Jan. 21, 1850, to House of Representatives that "the people of this territory still enjoy the benefit and protection of their municipal laws, originally derived from Mexico," see ante, § 48, n. 7.

"New Mexico was not an uninhabited territory or one occupied only by savages, colonized by an English-speaking people, bringing their common law with them. The Americans invaded a foreign territory and conquered a civilized people. The American military commander, proclaiming a code of laws for the conquered territory and people, long before the peace, did not establish the common law." Estate of Gabaldon, 38 N.M. 392, 34 P.2d 672, 94 A.L.R. 980. To the same effect, Barnett v. Barnett, 9 N.M. 205, 50 P. 337.

were to be enforced.[11] Indeed, a similar provision to that of Kearney's Code was enacted by the territorial legislature in 1851,[12] and the community property law was for many years determined solely by the law of Spain and Mexico upon that subject, no local statutes apparently being considered necessary and none being enacted,[13] with the exception of an occasional statute such as that enacted in 1852 relative to the right of a married woman to convey her realty by a conveyance executed by herself and her husband.[14] In 1876, it is true, the territorial legislature enacted that "In all the courts in this territory the common law as recognized in the United States of America shall be the rule of practice and decision."[15] This for a long period was construed by the New Mexico Supreme Court to have no effect upon the law of community property and to have made no change therein, that it provided nothing by which to ascertain the rights of spouses to property acquired during the marriage; and, accordingly, in view of that omission and where there was no statutory enactment bearing upon a question of community property involved, the law of Spain and Mexico must apply.[16] Statutes were enacted, however, to govern the descent both of community and separate property and designating the debts to which properties were subject before distribution, and these statutes appeared in the Compiled Laws of 1884.[17] In 1889, these statutes of descent governing community property were expressly repealed and replaced by others which, however, continued to recognize the existence of community property just as had the repealed statutes.[18] It is important to notice, because it was later made the basis of a decision by the New Mexico Supreme Court, that in 1887 the legislature enacted a law relating to descent of property which most obviously related only to separate property, for it made no reference to community property and indeed expressly provided that every

[11] Browning v. Browning, 3 N.M. (Gild.) 659, 9 P. 677; Estate of Gabaldon, 38 N.M. 392, 34 P.2d 672, 94 A.L.R. 980.

Formation of Territory of New Mexico, see Act of Sept. 9, 1850, Thirty-first Congress, First Session.

[12] N.M. Laws 1851, p. 176. And see Rev. Stats. and Laws 1865, p. 512; Comp. Laws 1897, p. 82; In re Chavez, 149 Fed. 73.

[13] See Chavez v. McKnight, 1 N.M. 148; Martinez v. Lucero, 1 N.M. 208.

[14] See Edgar v. Baca, 1 N.M. 613.

[15] N.M. Laws 1876, ch. 2, § 2.

Compare this legislative enactment with that in California which adopted the common law as the rule of decision where not repugnant to the state constitution which, of course, recognized the community property system. See ante, § 51.

[16] See Browning v. Browning, 3 N.M. (Gild.) 659, 9 P. 677; Barnett v. Barnett, 9 N.M. 205, 50 P. 337; Crary v. Field, 9 N.M. 222, 50 P. 342; Neher v. Armijo, 9 N.M. 325, 54 P. 236; Strong v. Eakin, 11 N.M. 107, 66 P. 539; Reade v. De Lea, 14 N.M. 442, 95 P. 131, rev'd Arnett v. Reade, 220 U.S. 311, 55 L. Ed. 477, 31 Sup. Ct. 424, as to interpretation of application of Act of 1901.

[17] N.M. Comp. Laws 1884, §§ 1410-1422.

[18] N.M. Laws 1889, ch. 90.

rule of descent or distribution prescribed in the act should be subject to existing provisions made in behalf of a surviving husband or wife.[19] That it had no effect or relation to the community property provisions of 1884 is shown by its own terms and by the fact that the act of 1889 which replaced that of 1884 found it unnecessary to make any reference to that of 1887 but confined itself to the express statement that it replaced that of 1884.[20] That the legislature never considered that the community property system was abolished by its enactment of 1876 as to the common law as a rule of decision is not only evidenced by the fact that it continued to accept during this period without demur the view of the territorial supreme court upon the matter, but also by the affirmative fact that it from time to time enacted legislation relative to the descent of community property. In 1901, however, we find the legislature enacting a very comprehensive statute as to community property,[21] and then repealing it and replacing it with another in 1907,[22] declared to be with a few exceptions an adoption of the California statutes,[23] which with little amendment remains the law today and is chiefly declaratory of the Spanish principles of the community.[24] The state constitution of 1912, the date of New Mexico's admission to statehood, made no change in the community of property.[25]

Yet in 1919, we find the Supreme Court of New Mexico holding that the enactment of 1876 had the effect of completely abrogating the civil law, including the community property system, in force in New Mexico except to the extent that it was preserved in statutory enactments. In holding that from 1876 the existence of the community property system must depend wholly upon statutory enactment, the court remarks that in any event the legislature enacted a statute in 1889 under which the territory "went back to the community property system."[26] Yet, as a matter of fact, this act of 1889 described by the

---

[19] N.M. Laws 1887, ch. 32.

[20] The statement, in Beals v. Ares, 25 N.M. 459, 185 P. 780, that this act of 1889 "specifically repealed" ch. 32, Laws of 1887, is untrue. It specifically repealed and replaced the provisions of the Comp. Laws of 1884, and both the repealed provisions and the new provisions recognized community of property.

[21] N.M. Laws 1901, ch. 42.

[22] N.M. Laws 1907, ch. 37.

[23] See Kirkwood, Historical Background and Objective of Law of Community Property in Pacific Coast States, 11 Wash. Law Rev. 1.

[24] While New Mexico statutes are largely adoption of California statutes

"this court has never followed the decisions of the California courts with respect to the interests of the spouses in the community property." McDonald v. Senn, 55 N.M. 198, 204 P.2d 990, 993, 10 A.L.R. 966.

[25] See N.M. Const. 1912, art. XXII, § 4.

[26] Beals v. Ares, 25 N.M. 459, 185 P. 790 (expressly overruling Barnett v. Barnett, 9 N.M. 205, 50 P. 337; Strong v. Eakin, 11 N.M. 107, 66 P. 539; Reade v. De Lea, 14 N.M. 442, 95 P. 131, in so far as they held that the civil law relating to marital property remained in force after the adoption of the common law and unless expressly abrogated by statute). And

court as taking the territory "back to the community property system" was by its own express terms in replacement of laws of 1884 which recognized the community property system as then existent as effectively as did the act of 1889 itself.[27] Since it is to be noticed that both the laws of 1884 and the act of 1889 by their very nature assumed the existence of a community property system to which they could relate, to assert that no community of property existed from 1876 to 1901 (when a comprehensive statute was enacted) except as established by statute would result, in view of the paucity of statutes upon various aspects of community property, in the recognition of the descent and distribution of a kind of property for the existence of which no provision was made, and similar absurd situations which could never have been in contemplation. As a matter of fact, in the period from 1876 to 1889 the territorial supreme court assumed, without question or action by the legislature, that the community property system was in force, an assumption that was indeed correct for it was verified by the action of the legislature in enacting the laws of 1884 which by their nature predicated an existing community property system was in force, an assumption that was indeed correct, for it was verified by the action of the legislature in enacting the laws of 1884 which by their nature predicated an existing community property system to which they attached.[28] The reason for the astonishing opinion of the New Mexico court may rest upon the fact that deciding the question before it according to the principles of the

see Laughlin v. Laughlin, 49 N.M. 20, 155 P.2d 1010.

Beals v. Ares, supra, relies heavily in its reasoning upon language of Routh v. Routh, 57 Tex. 589, which must be considered discredited language because of contrary views expressed in later Texas cases, such as Lee v. Lee, 112 Tex. 392, 247 S. W. 828, and upon the language of various California cases which of course are not dependable because of the constant misinterpretation and misunderstanding of community property principles shown by those cases.

Judge Lobingier seems to ignore this decision in remarking that the community property system has always been the law in New Mexico. Lobingier, History of Conjugal Partnership, 63 Am. Law Rev. 250; ibid., 14 Am. Bar Ass'n Jour. 211, although we agree with his statement, even with knowledge of this decision.

[27] The United States Circuit Court of Appeals for the Tenth Circuit, relying on Beals v. Ares, supra, erroneously describes the act of 1889 as repealing the act of 1887, whereas it specifically repeals laws of 1884 which, as said above, equally as did the act of 1889, recognized the existence of community property. See Hernandez v. Becker, 54 F.2d 542.

[28] "Contention is made that later legislative acts of the territory have eliminated or modified the foregoing rules [of community property]. In Strong v. Eakin, 11 N.M. 122, 66 P. 539, decided October, 1901, the Supreme Court reviewed the antecedent legislation of the territory, including the married women's act, and the statute pertaining more especially to descents and distributions, and controverted the proposition that these statutes had done away with the rule of community except as they furnished a rule for determining their devise, descent and distribution." In re Chavez, 149 Fed. 73.

Spanish law was distasteful to it, so that in effect it usurped the prerogatives of the legislature to amend the law, and in order to find an excuse for doing so denied what for generations had been accepted as true by the court itself, by the legislature and by the people of New Mexico.[29]

§ 50.   — Arizona.

Arizona, as a part of New Mexico until 1863, continued to have the community system as it had formerly existed under Spain and Mexico in that region.[30] In 1863 it became a separate territory[31] and in 1864 the first territorial legislature enacted legislation, including the adoption of the common law as the rule of decision, that has caused dispute as to its effect, that is, as to whether it abrogated the law of community property.[32]

The better reasoned view, as explained by John D. Lyons, a distinguished member of the Arizona bar, as a practitioner, a judge, and law school dean and professor, clearly establishes that the community property system did not prevail in the state in 1865.[33] In any event, at the next session in 1865 a law was enacted which definitely

---

[29] Curiously enough, after contending that the legislative act of 1876 made the English-developed common law the rule of decision except as to such matters of community property as were specifically expressed by statute, the court refused to apply the common law principle established by the Statute of Westminster II that living in adultery forfeited the wife's rights in the marital property, and did so on the ground that it was not applicable to community of property which was "altogether different" from common law dower right.

As to the question involved, forfeiture of the wife's right to the community property because of adultery, see post, §§ 189, 190.

[30] New Mexico, see preceding section.

[31] Thus, the enactment of the New Mexico territorial legislature in 1876 that the common law should be the rule of decision in New Mexico had no application to Arizona. See preceding section.

Provision for temporary government of Territory of Arizona, see Act of February 24, 1863, Thirty-seventh Congress, Third Session.

[32] Dean Kirkwood points out that at this session of 1864 the legislature repealed all laws and customs of Mexico, Spain and New Mexico, citing chap. LXI, § 1, and provided that the common law of England should be the rule of decision, citing chap. LXI, § 7, that there was no reference to community property and that, in fact, dower was provided for, citing chap. XXVII. Kirkwood, Historical Background and Objective of Law of Community Property in Pacific Coast States, 11 Wash. Law Rev. 1.

Judge Lobingier argues that although a statute adopting the common law appears in Ariz. Comp. Laws 1864, 1871, p. 524, § 7, such statute does not appear in the Ariz. Sess. Laws of 1864, and that neither that statute nor a statute providing for separate estate of married women enacted by Howell's Code 1864, chap. 32, are inconsistent with the continuance of the community property system. Lobingier, History of Conjugal Partnership, 63 Am. Law Rev. 250; ibid., 14 Am. Bar Ass'n Jour. 211.

[33] See Lyons, Development of Community Property Law in Arizona, 15 La. L. Rev. 512.

recognized the community system,[34] and it may be pointed out that the Supreme Court of Arizona has consistently held that the adoption of the common law was only to the extent that it was applicable to local conditions in Arizona,[35] and that it did not necessarily exclude the application of all principles of Spanish law, provided the latter are applicable to customs or enactments adopted from that law and not inconsistent with the laws and customs of the state.[36] While at one time the Arizona Supreme Court considered that the Arizona laws are analogous to those of Washington and some of its interpretations paralleled those of Washington,[37] more recently the Arizona court has pointed out that Arizona statutes are modeled after those of California and Texas. In the areas covered by the particular statutes, the respective law and decisions of those two states are considered now to be of weight.[38]

The community property system has continued to be the law of Arizona to the present day, and the state constitution of 1912 in no way affected the law of community property.[39]

§ 51.   — California.

At the outbreak of war in 1846 between Mexico and the United States, the latter immediately put under way plans for the conquest of California, then known as Alta (Upper) California. While it is true that some of the residents of Sonoma County rose against the Mexican authorities and proclaimed California an independent republic, seizure of the region was made chiefly by naval and military forces of the United States who held it in the name of the United States. The Treaty of Guadalupe Hidalgo in 1848 confirmed this possession.[40]

[34] Ariz. Laws 1865, p. 60.

[35] Hageman v. Vanderdoes, 15 Ariz. 312, 138 P. 1053, L.R.A. 1915A 491, Ann. Cas. 1915D 1197, holding that the common law rule of the husband's liability for his wife's torts was, in effect, abrogated by the married women's statutes.

"It is here plainly apparent that the legislative will was not to adopt the common law as it prevailed when the wife was the mere chattel of the husband." Luhrs v. Hancock, 6 Ariz. 340, 57 P. 605.

"At common law probably no such thing as an irrigating ditch was known. Under its provision the usufruct is the only extent of a claim in water. . . . But the common law has no application whatever to the use of water with us." Austin v. Chandler, 4 Ariz. 346, 42 P. 483.

[36] Pendleton v. Brown, 25 Ariz. 604, 221 P. 213, wherein the court, however, refused to apply the principle of Spanish law that adultery of the wife forfeits all her rights in the community property, before as well as after the adultery, in view of a local statute which provided only for forfeiture of her rights after the adultery.

[37] McFadden v. Watson, 51 Ariz. 110, 74 P.2d 1181.

[38] Mortensen v. Knight, 81 Ariz. 325, 305 P.2d 463.

[39] Besides the citation above to Dean Lyons, see Keddie, Community Property Law in Arizona, Phoenix, 1960; Smith and Tormey, Summary of Arizona Community Property Law, Tucson, 1964.

[40] As to this treaty, see Appendix IV, G, 1943 edition of this work.

Congress, however, other than appointing a collector of customs for the port of San Francisco, made no provision for a civil government, leaving the civil authority in the hands of the people, subject to the jurisdiction of the commanding general of the military department who acted as military governor. This post was held successively by General Kearney, Colonel Mason and General Riley.[41] Indeed, in 1849 General Riley issued a proclamation to the people stating that the military government actually ended with the war and that under the existing law of California he was not the military governor but *ex-officio* civil governor. Incidentally, he continued to act as such governor until the people formed the government (including the election of a governor) under which California was admitted to the Union. However, what is important to notice in his proclamation are the following words: "The laws of California not inconsistent with the laws, constitution, and treaties of the United States, are still in force and must continue in force until changed by competent authority. . . . The situation in California is almost identical with that of Louisiana; and the decisions of the Supreme Court in recognizing the validity of the laws which existed in that country previous to its annexation to the United States, where not inconsistent with the constitution and laws of the United States, or repealed by legitimate legislative enactments, furnish us a clear and safe guide in our present situation."[42] It is clear from this, as well as from preceding proclamations of Kearney and Riley stressing the same fact, that the formerly existing law, which included the community property system, was recognized and continued by the proper governmental authority during this period between the conquest of California and the taking effect of its constitution and admission as a state.[43] That the existing law remained in force until some change should be formally and validly made by the legislative body of the new government was recognized by the Supreme Court of the state in 1852.[44]

In the constitutional convention held in 1849 for the purpose of drafting a constitution for California, strong debate developed between the advocates of the common law and those of the civil law as to which should govern the marital property rights of husband and wife.

[41] See Shuck, History of Bench and Bar of California, pp. 3-32.

[42] Proclamation set out more fully, Appendix IV, I, 1943 edition, Principles of Community Property, de Funiak.

[43] See the Proclamations of Gen. Kearney and Col. Mason.

Although it may have been true, as alleged by McMurray, 3 Calif. Law Rev. 359, that many Americans in California, frequently men of prominence, were confused or doubtful as to what extent the Spanish-Mexican law was still in force in California during this period, their state of confusion or unfamiliarity with that law or their own individual preferences could obviously have no weight when placed against the consistent continuance of that law in force by the lawful governmental authority.

[44] See Fowler v. Smith, 2 Cal. 568.

The views of those advocating the continuance of the existing law of community property finally prevailed.[45] Accordingly, we find the Constitution of 1849, XI, § 14, providing as follows:

"All property, both real and personal, of the wife, owned or claimed by her before marriage, and that acquired afterward by gift, devise, or descent, shall be her separate property, and laws shall be passed more clearly defining the rights of the wife in relation as well to her separate property as to that held in common with the husband. Laws shall also be passed providing for the registration of the wife's separate property."[46]

The language of this provision itself as well as the views expressed in the debates in the Constitutional Convention of 1849 show conclusively that it was the intention to place in the framework of the constitution itself the Spanish system of community property; and to place it therein beyond the reach of the legislature, except to the extent that the legislature was empowered to define more clearly the rights of the wife in relation to her property rights and to provide for the registration of her separate property.[47] Pursuant thereto the first legislature, in 1850, enacted legislation defining the difference between community and separate property and continuing in effect the principles of the previously existing law of community property.[48]

In the same legislative session, argument continued between the advocates of the common law and the civil law as to which should govern or constitute the rule of decision in other matters than marital property rights. Governor Burnett, in his message to the legislature, recommended the adoption of codes which "would combine the best features of both the civil and the common law," but his recommendation was not followed.[49] Instead, the legislature enacted as law the following:

"The Common Law of England, so far as it is not repugnant to or inconsistent with the Constitution of the United States or the Constitution or laws of California, shall be the rule of decision in all courts of this state."[50]

---

[45] See Brown, Debates in Convention of California on Formation of State Constitution of 1849, pp. 258–260.

[46] Notice similarity in principle to Laws 1 and 2, Book 10, Title 4 of Novísima Recopilación.

Debates in constitutional convention show that by property "held in common with her husband" community property was meant. Brown, Debates in Convention of California on Formation of State Constitution of 1849, p. 257 et seq. See also Kirkwood, 11 Wash. Law Rev. 1.

[47] See Brown, Debates in Convention of California on Foundation of State Constitution of 1849, p. 257 et seq.; Burnett, Community Property Law, p. 40 et seq.

[48] Cal. Stats. 1850, chap. 95, p. 254. See also post, chap. VI.

[49] See Shuck, History of the Bench and Bar of California, pp. 47-53.

[50] See present Cal. Political Code, § 4468.

It is obvious that the common law as a rule of decision is repugnant to and inconsistent with the community property provisions and laws of the state which would naturally have to be determined and decided by community property principles. Indeed, this enactment expressly disclaimed any intention to interfere with the constitution.[51]

The state constitution of 1879, which superseded that of 1849, did not carry forward in the same language the provision of the former constitution respecting separate and community property, being content merely to define what constitutes separate property:

"All property, real and personal, owned by either husband or wife, before marriage, and that acquired by either of them afterwards by gift, devise, or descent, shall be their separate property."[52]

This virtually identical repetition of the Spanish law on the subject, by necessary implication effectively leaves all other acquisitions and gains by the spouses after marriage as community property, and leaves the Spanish community property system still firmly imbedded in the constitutional framework. Incidentally, existing legislative enactments were continued in force by the provision "That all laws in force at the adoption of this Constitution, not inconsistent therewith, shall remain in full force and effect until altered or repealed by the Legislature."[53] And the community property system has continued in effect to the present day.[54]

The statutory enactments of the legislature have, in the main, been consistent with the constitutional continuance of the existing Spanish system of community property. The courts, however, have

[51] Rather ingenuously, Professor McMurray, in 3 Cal. Law Rev. 359, points out that the legislature enacted the common law as the rule of decision on April 12 and enacted the community property law on April 17, and implies that during this five-day period the community property system was not in force in California. This is remarked on here merely because it is representative of the mistaken view of many that it was the action of the legislature which "adopted" the community property system in California. It should be apparent to any lawyer, however, that not only would the community property system, under principles of international law, continue to be the law of California until actually displaced by some action of a duly constituted government, but also that the existing law was expressly recognized and continued in force by the successive governors *and was recognized in the constitution of 1849.*

Thus, even the absence of any action by the legislature would not have affected the existence of the community property system, which would have continued in force just as it did in New Mexico in the absence of legislative action. Legislative action could only have the effect, so far as permitted by constitutional limitations, of defining certain provisions of the existing community property system.

[52] Const. 1879, art. XX, § 8.

[53] Const. 1879, art. XXII, § 1.

[54] California authorities on the subject are collected in California Jurisprudence, 2nd Ed., "Community Property," which attempts a historical discussion. See also Kirkwood, Historical Background and Objective of Law of Community Property in Pacific Coast States, 11 Wash. Law Rev. 1; Nicholas, California Community Property, 14 Calif. State Bar Jour. 9.

frequently so hacked away at the system as to leave it distorted almost beyond recognition. A recurring tendency has been to attempt the interpretation and definition of the community property system by common law concepts, although how the common law, which contains no recognition of and has no legal principles concerning community property, could serve as rule of decision as to community property is impossible to understand. Yet, beginning shortly after 1849, we find the California court, with what can be described only as startling obtuseness, attempting to do just that, determine a community property question by applying the common law.[55] Thus was inaugurated the series of confusing and conflicting decisions of the California courts respecting the law of community property which have so plagued that state.[56] On more than one occasion the legislature has been compelled to enact legislation to repeat or to clarify principles of the law muddled or misinterpreted by the courts.[57] However, the present day courts can be counted on to pursue the same consistent attitude toward the community system that has seemed to have animated the legislature. This tendency of the courts too frequently has been to ignore the provision of the Civil Code, which set out most of the community property provisions, to the effect that "The rule of the common law, that statutes in derogation thereof are to be strictly construed, has no application to this code. The code establishes the law of this state respecting the subject to which it relates and its provisions are to be liberally construed with the view to effect its objects and to promote justice."[58]

§ 52. — Nevada.

Nevada was originally part of the Utah territory, and while the civil law with its community property system was, of course, originally the law of that region, we have seen that the Utah Supreme Court considered that the common law had been adopted in Utah by the people in displacement of the civil law.[59] However, this determination of the Utah court came more than a decade after Nevada had been established as a separate territory. Accordingly, this pronouncement can hardly serve as a determinant of the law of Nevada. Although in 1861, after Nevada had become a separate territory, its legislature adopted the common law of England, with the usual qualification as to repugnancy and inconsistency,[60] and also an act defining the separate property of husband and wife,[61] neither of these enactments can be considered inconsistent with the continued existence of the com-

[55] See Van Maren v. Johnson (1860) 15 Cal. 308, per Field, J.; see also George v. Ransom (1860) 15 Cal. 322, 76 Am. Dec. 490.

[56] See post, § 107, for citation of California authorities.

[57] See 39 Harv. Law Rev. 762, 763.

[58] Cal. Civ. Code, § 4.

[59] See ante, § 49.

[60] Nev. Laws 1861, ch. 1.

[61] Nev. Laws 1861, ch. 55, § 323.

munity system any more than was the case in California,[62] and the inclusion in the state constitution of 1864, when Nevada was admitted as a state, of a provision similar to that of the California constitution of 1849, recognizing the existence of both separate and community property, shows that the community had been in existence prior thereto as well as being continued in force.[63] The legislation enacted pursuant thereto in 1865 was modeled after that of California.[64] A new enactment in 1873[65] has with some amendment remained the law up to the present.[66]

§ 53.   Other territorial acquisitions.

For some time after the Mexican war and its resultant Treaty of Guadalupe Hidalgo,[67] territorial accessions to the United States did not include areas having any form of community property. This was true, for example, as to Alaska and Hawaii, although the latter did later briefly embrace community of property.[68] However, the Spanish-American war did add, at least for a time, areas governed by a Spanish-derived law. This was true of the Philippine Islands,[69] but since the

---

[62] See ante, § 51.

[63] Nev. Const. 1864, art. IV, § 31.
Thus, as Lobingier has pointed out, there is little ground for various dicta that prior to the constitution of 1864 and the statute of 1865 the community had no legal existence and that the common law governed the property rights of husband and wife. See Lobingier, History of Conjugal Partnership, 63 Am. Law Rev. 250; ibid., 14 Am. Bar Ass'n Jour. 211 (critically citing Lake v. Bender (1884) 18 Nev. 382, 4 P. 711; Johnson v. Garner (1916) 233 Fed. 756). However, in an even earlier case, the Nevada Supreme Court, passing on the question directly, insisted that prior to 1865 the common law was in force governing the marital property rights. See Darrenberger v. Haupt, 10 Nev. 43. In Nixon v. Brown, 46 Nev. 439, 214 P. 524, however, the Nevada court said: "From a review of the entire subject, we are of the opinion that the state of Nevada, by constitutional and statutory enactment, adopted the community property law as it existed in Spain and Mexico, and as it existed in California at the time of its cession from Mexico."

[64] Nev. Laws 1864–5, ch. 76.

[65] Nev. Laws 1873, ch. 119.

[66] Concise presentation of Nevada community property law, see article by Shermack in 15 La. Law Rev. 559.
Nevada adopted the community property law almost as it was administered in Mexico, known as the Spanish-Mexican civil law, and as it was administered in California under the early statutes; it is therefore to those early California cases and to the original law that the Nevada Supreme Court must look for solutions. See Nixon v. Brown, 46 Nev. 439, 214 P. 524.

[67] See ante, § 48.

[68] See post, § 53.1.

[69] Generally, see Walton, Civil Law of Spain and Spanish America, Including Cuba, Puerto Rico and the Philippine Islands; Lobingier, History of Conjugal Partnership, 62 Am. Law Rev. 250, 270; ibid., 14 Am. Bar Ass'n Jour. 211; Howe, Roman Law and Civil Law in America, 16 Harv. L. Rev. 342; cf. Philippine Jurisprudence; Common Law or Civil Law? 16 Am. Bar Ass'n Jour. 80.
A more readily accessible source of information to most lawyers is the decision in Com'r of Int. Rev. v. Cadwallader, 9 C.C.A., 127 F.2d 547.

islands have become an independent republic we need not enter into any discussion of their law. Another area of importance is the Commonwealth of Puerto Rico.[70] It would appear that during our more immediate administering of the affairs of that island, American-law-trained judges made something of a hash of the community property system in force there.[71] Since Puerto Rico has administered its own affairs and its own law, as a more or less independent entity, it has been in a position to shape and interpret its laws in accordance with its own views.[72]

It is interesting to note that upon our purchase of the Virgin Islands from Denmark,[73] the Danish law of community property was in force there. Although the rules of the common law were subsequently declared by our Congress to be in force, it is to be borne in mind that rights to property which had vested under Danish law were not affected by the change of sovereignty or by substitution of the rules of the common law. Some of our available case law helps to clarify the matter for the American lawyer.[74]

§ 53.1. Temporary establishment for tax advantages.

During the period between 1939 and 1949, a number of our states temporarily adopted varying forms of marital community of property through legislative enactments. This was true of Hawaii (then a territory), Michigan, Nebraska, Oklahoma, Oregon and Pennsylvania.[75] In a great many other states, there were movements on foot to adopt community property and, while in some, passage of such legislation was defeated,[76] in others no doubt it would have taken place, given time.[77]

The reason for this was the advantage then to be obtained in the field of federal income taxes. Since spouses in a community property state equally owned the earnings of one spouse,[78] they could file separate returns and by dividing the earnings between themselves could get into lower tax brackets. The spouse in a non-community property state himself alone had to report all his earnings and was

---

[70] See citations in preceding note.

[71] See, e.g., Garrozzi v. Dastas, 204 U.S. 64, 51 E. Ed. 369, 27 Sup. Ct. 224.

[72] See Puerto Rican civil codes.

[73] Briefly as to Denmark, see ante, § 17.

[74] See, especially, Callwood v. Kean, 189 F.2d 565.

[75] Generally, see de Funiak, The New Community Property Jurisdictions (Dec. 1947) 22 Tulane L. Rev. 264; de Funiak (March 1948) The Community Property Trend, 23 Notre Dame Lawyer 293.

[76] E.g., in Indiana and Massachusetts.

[77] Strong movements were on foot in a number of diverse states, as, e.g., Kentucky and New York. In North Dakota, the movement was abandoned upon enactment in 1948 of the new federal tax law. See Bright, Community Property (April 1948) 24 North Dakota Bar Briefs 65.

[78] See post, Chap. VII, A.

in a higher tax bracket. Actually, to persons of moderate income the differences were slight, but in the area of larger incomes the differences were considerable.[79]

Oklahoma was the first state to enact a community property law. In 1939, by legislative enactment, community of property between spouses was provided for. This did not abrogate the previous laws, but left the matter to the election of the spouses as to which system they wished to govern their property during the continuance of the marriage.[80] Election to have the community property provisions apply to the marital property had to be by writing properly filed.

In 1943, Oregon followed with an act modeled after that of Oklahoma.[81] However, in 1945, the United States Supreme Court upheld the contentions of the Bureau of Internal Revenue that such an elective system of community property was not effective to entitle spouses to divide income for federal income tax purposes.[82] Oklahoma promptly repealed its law and enacted a new one, brief in form, which imposed community of property by operation of law on marital acquisitions of all spouses.[83] This was ultimately recognized by the bureau as placing Oklahoma in the same class as the old community property states.[84]

Oregon, however, discouraged by the Supreme Court decision, merely repealed its elective community property law[85] and took no further action until 1947 when it once more enacted a community property law, again modeled on that of Oklahoma.[86] In the meantime, in 1945, Hawaii, having observed the successful effect of the new Oklahoma act, also enacted a community property law.[87] Apparently, the success of Oklahoma and Hawaii in obtaining the benefit of the tax advantages of the community property system, plus the return of Oregon, encouraged other states to consider the enactment

[79] See, e.g., de Funiak, The Community Property Trend, 23 Notre Dame Lawyer 293.

[80] See Okla. Stats. Ann., Perm. Ed., Title 32, §§ 51-65, repealed in 1945.

Legislative history and effect of act, see Randolph, 10 Okla. State Bar Jour. 850; Campbell and Mosteller, 13 Okla. Bar Ass'n Jour. 49.

This written election required by the act has been described as following the German doctrine of community rather than that of France and Spain, where the community becomes operative by virtue of a legal marriage and must be contracted against if the parties do not desire it. See Daggert, 2 La. Law Rev. 575, 576.

[81] Ore. Laws of 1943, c. 440; Ore. Comp. Laws Ann., Title 63, c. 2A.

[82] Commissioner v. Harmon, 323 U.S. 44, 65 Sup. Ct. 103, L. Ed. 71 (1944), citing de Funiak, 1943 edition.

[83] Okla. Laws of 1945, H. B. 218; Okla. Stats. (Supp. 1945) Title 32, §§ 66-82.

[84] I. T. 3782. 1946-1 Cum. Bull. 84. And see de Funiak, The New Community Property Law, 14 Okla. Bar Jour. 1123.

[85] Ore. Laws of 1945, ch. 270.

[86] Ore. Laws of 1947, ch. 525, effective July 5, 1947. And see Dougherty, Some Initial Comments on the Oregon Community Property Law, 27 Ore. L. Rev. 1.

[87] Hawaii Laws of 1945, ch. 273; Hawaii Rev. Laws (1945) Title 32, ch. 301A, effective May 22, 1945.

of community property laws. This was true in Michigan,[88] Nebraska[89] and Pennsylvania.[90]

Early in 1948, Congress enacted a tax law, passing it again over the President's veto, whereby the tax advantage to the community property states was removed. Spouses in all states were allowed to divide earnings, whether such earnings were separate or community property.[91] This brought about a lack of interest in any further enactment of community property laws[92] and, in addition, resulted in the repeal of the laws already enacted in Hawaii,[93] Michigan,[94] Oklahoma,[95] Oregon[96] and Nebraska.[97] In Pennsylvania, the existing law had already been held invalid on constitutional grounds by the Supreme Court of that state.[98]

However, there can be problems in those states — except, of course, Pennsylvania — arising from the fact that for a brief period there was a creation of community property which could thus continue legally to exist. True, in all of the states, the repealing acts attempted to provide for this situation by creation of presumptions of abandonment or change of nature by agreement of the owners.[99] But this cannot be a sure cure-all and probable arising of problems in the future has been recognized by a number of writers [1] Indeed, litigation has already taken place since the repeals.[2]

---

[88] Mich. Acts of 1947, Pub. Act 317, effective July 1, 1947; Mich. Stats. Ann., §§ 26.216(1)-26.216(20).

[89] Neb. Laws of 1947, Leg. B. 410, effective Sept. 7, 1947.

[90] Pa. Laws of 1947, S. B. 615, effective Sept. 1, 1947.

[91] See 1948 and subsequent federal enactments.

[92] As in North Dakota as remarked by Bright, in 24 North Dakota Bar Briefs 65.

[93] Hawaii Laws 1949, ch. 242.

[94] Mich. Pub. Laws 1948, No. 39.

[95] Okla. Acts 1949, p. 229.

[96] Ore. Acts 1949, ch. 349.

[97] Neb. Acts 1949, ch. 129.

[98] Willcox v. Penn. Mut. Life Ins. Co. (1947) 357 Pa. 581, 55 A.2d 551, 174 A.L.R. 220, citing de Funiak, 1943 ed.; noted 46 Mich. L. Rev. 422. 34 Va. L. Rev. 341.

[99] See repealing acts cited above.

[1] See, e.g., Comment note, Epilogue to Community Property Scramble, (195) 50 Colum. L. Rev. 332; Trice, Community Property in Oklahoma, 4 S. W. L. Jour. 38. And this was foretold by de Funiak, in 23 Notre Dame Lawyer 293.

[2] In Hawaii, notice Bulgo v. Bulgo, 41 Hawaii 578; Yokochi v. Yoshimoto 44 Haw. 297, 353 P.2d 820; in Oklahoma, see Page v. Page, 341 P.2d 270.

CHAPTER V

INITIATION AND EXISTENCE OF MARITAL COMMUNITY

§ 54.   Conventional and legal community of property.

A primary division or classification of community property systems is based on the method of their creation. Within this polarization are found the conventional and the legal communities of property. Since essential differences exist between these two categories, one must know which type of community is under consideration in any given situation. Community problems can be solved only if this basic realization is kept in mind.

The term "convention" in the civil law is a general term comprehending all kinds of contracts, treaties, pacts, or agreements; the agreement of two or more persons to form with each other an engagement or to dissolve or change one which they had previously formed.[1] So, a conventional community of property is a community of property between spouses arising from an agreement between them that the marital property shall be held in some form of community. The agreement is usually contained in the marriage contract although it may be made during the marriage.

The conventional community is thus to be distinguished from the legal community which arises by operation of law upon the marriage of the parties. The latter may be arbitrarily imposed by law, or if the law allows the parties to agree to some other arrangement or to some

---

[1] Moore, Cyc. Law Dict.

modified form of that community of property provided by law, the legal community is assumed to become effective by the tacit or implied consent of the parties in the absence of any express agreement between them as to some other arrangement.[2]

The Spanish community of property was a legal community of property taking effect upon the marriage of the parties,[3] but it was not arbitrarily imposed, for the parties might at the time of contracting marriage or subsequently during marriage make some other agreement than that imposed by law whereby the husband and wife shared equally the earnings and gains during marriage. That is, the parties might contract to the effect that the wife renounced in whole or in part, generally or specially, her share in the marital profits, accepting some other arrangement.[4] We can note the same principles in France in the Custom of Paris and in the Napoleonic Code (the present Civil Code) in which the community property provisions of the Custom of Paris were incorporated. There the spouses might contract with respect to their marital property rights, but in the absence of any special agreement between them the law regulated the conjugal relations with respect to property.[5]

The form of community of property existing in all of our community property states is the legal community which by law becomes operative upon marriage of the parties.[6]

In most of those states, the parties may, however, make a marriage settlement containing stipulations contrary to the provisions of the legal community, but it is usually provided that such contracts must be in writing and recorded.[7]

§ 55.   Marriage as determinative factor.

As a basis for community of property between husband and wife there must, of course, be a marriage creating the status of husband

[2] The "modified legal community" sometimes referred to is, of course, the legal community provided by law which is modified in some way by agreement of the parties.

[3] See post, § 55.

[4] See Novísima Recopilación, Book 10, Title 4, Law 9. And see commentaries thereto, Appendix III, K, vol. 2, 1943 edition, Principles of Community Property.

Renunciation in general, see post, Chap. VIII.

Renunciation as releasing from liability for debts contracted during marriage, see post, Chap. IX.

Although the French legal community was displaced in the province of Louisiana by the Spanish legal community, the inhabitants were still enabled to enter into a conventional community on the French pattern. See Childers v. Cutter, 16 Mo. 41, 42; Cutter v. Waddingham, 22 Mo. 206, 257.

[5] See French Civil Code, art. 1387, De Nicols v. Curlier, [1900] App. Cas. 21.

That the same is true in the Province of Quebec, see Beaudoin v. Trudel, [1937] 1 D.L.R. 216.

[6] The original systems temporarily enacted in Oklahoma and Oregon were "conventional." See ante, § 53.1.

[7] See post, § 136.

and wife.[8] This, according to the Spanish law of community, could only result from the parties undergoing the ceremony of marriage and the wife going to live with the husband.[9] Mere betrothal, even if *de presenti,* was not sufficient.[10] The marriage, of course, was only the occasion for the partnership which the spouses had in the profits; the cause of the partnership was the law which established it.[11] Under some of the earlier and more primitive community property systems, the marriage was not considered to have begun, so as to share acquisitions, until the husband had carnally known the wife,[12] but this was not, of course, true of the Spanish community system, as we know it.[13] With them, the marriage ceremony and the act of the husband and wife going to live together constituted the beginning of the married state and the beginning of the community of property. This, substantially, is true with us,[14] except that in states where common-law marriages are recognized as valid, the agreement or intent of the parties would take the place of the marriage ceremony.[15]

[8] See, e.g., Jones v. Callery, (Tex. Civ. App.) 57 S. W. 2d 268, error ref.; Norvet v. Municipal Imp. Co., 119 La. Ann. 37, 21 So. 170.

Definition and nature of marriage as a relation or status, see the standard texts on family law.

[9] Azevedo's commentaries, No. 1 et seq., to Nov. Rec. Law 1, Book 10, Title 4. Matienzo, Gloss I, No. 41, to Nov. Rec. Law 1, Book 10, Title 4.

"Marriage is the conjunction of man and woman, made with the intention to live always together, and not to separate; observing fidelity one to the other, and not cohabiting with any other woman or man, living both together." Asso and Manuel, Institutes of Civil Law of Spain, Book I, Title 6, Cap. 1, § 2.

[10] Azevedo's commentaries, No. 1 et seq., to Nov. Rec. Law 1, Book 10, Title 4. See also Matienzo, Gloss I, No. 41, to the same.

And see French Civil Code, Cachard, Rev. Ed., § 1399: "Community, whether legal or conventional, commences from the day of the marriage contracted before the officer of civil status; it cannot be stipulated that it shall commence at any other time."

[11] Llamas y Molina, No. 14, to Nov. Rec. Law 8, Book 10, Title 4.

Nevertheless, the subsistence of the marriage was so entirely necessary for the existence of the conjugal partnership in the gains that Matienzo was undoubtedly justified in speaking of the marriage as the cause of the sharing and saying that if the cause ceased, the sharing must cease too. See Matienzo, Gloss I, No. 56, to Nov. Rec. Law 1, Book 10, Title 4.

[12] See Law of the Westgoths, according to the Manuscript of Eskil (Bergin's Translation), p. 59.

[13] "And this taking of the wife to her husband's house operated to such an extent that, even if the husband has not carnally known his wife, the profits acquired during marriage are shared, according to Aviles in the introduction of his chapter 'Praetorum' in no. 33." Azevedo, Nos. 3, 4, to Nov. Rec. Law 1, Book 10, Title 4.

[14] Necessity of cohabitation, see post, § 56.

See also Loveridge v. Loveridge, 52 N.M. 353, 198 P.2d 444, and Clark, Community of Property and the Family in New Mexico (1956), to the effect that only a valid marriage is required for a community of acquests and gains to come into effect in New Mexico.

[15] See following section.

§ 55.1.   — Ceremonial and common-law marriages.

The Spanish law of community property was based upon a ceremony of marriage. This usually comprised a civil contract relating to property matters and then, of course, a religious ceremony. Under that law there was no sanction of anything corresponding to the so-called common-law marriage.[16]

Currently, in Arizona, California, Louisiana, Nevada, New Mexico and Washington, a formal or ceremonial marriage is required.[17] A common-law marriage is wholly invalid if contracted and consummated in such states.[18] Of course, all of those states recognize a common-law marriage that was entered into in a jurisdiction which recognizes the validity of such marriages.[19]

It may be noticed that in early days in Louisiana expediency dictated that marriages were often recognized as valid without immediate religious ceremony because of the scarcity of priests. Usually a profession of intention was made before some civil officer and the actual religious ceremony performed later when a priest was available.

This was also true of Texas, but it was not so important there since Texas, like Idaho, recognizes the common-law marriage. In both of those states valid common-law marriages, duly established, will support marital community of property.[20] Notice that a valid common-law marriage requires an agreement between a man and a woman that they will presently be husband and wife, holding themselves out to the public as such, cohabitation, and the acquisition of

---

[16] Under the Spanish law, "secret marriages are forbidden for the just reasons set forth in Laws 1 and 5, tit. 3, Part. 4, as are also those which are celebrated without witnesses, without the permission of the father, mother, or relations to whose charge the woman betrothed is committed; or without giving notice of it in the parish church of which the contracting parties are parishioners, Law 1, tit. 3, Part. 4." Asso and Manuel, Institutes of Civil Law of Spain, Book I, Title 6, Cap. 1, § 2.

Not, of course, that a common law marriage is secret, since it depends on public reputation; it may, of course, be without witnesses or without prior notice.

[17] See statutes and codes.

[18] This was not always true in many of these states. In California common-law marriages were recognized until 1893. Nevada recognized them until much more recently, up to March 29, 1943. See Nev. Rev. Stat. § 122.010.

[19] See, e.g., Marsh, Marital Property in Conflict of Laws, Seattle, 1952.

Arizona, see Gradias v. Gradias, 51 Ariz. 35, 74 P.2d 53.

New Mexico, see In re Gabaldon's Estate, 38 N.M. 392, 34 P.2d 672, 94 A.L.R. 980.

Collections of cases on validity of common-law marriages in this country, see 39 A.L.R. 538; 60 A.L.R. 541; 94 A.L.R. 1000.

[20] As to Texas, see Oakes, Speer's Marital Rights in Texas, chap. II (1961). In Idaho, the matter is dictated by statute. See Idaho Code 1948, § 32-201; see also Brockelbank, The Community Property Law of Idaho (1962) chap. 2; Huff v. Huff, 20 Ida. 450, 118 P. 1080.

a reputation as being husband and wife.[21] It must be remarked, of course, that there is no common-law divorce.[22]

A primary reason why some states require the taking out of a marriage license and the performance of some sort of ceremony is to provide proof of the existence of the marriage. In Spain, of course, the requirements as to a religious ceremony were due to the influence of the Roman Catholic Church.

§ 56.   — Putative marriage and illicit relationships—In general.

A putative marriage, in the civil law, is a marriage which is forbidden but which has been contracted in good faith and in ignorance of the impediment on the part of at least one of the contracting parties.[23] While our American courts are more likely to use such terms as "attempted marriage" or "supposed marriage" or the like,[24] it is becoming more and more common for them to use the civil law term,[25] and because it is an apt term, it is used in this work. Our questions here then become those of what principles are applied and what results are reached where no valid marriage actually exists but there is a good faith belief by at least one party that there is a valid marriage.

The rule of the Spanish community property law that acquisitions during marriage by either spouse were common to both and divisible between them applied to a putative marriage as well as to a legal marriage.[26] Thus, where there was some legal disability to contract unknown to the parties who in ignorance thereof and in good faith entered into the marriage contract, the acquisitions of the parties nevertheless constituted community.[27] Even where one of the parties knew that there was a legal impediment to the marriage and the other in ignorance cohabited with the one having knowledge, the rule was

---

[21] See Vaughn, The Policy of Community Property and Interspousal Transactions, 19 Baylor L. Rev. 20, at p. 50.

[22] See, e.g., Huff v. Huff, 20 Idaho 450, 118 P. 1080.

[23] Moore, Cyc. Law Dict.

[24] E.g., "good faith marriage" as in Waterhouse v. Star Land Co., 139 La. 171, 71 So. 358.

[25] See, e.g., Vallera v. Vallera, 21 Cal. 2d 681, 134 P.2d 761: or, e.g., "putative wife" as in Barkley v. Dumke, 99 Tex. 150, 87 S. W. 1147.

[26] Matienzo, Gloss I, Nos. 4-7, to Nov. Rec. Law 1, Book 10, Title 4.

It was remarked, however, that there could be no community of property where there could be no

valid marriage, as between an infidel and a Christian. Matienzo, Gloss VIII, No. 1, to Nov. Rec. Law 2, Book 10, Title 4.

[27] Matienzo, Gloss I, No. 4, to Nov. Rec. Law 1, Book 10, Title 4; Azevedo, No. 5, to the same.

"Not alone in the legal or true marriage are the properties which they gain with their industry and work while it exists shared by the spouses, but also such as they acquire during a putative marriage, provided that in good faith and ignorance they believe that it is legitimate and not otherwise." Febrero, Librería de Escribanos, Cinco Juicios I, Book I, Cap. IV, § 1, No. 33.

Annulment of marriages, see post, § 222.

the same.[28] Where there were both a legal wife and a putative wife, the former having been abandoned and the latter having entered into marriage in good faith and in ignorance of the existing legal marriage, the Spanish law held that the legal wife did not lose her rights in one-half of the acquisitions of her husband because of the wrongful abandonment; likewise, the putative wife, having married in good faith, was entitled to one-half of the acquistions during the putative marriage. The husband, because of his wrongful conduct, forfeited his rights as against the just claims of the legal wife and of the putative wife.[29]

As between the two supposedly contracting parties, one who was not in good faith could claim no share in the acquisitions of the other, while the one in good faith could claim a share in the other's acquisitions. Of course, if both were not in good faith there was merely an illicit or meretricious relationship and no community of property existed at all.[30]

Most of the courts of our community property states, although they have not always termed it community property, have correctly allowed the man and woman to share equally the earnings and gains acquired by their joint efforts during the time they lived together where either or both in good faith entered into the attempted marriage and believed it a valid marriage although it was not in fact so.[31] The courts of a few of the states have continued to recognize the putative marriage of the civil law and hold that a lawful community of earnings and gains exists thereunder just as in the case of a valid marriage. This has been true of the courts of Louisiana[32] and sometimes in Texas, although among the latter courts conflicting decisions are to be found among the cases.[33] The courts of other community property states have taken the view that a valid marriage is absolutely essential to community of property, but nevertheless have allowed recovery, on the part of the one in good faith entering into the attempted marriage, of half of the earnings and gains acquired by the joint efforts of the parties;[34] frequently this has been allowed on the basis that a "partnership relation" existed between the man and woman.[35]

[28] Matienzo, Gloss I, No. 5, to Nov. Rec. Law 1, Book 10, Title 4.

Merely as a matter of interest it may be noticed that where one party was not aware of an impediment existing on account of which they should not marry, "in an instance of this kind the children will be legitimate, for the ignorance of one of them prevents it from being said that their children are not legitimate." Las Siete Partidas, Part 4, Title 3, Law 3.

[29] La Paz, Consultas Varias, pp. 483, 484, citing Covarrubias, Molina, etc., and quoted in Patton v. Philadelphia, 1 La. Ann. 98.

[30] See Matienzo, Gloss I, No. 5, to Law 1, Book 10, Title 4.

[31] See cases collected in 75 A.L.R. 732; California Jurisprudence, 2nd Ed. "Community Property," 31 Corpus Juris, pp. 18-20; 9 Calif. Law Rev. 68; Evans, Property Interests Arising from Quasi-Marital Relations, 9 Cornell Law Quart. 246.

[32] See post, § 56.4.

[33] Texas, see post, § 56.7.

[34] See California cases, post, § 56.2.

[35] See Washington cases, post, § 56.8. As to some Texas cases, see post, § 56.7.

Upon whatever ground recovery of half the earnings and gains is allowed, whether by recognition of the civil law putative marriage principle, or application by analogy of the community property rule, or by inferring or assuming a partnership relation, it must be noted that the essential element of good faith of one or both of the parties must be present.[36] It seems immaterial that the good faith involved rests upon mistake of fact or mistake of law.[37] Recovery has been allowed in the case of marriages absolutely void, as well as those voidable, if the essential element of good faith was present.[38] This has been true in the case of incestuous marriages,[39] and bigamous marriages,[40] and should, by the same reasoning, be true of miscegenous marriages.[41] However, strong application of local public policy will be present in this matter of miscegenous marriages, especially in Louisiana and Texas.[42]

Of course, where the man and woman are living together in a purely meretricious or illicit relationship of which both are aware, the situation is different,[43] although there have been exceptions even here. Thus, where the capital and labor of one party contributed to the gain, equitable principles have been held to entitle such party to share.[44] Or on the basis of an agreement between them to share, the

[36] See specific states in sections following. The good faith must be presumed and the presumption yields only to positive evidence to the contrary. McCaffrey v. Benson, 40 La. Ann. 10, 3 So. 393.

[37] See, for example, Succession of Buissiere, 41 La. Ann. 217, 5 So. 668; Knoll v. Knoll, 104 Wash. 110, 176 P. 22, 11 A. L. R. 1391.

[38] But cf. Texas view that marriage must be void, not merely voidable. See post, § 56.7.

[39] See, for example, Figoni v. Figoni, 211 Cal. 354, 295 P. 339: Succession of Buissiere, 41 La. Ann. 217, 5 So. 668.

[40] See, for example, Schneider v. Schneider, 183 Cal. 335, 191 P. 533, 11 A. L. R. 1386; Overton v. Brown, 3 La. App. 591; Texas Co. v. Stewart, (La. App.) 101 So.2d 222; Mathews v. Mathews (Tex. Civ. App.) 292 S. W. 2d 662.

Compare Beyerle v. Bartsch, 111 Wash. 287, 190 P. 239.

[41] To some extent this situation arose in Harris v. Hobbs, 22 Tex. Civ. App. 367, 54 S. W. 1085, where-in a negro woman claimed half the estate of a deceased white man with whom she had lived and by whom she had several children. The Texas court held that the evidence did not show any partnership relation between the parties and only that there was an illicit relation or concubinage.

[42] See Ryan v. Barthelmy, (La. App.) 32 So.2d 467; Harris v. Hobbs, 22 Tex. Civ. App. 367, 54 S. W. 1085. Cf. the situation in California where the Supreme Court of that state held the local miscegenation statute invalid.

[43] See, e.g., Parker v. Parker, 74 Cal. App. 646, 241 P. 581; Sims v. Matassa (La. App.), 200 So. 666; In re Sloan's Estate, 50 Wash. 86, 96 P. 684, 17 L. R. A. (N. S.) 960. And see Harris v. Hobbs, 22 Tex. Civ. App. 367, 54 S. W. 1085, Little v. Nicholson (Tex. Civ. App.), 187 S. W. 506.

And see specific states, in sections following.

[44] Thus, although a woman living in concubinage was said to have no right to share as a marital partner, where her capital and labor contributed toward the result, it was held

agreement has been sustained as a business or partnership agreement apart from the illicit relationship.[45] However, as to the latter situation, most courts are inclined to consider that the illicit relationship constitutes an immoral consideration and that public policy forbids giving the agreement effect.[46]

What is the situation, however, where there is a lawful wife and a putative wife? Cases have several times arisen where a man either consciously committed bigamy or married a second time in the honest but mistaken belief that he was divorced from his first wife, and the putative wife entered into the putative or attempted marriage in all good faith. Actually, no definite rule can be laid down, for much must depend upon the circumstances of the particular case as well as the views of the particular jurisdiction. For instance, if the lawful wife is not at fault, as where she has been deserted, and she still has the will to union, then her rights should be considered as well as those of the putative wife. Notice that here the husband cannot easily be characterized as being in good faith, so as to have rights. On the other hand, suppose the lawful wife has abandoned the husband or has committed adultery, does she have any rights? Certainly not in those gains acquired after her wrongdoing. To the extent that cases have arisen in the several states, the matter is considered in the sections following which deal with specific states.

§ 56.1.   — Arizona.

There are relatively few cases in Arizona dealing with putative marriage and illicit relationships. It has been stated as dictum that where one party is unaware of the invalidity of the marriage such innocent party may be allowed to recover his or her proportionate share.[47] There is also authority that in case of an invalid marriage there can be no acquisition of property rights based on a marital status but rather that the innocent party would have a cause of action for labor and money expended.[48] In this latter case, the indication is that both parties were in good faith.

Where both parties are aware that there is no valid marriage, there can be no community property since there is no valid marriage on which to base community. But nevertheless the court recognized and enforced a partnership agreement between the parties.[49]

that equity entitled her to half the property acquired. Delamour v. Roger, 7 La. Ann. 152. See also Hayworth v. Williams, 102 Tex. 308, 116 S. W. 43, 132 Am. St. Rep. 879. Conflicting decisions in California, see post, § 56.2.

[45] Conflicting cases in California, see post, § 56.2.

[46] See, e.g., California, Texas and Washington cases in following sections.

[47] Stevens v. Anderson, 75 Ariz. 331, 256 P.2d 712.

[48] In re Mortensen's Estate, 83 Ariz. 87, 316 P.2d 1106.

[49] Garza v. Fernandez, 74 Ariz. 312, 248 P.2d 869.

§ 56.2.   — California.

The California Supreme Court, with respect to what it now refers to by the civil law term of putative marriage,[50] has made the following most illuminating statement:

> In California, as in Texas, the common law is the general rule of decision, but in both states the law regulating the mutual property rights of married persons is radically different from that law; and while we do not wish to be understood as saying that the rule of the common law as to husband and wife apply to no case under our system, yet we agree with the Texas courts that the common-law rule as to the consequences of a void marriage upon the mutual property rights of the parties to it is inapplicable where the community property regime prevails. This conclusion is dictated by simple justice, for where persons domiciled in such a jurisdiction, believing themselves to be lawfully married to each other, acquire property as a result of their joint efforts, they have impliedly adopted . . . the rule of an equal division of their acquisitions, and the expectation of such a division should not be defeated in the case of innocent persons.[51]

On other occasions that court has said that, while strictly speaking there can be no community of property, the same rule will be applied by analogy as would obtain under a valid marriage.[52] The result has been that in every instance of a putative marriage, the community property laws are applied just as they are in the case of a valid marriage, so that in effect there is community of property. (Perhaps we could invent a term and call it "analagous community property.") So, unlike the results in Louisiana[53] and Texas,[54] the putative wife has been able to bring a wrongful death action as "heir" of the putative husband.[55] And just as in the case of a lawful wife, where the husband has not left his share of the community property by will, the putative wife can claim his share by descent, as well, of course, as her share by existing ownership.[56] And just as a lawful wife in a suit for divorce is entitled to the specified share of the community property, so the putative wife seeking to dissolve the marriage is entitled to the same share.[57] Of course, in a suit for divorce by the

---

[50] As in Vallera v. Vallera, 21 Cal. 2d 681, 134 P.2d 761.

Putative marriage defined, see Estate of Rayner, 165 Cal. App. 2d 715, 332 P.2d 416; Kunakoff v. Woods, 166 Cal. App. 2d 59, 332 P.2d 773.

[51] Schneider v. Schneider, 183 Cal. 335, 191 P. 533, 11 A.L.R. 1386.

[52] Coats v. Coats, 160 Cal. 671, 118 P. 441, 36 L.R.A. (N.S.) 844; Macchi v. La Rocca, 54 Cal. App. 98, 201 P. 143; Feig v. Bank of America, 5 Cal. 2d 266, 54 P.2d 3; Turknette v. Turknette, 100 Cal. App.

2d 291, 223 P.2d 495. And see 37 Cal. L. Rev. 671.

[53] See post, § 56.4.

[54] See post, § 56.7.

[55] Kunakoff v. Woods, 166 Cal. App. 2d 59, 332 P.2d 773.

[56] Estate of Krone, 83 Cal. App. 2d 766, 189 P.2d 741, noted 21 So. Cal. L. Rev. 385; Mazzenga v. Rosso, 87 Cal. App. 2d 790, 197 P.2d 778; Estate of Goldberg, 21 Cal. Rptr. 626.

[57] Turknette v. Turknette, 100 Cal. App. 2d 291; 223 P.2d 495.

supposed wife, upon it developing that the marriage is not a valid one, obviously no decree of divorce can be granted. What is or should be done is that the complaint is amended to seek an annulment of the supposed marriage, with the continuation of the request for the same division of property as in case of dissolution of a valid marriage.[58] Notice that in the former situation under the former California law, a lawful wife was entitled to more than half of the community property where the ground of divorce was adultery or extreme cruelty,[59] and the same recovery has been allowed to the putative wife where her suit began as one for divorce on the ground of adultery or extreme cruelty, although it then had to be amended to be a suit for annulment.[60] This is true of a suit for legal separation as well as of a suit for absolute divorce.[61]

Incidentally, while most cases involve the woman in good faith seeking her rightful share from the man, occasionally it turns out to be the man who has been victimized in some way.[62]

The essential element of good faith must be present on the part of the one seeking the aid of the court. If both parties are aware that there is or can be no valid marriage, it is merely an illicit or meretricious relationship and the court will not lend its aid [63] While on rare occasion the court has compelled a sharing on the basis of a partnership or joint venture agreement apart from the illicit relationship,[64] usually the courts consider the illicit relationship constitutes an immoral consideration for any such agreement and usually will not lend their aid.[65]

While many cases in California have considered and protected the interests of a putative wife, there has been relatively little case material relating to the rights or interests of the lawful wife or involving any dispute between the lawful wife and the putative wife. Attention may be called to the well-reasoned determination in one case which was a suit to quiet title between the lawful wife and the putative wife with regard to property accumulated during the putative marriage. The court decided entirely in favor of the putative wife, awarding her the entire property, half as being her share as her own and the other half as coming by descent from the putative husband who died intestate. Evidently the court was influenced by the fact

---

[58] See, e.g., Coats v. Coats, 160 Cal. 671, 118 P. 441, 36 L.R.A. (N.S.) 844. And see preceding note and following notes.

[59] See post, § 224 et seq.

[60] See cases supra, notes 57 and 58.

[61] Turknette v. Turknette, preceding note.

[62] See Feig v. Bank of America, 5 Cal. 2d 266, 54 P.2d 3.

[63] See, e.g., Vallera v. Vallera, 21 Cal. 2d 681, 134 P.2d 761: Latronica v. Gennoni, 205 Cal. 559, 271 P. 1054.

[64] Cline v. Kestersen, 128 Cal. App. 2d 380, 275 P.2d 149. And see Sutton v. Sutton, 145 Cal. App. 2d 730, 303 P.2d 21.

[65] Updeck v. Samuel, 123 Cal. App. 2d 264, 266 P.2d 822; Baskett v. Crook, 86 Cal. App. 2d 355, 195 P.2d 39.

that the lawful wife had evinced no interest in the husband for 34 years and that her interest was aroused only upon her discovering that he had died leaving considerable property.[66] This view would be even stronger today, in view of the recent statutory amendment providing that during the period of a wife's abandonment of her husband, his acquisitions during that period are his separate property.[67] This could be applied to defeat the claim of a lawful wife who can be considered to have abandoned her husband, but it could not properly be applied to defeat the claim of the putative wife who has been living with the husband. Moreover, the Arizona[68] and Washington[69] cases dealing with long separations between a husband and a lawful wife should have strong persuasive effect.

In another case of interest involving the lawful wife and the putative wife, the court was strongly influenced by the Louisiana view[70] and divided the property equally between the two women. There the husband was at fault and the lawful wife was not, in that he had deserted her and then entered into the putative marriage.[71] So, we have in these cases reached essentially the view followed in Louisiana and one in substantial accord with the civil law.[72] But attention should also be directed to a suggestion that the putative wife is entitled to one-half of the property acquired during the putative marriage and that the other half is divisible between the lawful wife and the husband.[73]

On another occasion, what began as an apparent dispute between a lawful wife and a supposed putative wife was disposed of in favor of the lawful wife when it was determined that the supposed putative wife was not in fact in good faith and so was living in an illicit relationship.[74]

Another feature of the putative marriage situation in California must be noticed. Evidently to meet the situation where the woman was in good faith but had been victimized by the fraud of the man and there was no substantial property available for division, the California Supreme Court recognized the right of the putative wife to

[66] Mazzenga v. Rosso, 87 Cal. App. 2d 970, 197 P.2d 770.

In the much-appealed case of Blache v. Blache, the case began with the tacit approval of a trial court division between the two women, then the court of appeal favored the lawful wife who had long been absent from the husband, awarding her everything on the apparent basis that there was a valid marriage and that flatly the lawful wife should take all. The state Supreme Court effectively overruled this view in granting a rehearing in 37 Cal. 2d 531, 233 P.2d 547. Moreover, the situation would now be controlled by Civil Code, § 5131.

[67] Cal. Civ. Code, § 5131.

[68] See ante, § 56.1.

[69] See post, § 56.8.

[70] See post, § 56.4.

[71] Estate of Ricci, 201 Cal. App. 2d 146, 19 Cal. Rptr. 739.

[72] See ante, § 56, post, § 56.4.

[73] See Estate of Williams, 36 Cal. 2d 289, 223 P.2d 248, 22 A.L.R. 2d 716.

[74] Estate of Rayner, 165 Cal. App. 2d 715, 332 P.2d 416.

sue the man for the value of her services. This was intended to be used only when there was not appreciable "community" property.[75] However, many of the Courts of Appeal have allowed the putative wife to have not only a division of appreciable property but also to recover damages on *quantum meruit* for her services.[76] This, in effect, gives a benefit to a putative wife that a lawful wife does not have. Certainly, both remedies should not be available and an election should be required of the putative wife. Moreover, the right to elect should only be available where the man is not in good faith.[77]

§ 56.3. — Idaho.

In his excellent work on the community property law of Idaho, Professor Brockelbank notes that with one recent exception there have been no putative marriage or illicit relationship cases in that state.[78] The one exception involved a case in which a married man had fraudulently induced a woman to marry him and live with him for two months. The court approved an award of damages in her favor for the fraud practiced on her.[79]

Professor Brockelbank discusses the general situation at length as it has arisen in the other states and strongly recommends the adoption of the putative marriage theory in preference to the partnership theory and the equitable division theory.[80]

§ 56.4. — Louisiana.

In most respects, Louisiana has followed the original civil law principles of putative marriage more closely than have the other states. Its courts recognize the putative marriage of the civil law and hold that a lawful community of earnings and gains exists just as in the case of a valid marriage.[81] Of course, the essential element of good faith of one or both of the parties must be present.[82] The good

---

[75] See discussion, 37 Cal. L. Rev. 671.

[76] See, e.g., Lazzarevitch v. Lazzarevitch, 88 Cal. App. 2d 708, 200 P.2d 49.

[77] See well-reasoned remarks in Spellens v. Spellens (Cal. App.) 305 P.2d 628, 640, but unfortunately decree was vacated by rehearing granted by supreme court in 49 Cal. 2d 210, 317 P.2d 613, holding husband estopped to deny validity of marriage.

[78] Brockelbank, The Community Property Law of Idaho (1962), pp. 49-70.

[79] McGhee v. McGhee, 82 Idaho

367, 353 P.2d 760.

[80] Brockelbank, p. 54.

[81] McCaffrey v. Benson, 40 La. Ann. 10, 3 So. 393; Jackson v. Lindlom, (La. App.) 84 So. 2d 101, noted in 31 Tulane L. Rev. 685; and see other cases cited in this section. For a detailed analysis of Louisiana cases on putative marriage, see Homes, The Putative Marriage Doctrine in Louisiana, 12 Loyola L. Rev. 89.

[82] McCaffrey v. Benson, supra, declaring that the good faith must be presumed and the presumption yields only to positive evidence to the contrary.

faith can rest either upon a mistake of fact or a mistake of law.[83] But one who is not in good faith has no right to share, although this has been departed from where the party's capital and labor have contributed toward the result.[84]

Although it might well be assumed that a putative wife would have all the same rights that would be true of a wife in a valid marriage, this has not always been the result. Thus, a putative widow was not entitled to recover for the wrongful death of the putative husband either on her own behalf or on behalf of the minor children,[85] similar to the result in Texas[86] but unlike that in California.[87]

In respect to claims made at the same time by a putative wife and by a lawful wife, a definite set of rules, based largely on the Spanish law, has been applied, unlike most of the other states where a sort of catch-as-catch-can situation has prevailed. Thus, in several of the cases the view has been followed that the lawful wife rightfully takes one-half and the putative wife one-half, leaving the husband nothing, upon the ground that by his conduct he has forfeited his rights in the community property acquired during the putative marriage.[88] However, more recently it has been pointed out that the foregoing result is reached only when the husband is in bad faith. Where he and the second or putative wife enter into the putative marriage in good faith, the court has applied the following division: one-half the community property to the husband (which is subject to inheritance by the children) and the other one-half of the property divided between the lawful wife and the putative wife, or, in short, one-fourth to

[83] Succession of Buissiere, 41 La. Ann. 217, 5 So. 668.

In Louisiana, it is provided by statute that "The marriage which has been declared null, produces, nevertheless its civil effects, as it relates to parties and their children, if it has been contracted in good faith." La. Civ. Code, art. 117. And also that "If one of the parties acted in good faith the marriage produces its civil effects only in his or her favor and in favor of the children born of the marriage." La. Civ. Code, art. 118. These provisions were taken from the French Code Napoleon, arts. 201, 202. Succession of Buissiere, supra, this note.

[84] In Delamour v. Roger, 7 La. Ann. 152, although a woman living in concubinage was said to have no right to share as a marital partner, where her capital and labor con- tributed toward the result, it was held equity entitled her to half the property acquired.

[85] Jackson v. Lindlom, (La. App.) 84 So. 2d 101, noted in 31 Tulane L. Rev. 685. But see United States v. Robinson (5 Cir.) 40 F.2d 14, as to putative wife taking under federal War Risk Insurance Act. Cf. Muir v. U.S., (Cal. D.C.) 93 F. Supp. 939.

[86] See post, § 56.7.

[87] See ante, § 56.2.

[88] This has been the view in Louisiana both under the Spanish law and the later statutes. See, among others, Waterhouse v. Star Land Co., 139 La. 171, 71 So. 358; Jerman v. Tenneas, 44 La. Ann. 620, 11 So. 80; Abston v. Abston, 15 La. Ann. 137; Hubbell v. Inkstein, 7 La. Ann. 252; Patton v. Philadelphia, 1 La. Ann. 98.

each.[89] This, of course, refers to the property acquired during the period of the putative marriage.

§ 56.5.   — Nevada.

There appear to be no Nevada cases dealing with the putative marriage situation. Certainly none is mentioned or cited in the text essays or articles dealing with the law of that state.[90]

§ 56.6.   — New Mexico.

No New Mexico case appears to have involved the matter of the putative marriage. The closest approach has been a case which points out that the common-law marriage is not the same thing as the civil law putative marriage.[91]

§ 56.7.   — Texas.

Prior to the adoption of the common law in Texas by act of the Congress of the Republic of Texas on February 20, 1840, the civil law doctrine that the putative marriage supported community of property was accepted.[92] The community property system was continued in Texas by constitutional and statutory provisions at the same time,[93] but shortly thereafter the Texas Supreme Court decided that the civil law as to putative marriages did not obtain after the adoption of the common law in 1840. The incident of community property was said to belong only to an actual and lawful marriage.[94] That case did not decide, however, how property acquired during the supposed marriage should be divided. Thereafter, many decisions followed the view that there could be no community of property but allowed a sharing of the gains acquired by the joint efforts of the parties on the ground that a "partnership relation" existed between them.[95]

In 1905, the entire doctrine and the cases were re-examined and it was held that the "putative wife" was entitled to recover one-half the property acquired during the supposed marriage, and "so long as

[89] Prince v. Hopson, 230 La. 575, 89 So.2d 128, noted in 11 S. W. L. Jour. 245, and distinguishing the Waterhouse and the Patton cases.

[90] See Shermack, Nevada Community Property Law, 15 La. Law Rev. 559; Clark, New Mexico and the Western United States, Part I, pp. 89-138, of Friedmann, Matrimonial Property Law, Toronto, 1955.

[91] In re Gabaldon's Estate, 38 N. M. 392, 34 P.2d 672, 94 A.L.R. 980, remarked on by Clark, Community of Property and the Family in New Mexico, 1956, p. 15.

[92] Smith v. Smith, 1 Tex. 621, 46 Am. Dec. 121.

[93] See ante, § 44.

[94] Routh v. Routh, 57 Tex. 589.

[95] See, e.g., Little v. Nicholson, (Tex. Civ. App.) 187 S. W. 506.

she acts innocently, has as to the property acquired during that time the rights of a lawful wife."[96] Subsequently, in 1910 it was again held that "Under repeated decisions of our higher courts, it is a settled principle of law that, when a marriage is held to be unlawful, the putative wife, who has assumed and sustained that relation, believing in good faith the marriage to be lawful, will be entitled to one-half of all property acquired by the joint labors of the two, even in the absence of proof of the extent of the labor contributed by each." But the court added that the putative marriage did not support community of property.[97]

In 1923, the Texas Supreme Court returned to the language of its 1905 decision that not only is the putative wife entitled to one-half of the acquisitions but that such acquisitions are community property.[98] However, there are subsequent decisions which deny that community of property actually exists, although allowing the putative wife to take one-half of the acquisitions.[99]

It may be noted that the issue of a putative marriage is legitimate,[1] that the putative marriage refers to one that is void and not merely voidable,[2] and that the putative marriage may arise from either a ceremonial or a common-law marriage.[3] But in line with the view that the property is not actually community and that the only right of the putative wife is to one-half of the acquired property, she has no cause of action for the wrongful death of the putative husband under either the Wrongful Death Act or the Workmen's Compensation Act;[4] nor is she entitled to homestead or other exemptions nor to allowances in lieu thereof, nor to rights of probate administration,

---

[96] Barkley v. Dumke, 99 Tex. 150, 87 S. W. 1147, placing reliance on Morgan v. Morgan, (Tex. Civ. App.) 21 S. W. 154 and Lawson v. Lawson, (Tex. Civ. App.) 69 S. W. 246.

[97] Fort Worth & Rio Grande Ry. Co. v. Robertson, 103 Tex. 504, 131 S. W. 400.

[98] Lee v. Lee, 112 Tex. 392, 247 S. W. 828, saying: "Texas, with just a few other states of the Union, has adopted as the basis of its laws relating to estates held by husband and wife the principles of the civil law, and our statutory enactments are in large measure declaratory of these principles. This is particularly true with reference to the laws relating to community property. Under the principles of this law, as recognized by numerous decisions of our courts, Mary Lee was the putative wife of Joseph H. Lee, and possessed all the rights and privileges of a lawful wife, to the extent of being entitled to an equal interest with Joseph H. Lee in all community property."

[99] Mathews v. Mathews, (Tex. Civ. App.) 292 S. W. 662, that property is jointly owned, separate property of each.

[1] Gravley v. Gravley, (Tex. Civ. App.) 353 S. W. 2d 333, error ref.

[2] Whaley v. Peat, (Tex. Civ. App.) 377 S. W. 2d 355. See Portwood v. Portwood, (Tex. Civ. App.) 109 S. W. 2d 515, err. dism.: "A merely voidable marriage must be treated as valid for all civil purposes until annulled by judicial decree." See also De Gurmond v. Smith, (Tex. Civ. App.) 168 S. W. 2d 899.

[3] See Pruett, The Requirements of a Marriage Ceremony for a Putative Relationship, 4 Baylor L. Rev. 343.

[4] Texas Employers' Ins. Ass'n v. Grimes, 153 Tex. 356, 269 S. W. 2d 332.

nor a widow's allowance, nor the prior right of guardianship of the putative husband.[5] The contrast with the California situation is most noticeable.[6]

As already indicated, the party seeking to recover on the basis of a putative marriage must in good faith believe that there is a valid marriage.[7] The good faith must be presumed and the presumption yields only to positive evidence to the contrary.[8]

In the situation where there is no good faith on either side and the man and woman are merely living together in an illicit relationship, the relationship itself provides no basis for a sharing.[9] There must be an agreement for such sharing of a partnership or joint venture nature or some contribution of labor or capital on which a right can be based. And since the moral sensibilities of the court are likely to be outraged by the illicit relationship, the court is disinclined to interpret the evidence favorably to such an agreement or situation.[10]

Despite the number of Texas cases in the field of the putative marriage, there seem to be hardly any involving the conflicting claims of a lawful wife and a putative wife, as has been true in California and Louisiana. In a case decided in 1882, the court awarded one-fourth of the property to the putative wife and one-half to the lawful wife. The other one-fourth went, of course, to the husband.[11]

§ 56.8.   — Washington.

A number of Washington cases have dealt with the putative marriage, although not usually by that name. Similarly to the view of some of the Texas cases,[12] the Washington courts have repeatedly held that there can be no community of property in the absence of a lawful marriage, but they have always allowed the woman, where she has been in good faith, to recover half the property acquired by their joint efforts. This has been put on the basis that there was a "partnership relation."[13] In other cases, in annulling a bigamous marriage at the suit of the innocent second wife, the court said that under its equitable powers it could divide the property that was jointly accumulated during the marriage.[14] And it has been held that property

[5] See Oakes, Speer's Marital Rights in Texas (1961), § 55.

[6] See ante, § 56.2.

[7] See this section and ante, § 56.

[8] See Papoutsis v. Trevino, (Tex. Civ. App.) 167 S. W. 2d 777, err. dism.

[9] See, e.g., Esparza v. Esparza, (Tex. Civ. App.) 382 S. W. 2d 162.

[10] See Hayworth v. Williams, 102 Tex. 308, 116 S. W. 43, 132 Am. St. Rep. 879.

[11] Routh v. Routh, 57 Tex. 589.

[12] See ante, § 56.7.

[13] Knoll v. Knoll, 104 Wash. 110, 176 P. 22, 11 A.L.R. 1391; In re Brenchley, 96 Wash. 223, 164 P. 913, L.R.A. 1917E 968; Powers v. Powers, 117 Wash. 248, 200 P. 1080. Review of Washington cases, see Poole v. Schricte, 39 Wash. 2d 558, 236 P.2d 1044.

[14] Buckley v. Buckley, 50 Wash. 213, 96 P. 1079, 126 Am. St. Rep. 900. Emphasis on the equity powers of the court to make the division is made in Poole v. Schricte, 39 Wash. 2d 558, 236 P.2d 1044.

acquired by a woman, who had in good faith entered into a bigamous marriage with a man who had a wife living, was her separate property.[15] Although putting stress on the fact that this was her separate property because there could be no community property without a lawful marriage, the court in this and in other cases has been, in effect, applying the civil law principles that the innocent party can share in the gains of the other but does not have to share his or her acquisitions with a wrongdoing party to the supposed marriage.[16]

In accord with the customary view, there must be good faith belief in a valid marriage to entitle one to the aid of the courts.[17] Of course, where neither party is in good faith there is merely an illicit relationship or, of course, if only one of the parties is in bad faith, as to that party the relationship is illicit. One in an illicit relationship has no right to share in the acquisitions even if they result from joint effort or the like,[18] unless it can be proved to the court's satisfaction that there was an agreement of a business nature in effect, which establishes the right.[19] No trust theory is recognized as to property acquired by joint effort and which is in the name of one of the parties.[20]

In the area of awarding shares of the property to a lawful wife and a putative wife, the only case appears to be one in which the court awarded one-fourth to the lawful wife, one-fourth to the putative wife, and one-half to the husband.[21]

§ 57.   Necessity of cohabitation.

It was a basic principle of the Spanish community property system that for acquisitions and earnings of the spouses to constitute community, the spouses must have been cohabiting as husband and wife at the time of the acquisitions or earnings.[22] This was because it was considered that it was the mutual loyalty, the mutual sharing of the burdens of marriage, the joint industry and labor of the spouses to further and advance the success and well-being of the marriage and of the family, which entitled them to share in the profits. But this did not mean that they had always to remain in the same house and never be apart. So long as the marriage actually continued to subsist, so long as there was the will to union, they were considered to be cohabiting

---

[15] Beyerle v. Bartsch, 111 Wash. 287, 190 P. 239; In re Sloan's Estate, 50 Wash. 86, 96 P. 684, 17 L.R.A. 960.

[16] See ante, § 56, as to civil law.

[17] Poole v. Schricte, 39 Wash. 2d 558, 236 P.2d 1044.

[18] In re Sloan's Estate, 50 Wash. 86, 96 P. 684, 17 L.R.A. 960; Poole v. Schricte, 39 Wash. 2d 558, 236 P.2d 1044.

[19] See cases, preceding and following notes.

[20] Creasman v. Boyle, 31 Wash. 2d 345, 196 P.2d 835; West v. Knowles, 50 Wash. 2d 311, 311 P.2d 684.

[21] Buckley v. Buckley, 50 Wash. 213, 96 P. 1079, 126 Am. St. Rep. 900.

[22] Matienzo, Gloss I, No. 41, to Nov. Rec. Law 1, Book 10, Title 4.

together, even if one of them was absent for business reasons,[23] or the husband absent for the purpose of seeking his fortune,[24] or the wife, for reasons of health, had to live elsewhere than where the husband was employed.[25] We have no difficulty in understanding such separations through necessity, of course, for these are matters that may exist with us without affecting the subsistence of a valid marriage or the right to share equally in the earnings and gains.[26]

Even if the wife was compelled to live apart through reason of the

---

[23] Matienzo, Gloss I, No. 42, to Nov. Rec. Law 1; Azevedo, No. 14, to the same.

[24] Matienzo, Gloss I, No. 43, to Nov. Rec. Law 1.

[25] "The conclusion set forth in the foregoing number, holds good and applies not only when the husband and wife cohabit in the same town and house, but even if they are in different places, provided the marriage subsists, and their mutual consent and union of wills, and no divorce has intervened, e.g., if the husband is employed, and the wife, because the climate is hurtful to her health, or for some other just cause remains in her country, or if she has therein some business, and the husband another business elsewhere; in these and other similar cases, the marriage, and the partnership and the union of wills subsist, although not that of their persons, so that all that one or the other or both gain, should be shared and divided in half; notwithstanding that some say that for this there is necessary the simultaneous cohabitation; but this opinion is rejected as destitute of a solid foundation." Febrero, Librería de Escribanos, Cinco Juicios I, Book I, Cap. IV, § 1, No. 2.

"It is required as a requisite condition, for this community of *gananciales* between spouses, that they should live together, according to Law 2 of the same title (Title 4, Book 10 of Novísima Recopilacíon). This should not be understood literally, so that this community of interests should be hampered by the absences of the spouses from each other, unless they have been

divorced." Llamas y Molina, No. 28, to Nov. Rec. Law 10.

[26] See Makeig v. United Security Bank & Trust Co., 112 Cal. App. 138, 296 P. 673.

In Succession of Dill, 155 La. 47, 98 So. 752, a husband moved to Louisiana, established his domicile there, and acquired movables. His wife did not accompany him, and the spouses lived separate, apparently because of the insanity of the wife, for subsequently she was committed to a New York asylum for the insane and her daughter appointed her guardian. By reason of the Louisiana decisions and statutes, the court determined that the movables acquired by the husband in Louisiana were community property of which the wife was entitled to half. To same effect, see Cole v. Cole's Ex'rs, 7 Mart. N. S. (La.) 41, 18 Am. Dec. 241; Dixon v. Dixon's Ex'rs, 4 La. 188, 23 Am. Dec. 478. On the other hand in Washington, where a husband came into the state unaccompanied by his wife and acquired property which was purchased from him in good faith by one unaware that he was married, it has been held that the wife could not claim half of the property as against the purchaser. Although the court decided the matter on the basis of the rights of an innocent purchaser for value, it might have been put on the ground that there can be no sharing where there is lack of cohabitation, assuming the wife wrongfully refused to accompany the husband. See Nuhn v. Miller, 5 Wash. 405, 31 P. 1031, 34 P. 152, 34 Am. St. Rep. 868; Daly v. Rizzuto, 59 Wash. 62, 109 P. 276, 29 L. R. A. (N. S.) 467.

fault of the husband, as by his cruelty, the marriage continued to subsist, so as to entitle the wife to half of the husband's acquests and gains, whether acquired before or during the separation,[27] although she did not have to-share her acquisitions with him.[28] On the other hand, where the spouses were separated through the fault of the wife, she was bound to share her acquisitions with the husband but was entitled to nothing from the property acquired by him, whether acquired before or after her abandonment of him.[29] Here it will be seen that the innocent spouse did not suffer for an absence of cohabitation which was not his or her fault. The foregoing presents the matter in brief. Since the right or absence of right to share in marital gains during a separation caused by the fault of one spouse was the same whether there was a mere living apart or whether a legal separation resulted, the question is discussed more fully in a subsequent chapter dealing with the effect of divorce.[30] It may be remarked here that aside from annulment of marriage, the only divorce recognized in the Spanish law was a legal separation as to cohabitation, in other words from bed and board.[31]

Statutes in many of our community property states have recognized the right of the wife to her own earnings and accumulations, as well as to those of the minor children living with her or in her custody, while she is living separate from her husband,[32] but if they specify no further than that they would appear not to place the mat-

---

[27] Matienzo, Gloss I, No. 45 et seq., to Nov. Rec. Law 1.

[28] Matienzo, Gloss I, No. 53, to Nov. Rec. Law 1.

[29] Matienzo, Gloss I, Nos. 54, 55, to Nov. Rec. Law 1.

See also post, § 189, as to misconduct depriving spouse of share of community property.

[30] Where the separation was by consent or due to the fault of neither, property acquired by one during such period of separation was not shared with the other. Matienzo, Gloss I, Nos. 56, 57, to Novísima Recopilacíon, Book 10, Title 4, Law 1.

[31] See post, Chap. X, C.

[32] Ariz. Rev. St. (1956) § 25-213; Cal. Civ. Code § 5118; Nev. Rev. St. (1956) § 123.180; N.M. St. (1953) § 57-3-7 (applies only to legal separation, Op. Atty. Gen. N.M., 1943-44, No. 4478); Rev. C. Wash. (1961) § 26.16.140. And see Evans, Primary Sources of Acquisition of Community Property, 10 Calif. Law Rev. 271; 126 Am. St. Rep. 115.

In Louisiana, as to earnings of wife living apart from husband, see La. Rev. Civ. Code, art. 2334. Earnings of minor children in her custody are not declared her separate property as is the case in the statutes of other states; possibly they belong to the child. See La. Civ. Code, art. 221; but cf. art. 229.

In Texas, the earnings of the wife while living apart from her husband continue to constitute community property. Carter v. Barnes, (Tex. Com. App.) 25 S. W. 2d 606. Furthermore, realty bought by wife has been held community property even though husband had abandoned her and had paid no part of consideration. Hitchcock v. Cassel, (Tex. Civ. App.) 275 S. W. 2d 205, err. ref., nre.

In Washington, property acquired by the husband almost four years after the spouses separated was denominated community property; it does not appear what caused the separation. Campbell v. Sandy, 190 Wash. 528, 69 P.2d 808. See also In re Towey's Estate, 22 Wash. 2d 212, 155 P.2d 273.

Acquisition by wife through occu-

ter on the same just and equitable basis that was true of the Spanish law of community. It may be inferred, however, that they are intended to apply to the situation where the wife is forced to live separate through fault of the husband and to the situation where the spouses separated by agreement. If viewed in that light they are more in accord with the Spanish principles of community than appears at first sight.[33]

Many of our courts have recognized the principle that where the spouses are living separate and apart through the fault of the wife, as by reason of adultery or abandonment on her part, that she forfeits her right to share at least in the husband's acquisitions during her period of misconduct.[34] Indeed, it has come to be recognized by statute, as in California, that the earnings of the husband during the period of unjustifiable abandonment by the wife, prior to any offer by her to return, are the husband's separate property.[35] So neither such earnings nor things purchased with them are community property and so do not need to be shared with the wife.[36] In such a situation, the burden is on the wife to show a good faith offer to return.[37]

It has also been recognized that a long continued absence of cohabitation may have the result of bringing an end to the conjugal partnership in the earnings and gains. There may well be considered to be an agreement or understanding that the partnership of sharing is terminated, so that what each earns is his or her separate property.[38]

Unfortunately, it must be admitted that there are cases where

---

pation and adverse possession of land, the title of which was in husband, after husband's abandonment of her, as "accumulation" within such a statute, see Union Oil Co. v. Stewart, 158 Cal. 149, 110 P. 313, Ann. Cas. 1912A 567. Recovery by wife for wrongful death of child in her custody held her separate property. Christiana v. Rose, 100 Cal. App. 2d 46, 222 P.2d 891.

[33] In California, the "living apart" referred to in the Code applies "to a condition where the spouses have come to a parting of the ways and have no present intention of resuming the marital relations and taking up life together under the same roof." Makeig v. United Security Bank & Trust Co., 112 Cal. App. 138, 296 P. 673. It has been held that under such a statute the husband's earnings during the separation were community property. Spreckels v. Spreckels, 116 Cal. 339, 48 P. 228, 36 L. R. A. 497, 58 Am. St. Rep. 170.

[34] Pendleton v. Brown, 25 Ariz. 604, 221 P. 213; Togliatti v. Robert-

son, 29 Wash. 2d 844, 190 P.2d 575. In Idaho and Texas, earlier views that the wife forfeited her interest in property acquired before as well as during her misconduct were modified to cover only property during the period of misconduct. See Bedal v. Sake, 10 Idaho 270, 77 P. 638, 66 L. R. A. 60; Peterson v. Peterson, 35 Idaho 470, 207 P. 425; Wheat v. Owens, 15 Tex. 241, 65 Am. Dec. 164; Routh v. Routh, 57 Tex. 583.

[35] Cal. Civ. Code § 5131.

And see Cal. Civ. Code § 5119, as to earnings by husband during interlocutory period of divorce. Similarly, in Washington as to interlocutory period of divorce, see In re Armstrong's Estate, 33 Wash. 2d 118, 204 P.2d 500.

[36] Norwich v. Norwich, 170 Cal. App. 2d 806, 339 P.2d 574.

[37] Polk v. Polk, (1st D.C.A.) 39 Cal. Rptr. 824.

[38] Togliatti v. Robertson, 29 Wash. 2d 844, 190 P.2d 575, followed in In re Armstrong's Estate, 33 Wash. 2d 118, 204 P.2d 500 and In re

there has been a failure to recognize the justice and equities of a situation and some courts have flatly held property to be community so as to be shared by a wrong-doing spouse.[39] Sometimes this has come about in the same jurisdictions in which other cases have recognized the proper application of the governing principles.[40] It can only be hoped that the courts in question will recognize their obligation to apply the correct and governing principles. It is no answer to try to put the obligation upon the legislature to enact specific legislation,[41] although such action would be helpful. Principles of equity alone, if nothing else, should sustain correct determinations.

Hewitt's Estate, (Alaska) 358 P.2d 579.

Where spouses living apart for seventeen years as if unmarried and without any regard to each other, survivor not entitled to statutory portion of decedent's estate. Pickens v. Gillam, 43 La. Ann. 350, 8 So. 928.

Estate, under Cal. Prob. Code § 640, could not be set aside to a widow who, because of her desertion, was not entitled to support of her husband at the time of his death, see Estate of Abila, 32 Cal. 2d 559, 197 P.2d 10.

Wife not questioning validity of Mexican mail order divorce and herself remarrying was estopped to claim any part of husband's earnings during his second marriage. Hengsen v. Silberman, 87 Cal. App. 2d 668, 197 P.2d 356.

[39] See Beals v. Ares, 25 N.M. 459, 185 P. 780; Loveridge v. Loveridge, 52 N.M. 353, 198 P.2d 444.

[40] As in Louisiana and Texas. Compare Cole's Widow v. His Executors, 7 Mart. N. S. (La.) 41, 18 Am. Dec. 41 with Pickens v. Gillam, 43 La. Ann. 550, 8 So. 928; also Hall v. Hall, (Tex. Civ. App.) 241 S. W. 624 with Wheat v. Owens, 15 Tex. 241.

[41] As was done by the court in Loveridge v. Loveridge, 52 N.M. 353, 198 P.2d 444.

CHAPTER VI

COMMUNITY AND SEPARATE PROPERTY

A.   INITIAL CONSIDERATIONS

§ 58.   In general.

Some American writers[1] have remarked that it is easier to define separate than community property and that the difficulty of defining the latter is avoided by saying that all that is not separate is community property; and they instance that only a few of our states by statute affirmatively define community property.[2] Such remarks as to the difficulty of defining community property only constitute criticism of the most heavily labored sort and are without adequate foundation. Indeed, they display a woeful ignorance of the source and basic principles of our community system. Our system is that inherited from Spain,[3] which is a community of the acquests and gains[4] by the spouses during the marriage[5] while they are living as husband and wife.[6] The phrase "community of acquests and gains" is sufficiently clear in itself. Indeed, the practice of the Spanish law from which our community system comes was to define the community property first and

[1] See Vernier, American Family Laws, vol. 3, p. 209, quoting Evans, Ownership of Community Property, 35 Harv. Law Rev. 47.

[2] See Ariz. R.S. 1956, § 25-211; Cal. Civ. Code, § 687; Idaho Code Ann. 1947, § 32-906; La. Civ. Code, arts. 2334, 2402.

[3] See ante, Chaps. I, IV.

[4] See ante, § 1.

"By the contract of marriage ownership and possession of property which the husband and wife owned at the time of the contract does not pass without delivery (unlike the case of a partnership in all goods, Dig. 17.2.1 and 2) although the fruits of such property are shared, see laws 4 and 5 below. For the partnership between husband and wife is not a partnership in all goods, but only a partnership in profits and acquisitions. This is shown by the fact that gifts, legacies and inheritances are not shared between husband and wife, see laws 3, 4, and 5 below, as they are in a partnership of all goods, Dig. 17.2.3.1, Dig. 17.2.73, laws 6 and 7, tit. 10 *de societate* part 5." Matienzo, Gloss 3, No. 10, to Nov. Rec. Law 1, Book 10, Title 4.

[5] Usually expressed in the Spanish laws, "durante el matrimonio" or "constante matrimonio."

[6] See ante, § 57.

As expressed in the Spanish laws, "estando de consuno." See Nov. Rec., Book 10, Title 4, Law 1, and the commentaries of Matienzo, Azevedo and Gutiérrez on this phrase in Appendix III, C, in vol. 2 of 1943 edition of this work.

then indicate the property which was excluded therefrom and was separate property. The first provision of the group of statutes of the Novísima Recopilación of 1805 relating to the community starts out by saying: "Everything the husband and wife may earn or purchase during union, let them both have it by halves; and if it is a gift of the King or other person, and given to both, let husband and wife have it."[7] It is only then that such code goes on to indicate what is not community property,[8] with the injunction that the presumption shall be that the property which husband and wife have shall be presumed common until proved otherwise.[9]

Thus, since our community property law is that developed in Spain, which clearly and sufficiently defines what is community property and provides as to the presumption relating thereto, there is in fact no necessity that our American statutes should have to define what is community property, for that is already clearly established.[10] The concern of our statutes with what constitutes separate property arises from an apparent anxiety to see that no misunderstanding exists as to what is the separate property of the spouses, and particularly of the wife; and because in many of our states the separate property has been broadened to include the earnings and income from the

---

[7] Nov. Rec., Book 10, Title 4, Law 1.

[8] Nov. Rec., Book 10, Title 4, Laws 1-3.

[9] Nov. Rec., Book 10, Title 4, Law 4.

Presumptions, see post, § 60.

[10] "Our lawmakers have not troubled themselves to define community property, other than to say that it shall include all property acquired by either husband or wife during marriage, except that which is the separate property of either one or the other. In many cases, and in the present one, no other definition is necessary." Lee v. Lee, 112 Tex. 392, 247 S. W. 828.

"All that either the husband or wife or both may acquire during the existence of the marriage, other than is specifically excepted, is an acquest of the community, and the presumption in all doubtful cases is strongly in favor of treating that which either spouse may own as community property." La Tourette v. La Tourette, 15 Ariz. 200, 137 P. 426, Ann. Cas. 1915B 70.

"It is not expressly declared [in the constitution of the state] what right or title she shall possess in the common property, nor is common property defined; but at the time of the formation of the Constitution, it was a term of well-known signification in the laws then in force, and a right on the wife's part in property of that character was recognized by the Constitution." Dow v. Gould & Curry Silver Mining Co., 31 Cal. 630.

"By the Mexican law in force in California prior to its acquisition by the United States, all property acquired by husband and wife during the marriage, and while living together, whether by onerous or lucrative title, and that acquired by either of them by onerous title, belonged to the community; while property acquired by either of them by lucrative title solely, constituted the property of the party making the acquisition. An onerous title, as defined by Mexican law authorities, was that which was created by the payment or the rendering of a valuable consideration for the property acquired. A lucrative title, by the same law, was that which was created by donation, inheritance or devise." Fuller v. Ferguson, 26 Cal. 546, 566.

separate property of each,[11] which earnings and income under the Spanish law were community.[12]

§ 59.   Effect of agreements, contracts or stipulations between spouses.

It was a cardinal precept of the Spanish community property system that the spouses could contract away the community edifice, by ante-nuptial or post-nuptial agreements, contracts or stipulations between themselves. The law operated on the thesis that it would not regulate the conjugal partnership unless the husband and wife failed to do so: the parties to the marriage were presumed to have adopted the community property laws unless they provided otherwise. Such agreement could provide for some other basis for the division, sharing, or ownership of the earnings and gains during marriage than that specified by law. Such agreements could have the effect of making separate property of what would otherwise be community property. This tenet of the Spanish community law has been unchanged from its Visigothic inception, and is an accurate reflection of the general feeling that husband and wife were so far regarded as separate persons that they could validly enter into onerous contracts between themselves. It has been continued by statutes in some of the community property jurisdictions of the United States. The statutes which are declaratory of that principle continue the right as to pre-nuptial and sometimes as to post-nuptial agreements. A more extensive and complete discussion of this matter will be found in a subsequent chapter treating of agreements and transactions generally between spouses.[13]

§ 60.   Presumptions as to spouses' property—In general.

The Spanish law of community expressly provided that the property which husband and wife had should be presumed to belong to both by halves, except that property which each one might prove to be his or hers separately.[14] This, indeed, seems to have been the

[11] See post, § 71.

[12] Nov. Rec., Book 10, Title 4, Law 3, providing that the fruits of the separate property of the husband or wife shall be common.

[13] See post, Chapter VIII. Conventional community, see ante, § 54.

Effect of such agreements on rights of creditors, see post, Chapter IX.

[14] Novísima Recopilación, Book 10, Title 4, Law 4. See also Novísimo Sala Mexicano, Sec. 2a, Title IV, No. 1.

If the wife denies that certain goods are profits (i. e., community property), she has the burden of proof for the presumption is against her; but such things will be given her if she is successful in her proof. See Azevedo, No. 3, to Nov. Rec. Law 4, Book 10, Title 4.

See Civil Code, art. 1407, in force in Cuba, Puerto Rico and the Philippines: "All the property of the marriage shall be considered as partnership property until it is proven that it belongs exclusively to the husband or to the wife," quoted in Garzot v. Rios De Rubio, 209 U.S.

presumption of the community property system from the time the Visigoths introduced the system into the Spanish peninsula, for a similar presumption is found in the Visigothic laws in other parts of Europe.[15] This presumption extended to all movable or immovable property, all rights and actions and all other things whatsoever.[16] The fact that the husband or the wife acquired the title in his or her own name, did not alter the presumption that property acquired during marriage was community property.[17] This presumption has generally been continued in our community property states as to property possessed or acquired during the marriage[18] or in possession of the spouses at the time of the dissolution of the marriage,[19] and while it

285, 52 L. Ed. 794, 28 S. Ct. 548.

This was not the presumption under the Roman, or civil, law in Spain. See post, § 104.

Presumption as to which died first where death of both spouses occurs approximately at same time, see post, § 192.

[15] See Law of the Westgoths, according to the Manuscript of Eskil (Bergin's Translation), p. 66.

[16] "Note that by the general custom of this realm, now confirmed by this law, all movable or immovable property, and all rights and actions and all other things whatsoever are presumed to be the common property of husband and wife, except such things as either of them proves to be his or her own property." Matienzo, Gloss II, No. 1, to Nov. Rec. Law 4, Book 10, Title 4.

Presumptions under Roman or civil law, see post, § 104.

[17] "Whether a purchase is made by the husband in his own name or by the wife, with the wife's money or with the husband's or with money belonging to them both, it immediately and automatically becomes common property with regard to ownership and possession." Matienzo, Gloss II, No. 3, to Nov. Rec. Law 1, Book 10, Title 4. The caution should be added that we are dealing with presumptions here. It might be adequately proven by the spouse that the use of his or her own money was to acquire property for his or her own separate use or benefit and which would be separate property in place

of the money so expended. See post, § 77.

See also Matienzo, Gloss III, No. 12, to Nov. Rec. Law 1, Book 10, Title 4, pointing out that the contrary was true according to the "imperial," i.e., Roman, law.

[18] La Tourette v. La Tourette, 15 Ariz. 200, 137 P. 426, Ann. Cas. 1915 B 70; De Marce v. De Marce, 101 Ariz. 369, 419 P.2d 726; Smith v. Smith, 12 Cal. 216, 73 Am. Dec. 533; Meyer v. Kinzer, 12 Cal. 247, 73 Am. Dec. 538; Gudelj v. Gudelj, 41 Cal. 2d 202, 259 P.2d 656; Mason v. Mason, 8 Cal. Rptr. 784; Bowman v. Bowman, 72 Ida. 266, 240 P.2d 487; Smalley v. Lawrence, 9 Rob. (La.) 211; Carlson v. McCall, 70 Nev. 437, 271 P.2d 1002, citing and following first edition; Lake v. Bender, 18 Nev. 361, 4 P. 711, 7 P. 74; Albright v. Albright, 21 N.M. 606, 157 P. 662, Ann. Cas. 1918 E 542; Huston v. Curl, 8 Tex. 240, 58 Am. Dec. 810; State ex rel. Marshall v. Superior Court, 119 Wash. 631, 206 P. 352. See also cases cited 126 Am. St. Rep. 120.

[19] Nilson v. Sarment, 153 Cal. 524, 96 P. 315; 126 Am. St. Rep. 91; La. Civ. Code, art. 2405; Brian v. Moore, 11 Mart. (La.) 26, 13 Am. Dec. 247; Tex. Family Code 1969, § 5.24; Tarver v. Tarver, (Tex.) 394 S. W. 2d 780, 783; McFaddin v. Com'r. of Int. Rev., (5 C.C.A.) 148 F.2d 570. See 1 Oakes, Speer's Marital Rights in Texas, (4th Ed., 1961), p. 575.

See Cal. Evidence Code (1967) § 164.5: "The presumption that property acquired during marriage is community property does not apply to any

is rebuttable,[20] if it is to be overcome it must be by adequate proof,[21] by what has been variously described as "clear and convincing" evidence or as "clear and cogent" evidence or "nearly conclusive" evidence or similar terms.[22] Of necessity, what is such evidence is dependent upon the force and circumstances of each case.[23] The basis of this presumption is a probability that the major part of the property of the husband and wife belongs to the community, and from the further fact that the real ownership is a matter peculiarly within the knowledge of the husband and the wife. This conclusion is sufficiently certain to provide a convenient rule of decision until rebutted or overcome by evidence to the contrary; any other rule would be inequitable towards creditors and purchasers who deal with the husband and whose means of knowledge are less ample.[24]

While the presumption in favor of community property is not conclusive, it has been stressed that it is a rule of property, a rule of

property to which legal or equitable title is held by a person at the time of his death if the marriage during which the property was acquired was terminated by divorce more than four years prior to such death." See also Cal. C.C.P. § 1963.40; comment note, 43 Cal. L. Rev. 687.

When a single family residence of a husband and wife is acquired by them during marriage, for the purpose of the division of such property upon divorce or separate maintenance only, the presumption is that such single family residence is the community property of said husband and wife. Cal. Civ. Code § 5110. This statutory presumption was not applicable to a joint tenancy deed of a motel. Gloden v. Gloden, 49 Cal. Rptr. 659.

[20] Kingsberry v. Kingsberry, 93 Ariz. 217, 379 P.2d 893; Rose v. Rose, 83 Ida. 395, 353 P.2d 1089; La. Civ. Code, art. 2405; Robinson v. Allen (La. App.) 88 So.2d 64; Campbell v. Campbell, 62 N.M. 330, 310 P.2d 66, citing and following first edition; In re Madsen's Estate, (Wash.) 296 P.2d 518; Welder v. Com'r of Int. Rev. (5 C.C.A.) 148 F.2d 583. And see Tarver v. Tarver (Tex.) 394 S. W. 2d 780; Clark, 25 So. Cal. L. Rev. 149.

[21] Huber v. Huber, 27 Cal. 2d 784, 167 P.2d 708.

[22] See, e.g., Porter v. Porter, 101 Ariz. 131, 416 P.2d 564; Stahl v. Stahl (Idaho) 430 P.2d 685; Succession of Ridley, 247 La. 921, 175 So.2d 265; Thaxton v. Thaxton, 75 N.M. 450, 405 P.2d 982; Tarver v. Tarver (Tex.) 394 S. W. 2d 780.

Showing that property was acquired by a spouse in a common-law jurisdiction, see Hall v. Tucker, (Tex. Civ. App.) 414 S. W. 2d 766 (Writ ref'd. n.r.e.).

It is not intended to require such a degree of proof as, excluding possibility of error, produces absolute certainty; generally moral certainty only is required, or that degree of proof which produces conviction in an unprejudiced mind. Freese v. Hibernia Savings & Loan Soc., 139 Cal. 392, 73 P. 172. In other words, the presumption should be overcome by a preponderance of the evidence. See Strong v. Eakin, 11 N.M. 107, 66 P. 539. See also Blackwell v. Mayfield (Tex. Civ. App.), 69 S. W. 659; Weymouth v. Sawtelle, 14 Wash. 32, 44 P. 109. General language implying more than this should be viewed with suspicion.

[23] Kingsberry v. Kingsberry, 93 Ariz. 217, 379 P.2d 893.

[24] See Brockelbank, The Community Property Law of Idaho (1962), p. 123; Speer, Law of Marital Rights in Texas, (1929) § 350.

substantive law, and is not just procedural, as a rule of evidence.[25]

In the absence of any statutory qualification,[26] this presumption in favor of community property is given effect regardless of whether the title to the property is taken in the name of one or the other or of both of the spouses.[27] Doctrines of the common law relative to presumptions existing when property is purchased by one spouse and taken in the name of the other or in the names of both are not entitled to recognition under a system in which the presumption is that an acquisition is community property of husband and wife.[28] So, taking title in the wife's name does not change the presumption, which is still in favor of community property, especially in the absence of language in the deed tending to show that the purchase was with the wife's separate funds and that the property was conveyed to her as her separate property.[29] Even recitals in the deed to a spouse that the consideration was paid with separate funds or property or that the conveyance was made to the spouse as the separate property of the spouse are, at the most, only prima facie and not conclusive evidence, so far as concerns rebutting the usual presumption.[30] This is based on

[25] Nilson v. Sarment, 153 Cal. 524, 96 P. 315, 126 Am. St. Rep. 91; Campbell v. Campbell, 62 N.M. 330, 310 P.2d 266, citing and following first edition; McFaddin v. Com'r of Int. Rev., (5 C.C.A.) 148 F.2d 570 (as to Texas).

[26] Statutory qualifications, see post, § 60.1.

[27] Stevens v. Stevens, 70 Ariz. 302, 219 P.2d 1045; Bowman v. Bowman, 72 Ida. 266, 240 P.2d 487; Fortier v. Barry, 111 La. 776, 35 So. 900; Zahringer v. Zahringer, 76 Nev. 21, 348 P.2d 161. See also Carmichael v. Williams, (Tex. Civ. App.) 268 S. W. 502.

"Ownership and possession pass with regard to property acquired before the making of the contract of [business] partnership forthwith on the formation of the partnership and with regard to property subsequently acquired they pass when the property is acquired, as I showed in Nos. 8 and 9 above. The same rule must apply to the partnership which is by royal law implied between husband and wife; such partnership includes future profits (see this law and the next) and so at the date when they are acquired they will be deemed to be transferred (also) to the wife, even though it is in his own name that the husband purchases them or acquires them by some other title, as is abundantly clear from what I have said." Matienzo, Gloss III, No. 19, to Nov. Rec. Law 1, Book 10, Title 4.

[28] Parker v. Chance, 11 Tex. 513, 519.

It is necessary to note, however, that there are many cases to the effect that property purchased by the husband with community funds and directed by him to be conveyed to the wife is deemed to be a gift by the husband to the wife. See post, § 141, and criticism thereof.

[29] Brick & Tile, Inc. v. Parker, 143 Tex. 383, 186 S. W. 2d 66.

[30] See cases cited, 126 Am. St. Rep. 124; 31 Corpus Juris 67.

In Louisiana, when title to realty is taken in husband's name, without a declaration in the deed that property is bought with his separate funds and is his separate property, the presumption cannot be contradicted by him to the prejudice of the wife or her heirs. See Bruyninckx v. Woodward, 217 La. 736, 47 So.2d 478. Exception, see Slaton v. King, 214 La. 89, 36 So.2d 648. But the contrary is true where the title, in such circumstances, is taken in the name of the wife. Suc-

the primary principle of the Spanish law of community property that ownership is the important matter, rather than in whose name title is. Indeed, the civil law generally has given primary consideration to the question of ownership, in contradistinction to the English common law which developed to such an extent the technical importance of title that it had to be offset by the development of equitable principles.

It should be mentioned that the California courts have frequently announced that the presumption in favor of community property has less weight where the marriage is of short duration or, alternatively, that the shorter the marriage the weaker the presumption.[31] This is a somewhat cryptic assertion and evidently is intended to mean that evidence of less weight than usual will suffice; it should not, however, shift the burden of proof.[32] Somewhat similarly, in Texas, it has been said the presumption is not applicable where the property has been acquired immediately after the marriage takes place.[33]

Some jurisdictions have stressed that self-serving declarations of one spouse that the property in question is that spouse's separate property by reason of having been purchased with separate funds or that separate funds were available do not meet the requirement for clear and satisfactory evidence.[34] Statements that property purchased with separate funds is separate property[35] should be taken with several grains of salt. Merely showing the source of the funds as separate should not rebut the presumption in favor of community property. The conduct, the declarations of the parties, and the use to which the property is put, should all be looked to for a determination.[36]

§ 60.1.   — Statutory presumptions.

Statutory qualifications have been added to the effect that property acquired by a husband and wife by an instrument describing them as husband and wife is presumed community unless a different

cession of Farley, 205 La. 972, 18 So.2d 586. What is necessary to establish that property in name of wife is her separate property, see Howell v. Harris (La. App.), 18 So.2d 668; Lotz v. Citizens Bank & Trust Co. (La. App.), 17 So.2d 463; Succession of Davis (La. App.), 21 So.2d 641. Generally, see also Capillon v. Chambliss, 211 La. 1, 29 So.2d 171.

Somewhat different approach in Texas, see Hodge v. Ellis, 154 Tex. 341, 277 S. W. 2d 900.

[31] See, e.g., Fidelity & Casualty Co. v. Mahoney, 71 Cal. App. 2d 65, 161 P.2d 944; Falk v. Falk, 48 Cal. App. 2d 762, 120 P.2d 714.

[32] As seems to have been done in Fidelity & Casualty Co. v. Mahoney, supra.

[33] Riddle v. Riddle, (Tex. Civ. App.) 62 S. W. 2d 970.

[34] Berol v. Berol, 37 Wash. 2d 380, 223 P.2d 1055. Evidence of wife insufficient to show property standing in her name was purchased with her separate funds, see Stafford v. Sumrall (La. App.), 21 So.2d 83.

[35] As in Blackman v. Blackman, 45 Ariz. 374, 43 P.2d 1011.

[36] Consideration given to intention of spouses at time of acquisition of property, the length of the marriage, the purchase with community funds and that it was intended as a "home." In re Collins, 141 F. Supp. 25.

intention is expressed in the instrument,[37] that property acquired by a married woman by an instrument in writing is presumed her separate property, that property acquired by a married woman and any other person by instrument in writing is presumed to be acquired by her as a tenant in common, unless a contrary intention is expressed.[38]

These statutory presumptions are rebuttable except as against purchasers, encumbrancers, or others dealing with the married woman in good faith and for valuable consideration.[39] These statutory qualifications superimpose the common law technical reliance on title upon the community property reliance upon actual ownership and the presumptions relating thereto.

While these statutory presumptions are rebuttable, as remarked, the rebuttal must be by what is frequently described as "clear and satisfactory" evidence or by terms of a similar nature.[40] If it is sought to be shown that the property is held in joint tenancy rather than by tenancy in common or as community property, there must be sufficient evidence to show the joint tenancy holding. In the case of realty, the recital in the deed of a joint tenancy may be sufficient but is not conclusive evidence,[41] for it may be shown, despite the recital, that the property was not intended by the parties to be so held.[42] And it may help to establish this intention by showing that the property was

---

[37] Cal. Civ. Code § 5110; N.M. Stats. Ann. 1953, § 57-4-1.

In a contract for the sale and purchase of realty where the purchasers were described as "husband and wife," the presumption was applied that the property was their community property (there being a property right under the contract, of course). Bensinger v. Davidson, (S.D. Cal.) 147 F. Supp. 240, distinguishing Peiser v. Bradbury, 138 Cal. 570, 72 P. 165, as decided under prior wording of C.C. § 164 (after January 1, 1970, § 5110).

[38] See Cal. Civ. Code § 5110; N.M. Stats. Ann. 1953, 57-4-1; In re Chavez, 34 N.M. 258, 280 P. 241, 69 A.L.R. 769; Laughlin v. Laughlin, 49 N.M. 20, 155 P.2d 1010.

Generally as to spouses holding property as tenants in common of joint tenants, see post, § 134.

[39] Cal. Civ. Code § 5110; N.M. Stats. Ann. 1953, 57-4-1.

See Clark, Presumptions in New Mexico Community Property Law: The California Influence, 25 So. Cal. L. Rev. 149, at p. 156.

It will be noticed that the statutes make no provision as to presumption in case of conveyance to the husband alone; undoubtedly the presumption remains that such property is community property. See Dunn v. Mullan, 211 Cal. 583, 296 P. 604, 77 A. L. R. 1015. In California, where title is in the name of the husband only and one purchases from him in good faith without knowledge of the marriage, the husband's title is presumed to be good, but this presumption is rebuttable by wife on bringing suit to set aside the conveyance within one year from the date of its recordation, Cal. Civ. Code, § 5127. And notice particularly that what would be good faith and lack of knowledge of the marriage would, under the California view, require more than mere examination of the title.

[40] As to nature of such evidence, see ante, § 60.

[41] Bowman v. Bowman, 149 Cal. App. 2d 443, 308 P.2d 906. As to holding property other than in community, see post, § 134.

[42] Party claiming it is not joint tenancy has burden of overcoming joint tenancy presumption. Bowman v. Bowman, supra.

purchased with community funds and intended to be held as community property,[43] although the mere purchase with community funds has been said not to be sufficient in itself to rebut the joint tenancy declaration.[44] Proof that the property was not intended, either originally or by later decision, to be held in joint tenancy, may be established by parol evidence of the parties' intention, as well as by written evidence.[45]

As to personal property, a joint tenancy thereof may by some statutes be created only by a "written transfer, instrument or agreement" and it must be expressly declared that it is a joint tenancy. Thus, where an automobile registration certificate did not expressly declare a joint tenancy and merely listed the names of the husband and the wife joined by the word "or," this could not be properly interpreted as an expression of such a declaration and so the automobile had to be held either as community property or by tenancy in common.[46] Under the aforementioned statutory presumption of a wife holding with another as being a tenant in common, the automobile is held under a tenancy in common, in the absence of sufficient evidence to rebut this statutory presumption and to show that a holding in community was intended.[47]

Notice that the written transfer of property by the husband to the wife or the written transfer by a third person to the wife, arranged by the husband, comes within the statutory presumption that the property is the separate property of the wife. It is frequently stated, in addition, that it is presumed that the husband is making a gift to the wife.[48] This presumption of a gift, borrowed from the common law, has been applied in community property jurisdictions which do not have the statutory presumptions in question.[49] In California, where

[43] Gudelj v. Gudelj, 41 Cal. 2d 202, 259 P.2d 656.

[44] Bowman v. Bowman and Gudelj v. Gudelj, supra.

[45] Tomaier v. Tomaier, 23 Cal. 2d 754, 146 P.2d 905.

Evidence of conduct and declarations of parties may establish this intention. Socol v. King, 36 Cal. 2d 342, 223 P.2d 627.

Evidence of a previous *express* agreement is not necessary to support finding and judgment in favor of community property. Galloway v. Woenie, 15 Cal. Rptr. 147.

[46] Cooke v. Tsipouroglou, 59 Cal. 2d 660, 31 Cal. Rptr. 60, 381 P.2d 940, necessarily overruling any prior decisions that the automobile registration certificate is not a writing within Cal. C. C. § 5110.

That a stock certificate in name of wife is not an instrument in writing within meaning of said § 5110, see Vogel's Estate v. Com'r of Int. Rev., (9 C.C.A.) 278 F.2d 548, in concurring opinion. However, it refers, for support, to now overruled view as to automobile registration certificate.

[47] Cooke v. Tsipouroglou, supra. And see post, § 134.   ,

[48] Gifts between spouses, see post, § 140 et seq.

In Idaho, statute now provides for presumption in favor of separate property of either spouse where other conveyed realty to such spouse. Idaho Code Ann. § 32-906, as amended by Laws, 1943, ch. 23, p. 51.

[49] Weeks v. Weeks, 72 Nev. 268, 302 P.2d 750; Peardon v. Peardon, 65 Nev. 717, 201 P.2d 309. See also Jones v. Rigdon, 32 Ariz. 286, 257 P. 639.

property is transferred by the husband to the wife, but not in writing, the presumption continues that the property is community property.[50] The most that is presumed is that the husband is transferring the management of the property to the wife.[51]

The presumption that property in the name of the wife is her separate property, even where also presumed a gift by the husband, may be rebutted, of course.[52] In some jurisdictions this may be by the testimony of the husband alone, if believed credible by the court,[53] but in other jurisdictions some evidence to corroborate the husband may also be required.[54] This corroboration may include, for example, the fact that community funds were used to purchase the property,[55] bearing in mind, again, that this alone may not suffice in itself.

Some states have statutes to the effect that bank deposits or accounts in the name of one spouse are presumed to be the separate property of that spouse in whose name deposited,[56] but this is primarily for the protection of the bank and does not supplant the presumption in favor of community property.[57]

§ 60.2.   — Official record.

In the Spanish law, to avoid confusion as to what was community and what separate property, and to facilitate proof as to what was separate property, the recommendation generally made was that at the time of the marriage contract an official record of an inventory should be made of all the goods brought by either spouse to the marriage, since such property, of course, was always separate property.[58]

[50] Estate of Walsh, 66 Cal. App. 2d 704, 152 P.2d 750, where statement of rule is correct but one might interpret particular factual situation as showing intention to make a gift. More fully as to such gifts between spouses, see post, § 140 et seq.

[51] See Odone v. Marzocchi, 34 Cal. 2d 431, 211 P.2d 297, noted 23 So. Cal. L. Rev. 83.

[52] Property in wife's name at time of her death shown to be community property, see Estate of Wilson, 64 Cal. App. 2d 123, 148 P.2d 390.

[53] Estate of Baer, 81 Cal. App. 2d 830, 185 P.2d 412.

Statutory presumption of separate property of wife, rebutted by husband as against trustee in bankruptcy of wife, see Steward v. Paige, 90 Cal. App. 2d 820, 203 P.2d 858.

Uncorroborated testimony of one spouse as sufficient, see Nilson v. Sarment, 153 Cal. 524, 96 P. 315, 126 Am. St. Rep. 91; Albright v. Albright, 21 N.M. 606, 157 P. 662, Ann. Cas. 1918 E 542.

[54] Peardon v. Peardon, 65 Nev. 717, 201 P.2d 309, to effect that husband's statement was mere conclusion of law and should not be received.

[55] See, e.g., Petition of Fuller, 63 Nev. 26, 159 P.2d 570, citing first edition.

[56] See, e.g., Texas Family Code 1969, § 5.24; Callaway v. Clark (Tex. Civ. App.) 200 S. W. 2d 447, wrt ref'd. And see Deering's Cal. Gen. Laws, Act 652, § 15a.

[57] Phillips v. Vitemb, (5 C.C.A.) 235 F.2d 11, as to Texas statute.

[58] "It is there suggested that the best plan is that at the time of the marriage contract an official record of an inventory should be made of all the goods brought by either spouse to the marriage." Matienzo, Gloss II, No. 2, to Nov. Rec. Law 4, Book 10, Title 4. See also Escriche, Diccionario, "Bienes Gananciales."

This wise recommendation, which from the extent of its repetition by the various Spanish jurisconsults undoubtedly became customary,[59] and has been followed in Mexico,[60] has been reinforced in several of our community property states by express statutory provision sanctioning such an official recording.[61] Indeed, some of the state constitutions have expressly enjoined that laws shall be passed providing for the registration of the wife's separate property.[62]

It may be noticed that the California statute authorizes the husband or the wife to file such an inventory, while the Idaho and Nevada statutes relate only to the wife. From a practical standpoint, the availability of filing should relate to either spouse, since the right is as valuable to the husband as to the wife. In Nevada, the statute relating to the filing of an inventory by the wife is described as mandatory, in contrast to the permissive provisions of the other states' statutes.[63] But while mandatory, the failure of the wife to file does not forfeit her right or ability to establish that the property is her separate property, although the failure does constitute a circumstance that may be considered with other evidence in making a *prima facie* case that the property is not the wife's separate property.[64]

§ 61.   — Intermingling of community and separate property.

This presumption of the Spanish law that the property which husband and wife had should be presumed common necessarily arose in the case of intermingled properties, and such intermingled properties were considered community properties where they were so mixed that it could not be known to which of them they belonged and neither could prove his or her right of ownership; a reason, it was pointed out,

[59] "And so it is most useful for husbands and wives to make, in the presence of a notary and witnesses, a public inventory of the property which each brings to the marriage, as was advised by Matienzo hereon glos. 2 no. 2." Azevedo, No. 3, to Nov. Rec. Law 4, Book 10, Title 4.

[60] "Thus they are presumed to be community, if they are not proved otherwise, and upon this is founded the necessity or convenience of executing a public instrument at the time of contracting marriage in which is set forth the properties which each one brings." Novísimo Sala Mexicano, Sec. 2a, Title IV, No. 1.

[61] See, e.g., Cal. Civ. Code, § 5114; Idaho Code Ann. 1948, §§ 32-907, 32-908; Nev. Rev. St. 1966, §§ 123.140, 123.160. Earlier Texas statutes made similar provision but are now replaced by Texas Family Code 1969, § 5.03, which merely makes filing of schedule notice to purchasers and creditors. Arizona and Washington recording statutes allow the wife to record but do not direct manner or effect.

[62] Cal. Const. 1849, art. XI, § 14; Nev. Const. 1864, art. IV, § 31.

[63] Thomas v. Nevans, 67 Nev. 122, 215 P.2d 244.

[64] Bowler v. Leonard, (Nev.) 333 P.2d 989; Thomas v. Nevans, 67 Nev. 122, 215 P.2d 244; Petition of Fuller, 63 Nev. 26, 159 P.2d 579.

Effect of former Texas statutes which were permissive, see Le Gierse v. Moore, 59 Tex. 470.

for executing a public written instrument upon contracting marriage, showing which property each consort had.[65] In our own community property states this intermingling of the properties of the spouses and the intermingling of community with separate property may result in the whole being considered community property, the mode of handling having been such as to render it impossible to distinguish which is which.[66] Stress must be placed on the fact the presumption from intermingling is in the absence of identification and does not result from the mere fact of intermixture.[67] It is obligatory upon the husband, as the one having the management of the community property, to keep the community and separate property segregated, and he must assume the consequences for failure to do so.[68] However, this rule operates as well against the wife where she is the manager of the community.[69]

This presumption is not merely procedural but is a part of the substantive law.[70] The burden is on the one claiming that the property or some part of it is separate property to prove that fact and the amount by clear and satisfactory evidence.[71]

Some cases have stated that the commingling must be so extensive

[65] "Since in some cases doubts may arise as to whether certain properties are of this class (i.e., ganancial) or not, it is necessary to keep in mind, for better clearness of some points which occur, that the following are considered to be common properties: The private properties of the husband or of the wife which are found so intermingled or so mixed in such manner that it cannot be determined to which of them they belong, and neither of them can prove his or her right of ownership." Escriche, Diccionario, "Bienes Gananciales."

[66] Laughlin v. Laughlin, 61 Ariz. 6, 143 P.2d 336; Estate of Woods, 23 Cal. App. 2d 187, 72 P.2d 258; Fisher v. Fisher, 86 Ida. 181, 383 P.2d 840; Slater v. Culpepper, 233 La. 1671, 99 So.2d 348; Fox v. Fox, 81 Nev. 186, 401 P.2d 53; Ormachea v. Ormachea, 67 Nev. 213, 217 P.2d 355, citing and following first edition; Stroope v. Potter, 48 N.M. 404, 151 P.2d 148; Tarver v. Tarver, (Tex. Civ. App.) 378 S. W. 2d 381, aff'd (Tex.) 394 S. W. 2d 780; Graham v. Radford (Wash.) 431 P.2d 193.

Acquisition or purchase of other property with commingled separate and community property, see post. § 77.

[67] Kingsberry v. Kingsberry, 93 Ariz. 217, 379 P.2d 893.

[68] White v. White, 26 Cal. App. 2d 524, 79 P.2d 759; Ormachea v. Ormachea, 67 Nev. 213, 217 P.2d 355, citing and following first edition; Fox v. Fox, 81 Nev. 186, 401 P.2d 53.

[69] Franklin v. Franklin, 75 Ariz. 151, 253 P.2d 337.

[70] See McFaddin v. Commissioner of Internal Revenue (5 C. C. A.), 148 F.2d 570, in regard to Texas law and stating that the court has held likewise as to Louisiana law in Howard v. United States (5 C. C. A.), 125 F.2d 986.

[71] Laughlin v. Laughlin, 61 Ariz. 6, 143 P.2d 336; Fisher v. Fisher, 66 Ida. 131, 383 P.2d 840; Slater v. Culpepper, 233 La. 1071, 99 So.2d 348; Fox v. Fox, 81 Nev. 186, 151 P.2d 748; Stroope v. Potter, 48 N.M. 404, 151 P.2d 748; Tarver v. Tarver, (Tex. Civ. App.) 378 S. W. 2d 381, aff'd (Tex.) 394 S. W. 2d 780; Graham v. Radford (Wash.), 431 P.2d 193. See also § 60.

as to render segregation impracticable for the presumption of community property to arise. This is really no different from the general rule but is only a more elaborate statement of it.[72]

It is usual to state that where the amount of property commingled is very unequal in that the amount of the community property is inconsiderable as compared with the separate property, then the presumption in favor of community property is not applied.[73]

In the matter of intermingled funds, particularly bank accounts, even where the respective separate and community amounts are identifiable, question may arise as to withdrawals. In California, for example, when community or family expenses are paid from such a bank account it is presumed that they have been paid from the community funds. If, at the time of such payment, no community funds are on deposit, the payment is of course being made from separate funds and reimbursement therefor is to be made from any subsequent deposit of community funds. In the event that the amount of community expenses paid from a composite account exceeds the amount of community funds deposited therein, the balance of the money deposited, whether remaining in the account or transmuted to another form, is separate property. Somewhat similarly where withdrawals are established to be for separate purposes, they are charged off against the separate funds deposited.[74] While other states have also indulged the presumption that payments from the composite account for separate charges are paid from the separate funds, this presumption cannot be indulged where the payment is for the purchase of property, for such property must be presumed to be community property. This situation would also cover increase in the cash value of life insurance policies due to the payment of premiums during marriage from such commingled funds.[75]

§ 62.   Onerous and lucrative titles.

At the risk of infringing on the fuller discussions in the following sections on acquisitions during the marriage and their nature as com-

---

[72] See Evans v. Evans, 79 Ariz. 284, 288 P.2d 775; Mumm v. Mumm, 63 Wash. 2d 349, 387 P.2d 547.

[73] Gudelj v. Gudelj, 41 Cal. 2d 202, 259 P.2d 656; Abraham v. Abraham, 230 La. 78, 87 So.2d 735; Burlingham v. Burlingham, 72 N.M. 433, 384 P.2d 699.

[74] See particularly Hicks v. Hicks, 211 Cal. App. 2d 144, 27 Cal. Rptr. 307, classifying and citing California cases.

[75] Blaine v. Blaine, 63 Ariz. 100, 159 P.2d 786; Gibson v. Gibson, (Tex. Civ. App.) 202 S. W. 2d 288.

In Blaine case, upon division of community property on dissolution of marriage, husband was given credit for separate funds intermingled with community funds as offset to charges against him for community funds used by him for his separate purposes. Compare Gulstine's Estate, 166 Wash. 325, 6 P.2d 628, where husband's estate was refused credit for alleged expenditures of separate property to improve community property.

munity or separate property, it is necessary at this point to distinguish between property and goods acquired by onerous title and property and goods acquired by lucrative title. These were important definitive elements in the Spanish community property law and are no less so in our community property law although too frequently ignored in the decisions of our courts.[76]

That property acquired by husband and wife during the marriage through their labor or industry or other valuable consideration is said to be acquired by onerous title. Other valuable consideration might consist of payment of money, rendition of services, performance of conditions, payment of charges to which the property was subject, and the like.[77] With the exception that property acquired through valuable consideration which is wholly the separate property of one spouse naturally retains the character of separate property,[78] property acquired by onerous title is always community property. This is so because it is acquired by the labor and industry of members of a form of partnership, that is, a marital partnership, or is acquired for valuable consideration which had previously been acquired by the industry and labor of the marital partnership, and whatever is earned or gained by one marital partner during the existence of the marital partnership must accrue to the benefit of both marital partners, who share equally in such earnings and gains.[79] Such earnings and gains, even if by one spouse alone,[80] are necessarily for the maintenance and furtherance of the marital society. They are earned or gained at the expense of the community in that the one making the earnings or gains is furthered therein by the use of community property or by the joint efforts of the other spouse, joint efforts on the part of the other spouse which may consist, as in the case of the wife, in maintaining the home and rearing the children, for that is a sharing of the burdens of the marital partnership and a contribution to the community effort.[81]

[76] The terms themselves are little used in our statute and case law, although they would have value as distinguishing and defining the method of acquisition. Notice that early New Mexico statutes used these terms for definition.

[77] Escriche, Diccionario, "Oneroso."

[78] See post, § 77.

[79] "Palacios Ruvios affirms in Commentary No. 5 to the present law, that as the property acquired during marriage originates in the work and industry of the contracting parties, it should be considered as obtained not under a lucrative but an onerous title; he adds that he assisted in the drafting of the law, and that he recommended its adoption, as he had previously advised." Llamas y Molina, Commentaries, No. 3, to Nov. Rec. Law 6, Book 10, Title 4.

"Community property is all that which is increased or multiplied during marriage. By multiplied is understood all that is increased by onerous cause or title, and not that which acquired by a lucrative one, as inheritance, donation, etc." Asso and Mañuel, Institutes of Civil Law of Spain, Book I, Title VII, chap. 5, § 1.

[80] See post, § 67.

[81] "They adopt a false premise when they say that one of the spouses contributes nothing to such a partnership, neither money nor work. The wife can work and take care of and preserve the family property. . . . Fre-

127

Property acquired by lucrative title is that acquired through gift, succession, inheritance or the like.[82] It has its basis in pure donation on the part of the donor. It may or may not be community property, depending on whether the donor intends it to be for the benefit of both spouses or to be for one of them alone. While on occasion it is difficult to interpret the intent of the donor, usually the instrument or terms by which the donation is made clearly indicate whether the donation is for both spouses, and thus community property, or whether it is intended for one spouse alone, and thus his or her separate property.[83]

One of the difficulties arising in considering the question of onerous and lucrative titles has been whether a so-called reward, gift or the like is actually a pure donation given to one spouse alone in recognition, for example, of that spouse's peculiar or individual merits, and thus that spouse's separate property, or whether it is given in remuneration of certain services rendered by the spouse, and thus actually acquired by onerous title and coming within the earnings and gains which constitute community property. This has been a matter which has resulted in many conflicting decisions by our courts because of their frequent failure to distinguish between property acquired by onerous or lucrative title and their frequent inability to differentiate between a pure donation and one actually remunerative in nature.[84]

In addition, our courts have been extremely prone to be misled by a literal interpretation of their local statutes providing that all property acquired during marriage, except that acquired by gift, bequest, devise or inheritance, is community property. Overlooking or not comprehending the fact that one of the basic principles of community property law is that by "property acquired during marriage" is primarily meant property acquired by onerous title, they have frequently tended, without adequate analysis, to hold any property acquired during marriage to be community property, just so long as it was not acquired by gift, bequest, devise or inheritance. This has

---

quently the poorer spouse by work and labor makes up the deficiency in his or her estate." Matienzo, Gloss I, No. 8, to Nov. Rec. Law 1.

"With regard to community of goods the law has regard to the industry and common labor of each spouse and to the burdens of community and partnership. . . . [The] principle in accordance with which it was enacted by royal law that profits should be shared between husband and wife . . . being the fact while the one spouse supplies work and labor the other supplies money or other property, the fact of their individual habit of life ordained by both natural and divine law, the fact of the mutual

love between husband and wife which should be encouraged. . . ." Matienzo, Gloss I, Nos. 6, 13, to Nov. Rec. Law 1.

[82] Escriche, Diccionario, "Lucrativo."

"An onerous title, as defined by the Mexican law authorities, was that which was created by the payment or the rendering of a valuable consideration for the property acquired. A lucrative title, by the same law, was that which was created by donation, inheritance or devise." Fuller v. Ferguson, 26 Cal. 546, 566.

[83] See post, § 69.

[84] Remuneratory gifts, see post, § 70.

been true of rights of action for personal injury to a spouse,[85] money or property obtained upon the personal credit or security of a spouse,[86] and other instances of property not actually acquired by onerous title. They have even been disturbed over holding that property acquired in exchange for separate property is also separate property, just because it has been "acquired during marriage."[87] There is no excuse for this,

The fact that community property is basically that property acquired by the industry, labor or talent of either or both spouses is often well recognized, however. This has been especially true in Nevada[88] and has also been recognized in many of the California decisions in which the court credits some part of income from separate property to the community, on the basis of the community effort or labor which contributed to producing it.[89] Other courts have been similarly perceptive.[90]

B. TIME, METHOD AND TYPE OF ACQUISITION

§ 63. Property owned or acquired prior to marriage.

Since the Spanish law of community was one of acquests and gains during the marriage, whatever properties either spouse had before the marriage continued to remain, after the marriage, his or her separate property;[91] and this, incidentally, continued to be the law in the Mexican republic.[92] Indeed, as has been previously stated, the recommendation of the Spanish jurisconsults was that an official record of an inventory of all such properties be made at the time of the marriage contract.[93] Such properties might comprise not only realty and tangible

---

[85] See post, § 82.

[86] See post, § 78, especially as to view of the Washington courts.

[87] See post, § 77, especially as to the misgivings of the New Mexico court.

[88] Frederickson & Watson Construction Co. v. Boyd, 60 Nev. 117, 102 P.2d 627.

See also Daggett, The Community Property System of Louisiana (1931), p. 9 et seq.; Oakes, Speer's Marital Rights In Texas, (4th Ed.) chap. 22; Soto v. Vandeventer, 56 N.M. 483, 245 P.2d 826, 35 A.L.R. 2d 1190, citing and following first edition.

[89] See post, § 71 et seq.

[90] See post, § 66 et seq.

[91] Novísima Recopilación, Book 10, Title 4, Law 3.

"The following are not counted among the ganancial properties: Those which the spouses had before contracting the marriage, law 3, tit. 4, lib. 10, Nov. Rec." Escriche, Diccionario, vol. 2, "Ganancial Properties."

"A wife can have property of three kinds, dowry, paraphernalia and private property of which the husband has not the right of administration . . . To this you should add a fourth kind, viz., property acquired during marriage, (i.e., as her own, as by gift, etc.)." Matienzo, Gloss IV, to Nov. Rec. Law 11, Book 10, Title 4. As to the wife's separate property, see also post, § 112.

[92] "There are not considered as properties of the (marital) partnership, commonly called *gananciales*, those which the spouses had before the marriage, which remain the property of the one to whom they belonged." Novísimo Sala Mexicano, Sec. 2a, Title IV, No. 4.

[93] See ante, § 60.2.

personalty but also intangibles and choses in action.[94] As a necessary integral part of any community system confined to community of acquests and gains, this of course continues as the law of our community property states and is most strongly emphasized by constitutional and statutory provisions.[95]

§ 64.   — Initiation of acquisition before and completion during marriage.

It was clearly established in the Spanish law of community that where one spouse had initiated the acquisition of title and ownership of property before marriage, and completed that acquisition after marriage, such property was the separate property of that spouse.[96] Thus, if a spouse, before marriage, had acquired ownership of property without the usufruct thereof, and after marriage the usufruct was consolidated with that ownership, the usufruct actually had its origin in the time preceding the marriage and was the separate property of that spouse.[97] Likewise, where a spouse before marriage had sold property with a pact to repurchase or with a right of redemption, and

[94] See Escriche, Diccionario, "Bienes Gananciales," listing among others shares in partnerships and companies, rights of action, etc.

"Note that by the general custom of this realm, now confirmed by this law, all movable or immovable property, and all rights and actions and all other things whatsoever are presumed to be the common property of husband and wife, except such things as either proves to be his or her own property." Matienzo, Gloss II, No. 1, to Nov. Rec. Law 4, Book 10, Title 4.

[95] Nev. Rev. Stats., § 123.060; N.M. Stats. 1953, § 53-3-3. And see Idaho Code 1948, § 32-903.

But neither can be excluded from the other's dwelling. Cal. Civ. Code, § 5102; N.M. Stats., 1953, § 57-3-3.

[96] See Gutiérrez, Quaestio CXVI, to Nov. Rec. Law 1, Book 10, Title 4.

"I ask further, if a husband before marriage buys something and postpones the date of payment and that date occurs after the marriage has been performed and the wife has been taken to her new home, whether in such a case a moiety of the goods so bought will be due to the wife and her heirs. This question is discussed by Cassaneus in [his Customs of Bur-gundy]. There he seems to hold the negative. . . . Likewise I say that goods so bought are not shared, although the expense involved by payment for them during marriage after the wife has been taken to her new home must be shared, if that amount is taken from the common property. This is so unless the husband paid with private money brought by him to the marriage; for in that case the wife will profit nothing from their price. The same rule applies if in payment for such goods the husband offers an inheritance or an estate from his capital or if he sells such an estate and with the proceeds pays the price of the goods purchased before and paid for during marriage." Azevedo, No. 16, to Nov. Rec. Law 1, Book 10, Title 4.

In a community property system where income, rents, profits, etc. from separate property of a spouse are common property, crops or ripe fruits which were sown before marriage but harvested after marriage are not common property. See Asso and Mañuel, Institutes of Civil Law of Spain, Book I, Title VII, Cap. 5, § 1.

[97] Gutiérrez, Quaestio CXVI, to Nov. Rec. Law 1, Book 10, Title 4; Azevedo, No. 23, to the same; Matienzo, Gloss I, No. 87, to the same.

after marriage exercised his right to regain the property, even though the property was worth much more than when originally sold, that profit remained the separate property of the spouse in question. Of course, if the repurchase or redemption was made with community funds, the other spouse had the right to be reimbursed to the extent of half the price paid from the common funds.[98]

So far as our American courts are concerned, it is necessary to recognize that there are differences of view in some areas of this general situation. Certainly our community property states are all in accord that if the right of a spouse to the property is initiated before marriage, the nature of the property is fixed at that time as separate property and it comes into the marriage, so to speak, as of that nature.[99] Especially is this true where the consideration was completely paid and the title transferred before marriage.[1] But this is a presumption which is actually rebuttable by showing that the spouses-to-be intended that it should belong to the family during the marriage or, in other words, that it was intended to be community property once the marriage took place.[2] This may be more effectively established where it is shown that both contributed from their respective estates of funds to acquire the property or that title was taken in the names of both or that both of these things

---

[98] Gutiérrez, Quaestio CXVI, to Nov. Rec. Law 1, Book 10, Title 4.

"The price of land, which the husband has sold before marriage with stipulation for repurchase, and after marriage recovers it by virtue of such stipulation, belongs to both spouses, but not the land itself; and in the partition the latter should go to the husband, because therein the wife has no right, but only to one-half of the price with which it was redeemed, if it came from community funds." Febrero, Librería de Escribanos, Cinco Juicios I, Book I, Cap. IV, § 1, No. 23.

Whether a *retractus* through kinship was a profit in which the wife took a half share was apparently a subject of disagreement. Azevedo, No. 23, to Nov. Rec. Law 1, Book 10, Title 4. Gutiérrez, Quaestio CXVI, to the same.

[99] Obtaining before marriage a fixed contract right to acquire lands by compliance with the conditions of the contract is an inception of title or property right fixing the nature of the land as separate property when acquired subsequently during marriage. Welder v. Lambert, 91 Tex. 510, 44 S. W. 281.

The California court has said that the right of an heir to transfer his inheritance, even though a will or purported will was in existence, is recognized; that consequently, upon the instant of the death of a son who left a will, his father had a property right which he could assign or transfer or surrender for a consideration, and also a statutory right, which of itself was a property right, to contest his son's will. Since that right vested in the father prior to his marriage (a second marriage), it was therefore his separate property, and a considerable sum of money he later realized during marriage from compromising the will contest constituted separate property. Estate of Clark, 94 Cal. App. 453, 271 P. 542.

Note that the Texas statutes describe as separate property all property of the spouse owned or *claimed* before marriage. Texas Family Code 1969, §§ 5.01, 5.21, 5.61.

[1] See ante, § 63.

[2] Agreements between spouses, see post, § 136 et seq.; transfer of separate property to the community, see post, § 144.

transpired.[3] Where there is such an intention, it is immaterial whether the spouses contributed proportionate shares,[4] disproportionate amounts,[5] or that one contributed all the consideration.[6]

The situation may also result that the right to the property is initiated prior to marriage, the consideration is entirely paid by one party prior to the marriage, but for some reason the mere transfer of title to the one so concerned is not accomplished until after the marriage takes place.[7] While this may raise a presumption that it is community property because technically acquired during marriage, this presumption is rebuttable by showing the facts involved along with evidence that there was no intention of anything other than separate property. This rebuttal may present little difficulty.[8]

The situation begins to present more difficulty, though, when the right to the property is initiated before marriage, part of the consideration is paid before marriage, then the marriage takes place and the acquisition is completed during the marriage with the payment of the rest of the consideration made during the marriage.[9] Of course, if the consideration paid during the marriage continues to be from the separate estate of the initiator of the acquisition, with no intention that the property should be other than such party's separate estate, naturally all community property states will recognize its separate property nature. But it must be borne in mind that there is a presumption in favor of it being community property because its acquisition is completed during the marriage. The burden is then placed on the one claiming it to be his or her separate property to establish that fact. This, again, may be relatively simple through showing the initiation of the right before marriage and that all the consideration came from such party's separate estate. It then presumably is the separate property of such party. However, this in turn is rebuttable by showing that during the marriage some part of this consideration came from community funds, either for the purpose of establishing that the property is in part

[3] See, e.g., Vieux v. Vieux, 80 Cal. App. 222, 251 P. 640; In re Buchanan's Estate, 89 Wash. 172, 154 P. 129. And see preceding note.

[4] As in Mooney v. Mooney, 91 Cal. App. 2d 118, 204 P.2d 630; Estate of Wahlefeld, 105 Cal. App. 770, 288 P. 870.

More fully as to agreements and transactions between spouses, see post, chap. VIII.

[5] As in Stanger's Estate, 75 Ariz. 399, 257 P.2d 593.

[6] As in Estate of Raphael, 91 Cal. App. 2d 931, 206 P.2d 391.

[7] See cases, Tiffany, Real Property, 3rd Ed., 439; 126 Am. St. Rep. 101;

41 Corpus Juris Secundum, p. 1025 et seq. See also Oakes, Speer's Marital Rights in Texas, 4th Ed., § 388.

[8] Hollingsworth v. Hicks, 57 N.M. 336, 258 P.2d 724, quoting and following first edition. See also cases cited in Tiffany, Real Property, 3rd Ed., § 439; 126 Am. St. Rep. 101; 41 Corpus Juris Secundum, p. 1025 et seq.; Oakes, Speer's Marital Rights in Texas, 4th Ed., § 388.

[9] As in Barrett v. Franke, 46 Nev. 170, 208 P. 435.

See also Hollingsworth v. Hicks, 57 N.M. 336, 258 P.2d 724, quoting and following first edition and stressing unalterable fixing of nature of property as separate property.

community property or for the purpose of obtaining reimbursement for the community, dependent upon the view in the state,[10] or, of course, by proving an intention by the spouses that the property should be community.[11]

Again, we may have the situation of the right to the property being initiated before marriage by one party, part of the consideration paid from such party's separate estate during such period and then the completion of the acquisition during marriage by the payment of the rest of the consideration during the marriage, with such consideration definitely coming from community property.[12] Here we have a definite split of authority. According to the New Mexico and Texas view, which closely follows the Spanish law, the nature of the property having been once fixed, before marriage, as separate property, it thereafter continues to retain that nature unaffected by any payment from community property but subject to the right of the community to be reimbursed in the amount of the community property used to complete the acquisition.[13] It makes no difference in those states when legal title is actually transferred. It is the situation when the right to the property is initiated that is important. But Louisiana varies somewhat by putting determination of the nature of the property as of the time that legal title is transferred. Thus, if part of the consideration is paid before marriage and the legal title then transferred, with the remainder of the consideration paid during marriage, although from community property, the property is separate and remains separate, but with a right of reimbursement in the community, similarly to New Mexico and Texas.[14] But if the right is initiated prior to the marriage, part of the consideration paid at that time, then during marriage the rest of the consideration is paid from community and the legal title is transferred, the property is community in nature, but here with a right of reimbursement in the spouse for the amount of the separate property of such spouse previously paid as consideration.[15]

In California, Idaho, Nevada and Washington, whatever the nature of the property as originally fixed, it is held that if separate and community property are used to acquire the property, then such property so acquired is part separate and part community in nature, in pro-

[10] As in Barrett v. Franke, supra, where evidence failed to show that any part of payment during marriage was from community funds.

[11] Agreements between spouses, see post, Chap. VIII.

[12] Bear in mind that "payment" can come from labor or industry of one or both spouses. See post, § 66.

Initiation of right to property during marriage and completion of right after dissolution of partnership, see post, § 68.2.

[13] Hollingsworth v. Hicks, 57 N.M. 336, 259 P.2d 724; Laughlin v. Laughlin, 49 N.M. 20, 155 P.2d 1010; Langhurst v. Langhurst, 49 N.M. 329, 164 P.2d 204; Colden v. Alexander, 141 Tex. 134, 171 S. W. 2d 328.

[14] Baker v. Baker, 209 La. 1041, 26 So.2d 132.

See Oppenheim, Comparative Study of Community Property Systems, 21 Temple L. Q. 235.

[15] Succession of Siver, 167 La. 383, 119 So. 399.

portion to the amount of the respective properties used.[16] Actually, the proportions or respective interests can change with each payment, but it is the proportions or interests at the time the matter is brought into dispute that is important.[17]

As to Arizona, the cases present some confusion. There are cases which state that once the nature of the property as separate property is fixed — as upon initiation of the right thereto — that it retains that nature until changed by the intention of the spouses,[18] even though community property or separate property of the other spouse is later used,[19] with a right of reimbursement in the amount of the property so used.[20] But there is also authority that property purchased in part with community funds is community to the extent of the funds so used[21] and that if the property is purchased with the separate funds of both spouses that they are tenants in common of proportionate shares.[22] Perhaps the courts of that state will one day clarify the matter as to which "camp" the state is in.[23] Where reimbursement is recognized as obtainable, whether in the area of purchase or in the area of improvement of separate property with community funds, some cases hold that the amount of reimbursement is to be based on the amount of community property used,[24] but other authority has placed the recovery on the increase in value of the property from the use of community funds.[25]

In the various states, a large number of cases have involved life insurance policies taken out by a spouse prior to marriage, then later the payment of premiums during marriage from community funds. Of course, in such states as California and Washington, the policy and its proceeds are part separate and part community in nature, in the proportions represented by the amount of the premium paid.[26] In

[16] Forbes v. Forbes, 118 Cal. App. 324, 257 P.2d 721, quoting first edition; Vieux v. Vieux, 80 Cal. App. 222, 251 P. 640 (a leading case); Gapsch v. Gapsch, 76 Ida. 44, 277 P.2d 278, 54 A.L.R. 2d 416; Shermack, Nevada Community Property Law, 15 La. L. Rev. 559; Jacobs v. Hoitt, 119 Wash. 283, 205 P. 414. Cf. Fisher v. Fisher (Ida.) 383 P.2d 840.

[17] Consider Vieux v. Vieux, supra, preceding note.

[18] See, e.g., Lawson v. Ridgeway, 72 Ariz. 253, 233 P.2d 459.

[19] Flynn v. Allender, 75 Ariz. 322, 256 P.2d 560.

[20] Kingsberry v. Kingsberry, 93 Ariz. 217, 379 P.2d 893; Stauss v. Stauss, 82 Ariz. 268, 312 P.2d 148.

[21] Horton v. Horton, 35 Ariz. 378, 278 P. 370.

[22] Blackman v. Blackman, 45 Ariz. 374, 43 P.2d 1011.

[23] Arizona commentators supply no definitive answer. See Keddie, Community Property Law in Arizona (1957); Smith & Tormey, Summary of Arizona Community Property Law (1964); Demson, Summary of Arizona Law (1967).

[24] Kingsberry v. Kingsberry, 93 Ariz. 217, 379 P.2d 893.
Improvements of separate property, see post, § 142.

[25] Lawson v. Ridgeway, 72 Ariz. 253, 233 P.2d 459.

[26] Estate of Webb, Myr. Prob. Law (Cal. 1875); Modern Woodmen v. Gray, 113 Cal. App. 729, 299 P. 754; Coffey's Estate, 195 Wash. 379, 81 P.2d 283.

others, such as New Mexico and Texas, there is a right of reimbursement in the community for the amount of the community property used to pay premiums,[27] and this view has been followed in Arizona.[28]

§ 64.1.   — Public lands.

Grants of public land or acquisitions of public land are usually governed by statute and there may be, of course, differences among the statutes.[29] Usually there is some sort of formal filing of intention and an entry upon the land sought to be acquired, and this may be accompanied by the issuance of a certificate of some sort to the entrant. Upon his completion of a prescribed period of occupancy, accompanied by the making of specified improvements or the expenditure of specified sums, or the like, a deed — usually termed a "patent" — is issued to the entrant.[30] If all of this takes place prior to marriage or during marriage, there is usually no difficulty.[31] Even where the entry and all or substantially all of the occupancy and improvements or expenditures take place prior to marriage, with the more or less mechanical issuance of the patent coming after the marriage takes place, the public land may be classed as separate property, whatever the jurisdiction.[32]

However, where the entry and part of the occupancy take place prior to marriage and then part of the occupancy and the issuance of the patent come during marriage, question as to the nature of the land as separate or community may arise.[33] In New Mexico and Texas, the initial filing and entry is considered the initiation of the right to the land and it is classed as separate property and continues to remain so, despite the issuance of the patent during the marriage.[34] This is pursuant to their usual views, as previously discussed.[35] But if during the marriage, labor and industry of the spouses or the expenditure of community funds go into the improvement of the land, this entitles the community to reimbursement therefor.[36]

Likewise, in Louisiana the view as to such acquisition of public

---

[27] See New Mexico and Texas citations, supra.

[28] Rothman v. Rumbeck, 54 Ariz. 443, 96 P.2d 755.

[29] See post, § 75.

[30] See "Public Land," 42 Am. Jur., § 19-41; 73 C.J.S., §§ 45-53.

[31] See, e.g., ante, § 63.

[32] As in Humbird Lumber Co. v. Doran, 24 Ida. 507, 135 P. 66, where there was substantial completion of statutory requirements before marriage.

[33] See note, 24 So. Cal. L. Rev. 195;

Evans, Community Property in Public Lands, 9 Cal. L. Rev. 267; annotations, 96 Am. St. Rep. 916, 126 Am. St. Rep. 116.

[34] McDonald v. Lambert, 43 N.M. 27, 85 P.2d 78; Citizens' National Bank v. Ruley, 29 N.M. 662, 226 P. 416; Stiles v. Hawkins (Tex. Com. App.) 207 S. W. 89. See also Creamer v. Briscoe, 101 Tex. 490, 109 S. W. 911, 130 Am. St. Rep. 869, 17 L.R.A. (N.S.) 154.

[35] See ante, § 64.

[36] Stiles v. Hawkins, (Tex. Com. App.) 207 S. W. 89.

lands seems to be in accord with their usual views.[37] That is, it is the acquisition of the legal title, through the patent, during the period of marriage that governs, in that it fixes the nature of the land as community property.[38] This also seems to be the view indicated in Arizona.[39]

It is in the states of California, Idaho and Washington that we find the most conflict of views, sometimes within the same jurisdiction. Several decisions have placed all the weight on the situation at the time of entry; if the party was unmarried at that time the property is separate in nature, and remains so.[40] The delivery of the patent during the period of marriage has no effect;[41] even the fact that industry of both spouses or the expenditure of community funds, or both, contributed to the receipt of the patent has been held to give the community no interest in the property or entitle it to right of reimbursement.[42] There are other cases which put the determination of the nature of the property upon the situation existing at the time when the patent is issued so that, for example, the property is community if the patent is issued during marriage.[43]

Of course, it may well be that the one entitled — under the local view — to claim the property to be his or her separate property may have changed it into community property by appropriate conduct, such as consenting thereto.[44] Or one spouse may consent that the use of community funds shall inure to the separate benefit of the other spouse who had initiated a right by entry prior to marriage.[45]

[37] See ante, § 64.

[38] Doucet v. Fontenot, 165 La. 458, 115 So. 655.

[39] Valley Nat. Bank v. Battles, 62 Ariz. 204, 156 P.2d 244, evidently on basis that title taken during marriage renders property so taken presumably community property. See also Molina v. Ramírez, 15 Ariz. 249, 138 P. 17.

[40] Estate of Rupley, 174 Cal. App. 2d 597, 345 P.2d 11; Estate of Lamb, 95 Cal. 397, 30 P. 568; Harris v. Harris, 71 Cal. 314, 12 P. 274; Boggs v. Seawell, 35 Ida. 132, 205 P. 262; Card v. Cerini, 86 Wash. 419, 150 P. 610; Teynor v. Heible, 74 Wash. 222, 133 P. 1.

[41] See, e.g., Boggs v. Seawell, preceding note, that fixing of nature as separate property while single "is not affected by subsequent marriage."

[42] Meyer v. Meyer, 82 Cal. App. 313, 255 P. 767; Harris v. Harris, (Cal.) supra; Boggs v. Seawell (Ida.), supra.

[43] In Ellis v. Ellis, 97 Cal. App. 2d 808, 218 P.2d 823, noted in 24 So. Cal. L. Rev. 195, although on a case where entry was made during marriage, requirements substantially met during marriage, and patent issued after marriage terminated, court held issuance of patent at time no marriage existed made property separate property. And see post, § 68.1, as to entry during marriage and patent issued after dissolution of marriage.

[44] Peterson v. Peterson, 35 Ida. 470, 207 P. 425.

[45] See Harris v. Harris, 71 Cal. 314, 12 P. 274, where the wife had made the entry prior to marriage and the husband was said to have "consented" to the use of community funds so as to inure to her benefit.

[46] See, e.g., Harris v. Harris (Cal.); Boggs v. Seawell (Ida.); Card v. Cerini (Wash.); all supra.

[47] See discussion in note 43 supra, 24 So. Cal. L. Rev. 195.

[48] See ante, § 64.

While several of the California, Idaho and Washington cases express the view that entry confers a definite title of interest of an equitable nature which is completed by the issuance of the patent,[46] other authority, especially in California, says that entry merely gives a possessory right and that no equitable interest or title is acquired until compliance with all the statutory requirements essential for obtaining a patent.[47] It is regrettable that these inconsistencies exist and particularly inconsistency between cases of these states in the public land area and their cases otherwise dealing with property acquired partly with separate consideration and partly with community consideration.[48] We can only hope that these inconsistencies will be ironed out in the future.

§ 65.   — Prescription or adverse possession.

The nature of property acquired by adverse possession (or prescription, according to the civil law terminology), is determined by application of the inception of title doctrine. Clearly, if adverse possession is begun and completed during the marriage, the property will take on a community status.[49] There the title had its inception during the marriage, since the adverse possession was both begun and completed while the marriage relation subsisted. A more complex problem is presented, however, when possession is taken before marriage but title is perfected during marriage by the lapse of the statutory period, or where possession is taken during marriage but title is perfected after a dissolution of the marriage. In those instances it is necessary to determine when the title had its inception to determine the nature of the property. Two situations present themselves. One, where the possession is originally taken in good faith under color of title, and two, where the possession is not taken under color of title, and is a pure disseisin.[50] In the first situation, where entry was made in good faith under color of title, the inception of title is at the time of entry. This is true even though the right to the property is perfected by prescription or adverse possession through lapse of time. In the second situation, however, where the possession is not taken under any color of title and is entirely contingent upon or dependent upon continuation of the possession for a prescribed period and is thus so precarious that it is subject to be defeated at any moment by the rightful owner, the right of title to the property rests entirely upon the perfection of the right or title thereto,

---

[49] Villescas v. Ariz. Copper Co., 20 Ariz. 268, 179 P. 963. See also Evans, Some Sources of Acquisition of Community Property, 31 Yale L.J. 734.

[50] In the Spanish law for prescription to run the property must have been acquired in good faith under color of title, in order to obtain it in the statutory period of three years. However, where one had obtained property without good faith, by a pure disseisin, it was necessary to possess it continuously for a period of thirty years. Las Siete Partidas, Part. 3, Title 29.

and the nature of the property as community or separate will be determined in recognition of the marital status of the parties at the time of perfection.

These distinctions, which incidentally seem to be recognized in several of our community property states, were the subject of an excellent exposition by the Spanish jurisconsult, Didacus Perez, who asks: "What will the situation be, when the husband before marriage bought a house with title and in good faith from one not the owner, then acquired it during marriage by prescription through lapse of time, is it to be shared with the wife?" After noting that Joannes Lupi said that it is to be considered common property because, of its own force through lapse of time with possession, the ownership and acquisition is attained during marriage, Perez points out that on close inspection it is from what point the contract has its inception that ought to determine the matter conclusively. The prescription which comes after, so as to confirm the ownership, does so by virtue of a contract executed before marriage. Therefore it should be the separate property of the husband, so long, of course, as there has been no new or modified contract and the price was paid from the husband's separate property and not from the capital of the community.[51] This view, as already noted, was not held by Joannes Lupi, but the latter seems alone in his disagreement. Perez cites Tiraquellus as following the same view that Perez maintained, and it is clear that Covarruvias also approved the same view,[52] as did also, it may be inferred, the jurisconsult Azevedo,

[51] Didacus Perez, Glosses on Ordenanzas Reales de Castilla, Book 5, Title 4, where he says: "Quid autem erit, cum maritus emit domum ante matrimonium cum titulo et bona fide a non domino, quam matrimonio constante cursu temporis praescriptione acquisivit, utrum sit cum uxore communicanda? Lupi . . . dicit communem censendam esse, ex, eo, quia suam vim ex cursu temporis cum possessione dominium ipsius et acquisitio contingit constante matrimonio. Sed videtur tenendum contrarium, inspecta cause prima, a qua initium sumpsit contractus, et pariformiter debet judicari in fine. [Citing Tiraquellus], tractat, confirmari posterit ista praescriptio inchoata virtute contractus celebrate ante matrimonium posuit quondam rei irrevocabilitatem, firmitatem, et securitatem, non tamen induxit novum contractum, nec augmentum, cum˜ res succedat solo pretii soluti ab ipso marito, quod fuit proprium ipsius, capitale adductum in societate."

[52] Covarruvias, Opera Omnia, De Matrimonio, Pars II, Cap. VII, § 1, No. 13, stating, in part: "Tertio subinde deducitur, non esse uxori et viro, communem rem, quam usucapere vir coeperat ante matrimonium, completa postmodem, matrimonio constante, usucapioni. . . . Hoc tamen cogitandum relinquit Joan. Lupi. . . . Quamvis non ausim a priori opinione dissedere." [Thirdly, it is to be deduced therefrom (i. e., from a preceding discussion of inception of title before marriage), not to be the common property of wife and husband what the husband began before marriage to acquire by prescription and afterwards completed by the prescription during marriage. . . . Joan. Lupi does not follow this view. . . . However that may be, I do not venture to disagree with the first opinion.]

who although forbearing to discuss the matter, does so on the ground that consideration of the matter by him was unnecessary since it had been fully discussed by Palacios Ruvios, Covarruvias and Perez.[53]

The same view finds substantial support, also, in the decisions of many of our courts. Thus, the Texas courts seem to consider that where there is entry, before marriage, without color of title or apparent right and completion of title during marriage, the character of the property is determined as of the time of acquisition of title by completion of the adverse possession, and the property is community.[54] Somewhat similarly, in California, a mere squatter who without right was occupying land, before marriage, obtained thereby no separate property right, and when, during marriage, he surrendered possession to the real owner in consideration of a conveyance to himself of part of the land, such land so received was held to be community property.[55] And in Louisiana it has been held that where possession taken before marriage continued to be precarious and the title was inchoate, entirely dependent on the continued possession and subject to be defeated at any time by the rightful owner, and the prescriptive period was completed during marriage, the title was acquired for the benefit of the community.[56] On the other hand, in Texas, where the entry is under color of title, however defective, the status of the property as community or separate property is determined as of the time when the title had its inception rather than by the time of completion of title by bar of statute.[57] This has also been the result in California where entry in possession, before marriage, under claim of right, and acquisition of title by adverse possession during marriage constituted such property separate property.[58] To repeat, it will be noticed that the distinction rests on whether it can be said that there was a valid inception of title before marriage to which perfection of title will relate back.[59]

It is pertinent to state at this point, as to property to which title is

<hr />

[53] Azevedo refers to this problem, in No. 24 to Nov. Rec. Law 1, Book 10, Title 4, but refrains from answering it on the ground that the other commentators to whom he refers have disposed of the problem.

[54] See cases collected, 23 Tex. Jur. 137; Oakes, Speer's Marital Rights in Texas, 4th Ed., § 443; McKay, Community Property, 2nd Ed., chap. 35. This view results from the interpretation given the Texas statutes. See also Strong v. Garrett, 148 Tex. 265, 224 S. W. 2d 471; Scott v. Washburn (Tex. Civ. App.) 324 S. W. 2d 957, writ ref'd n.r.e.

[55] Pancoast v. Pancoast, 57 Cal. 320.

[56] Crouch v. Richardson, 158 La. 822, 104 So. 728.

[57] Oakes, Speer's Marital Rights in Texas, 4th Ed., § 443.

[58] Siddall v. Haight, 132 Cal. 320, 64 P. 410, where possession and adverse title originated in parol gift to woman who later married. This case has been criticized by Evans, 31 Yale Law Jour. 734, on the ground that parol gift does not alone give color of title.

[59] The difference in the result, depending on which of the situations is involved, seems to have gone unnoticed in the standard encyclopedias when treating of this matter. And McKay, Community Property,

perfected after dissolution of the marital community, although inception of title, entry or possession took place during marriage, that the same principles should apply in determining whether it is community or separate property, and this is true even where title is perfected by adverse possession.[60]

§ 66.   Acquisitions, earnings and gains during marriage.

Here we come to the very nub of the Spanish community property system and hence of our own system. This was a community of property in acquests and gains by the spouses during marriage, and not a universal partnership in the sense that separate properties owned before marriage became community property or in the sense that anything obtained by one spouse by lucrative title during marriage was shared with the other spouse.[61] Ordinarily, whatever was acquired, earned, gained or purchased by the husband and wife during the marriage belonged to both by halves.[62] No distinctions were made between husband and wife, the husband being as much entitled to share equally in acquisitions by the wife through her industry as she was entitled to share equally in acquisitions by the husband.[63] It was not necessary

2nd Ed., chaps. 34, 35, seems aware of it only as relates to Texas (of which Judge Speer is, naturally, aware in his Treatise on Law of Marital Rights in Texas, 3rd Ed.); McKay seems to argue, on the basis of common law authorities, that in any event, if possession is established before marriage, the property should be separate property. See, however, Evans, Sources of Acquisition of Community Property, 31 Yale Law Jour. 734; Burby's Cas. on Com. Prop., 4th Ed., p. 78.

[60] See post, § 68.2.

[61] The communal sharing is in profits and acquisitions during marriage. Matienzo, Glosses I and II, to Nov. Rec. Law 3, Book 10, Title 4.

"Ganancial property (bienes de ganancias) is all that which is increased during marriage. By increased, is understood all that is increased by onerous cause or title, and not that which is acquired by a lucrative one, as inheritance, donation, etc." Asso and Mañuel, Institutes of the Civil Law of Spain, Book 1, Title VII, Cap. 5, § 1.

[62] See Novísima Recopilación, Book 10, Title 4, Law 1 et seq., and Commentaries, vol. 2, 1943 edition of this work.

"And thus we should say that if a husband and a wife admit in a deed the receipt of one hundred crowns by such and such a sale, each is understood to have received a half share thereof, according to Palatius Rubeus on Dig. 45 2.11, where his note cites other authorities." Azevedo, No. 14, to Nov. Rec. Book 10, Title 3, Law 4.

Earnings while separated, see ante. § 57.

Remuneratory gifts, see post, § 70.

[63] See Novísima Recopilación, Book 10, Title 4, Law 2. "What above is said of the earnings of husbands, let the same be as regards those of wives." See Azevedo's commentaries, No. 13, to Nov. Rec. Law 1, Book 10, Title 4, especially drawing attention to this right of the husband. He pointed out that the principles of the Roman law and the view of the commentators on the Roman law that acquisitions by a wife through her own industry were her own "is contrary to our law and precedent and so not to be held in our kingdom."

"The reason is that the one spouse is deemed to be appointed business agent by the other, just as two part-

that an acquisition or purchase be made jointly; the spouses shared equally though the acquisition or purchase was made by one alone, provided of course that they were living together,[64] or still had the will to union although temporarily separated by exigencies of life.[65] Certain exceptions existed, of course, as where it was clearly evidenced that acquisitions or gains of one spouse came from gifts or inheritances or the like intended for that spouse alone, or that property purchased was paid for with the separate property of the purchasing spouse, or that agreements or stipulations of the spouses affected their rights. These matters, however, will be dealt with in the sections following, in

ners carrying on different businesses are deemed to be mutual agents of each other, so that what one does benefits or hurts the other (citing authorities). But a wife must act only with the leave and consent of her husband if her acts are to be valid and her purchases and acquisitions are to be shared. . . . Whether a purchase is made by the husband in his own name or by the wife, with the wife's money or with the husband's or with money belonging to them both, it immediately and automatically becomes common property with regard to ownership and possession." Matienzo, Gloss II, Nos. 2, 3, to Nov. Rec. Law 1, Book 10, Title 4.

[64] Novísima Recopilación, Book 10, Title 4, Law 1; Matienzo, Gloss II, Nos. 1, 3, to Nov. Rec. Law 1.

Llamas y Molina, in Nos. 58-60, to Nov. Rec. Law 8, Book 10, Title 4, goes thoroughly into the matter, explaining that the words *compraren de consuno* appearing originally in the law in the Fuero Real of 1255 meant "is purchased while living together," that is, the spouses shared equally anything acquired "while living together" and that it was sufficient that the acquisition be made by one of them only, while they were living together. He disapproved the argument of an early commentator, Tello, that *de consuno* meant "conjointly" and that the meaning of the law was that the acquisition had to be by both spouses "conjointly." Tello appears to have been virtually alone in so contending, and in any

event, to remove the question from all doubt, the law by 1567 was enlarged to read *compraren estando de consuno,* which clearly means "purchased during union," that is, while living together. In other words, the purchase or acquisition which is shared is one made by both spouses or by either spouse while they are living together and not merely a purchase or acquisition made by them conjointly. Matienzo made note of the same matter, in Gloss II, No. 1, to Nov. Rec. Law 1, saying: "In the law *fori et ordinationum,* from which this law is taken, the words used were *compraren de consuno* as if it were necessary, in order to render property acquired during marriage shareable between spouses, that the property should be purchased jointly by them. But this was not admitted by the Doctors. It was enough, according to them, for the property to be acquired by one spouse; and sharing would then take place. This was approved by Segura. But clearer still are the words of the present law to this effect. It says '*que compraren estando de consuno*', i.e., it is not necessary that they should purchase together, but they must live together according to the principles set out in gloss I, nos. 41 and 42 above. And this is correct, whatever may have been inadvertently said to the contrary by Tellius (i.e., Tello) Fernandez."

Property acquired by husband or wife alone is mutually shared, see also Matienzo, Gloss IX, No. 1, to Nov. Rec. Law 5, Book 10, Title 4.

[65] See ante, § 57.

order to avoid confusion, and we confine ourselves here to consideration of acquisitions, earnings and gains through labor and industry of the spouses. But note particularly that we say acquisitions, earnings and gains through labor and industry, that is, by onerous title.[66] Our courts have been too prone to fail to comprehend this qualification.[67]

It is important to notice that the wife's ownership and possession in half of these earnings and gains during marriage passed to her automatically *ipso jure* without the necessity of delivery. And her ownership and possession in half of these earnings and gains did not depend upon any mere physical fact of placing the earnings or gains in the husband's hands but related, just as the husband's ownership did, to the very inception of the right to such earnings and gains.[68]

In many early forms of community of property, the acquisitions, earnings and gains during the marriage were not shared equally between the spouses but rather in proportion to the amount of property each had brought or contributed to the marriage.[69] This was originally true of

---

[66] "With regard to the community of goods, the law has regard to the industry and common labor of each spouse and to the burdens of partnership and community." Matienzo, Gloss I, No. 6, to Nov. Rec. Law 1, Book 10, Title 4.

"Palacios Ruvios affirms in Commentary No. 5 to the present law, that as the property acquired during marriage originates in the work and industry of the contracting parties, it should be considered as obtained not under a lucrative title but an onerous title; he adds that he assisted in the drafting of the law, and that he recommended its adoption, as he had previously advised." Llamas y Molina, No. 3, to Nov. Rec. Law 6, Book 10, Title 4.

[67] See criticisms, ante, § 62.

"The fact that such a share accrues by law to either spouse is due to the existence of the conjugal partnership, since such property is deemed to have been acquired by the industry and labor of both spouses and so accrues by onerous rather than by lucrative title." Matienzo, Gloss I, No. 2, to Nov. Rec. Law 6, Book 10, Title 4.

"It is a fundamental postulate of the community property system that whatever is gained during coverture, by the toil, talent, or other productive faculty of either spouse, is community property." Hammonds v. Commissioner of Internal Revenue, 10 C. C. A., 106 F.2d 420 (property acquired in Texas by Oklahoma domiciliary in return for personal services). To same effect, see In re Wilson's Estate, 56 Nev. 353, 53 P.2d 339; Logan v. Logan, (Tex. Civ. App.) 112 S. W. 2d 515, w/e dis.; Friedlander v. Friedlander, 56 Wash. 2d 288, 362 P.2d 352.

[68] See Gutiérrez, Quaestio CXVIII, No. 4, to Nov. Rec. Law 1, Book 10, Title 4; Matienzo, Gloss III, No. 2, to Nov. Rec. Law 1; and commentaries generally. And see also especially post, Chap. VII, A, as to wife's ownership.

"In the second place you should note from the words *'ayanlo ambos de por medio'* [let them both have it by halves] that ownership and possession of a moiety of the property acquired during marriage passes automatically to the wife without delivery and the wife is owner even during marriage of the share which belongs to her." Matienzo, Gloss III, No. 2, to Nov. Rec. Law 1, Book 10, Title 4.

And see post, Chap. VII, A.

[69] Thus, in ancient Ireland, natural gains during marriage were owned jointly by husband and wife, the

the Spanish community property system, as appears from the provision of the Fuero Juzgo in the year 693.[70] But by the time of the thirteenth century we find the Spanish law providing that the spouses should share in these things equally, that is by halves, irrespective of whether one spouse was richer than the other, and this continued thereafter unchanged.[71] It thus has been the principle for centuries that the spouses share equally, regardless of the fact that one, being richer than the other, may have brought more property into the marriage,[72] a principle that has governed the community system both in Mexico[73] and in our American community property states.[74]

That the earnings of the wife as well as of the husband during the subsistence of the marriage are community property, one of the primary principles of the Spanish law of community, has been continued almost without question in all our community property states,[75] although it is

---

wife's share being a proportion based on the amount of property she brought into the marriage. Joyce, Social History of Ancient Ireland, 2nd Ed., vol. 2, pp. 8-12.

See also ante, Chap. II.

[70] Fuero Juzgo, Book 4, Title 2, Law 17.

In the Law of the Visigoths in Sweden, circa 1200 A.D., upon division of the common property upon the husband's death, the wife's share was one-third. Law of the West Goths, according to the Manuscript of Eskil (Bergin's Translation), p. 54.

[71] It was so provided in the Fuero Real in 1255, Book 3, Title 3, Law 1, which provisions were carried into successive codes ending with the Novísima Recopilación of 1805. See Novísima Recopilación, Book 10, Title 4, Law 1.

According to the law of the West Goths in Sweden, circa 1200 A.D., we find a similar provision that if land was secured and surveyed during marriage it belonged to both spouses. Law of the West Goths, according to the Manuscript of Eskil (Bergin's Translation), p. 66.

[72] "Although the husband may have more than the wife, or the wife more than the husband, in realty or in personalty, let the fruits be common to both." Novísima Recopilación, Book 10, Title 4, Law 3.

This law "prescribes that although the husband may have more property than the wife, or she more than he, the benefits are common to both of them." Llamas y Molina, No. 15 to Nov. Rec. Law 6, Book 10, Title 4. See also Matienzo, Gloss I, No. 8, to Nov. Rec. Law 1, Book 10, Title 4, who points out that frequently the poorer spouse by work and labor makes up for the deficiency in his or her estate.

[73] "The ownership of the gananciales is common equally in halves to the husband and wife, without consideration as to whether one brought more properties than the other into the marriage." Novísimo Sala Mexicano, sec. 2a, Title IV, No. 5.

[74] See Ariz. R.S. 1956, § 25-211; Ida. Code 1948, § 32-906; La. Civ. Code, art. 2334; Nev. R.S. 1956, § 123.220; N.M. Stats. 1953, 57-4-1; Texas Family Code 1969, §§ 5.01, 5.21, 5.61.

[75] See Shaw v. Greer, 67 Ariz. 223, 194 P.2d 430; Smith v. Furnish, 70 Cal. 424, 12 P. 392; Ahlstrom v. Tage, 31 Ida. 459, 174 P. 605; Fazzio v. Krieger, 226 La. 571, 76 So.2d 713; Ormachea v. Ormachea, 67 Nev. 213, 217 P.2d 355 (citing 1st ed.); Clark, Community of Property and the Family in New Mexico (1958), p. 21; Moss v. Gibbs, (Tex.) 370 S. W. 2d 452; Colagrossi v. Hendrickson, 50 Wash. 2d 266, 310 P.2d 1072.

The jurisconsult Gutiérrez discusses at length the situation of the wife

143

frequently provided that she shall have the management and control of her earnings and wages received for her personal labor and services, including the right to maintain action therefor in her own name.[76] No difficulties should arise in the determination of this matter if principles of the law of community are properly applied, including the yardstick of acquisition by onerous title.[77] Any so-called community property system of acquests and gains which made the earnings and gains of the husband community property but not those of the wife community property would be parading under a false mask and would constitute nothing more than a pretense of being a community property system.[78] However, difficulty has sometimes arisen over the apparent attempt to

under the Roman law, pointing out that under that law her labors imposed by family duty were owed to the marriage but that her earnings from any skill or trade belonged to herself, and concludes by stating that under the Spanish law of community property it was otherwise as to such earnings of hers for by that law "gains by man and wife whilst living together are equally shared between them and divided, except in the case of gifts by kinsmen." Gutiérrez, Quaestio CXX, No. 3, to Nov. Rec. Law 2, Book 10, Title 4.

Earnings of the spouses, see also Evans, 10 Calif. Law Rev. 271; Oakes, Speer's Marital Rights in Texas, 4th Ed., § 421.

Earnings of wife while living separate from her husband, see ante, § 57.

[76] See post, § 114.

Power conferred on wife to manage her own earnings does not make such earnings her separate property. See McMillan v. United States Fire Ins. Co., 48 Idaho 163, 280 P. 220.

Statute exempting earnings of wife from liability for debts of husband as not constituting such earnings the separate property of the wife, see Street v. Bertolone, 193 Cal. 751, 226 P. 913; Albright v. Albright, 21 N.M. 606, 157 P. 662, Ann. Cas. 1918 E 542. See likewise, Arnold v. Leonard, 114 Tex. 535, 273 S. W. 799.

[77] "Earnings" and "accumulation" defined, see Phoenix v. Dickson, 40 Ariz. 403, 12 P.2d 618.

Interest in oil and gas leases received by wife in exchange for her personal services as community property, see Hammonds v. Commissioner of Internal Revenue, 10 C. C. A., 106 F.2d 420 (under Texas law). And see post, § 71.1.

In Smith v. Furnish, 70 Cal. 424, 12 P. 392, a claim against a decedent's estate for services rendered by a married woman to the decedent as a nurse, while she was living with her husband, was properly held community property.

Cf. Evans, 10 Calif. Law Rev. 271, who remarks that what is meant by "earnings for personal services" as used in various statutes has never been accurately determined and that it is not easy to show what the legislatures intended to include.

[78] "Section 168 (after January 1, 1970, Cal. Civ. Code, § 5117) does not provide that the earnings of the wife are her separate property, but that they are not liable for the debts of the husband. They continue to be community property for the purposes of administration and for the purposes of investment and other management by the husband." Street v. Bertolone, 193 Cal. 751, 226 P. 913.

In 1912 the Louisiana legislature enacted a statute containing two clauses, the first providing that the earnings of the wife when living separate from her husband although not separated by judgment of court should be her separate property, the second clause providing that her earnings when carrying on a business, trade, occupation or industry should be her separate property. This second clause was construed by Louisiana

distinguish, especially in the case of the wife, ordinary earnings in the way of salary or wages from profits of some business carried on. Leaving aside the question of a business owned by a spouse before marriage,[79] there should be no distinction whatsoever between ordinary earnings in the way of salary or wages and profits from the conduct of a business. Whether gained by husband or wife they should fall into the communal property. It is another matter, of course, if some agreement between the spouses permits one of them to retain, as separate property, wages or profits,[80] or if the wife is able to qualify as a "sole trader" in the conduct of a business, under statutory provisions, whereby her earnings and profits therefrom are to constitute her separate property.[81]

Since this work is concerned primarily with principles of community property law, no effort is made to illustrate every conceivable kind of earnings, gains or acquisitions which may constitute property of the marital community. Once the principles are understood, their application to whatever factual situation arises should be readily possible.[82] Some few types of property or property interests are considered, however, particularly those, such as life insurance, which have developed in importance in our own day.[83] Lawyers will undoubtedly be interested in cases involving legal fees and compensation as community property.[84]

commentators to mean that a wife although living with her husband was entitled to earnings from carrying on a business, etc. See 4 Tulane Law Rev. 281; 11 Loyola Law Jour. 28; Daggett, Community Property System in Louisiana, p. 8. However, the Louisiana Supreme Court has interpreted the second clause to refer to situations where the wife is living separate and apart from her husband and was intended by the legislature to be merely explanatory of the first clause. Houghton v. Hall, 177 La. 237, 148 So. 37. Such an interpretation is certainly in accord with proper principles of community property, for it would be a peculiar system which made the husband's earnings community but not the wife's, while they are living together.

[79] See post, § 72. See also Vaughn v. Vaughn, (Ida.) 428 P.2d 50; Kolmorgan v. Schaller, 51 Wash. 2d 194, 67 A.L.R. 2d 704, noting Houghton v. Hall at p. 722.

[80] See post, § 142.

Validity of such agreement, see post, §§ 136, 142.

Savings effected by the wife from community funds turned over to her for running the household remain community property. Milisich v. Hillhouse, 48 Nev. 166, 228 P. 307; Abbott v. Weatherby, 6 Wash. 507, 33 P. 1070, 36 Am. St. Rep. 176. See also Worker v. Knox, 197 Wash. 453, 85 P.2d 1041; annotation, 67 A.L.R. 2d 708.

[81] See post, § 149.

[82] See, e g , Stevens v. Stevens, 70 Ariz. 302, 219 P.2d 1045, dealing with a permit to graze cattle on public lands that was issued to husband during marriage. On divorce, it was treated as community property of which wife held an undivided half-interest.

Winnings of wife in puzzle contest as community property, see Estate of Baer, 81 Cal. App. 2d 830, 185 P.2d 412.

[83] See post, this chapter.

[84] In re Monaghan's Estate, 60 Ariz. 342, 137 P.2d 393 (fees during and after marriage); Waters v. Waters, 95 Cal. App. 2d 265, 170 P.2d 494, noted 20 So. Cal. L. Rev. 281 (contingent fee not collected

§ 67.   — Greater earnings or gains by one spouse or earnings or gains by one spouse alone.

The right of the spouses to share equally in the acquisitions, earnings and gains of each other was in no way dependent upon any necessity that the acquisitions, earnings and gains of each should be equal. Each spouse owned half of all that was earned or gained, even though one earned or gained more than the other,[85] or even though one actually earned or gained nothing.[86] This latter situation would result most frequently, of course, from the fact that the wife made no actual earnings or gains. Nevertheless, she had an ownership of half of the earnings and gains of the husband, for it was rightfully considered that the services, industry and labor she contributed to the conjugal partnership were as important thereto as that contributed by the husband.[87]

until after divorce decree). And see Drysdale v. Com'r of Int. Rev., (6 Cir.) 232 F.2d 633. See discussion by Brockelbank, The Community Property Law of Idaho (1962), pp. 157-161.

[85] "The ganancial properties are in common of the husband and wife, and belong to each of them in half, . . . even though one gains more afterwards than the other." Escriche, Diccionario, "Ganancial Properties."

[86] "And so if the husband or the wife acquires alone, what they acquire is mutually shared." Matienzo, Gloss IX, No. 1, to Nov. Rec. Law 5, Book 10, Title 4.

"The ganancial properties are in common of the husband and wife, and belong to each of them in half, . . . even though only one may acquire them trafficking or working; because there is established between the spouses a legal partnership, different from the others, whereby their acquisitions are reciprocally shared by each other." Escriche, Diccionario, "Ganancial Properties."

"The same (i. e., division by halves) applies, whether gained by both or by one only during the marriage, because though one may not work at all, that one would not thereby be unable to participate in the profits, because by this unique effect through legal concession, they are partners of a universal partner-

ship, so that neither the association nor the participation in the profits is barred by reason of one doing business and working, and the other doing nothing as concerns the doing of business with the capital and in the name of both, although only one acts, since to that end they are in legal contemplation a single unit." Febrero, Librería de Escribanos, Cinco Juicios I, Book I, Cap. IV, § 1, No. 3.

[87] See Matienzo, Gloss I, No. 8, to Nov. Rec. Law 1.

Notice that there is no sharing of marital earnings and gains when the wife remains in her house and does not live with the husband "as then she has given no work or care in its increase and conservation (which is one of the reasons for which the half is granted to the wife." Febrero, Librería de Escribanos, Testamentos y Contratos I, Cap. I, § 22, No. 242.

"Viewed solely as a matter of economy, the labor, pain, and drudgery required of the mother in sustaining the home, giving birth to and rearing the children will often more than offset the contribution of the father to the family budget." Terrell, J., in Strauss v. Strauss, 148 Fla. 23, 3 So.2d 727, speaking with approval of the community property system.

See Vaughn, The Policy of Community Property and Interspousal Transactions, 19 Baylor L. Rev. 20, at p. 55. See also Evans, 10 Calif. L. Rev. 270.

There certainly should not be any confusion about the foregoing matters so far as our courts are concerned and, happily, on the whole it is well understood by them.[88]

§ 68. — Benefits from workmen's compensation acts, unemployment compensation, employees' group insurance, pension plans and the like.

Since personal earnings of the spouses, in the absence of some agreement to the contrary, are community property,[89] payments made to a spouse in lieu of those earnings that were themselves community property are generally held to belong to the community.[90] Thus, compensation awarded under workmen's compensation acts is community property. It is in substitution of damages ordinarily recovered because of the death or injury of an employee and, being measured by the current wages of the employee, is to all practical purposes in lieu of earnings of the employee which were themselves community property.[91] Unemployment compensation to a spouse would have the same nature, since the purpose of the payments is to replace lost wages or salary.[92]

So-called fringe benefits which are included as an essential part of the contract of employment and are a part of the consideration for the employee's services take on the same character as the wages or salary.[93] To provide the benefits, sometimes there are deductions from the employee's wages or salary, sometimes there are such deductions plus some additional amount contributed by the employer and sometimes there is no deduction from the wages or salary but only a contribution by the employer. But even if the employee contributes

---

[88] That whatever is earned or gained by the efforts of both spouses or of one spouse alone is community property, see cases cited, 126 Am. St. Rep. 102, 103; 41 Corpus Juris Secundum, Husband and Wife, § 475.

[89] See ante, § 66.

[90] See cases, infra.

[91] Dawson v. McNaney, 71 Ariz. 79, 223 P.2d 907, citing and following de Funiak, 1st Ed.; Estate of Simoni, 220 Cal. App. 2d 339, 33 Cal. Rptr. 845, noted 4 Santa Clara Lawyer 236; Pickens v. Pickens, 125 Tex. 410, 83 S. W. 2d 951; Texas Employers' Ins. Ass'n v. Boudreaux, (Tex. Com. App.) 231 S. W. 756; Piro v. Piro (Tex. Civ. App.) 327 S. W. 2d 335. But cf. Brownfield v. Southern Amusement Co. (La. App.)

198 So. 670, dism. on rehearing 196 La. 73, 198 So. 656; Richards v. Richards, 59 N.M. 308, 283 P.2d 881, conceding general rule to be that stated by de Funiak, 1st Ed., § 68, but attempting to distinguish cases there cited and holding the contrary.

[92] No current cases in this area have been noted. But see Cal. Welfare & Institutions Code, § 460 (1963), that the earnings of a spouse of an applicant for welfare aid up to the amount of $200 a month, after expenses, shall not be community property.

[93] Interest in profit-sharing plan as community property, see Herring v. Blakeley (Tex.) 385 S. W. 2d 843.

nothing directly from his compensation, the benefit to him is part of the consideration paid for his services.[94]

These benefits may include the benefits or protection accruing from various group insurance policies,[95] such as those providing benefits, payments or protection generally in cases of sickness, accident, hospital confinement and the like.[96] Death benefits to the employee's family may also be provided for[97] and also retirement or pension plans of one kind or another may be set up for the employee's benefit.[98] In addition, there is, of course, the federal Social Security program to provide for retirement payments or pensions to the elderly and their families.[99] To the extent that deductions come from the pay of the employee and by contributions from the employer during the employee's marriage, the payments later made from the fund or rights built up are community property in nature.[1] Incidentally, frequently a private employer's retirement or pension plan takes into account what will be received from Social Security.

To determine if these various benefits or rights are community or separate property in nature, the status of the employee at the time

---

[94] Such benefits are thus a "gain" added to the common property of the marital partnership as the direct result of the spouse's labor. Lee v. Lee, 112 Tex. 392, 247 S. W. 828; Reedy v. Jones (Tex. Civ. App.) 41 S. W. 2d 1044.

[95] Interest in group insurance policies, see Messersmith v. Messersmith, 229 La. 495, 86 So.2d 169.

[96] Sick-pay benefits, see Doyle v. Doyle, 44 Cal. App. 259, 186 P. 188.

Disability benefits, see Easterling v. Succession of Lamkin (La.) 31 So.2d 220.

[97] Death benefits under union welfare and pension plan, see Boyd v. Curran (D.C., S. D. N. Y.) 166 F. Supp. 193, applying California law as being matrimonial domicile.

[98] In ordinary course of events, that the amount payable from employees' retirement fund represents earnings and thus would constitute community property, see Cheney v. City and County of San Francisco, 7 Cal. 2d 565, 61 P.2d 754. (However, rule nullified by spouses' agreement to contrary.)

Pension plans of corporations and other employers, see discussion by Kent, Pension Funds and Problems Under California Community Prop-

erty Laws, 2 Stanford Law Rev. 447; comment, 37 So. Cal. L. Rev. 594. Pensions and retirement pay to military personnel, see post, § 75.

Illustrative pension cases, see Kemp v. Metropolitan Life Ins. Co., 205 F.2d 857; Succession of Scott, 231 La. 381, 91 So.2d 574; Daigre v. Daigre, 228 La. 682, 83 So.2d 900; Succession of Rockvoan (La. App.) 141 So.2d 438.

No power to name beneficiary of pension rights without other spouse's consent, see Jorgeman v. Cranston, 27 Cal. Rptr. 297.

[99] See Social Security Act, U.S. Code. Some states provide for a Social Security program by that name.

[1] See In re Ney's Estate, 28 Cal. Rptr. 442.

In Christiansen v. Department of Social Security, 15 Wash. 2d 465, 131 P.2d 189, it was said that a destitute husband had no enforcible right of action against his wife to compel his support from her separate property, and thus he had no resources which disqualified him from receiving aid from the state Department of Social Security. No question was raised, however, as to whether the aid so received would represent community or separate income.

the right is acquired becomes important. If the right was acquired or has accrued before marriage, it is separate,[2] even though payment pursuant to the right is not received until during marriage.[3] If the right is acquired or accrued during marriage, it is community property,[4] even though payment pursuant to the right is not received until after termination of the marriage.[5]

Problems sometimes arise where the spouse was employed while single and then later married. Many cases have held that the sums later received are considered both community property in part and separate property in part in the proportion to the amounts of wages or salary while single and while married that went into the securing of the right or benefit.[6] It has otherwise been expressed as in proportion to the number of years worked while single and while married.[7] It has sometimes been argued that the employee actually had no contract or property right in the fund involved and that the right cannot accrue until the happening of an event upon which payment is contingent. Thus, upon division of property upon divorce, is there a right or interest to be considered? The answer has been that there is a valuable right which has been purchased with the community funds or community labor and the right or interest is community property and is to be valued by what went into earning it. The foregoing has been particularly true in some pension fund cases.[8] What happens if, upon divorce, as sometimes has happened, counsel overlooks such rights or interest in arranging for division of community property and the ex-husband then dies first? (Indeed, he may even have remarried and then die before his ex-wife.)[9] An interesting California discussion contends that the current California view is that the ex-wife has no right or interest and this is said to be based on some one of three rationales: (a) the ex-wife has no enforceable right after dissolution of the community, (b) the ex-wife's death benefit is community property, but if there was no distribution of community property upon divorce she then loses her property interest upon the death of the ex-husband, or (c) that a new class of community property has been created which vests in the community so long as the community exists but is not vested in the individual members so that no rights are assertable after dissolution of the community.[10]

[2] See ante, § 63.

[3] See ante, §§ 63, 64.

[4] See ante, § 66.

[5] See ante, § 68.2.

[6] See, e.g., Gettman v. City of Los Angeles, 87 Cal. App. 2d 862, 197 P.2d 817.

[7] See Kirkham v. Kirkham, (Tex. Civ. App.) 335 S. W. 2d 393.

[8] See, e.g., Crossan v. Crossan, 35 Cal. App. 2d 39, 94 P.2d 609. But cf. Williamson v. Williamson, 21 Cal. Rptr. 164, attempting to distinguish the Cheney and Crossan cases.

[9] Consider who is the "widow"? As not being "widow" of deceased at time of his death, see Benson v. Los Angeles, 27 Cal. Rptr. 484.

[10] See Comment, The Community Property Status of the Pension and the Widow's Death Benefit, 37 So. Cal. L. Rev. 594.

In our view these are all erroneous rationales: undivided community property is owned by the ex-spouses as tenants in common and the enforceable rights of the ex-wife should be recognized.[11]

In conclusion, it may be noted that in those jurisdictions which permit it,[12] agreements between the spouses may provide that the earnings of a spouse are to be that spouse's separate property and this will result in the benefits obtained through those earnings also being separate property.[13] Or the agreement may relate directly to the benefits themselves.[14]

§ 68.1.   — Earnings of minor children.

It will be recalled that under Anglo-American common law, the earnings of unemancipated minor children are declared to belong to their parents.[15] Authority to this same effect exists in several of our community property states, namely, California,[16] Idaho,[17] Louisiana,[18] Texas[19] and Washington.[20] While the manner in which the parents hold these earnings has not been clearly expressed in Idaho, Louisiana and Washington, it is clearly indicated in Texas that they hold it as community property, and this seems to be indicated to be the case in California.[21] Under the presumption in favor of community property,[22] certainly it must be presumed that this is the manner in which the parents do hold it together, and this must be accepted as the rule.[23]

This view in our community property states that the earnings in question belong to the parents is a graft upon the community property system of the common-law rule that the earnings of minor children belong to the parents or, perhaps it should be said, more specifically, to the father. It is not difficult to trace this grafting process. It was most probably considered by the courts that if, pursuant to the com-

---

[11] Such a view is recommended in the preceding comment at p. 602 et seq.

[12] See post, §§ 135-139.

[13] Cheney v. City and County of San Francisco, 7 Cal. 2d 565, 61 P.2d 754.

[14] Sullivan v. Union Oil Co., 16 Cal. 2d 229, 105 P.2d 922.

[15] See, e.g., Vernier, American Family Laws, Stanford Univ. Press, 1935.

[16] See Cossi v. Southern Pac. Co., 110 Cal. App. 110, 293 P. 663.
"The father and mother of a legitimate unmarried minor child are equally entitled to its custody, services and earnings." Cal. Civ. Code, § 197 (in part).

[17] McLean v. Lewiston, 17 Ida. 63, 104 P. 1015.

[18] See La. Civ. Code, arts. 221, 229; Lewis v. Southern Advance Bag & Paper Co. (La. App.) 147 So. 532.

[19] See Insurance Co. of Texas v. Stratton, (Tex. Civ. App.) 287 S. W. 2d 320, writ ref. n.r.e.; Messimer v. Echols, (Tex. Civ. App.) 194 S. W. 1171.

[20] Hines v. Chesire, 36 Wash. 2d 467, 219 P.2d 100.

[21] See statutes and cases cited supra, this section.

[22] See ante, § 60.

[23] This is stated as the rule, without citation of authority by McKay, Community Property, 2d Ed., § 296.
Personal injury to minor child, recovery by parents for loss of child's services or earnings as community property, see post, § 85.

mon-law rule, the earnings of minor children belong to the parents, and if, under community property statutes everything acquired by the spouses during marriage is community property, except that acquired individually by gift, inheritance, bequest or devise, then the minor children's earnings were acquired during marriage, and not by gift, etc., and so must constitute community property. This may have seemed logical reasoning, but it overlooked the basic principle of the community property system that what is community property is that which is acquired by the spouses themselves, by onerous title, or which is given, bequeathed, etc., to both of them. If the courts had resorted to the principles of community property, instead of to the common law, to determine what is and what is not community property, they would have discovered that the earnings of minor children were not community property but belonged to the children themselves, except where the earnings were made through the use of property of the father, in which case the earnings belonged to the father.[24]

In the case of minor children by a former marriage who are living with their surviving parent and the second spouse of the latter, it has been said by our courts both that their earnings are the separate property of their surviving parent,[25] and that their earnings are community property of the second marriage.[26]

§ 68.2 — Initiation of acquisition during marriage and completion after dissolution of partnership.

Attention has already been given to the situation where the acquisition of property is initiated prior to marriage and the acquisition

---

[24] Las Siete Partidas, Part. 4, Title 17, Laws 5-7; Fuero Real, Book 3, Title 4, Law 7.

According to the Partidas, there were three kinds of earnings obtained by children while under the control of the father; the profectitious earnings by means of the father's property and which belonged to the father; the adventitious earnings which were all those earned by the labor of the child's hands, by means of some trade or profession or through any other knowledge possessed by the child, or in any other manner, and included as well gifts received by will or inheritance, etc., and treasure or other property accidentally found, all of which adventitious earnings belonged to the child but were to be preserved and cared for by the father, who enjoyed the usufruct thereof until emancipation of the child; and thirdly those earnings in the army or service of the king which belonged also to the child and also remained entirely under his control. See also Asso & Mañuel, Institutes of Civil Law of Spain, Book I, Title VIII, Cap. 2. Schmidt, in his Civil Law of Spain and Mexico, at p. 22, deals very inadequately with this subject and fails not only to distinguish the three kinds of earnings, but also fails to distinguish between ownership by the father and mere administration by him for puposes of preservation.

The Fuero Real also provided that property acquired by the labor of the minor child or through gift from anyone became the minor's property; however, if acquired through the use of the father's properties it became the father's property. Fuero Real, Book 3, Title 4, Law 7.

[25] Santos v. Santos, 32 Cal. App. 2d 62, 89 P.2d 164.

[26] See Davis v. Campbell-Root Lumber Co. (Tex. Civ. App.), 231 S. W. 167.

becomes complete during the marriage. We saw that determination of the nature of the property as separate or community may become important where part of the consideration is paid prior to marriage and part during the marriage.[27] Somewhat similarly, some cases have arisen where the right to the property was initiated during the marriage, with payment of some of the consideration during that period, and completion of the acquisition with payment of the rest of the consideration after the marital partnership has terminated,[28] whether that termination be by some agreement of the spouses[29] or by reason of the termination of the marriage itself.[30]

If this initiation of a right to the property constitutes the acquisition of a property right — as for instance an equitable right[31] — it is presumably community property.[32] This presumption can be rebutted by evidence of such matters as the wording of the title, the nature and source of the consideration, or the intention of the party,[33] so that the completion of the acquisition after termination of the marital partnership definitely results in the property being entirely separate in nature.[34] Or, of course, if the initiation during marriage does not amount to or constitute a right of property and no acquisition takes place until afterwards, it may then very well be that the property is acquired completely as separate property.[35]

Of course, intention and the nature of the consideration can always be of weight.[36] And it must be borne in mind that in jurisdictions such as California, Idaho, Nevada and Washington, where property can be acquired as partly community and partly separate in the proportion to the consideration used,[37] acquisition in part during marriage with community consideration and completion of acquisition afterwards with separate consideration can produce a property that is part community and part separate.[38] In jurisdictions which consider that the initiation of a property right fixes the nature unalterably, this initiation during marriage renders the property community property,[39] although, of course, with the possibility of reimbursement for separate funds later used to complete the acquisition.[40] And in

[27] See ante, § 64.

[28] See cases cited infra, this section.

[29] As to right of spouses, in some states, to agree to terminate the sharing in acquests and gains, although the marriage continues, see post, § 135-139, 187.

[30] See post, Chap. X.

[31] See ante, § 66.

[32] Presumptions, see ante, §§ 60-61.

[33] See ante, §§ 60-61.

[34] And see post, §§ 77-79.

[35] See In re Kuhn's Estate, 132 Wash. 678, 233 P. 293, that a contract of purchase of realty that is executory and forfeitable gives neither legal nor equitable title or interest so as to represent inception or initiation of a property right. This particular view would seem to be overruled by In re Binge's Estate, 5 Wash. 2d 446, 105 P.2d 689.

[36] See ante, §§ 59-61; post, §§ 77-79.

[37] See ante, §§ 64-66.

[38] See generally this chapter.

[39] Creamer v. Briscoe, 101 Tex. 490, 109 S. W. 911, 130 Am. St. Rep. 869, 17 L.R.A.N.S. 174; Bishop v. Lusk, 8 Tex. Civ. App. 30, 27 S. W. 306.

[40] In re Kuhn's Estate, supra, hold-

Louisiana, the situation when the legal title is received is determinative,[41] unless it is a mere formality following actual completion of acquisition during the marriage.[42] Of course, in any jurisdiction, where the acquisition is actually, even substantially, completed during marriage, the mere receipt of the title later is a mere formality not affecting the already-acquired community character of the property.[43]

§ 68.3. — Quasi-community property.

Presently, in California, a type of property has been introduced by statute called "quasi-community property."[44] This is defined as all personal property wherever situated and all real property situated in California which has been acquired by either spouse while domiciled elsewhere — during the marriage, of course — which would have been community property of the husband and wife had the spouse acquiring the property been domiciled in California at the time of its acquisition.[45] It also includes property received in exchange for real and personal property, wherever situated, acquired other than by gift, devise, bequest or descent during the marriage while domiciled elsewhere.[46] Leasehold interests in real property are defined as real property and not as personal property.[47]

Since this is property sent into or brought into the state, usually on a change of domicile, it is discussed more appropriately in the following subdivision which deals with conflicts-of-laws problems.[48] Control, transmissibility on death, division on divorce and other such matters are also dealt with subsequently.[49]

§ 69. Property acquired through gift, inheritance, bequest or devise.[50]

The statute laws of Spain, from the time of the promulgation of

ing that property was not acquired until after termination of marriage but allowing reimbursement for community funds used.

[41] See Oppenheim, Comparative Study of Community Property Systems, 21 Temple L. Q. 235, especially as to passing of title of realty and personalty in Louisiana.

[42] Smith v. Anacoco Lumber Co., 157 La. 466, 102 So. 574.

[43] Similarly, in Ahern v. Ahern, 31 Wash. 334, 71 P. 1023, 96 Am. St. Rep. 912, as to public land where everything required by law to acquire land had been done by the spouses prior to death of wife, so that equitable title vested in spouses. Compare Ellis v. Ellis, 97 Cal. App. 2d 808, 218 P.2d 823, noted in 24 So. Cal. L. Rev. 195, taking contrary view as to public lands under similar facts

and holding issuance of patent to husband just after interlocutory decree of divorce made the land the husband's separate property.

[44] Actually separate property by the law of the place of acquisition but to be dealt with in California as if it were community property.

[45] Cal. Civ. Code, § 4803; Rogers v. Cranston, 53 Cal. Rptr. 572.

[46] Cal. Civ. Code, § 4803(b). Exchanges of property, see post, § 77; property acquired through gift, etc., see post, § 69.

[47] Cal. Civ. Code, § 4803. Leases and leasehold interests, see post, § 118.

[48] See post, § 92.1.

[49] See, e.g., post, §§ 123.1, 201.1, 227.1.

[50] Gifts of public lands, etc., see post, § 75.

the Fuero Juzgo in 693,[51] have explicitly made provision as to property acquired by the spouses during marriage by gift, inheritance, devise or bequest and have been most careful in protecting each spouse in his or her right to have such acquisition as separate property when it was given to such spouse alone.[52] This was fully recognized and thoroughly discussed by the Spanish jurisconsults.[53] Property so acquired was not acquired by labor, skill or industry so as to have been acquired by onerous title and, consequently, shared between spouses. Thus, it did not come under the head of acquisitions, dealt with by the laws, which were to be shared.[54] It was perfectly permissible for spouses to contract, however, that their sharing should relate to gifts and inheritances and the like as well as to those things acquired by onerous title.[55] Of course, if the gift, inheritance, devise or bequest was made to both spouses, they both took it as community property;[56] but if it was made to one alone it was the separate property of that spouse.[57]

Constitutional and statutory provisions of our community property

[51] Fuero Juzgo, Book 4, Title 2, Law 17.

[52] Novísima Recopilación, Book 10, Title 4, Law 1 et seq.

[53] See Commentaries of Matienzo, Azevedo and Gutiérrez to this law, and those of Llamas y Molina, Nos. 19-24 to Novísima Recopilación, Book 10, Title 4, Law 10. See likewise, Febrero, Librería de Escribanos, Testamentos y Contratos I, Cap. 1, XXII, No. 244. "For the partnership between husband and wife is not a partnership in all goods, but only a partnership in profits and acquisitions. This is shown by the fact that gifts, legacies, and inheritances are not shared between husband and wife." Matienzo, Gloss III, No. 10, to Nov. Rec. Law 1, Book 10, Title 4.

"But if either of them prove that those things which he or she inherited by will, or by intestate succession, or was donated by devise in the manner stated, whether they be movables, realty, or other kind without exception, they shall be his or hers privately, and should be separated and given to him or her, because the acquisition arising from the succession, does not belong to the (marital) partnership, as is provided by law." Febrero, Librería de Escribanos, Cinco Juicios I, Book I, Cap. IV, § 1, No. 4.

[54] "It is not by industry, labor or skill that an inheritance is acquired by husband or wife when they accept an inheritance from father, mother, other relative, or friend; and so it is not strange that such inheritances are not shared between husband and wife, whether they devolve by will or on intestacy, see Cod. 4.37.4. Thus an inheritance does not come under the head of acquisitions, Dig. 17.2.9 and the gloss of Dig. 17.2.8. In this way you can distinguish between contracts and quasi-contracts on the one hand and gifts and dying wishes on the other. Property acquired by onerous contracts is shared; but it is not so in the case of profits coming by gift without consideration (see the foregoing law and this law) or by will or on intestacy, according to our law." Azevedo, No. 2, to Nov. Rec. Laws 2 and 3, Book 10, Title 4.

It is necessary to keep in mind the difference between property acquired by "onerous" title, that is, by labor or other valuable consideration, and that acquired by "lucrative" title, that is, by gift, inheritance and the like. See ante, § 62.

[55] Azevedo, No. 4, to Nov. Rec. Laws 2 and 3, Book 10, Title 4.

Agreements between spouses, see ante, § 54; post, Chap. VIII.

[56] Novísima Recopilación, Book 10, Title 4, Law 1 et seq.

[57] Novísima Recopilación, Book 10, Title 4, Law 1 et seq.

"Note also from this and the following laws that a gift by the king or

states have been most careful to specify, particularly as to the wife, that property acquired by her during the marriage by gift, inheritance, devise or bequest shall be her separate property.[58] These do nothing more, actually, than continue the well-established principles of the Spanish community property system, but it is probable that their adoption or enactment resulted from the too frequent misconception of the Spanish community property principles and the mistaken idea, resulting from training in the English common law, that gifts or the like to the wife during the marriage, or at least half of them, would pass into the husband's hands if there were not explicit provisions relating thereto. With or without these constitutional and statutory provisions, the principles of the Spanish law of community are equally applicable now, that is, that a gift, inheritance, devise or bequest to one spouse alone during the marriage is the separate property of that spouse, but if made to both spouses they both take it as community property.[59] If spouses hold property together, the presumption in favor of community property must govern, and such property must be held as community property.[60] This is particularly true in jurisdictions which give little or no recognition to common-law tenancies[61] or which do not favor such tenancies.[62] Where common-law tenancies between the spouses are permitted, of course, express language of the instrument transferring the property may specifically rebut a holding in community.[63] But despite the foregoing, it would appear that in Texas there can be no gift to the community and a gift to the spouses jointly will be held by them as tenants in common, the interest of each being a separate property interest.[64] A similar expression of view has appeared in California, but without any reasons being given and actually in opposition to the ruling presumption in favor of community property.[65]

by any other person to one of the spouses becomes the private property of the donee and need not be shared, unless it was a gift to both spouses." Matienzo, Gloss IV, No. 2, to Nov. Rec. Law 1, Book 10, Title 4.

[58] Ariz. Rev. Stat. 1956, § 25-213; Cal. Civ. Code, § 5108; Idaho Code 1948, § 32-903; La. Civ. Code, art. 2334; Nev. Rev. Stat. 1956, § 123.130; N.M. Stats. 1953, §§ 57-3-4, 57-3-5; Texas Family Code 1969, §§ 5.01, 5.21, 5.61.

[59] See, e.g., In re Salvini's Estate, 65 Wash. 2d 442, 397 P.2d 811, quoting and following 1 de Funiak, § 69 (1943) and refusing to be bound by or to follow a contrary federal decision as to Washington law in Stockstill v. Bart, 47 Fed. 231.

See Vaughn, The Policy of Community Property and Interspousal Transactions, 19 Baylor L. Rev. 20, at p. 57.

[60] Presumptions, see ante, §§ 60, 60.1.

[61] As in Louisiana. See, e.g., Midstate Homes, Inc. v. Davis, (La.) 172 So.2d 326, as to gift to community if this is the donor's 'intention. See also La. Civ. Code, art. 2402.

[62] As in Arizona and Washington. See ante, §§ 60, 60.1; post, § 134.

[63] See ante, § 60.1; post, § 134.

[64] See Bradley v. Love, 60 Tex. 472; Ramwower v. Pieper, (Tex. Civ. App.) 114 S. W. 2d 1188.

[65] See, e.g., Andrews v. Andrews, 81 Cal. App. 2d 621, 186 P.2d 744, where relative of husband made wedding gift of a home to the spouses, executing deed in name of husband.

Many laymen become concerned over the matter of wedding gifts, especially where the marriage breaks up and a divorce follows. It is interesting to notice that many of the ladies who give advice on etiquette or advice to the lovelorn appear to think that wedding gifts belong to the bride, and they frequently assert that this is the "law."[66] Of course, if the gifts are intended for both by the donor, they belong to both in the manner discussed in the preceding paragraph.[67]

The important point about property received through gift, inheritance, bequest or devise is that it is considered gained or acquired through lucrative and not through onerous title; that is, no labor or industry has been expended on the part of the community to earn or gain such property.[68] But we must not be blinded or bemused by the mere words "inheritance, bequest or devise," for it is possible sometimes that they may actually cover something gained by onerous title. For example, suppose that a parent agrees to leave his son certain property in return for the son caring for and maintaining the parent during the last years of the latter's life. If the son is married and the care and maintenance supplied involves expense to the community, requires labor and industry by the son's wife as well as by the son, we have a definite case of property being earned by onerous title and the property should be considered community property.[69] The Spanish jurisconsult, Azevedo, in remarking that property received by one spouse by way of gift was not shared between the spouses, describes such gift as "without consideration."[70]

[66] The pronouncement of the late Emily Post in her work on etiquette is amusingly referred to by a judge in a lower court case in New York. See Avnet v. Avnet, 124 N.Y.S.2d 517.

And Mrs. Ann Landers, in the now defunct *San Francisco News-Call-Bulletin* of March 28, 1964, made a similar pronouncement as to "wedding gifts" but then recommended that a lawyer be consulted as to "checks" received, since these might be "considered community property" in some states. No explanation is given as to why a difference might exist between tangibles and intangibles or between community states and common-law states as to common or joint ownership.

[67] See, e.g., Andrews v. Andrews (Cal.), supra.

[68] Lucrative and onerous titles, see ante, § 62.

[69] See Andrews v. Andrews, 116 Wash. 513, 199 P. 981, wherein it was said: "The testimony was that the services to be performed in payment of the property to be acquired were performed by the appellant and his wife. It was their community property which housed and sheltered Joshua Andrews; it was the community money of the appellant and his wife which furnished, and was to furnish, the table from which Mr. Andrews, Sr., was to eat. The testimony shows that the appellant's wife did the housework and cooked the food, and did the other usual duties in the maintenance of the home, and in the care and attention given to Mr. Andrews, Sr. Everything that went into his maintenance was the joint effort of the appellant and his wife."

Similarly, in Frymire v. Brown, 94 Cal. App. 2d 334, 210 P.2d 707, where wife received property from father's estate for services, pursuant to agreement, court held property represented earnings of wife during marriage and was community property.

[70] See Azevedo, No. 2, to Nov. Rec. Laws 2 and 3, Book 10, Title 4. Remuneratory gifts, see the next section.

Attention is called to the matter of a spouse receiving during the marriage money or property pursuant to a compromise agreement growing out of litigation in which the spouse asserted a right of inheritance. Since the right of inheritance, if regarded as a property right, is separate property, absent any question of consideration for the claimed inheritance, whatever is received through the inheritance, as by way of a compromise agreement, is also separate property. It is immaterial whether the right of inheritance accrues before marriage[71] or during the marriage.[72]

§ 70. — Remuneratory gifts.

So far, in treating of gifts, we have been considering the simple gift or pure donation, such as is made from liberality, charity, affection or the like. The community property provisions of the Spanish codes relating to gifts to one or both spouses[73] were commonly interpreted as meaning that type of gift,[74] and were not applicable to a remuneration gift,[75] which was said not to be properly a gift, since it was by way of reward or remuneration.[76] The question then arose as to whether a remuneratory gift was acquired by lucrative title so as to remain the separate property of the donee or whether it was acquired by onerous title so as to be community property.[77] Interpretation of the views of the Spanish jurisconsults presents some difficulties because they were not entirely in accord in this matter of remuneratory gifts; some of the conflict of views pertains, however, only to the situations to which the term was applicable.[78] The majority applied the term to a gift, particularly a gift by the king, on account of or in appreciation of some antecedent or individual merit of the donee; and likewise to

[71] As in Estate of Clark, 94 Cal. App. 453, 271 P. 542.

[72] As in Succession of Land, (La.) 31 So.2d 609. See also Orr v. Pope, (Tex. Civ. App.) 400 S. W. 2d 614.

[73] See Novísima Recopilación, Book 10, Title 4, Laws 1, 2 and 5.

[74] Matienzo, Gloss VI, No. 4, to Nov. Rec. Law 2, Book 10, Title 4. Gutiérrez, Quaestio CXIX, No. 2, to the same.

[75] Matienzo, Gloss VI, No. 4, to Nov. Rec. Law 2, Book 10, Title 4.

[76] Matienzo, Gloss VI, No. 4, to Nov. Rec. Law 2, Book 10, Title 4. Gutiérrez, Quaestio CXIX, No. 2, to the same.

"This law, law 2 above and law 5 below [which were laws 1 and 5 in the Novísima Recopilación] relate only to mere and simple gifts, such as are made out of mere liberality and under no compulsion. Dig. 39.5.1. And so

they should not be applied to remuneratory gifts, which are not gifts properly so called. Words simply used must be interpreted according to their natural meaning." Matienzo, Gloss VI, No. 4, to Nov. Rec. Law. 2, Book 10, Title 4.

[77] Onerous and lucrative titles, see ante, § 62.

[78] See Llamas y Molina, No. 19 et seq. to Nov. Rec. Law 10, Book 10, Title 4.

"There are not reputed as properties of the partnership, commonly *gananciales*, . . . the inheritances and donations which may be made to one of them, although the remuneratory, if they are from service rendered by both, in the opinion of Gutiérrez, belong to the partnership; according to García in every case, and according to Matienzo in none." Novísimo Sala Mexicano, sec. 2a, Title IV, No. 4.

a gift in reward or remuneration of services rendered. In the former case they considered that the gift being given to the donee solely on account of his own merits was clearly his separate property.[79] In the latter case, they distinguished two situations. If the remuneratory gift was actually made to a spouse in reward for services rendered wholly at his separate expense and not at the expense of the community, a situation frequently existing where one rendered services to the king, it was the separate property of that spouse, since this was in the nature of a real gift, intended for the beneficiary alone (though its fruits were common property).[80] But where the gift was in remuneration of services rendered at the common expense of the spouses, it was considered not a gift in the true sense but as acquired by the community by onerous title,[81] on the basis that everything acquired by both spouses during the marriage by labor and industry belonged to both by halves.[82] That the wife, at the time the husband rendered the services, remained at home ruling the home, bearing the children and preserving the common goods was also a factor which was considered.[83] However, the view of the jurisconsults, that in this latter situation the gift received was community property, was confined to cases where the gift did not exceed in value the services rendered, but was commensurate with the services. If the gift exceeded the value of the services, it was said not to be shared since it was the result of liberality.[84]

The view of other jurisconsults, as expressed by Matienzo, was that a gift on account of some merit of the donee was not in the class

[79] "The following are not counted among the ganancial properties: . . . The remuneratory gifts which are made to one spouse by reason of individual merits." Escriche, Diccionario, vol. 2, "Ganancial Properties."

[80] "What view should we hold? For a true answer, two cases must be distinguished. The first when a husband receives a reward from the king or some prince for services rendered at the expense of the beneficiary himself, and then without doubt the gift although made by way of reward, will be the peculiar property of the husband to whom the gift is made, though the fruits may be common." Gutiérrez, Quaestio CXIX, No. 3, to Nov. Rec. Law 2, Book 10, Title 4.

Public grants and pensions, see post, § 75.

Fruits of separate property as community property, see post, § 71.

[81] "The second case is where the husband, who received the gift for his services, rendered them at the common expense of himself and his wife.

In this case it seems that the gift is to be shared equally between man and wife, since the expense was borne jointly by the property of each." Gutiérrez, Quaestio CXIX, No. 6, to Nov. Rec. Law 2, Book 10, Title 4. See also Azevedo, No. 14 to Nov. Rec. Laws 2 and 3, same.

[82] See Novísima Recopilación, Book 10, Title 4, Laws 1 and 5.

"There is also shared by the spouses any remuneratory gift made to one of them during the marriage for services and merits rendered during that period; it is not properly a mere and pure lucrative donation but satisfaction for work done or benefit received." Febrero, Librería de Escribanos, Cinco Juicios I, Book I, Cap. IV, § 1, No. 19.

[83] Gutiérrez, Quaestio CXIX, Nos. 2 and 7, to Nov. Rec. Law 2, Book 10, Title 4; Azevedo, No. 14, to Nov. Rev. Laws 2 and 3, same.

[84] See Matienzo, Gloss VI, No. 5 et seq., to Nov. Rec. Law 2; Gutiérrez, Quaestio CXIX, No. 2, to the same.

of remuneratory gifts but in the class of simple gifts or pure donations, which were always, so they argued, made on account of the merit of the donee.[85] However, since they considered such a gift on account of some merit of the donee as constituting separate property of the recipient, their only disagreement with other jurisconsults would seem to be a matter of terminology. Their view, as expressed by Matienzo, was that a remuneratory gift was properly to be considered only as one given in reward for services, in the sense that it was given in appreciation of the merit of the donee, and therefore, like any simple gift given on account of the merit of the donee was acquired by him by lucrative title and was not to be shared between the spouses.[86] It is to be borne in mind, however, that neither Matienzo nor those in accord with him questioned the fact that a gift clearly given to both spouses was community property or the fact that property earned by a soldier serving without pay was community property.[87]

When one considers the foregoing, it is not surprising to find our courts and writers frequently confused over the matter of gifts, so-called, given in return for services.[88] But despite the disagreement among some of the jurisconsults, it is not difficult to formulate the correct principles applicable, basing it on the view of the majority which seems the better reasoned. Thus, where the gift is actually remuneratory of services rendered or to be rendered by one spouse, and such services are at the expense of the community, for example in that they represent the expenditure of labor and industry and time to which the marital partnership is entitled and which in other channels would have advanced the interests of the marital partnership, it is clear that the remuneratory gift is the equivalent of any other property earned through labor and industry and is community property. This should be true even where the donor is not obligated to make

[85] Matienzo, Gloss IV, No. 3, to Nov. Rec. Law 2, Book 10, Title 4.
"Gifts by the king to one spouse go to that spouse alone, see law 2 (i.e., Law 1 of Novísima Recopilación, Bk. 10, Tit. 4) above at the end; for, as I have said many times, a gift is always presumed to have been made in consequence of antecedent merit, see Dig. 17.2.9 and 10, which says 'it does not accrue without any reason, it is presented on the ground of some desert in the party'." Matienzo, Gloss VI, No. 2, to Nov. Rec. Law 2.

[86] Matienzo, Gloss VI, Nos. 2, 7, to Nov. Rec. Law 2, Book 10, Title 4.
Notice particularly the discussion by Llamas y Molina, No. 19 et seq. to Nov. Rec. Law 10, Book 10, Title 4.

[87] Matienzo, Gloss VI, Nos. 1, 9, to Nov. Rec. Law 1, Book 10, Title 4.
Rewards or gains from military service, public grants, and the like, see post, § 75.

[88] In Fisk v. Flores, 43 Tex. 340, land deeded to the wife, the deed reciting that it was made in compensation for various services, was held to be the wife's separate property. The court waved aside the contention that the land was acquired by onerous title and thus community property and declared it a donation or gift pure and simple, basing its decision on quotations from a number of authorities (some of them on Roman law, a different thing from Spanish statutory law of community) defining donations made gratuitously and from liberality, and on Escriche's classification of a donation because of the recipient's individual merits as separate property.

the remuneratory gift.[89] On the other hand, a gift which, although in recognition or appreciation of some individual merit, is actually in the nature of a simple gift inspired by charity, affection, liberality or the like, is undoubtedly the separate property of the one to whom it is given. The first is acquired by onerous title, the latter by lucrative title.[90] But if the remuneratory gift apparently given, without compulsion, in reward of services is so in excess of the value of the services as to indicate that it is inspired by liberality rather than to remunerate the actual value of the services, it should be considered that the gift falls into the class of a pure donation.[91]

§ 71.   Fruits and profits of separate property.

In respect to the fruits and profits of separate property of the spouses we come to a matter wherein one of the principles of the Spanish community system has been radically modified in most, though not in all, of our community property states. Under the Spanish law of community property, no matter whether the separate property of one spouse was the spouse's separate property at the time of the marriage or was acquired as separate property by that spouse after the marriage, the fruits and profits of that separate property were community property, belonging to both of the spouses by halves.[92]

The decision fails to analyze the situation or grasp the distinction between a pure donation and remuneration for services rendered. If given in return for services and reasonably commensurate with the value of the services, it was not a pure donation but something earned by labor and industry and therefore community property.

See also Daigre v. Daigre, 228 La. 682, 83 So.2d 900, where a pension payable to the husband was held to be his separate property on the basis that since it was terminable at the will of the company it was a gratuity and did not arise out of his contract of employment.

And McKay remarks, that the "civil law authorities" do not make it very clear whether a remuneratory gift which is but little superior in value to the services rendered is community or separate property. McKay, Community Property, 2nd Ed., § 265. On the contrary, it would seem clearly to be shown that it would be community.

[89] Note that the Louisiana Civ. Code, art. 1525, provides: "The remunerative donation is not a real donation, if the value of the services to be recompensed thereby being appreciated in money, should be little inferior to that of the gift."

[90] And see Scott v. Ward, 13 Cal. 458.

Onerous and lucrative titles, see ante, § 62.

[91] While a somewhat exaggerated example, variations on the following time-worn theme spring to mind: the poor but kindhearted newspaper vendor who always helps the old blind lady across the street and one day finds himself the recipient of a gift or legacy of several thousand dollars in appreciation; obviously the gift is far in excess of the value of the services and springs from liberality.

[92] Novísima Recopilación, Book 10, Title 4, Laws 3 and 5.

"Let the fruits of the separate property of the husband or of the wife be common." Novísima Recopilación, Book 10, Title 4, Law 3.

Effect of Law 5 was that the returns and fruits of everything whatsoever which was the private property of either spouse had to be shared. Matienzo, Gloss V, No. 2, to Nov. Rec. Law 5. Text cited in Willcox v. Penn. Mut. L. Ins. Co., 357 Pa. 581, 55 A.2d 521, 174 A.L.R. 220.

This provision of the law is found as early as the year 1255 in the royal code of laws, the Fuero Real,[93] and was undoubtedly an original feature of the Visigothic system of marital community of property, for it appears among the Visigothic laws and custom in other parts of Europe.[94] This was based on the conception that, although each spouse retained ownership of his or her separate property, each unselfishly and unhesitantly had at heart the success and well-being of the marital union and that, accordingly, the fruits and income of all property of each naturally were to be devoted to the benefit of the marital union.[95]

As indicated above, the principle of the Spanish community property system that fruits and profits of the spouses' separate property are community property remains the law of some of our community property states, specifically in Idaho,[96] Louisiana,[97] and Texas;[98] and likewise, it may be mentioned, in Puerto Rico and the Philippines.[99]

[93] Fuero Real, Book 3, Title 3, Law 3.

[94] According to the Law of the West Goths in Sweden, *circa* 1200 A.D., if cattle or horses or the like were inherited by one spouse they belonged to the spouse inheriting them, but the increase thereof belonged to them both. The same was true as to crops of a farm inherited by either spouse. Law of the West Goths, according to the Manuscript of Eskil (Bergin's Translation), p. 53.

Text quoted in Bulgo v. Bulgo, 41 Hawaii 578, at 581.

[95] "For a wife is given a share of the fruits resulting from property which is not shared with the wife, just as she is entitled to a share of the fruits of all other goods whatsoever, acquired during the marriage, as is shown by the foregoing law." Azevedo, No. 5, to Nov. Rec. Law 5.

[96] Idaho Code Ann. 1948, § 32-906; Shovlain v. Shovlain, 78 Ida. 399, 305 P.2d 737.

However, the statute permits the instrument by which separate property is acquired by the wife to provide that the rents and profits thereof shall be applied to her sole and separate use, in which case she has the management and disposal of them. Rents and profits means income only. And see Malone v. Malone, 64 Ida. 252, 130 P.2d 674, stating that rents and profits means net profit, not gross income. See also Kohny v. Dunbar, 21

Idaho 258, 121 P. 544, Ann. Cas. 1913D 492, 39 L.R.A. (N.S.) 1107.

[97] La. Civ. Code, arts. 2386, 2402, provide that rents, issues and profits from husband's and wife's separate properties are community property with one exception, which exists with respect to wife's paraphernal property if she has declared by written instrument, duly notarized and witnessed that she reserves such property as her separate property. Prior to 1944 income from this paraphernal property was her separate property if she managed the paraphernal property. See Helberg v. Hyland, 168 La. 493, 122 So. 593. And see Oppenheim, 19 Tulane L. Rev. 200; Daggett, 6 La. L. Rev. 1.

[98] The uniform construction given Tex. Const. 1876, Art. 16, § 15 and Texas Family Code 1969, §§ 5.01, 5.21, 5.61, is that income from separate property is community property. See Frame v. Frame, 120 Tex. 61, 36 S.W. 2d 152, 73 A.L.R. 1512, also holding status of such rents and revenues could not be changed by agreement of spouses previous to their acquisition. As to such an agreement, see also Dixon v. Sanderson, 72 Tex. 359, 10 S.W. 535, 13 Am. St. Rep. 101, as to winnings of wife after using one dollar of her separate property to buy ticket on Louisiana State Lottery.

[99] See Civil Code, art. 1401, in force in Cuba, Puerto Rico and the Philippine Republic: "To the conjugal part-

But in the other community property states express statutory enactments have radically modified or changed this principle and provide that fruits and profits of separate property of a spouse shall also be the separate property of that spouse.[1] However, in Arizona the statute tends to be given a different interpretation and that state now more closely follows the Spanish law under which all of the increment of property during marriage, including earnings from the separate estate, was regarded as community.[2] The application of an "all or none" rule as to earnings or income from a separate business is discussed in a following section.[3]

Formerly in California, the Act of 1850, § 9, provided that "The rents and profits of the separate property of either husband or wife shall be deemed common property," but this provision was held unconstitutional and void by the state Supreme Court. It was said: "We think the legislature has not the constitutional power to say that the fruits of the property of the wife shall be taken from her and given to the husband or his creditor. This term 'separate property' has a fixed meaning in the common law, and had in the minds of those who framed the Constitution, the large majority of whom were familiar with, and had lived under that system. . . . It is not perceived that property can be in one, in fixed and separate ownership, with a right in another to control and enjoy all its benefits."[4] This quotation illustrates only too well the tendency of that court to interpret community of property by the common law, as well as the misconception as to the true meaning of community of property. It is patent that the court misunderstood what community property was and reckoned

---

nership belong: . . . 3. The fruits, income, or interest collected or accrued during the marriage from the partnership property, or from that which belongs to either one of the spouses."

Similarly, in the temporary community property states of Hawaii, Michigan, Nebraska, Oklahoma and Oregon, as to which, see ante, § 53.1.

[1] Ariz. Rev. St. 1956, § 25-213; Cal. Civ. Code, §§ 5107, 5108; Nev. Rev. St. 1956, § 123.130; N.M. St. 1953, §§ 57-3-4, 57-3-5; Wash. Rev. Code 1961, §§ 26.16.010, 26.16.020.

Rents, issues and profits of separate property, see Evans, 10 Calif. Law Rev. 271, 276; 126 Am. St. Rep. 112. See also Estate of Pepper, 158 Cal. 619, 112 P. 62, 31 L.R.A. (N. S.) 1092.

[2] See Nace v. Nace (Ariz. App.) 432 P.2d 896, citing 1 de Funiak (1943).

[3] See post, § 72.

[4] George v. Ransom, 15 Cal. 322, 324.

In Boyd v. Oser, 23 Cal. 2d 613, 145 P.2d 312, the California Supreme Court again referred to the decision in George v. Ransom and defended the holding therein.

In Laughlin v. Laughlin, 49 N.M. 20, 155 P.2d 1010, the court notices criticism of George v. Ransom in 1943 edition of this work, particularly with reference to the California court's reliance upon the common law to interpret community property principles and definitely refuses to fall into that error. To give separate property its common-law meaning would result in all separate property of the wife becoming the property of the husband, where personalty, and virtually the property of the husband, where realty, so as to be subject to his debts.

that just because it was under the husband's administration it was entirely his property (and, incidentally, as such, subject to the claims of his separate creditors).[5] Actually, the court was constitutionally bound to determine what was community and what was separate property, not by the common law, but by principles of the Spanish community property system which had been incorporated into the framework of the state constitution.[6] Under the principles of that system as incorporated into the constitutional framework, the terms "separate property" and "common property" had meanings as fixed as any meaning of "separate property" in the common law, and such meanings in the community property system were to be interpreted by its own principles and not by common law principles or concepts repugnant and alien to the community property system. The common law was adopted only insofar as it was not repugnant to the constitution.[7] It is only too plain that the court confused mere adminis tration by the husband of property equally owned by the spouses with the common law concept that "control" by the husband carried with it virtual ownership and the exclusive right of enjoyment. That the husband does not "enjoy" all the "benefits" of community property is a basic principle of the law of that subject.[8] The court fell into the error of depriving the husband of what was his share of the community property, according to the law in force at the time of the formation of the constitution and which was continued by the constitution, and fell into such error in order to avoid its previous error that community property is subject to the claims of separate creditors of the husband.[9]

§ 71.1. — Mineral Interests.

The importance of natural resources in the community property states requires that some special consideration be given these assets. As a general rule, the constituents of property take on the same

---

[5] This tendency to judge the control of the husband under the community property system, which is merely administrative and can be exercised only for the joint benefit of husband and wife, with the control of the husband at common law which gives him virtual right to enjoy all the benefits of the wife's property himself, is a common error. See post, Chaps. VII, VIII, XI.

This view of the community property as subject, in toto, to the claims of husband's separate creditors still prevails among the California courts, despite all enactments by the legislature. See post, Chap. IX.

[6] "It is not expressly declared [in the state constitution] what right or title she shall possess in the common property, nor is common property defined; but at the time of the formation of the Constitution, it was a term of well-known signification in the law then in force, and a right on the wife's part in property of that character was recognized by the Constitution." Dow v. Gould & Curry Silver Mining Co., 31 Cal. 630.

[7] See ante, § 51.

[8] See post, Chaps. VII, VIII, XI.

[9] Community property correctly subject to liability only for community debts, see post, Chaps. IX, X.

character as the property itself, so that proceeds derived from the sale of timber, sand, gravel, stones, minerals and the like are of the same character as the property from which the items were derived.[10] Relating this to mineral leases, three types of payments must be considered. Bonuses and royalties are not considered income or fruits of the property and money received in payment for them takes on the same character as the property sold.[11] On the other hand, delay rentals, sums paid by the lessee for the privilege of delaying his obligation to develop, are regarded as income and hence community property.[12]

§ 71.2.   — Trust property.

The eternal conflict between community property principles and common law principles is very evident when dealing with the law of trusts. It is settled that no community interest exists in property which one spouse holds or has title to as trustee.[13] The most difficult area is that of determining the ownership of trust income in the states in which income from separate property is community property. The principal question there is whether or not the payment from the trust is income from separate property, and hence takes on a community nature, or is itself a gift which the beneficiary received from the settlor, and hence separate property.

Although cases of this nature arising in Louisiana are few, it would appear to be settled there that income from a trust estate constitutes community property.[14] The authorities in Texas are not in accord, however. The earlier cases take the position that the income from the trust estate is the separate property of the beneficiary.[15] However, the later cases consider the collective rights of the beneficiary as the "property" from which the income flows, and the income from that property is community.[16]

[10] See Welder v. Commissioner of Internal Revenue, 148 F.2d 583, quoting Speer, Law of Marital Rights in Texas, 3rd Ed., § 411.

[11] Commissioner of Internal Revenue v. Gray, 159 F.2d 834 and United States v. Harang, 165 F.2d 106; Hager v. Stakes, 116 Tex. 453, 294 S. W. 835, and Tirado v. Tirado, 357 S. W. 2d 468 (Tex. Civ. App., writ dism.).

In Oklahoma, such royalties were community property.

[12] See Texas Co. v. Parks, 247 S. W. 2d 179 (Tex. Civ. App., writ ref'd, n.r.e.).

[13] Leslie v. Midgate Center Inc., 436 P.2d 201.

[14] United States v. Burglass, 172 F.2d 960, pointing out that "under Louisiana law, as now written, the fruits and issues of the separate property of the spouses fall into the community, the sole exception being where the wife has executed and placed of record a written instrument in accordance with the requirements of the 1944 act."

[15] Hutcheson v. Mitchell, 39 Tex. 488; Sullivan v. Skinner, (Tex. Civ. App.) 66 S. W. 680.

[16] See Mercantile National Bank v. Wilson, 279 S. W. 2d 650 (Tex. Civ. App., writ ref'd, n.r.e.) and Branscomb and Miller, Community Property and the Law of Trusts, 20 S. W. L.J. 699. But cf. Newman, Income

Where various married persons living in Texas were made beneficiaries of spendthrift trusts created in New York, administered in New York, and consisting of personal property, stocks and bonds, Judge Hutcheson of the Fifth Circuit pointed out that the controlling principle is that the interest of one spouse in movables acquired during marriage by the other spouse is determined by the law of the domicile of the parties when the movables are acquired. He further argued that, although the interest in the trust fund might be separate property of the beneficiary, the income therefrom was community property since under Texas law all income from separate property is community property. While not deciding that a trust could or could not be validly made upon terms giving income to a wife or husband for life as her or his separate property, he held that there was no language in the trusts involved to show any intention other than that the ordinary results of the law should take effect.[17] While the principle invoked by Judge Hutcheson is undoubtedly the correct one to be applied in such cases as these here in question, one criticism may be made. The only actual gift involved is a gift of trust income itself to a married person. Since this is given to a named married person it would seem to be given to such married person as separate property. Any so-called equitable interest in the trust has no value to the beneficiary since by the very nature of the trust as a spendthrift trust, it could not be sold or otherwise disposed of. All that is given, to repeat, is certain income and it would appear to be plainly the separate property of the recipient.[18] Of course, if this income which is separate property is invested by the Texas domiciliary and itself earns income, then such latter income is definitely community property under the Texas law.

§ 72.   — Difficulty arising from alteration of community property principle.

Difficulty has sometimes arisen over the case of profits of a business which was the separate property of one spouse before the marriage. In jurisdictions where the rents, profits and increases of separate property are community property, naturally profits after marriage from such a business are community property.[19] But in

Distributions from Trusts: Separate or Community Property?, 29 Texas Bar Journal 449, which reaches the conclusion that the income from the trust is separate property in reliance on the older cases. See also Davis, Income Arising from Trusts During Marriage is Community Property, 29 Texas Bar Journal 901, which pointedly refutes the Newman article.

[17] Com'r of Internal Revenue v. Porter, 148 F.2d 567; Commissioner of Internal Revenue v. Snowden, 148 F.2d 569; see also McFaddin v. Commissioner of Internal Revenue, 148 F.2d 570; Commissioner of Internal Revenue v. Sims, 148 F.2d 574.

[18] See ante, § 69.

[19] See Rigors v. Rigors, (Ida.) 347 P.2d 762; Peltier v. Beglevitch, 239 La. 238, 118 So.2d 395; Mehnert v. Dietrich, 36 La. Ann. 390; Gifford v. Gavord, (Tex. Civ. App.) 305 S. W. 2d 668.

jurisdictions when the profits from separate property are also separate property, there has been considerable disagreement as to the character of profits from a business which was the separate property of the owning spouse before marriage.[20] Theoretically, it would seem that such profits should continue to be separate property after marriage just as they were before marriage. But this overlooks the fact that after marriage the labor and industry of the other spouse perhaps contributes in some degree to the operation of the business, as well as the principle that gains through the industry of either spouse are community property. Certainly, if the business was the separate property of the husband before marriage and after marriage is the only source of income for the support of the husband and wife, we may have as a result that the only earnings or income of the husband are his separate property while the wife's services go to benefit the marital community. Her contribution to the marital partnership should certainly be offset by some contribution from the husband, for his labor and industry should certainly be credited in some way to the benefit of the community.[21]

The view taken by many of the courts is that each case must be determined with reference to its surrounding facts and circumstances and that therefrom must be determined what amount of the income is due to personal efforts of the spouses and what is attributable to the separate property employed. Dependent upon the nature of the business and the risks involved, it must be reckoned what would be a fair return on the capital investment as well as determined what would be a fair allowance for the personal services rendered.[22] Some

[20] See annotation, Profits from business operating on spouse's separate capital as community or separate property, 29 A.L.R. 2d 530; King, The Challenge of Apportionment, 37 Wash. L. Rev. 483.

[21] While in most of the cases the separate property or business is that of the husband, occasionally it is that of the wife, as in Balkema v. Deiches, 90 Cal. App. 2d 427, 202 P.2d 1069. The same principles must govern in either case.

[22] See In re Torrey's Estate, 54 Ariz. 369, 95 P.2d 990; Estate of Gold, 170 Cal. 621, 151 P. 12; Estate of Neilson, 57 Cal. 2d 733, 22 Cal. Rptr. 1, 371 P.2d 745; Jones v. Jones, 67 N.M. 415, 356 P.2d 231; Laughlin v. Laughlin, 49 N.M. 20, 55 P.2d 1010, quoting with approval similar language of first edition; State v. Sailors, 180 Wash. 269, 39 P.2d 397.

In Lake v. Lake, 4 West Coast Reporter 159, the Nevada court faced this problem and said, in part, "Under our statute the sole question is, whether property claimed by either spouse belonged to him or her at the time of marriage, or has since been acquired by gift, devise, or descent, or has come from the rents, issues, or profits of separate estate. And in this or any other case, if profits come mainly from the property rather than from the joint efforts of the husband and wife, or either of them, they belong to the owner of the property, although the labor and skill of one or both may have been given to the business. On the other hand, if profits come mainly from the efforts or skill of one or both, they belong to the community. It may be difficult in a given case to determine the controlling question, owing to the equality of the two elements mentioned, but we know of no

of the courts have decided that if the spouse contributing personal services takes a salary from the business, such salary shall be considered community property and the balance of the income the separate estate of the spouse owning the business or capital investment.[23] Somewhat similarly, it has been determined what would be the salary of one managing a similar business and that amount from the income has been determined to be community property and the amount beyond that determined to be separate.[24] Others have restricted the return from the separate property to the legal rate of interest with the balance regarded as community income unless the spouse owning the separate property can establish that a higher investment yield is warranted by the circumstances.[25]

While some of the cases, especially earlier cases, in Arizona, Nevada and Washington, have spoken in terms of apportioning the earnings between the community and the separate estates,[26] the more recent cases in those states have tended to favor the community by attributing the income entirely to the community where there has been any community industry involved. This has frequently been put on the basis of the presumption in favor of community property where community and separate properties are intermingled and the evidence is insufficient to show what amount is to be attributed to the separate estate.[27] Arizona is in the position of rather closely following the original Spanish law, under which all the increment in property

other method of determining to whom profits belong. In the use of separate property, for the purpose of gain, more or less labor or skill of one or both must always be given, no matter what the use may be; and yet the profits of property belong to the owner, and in ascertaining the party in whom the title rests, the statute provides no means of separating that which is the product of labor and skill from that which comes from the property alone." And see id., 18 Nev. 361, 4 P. 711, 7 P. 74.

In Witaschek v. Witaschek, 56 Cal. App. 2d 277, 132 P.2d 600, the court, citing previous authorities, declares that it is a question for the court to determine what portion of profits arising from capital which is separate property of the husband arises from the use of this capital and what part arises from his activity and personal ability; and it repeats that what is due to "personal character, energy, ability and capacity of the husband" is community property.

[23] See Van Camp v. Van Camp,

53 Cal. App. 17, 199 P. 885; Katson v. Katson, 43 N.M. 214, 89 P.2d 524; In re Herbert's Estate, 169 Wash. 402, 14 P.2d 6.

[24] Gilmore v. Gilmore, 45 Cal. 2d 142, 287 P.2d 769; Huber v. Huber, 27 Cal. 2d 784, 167 P.2d 708. These cases indicate that this method is to be used if possible and only if not usable then the capital investment method.

[25] See Pereira v. Pereira, 156 Cal. 1, 103 P. 488, 23 L.R.A. (N. S.) 880, 134 Am. St. Rep. 107, attempting to reach a solution of some of the problems involved. And see cases cited and discussed, 10 Calif. Law Rev. 271 at 279-284.

[26] See cases, preceding notes.

[27] Evans v. Evans, 79 Ariz. 284, 288 P.2d 775; Nace v. Nace (Ariz. App.) 432 P.2d 896 (citing 1 de Funiak, § 71); Ormachea v. Ormachea, 67 Nev. 273, 217 P.2d 355, 367 (citing 1 de Funiak, §§ 61, 77); Hamlin v. Merlino, 44 Wash. 2d 851, 272 P.2d 125; Le Sourd, Income from Busi-

during marriage, including earnings from the property, is community property.[28] Indeed, with the exception of California, all the states seem to favor the community by putting the burden of proof on the one seeking to establish that some part of the income is separate.[29] The California cases, with what seems to be one exception,[30] put the burden of proof on the party seeking to establish that some part of the income is to be credited to the community.[31]

With respect to particular kinds of property, attention may be called to agricultural lands. The rental value of such property can represent a normal return from such separate property which would also be separate property. Any amount in excess of such rental value while the property is under the management of the owner spouse should be attributed to the labor and industry of the spouse and should be credited to the community.[32] Certainly a fair return on the investment must be allocated to the separate property and any excess allocated to the community.[33]

§ 73.   — Improvements and increases in value.

Under the Spanish system, where the separate property of a spouse during the marriage increased in value for some intrinsic reason, such intrinsic increase was not shared with the other spouse as were fruits and income of the separate property.[34] Likewise, improvements to the property of one spouse made wholly at the

ness Involving Personal Services, 22 Wash. L. Rev. 19. And see Moore v. Moore, 71 N.M. 495, 379 P.2d 784.

[28] Nace v. Nace (Ariz. App.) 432 P.2d 896, 902 (citing with approval 1 de Funiak, § 71), and remarking that "In absence of a clear showing that a fair salary for the husband's efforts have been set, Arizona decisions have followed an 'all or none' rule, placing the earnings either all in the community or all in the separate estate, depending upon the nature of the property, with every presumption being in favor of the community."

[29] See cases cited, this section.

[30] Mueller v. Mueller, 144 Cal. App. 2d 245, 301 P.2d 90 (3rd District), also applying intermingling presumption.

[31] See, e.g., Cozzi v. Cozzi, 81 Cal. App. 2d 229, 183 P.2d 739, followed in Estate of Ney, 28 Cal. Rptr. 442. And see other California cases supra, this section.

[32] Laughlin v. Laughlin, 49 N.M. 20, 155 P.2d 1010; Conly v. Quinn, 66 N.M. 242, 346 P.2d 1030; Jones v. Jones, 67 N.M. 415, 356 P.2d 231; In re Witte's Estate, 21 Wash. 2d 112, 150 P.2d 595.

[33] Estate of Neilsen, 57 Cal. 2d 733, 22 Cal. Rptr. 1, 371 P.2d 745, overruling Estate of Pepper, 158 Cal. 610, 112 P. 62, 31 L.R.A. (N.S.) 1092, and followed in Mayhood v. La Rosa, 24 Cal. Rptr. 837, 374 P.2d 805 and Machado v. Machado, 25 Cal. Rptr. 87, 375 P.2d 55.

[34] See Matienzo, Gloss I, No. 88 et seq., to Nov. Rec. Law 1, Book 10, Title 4; Gutiérrez, Quaestio CXVI, No. 1, to the same; Azevedo, No. 8 et seq., to the same.
"The following are not counted among the ganancial properties: . . . the improvements or increases which the properties of either of them receive solely from the benefit of nature or of time, without industry or work." Escriche, Diccionario, vol. 2, "Ganancial Properties."

expense of that spouse through the use of that spouse's other separate property remained the property of the spouse making them.[35] But improvements to and increases of the property of either spouse, if originating from industry or labor or if due to the use of community property, pertained to the community.[36] However, since in the case of improvements it would be difficult or not feasible to separate them from the property to which they were made, such improvements continued during the marriage to belong to the spouse owning the separate property to which they were made, in the sense that they were necessarily subject to that spouse's control and disposition along with the separate property itself; but the value of the improvements were shared, in the sense that the other spouse owned a half interest in the value of such improvements, or was entitled to reimbursement to the extent thereof.[37] The valuation of the expenses or improvements, it has been said, was to be made on the basis of the time at which the expense was incurred or the improvement made,[38] and not on the greater value of the property resulting from the expenditure or improvement.[39] However, some of the commentators made a distinction between improvements that related to sowing or planting on separate land of a spouse and improvements that related to the erection of buildings on the land.[40]

The principle of the Spanish law of community has been largely followed in this country with respect to increases in value, during marriage, of the separate property of one of the spouses. If the

[35] Escriche, Diccionario, "Ganancial Properties."

[36] "The improvements and increases of the properties of either of them, if they have originated from industry or work, pertain to the partnership; but not if they are the work of time, as if to the land of the husband something has been added by alluvion." Novísimo Sala Mexicano, Sec. 2a, Title IV, No. 4.

[37] See Azevedo, No. 4, to Nov. Rec. Law 5, Book 10, Title 4, No. 8 et seq., to Nov. Rec. Law 1.

Money expended in improving separate property of a spouse gives the community a claim for the amount so spent but gives the community no claim to the property itself. Schmidt, Civil Law of Spain and Mexico, art. 48.

[38] Azevedo, No. 4, to Nov. Rec. Law 5.

[39] "This doctrine of the improvements, in the opinion of Febrero, is understood only as regards what is spent in making them, and not as regards the greater value of the land." Novísimo Sala Mexicano, Sec. 2a, Title IV, No. 4

[40] It has been said "that the improvements made of plantation, building, etc., are divided, with the difference that if the planting should be done in the particular land of either of the spouses, it shall be divided, deducting first the value of the land before it was planted, and giving or allowing that to the owner; but if a house has been built, or an oven or a mill has been erected on the land of one of them, the person on whose land the building or erection is made, shall have the benefit of it, and shall pay to the other the moiety of what the building cost." Asso and Mañuel, Institutes of the Civil Law of Spain, Book I, Title VII, Cap. 5, § 2.

Recompense under the French customs, see Brissaud, History of French Private Law, p. 849 et seq.

increases follow from general economic forces and not from any labor or industry, such increases belong wholly to the owner of the separate property. It is otherwise, of course, if the spouses' labor or industry or property have contributed to the increase, for then the community should share in the increase in the proportion to which the community contributed to the increase.[41] In other words, the distinction is between the increase in the capital value and the income. If the increase is a part of the capital value it will take on the same character. Thus, the natural increment of the value of a stock certificate takes on the same character as the basic certificate,[42] unless of course it conceivably could be shown that the activities of the owning spouse brought about this increase,[43] or some part of it,[44] as where he has actively managed the affairs of the corporation, so as to be responsible for the increased value.[45] Similarly, stock dividends and stock splits have been construed to have the same character as the original stock on the theory that the new stock effects no change in the corporate structure or in the actual interest of the stockholder.[46] As to cash dividends from stock, the view varies. In a state wherein income from separate property is community property,[47] the cash dividends are community property.[48] In a jurisdiction where the

[41] Gapsch v. Gapsch, 76 Ida. 44, 277 P.2d 278; Beal v. Fontenot, 111 F.2d 956, decided under La. Civ. Code 1870, art. 2408; Campbell v. Campbell, 62 N.M. 330, 310 P.2d 266; Johnson v. First Nat. Bank, (Tex. Civ. App.) 306 S. W. 2d 927; Conley v. Moe, 7 Wash. 2d 355, 110 P.2d 172, 133 A.L.R. 1089. Compare In re Buchanan's Estate, 89 Wash. 172, 154 P. 129. And see also Gump v. Commissioner of Internal Revenue, 124 F.2d 543 (California).

In Texas, where the statute provides that rents, issues and profits of separate property are community property, "increases of land" are excepted therefrom, Vernon's Tex. Stats. 1936, arts. 4613, 4614. Both as to land and personalty the Texas courts have distinguished increases in value due to community effort from increases due to intrinsic or economic reasons. Incidentally, oil and gas royalties from separate property are regarded by the Texas courts as separate property, as representing the proceeds of a sale of a part of the property, and not rents or profits. See ante, § 71.1.

[42] Kershman v. Kershman, 13 Cal. Rptr. 288; Gump v. Com'r of Int. Rev., 124 F.2d 540 (California).

[43] Where husband spent all his time managing his securities, some part of the increased value of his holdings must be attributed to his talent and skill. Witaschek v. Witaschek, 56 Cal. App. 2d 277, 132 P.2d 600. Cf. Kershman v. Kershman (Cal.) in preceding note.

[44] Weinberg v. Weinberg, 67 Cal. 2d 557, 63 Cal. Rptr. 13, 432 P.2d 709.

[45] See Buchanan's Estate, 89 Wash. 172; 154 P. 129.

Although husband owning stock was manager of corporation, stock's increased value not credited to him. Van Camp v. Van Camp, 53 Cal. App. 17, 199 P. 885.

[46] Daigre v. Daigre, 228 La. 682, 83 So.2d 900, noted in 30 Tulane L. Rev. 589; Tirado v. Tirado, (Tex. Civ. App.) 357 S. W. 2d 468, writ dism.; Duncan v. U.S., 247 F.2d 845 (Texas); Scofield v. Collector of Int. Rev., 131 F.2d 631 (Texas).

[47] See ante, § 71.

[48] See Scofield v. Collector of Int. Rev., 131 F.2d 631 (Texas).

statute provides that income from separate property is also separate property,[49] such cash dividends are separate property,[50] unless it can be shown that the dividends are wholly or in part produced by the spouse's labor or industry in which case to that extent the dividends will be community in character.[51]

The principle of the Spanish law of community in respect to improvements during the marriage to the separate property of one spouse at the expense of the community has, in effect, been fairly closely followed in this country. That is, that while the improvements made at the expense of the community, as with community funds or through labor and industry, belong to the spouse owning the separate property, nevertheless the value of such improvements is shared in the sense that the other spouse, or the heirs of such spouse, is entitled to reimbursement to the extent of half the enhanced value of the property. To what extent this right of the community to reimbursement is to be deemed a lien or charge or merely an equitable interest, the courts of the different jurisdictions are not in entire accord.[52]

With respect to the foregoing, it may be noted that both at common law and under the civil law, improvement of realty passes no form of title to the realty by reason of the improvement.[53] The improvement takes the same nature as the realty to which it is affixed, in the absence of any agreement to the contrary.[54] However, the civil law recognized a right of reimbursement in favor of the one whose

---

[49] See ante, § 72.

[50] Porter v. Porter, 67 Ariz. 273, 195 P.2d 133; Hicks v. Hicks, 27 Cal. Rptr. 307.

[51] Although husband worked for corporation, dividends did not result from any unusual talents or skill of husband. Porter v. Porter, preceding note.

[52] For adequate collections of cases, see 41 C.J.S., Husband & Wife, § 510; Oakes, Speer's Marital Rights in Texas, § 414; annotations, 77 A.L.R. 1021; 54 A.L.R. 2d 429. See especially, de Funiak, Improving Separate Property or Retiring Liens or Paying Taxes on Separate Property with Community Funds, 9 Hastings L. J. 36.

California and some jurisdictions influenced by California decisions, seem to make the distinction, however, that when the husband uses community funds to improve the separate property of the wife, in the absence of a specific agreement, his intention is presumed to be that such improvements are to become a part of the separate property of the wife without any interest therein on his part. Shaw v. Bernal, 163 Cal. 262, 124 P. 1012; Dunn v. Mullan, 211 Cal. 583, 296 P. 604, 77 A.L.R. 1015; Lombardi v. Lombardi, 44 Nev. 314, 195 P. 93. See also Bank of Orofino v. Wellman, 26 Idaho 425, 143 P. 1169; Tilton v. Tilton, 85 Idaho 245, 378 P.2d 191. And see post, § 142.

Right of creditors of community to reach such improvements as community property, see post, § 174.

[53] Kingsberry v. Kingsberry, 93 Ariz. 217, 279 P.2d 893; Shaw v. Bernal, 163 Cal. 262, 124 P. 1012; Dunn v. Mullan, 211 Cal. 583, 296 P. 604, 77 A.L.R. 1015; also Peck v. Brummagin, 31 Cal. 440, 89 Am. Dec. 195; de Funiak, 9 Hastings L. J. 36.

[54] See Brown v. Brown, 58 Ariz. 33, 119 P.2d 198; Shaw v. Bernal, preceding note.

funds were used without consent.[55] Likewise, our common law severity is softened or offset by equitable principles.[56] Thus, while the common law might recognize no title in the realty on the part of one whose funds were used to improve it, equity would provide a means of relief. In equity, one in a fiduciary relation, in that funds of another are in his control, who uses such funds for his own private ends, would find a constructive trust or equitable lien imposed to protect the one whose funds were so used.[57] When we consider that a spouse managing community funds occupies fiduciary relation to the other spouse and must not act in fraud or prejudice of the rights of such other spouse,[58] the improvement of his or her own separate property with community funds is fraudulent or prejudicial to the rights of the other.[59] Therefore an equitable lien is authorized in favor of the other spouse at least to the extent of that spouse's share in the community funds used or,[60] in order to prevent profit to the wrongdoer, more properly a constructive trust to the extent of the enhanced or increased value of the separate property brought about by the use of the community funds should be imposed.[61] All of the community property states take the position that improvements to separate property at the expense of the community property do not change the nature of the property so improved. All do recognize some right on the part of the community for reimbursement. In some, this is limited to the amount of the funds expended.[62] In others, the community is entitled to reimbursement in the amount by which the use of the community assets increased or enhanced the value of the property improved.[63] The

[55] See Buckland & McNair, Roman Law and Common Law; Dawson, Unjust Enrichment.

[56] See Dawson, Unjust Enrichment; de Funiak, Handbook of Modern Equity.

[57] Bogert, Trusts & Trustees, § 492 (1946); 4 Scott, Trusts, § 514.2 (2d Ed., 1956); Rest. Trusts, § 201.

[58] See post, § 113 et seq.

[59] See post, Chap. VII, B.

[60] See, e.g., Lawson v. Ridgeway, 72 Ariz. 253, 233 P.2d 459; Conley v. Moe, 7 Wash. 2d 355, 110 P.2d 172, 133 A.L.R. 1089; Jones v. Davis, 15 Wash. 2d 567, 131 P. 2d 433.

[61] See Bogert and Scott, cited supra.

[62] Kingsberry v. Kingsberry, 93 Ariz. 217, 379 P.2d 893; Rothman v. Rumbeck, 54 Ariz. 443, 96 P.2d 555. Cf. Lawson v. Ridgeway, supra, recognizing increase in value.

[63] Shaw v. Bernal (Cal.) and Dunn v. Mullan (Cal.), supra; Tilton v. Til-ton, 85 Ida. 245, 378 P.2d 191; Gapsch v. Gapsch, 76 Ida. 44, 277 P.2d 278; Succession of Singer, 208 La. 463, 23 So.2d 184; Williams v. Williams, (La. App.) 199 So.2d 401; Boyer's Succession, 36 La. Ann. 506; La. Civ. Code, art. 2408; Campbell v. Campbell, 62 N.M. 330, 310 P.2d 266; Lindsay v. Clayman, 151 Tex. 593, 254 S. W. 2d 777; Waheed v. Waheed, (Tex. Civ. App.) 423 S. W. 2d 159; Birch v. Rice, 37 Wash. 2d 185, 222 P. 2d 847.

But see Depas v. Riez, 2 La. Ann. 30; McClelland's Succession, 14 La. Ann. 776; and La. Civ. Code, art. 507, providing: "If the owner of the soil has made constructions, plantations and works thereon, with materials which did not belong to him, he has the right to keep the same, whether he has made use of them in good or bad faith, on condition of reimbursing their value to the owner of them and paying damages, if he has thereby caused him any injury or damage."

value in point is that existent when the question or controversy arises.[64]

Most of the community property states take the view that the same principles apply whether a managing husband improves his own separate property or the wife's separate property with community assets.[65] So, for example, in Washington, the same equitable lien is applicable in either event.[66] But in California[67] and in Idaho[68] and Nevada,[69] which follow the California view, if the husband uses community funds to improve the wife's separate property, it is presumed that he intends to make a gift to her of his interest in such funds. In the absence of any agreement to the contrary, the title to the improvements follows the title to the separate property and is in the wife. The presumption may be rebutted, of course, and if rebutted successfully, there is the right to reimbursement to the extent of the value added by the improvements.[70]

Similarly, also, to the principles of Spanish community property law, improvements upon separate property of a spouse made with the separate property or proceeds of the separate property of that spouse are likewise that spouse's separate property.[71] In addition to the foregoing, a third situation arises where one spouse improves his or her own separate property with or by means of the separate property of the other spouse. Thus, where the husband improves his separate property through the use of the separate property of the wife, the wife, or her heirs, is entitled to reimbursement to the extent of the value of her separate property so used.[72] If, however, separate property of the husband is used to improve the wife's separate property there is some conflict in the views of the various jurisdictions, one view being that the husband is entitled to reimbursement to the extent of the value of his property so used,[73] the other view being that in the absence of evidence showing definitely otherwise, as in the absence of a specific agreement, the use of the husband's separate property is presumed to be a gift to the wife and to become a part of the separate property of the wife without any interest therein on his part.[74]

---

[64] Value at date of dissolution of marriage, see, e.g., Boyer's Succession, 36 La. Ann. 506.

[65] See cases cited above.

[66] See Conley v. Moe, supra.

[67] Dunn v. Mullan, supra.

[68] Shovlain v. Shovlain, 78 Ida. 399, 305 P.2d 737; Bank of Orofino v. Wellman, 26 Ida. 425, 143 P. 1149.

[69] Lombardi v. Lombardi, 44 Nev. 314, 195 P. 93.

[70] For an agreement as to improvement, see Wheeland v. Rogers, 20 Cal. 2d 218, 124 P.2d 816; Shaw v. Bernal (Cal.), supra.

[71] See Brown v. Brown, 58 Ariz. 333, 119 P.2d 938; Seligman v. Seligman, 95 Cal. App. 683, 259 P. 984; Mackenroth v. Pelkey, 171 La. 842, 132 So. 365; Glaze v. Pullman State Bank, 91 Wash. 187, 157 P. 488.

In Evans, 31 Yale Law Jour. 734, 741, this situation is omitted from the classifications attempted.

[72] See Parrish v. Williams (Tex. Civ. App.), 53 S. W. 79.

[73] See Brady v. Maddox (Tex. Civ. App.) 124 S. W. 739.

[74] Carlson v. Carlson, 10 Cal. App. 300, 101 P. 923.

In virtually all of the cases covering the points discussed in this section, the husband has been the manager. But it should logically follow, of course, that the same principles must apply where the wife is the manager of the community property.[75]

Another matter requiring notice is the fact that when the managing spouse applies community assets to improve separate property, such manager may be removing from the reach of creditors assets which were subject to their claims and placing them in property not ordinarily subject to their claims. This is discussed subsequently.[76]

§ 74.   Public or governmental offices and their income.

Many public offices in Spain were of the kind that could not be purchased, sold or assigned, such as offices of justice. They ended with the life of the holder or at the will of the king; not being property they were not shared between the spouses. Nevertheless, the fruits and salaries of such offices were subject to be shared between the spouses, just as were the fruits of other things.[77] On the other hand, pursuant to the European practices of that day, many royal offices or offices of a public nature had a value in themselves, frequently being acquired by gift of the king or by purchase, and if acquired by a spouse before marriage, or if obtained after marriage by gift to that spouse alone or by purchase wholly with separate property of that spouse, the office remained the separate property of that spouse but, it is to be specially noted, its income and fruits were common property. However, if it was purchased or obtained with common funds, or was a gift to both or a gift in consideration of services actually rendered at the common expense, the office as well as its income and fruits was common property of the spouses.[78] This is not a problem that is of importance to us today under our form of government, in which public office is not "property" so as to be "owned" by the occupant but is in the nature of a public trust.[79] With

[75] Wife as manager, see post, § 113 et seq.

[76] See post, §§ 167, 168.

[77] See Azevedo's Commentaries, No. 1 to Nov. Rec. Law 5, Book 10, Title 4.

[78] See Novísima Recopilación, Book 10, Title 4, Laws 1, 2, and 5, commentaries of Matienzo, Gloss VI to Nov. Rec. Law 2, Glosses I-IV to Nov. Rec. Law 5; Azevedo, No. 25 to Law 1, Nos. 14, 15 to Laws 2 and 3, No. 1 et seq. to Law 5; Gutiérrez, Quaestio CXIX to Law 2.

"In the same manner as whatever the husband acquires in war is shared by the wife in the case propounded, so likewise what he gains with the offices of judge, lawyer, notary or others similar, during the marriage; as these offices are quasi-castrenses, and whatever they produce are fruits which, whatever their nature may be, belong to them by halves . . . but their ownership, which are the offices themselves, or the authority to exercise them, if the king grants them to the husband, belong to him separately, and so the wife takes nothing therein." Febrero, Librería de Escribanos, Cinco Juicios I, Book I, Cap. IV, § 1, No. 22.

[79] "In our form of government it is fundamental that a public office is a public trust . . . and not a vested property right." McQuillin, Municipal Corporations, § 436.

Nevertheless, it seems that the mari-

us, the salary or fees of a public officer constitutes community property just as any other earnings.[80]

Since the wages or salaries earned by either spouse are community property in which the other spouse has an ownership interest, a spouse who is a public officer and employs the other as an assistant in the public office thereby receives compensation in addition to his or her salary as a public officer in violation of law. While an agreement might be entered into between the spouses that the wages or salary of the assistant or employee is to be the separate property of the latter, the actuality and validity of such agreement must be established by the evidence.[81]

§ 75. Rewards or gains from military service, public grants, military pensions and the like.

These matters are dealt with here purely for purposes of convenience.[82] Actually, they might be classifiable as acquisitions or gains by onerous title or classifiable as donations or gifts acquired by lucrative title, dependent upon the circumstances of the individual case. Under the Spanish law of community property, whatever a soldier earned or gained while serving in the army with pay became his separate property, but if he was serving without pay, anything then earned or gained was community property.[83] The reason for this was that as a paid soldier he was supporting himself, paying his own expenses and drawing nothing from the community, while if serving without pay he was necessarily supporting himself and paying his expenses from the common property, and anything gained in the latter situation inured to the community which was bearing the expenses.[84] Apparently, if a paid soldier, his pay was not considered

tal community may engage in the business or calling of notary public if it chooses, and can obtain authority for one of its members so to act, just as it may as to the practice of law or medicine; although it cannot be elected to an office and discharge the duties of that office. Kangley v. Rogers, 85 Wash. 250, 147 P. 898.

[80] See Kangley v. Rogers, 85 Wash. 250, 147 P. 898; Moore v. Moore, 71 N.M. 495, 379 P.2d 784.

[81] State v. Miller, 32 Wash. 2d 149, 201 P.2d 136, where agreement not established by evidence, salary expended on vacations and for children, since these things benefited the community.

[82] Pensions of employees generally, see ante, § 68.

[83] Novísima Recopilación, Book 10, Title 4, Laws 2 and 5.

[84] Matienzo, Gloss V, to Nov. Rec. Law 2, and Gloss III to Law 5; Febrero, Librería de Escribanos, Cinco Juicios I, Book I, Cap. IV, § 1, No. 21.

"Under the rule announced in Hughey v. Barrow, 4 La. Ann. 248, a pension awarded the husband for military services rendered the sovereign would fall into the community, if the husband served without pay and the community supported him in whole or in part during the term of the service. The reason for so holding is obvious. The community was being deprived of his services to it, and the remuneration given in satisfaction thereof was but an acquirement of the community, as would be the case had the services been rendered to an individual." Howard v. Ingle (La. App.), 180 So. 248.

earnings or gains which fell into the community, on the ground that his services as a soldier were not for the furtherance of the interests of the marital partnership but the interests of his king and country and the pay was given him as his separate property the better to insure this.[85]

A comparable situation with us is the one in which a soldier serving with pay (as is usually the case with us)[86] is made the recipient of a donation ("bonus") of public land or money, or a pension, in reward for his services. Whether placed on the ground just discussed or on the ground of a donation made to one person and intended for him alone, a number of cases in this country have held that a donation of public land or the like to a soldier for his services to his country was not acquired by onerous title and was his separate property.[87] But in some cases where land is offered to those who would volunteer to serve their country, it was held that the land was earned by onerous title under a contract for services and was thus community property.[88] In addition, in the latter cases, there may be some ground for arguing that, under the aforementioned Spanish principles of community property law, the service as a volunteer without pay made the property so gained community property.[89] Of course the bonus or additional compensation may have been given for military services rendered prior to marriage, so that although not actually received until after marriage it constitutes separate property.[90]

In the matter of a military pension much is dependent, of course, upon the circumstances of each individual case. The pension may have been intended as a gift to the recipient alone or may have been awarded for services rendered prior to marriage.[91] In the more recent

[85] "Our law says that not only do pay and allowances coming from the King or on active service, when a husband is engaged in war or the King's service for a salary, belong to the husband alone, but so also do all other profits which he makes therein over and above salary." Azevedo, No. 14, to Nov. Rec. Laws 2 and 3.

"But whatever he saves of his salary outside of the campaign, whether or not he be pensioned or retired from the service, and whatever he purchases and gains therewith, shall be shared by both." Febrero, op. cit., as in preceding note.

[86] With us, of course, pay received by a spouse while in the armed services is community property. See McElroy v. McElroy, 32 Cal. 2d 828, 198 P.2d 683.

[87] See cases cited, 96 Am. St. Rep. 922; Am. St. Rep. 116.

[88] Barret v. Spence, 28 Tex. Civ. App. 344, 67 S. W. 921; Kircher v. Murray, 54 Fed. 617, aff'd 60 Fed. 48, 8 C. C. A. 448.

[89] See Hughey v. Barrow, 4 La. Ann. 248.

[90] See Succession of Lewis, 192 La. 734, 189 So. 118, and cases cited post.

Generally, see ante, § 64.

[91] See Johnson v. Johnson (Tex. Civ. App.), 23 S. W. 1022, where a pension was given to a husband by the federal government for services as a soldier in the Civil War. Not only did the statute granting the pension (U.S. Rev. Stat. § 4747) provide that it inured wholly to the benefit of the pensioner, but even if it was considered as earned it would be separate property because his war services were rendered before marriage. However, the court elected to base its

cases, the rule appears to be followed that if the services giving rise to the grant or pension were performed during marriage, the property received in return for such services is community property.[92] There is even authority that if the pension or grant is received during marriage, it is community property, and this regardless of the unmarried status of the recipient at the time he rendered the military services.[93]

In the sense that "retired pay" of one who has been in the armed service of his country is compensation for services rendered in the past it is community property (if the services were rendered during marriage), but the mere right to retirement pay in the future is a mere expectancy which is not subject to division as community property, according to dictum of the California court in holding that "reserve pay" of one transferred to the naval reserve was community property as to that amount of it as was received up to the time of dissolution of the marital community.[94]

When we consider grants of public land (apart from those made for military services), we are faced again with the question whether it is a pure donation, intended for the recipient alone, in which case it is his separate property, or whether it is a pure donation, but intended for both spouses, in which case it is community property, or, finally, whether it has actually been gained or acquired at the community expense and is thus community property.[95] This was a

decision on the ground that the pension was purely a gift from the federal government, and as such under the Texas statute was his separate property. As to pension, see also Llamas y Molina, Nos. 25, 26, to Nov. Rec. Law 10, Book 10, Title 4.

The Texas courts now recognize military pensions as community property if earned during marriage, or at least to the extent earned during marriage.

See also Howard v. Ingle (La. App.), 180 So. 248, as to pension granted for military services rendered prior to marriage. Moore v. Moore (Tex. Civ. App.), 192 S. W. 2d 929, as to bonus received during marriage for services rendered before marriage.

[92] See, e.g., Succession of Scott, 231 La. 381, 91 So.2d 574.

Where federal statute provided for continuing payment of wages to civilian employee of navy during period he was prisoner of war of enemy, such payments were not a gift but were compensation for a consideration so as to make them community property and distributable

as such upon his death. Estate of Worley, 87 Cal. App. 2d 760, 197 P.2d 773.

[93] See Sullivan v. Albuquerque Nat. Trust & Sav. Bank, 51 N.M. 456, 188 P.2d 169.

[94] See French v. French, 17 Cal. 2d 775, 112 P.2d 235, 134 A. L. R. 366. But cf. Johnson, Retirement Benefits as Community Property on Divorce Cases, 14 Baylor L. Rev. 284, in which a contrary conclusion is reached.

[95] "There are several sources of grants of public land: e.g., the homestead and the pre-emption acts; stone and timber, mining, and coal land acts; grants by the Federal government for military services, and similar grants by a state, as in Texas; Texas headright certificates and homestead acts; and the Mexican colonization act." Evans, Community Property in Public Lands, 9 Calif. Law Rev. 267, an excellent analysis of the various situations involved. See also 96 Am. St. Rep. 916; 126 Am. St. Rep. 116.

In Ahern v. Ahern, 31 Wash. 334, 71 P. 1023, 96 Am. St. Rep. 912,

question which had to be determined in the case of Spanish and Mexican land grants,[96] and equally as well to grants by our federal or state governments. Our American cases are not always in accord, but it is clear from a study of them that differences in result have usually arisen from statutory differences and that there has been a commendable effort to determine, and the basing of the decision on such determination, whether the public land is acquired wholly by one spouse, as by donation of the government or at his own expense, or whether, as has sometimes been the case of acquisition of homesteads, whether the public land is acquired for the benefit of both spouses or at the expense of the community. By "statutory differences," just referred to, is meant the fact that the language of the particular statute is often of importance, since by its terms it may clearly provide that the grant is to inure wholly to the benefit of the one to whom granted; or the statute may indicate that there is no inception of title from mere occupancy or possessory right to which perfection of title would relate back.[97] Nevertheless, it has been said by the United

---

where a homestead entry was made by a husband during the life of the wife but the patent was not obtained until after her death, it was held that the homestead was actually acquired by the combined efforts of the spouses, that everything actually required by law to earn the title had been done, and that equitable title had vested in the community. See also Doucet v. Fontenot, 165 La. 458, 115 So. 655. Compare McDonald v. Lambert, 43 N.M. 27, 85 P.2d 78, 120 A. L. R. 250.

Acquiring public lands partly during marriage and partly before or after marriage, see ante, §§ 64.1, 68.2.

[96] See Novísima Recopilación, Book 10, Title 4, Laws 1, 2, 3 and 5, post Appendix I, E, 2; and ante, § 69. See also Halleck, Collection of Mining Laws of Spain and Mexico; Rockwell, Compilation of the Spanish and Mexican Law, in relation to mines and titles to real estate; White, New Collection of Laws, Charters and Local Ordinances.

As to Spanish or Mexican grants passed upon by our courts, see Scott v. Ward, 13 Cal. 458; Noe v. Card, 14 Cal. 576; Boissier v. Metayer, 5 Mart. (La.) 678; Gayosa De Lemos v. García, 1 Mart. N. S. (La.) 324; Frique v. Hopkins, 4 Mart. N. S. (La.) 212; Heirs of Rouquier v.

Executors of Rouquier, 5 Mart. N. S. (La.) 98; Hughey v. Barrow, 4 La. Ann. 248; Yates v. Houston, 3 Tex. 433.

In McKay, Community Property, 2nd Ed., § 272, the impression is given, based on quotations from the Fuero Juzgo, that grants or gifts from the king were always the separate property of the recipient, except where given to a soldier serving without pay. But it must be borne in mind that the king might intend the grant or gift for both spouses, in which case it was clearly provided that it should be community property. See Novísima Recopilación, Book 10, Title 4, Law 1. Grants or gifts to the husband which were intended for him alone were usually those given for military services. See Novísima Recopilación, Book 10, Title 4, Law 5.

[97] See cases collected, 96 Am. St. Rep. 916; 126 Am. St. Rep. 116; 41 C.J.S., Husband and Wife, § 486; Evans, Community Property in Public Lands, 9 Calif. Law Rev. 267.

Property acquired under Federal Stone and Timber Act as separate property of grantee, see Guye v. Guye, 63 Wash. 340, 115 P. 731.

Federal pension statute providing that pension was to inure wholly to benefit of recipient, see Johnson v. Johnson (Tex. Civ. App.), 23 S. W. 1022, ante, n. 84.

States Supreme Court that although the question of whether title to land which had been the property of the United States has passed is to be resolved by the laws of the United States, whenever according to those laws title has passed, then like all other property in the state it is subject to state law.[98]

§ 76.   Unlawful earnings or gains.

One very definite exception in the Spanish law of community of acquests and gains existed in the case of ill-gotten acquisitions, that is, those unjustly, dishonestly or unlawfully gained by one spouse. There was no right in the other spouse to share in such acquisitions.[99] Statutes relating to the sharing of property acquired were interpreted to refer only to property justly acquired.[1] Moreover, it was considered that there could be no contract of partnership with a dishonest object, and accordingly profits therefrom could not be shared.[2] The presumption, however, was that acquisitions were justly made unless the contrary was clearly shown. And if the wife's heirs, after her death, claimed her half of the community, the husband was estopped to claim that the acquisitions were unlawfully made by setting up his own wrong.[3] For this latter reason, once unlawful acquisitions were actually put into the common stock, they were subject to be divided equally between the spouses and their heirs except as against the claims of the true owners, to whom, of course, satisfaction had to be made from the whole of the wrongdoer's property. Indeed, the spouse who had not made the wrongful acquisitions might be subject to a penalty if knowing that the property belonged to some one else or was unlawfully acquired; but if ignorant of this, the spouse only had to restore the unlawful acquisitions from the common stock.[4]

The spouse making the unlawful acquisitions could during his lifetime restore such unlawful acquisitions before they were put into the common stock without the necessity, of course, of the consent of the other spouse.[5]

This situation as to unlawful earnings and gains seems one that

---

[98] Wilcox v. McConnell, 13 Pet. (U. S.) 517, 10 L. Ed. 264.

Mere oral agreement made by entryman, before title had passed to him by patent, made to his prospective wife that property should be community property was said by New Mexico court to have no validity. McDonald v. Lambert, 43 N.M. 27, 85 P.2d 78, 120 A.L.R. 250. But consider overruling effect of Chavez v. Chavez, 56 N.M. 393, 244 P.2d 781, discussed by Clark, Community of Property and the Family in New Mexico, 14, 15.

[99] Matienzo, Gloss I, Nos. 61-64, to Nov. Rec. Law 1, Book 10, Title 4; Azevedo, Nos. 6, 7, to the same.

[1] Matienzo, Gloss I, No. 61, to Nov. Rec. Law 1.

[2] Matienzo, Gloss I, No. 62, to Nov. Rec. Law 1.

[3] Matienzo, Gloss I, No. 63, to Nov. Rec. Law 1.

[4] Matienzo, Gloss I, No. 64, to Nov. Rec. Law 1.

[5] Azevedo, No. 7, to Nov. Rec. Law 1. See also Matienzo, Gloss I, No. 64, to the same.

has generally been overlooked by writers in this country.[6] Nevertheless, it is a situation that has arisen here, and undoubtedly will arise again. Therefore, care should be taken to keep in mind the principles of the law of community property in this matter.[7]

§ 77.   Property acquired through the use of separate or community property.[8]

We have already seen that under the Spanish codes "everything the husband and wife may earn or purchase during union" they both owned by halves.[9] But in considering this it is also necessary to bear in mind that it was also provided by statute that the realty or other things owned as separate property before marriage remained the separate property of the spouse after marriage.[10] What was the situation, then, where after marriage such separate property was exchanged, for, or used for the purchase or acquisition of, other property? It was unquestioned that where such property was exchanged for other property, the property received in exchange took the place of that originally owned and was the separate property of the spouse. Similarly, where after marriage the spouse sold his or her separate property and used the proceeds of the sale to buy other property, the latter property took the place of the former and was the separate

[6] McKay, Community Property, 2nd Ed., is an exception. See chapter 21 thereof.

[7] In Estate of Gold, 170 Cal. 621, 151 P. 12, a proceeding to determine heirship to the estate of a decedent and whether profits made by him after marriage were community or separate property where they were derived from winnings in a gambling partnership, it was held that under the Cal. Civ. Code, § 163 (§ 5108 as of January 1970), any property acquired by a husband during marriage, other than by gift, bequest, devise or inheritance, was community property and that accordingly these gambling winnings were community property. While we may well question whether, under correct community property principles, such statute could be construed to include other than lawfully acquired gains, it would appear that despite itself the court reached the correct conclusion if we consider that once unlawful acquisitions are placed in the common stock, the wrongful acquisition cannot be set up to defeat the rights of heirs.

In McGregor v. Johnson, 58 Wash. 78, 107 P. 1049, the plaintiff had been fraudulently bled by a real estate broker of more commissions than she should have had to pay; she brought action against the broker and his wife to recover from the community the excess so fraudulently obtained from her. It was defended that any liability incurred by the wrongful act of the broker was his separate obligation and not that of the community. It was held that the unlawful acquisition had inured to the benefit of the community, in that under the statute it became community property, and that accordingly the community was estopped to deny its liability. Note that here, too, the statute is evidently construed to include unlawful acquisitions, thus viewing the statute as sanctioning a marital partnership in illegal acquisitions and the right of each spouse to share in illegal acquisitions. Is any statute enacted with such an immoral purpose in view?

[8] Property improved by the use of community or separate property or funds, see ante, § 73.

[9] See ante, § 66.

[10] See ante, § 63.

property of the spouse.[11] This unquestionably was a well understood feature of the community property system in Spain from the time of the introduction of that system by the Visigoths (West Goths), for the same feature appears in Visigothic customs and laws in other parts of Europe.[12]

However, an understandable difficulty of interpretation arose as to the situation where, during the marriage, one spouse purchased property with money which had belonged to that spouse before marriage. Thus, Roderic Xuarez stated that if the husband during marriage purchased land with his own money and proved it by proper evidence, the land was his own and was not shared with his wife. Others of the jurisconsults, notably Joannes Lupi, Palacios Rubios, Matienzo and Gutiérrez, pointed out that such rule should not apply when it was with money brought by one of the spouses to the marriage that land or other property was purchased, if the money was brought to the marriage for the common benefit of the spouses, for then property purchased therewith should be common property.[13] It is apparent at once that the question is entirely one of evidence rather than a conflict of opinion. If the evidence is clear that a spouse is using his or her own money to purchase property for the spouse's own benefit, the property so purchased is separate property. On the other hand, if the evidence shows that the spouse bringing the money to the marriage is devoting the result of the purchase to, or making the purchase for, the benefit of both spouses, the property so purchased is naturally community property, on the basis of a gift to the community.[14] Even those espousing the view that whatever property

---

[11] Matienzo, Gloss II, Nos. 1-6; Azevedo, No. 16; Gutiérrez, Quaestio CXVII; all to Nov. Rec. Law 1, Book 10, Title 4.

Property acquired in exchange for other property belonging to one of the spouses and that acquired by the produce of the sale of property belonging exclusively to one of the spouses does not belong to the community. Schmidt, Civil Law of Spain and Mexico, p. 13.

[12] According to the Law of the West Goths in Sweden, *circa* 1200 A.D., if a husband or wife sold his or her own land and did not add the price received to the common stock but instead purchased other land, such land continued to be the separate property of the spouse in question. Law of the West Goths, according to the Manuscript of Eskil (Bergin's Translation), p. 66.

Visigoths responsible for introducing community property system into the Spanish peninsula, see ante, Chaps. II, III.

[13] Matienzo, Gloss II, Nos. 1-6; Gutiérrez, Quaestio CXVII; both to Nov. Rec. Law 1. Azevedo would appear to agree with the opinion of Xuarez. See Azevedo, No. 16, to Nov. Rec. Law 1.

[14] Thus Febrero, in discussing intrinsic increase in value of an office belonging to one spouse as also belonging to the owner of the office, declared that the same applied "when it appears that one of the spouses took into the marriage money in specie sufficient to purchase some office or property, and the other spouse none, nor properties from the sale of the products of which it might be purchased, or even if having properties they exist unsold, and after a short time married, the first spouse purchases the office or property, e. g., for twenty, expressing it to be that money, and upon the death of one

181

was purchased with the money of one spouse was common property — under the belief, no doubt, that it was to be presumed that the purchase must have been made for the common benefit — added the qualification that such spouse was entitled to be reimbursed in full, for the money so spent, from the common stock of properties when division thereof took place.[15] It must be remembered that the presumption was (as it still is with us) that all property acquired during the marriage by either spouse was community property until it was proved otherwise.[16]

There was no question in the Spanish law, of course, that upon the acquisition or purchase of other property through the use of community property, the property so acquired or purchased was also community property; the same was true of property acquired or purchased by a husband or wife through the use of money of the husband or wife, where such money was earned or gained during the marriage since it constituted community property.[17]

It is undoubted that our community property states attempt to follow the rule of the Spanish community property law and that it is considered that the property or thing acquired or purchased partakes of the same nature as the nature of the property or funds used to acquire or purchase it.[18] This rule our courts have continued to apply,[19]

spouse, it is valued at sixty; for though it appears that this intrinsic increase should be shared by the partnership, because the purchase was made during the partnership, the contrary is true, and it will therefore go to the owner of the money only, because it is seen that it was bought by him and subrogated in his place; and the other spouse not having had the wherewithal to purchase it, nor placed any work in its increase in value will have no right to anything, nor will he share in the decrease if it should suffer it from time to time; unless both stipulate otherwise." Febrero, Librería de Escribanos, Cinco Juicios I, Book I, Cap. IV, § 1, No. 18.

Gifts of separate property to the community generally, see post, Chap. VIII.

[15] Matienzo, Gloss II, No. 6, to Nov. Rec. Law 1; Novísimo Sala Mexicano, Sec. 2a, Title IV, No. 4.

[16] See ante, § 60.

Two early cases in this country (Davenat v. Blocton, 1 La. 520; Scott v. Maynard, Dallam (Tex.) 548) seem to have been misconstrued

as stating flatly that the rule in Spain and Mexico was that property purchased with the money of one of the spouses was community property, but what they state is that such property was to be considered common property unless it was established otherwise by certain and positive evidence. This should be borne in mind when reading such statements as those appearing in 86 Am. Dec. 629 and 11 Am. Jur. 190, § 26.

[17] See Matienzo, Gloss II, No. 3; Gutiérrez, Quaestio CXVII; both to Nov. Rec. Law 1; In re Trimble's Estate, 57 N.M. 51, 253 P.2d 805, quoting 1 de Funiak § 77 but recognizing existence of common law estates in New Mexico.

[18] See cases cited, 64 A. L. R. 246; 126 Am. St. Rep. 104, 105; 15 Am. Jur. 2d, Community Property, §§ 27, 28; 41 C.J.S., Husband and Wife, § 485.

Property held by spouses as joint tenants or tenants in common, see post, § 134.

[19] Lincoln Fire Ins. Co. v. Barnes, 53 Ariz. 264, 88 P.2d 533; Kohny v. Dunbar, 21 Ida. 258, 121 P. 544;

although frequently with some misgivings as to how the "absolute letter" of the statute should apply to property received during marriage in exchange for separate property.[20] They need have no such misgivings. The rule was consistently followed in the Spanish law of community, because it was realized that consistency, logic and common sense would permit of no other conclusion.[21] So far as the separate funds or separate property of a spouse are employed in a manner to benefit the marital community, it may well be intended that such funds or property are meant to be a gift to the marital community. On the other hand, although it may have been intended to use such funds or property to acquire something for the benefit of the marital community, so that what was acquired thus has the character of community property, the evidence may show that the donor intended to or expected to be reimbursed subsequently from the common stock of goods for such expenditure.[22]

Kittredge v. Grau, 158 La. 154, 103 So. 723; Lake v. Bender, 18 Nev. 361, 4 P. 711; Burlingham v. Burlingham, 72 N.M. 433, 384 P.2d 899; Bates v. Bates (Tex. Civ. App.), 270 S. W. 301; In re Hebert's Estate, 169 Wash. 402, 14 P.2d 6.

The definition of separate property in Cal. Civ. Code, § 5108 (formerly § 163) includes "property taken in exchange for, or in the investment, or as the price of the property so originally owned or acquired." Meyer v. Kinzer, 12 Cal. 247, 73 Am. Dec. 538; Smith v. Smith, 12 Cal. 216, 73 Am. Dec. 533.

The La. Civ. Code, art. 2334, defines separate property, among others, as that "acquired during marriage with separate funds."

[20] "The doctrine that property acquired during marriage by exchange therefor of separate property remains separate property is contrary to the absolute letter of the statute, and was no doubt formulated by the courts out of necessity, and to render the right to separate property effective. If 'all other property acquired after marriage . . . is community property,' as is declared by the letter of the statute, then neither husband nor wife during coverture can acquire separate property except by gift, bequest, devise, or descent. If they have separate property, they must keep it just as it is, else if they sell or exchange

it and invest in other property, the property so acquired will become common property. The letter of the statute would bring about this result. But the courts wisely ingrafted upon the doctrine the principle that where property is acquired during marriage by the sale or exchange of separate property, it remains separate property." Morris v. Waring, 22 N.M. 175, 159 P. 1002. See also Roberts v. Roberts, 35 N.M. 593, 4 P.2d 920. One may well raise an eyebrow over the somewhat smug assumption of the New Mexico court that it "wisely ingrafted" a principle which had actually been recognized for hundreds of years in the Spanish-Mexican community property law.

[21] See criticism of our courts, ante, § 62.

[22] And see post, § 78.

In Meng v. Security State Bank (Wash.), 133 P.2d 293, husband and wife changed their domicile from a noncommunity property state to Washington. The husband owned only some old farm machinery, and the wife had $800 saved from a boarding house venture of hers. This money was invested in the purchase of some cows and the lease of a farm with which they prosecuted a dairy business for some years, both giving all their time to it and putting back into the business whatever was gained from it. Without giving its reasons

The rule is also usually correctly followed by the courts of our community property states that property acquired during marriage through the use of community property also is community property.[23] Since the earnings of the spouses are community property,[24] property purchased with the earnings of the husband and wife or with the earnings of either of them is also community property.[25] This would not be true, of course, as to earnings of the wife which are declared by statute to be her separate property when acquired by her while living separate and apart from her husband or when constituted her separate property by reason of agreement with or gift by the husband.[26]

One might assume in view of the foregoing matters that, under the Spanish law of community, if property was acquired through the use partly of community property and partly of separate property, the property so acquired would also be community and separate property in the proper proportions. Theoretically, that might have been so,[27] but other factors must be taken into consideration, for example, that the statutory presumption was that the property which the husband and wife had was presumed to belong to both by halves except that which each might prove to be his or hers separately, as well as the necessary concomitant that where community and separate property was so intermingled that it could not be known or proved to which of them the property belonged it was necessarily all presumed community.[28] Thus, it is a matter of evidence, and it is naturally very

therefor, the court termed the dairy business community property, so as not to be subject to a separate obligation of the husband. It may undoubtedly be assumed that the wife used her money to benefit the marital community so that whatever was purchased with her money was community property, but whether she made a gift of the $800 to the marital community or was entitled to be reimbursed therefor was not necessary to decide for the purposes of the case.

[23] See, e. g., Anderson v. Anderson, 65 Ariz. 184, 177 P.2d 227; Steward v. Paige (Cal. App.), 203 P.2d 858; Farmers Ins. Exchange v. Wendler (Ida.), 368 P.2d 933; Betz v. Riviere, 211 La. 43, 29 So.2d 465; In re Wilson's Estate, 56 Nev. 353, 53 P.2d 339; In re Trimble's Estate, 57 N.M. 51, 253 P.2d 805, quoting 1 de Funiak, § 77; Campbell v. Campbell, 62 N.M. 330, 310 P.2d 266; Hilley v. Hilley (Tex.), 342 S. W. 2d 565; Pain v. Morrison, 125 Wash. 267, 216 P. 29; Free v. Bland, 82 S. Ct.

1089.

Property acquired with community credit, see post, § 78.

[24] See ante, § 66.

[25] See Winchester v. Winchester, 175 Cal. 391, 165 P. 965; Cox v. Kaufman, (Cal. App.) 175 P.2d 260; Ahlstrom v. Tage, 31 Idaho 459, 174 P. 605; Fleury v. Fleury, (La.) 131 So.2d 355; Marsh v. Fisher, 69 Wash. 570, 125 P. 951.

[26] See In re Wilson's Estate, 56 Nev. 353, 53 P.2d 339.

[27] For example, the law of the West Goths in Sweden, *circa* 1200 A.D., provided that if the husband purchased anything by the use of his separate property but paid something additional on the price from the common property, the value of so much of the common property as was used had to be restored upon division of the common property. Law of the West Goths, according to the Manuscript of Eskil (Bergin's Translation), p. 66.

[28] See ante, §§ 60, 61.

frequently difficult to prove that acquired or purchased property is partly community and partly separate property where its acquisition or purchase has been made partly with community and partly with separate property or funds. Certainly this difficulty has arisen with us of attempting to disentangle the intereste raised by the intermingled use of community and separate property or funds in acquiring or purchasing other property or interests.[29] However, where the acquisition or purchase of property during marriage is effected by the use partly of community and partly of separate property or funds and the community and separate property or funds are not so intermingled as to make identification impossible or too difficult, the character of the acquired or purchased property may, under some views, be separated according to the proportions of the separate and community property or funds used to acquire it.[30] But while such separation is favored in some of our community property states, it must be remembered that this is not so in others, especially where acquisition is initiated prior to marriage and completed during marriage[31] or initiated during marriage and completed after termination of marriage.[32]

§ 78.   — Acquisitions on credit and security.

A determination of the community or separate status of borrowed money or property purchased on credit necessarily involves a qualitative consideration of several factors. The first, of course, is the very general rule that property acquired during marriage by industry or labor of the spouses is community[33] and its concomitant presumption that all property on hand is community rather than separate.[34] Another is the basic policy force that during the marriage the community has a claim to the energy and activity of the spouses, and that property acquired by such effort is community.[35] On the other hand, is the equally viable principle that property acquired by mutations of existing separate property is itself separate.[36]

To resolve this classification question, two situations must initially be segregated — the acquisition on open credit where no security is given and the acquisition on secured credit where property is mortgaged. Final consideration must be given the situation where the parties make some specific agreement as to the nature of the property.

In Arizona, property acquired on credit secured by a pledge of separate property is itself separate.[37] It would be community if com-

[29] See In re Gulstine's Estate, 166 Wash. 325, 6 P.2d 628. And see Ormachea v. Ormachea, 67 Nev. 213, 217 P.2d 355, citing and following first edition, de Funiak. And see ante, § 61.

[30] See e.g., Faust v. Faust, (Cal. App.) 204 P.2d 906. See cases, 64 A. L. R. 249; 126 Am. St. Rep. 104.

[31] See ante, § 64.

[32] See ante, § 68.2.

[33] See supra, § 62.

[34] See supra, § 60.

[35] Vaughn, The Policy of Community Property and Interspousal Transactions, 19 Baylor L. Rev. 20.

[36] See supra, § 77.

[37] Malich v. Malich, 23 Ariz. 423, 204 P. 1020.

munity property were pledged or if the acquisition was made on open credit.[38] This follows from the general rule that money borrowed on the personal credit of either spouse is community property. However, if the property is bought on credit and it is agreed that only the separate estate is to be liable, the property so purchased becomes itself separate property even though community funds are actually used to pay the obligation.[39] Similarly, if the community assumes payment of part of the deferred obligation, the property is community in the proportion that the community funds actually spent bear to the total price.[40] Thus, if property has a separate status at the time of its initial acquisition it can never lose this.[41] On the other hand, property acquired partly with separate funds and community credit takes on a community character only to the actual extent of community funds spent.

In California, when money is borrowed on the credit and faith of or on security of community or separate property and used to acquire or purchase other property, usually the property so acquired or purchased partakes of the nature of the property upon which the credit was given or which was given as security. Thus, if money is borrowed upon the sole credit and faith of or on the security of separate property of the wife and used to purchase other property, the property so purchased is the separate property of the wife, if it is evident that she purchased it for her own benefit or private purposes and not for the benefit of the marital community.[42]

But unless the money borrowed by the married woman is borrowed on the credit of her existing separate property, the California courts view the borrowed money as community property.[43] Of course money borrowed by the husband is ordinarily community property also,[44] unless it is shown to have been lent on the security of his separate property.[45]

Idaho has not considered these problems in great detail. The available cases indicate that money borrowed, or property bought on credit, on the security of the separate estate of either spouse, becomes the separate property of the spouse whose property is the security.[46]

[38] Malich v. Malich, supra.

[39] Lincoln Fire Ins. Co. v. Barnes, 53 Ariz. 264, 88 P.2d 533.

[40] Horton v. Horton, 35 Ariz. 378, 278 Pac. 370; Porter v. Porter, 67 Ariz. 273, 195 P.2d 132.

[41] Flynn v. Allender, 75 Ariz. 322, 256 P.2d 560.

[42] Dyment v. Nelson, 166 Cal. 38, 134 P. 688 (money lent by bank on sole credit and faith of wife's separate property and used to purchase a yacht).

[43] See Moulton v. Moulton, 182 Cal. 185, 187 P. 421, and cases cited therein; Guerin v. Guerin, (Cal. App.) 313 P.2d 902.

[44] Usually lent on his personal credit, a community asset, or on security of community property.

[45] Estate of Ellis, 203 Cal. 414, 264 P. 743.

[46] Shovlain v. Shovlain, 78 Ida. 399, 305 P.2d 737; Gapsch v. Gapsch, 76 Ida. 44, 277 P.2d 278, 54 A. L. R. 2d 416.

Brockelbank suggests that the proper approach is to determine factually on whose credit the loan was made and the purpose of it.[47] This follows the typical Idaho position that the crucial question in determining whether property is community or separate is the actual source of the funds used to make the purchase.[48]

Louisiana adheres to the usual presumption of community status, but allows proof of separate status.[49] A married woman can show that property bought on credit is her separate property by proving that it was purchased with separate funds, that she individually administered the property, that she invested the money, that the down payment was made from her separate property, and that she had sufficient separate property at time of purchase to be able to meet the deferred payments with reasonable certainty.[50] These recitals may be in the instrument by which the married woman acquires the property; but the failure to make such recitations does not preclude proof of separate status at a later time, nor does the inclusion of such recitations preclude proof of community status.[51] Quite to the contrary, a married man buying realty is precluded from proving that it is his separate property unless the instrument recites that the property is bought with the separate funds of the husband and for his separate estate.[52]

There is little Nevada authority in this area,[53] but it may reasonably be assumed that the Nevada courts would follow the California views where they lack authorities from their own state.

The New Mexico cases are also few, but generally indicate that property bought on credit secured by separate property is itself separate.[54] Also, the husband's credit presumptively belongs to the community and there is a presumption that property he purchases on credit is community; but he may contract a separate debt based upon his separate credit, and assets acquired in such manner are his separate property.[55] On the other hand, this presumption may not exist as to purchases by the wife. In fact it may be quite the contrary.[56]

The Texas courts have considered this question many times and have formulated a thorough approach.[57] Either spouse may borrow

---

[47] Brockelbank, The Community Property Law of Idaho, § 3.5.3.

[48] Rose v. Rose, (Idaho) 353 P.2d 1089.

[49] See supra, § 60.

[50] Graves v. U. S. Rubber Co., (La.) 111 So.2d 752; Monk v. Monk, (La.) 144 So.2d 384.

[51] Stevens v. Johnson, (La.) 81 So.2d 464; Southwest Natural Production Co. v. Anderson, (La.) 118 So.2d 897.

[52] Smith v. Smith, (La.) 89 So.2d 55.

[53] Zahringer v. Zahringer (Nev.) 348 P.2d 161, where husband borrowed money from his parents and bought stock which was presumed community.

[54] McElyea v. McElyea, 49 N.M. 322, 163 P.2d 635.

[55] Campbell v. Campbell, 62 N.M. 330, 310 P.2d 266.

[56] Morris v. Waring, 22 N.M. 175, 159 Pac. 1002; Laughlin v. Laughlin, 49 N.M. 20, 155 P.2d 1010.

[57] See Oakes, Speer's Marital Rights in Texas, §§ 440, 441, 442 and 41 Texas L. Rev. 1.

money on his or her separate account. But money borrowed after marriage, and the property bought with it, is presumed to be for the benefit of the community.[58] Furthermore, the character of property as community or separate is determined as of the time of its acquisition, and this character cannot be changed even if payment is later made from property of contrary status.[59] To render the property separate if it is acquired during marriage the vendor must agree to look to the separate estate of the vendee only.[60] If no such agreement is made the property is proportionately community and separate based on the relative amounts of each type of fund used to constitute the purchase price.[61] If such an agreement is made the community would have only a right of reimbursement, but would not own part of the property, if community funds were actually used to discharge the obligation.[62] Similarly, if the property takes on a community status at the time of acquisition, the use of separate property to finish paying the cost does not transform the asset into separate property but merely creates a right of reimbursement in the separate estate.[63]

Washington cases have taken an unusual approach to this question. Generally, the community is entitled to the credit of the spouses, and property purchased on credit is community property, in the absence of an agreement to the contrary.[64] Early cases, however, felt that if one spouse used his separate estate as security for a new acquisition, the new acquisition was community property.[65] The courts do not appear likely to change this rule.[66]

In most of the foregoing jurisdictions, where a spouse borrows money on his or her personal credit or the faith and credit or security of his or her separate property to be used for his or her own separate benefit, and it is clear that the loan was made on the sole credit of that spouse, it is immaterial that the evidence of indebtedness to the lender was executed by both spouses.[67]

---

[58] Hamilton v. Charles Maund Oldsmobile-Cadillac Co., 347 S. W.2d 944 (Tex. Civ. App., writ ref'd, n.r.e.).

[59] Colden v. Alexander, 141 Tex. 134, 171 S. W. 2d 328.

[60] Dillard v. Dillard, (Tex. Civ. App.) 341 S. W. 2d 668, writ ref'd, n.r.e.

[61] Carter v. Brabeel, 341 S. W. 2d 458 (Tex. Civ. App.).

[62] Holdg v. Ellis, 268 S. W. 2d 275, 154 Tex. 341, 277 S. W. 2d 900. And as to Texas, see excellent note in 26 Tex. L. Rev. 93, to Hudspeth v. Hudspeth (Tex. Civ. App.) 198 S. W. 2d 768, error refused.

[63] Broussard v. Tian, 156 Tex. 371, 295 S. W. 2d 405, cert. denied 353 U.S. 941, 1 L.Ed. 2d 941, 77 S. Ct. 811.

[64] In re Dougherty's Estate, 27 Wash. 2d 11, 176 P.2d 335.

[65] Heintz v. Brown, 46 Wash. 387, 90 P. 211, 123 Am. St. Rep. 937.

[66] Finley v. Finley, (Wash.) 287 P.2d 475.

[67] Porter v. Porter, 67 Ariz. 273, 195 P.2d 132; Dyment v. Nelson, 166 Cal. 38, 134 P. 988. Stewart v. Weiser Lumber Co., 21 Idaho 340, 121 P. 775 (purchase money mortgage executed by husband and wife though property purchased by wife as her separate property); Finn's

Money, of course, may be borrowed on the credit of community property and used for the separate benefit of one of the spouses, subject again to principles concerning gifts of the community property to one of the spouses.[68]

The following situation may arise: A person, either before marriage or even during marriage acquires property, taking title in his name, paying part of the purchase price with his separate funds and intending the property to be his separate property, but necessarily having to borrow the rest of the purchase price from a lender, perhaps giving a mortgage, pledge or deed of trust on the purchased property as security for the loan. Since the property is intended to be separate property, the loan is necessarily made on the security of separate property, and the money borrowed is separate property. The fact that this loan or some part of it is later paid off with community funds does not make any part of the purchased property itself community. It has already been completely acquired as separate property, and the title has passed, and the repayment of the loan in question is apart from that. The most that is due the community is a right of reimbursement for the community funds so used.[69]

§ 79.   — Insurance policies and their proceeds.

While the insurance of property and business risks was known to the old Spanish law,[70] that was not the case as to life insurance, which has become so highly developed in our economy of life. While it cannot be truthfully said that our courts always resort to the basic principles of the Spanish community property law for enlightenment, nevertheless the lack of guiding authority from the Spanish sources may have contributed to some extent to the conflict and confusion among our courts when they try to determine the nature of and the interests in the proceeds of life insurance policies upon which the

Estate, 100 Wash. 137, 179 P. 103

In Washington, however, it is said that the nature of property purchased is fixed at the time of its purchase, and the view seems to be that if at the time of purchase title is taken in the names of both spouses the property is community property, regardless of what funds may have gone into its purchase. See Walker v. Fowler, 155 Wash. 631, 285 P. 649.

[68] See Union Securities Co. v. Smith, 93 Wash. 115, 160 P. 304.

Gifts generally, see post, Chap. VIII.

[69] See language of Walker v. Fowler, supra.

Cf. questionable language of some

of Arizona cases, especially Porter v. Porter, supra.

Where wife borrowed $2,000 on the strength of her separate credit and paid it down on a piece of property sold for $13,500 and title thereto was taken in her and her husband's names as joint tenants, she was entitled to priority in payment of this amount from the proceeds of the sale of the property, sold on order of the court upon their divorce. Searles v. Searles, 99 Cal. App. 2d 869, 222 P.2d 938. See also Nichols v. Nichols, 84 Ida. 379, 372 P.2d 758.

[70] See Asso and Mañuel, Institutes of the Civil Law of Spain, Book II, Title XVII.

premiums have been paid wholly or in part from community property. Admittedly, the problems arising are frequently extremely varied and frequently complex and such as to tax the ingenuity of the courts to the utmost.[71]

As we have seen, the proper principle is that where separate or community property is used to acquire other property, the latter partakes of the same nature as that of the property used for its acquisition.[72] However, this principle does not always seem to be followed in cases of the use of community property to pay premiums upon life insurance policies so as to make the proceeds or part of the proceeds community property. Frequently, the courts seem to proceed on the theory that the use of community funds to pay life insurance premiums is analogous to the use of community property to make improvements on land which is the separate property of one spouse, wherein the principle followed in this country is usually that the improvements so made follow the property, although there is a right of reimbursement to the community for the value of the community property so expended.[73] It has sometimes been said that whether the insured took out the policy before or during marriage determines whether the policy represents separate or community property,[74] and where one, before marriage, insured his life and after marriage premiums were paid with community funds, the proceeds of the policy were held not to be community property although reimbursement was allowed the community for the amount of the community funds paid for premiums.[75] Actually, since the community property has contributed to the creation of the sum representing the proceeds of the life insurance policy,

[71] For collection of cases on problems arising under community property system with respect to life insurance policies, see 114 A. L. R. 545, 168 A. L. R. 342.

See also Catlett, Status of Proceeds of Life Insurance Under Community Property System, 5 Wash. Law Rev. 45; Huie, Community Property Laws as Applied to Life Insurance, 17 Tex. Law Rev. 121, 18 Tex. Law Rev. 121; Schimke, Problems in Community Property Law in Relation to Life Insurance, 16 Idaho S. B. J. 101; Evans, Some Secondary Sources of Acquisition of Community Property, 11 Cal. Law Rev. 156; Stephens, Life Insurance and Community Property in Texas: Revisited, 10 S. W. L. J. 343; Comment, The Community Property Life Insurance Policy, 18 Baylor L. Rev. 627; Hokanson, Life Insurance Proceeds as Community Property, 13 Wash. Law Rev. 321;

Luccock, Life Insurance as Community Property, 16 Wash. Law Rev. 687. Of the foregoing, the articles of Professor Huie are to be highly recommended.

Divorce of insured and beneficiary as affecting latter's rights, see post, Chap. X.

[72] See ante, § 77.

[73] See ante, § 73.

[74] See In re Moseman, 38 La. Ann. 219. And see In re Castagnola, 68 Cal. App. 732, 230 P. 188; In re White, 41 N.M. 631, 73 P.2d 316.

Rule applicable to life insurance and not to disability insurance. Easterling v. Succession of Lamkin (La.) 31 So.2d 220.

[75] In re Moseman's Estate, 38 La. Ann. 219. See also Vernuille's Succession, 120 La. 605, 45 So. 520.

In In re White's Estate, 45 N.M. 202, 89 P.2d 86, in following rule

the community should be entitled to such proportion of such proceeds as the community property used in payment of premiums bears to the whole amount paid in premiums.[76] This is in correct accord with the principles of community property that where community property or labor is used to increase the value of separate property, the value of the increases should be shared by the community.[77]

As indicated in the preceding paragraph, it is usually considered by most courts that, when a spouse, during marriage, takes out a policy on his or her own life and the premiums are paid from community funds, the policy represents community property.[78] But this situation is much complicated by the question of who is named as beneficiary. If the husband, during the marriage, insures his own life, names some third person as beneficiary, and the premiums are paid with community funds, what are the rights of the surviving wife? This virtually amounts to making a gift of the community property and the extent to which the husband can do this without the wife's consent is matter upon which the courts are in conflict. However, the question comes more appropriately under the discussion of the husband's power

that time of taking out policy determines whether it and the proceeds are separate or community, the reinstatement during marriage of a policy originally taken out before marriage was held to be merely a continuation of original policy and proceeds were held separate property. To same effect, see Succession of Lewis, 192 La. 734, 189 So. 118, as to War Risk Insurance.

[76] Webb's Estate, Myrick Prob. (Cal.) 93 (one-third of premiums paid from separate estate before marriage, two-thirds from community funds after marriage; proceeds held to belong to separate and community estates in same proportion); Modern Woodmen v. Gray, 113 Cal. App. 729, 299 P. 754; In re Coffey's Estate, 195 Wash. 379, 81 P.2d 283; Wilson v. Wilson (Wash.) 212 P.2d 1022. See ante, § 73.

[77] This view is objected to by some writers (see Catlett, 5 Wash. Law Rev. 45), on the ground that the policy when taken out was separate property and that the proceeds should also be separate property, subject at the most to having to reimburse the community for the amount of the community funds used to pay premiums. This view would justify the act of the husband, by virtue of his power to manage and

control the community property, in using it to further his own ends, in much the same way that any fiduciary might wrongfully use the funds in his control to increase the value of his own holdings.

[78] See In re Castagnola's Estate, 68 Cal. App. 732, 230 P. 188; In re White's Estate, 41 N.M. 631, 73 P.2d 316; Salvato v. Volunteer State L. Ins. Co. (Tex. Civ. App.) 424 S. W. 2d 1; In re Brown's Estate, 124 Wash. 273, 214 P. 10; Manufacturers L. Ins. Co. v. Moore, 116 F. Supp. 171, quoting first edition but limiting recovery by spouse causing other's death (see post, § 153).

But notice the language of a court in Louisiana that a policy of insurance is not property but merely evidence of a contract that a certain sum of money will be paid to a particular person named in the policy upon the happening of a certain event. Succession of Hearing, 26 La. Ann. 326. Nevertheless, the Louisiana courts have usually followed the same rules as other courts by which the character of property is to be determined as applicable to insurance policies. See Nabors, Civil Law Influences Upon Law of Insurance in Louisiana, 6 Tulane Law Rev. 515.

of control and management of the community property and is dealt with in a subsequent chapter.[79]

In the situation where the husband during marriage insures his own life, making the proceeds payable to his estate or to his executors, administrators or assigns, and the premiums have been paid with community funds, the proceeds are said to belong to the community, and this is sometimes explained on the ground that the husband cannot make a gift to himself from the community property.[80]

The courts seem fairly uniform in the view that when the husband takes out a policy, during marriage, on his own life naming the wife as beneficiary, the policy and the proceeds thereof are the separate property of the wife, although the premiums were paid from community funds. This seems to rest upon the presumption that the husband has made her a gift of his interest in the community funds.[81] Thus, even where the wife died before the husband, and the insurer's obligation did not arise until the subsequent death of the husband, the proceeds were considered separate property, on the ground that the wife had during the marriage by gift the ownership of the chose in action represented by the policy.[82] Must the foregoing have depended on the fact that the policy was payable to the wife without any reservation by the insured of the right to change the beneficiary? Seemingly, it should be dependent on that fact. The failure to reserve the right to change the beneficiary makes the gift effective at once. Otherwise it does not become fully complete until the husband dies without changing the beneficiary. But even if the husband has reserved the right to change the beneficiary and does do so, still the wife should properly and correctly be entitled to claim half the proceeds of the policy as community property, although admittedly this is dependent on the interpretation of the extent of the husband's power to give away community property without the consent of the wife.[83]

---

[79] See post, Chap. VII.

Consider effect of husband dying testate or intestate; see §§ 198, 199.

[80] In re Castagnola's Estate, 68 Cal. App. 732, 230 P. 188; Berry v. Franklin State Bank & Trust Co., 186 La. 623, 173 So. 126; Succession of Buddig, 108 La. 406, 32 So. 361; Le-Blanc's Succession, 142 La. 27, 76 So. 223, L.R.A. 1917 F 1137; In re White's Estate, 41 N.M. 631, 73 P.2d 316; Aetna Life Ins. Co. v. Osborne (Tex. Civ. App.), 224 S. W. 815; Lee v. Lee, 112 Tex. 392, 247 S. W. 828; In re Brown's Estate, 124 Wash. 273, 214 P. 10; In re Towey's Estate, 22 Wash. 2d 212, 155 P.2d 273. See case note, 20 Wash. L. Rev. 167.

[81] In re Dobbel, 104 Cal. 432, 38 P. 87, 43 Am. St. Rep. 123; Nulsen v. Herndon, 176 La. 1097, 147 So. 359, 88 A.L.R. 236; Evans v. Opperman, 76 Tex. 293, 13 S. W. 312. Statute in Washington, see Wash. Rev. Stats. § 7230. Rem.

[82] In re Dobbel's Estate; Evans v. Opperman; both ante, preceding note. And see Comment, 18 Baylor L. Rev. 627, at 629; Kemp v. Metropolitan L. Ins. Co., (5 C.A.) 205 F.2d 857, citing first edition, involving failure to notify insurer of intention to change beneficiary.

[83] This question is more properly dealt with in the chapter on the control and management of the community property. See post, Chap. VII.

Conversely to the preceding situation, it has been held in Texas that when the husband insures the life of the wife in his favor and the premiums are paid with community funds, the proceeds of the policy are not community property but part of his separate estate. This view seems to be based on the theory that the husband as manager of the community property has the power so to divert community funds.[84] Actually, this puts it in the power of the husband to make gifts to himself from the community property, a thing that no court should sanction, unless there is clear evidence of the wife's consent with full knowledge of the consequences of such consent. In the absence of any satisfactory showing to that effect, the proceeds of such a policy should definitely be community property.[85] The present Texas view that the right to receive insurance proceeds at a future but uncertain date is property[86] appears to modify the situation, for the previous holding was based on the view that the "proceeds right" was not property and so the husband was not acting in fraud of the wife's rights in awarding them to himself.[87]

A situation in which there has been a paucity of cases is that wherein during the marriage the life of the spouses' minor child is insured. The right to the proceeds is a chose in action which is community property in nature. Hence, even though only one spouse is named as beneficiary, the other has a half interest in the proceeds.[88] If the spouses are divorced without any division of this chose and without any agreement as to it, they continue to own their respective interests as tenants in common,[89] in accord with the usual view in such situations.[90]

However, see especially, In re Towey's Estate (Wash.), supra.

In California, even where the policy reserves the right to change the beneficiary, where the husband has insured his life and made his estate or his wife the beneficiary and paid the premiums with community funds, he cannot change the beneficiary without the wife's consent. Dixon Lumber Co. v. Peacock, 217 Cal. 415, 19 P.2d 233; New York Life Ins. Co. v. Bank of Italy, 60 Cal. App. 602, 214 P. 61. As inchoate gift to wife, see Travelers' Ins. Co. v. Fancher, 219 Cal. 351, 26 P.2d 482. Other California cases seem to indicate that such a policy does not make a gift to the wife, unless the right to change the beneficiary is never exercised. See Blackburn v. Merchants Life Ins. Co., 90 Cal. App. 362, 265 P. 882; Jenkins v. Jenkins, 112 Cal. App. 402, 297 P. 56.

[84] Martin v. McAllister, 94 Tex. 567, 63 S. W. 624, 56 L.R.A. 585. And see Gristy v. Hudgens, 23 Ariz. 339, 203 P. 569, as to power of husband to dispose of personalty.

[85] See Huie, Community Property Laws as Applied to Life Insurance, 17 Tex. Law. Rev. 121, 128 et seq. Consider effect, in some states, of husband dying testate or intestate. See post, §§ 198, 199.

[86] Tex. Rev. Civ. Stats. 1925, Art. 23 (1), as amended in 1957; Brown v. Lee (Tex.) 371 S. W. 2d 694; Kemp v. Metropolitan L. Ins. Co. (5 C.A.) 205 F.2d 857, 860, citing 1 de Funiak, § 79.

[87] See Comment, 18 Baylor L. Rev. 627, at p. 632.

[88] Hickson v. Herrman, 77 N.M. 68, 427 P.2d 36.

[89] Hickson v. Herrman, supra.

[90] See post, §§ 229, 231.

A different situation than any of the foregoing is presented, of course, where some third person insures his life in favor of one of the spouses. The proceeds come to the spouse by way of gift or the like and are the separate property of the spouse.[91] This is so unless other factors change the complexion of affairs. For example, a spouse may be made the beneficiary in consideration of both spouses giving the insured care and support, or community funds may be devoted to paying premiums on the policy of the insured, and so on. The presence of one or more of these factors may serve to constitute the proceeds in whole or in part community property,[92] as gained by industry or labor.[93]

In the case of property insurance it has been said that the proceeds follow the nature of the property as a matter of course.[94] Nevertheless, if a husband should, for example, divert community funds to the payment of premiums on insurance on his separate property, the community should be entitled to reimbursement either from the property or the proceeds to the extent of the value of the funds so used.

§ 80.   Property in and profits from business partnership.

A discussion of the laws and principles applicable to business partnerships is no part of the scope of this work, and the extent to which the subject can be considered here must necessarily be brief.[95] The questions presented where one of the spouses is a member of a business partnership are not, as a rule, different from those ordinarily presented,[96] although admittedly at times the principles and laws applicable to partnerships, particularly the Uniform Partnership Act, introduce some complicating factors.

Where the interest in the partnership was acquired before marriage it is the separate property of such partner and remains so after

---

[91] This should be obvious.

[92] See Bellinger v. Wright, 143 Cal. 292, 76 P. 1108.

[93] See ante, §§ 66, 73.

[94] McMillan v. United States Fire Ins. Co., 48 Ida. 463, 280 P. 220; In re Hickman's Estate, 41 Wash. 2d 519, 250 P.2d 524, citing and following 1 de Funiak, § 79. See Evans, Some Secondary Sources of Acquisition of Community Property, 11 Calif. Law Rev. 156, 160.

Married woman insuring property, representing herself as sole and unconditional owner, although property paid for with community funds, see Germania Fire Ins. Co. v. Bally, 19 Ariz. 580, 173 P. 1052, 1 A.L.R. 488.

Insurable interest of husband in barn belonging to wife where barn was on farm used by spouses to obtain their livelihood and wherein was stored hay which was their community property, see Washington Fire Relief Ass'n v. Albro, 137 Wash. 31, 241 P. 356.

[95] Generally, see Mechem, Elements of Partnership; Uniform Partnership Act.

[96] For discussion, under the Spanish law, of the rights of the widow of one who was member of a business partnership, see Matienzo, Gloss I, No. 17 et seq., to Nov. Rec. Law 1, Book 10, Title 4.

Spouses as commercial partners of each other, see post, § 148.

marriage.[97] The profits and gains therefrom are, however, community property in those jurisdictions which consider the profits and gains from separate property as community property; but are separate property in those jurisdictions which have amended the Spanish community property law and now provide that profits and fruits of separate property are also separate property.[98] In this latter situation we may be presented with the problem that if the husband is the one owning the partnership interest and that is the only business he has bringing in profits and gains, then everything he gains during the marriage is his separate property, while the wife must contribute her services to the community without the husband contributing anything. The obvious injustice of such a situation has already been referred to.[99]

Naturally, where community property has been invested in a business partnership of which one of the spouses is a partner, such property remains community property even though converted into other forms, although naturally subject to the claims of the creditors of the business partnership and to the adjustment of the equities between the business partners before the rights of the spouses, or of claims of ordinary community creditors, are considered.[1] However, so far as claims of creditors are concerned, whether ordinary creditors of the marital community or creditors of the business partnership, consideration of such matters is postponed to the chapter dealing more fully with debts and obligations of the spouses.[2]

The Uniform Partnership Act, § 25 (2) (e), which provides that "A partner's right in specific property is not subject to dower, curtesy, or allowances to widows, heirs, or next of kin," as adopted in California has been amended to add "and is not community property."[3] This amendment is most puzzling. If it were not for the fact that the statute was enacted in 1929, two years after the state legislature had decisively, as it believed, disposed of the California Supreme Court's frequent assertions that the wife's interest in the community property was only an expectant interest in the nature of a dower right at

---

[97] Guthrie v. Guthrie, 73 Ariz. 423, 242 P.2d 549; Kittredge v. Grau, 158 La. 154, 103 So. 723; Norris v. Vaughn (Tex.) 260 S. W. 2d 676.

[98] See ante, § 71.

[99] See ante, § 72.

[1] See Cummings v. Weast, 72 Ariz. 93, 231 P.2d 439; Malich v. Malich, 23 Ariz. 423, 204 P. 1020; Coe v. Winchester, 43 Ariz. 500, 33 P.2d 286; McCall v. McCall, 2 Cal. App. 2d 92, 37 P.2d 496; Adams v. Blumenshine, 27 N.M. 643, 204 P. 66, 20 A.L.R. 369; Attaway v. Stanolind Oil & Gas Co., 232 F.2d 790.

Wife as member of partnership and the community as entitled to profits and liable for debts, see Hulsman v. Ireland, 205 Cal. 345, 270 P. 948.

Husband as a member of one business partnership and wife as member of another, see Strong v. Eakin, 11 N.M. 107, 66 P. 539.

[2] See post, § 172.

Federal income tax upon income from partnership in which one spouse is a partner, see Black v. Commissioner of Internal Revenue, 114 F.2d 355 and cases cited therein.

[3] See Cal. Civ. Code § 2419, subd. (2) (e).

common law, it might be assumed that there was in the legislature's mind that an ownership in community property was something expectant in the nature of dower, or, for that matter, curtesy. It would be an extremely odd situation if the act of a spouse having the management of certain community property in investing it in a commercial partnership thereby defeated the rights of the other spouse in the community property. But notice that this statute says "specific" property. Certainly if the partnership interest was acquired with community property, upon dissolution of the partnership or upon conversion of the partner's interest into something else, such as shares of stock of a corporation, what remains to the partner after payment of partnership creditors and adjustment of equities between the partners or what the erstwhile partner possesses from conversion of his partnership interest into something else now represents community property in which the wife has a half ownership.[4] Since it involves a law partnership, readers may be interested in the following somewhat puzzling case.[5] At the time of marrying and during marriage the husband was a member of a partnership engaged in the practice of law, with a right to share in the profits. His partnership interest was thus separate property, but it would follow, in California, that his efforts during the marriage in the law partnership would result in some part of the profits therefrom being community property.[6] Actually, in the accounting upon divorce, all of his profits during marriage from this partnership interest were treated as community property. In addition, the wife claimed that the capital assets of the partnership had been increased during the marriage by the use of community funds, and sought to be awarded an interest in such additions to the capital assets.[7] The court pointed out that, under Cal. Civ. Code § 2419 (2) (e), a partner's right in specific partnership property is not community property and is not subject to division. His interest is described as an equitable one, only determinable upon accounting and that therefore he has a mere expectancy not subject to division as community property. However, it is difficult to see how a present equitable interest to future division of profits or assets is describable as a mere expectancy. Some effort could be made to determine the extent of the husband's partnership interest to the

---

[4] See Estate of Duncan, 9 Cal. 2d 207, 70 P.2d 174; Wood v. Gunther, 89 Cal. App. 2d 718, 201 P.2d 874. at law, the administratrix and the in- a partnership was acquired during marriage and was presumed to have been acquired with community funds, and no evidence rebutted that presumption. It was declared that while the interest of the partner in the partnership was not, as such, community property, yet among the surviving spouse, the heirs at law, the administratrix and the individual creditors of the deceased partner's estate, it was governed by community property rules.

See, especially, Mullin, The Partner's Problems Augmented: His Wife Writes a Will, Los Angeles Bar Bulletin, Aug. 1947; also issued as Reprint No. 20, Committee on Continuing Education, Calif. State Bar.

[5] Hill v. Hill, 82 Cal. App. 2d 682. 187 P.2d 28.

[6] See ante, §§ 72, 73.

[7] See ante, § 73.

extent that it has been increased by use of community funds, or in other words in the community interest in the partnership, and half the value thereof awarded the wife from other available community property. At least, she should be entitled to reimbursement for half the value of community funds used to increase the capital assets of the partnership if the husband's interest in the partnership is actually his separate property, owned before marriage.

C. RIGHTS OF ACTION, AND DAMAGES OR COMPENSATION FOR INJURIES

§ 81.   The delict of the Spanish law.

The *delictus* of the Roman law, that is, a delict or wrong, may be described briefly and roughly as the equivalent of our tort. It comprised wrongs against person and property, for which actions for damages would lie.[8] When we come to the old Spanish law we find the corresponding term *delito* defined as "every bad act done or committed wilfully by one to the damage (*daño*) or discredit (*deshonra*) of another," and including what we would describe as a crime as well as a wrong in the sense of a tort. Thus *delito* might indicate a delict or wrong that constituted a crime, being termed more specifically a *delito verdadero* (real or true wrong, i.e., a crime) or *malfetria* (offense), or it might indicate a private wrong in the sense of a tort.[9] Leaving aside the *delito verdadero* or crime, we may note briefly that the wrong which consisted of damage or trespass (*daño*) or of injury by deed, word or writing (*injuria*) to an individual were matters for which all damages had to be made good by him causing it. Whether the damage was to person or property, whether committed by word or deed, it was said that all persons injured or owning the thing injured might institute action against the wrongdoer to compel him to make good the damage.[10] There is no question that this included

[8] See Buckland & McNair, Roman Law and Common Law, Chaps X, XI; Sherman, Roman Law in the Modern World, vol. 2, Titles IV, V.

[9] Asso and Mañuel, Institutes of the Civil Law of Spain, Book II, Title XIX, Cap. 1, § 1.

Notice the provisions of the Novísima Recopilación, Book 10, Title 4, Laws 10 and 11, relating to the question of whether one spouse should be deprived of ganancial properties for the delict of the other spouse, etc. See also post, § 181, et seq.

[10] See Asso and Mañuel, Institutes of the Civil Law of Spain, Book II, Title XIX, Cap. 3. And see De Witt, Law of Torts in the Spanish System, 6 Mich. Law Rev. 136.

"*Injuria* in Latin means in Castilian, dishonor (or discredit) done or said to another person wrongfully, or by way of contempt for him; and although there are many kinds of dishonor, still, they are derived from two sources: first, that of speech; second, that of deeds." Las Siete Partidas, Part. 7, Title 9, Law 1, which proceeds to define a wrong by way of speech and which constituted what we term slander or injury to reputation or the like. Law 6 of the same prescribes how one injures or dishonors another by acts or deeds, which included striking another, or wronging or dishonoring another "in many other ways; as, for instance, when one runs after another, or pursues him with the

the wife as a person wronged or the owner of property injured as well as the husband, with the right to be made whole so nearly as was possible, for it was provided that "when one party wrongs or dishonors another in any of the ways aforesaid or any other similar to them, he shall make reparation therefor according to the nature of the wrongs which he committed" and the one wronged "may bring suit for damages in court, and the other party is bound to make reparation to him with the approval of the judge,"[11] and the "Wrong or dishonor can be committed against any male or female of any age whatsoever."[12] Thus, the injury to the person of a wife was compensable to her to the extent that she was wronged or dishonored by such injury, and the injury to the property of the wife was compensable to her to the extent that her property was injured or destroyed. Originally, however, it seems that it was the place of the husband to maintain the action,[13] but subsequently by the sixteenth century the wife was entitled to bring the delictual proceeding herself and without the necessity of obtaining the husband's consent to do so.[14] Naturally, it was the husband's place to sue, as manager of the marital community, where an injury was done to community property.[15]

§ 82.   Injuries to person, reputation or the like.

What is the situation where a spouse during marriage sustains injury to his or her person, reputation or the like? The right of action is property as are the damages recovered in compensation for the injury. Is this property community or separate in character?[16] Formerly, most of our community property states considered that the property was community property in character, whether the injury was to the husband or the wife.[17] This was frequently put on the ground

intention of striking him or seizing him; or when he locks him up in some place; or enters his house by force; or when he arrests him, or takes any of his property by violence and against his will," etc. And Part. 7, Title 15, covered injuries to property of others, describing in Law 1 thereof "injury is the diminution or depreciation in value, or destruction which a man sustains in person and property, through the fault of another," and declaring in Law 2 thereof "The owner of the property which is damaged can demand reparation therefor."

[11] Las Siete Partidas, Part. 7, Title 9, Law 6, relating only to injuries to the person, but it will be noticed that Part. 7, Title 15, Law 2, declares that "The owner of property which is dam-

aged can demand reparation therefor."

[12] Part. 7, Title 9, Law 9.

[13] Part. 7, Title 9, Law 9.

[14] Llamas y Molina, No. 17, to Law 55 of Leyes de Toro, and citing Azevedo in agreement. See also Asso & Mañuel, Institutes of Civil Law of Spain, Book III, Title III, Cap. 1.

[15] See post, § 124.

[16] Discussion and cases, see 1943 edition, 1 de Funiak, § 82; annotation, 35 A.L.R. 2d 1190; 41 C.J.S., Husband and Wife, § 473; 11 Cal. Law Rev. 161; 11 Wash. Law Rev. 229; 1 Idaho Law Jour. 38; 6 A.L.R. 1059; 126 Am. St. Rep. 119.

[17] See 1943 edition, 1 de Funiak, § 82. As to Arizona, Idaho and Washington cases, see infra, this section. As

that this was property acquired during the marriage but was not separate property within the usual statutory definition that separate property is that acquired by gift, descent, devise or the like and that everything else is community property.[18] Another basis for such a view has been that any act by which either spouse is deprived of the capacity to render services diminishes the capacity to accumulate community property.[19] But a frequently expressed dissatisfaction with the foregoing view[20] now leaves only Arizona, California, Idaho and Washington in full support of the view that the right of action and all the damages recovered therefor are community property.[21] But even in those four states, if the wife while the marriage is still existent is living separate and apart from the husband, under the statute applicable to her "earnings and accumulations" while living separate and apart, the right of action and the damages therefor are her separate property.[22] But the husband's right of action and the damages therefor while so living separate and apart have been held to be community property,[23] in the absence of any similar statute relating to him.[24]

Where the right of action is classified as community property, the fact that the action is not brought until after the dissolution of the marriage does not alter the equivalent interests of the former spouses, or those standing their place, in the recovery.[25]

Presently and most importantly, in the other community property

---

to Louisiana and Texas cases under former view, see, e.g., Wilson v. Pope Mfg. Co., 52 La. Ann. 1417, 27 So. 851, 50 L.R.A. 816, 78 Am. St. Rep. 390; Ft. Worth & R. C. R. Co. v. Robertson, 103 Tex. 504, 121 S. W. 202, 131 S. W. 400, Ann. Cas. 1913 A 231. As to California, see post, § 83.1.

[18] See, e.g., McFadden v. Santa Ana, Orange & Tustin Ry. Co., 87 Cal. 464, 25 P. 681, 11 L.R.A. 252.

[19] Dawson v. McNaney, 71 Ariz. 79, 22 P.2d 907.

[20] See 1943 edition of this work, 1 de Funiak, § 82, quoted in full in Soto v. Vandeventer, 56 N.M. 43, 245 P.2d 846, 35 A.L.R. 2d 1190.

[21] Tinker v. Hobbs, 80 Ariz. 166, 294 P.2d 659; Labonte v. Davidson, 31 Ida. 644, 175 P. 588; Schneider v. Biberger, 76 Wash. 504, 136 P. 701, 6 A.L.R. 1056. California, see post, § 83.1.

Husband or wife as proper person to bring action to recover for personal injuries to wife, see post, § 125.

[22] City of Phoenix v. Dickson, 40 Ariz. 403, 12 P.2d 618; Lorang v. Hays, 69 Ida. 440, 209 P.2d 733.

Wife absent on a visit but not living separate and apart, see Schneider v. Biberger, 76 Wash. 504, 136 P. 701, 6 A.L.R. 1056.

[23] See Ligon v. Ligon, 39 Tex. Civ. App. 392, 87 S. W. 838, under old view.

[24] Notice such a statute as Cal. Civ. Code, § 5131, as to earnings of husband during period that wife has unjustifiably abandoned him. And see ante, § 57.

[25] Fordyce v. Fordyce, 70 Tex. 694, 8 S. W. 504; Lamar & Smith v. Stroud, (Tex. Civ. App.) 5 S. W. 2d 824; Schneider v. Biberger, 76 Wash. 504, 136 P. 701, 6 A.L.R. 1056; O'Toole v. Faulkner, 34 Wash. 371, 75 P. 975.

Death of husband while action pending against wrongdoer; substitution of husband's administratrix as a party plaintiff, Fox Tucson Theatres Corp. v. Lindsay, 47 Ariz. 388, 56 P.2d 183. Similarly, see Gomez v. Scanlan, 2 Cal. App. 579, 84 P.50.

states, specifically in Louisiana, Nevada, New Mexico and Texas, there has been a departure from the flat view in favor of the community property nature of such a right of action and the damages therefrom, a change brought about sometimes by statute, sometimes by judicial decision, sometimes by a combination of both.[26]

Thus, in 1915 the Texas legislature enacted a statute providing that all property or monies received as compensation for personal injuries sustained by the wife should be her separate property.[27] However, this statute was quickly held unconstitutional by the Texas courts, on the theory that the statute was an invalid attempt by the legislature to enlarge the constitutional definition of the wife's separate property.[28] In 1967 the Texas legislature enacted a new statute providing that the recovery awarded for personal injuries sustained by either spouse during marriage shall be the separate property of that spouse except for any recovery for loss of earning capacity during marriage.[29] The basic theory of this statute is that physical well-being is an asset which a spouse brings into the marriage. Property which is owned by the spouse before marriage is regarded as separate property. Items which are in replacement of such property are regarded as separate property. Therefore, it should be possible that compensation for the loss of physical well-being could be made separate property also. The statute so provides, with the exception of recovery for loss of earning capacity during marriage. The earning capacity as such, would presumably be translated into earnings during the marriage, which would be community property.[30] At the time of this writing there were no cases on the new statute, and it was not known what position the courts would take when they did begin to consider it.

The Louisiana Code in 1902 adopted a similar provision that damages resulting from personal injuries to the wife should be her separate property,[31] and although the language of an amendment of another article of the code in 1912 described as the separate property of the wife "actions for damages resulting from offenses and quasi-offenses and the property purchased with all funds thus derived,"[32] it would seem that the two provisions may be read together without inconsistency.[33]

California, which was temporarily in the modern field and then

---

[26] See discussions of specific states, following.

[27] Art. 4615, Tex. Rev. Civ. Stat. as adopted in 1915.

[28] Northern Texas Traction Co. v. Hill, 297 S. W. 778 (Tex. Civ. App., *writ ref'd*). This case relies on Arnold v. Leonard, 114 Tex. 540, 273 S.W. 801.

Decision prior to the statute, see Ft. Worth & Rio Grande Ry. Co. v. Rob-

ertson, 103 Tex. 504, 121 S. W. 202, 131 S. W. 400.

[29] Tex. Family Code 1969, § 5.01.

[30] McSwain, A Survey of the New Marital Property Statutes, 2 Newsletter of the Family Law Section of the State Bar of Texas 3.

[31] La. Civ. Code, art. 2402.

[32] La. Civ. Code, art. 2334.

[33] See Louisiana cases, infra, this section.

retrograded, is discussed in the section following.[34] Judicial decisions appear to have established the modern view in New Mexico[35] and in Nevada[36] plus the fact that in Nevada a statutory provision can be considered to buttress the judicial decisions.[37]

The frequently evident dissatisfaction with the frequently inadequate reasons given for the doctrine that compensation for personal injuries to a spouse is community property lie in an incomplete understanding of the true principles of community property. This incomplete understanding in itself often leads to a too literal interpretation of the local statutes. The misgivings of some courts in respect to exchange during marriage of separate property for other property have already been instanced; that is, they have sometimes felt that the property received in exchange should also be separate property, but yet when they view the local statutes with provisions to the effect that all property acquired during marriage is community property except that received by gift, bequest, devise or inheritance, they become worried. Property received by way of exchange, they reason, is not received through gift, etc., and is acquired during marriage, therefore doesn't the statute require by its absolute letter that property received by way of exchange be considered community property? Their usual decision to consider the property received in exchange for separate property as taking the character of separate property is a fortunate triumph of common sense over a lack of understanding of the principles of community property.[38] But apparently the courts are inclined to apply a similar reasoning to the right of action for personal injuries and to the compensation received; that is, it is property acquired during marriage and is not acquired by gift, etc., therefore it must be community property. But this overlooks the principles of onerous and lucrative titles and other pertinent principles. Except for gifts clearly made to the marital community, community property only consists of that which is acquired by onerous title, that is, by labor or industry of the spouses, or which is acquired in exchange for community property (which, of course, was acquired itself by onerous title, again with the exception as to the gift). It must be plainly evident that a right of action for injuries to person, reputation, property, or the like, or the

[34] See post, § 82.1.

[35] Soto v. Vandeventer, 56 N.M. 482, 245 P.2d 826, 35 A.L.R. 2d 1190. And see Richards v. Richards, 59 N.M. 308, 283 P.2d 881.

[36] Frederickson & Watson Const. Co. v. Boyd, 60 Nev. 117, 102 P.2d 627. See also Underhill v. Anciaux, 68 Nev. 69, 226 P.2d 794; Meagher v. Garvin, (Nev.) 391 P.2d 507; King v. Yancey, (9 C.A.) 147 F.2d 379; Choate v. Ransom, (Nev.) 323 P.2d 700.

[37] Nev. Rev. St. 1956 § 41.170, formerly Nev. Comp. Laws Ann. § 3389.01 (Supp. 1949), providing that husband and wife may sue jointly and that damages are then to be segregated, those by reason of wife's personal injury and pain and suffering being awarded to wife as her separate property, while those for loss of services and for hospital and medical expenses, etc., are awarded to husband (as manager of the community property, of course).

[38] See ante, § 77.

compensation received therefor, is not property acquired by onerous title. The labor and industry of the spouses did not bring it into being. For that matter, it is not property acquired by lucrative title either.[39] What then, is it? Since the right of action for injury to the person, or for that matter, to the reputation, is intended to bring about compensation for the injury, and the compensation is intended to repair or make whole the injury, so far as is possible in such a case, the compensation partakes of the same character as that which has been injured or suffered loss.[40] In this respect, the situation is very similar to an exchange of property during marriage. But what or who has been injured? Is it the marital community or is it the separate individuality of the spouse? In actuality, both. The physical injury to the spouse, the pain and suffering of the spouse therefrom is an injury to the spouse as an individual.[41] If the spouse also suffers monetary loss to separate property or from inability to pursue allowable separate projects, that also is a loss to the spouse separately and as an individual.[42] But on the other hand, if the injury deprives the marital

[39] The Nevada Supreme Court has been aware of the fact that "property acquired" during marriage more properly means "wages, salaries, earnings or other property acquired through the toil or talent or other productive faculty of either spouse" and does not properly include compensation to a married woman for personal injury; such compensation, says the court, takes the place of the right of personal security which was violated and belongs to the wife. Frederickson & Watson Const. Co. v. Boyd, 60 Nev. 117, 102 P.2d 627. Similarly, in New Mexico, see Soto v. Vandeventer, 56 N.M. 43, 245 P.2d 826, 35 A.L.R. 2d 1190.

Onerous and lucrative titles, see ante, § 62.

See also criticism by Horowitz, 11 Wash. Law Rev. 228, 229.

[40] See Frederickson & Watson Const. Co. v. Boyd; Soto v. Vandeventer, preceding note.

Where the injury is to property the question whether the injury is to one spouse separately or to the marital community is, of course, easier to determine, since it is dependent upon the character of the property injured. See post, § 86.

[41] See Frederickson & Watson Const. Co. v. Boyd; Soto v. Vandeventer, supra.

The Arizona court, in discussing the necessity that the husband as head of the marital community bring the action for injury to the wife, actually gets to the point of recognizing that the cause of action does not really belong to him but to the wife who was injured, that the injury was personal to the wife, that it was her body that was bruised, that it was she who suffered the agonizing mental and physical pain, but the court still remains blind to the fact that therefore the recovery therefor should belong to the wife and continues to consider the recovery as community property. See Fox Tucson Theatres Corp. v. Lindsay, 47 Ariz. 388, 56 P.2d 183.

[42] In Scoville v. Keglor, 27 Cal. App. 2d 17, 80 P.2d 162, although the former California rule was repeated that all general damages for personal injuries to both spouses were community property, including damages for loss of time and impairment of the husband's earning power, there was evidently a finding segregating from the damages $600 for the demolition of an automobile as the separate property of the wife. So far as concerned the damages for the husband's loss of earning power and the demolition of the wife's separate property, these were correctly community and separate property respectively.

community of the earnings or services of the spouse, that is an injury to the marital community;[43] likewise there is loss to the community where the community funds are expended for hospital and medical expenses, etc.[44] Since the husband is usually the breadwinner, contributing definite earnings, the loss to the marital community resulting from an injury to him is more obvious and more easily calculable in monetary figures. Therefore, there is usually little question that an injury depriving the community wholly or partly of his earnings is an injury to the community.[45] If the wife is contributing earnings to the marital community, any injury interrupting or lowering these earnings is equally, as in the case of the husband, an injury to the community, and a cause of action for such injury is property of the community.[46] This has been recognized in Louisiana where the statute makes damages resulting from personal injury to the wife the separate property

[43] See Simon v. Harrison (La. App.), 200 So. 476; Kientz v. Charles Dennery, Inc. (La. App.), 17 So.2d 506 (in both cases earnings were those of wife); Martin v. Huff Truck Line, Inc. (La. App.), 32 So.2d 49; Glen Falls Ins. Co. v. Yarbrough (Tex. Civ. App.) 369 S. W. 2d 640.

[44] Medical expenses, etc., see post, this section.

Notice that upon injury to a person before marriage, the damages, although recovered during marriage, are held to be the separate property of the person injured. See St. Louis & S. W. Ry. v. Wright, 33 Tex. Civ. App. 80, 75 S. W. 565; Finley v. Winkler, 99 Cal. App. 2d 887, 222 P.2d 345; Morrissey v. Kirkelies, 5 Cal. App. 2d 183, 42 P.2d 361.

[45] As to the so-called civil damage statutes giving a wife the right to sue on a liquor dealer's bond because of his wrongful sale of liquor to her husband, see Hahn v. Goings, 22 Tex. Civ. App. 576, 56 S. W. 217, a frequently cited case. There the money recovered was said to be the separate property of the wife because the statute gave her the right to bring the action. This is an inadequate reason. If the wrongful sale results in an injury to the husband or otherwise results in the husband's earning power being impaired, the injury is actually to the marital community. It is reasonable to assume that the statute merely makes the wife the agent of the mari-

tal community to collect the sum, as in the case of the California statute which permits the wife to bring the action to recover for personal injuries to herself. In Arizona, even in the absence of a civil damage statute, a wife was allowed to prosecute an action against and recover damages from one who sold intoxicating liquor to her husband with knowledge that the husband was a habitual drunkard. The court declared the wife had a right of action for the loss of consortium which was a property right belonging to her individually. Pratt v. Daly, 55 Ariz. 535, 104 P.2d 147, stating that this was so, regardless of whether the damages recovered would become community property.

[46] As in Simon v. Harrison and Kientz v. Charles Dennery, Inc. (La.), supra. And see Giffen v. Lewiston, 6 Ida. 231, 55 P.2d 545.

Likewise, as to medical and hospital expenses paid by husband on behalf of injured wife as expenses incurred by community, for which action is to be brought by husband on behalf of the community, see White v. Coca Cola Bottling Co. (La. App.), 16 So.2d 579; Kientz v. Charles Dennery, Inc. (La. App.), 17 So.2d 506.

Right to recover amount expended for hire to servant employed to do household work which personal injury to wife incapacitated her from doing, see Martin v. Southern Pac. Co., 130 Cal. 285, 62 P. 515; Lively v. State (La. App.), 15 So.2d 617.

of the wife.[47] Even if the wife is not contributing earnings to the marital community, her services are a definite asset of the marital community, and the community, if wholly or partly deprived of them, suffers a loss which should render the right of action and the compensation therefor the property of the community. It is not alone the question of hospital and medical bills involved, although these are definitely a drain on the community property; it may be necessary to employ someone to keep house, to look after the children, the expenses for which definitely tend to indicate the value of the wife's services to the marital community and the loss thereto by deprivation of her services.[48]

The only logical conclusion, therefore, is that a personal injury to a spouse, or for that matter an injury to reputation or the like, may give rise to a cause of action in the injured spouse and also in the marital community.[49] This should be so without the necessity of stat-

---

[47] See Simon v. Harrison (La. App.), 200 So. 476, which consolidated suits by a husband and a wife to recover damages for personal injuries resulting from a collision of automobiles. The appellate court allowed an award to the wife for the actual injuries suffered to her person but refused to allow an award made her in the trial court for loss of earnings resulting from impairment of her ability to follow her profession of acrobatic dancer, adding that "we do not think that it is properly allowed for the reason that any earnings produced by Mrs. Simon from her professional ability necessarily fell into the community of acquests and gains which existed between her and her husband, C. C. art. 2402, and any loss sustained therefrom would be a loss recoverable by the community which would have to be demanded by the husband as head and master of the community."

[48] Although the damages recovered for the personal injuries sustained by the wife are, in Louisiana, the separate property of the wife, items of damages for doctor bills, nurse bills, drug bills, and the like are expenses of the community for which the husband alone can recover. Shield v. F. Johnson & Son Co., 132 La. 773, 61 So. 787, 47 L. R. A. (N.S.) 1080.

"Note from this law that just as profit is shared between husband and wife, so are losses and expenses in-

curred by reason of the partnership, e.g., doctor's fees, the price of medicines, traveling expenses." Matienzo, Gloss VII, No. 1 to Nov. Rec. Law 2, Book 10, Title 4.

Note that former Texas statute, ante, n. 27, although providing that damages for personal injuries to the wife shall be her separate property, made an exception as to hospital and medical bills and all expenses incident to collection of the compensation. Tex. Rev. Civ. Stats. 1925, art. 4615.

[49] Injury to the husband and injury to the marital community from the same act has been recognized as ground for two separate actions. Lindsay v. Oregon Short Line R. Co., 13 Idaho 477, 90 P. 984, 12 L. R. A. (N.S.) 184, where, however, with much inconsistency the court seems to take the attitude that the injury to the husband gives rise to a cause of action that is his separate property, while injury to the wife from the same act gives a cause of action that is community property. This, of course, is not a logical separation of what is separate and what is community property; it seems merely a variation, because of lip service to community property principles, of the common law rule that everything acquired by the husband is his and everything acquired by the wife is also the husband's.

In the case of injury to a minor it

utory intervention. Indeed, it is probable that such statutes as have been enacted in some of the states result from a hazy idea of the true state of affairs. Louisiana, by statute and judicial decision combined, has arrived at the correct understanding of the situation,[50] and much the same may be said of Nevada[51] and New Mexico.[52]

The courts which declare that the injury to one spouse gives the other spouse a right of action for loss of consortium and that the right of action is an individual property right belonging to the latter spouse,[53] are being governed entirely by common law considerations. In the old common law the wife being virtually the property of the husband, her society and services were valuable property rights of his for which he was entitled to recover compensation when they were lost to him through injury to the wife.[54] Such a view, even the liberalized version of it at the present day, has no application to a system such as the community property system where the spouses are united in a conjugal partnership in the gains and earnings during marriage so that the services and labors of each are assets of the conjugal partnership itself and where the injury to one of the spouses depriving the conjugal partnership of the loss of that spouse's services is a loss to the conjugal partnership.[55]

§ 83. — Contributory negligence.

This brings us to a consideration of what has often been a controversial matter, that of the contributory negligence of one spouse as affecting the right of recovery for injuries to the other spouse. Courts flatly applying the doctrine that a right of action for personal injuries to one spouse belongs to the community usually hold that, if the negligence of the other spouse contributed to the injuries of the injured spouse, such contributory negligence must be attributed to the community, thus barring recovery on behalf of the community.[56]

---

is recognized that two causes of action may arise, one in favor of the minor for the pain and suffering and the permanent injury and one in favor of the parents for the loss of the child's services during minority. See, e.g., Harris v. Puget Sound Electric R. Co., 52 Wash. 289, 100 P. 838.

[50] See Louisiana cases and statutes cited ante, nn. 31, 32, 43, 47.

[51] See Frederickson & Watson Const. Co. v. Boyd, 60 Nev. 117, 102 P.2d 627.

[52] See Soto v. Vandeventer, 56 N.M. 43, 245 P.2d 826, 35 A.L.R. 2d 1190.

[53] See, e.g., Pratt v. Daley, 55 Ariz. 535, 104 P.2d 147.

[54] See 3 Blackstone's Com. 140.

[55] Notice that in California, husband has been entitled to recover on behalf of the community for the loss to it of wife's services but not entitled to recover for loss of wife's consortium. West v. San Diego, 54 Cal. 2d 469, 6 Cal. Rptr. 289, 353 P.2d 929. Same view in Louisiana, see 88 F. Supp. 908. Likewise, wife had no cause of action for loss of husband's consortium. Deshotel v. Atchison, etc., Ry. Co., 50 Cal. 2d 64, 328 P.2d 444, noted 6 UCLA Law Rev. 161.

[56] See cases cited, 59 A.L.R. 161; 110 A.L.R. 1103; 35 A.L.R. 2d 1190.

As an illustration, a frequent occurrence is that the husband and wife are riding in the family conveyance with the husband driving, and a collision occurs with a train or another conveyance, and the wife is injured. If the negligence of the husband contributed to the collision, this contributory negligence has usually been attributed to the community on behalf of which the action is brought and the recovery sought.[57] But if we apply the principles formulated in the preceding section, it should be apparent that the cause of action does not pertain entirely to the community. The wife is properly entitled to a cause of action to the extent at least of her pain and suffering and any monetary loss to her separate property that she has sustained. Of course, if the husband's negligence was the sole cause of the accident and there has been no negligence on the part of the third person, the wife should have no cause of action against such third person.[58] But if, aside from the husband's negligence, there has been some negligence on the part of the third person contributing to bring about the injury to the wife, he should be liable to her to the extent that his negligence imposes liability upon him,[59] and the husband's contributory negligence should not defeat the right of the wife to recover against such third person who has himself been guilty of negligence.[60] Naturally, the contributory negligence of the husband must be attributed to the marital community so far as affects any right of action on behalf of the marital community.[61]

In a jurisdiction which still adheres to the view that the right of action and the proceeds are community property in all aspects, the fact that the injured spouse does not sue until after dissolution of the marriage has not affected the view that the other spouse's contributory negligence defeats the recovery.[62] This could even be so held where the injury occurs while the spouses are living separate and apart but undivorced, if the right of action is still classed as community prop-

[57] See, e.g., Tinker v. Hobbs, 80 Ariz. 166, 294 P.2d 659. Under old rule in California, see McFadden v. Santa Ana, etc., R. Co., 87 Cal. 464, 25 P. 681, 11 L.R.A. 252; Basler v. Sacramento Gas, etc., Co., 158 Cal. 514, 11 P. 530.

[58] Discussion of right of action in tort by one spouse against the other, see post, § 153.

[59] As to damages recovered for an injury inflicted on the wife by the husband and a third person as separate property of the wife, see Nickerson v. Nickerson, 65 Tex. 281, for an interesting discussion.

[60] This was recognized in Frederickson & Watson Const. Co. v. Boyd, 60 Nev. 117, 102 P.2d 627; Vitale v. Checker Cab Co., 166 La. 527, 117 So. 579, 59 A.L.R. 148; Elba v. Thomas (La.) 59 So.2d 732; King v. Yancey (9 C.A.) 147 F.2d 379.

[61] Kientz v. Charles Dennery, Inc. (La. App.), 17 So.2d 506.

In Louisiana, when the damage or loss results from injury in the operation of an automobile owned by the community on a mission for the community benefit, and there has been contributory negligence by one of the spouses, there can be no recovery by the community for the loss or damage. Levey v. New Orleans & Northeastern R. Co. (La. App.), 21 So.2d 155.

[62] Timber v. Hobbs, 80 Ariz. 166, 294 P.2d 659, where husband was injured spouse and sued after a divorce. In California, see post, § 83.1.

erty.[63] But this should not be true where it is classed as the separate property of the injured spouse.[64]

In the Spanish law, contributory negligence of the person injured defeated his or her right of recovery,[65] but since husband and wife were treated as separate individuals in their own right, the contributory negligence of one spouse could not defeat the other spouse's right of recovery.

§ 83.1.   — California.

In California, up to the year 1957, the cause of action and the damages recovered therefor for personal injury to a spouse during marriage were considered to be entirely community property. Even where it was the wife who was injured, the item of damages for her pain and suffering was originally to be recovered in an action by the husband along with other damages, since he was the manager of the community property. And it may be noticed that his contributory negligence could defeat the cause of action in its entirety, even the recovery of damages for the pain and suffering of the wife.[66] However, in the course of time the courts came to recognize that some sort of distinction existed between the damages for the wife's pain and suffering and the damages for the loss to the community arising from payment of medical expenses and the like, loss of any earnings, costs of employing a housekeeper or cook or nurse to perform household functions and other such expenses. This recognition did not extend to any view that there was a separate property cause of action in the wife but rather that two actions might lie on the same cause of action, one by the wife to recover the damages for her pain and suffering[67] and one by the husband to recover for the actual losses to the marital community.[68] These actions might be brought separately

---

[63] Consider discussion, ante, § 82.

[64] Lorang v. Hays, 69 Ida. 440, 209 P.2d 733. Similarly, in actions for wrongful death of minor child, see post, § 84.

[65] Las Siete Partidas, Part. 7, Title 15, Law 6.

[66] See, e.g., McFadden v. Santa Ana, O. & T. St. Ry. Co., 87 Cal. 464, 25 P. 681, 11 L.R.A. 252; Basler v. Sacramento Gas & Electric Co., 158 Cal. 514, 111 P. 530, Ann. Cas. 1912 A 642.

[67] Indeed, in Sanderson v. Niemann, 17 Cal. 2d 563, 110 P.2d 1025, the wife was declared to be the indispensable party plaintiff, although the husband might be joined with her. Cal. Code Civ. Proc. § 370, which

now gives the wife the right to sue alone for personal injuries sustained by her, did not change the rule in California that the damages recovered were community property. See Giorgetti v. Wollaston, 83 Cal. App. 358, 257 P. 109. This merely had the effect of making the wife the agent of the community for the collection of such damages.

[68] See Sanderson v. Niemann, preceding note.

However, wife could sue for both types of damages, without the husband being joined, under the theory that he had delegated authority to her to sue for loss to community. Louie v. Hagstrom's Food Stores, Inc., 81 Cal. App. 2d 601, 184 P.2d 708.

or joined,[69] but when brought separately, decisions in the first would be binding in the second.[70] Thus, the contributory negligence of the husband could, in any event, defeat the wife's recovery of damages for her own pain and suffering.[71] The state supreme court sought in various ways to do away with this latter result, such as deciding that if the wife brought her action after the husband's death or after a divorce that his contributory negligence would no longer be effective to defeat her claim for damages for her pain and suffering.[72]

Of course, the foregoing devices did not reach many cases and dissatisfaction undeniably existed over this fact of the wife's attempt to recover damages for her pain and suffering being subject to be defeated by this contributory negligence. Hence, in 1957, the legislature enacted a new statute, providing that all damages, general and special, recovered by a spouse for personal injuries were the separate property of such spouse.[73] This statute, far removed from the legislation recommended by the state bar, would appear to be ambiguous. On its face it would seem to be trying to make the entire damages, even those allowed for the loss to the community, the separate property of the injured spouse.[74] The hope of those critics of this legislation was that the state supreme court would interpret the situation as still recognizing a cause of action also in the marital community.[75]

Or it was hoped that the legislature would clarify the situation, by following the modern views now effective in Louisiana, Nevada, New Mexico and Texas.[76] However, in July 1968, the legislature suddenly enacted legislation setting the situation back to where it had been twelve years before, declaring the entire recovery of damages to be community property,[77] but with a confused situation that would seem to place the duty on the injured wife to sue for the entire recovery, whereupon the husband then seeks to recover from her

---

[69] See cases cited in preceding notes.

[70] See, e.g., Zaragosa v. Craven, 33 Cal. 2d 315, 202 P.2d 73.

[71] See Zaragosa v. Craven, preceding note.

[72] See, e.g., Washington v. Washington, 47 Cal. 2d 249, 302 P.2d 569, citing de Funiak, 1943 edition; Flores v. Brown, 39 Cal. 2d 692, 248 P.2d 922.

Lack of effect of agreement whereby husband guilty of contributory negligence sought to relinquish his community interest to injured wife, see Kesler v. Pabst, 43 Cal. 2d 254, 273 P.2d 257.

[73] Cal. Civ. Code, § 5109. Statute not retroactive. Ferguson v. Rogers, 68 Cal. App. 2d 486, 336 P.2d 234.

Award by state industrial accident commission not within meaning of statute. Estate of Simoni, 220 Cal. App. 2d 339, 33 Cal. Rptr. 848, noted 4 Santa Clara Lawyer 236.

[74] See 1957 Cal. State Bar Jour.

[75] Generally, see Judge Brunn, California Personal Injury Damage Awards to Married Women, 13 UCLA Law Rev. 587; de Funiak, Personal Injuries Under the California Community Property Law, 3 Cal. West. L. Rev. 69.

[76] See ante, § 83.

[77] See Cal. Civ. Code, §§ 4808, 5109, 5112, 5113, 5117, 5122, 5124.

reimbursement for the community expenditures on account of her injury.[78] On the matter of the contributory negligence of the husband, part of the legislation relates to that and would appear to release the whole from defeat because of the husband's contributory negligence — certainly so long as it is the wife who sues.[79]

Further portions of this legislation make the damages the separate property of the injured spouse if it is received after decree of separate maintenance, interlocutory divorce, or of an injured wife if she is living separate and apart from the husband, or of the injured husband if the wife has unjustifiably deserted him.[80] There is a right of reimbursement to the other spouse for expenses paid from his or her separate property or from community property subject to his or her control.[81]

It seems to the authors that the simple solution to the whole problem would have been merely to clarify the 1957 statute by making it clear that two causes of action exist, one in the injured spouse for pain and suffering and one in the marital community for its expenses and losses.

§ 84. Wrongful death.

What is the situation when the personal injuries result in or cause the death of the injured spouse? Is a recovery under the wrongful death statutes also community property? The courts have frequently extended the doctrine that injury to one spouse gives a right of action to the marital community to the situation of wrongful death, and have held that the right of action for wrongful death of a spouse and the compensation or damages received therefor belong to the marital community.[82] The extension of the doctrine to wrongful death cases has been strongly attacked, and it has been argued that community property is property acquired during the existence of the marital relation, that damages for wrongful death cannot be recovered during the marital relation and thus cannot be community property.[83]

[78] See Cal. Civ. Code, §§ 5117, 5126.

[79] See Cal. Civ. Code, § 5112.

[80] See Cal. Civ. Code, § 5126.

[81] See Cal. Civ. Code, § 5126.

[82] A much cited case is Ostheller v. Spokane & Inland Empire R. Co., 107 Wash. 678, 182 P. 630, in which, however, the court said that the contributory negligence of the husband was the negligence of the community so as to bar recovery both for the deaths of the husband and the wife.
Wrongful death of minor child, see post, § 85.

[83] See Redfield v. Oakland Consol. St. Ry. Co., 110 Cal. 277, 42 P. 822; Blackwell v. American Film Co., 189 Cal. 689, 209 P. 999.
See also Jacob, Law of Community Property in Idaho, 1 Idaho Law Jour. 1, 40, who points out that in Spokane & Inland Empire R. Co. v. Whitley, 237 U. S. 487, 59 L. Ed. 1060, 35 S. Ct. 655, L.R.A. 1915 F 736, aff'g 23 Idaho 642, 132 P. 121, it was held that the right of action given by the Idaho wrongful death statute had nothing to do with the estate of the decedent or the right of the decedent but was an entirely independent right given to someone else ("heirs or personal representatives") and gave no

Nevertheless, the community may have been injured by the wrongful death to the extent of having been deprived of the earnings or services of the dead spouse for the period of the normal life expectancy of that spouse.[84] But, assuming death was not instantaneous, any pain or suffering on the part of the spouse between the time of the injury and the death resulting therefrom would not pertain to the marital community. Admittedly, however, much is dependent upon the provisions of the particular statute as to who has the right of recovery.

In the civil law, it may be remarked, a right of action in the heirs has almost uniformly been recognized, dating back to the Roman law.[85] And the right of recovery included not only the amount of expenses which might have been incurred for medical attendance but also compensation to those such as his children, wife or parents who had a right to be maintained by the deceased, based on consideration of the age, fortune and employment of the deceased.[86]

§ 85.   Injuries to or death of minor child.

In the case of damages recovered by parents for personal injuries to or for the death of their minor child, such damages are usually said to be community funds.[87] If the marital community as represented by the parents is entitled to the services of the child and suffers a loss

right of recovery that would be assets of the decedent's estate. But suppose the statute does give the right of action to the decedent's estate?

Where the husband killed the wife, the recovery by the heirs for the wrongful death was not community property. Russell v. Cox, 65 Idaho 534, 148 P.2d 221.

That mental suffering of wife after husband's death was not community property, see Western Union Tel. Co. v. Kelly (Tex. Civ. App.), 29 S. W. 408.

[84] See Blackwell v. American Film Co., 189 Cal. 689, 209 P. 999, but to the effect, however, that the money recovered should not go directly to the widow and children but to the estate as an asset for payment of debts, the balance to go to the widow and children.

[85] This fact seems to have been misunderstood by the Louisiana court in Hubgh v. New Orleans & C. R. Co., 6 La. Ann. 495; subsequently, however, in Hermann v. New Orleans & C. R. Co., 11 La. Ann. 5, it indicated that it might have been mistaken but seemed to consider itself bound by the stand first taken.

[86] See Lobingier, "Modern Civil Law," 40 Corpus Juris 1327, 1328, and authorities cited.

[87] See Flores v. Brown, 39 Cal. 2d 622, 248 P.2d 922; Fuentes v. Tucker, 31 Cal. 2d 1, 10, 187 P.2d 752; Abos v. Martyn, 10 Cal. App. 2d 698, 52 P.2d 987; Hawkins v. Schroeter (Tex. Civ. App.) 212 S. W. 2d 843; Chicago, R. I. & G. Ry. Co. v. Oliver, (Tex. Civ. App.) 159 S. W. 853. But see Sutton v. Champagne, 141 La. 469, 75 So. 209, where husband and wife joined in action for son's wrongful death and court held that recovery by wife was her separate property by virtue of statute giving her a right of action for offenses and quasi-offenses; Baca v. Baca, 71 N.M. 468, 379 P.2d 765, holding right of action and proceeds not community property; evidently divisible as separate property of each spouse, so contributory negligence of one not bar to action by other spouse.

of those services from the personal injuries or death, it is evident that here there is an ascribable loss to the marital community. Explaining it, as some courts do, merely on the ground that the compensation recovered is "property acquired during marriage" and thus community property, is a totally inadequate explanation. The question of earnings of a minor child as community property has been discussed previously.[88]

Where the spouses have been divorced, that one who has been awarded the custody of the minor child is entitled to the services and earnings of the child and so, of course, the right of action and the recovery therefrom for the injury to or wrongful death of the child is the separate property of that spouse.[89] And where a wife had been living separate and apart from the husband, though not divorced, and she sued for and recovered for the wrongful death of the minor child of whom she had the immediate custody, such recovery was said to be an "accumulation" within the meaning of the local statute that earnings and accumulations of a wife while living separate and apart are her separate property.[90] While custody in such situation might result from some court order, it may also result from some agreement or understanding on the part of the spouses; this might well be interpreted as consent that the spouse having custody, whether husband or wife, is entitled to the services and earnings of the child.[91]

Subject to the rules governing as to contributory negligence,[92] where the negligence of one or both parents contributes to the injury or death of the child, this will bar a recovery since the negligence is imputed to the marital community.[93] But where the parent contributing to the injury or death of the child has died, recovery by the surviving spouse has not been barred by such contributory negligence.[94]

§ 86.   Property injuries.

Whether a right of action for injuries to property, or the damages or compensation received therefor, is separate or community property necessarily depends upon the nature of the property injured. If the injury is to community property, the right of action therefor, or the compensation recovered, is also community property; if for injuries to separate property, the damages recovered are, of course, separate

[88] See ante, § 68.1.

[89] Divorce generally, see post, Chap. X, C.

[90] Christiana v. Rose, 100 Cal. App. 2d 46, 222 P.2d 891.

[91] Agreements between spouses, see post, Chap. VIII.

[92] See ante, § 83.

[93] Cossi v. Southern Pac. Co., 110 Cal. App. 110, 293 P. 263.

Similarly, as to attempt to recover for wrongful death of adult child, see Cervantes v. Maco Gas Co., 2 Cal. Rptr. 75.

Cf. Baca v. Baca (N.M.), supra, this section.

[94] Flores v. Brown, 39 Cal. 2d 622, 248 P.2d 922; M-K-T R.R. v. Hamilton (Tex. Civ. App.) 314 S. W. 114, error ref'd, n.r.e., noted 13 S. W. Law Jour. 295.

property.[95] Nevertheless, even where the property is community property, a tort in relation to such property may injure one of the spouses separately and individually as well as the marital community. For example, the illegal seizure of community property has been said to be definitely a wrong to the marital community and the right of action therefore is the property of the community, but the illegal seizure may also be a wrong to the wife who is in peaceful possession of the property and is thus wrongfully deprived of its use.[96]

D. CONFLICT OF LAWS

§ 87.   Importance of application of principles.

The application of principles of conflict of laws to marital property becomes of importance in several particulars: a man and a woman, at the time of marrying in one jurisdiction, own property in other jurisdictions; the spouses while living in one jurisdiction acquire property in other jurisdictions; spouses married in one jurisdiction, making at the time an express or implied agreement as to the nature of their interests in property to be acquired, move to another jurisdiction, taking their property with them or acquiring property there after arrival. What is the nature of the property which may be owned by a man and woman at the time of marriage or acquired by them after marriage? Is it community or separate property, and by what law is such question to be determined? With our fifty states, some of them having the community property system and some not, with our frequent tendency to change our domiciles from one state to another, our acquisitions of property in one state while domiciled in another, the question of what law governs the nature of the property acquired by spouses, whether it is community or separate property, is frequently one of considerable difficulty.[97]

§ 88.   Spanish views.

It might be thought that questions of conflict of laws in relation to the nature of marital property rights did not constitute a question

---

[95] The rule is well established by the cases. See, e.g., Lorang v. Hayes, 69 Ida. 440, 209 P.2d 773; Peltier v. Begovich, 39 La. 238, 118 So.2d 395; Polk v. New York Fire & Marine Underwriters, Inc. (La.) 192 So.2d 667; Frederickson & Watson Const. Co. v. Boyd, 60 Nev. 117, 102 P.2d 627; Garrett v. Reno Oil Co. (Tex. Civ. App.) 271 S. W. 2d 674, writ ref'd, n.r.e.; Gillam v. City of Centralia, 14 Wash. 2d 523, 128 P.2d 661.

"The party who caused the damage must make reparation to the party who sustained it." Las Siete Partidas, Part. 7, Title 15, Law 3.

[96] See Rogers v. Burglass (La. App.), 171 So. 106.

Right of wife abandoned by husband to bring action for wrongful seizure of community property, see Leeds v. Reed (Tex. Civ. App.), 36 S. W. 347. See also post, § 126.

[97] Conflict of laws with relation to prosecution of civil actions, see post, § 120.

of much import in the Spanish law of community property. But in Las Siete Partidas of 1263 we find the provision that when a man and woman marry, making at the time an agreement as to the manner in which they shall hold the property earned by them during the marriage, and thereafter go to live in another country having customs contrary to that of the agreement, upon the death of one of them the agreement that they made should be given effect; indeed, it provided further that even if they entered into no agreement, the custom of the country where they contracted the marriage should be given effect and not that of the place to which they removed.[98] And we find the Spanish jurisconsult, Matienzo, discussing at considerable length, three hundred and fifty years ago, the views and authorities upon the subject of conflict of laws.[99] In regard to the law that property acquired during the marriage is common property and must be divided equally between the spouses and their heirs, he remarks that one of the limitations "which should be put upon this law is that it applies so long as there is no different custom in force in any particular state or province of this realm. . . . There is still such a [different] custom in the state of Cordova where this law is not received and there is no sharing of property between husband and wife."[1] He then points out that "With regard to this limitation a nice question arises. Suppose that in the domicile of the husband it is the custom according to our law to divide property acquired during marriage, and that in the place where the marriage is contracted, say at Cordova, or in some other place outside this realm, such division or sharing of profits between spouses does not take place. Which law should be followed if a case arises in which a claim for division is made . . .? Must regard be had to the place where the marriage was contracted or to the place of the husband's domicile or to the place whither they have betaken themselves to reside or to the place where the property is situate?"[2] Leaving aside for the moment questions concerning the situs of property, in the absence of any express agreement between the parties as to how marital acquisitions should be divided,

---

[98] Las Siete Partidas, Part. 4, Title 3, Law 24.

"Only in the case of there being an agreement between the contracting parties, or the custom of the locality, introducing this community of interests, does Law 24, Title 11, Partida 4 provide that the property acquired during marriage be divided between husband and wife." Llamas y Molina, No. 4, to Nov. Rec. Law 6, Book 10, Title 4.

[99] Matienzo, Gloss I, Nos. 65–86, to Nov. Rec. Law 1, Book 10, Title 4.

Generally, see de Funiak, Some Aspects of Conflict of Laws in the Old Spanish Jurisprudence, 35 Ky. Law Jour. 175.

[1] Matienzo, Gloss I, No. 65 to Nov. Rec. Law 1, who remarks that formerly in the state of Hispala there had been a custom similar to that of Cordova.

In 1802, however, this custom of Cordova was abolished and the community of property made the law. See Novísima Recopilación, Book 10, Title 4, Law 13.

[2] Matienzo, Gloss I, No. 66, to Nov. Rec. Law 1.

"If the laws enacted or the customs adopted, with regard to the sharing or division of property acquired during marriage or with regard to anything else, in the place of the husband's domicile differ from those in force in the place where the marriage was contracted, the law to be observed is that of the husband's domicile and not that of the wife's domicile when the marriage was contracted." This was true although the husband changed his domicile by going to some new residence, for the parties were presumed to have contracted the marriage with intent to follow the husband's domicile.[3] The foregoing applied, however, only "in a case where the husband makes the marriage contract as a foreigner in the place of his wife's domicile without intending to stay and remain there and with the intention of returning at once to the place where he is domiciled and resides. In such a case it is natural to have regard to the customs not of the place where the marriage is contracted but of the place to which they betake themselves. . . . The case is different, however, if they make the contract of marriage with intent that they should reside as husband and wife in the place of the wife's domicile where the marriage contract was made. In that case, as the husband intends to live with his wife in the place of her domicile, the laws of her domicile must be followed."[4] The law of the Partida referred to above, in providing that if the spouses entered into no agreement the law of the place of contracting marriage should be given effect as regards their earnings, was considered to apply to cases only where the marriage was contracted with intent that the spouses should live in that place and reside there permanently but subsequently changed their minds. It had no application where the man contracted marriage in another jurisdiction than that of his domicile with the intent to return to that domicile again and reside there.[5]

When we come to the case of an express agreement between the spouses regarding their earnings during mariage, the agreement being made at the place where the marriage was contracted and where they

---

[3] Matienzo, Gloss I, No. 70, to Nov. Rec. Law 1.

According to Matienzo, a wife was charged with knowledge of the law of her husband's domicile and could not plead ignorance thereof to defeat its application to the earnings during the marriage. Only if she could prove that she believed in good faith that he was domiciled in the same state as herself and that the laws of that state were to govern the marital acquisitions could she obtain relief. Matienzo, Gloss I, No. 86, to Nov. Rec. Law 1.

[4] Matienzo, Gloss I, No. 71, to Nov. Rec. Law 1.

Judge Story followed this view in defining the matrimonial domicile to be "the domicile of the husband, if the intention of the parties be to fix their residence there; and of the wife, if the intention is to fix their residence there; and if the residence is to be in some other place, as in New York, then the matrimonial domicile would be in New York." Story, Conflict of Laws, 8th Ed., § 194.

Note that if the husband intends to reside at the domicile of the wife, this becomes his domicile, so that it is really the husband's domicile that still controls.

[5] Matienzo, Gloss I, No. 73, to Nov. Rec. Law 1.

intended to reside permanently, but subsequently they move to another jurisdiction which has laws contrary to that of their agreement, the case was governed by the law of the Partida, already referred to, that their express agreement should be recognized and given effect. Even if the express agreement was made according to the laws of the place where the marriage was contracted, and the spouses did not intend to reside there but to return to the husband's domicile where the law might be different, the express agreement was given effect. "If in the marriage contract there is an express agreement that such property is to go in whole or in part to one spouse or to the other or to both of them, such an agreement must be observed and all distinctions of places or customs are irrelevant. For such agreements are not contrary to good morals and indeed are actually approved of by the laws."[6] That is, since the Spanish law of community itself recognized the right of intending spouses to contract that their earnings and gains should be governed by some other arrangement than the provisions of the community property law, it was not against public policy to recognize such an agreement when entered into elsewhere. The fact that a man domiciled within the jurisdiction of the Spanish law went elsewhere to be married and returned to his domicile, having made a contract for other than equal division or sharing of earnings, was not an attempt to evade the Spanish laws or against the policy expressed by those laws, since he could make such an express agreement under the Spanish laws themselves.

Despite the foregoing, it was recognized that the law of the situs of property was an important factor and that property must be dealt with according to the law or custom of the place where situated and that the law or custom of another jurisdiction could not extend beyond its own territory to govern property situated elsewhere, least of all to govern property situated where different or contrary laws or customs were in force.[7] Some of the earlier commentators on the Roman codes made a distinction between a law *in personam* and one *in rem*, that is, that a law relating only to the persons of the spouses would control them in respect to their acquisitions in other jurisdictions, but the sounder view followed by the Spanish commentators was said to be that whether a statute spoke *in rem* or *in personam* it did not apply to property situated outside the jurisdiction acquired by the spouses.[8] In any event, it was pointed out, the Spanish statute providing for the equal sharing of earnings and gains was *in rem* in that it related

[6] Matienzo, Gloss I, No. 67, to Nov. Rev. Law 1.

[7] Matienzo, Gloss I, No. 74, to Nov. Rec. Law 1.

[8] Matienzo, Gloss I, No. 74, to Nov. Rec. Law 1, who declares, citing authorities, that this was also the view in France under the customs relating to division of property between spouses.

An excellent discussion of real and personal statutes and of the views of the jurisconsults of Holland and France on the subject is given in the opinion of Porter, J., in Saul v. His Creditors, 5 Mart. N. S. (La.) 569, 16 Am. Dec. 212.

directly to the property acquired during marriage and could have no extraterritorial application to property situated outside the jurisdiction.[9]

In regard to immovables, there was no question that they were subject to the law of the place where situated. In the case of movables, despite the principle of the Roman law that movables followed the person of their owner and thus were subject to the law of his domicile, "the contrary view is sounder and more popular, viz., that movable property is presumed to belong to the territory in which it is situate. . . . But you must understand this generally accepted rule as applying only when movable property is permanently and not merely temporarily situate in a place."[10] Thus "property which is in a place for a period and on its expiry is to be taken back to another place is not deemed to belong to the place where it is, but to the place whither it is to be taken. It is not deemed to be where it is found but rather belongs to the place of its destination and it should be dealt with according to the laws and customs of that place."[11] Accordingly, with regard to movable property acquired during the marriage "it is shared between husband and wife if it is situate in a place where there is in force a custom to this effect, or, alternatively, if it was intended by the acquiring spouse to be taken to such a place even though it was at the time of the marriage actually situate at Cordova or in some other place where no such custom is in force."[12]

"Now let us see what should be said with regard to annual returns and real rights such as the rent of a permanent lease (emphyteusis) or tax payments, mortgage-rent, land-rent or other annual returns. It is clear that such annual rents attach to the land which is subject to the rent and partake of its nature. . . . The principle is that such annual rents even if they are redeemable are reckoned as immovable property. . . . But with regard to rents which are not perpetual but only temporary we should say that the rule is the same as that as to movable property."[13]

In the case of debts and rights of action, after reviewing the authorities, it was pointed out that they were not confined to any certain place and could not be called property definitely situate in any place, but so far as regards their effective enforcement which was only possible in a definite place they were property in that place. So that in regard to the sharing and division of such rights of that nature as had been acquired during marriage, it was the law or custom of the place at which they could be enforced that had to be considered.[14]

[9] Matienzo, Gloss I, No. 75, to Nov. Rec. Law 1. And see Saul v. His Creditors, 5 Mart. N. S. (La.) 569, 16 Am. Dec. 212.

[10] Matienzo, Gloss I, Nos. 79, 80, to Nov. Rec. Law 1.

[11] Matienzo, Gloss I, No. 80, to Nov. Rec. Law 1.

[12] Matienzo, Gloss I, No. 81, to Nov. Rec. Law 1.

[13] Matienzo, Gloss I, Nos. 82, 83, to Nov. Rec. Law 1.

[14] Matienzo, Gloss I, Nos. 84, 85, to Nov. Rec. Laws 1.

§ 89.   American views.

In all of the community property states, property owned by each of the spouses at the time of contracting the marriage remains the separate property of that spouse.[15] And in all of our noncommunity property states statutes have now been enacted, in derogation of the common law, providing more or less to the same effect. As things stand now it is clear that there is little ground for conflict as to the nature of the spouse's ownership of his or her antenuptial property. The chief difficulty is in determining what law governs in determining the respective rights and interests of the spouses in property acquired during the marriage, in view of the conflict that must necessarily arise between the laws of the community property states on the one hand and the law of the noncommunity property states on the other.[16]

§ 90.   — Express agreements or contracts.

Where the spouses at the time of the marriage, or even after the marriage, enter into an express contract governing their rights and interests in property to be acquired there is no reason why such an express agreement should not govern and be recognized in other states than that in which it is made, provided that it was valid where made and provided that its recognition and enforcement are not against the public policy of the forum. So far as our community property states are concerned, most of them recognize the right of their own citizens to make prenuptial agreements or contracts that their marital property rights shall be governed by some other arrangement than the community of property provided for by the local law, and many recognize the same right as to postnuptial agreements or

---

[15] See ante, § 63.

[16] Discussions of the matter are naturally very numerous. The authors of this work naturally recommend their own writings in this field, including de Funiak, Conflict of Laws in the Community Property Field, 7 Ariz. L. Rev. 50; de Funiak, Commonwealth v. Terjen: Common Law Mutilates Community Property, 43 Va. L. Rev. 49. They also recommend the excellent work by Harold Marsh, Marital Property in Conflict of Laws, Univ. of Wash. Press, 1952. Other discussions, some good and some indifferent, and adequate citations of cases will be found in the following: Thomas, Community Property and the Conflict of Laws: Recapitulation, 4 S. W. L. Jour. 46; Conflict of Laws: Rules on Marital Property, 18 La. L. Rev. 557; Lay, Property Rights Following Migration from Community Property States, 19 Ala. L. Rev. 298; Ibid., 41 Temp. L. Q. 1; Marsh, Community Property and Conflict of Laws: Problems of the Oil and Gas Investor and Operator, 105 S. W. L. Jour. 368; Deering, Separate and Community Property and the Conflict of Laws, 30 Rocky Mt. L. Rev. 127; Leflar, Community Property and Conflict of Laws, 21 Calif. Law Rev. 221; Horowitz, Conflict of Laws: Problems in Community Property, 11 Wash. Law Rev. 121, 212; Harding, Matrimonial Domicile and Marital Rights in Movables, 30 Mich. Law Rev. 61; and see 92 A.L.R. 1347; 57 L.R.A. 353.

contracts;[17] accordingly, it could not be in any violation of the public policy of such states to recognize and give effect to such marital agreements or contracts made elsewhere even though they would have the effect of making earnings or gains acquired in community property states not community property.[18] As a matter of fact, marital property contracts have frequently been given effect by the courts of the community property states and as well by courts of noncommunity property states,[19] although in some cases the contracts have been most strictly construed from the standpoint that unless they were made with a change of domicile in view they did not affect property acquired after a change of domicile, with the result that the spouses' rights and interests in the property were held to be governed by the law of the new domicile despite the terms of the contract.[20]

§ 91.   — Absence of express contract; changes of domicile.

In the absence of an express agreement or contract between the spouses to govern their rights and interests in property acquired during the marriage,[21] the determination of what law governs their interests in such property has sometimes been a matter of confusion; but the application of the following principles should remove much of this confusion. If the spouses are married in the jurisdiction which they intend to be their matrimonial domicile, the law of that jurisdiction should naturally govern as to property there acquired.[22]

But if the spouses marry in a certain jurisdiction for purposes of convenience but do not intend to make that place their domicile, there is absolutely no reason why the law of that jurisdiction should

[17] See Ariz. Rev. St. 1956, § 25-201; Cal. Civ. Code, § § 5103, 5134–5136; Idaho Code 1948, § 32-916; La. Civ. Code, art. 2325; Nev. Rev. St. 1956, §§ 123.070, 123.080; Wash. Rev. Code 1961, § 26.16.120.

See also N.M. St. 1953, § 57-2-6; Tex. Family Code 1969, § 5.41. In those states policy opposes spouses entering into agreement contrary to community property regime. Texas, see Vaughn, The Policy of Community Property and Interspousal Transactions, 19 Baylor L. Rev. 20, at p. 67.

See post, § 135.

[18] As to effect of local statutes providing as to property acquired in the state by outsiders or by those moving to the state, see post, §§ 91, 92.

[19] See cases cited, Marsh, Marital Property in Conflict of Laws; Leflar, 21 Calif. Law Rev. 221, 224; Horo-witz, 11 Wash. Law Rev. 212: note, 27 Ill. Law Rev. 202. But compare the view of the federal government where federal income taxes are concerned. Blumenthal v. Commissioner of Internal Revenue, 60 F.2d 715.

[20] See, e.g., Hoefer v. Probasco, 80 Okla. 261, 196 P. 138 (reviewing many cases); Castro v. Illies, 22 Tex. 479, 73 Am. Dec. 277; Clark v. Baker, 76 Wash. 110, 138 P. 1025.

[21] As indicated at the beginning of § 89, laws relating to property already owned at the time of the marriage are now fairly uniform.

[22] Property acquired outside of the matrimonial domicile, see post, this section.

"Matrimonial domicile" as used in this section means the place which the spouses select as their home and in which they intend to live and do live.

control or govern.[23] The law which should govern is that of the husband's domicile to which the parties return after the marriage ceremony.[24] It has frequently happened, however, that the spouses did not plan to return to the domicile of the husband but to acquire a new domicile and this situation has caused some confusion among judges and legal writers. That is, should the marital property rights of the spouses be governed by the law of the husband's domicile at the time of the celebration of the marriage, a domicile they intend to abandon immediately thereafter, or should those rights be governed by the law of the new domicile they intend to acquire but have not yet actually acquired by physical presence which will complement their intent, but which is undoubtedly the jurisdiction in which their acquisitions and controversies relative thereto will accrue? If any agreement or tacit consent is to be implied between them as to what law they intend to govern their marital property rights, the application of common sense would indicate that they intended the law of the intended domicile to apply in preference to that of the husband's former domicile where they had no intention of living, or for that matter in preference to the law of the place of marriage which was merely fortuitous. In any event, the court of the new domicile would have jurisdiction of the parties and the property acquired there, by reason of their domicile there, and certainly should apply its law in preference to that of a place which was never the matrimonial domicile.[25] In the unusual event of movable property being acquired while the spouses are en route from the place of the celebration of the marriage to the intended new domicile, the law of the new domicile should be applied to determine the nature of the spouses' interests in the property, not only because if any contract at all is to be implied between the spouses as to what law shall govern their rights it must be the law of their intended domicile,[26] but also because movable property, according to the Spanish principles in such a case, belonged

[23] See Allen v. Allen, 6. Rob. (La.) 104, 39 Am. Dec. 553; Percy v. Percy, 9 La. Ann. 185; Connor v. Connor, 10 La. Ann. 440, aff'd 18 How. (U.S.) 591, 15 L. Ed. 497.

[24] See Ford's Curator v. Ford, 2 Mart. N. S. (La.) 574, 14 Am. Dec. 201; Allen v. Allen, 6 Rob. (La.) 104, 39 Am. Dec. 553. See also Brien Dit Desrochers v. Marchildon (Rap. Jud. Que.) 15 C. S. 318 (marriage celebrated in New Hampshire; husband's domicile in Quebec).

[25] Some interesting if academic discussions of this variation are contained in Leflar, Community Property and Conflict of Laws, 21 Calif. Law Rev. 221; Horowitz, Conflict of Laws: Problems in Community Property, 11 Wash. Law Rev. 121, 212; Harding, Matrimonial Domicile and Marital Rights in Movables, 30 Mich. Law Rev. 859; note, 43 Harv. Law Rev. 1286. Generally as to domicile, see Marsh, Marital Property in Conflict of Laws, Chap. 2.

[26] See Ford's Curators v. Ford, 2 Mart. N. S. (La.) 574, 14 Am. Dec. 201; Le Breton v. Nouchet, 3 Mart. N. S. (La.) 60, 5 Am. Dec. 736; Hayden v. Nutt, 4 La. Ann. 65; Arendell v. Arendell, 10 La. Ann. 566; Story, Conflict of Laws, 5th Ed., Chap. VI.

Texas v. Barrow, 14 Tex. 179, also presented a situation of this kind;

not to the place where it was temporarily but to the place whither it was to be taken and should be dealt with according to the laws of that place.[27] If it is immovable property which is involved, the law of the place of its situs can be applied.

But suppose spouses who have made no express agreement or contract in relation to marital property acquire a new domicile, not immediately after the marriage ceremony but after for some time having had a matrimonial domicile elsewhere. Are the courts of the new domicile to assume that they had impliedly or tacitly agreed that the law of the old matrimonial domicile should govern all future acquisitions of property even after they have moved to a new domicile having contrary laws or customs? According to the view of many jurists and writers, especially in Europe, this is what should be assumed and their acquisitions in the new domicile should continue, as was the case in the former domicile, to be governed by the laws and customs of the former domicile.[28] This view that such former law constituted an implied contract between the spouses, in relation to all their after-acquired property, which was effective even when they changed their domicile to a jurisdiction where a contrary law as to marital property rights prevailed, was applied in the famous English cases of *De Nicols v. Curlier*[29] and *In re De Nicols*.[30] There spouses, married in France under the French Civil Code providing that acquisitions during marriage were community property unless the spouses otherwise expressly contracted or stipulated, subsequently moved to England to live and acquired both movables and immovables. It was held that the French law constituted an implied contract between the spouses which governed their rights in the property acquired in England, rather than English law.

Exactly the same result was reached by the Ontario Court of Appeal in respect to property acquired in Ontario by spouses who had moved to Ontario from Quebec where they were married under laws similar to those of France.[31]

However, while in this country the view is followed that the spouses impliedly contract according to the law of the place of their

spouses domiciled in Mississippi decided to change their domicile to Texas and stopped in Tennessee while en route, and in that state the wife was given a slave by a relative; by Mississippi and Texas law the gift represented separate property of the wife, by Tennessee law it would be the husband's property; the Texas court held that the law of the intended domicile, Texas, must govern even though they had not yet come to Texas. Cf. McIntyre v. Chappell, 4 Tex. 187; Giddings v. Steele, 28 Tex. 732, 91 Am.

Dec. 336.

Principle discussed in Latterner v. Latterner, 121 Cal. App. 298, 8 P.2d 870, but seemingly not applicable to the facts.

[27] See ante, § 88.

[28] See Burge, Colonial and Foreign Laws, vol. 1, pp. 619–622.

[29] [1900] A. C. 21.

[30] [1900] 2 Chap. 410.

[31] Beaudoin v. Trudel, [1937] 1 Dom. Law Rep. 216.

matrimonial domicile, it is not considered that their implied contract makes that law govern their after-acquired property when they have subsequently changed their domicile to a jurisdiction where a contrary law governs marital property rights. The property acquired in the new domicile is considered controlled by the law of that jurisdiction, in the absence of any express and effective agreement between the spouses.[32] The leading American case on this subject, *Saul v. His Creditors*,[33] which early established this principle, has been followed "in literally hundreds of American cases," as one writer puts it, and who ascribes this to the fact that its result is so consonant with American common-law ideas despite an opinion based on authorities strange to common-law lawyers.[34] As a matter of fact, it appears that Judge Porter, in *Saul v. His Creditors,* in basing his decision upon the Spanish law as authority therefor, in part at least misread the interpretations of the Spanish jurisconsults as to the Spanish law. A careful study of the law of the Partida in question,[35] and of the commentaries of Matienzo and Llamas y Molina,[36] indicates that such law was a declaration of the policy to be followed in Spain, that is, that upon a removal to that jurisdiction by spouses who had married and lived elsewhere, the laws and customs of their matrimonial domicile as to marital earnings would be given effect in Spain; it was recognized, however, that the Spanish law in question could have no extraterritorial effect, and that the common principle was that property was usually dealt with according to the law or custom of the place where it was situate. At any rate, in Louisiana the matter is now governed by statute which provides that upon spouses moving to Louisiana their marital property rights are to be governed by the

---

[32] Notice In re Majot's Estate, 199 N.Y. 29, 92 N. E. 402, 29 L.R.A. (N. S.) 780, where despite a marriage under the French law, the New York court held that property acquired in that state after the spouses moved there was controlled by its laws. Cf. Bonati v. Welch, 24 N.Y. 157. And see Kashaw v. Kashaw, 3 Cal. 312, where spouses were domiciled in New York, husband went to California, and wife followed him several months later and claimed and received half the property he had acquired in California. See also In re Gulstine's Estate, 166 Wash. 325, 6 P.2d 628, as to a commingling.

Suppose only one spouse changes his or her domicile? See Succession of Dill, post, n. 37. And see In re Florance's Will, 7 N.Y.S. 578; Bonati v. Welch, 24 N.Y. 157 (where husband at time of his death was domiciled in New York and wife in France, which had been the matrimonial domicile; the rights she acquired under the law of her domicile were not lost or impaired by the husband's change of domicile).

[33] 5 Mart. N. S. (La.) 569, 16 Am. Dec. 212.

[34] Leflar, Community Property and Conflict of Laws, 21 Calif. Law Rev. 221, 223; see also Horowitz, Conflict of Laws: Problems in Community Property, 11 Wash. Law Rev. 121, 212; Harding, Matrimonial Domicile and Marital Rights in Movables, 30 Mich. Law Rev. 859; all of which cite numerous cases.

[35] See Law 24, Title 11, Part. 4. See also ante, § 88.

[36] See ante, § 88.

local law of acquests and gains.[37] Similar statutes are also in force in Texas,[38] Arizona,[39] and formerly in California and Washington,[40] and in the absence of statute, judicial decisions have established the same rule elsewhere. The usual view is that the community property laws of the state are real statutes and not personal statutes, that is, that they attach to and govern the property acquired in the state rather than affecting the persons of the spouses who may, as a matter of fact, at the time of marriage have been domiciled elsewhere where other laws were in force respecting marital property. The effectiveness of these laws usually relates to realty or interests therein acquired in the state, although they also relate to personalty acquired in the state after the spouses have removed their domicile to the state. These statutes should not, of course, apply to spouses moving to the state who have an express agreement or contract between them as to how their future acquisitions should be shared. Where other statutes of these states permit their own residents to make such contracts as to marital acquisitions, it would be extremely inconsistent to deny the same privilege of recognition to the already executed contracts of spouses moving into the state.[41]

An interesting point is that where a spouse enters into a contract of employment in a noncommunity property jurisdiction and subse-

---

[37] La. Civ. Code, art. 2401.

See Succession of Dill, 155 La. 47, 98 So. 752, wherein the husband alone moved to Louisiana, established his domicile there, and acquired movables. It was not explained why the wife never accompanied him, but it appeared that some years later she was committed to a New York asylum for the insane and her daughter appointed her guardian and such insanity, no doubt, is the answer. Upon the husband's death the court held, after reviewing the Louisiana cases and statutes, that the property acquired by the husband in Louisiana was community property. See also Cole v. Cole's Ex'rs, 7 Mart. N. S. (La.) 41; 18 Am. Dec. 241; Dixon v. Dixon's Ex'rs, 4 La. 188, 23 Am. Dec. 478. Cf. Kashaw v. Kashaw, 3 Cal. 312, post, this section.

[38] Tex. Family Code 1969, § 4.01.

[39] Ariz. Rev. St. 1956, § 25-217.

[40] And see Kashaw v. Kashaw, 3 Cal. 312, where spouses were domiciled in New York and husband went to California in 1850 to better his condition. He failed to provide for the wife and entered into an unlawful marriage with another woman. Several months later the wife followed him to California and claimed half the common property he had acquired there. The court held that her complaint was not demurrable, and that since a wife's domicile is that of her husband, her domicile had been California all the time the husband was in California.

Quasi-community property in California, see post, § 92.1.

[41] Such view seems to find support, obiter, in Succession of Dill, 155 La. 47, 98 So. 752. However, the Louisiana statutes, while providing that its law shall govern acquisitions of property by spouses moving to that state, give such spouses a year within which to contract between themselves as to how their acquired property shall be held.

Nevertheless, in Blumenthal v. Commissioner of Internal Revenue, 60 F.2d 715, where spouses were not only married in a community property jurisdiction—Alsace-Lorraine —but entered into an express ante-

quently removes his domicile to a community property state where compensation is received for his services, pursuant to the contract. Although the contract was entered into in a noncommunity property state that should not alter the fact that the compensation received for his services while domiciled in a community property state constitutes community property.[42] The converse should be true where the contract of employment is entered into in a community property state and subsequently the spouse removes to a noncommunity property state and receives compensation under the contract for services rendered in the latter state. This situation should not be confused, however, with that in which he remains domiciled, for example, in a community property state and earns money in noncommunity property states into which his business carries him. The law of his domicile, to which he intends to take the earnings, should govern their nature and character.[43]

It is well settled in this country that a change of domicile does not affect the nature of property which had already been acquired by the spouses at the time of the change of domicile.[44] Thus, property which is separate property under the law of the noncommunity property state under which it was acquired remains separate property when the spouses move to a community property state, whatever may be the situation as to the nature of property acquired by them thereafter in the community property state;[45] likewise, community property according to the law of the community property state in which it

---

nuptial contract that property acquired during the period of the marriage should be jointly held, earnings by the husband in New York at a subsequent period were said to be his separate property under the law of New York. The effect of the express contract was dismissed as being an assignment of future interests and not a transfer *ex proprio vigore* from the moment the earnings arose.

[42] See Fooshe v. Commissioner of Internal Revenue, 132 F.2d 686, as to compensation received for services while domiciled in California, under contract of employment entered into in Missouri. In Mounsey v. Stahl, 62 N.M. 135, 306 P.2d 258, court seems to apply immovables rule to realty purchased with earnings. Although conflicts rule is wrongly stated and Marsh wrongly cited and applied, presumption in favor of community may be applied as added reason for result.

[43] See post, § 92.

[44] Qualification as to quasi-community property, see post, § 92.1.

[45] See Estate of Allshouse, 13 Cal. 2d 691, 81 P.2d 169; Douglas v. Douglas, 22 Idaho 336, 125 P. 796; Saul v. His Creditors, 5 Mart. N. S. (La.) 569, 16 Am. Dec. 212, stating that this was the effect in Spain of Law 24, Title 3, Part. 4 of Las Siete Partidas; Brookman v. Durkee, 46 Wash. 578, 90 P. 914, 123 Am. St. Rep. 944, 13 Ann. Cas. 839, 12 L. R. A. (N. S.) 921; Rustad v. Rustad, 61 Wash. 2d 176, 377 P.2d 414; Payne v. Com'r of Int. Rev., 141 F.2d 398; see also cases collected, 92 A. L. R. 1347, 1348.

See, however, In re Gulstine's Estate, 166 Wash. 325, 6 P.2d 628, where money brought into the state by the husband as his separate property was so intermingled with subsequently acquired community property that it also became community property under the local statute that when separate and com-

was acquired will be recognized as the property of both spouses in a noncommunity property state to which they thereafter remove, and though the title may be in the name of one only of the spouses, the courts will effectuate the equal ownership by evoking the "trust" theory.[46] The foregoing is true even though the form of the property is changed after it is brought to the new domicile.[47]

§ 92.   — Property removed to or acquired in state other than domicile.

Where the spouses without changing their domicile send or remove property to another state, it is recognized in the latter state that it

munity property are intermingled the whole becomes community.

And in community property states in which the proceeds of separate property are community property, undoubtedly as to separate property brought into the state, the proceeds would thereafter be community property. See Oliver v. Robertson, 41 Tex. 422; and ante, § 71.

An attempt by statute to declare that separate property acquired in a noncommunity property state and brought into a community property state upon change of domicile to the latter shall become community property, if it would not have been separate property if acquired while the spouses were domiciled in the latter state, is unconstitutional. Estate of Thornton, 1 Cal. 2d 1, 33 P.2d 1, 92 A. L. R. 1343. But see § 92.1.

[46] See cases collected: 92 A. L. R. 1347, 1352; and see Doss v. Campbell, 19 Ala. 590, 54 Am. Dec. 198 (change of domicile from Texas to Alabama); Kessler's Estate (Ohio), 203 N. E. 2d 221; People v. Bejarano (Colo.) 38 P.2d 866, citing de Funiak, 43 Va. L. Rev. 49; Rozan v. Rosen (Mont.) 431 P.2d 870; Popp's Succession, 146 La. 464, 83 So. 765; Johnson v. Com'r of Int. Rev., 105 F.2d 454; Warbury's Estate, 237 N. Y. S. 2d 557.

[47] Koprian v. Mennecke, 53 N.M. 176, 204 P.2d 440; Scott v. Currie, 7 Wash. 2d 301, 109 P.2d 526; Brookman v. Durkee, 46 Wash. 578, 90 P. 914, 123 Am. St. Rep. 944,

13 Ann. Cas. 839, 12 L. R. A. (N. S.) 921. See also post, § 92, as to property sent or removed to another state, without change of domicile.

In Depas v. Mayo, 11 Mo. 314, 49 Am. Dec. 88, husband domiciled in Louisiana married in New York and the spouses returned to Louisiana to live, where community property was acquired; they then changed their domicile to Missouri where husband converted community funds into realty. The court held that while as to realty, all title thereto, either legal or equitable, must be determined by the law of the situs of the realty, the husband would be regarded as a trustee for the wife to the extent of her half interest. To same effect, see Edwards v. Edwards, 108 Okla. 93, 233 P. 477, where spouses domiciled in Texas and acquiring property there then moved to Oklahoma.

In Louisiana, where husband purchases property after spouses have changed their domicile to that state, the presumption is that he is buying it for the benefit of the community in the absence of anything in the instrument rebutting such presumption. See Fleming v. Fleming, 211 La. 860, 30 So.2d 860.

In an unusual and obviously erroneous decision in Succession of Packwood, 9 Rob. (La.) 438, 41 Am. Dec. 341, it appeared that spouses long domiciled in Louisiana had acquired much community property there, including a sugar plantation. They then changed their domicile to

retains the same nature it had when sent or removed from the domicile of the spouses. Thus, property which is separate property in the noncommunity property domicile of the spouses is recognized as separate property if sent or removed to a community property state,[48] and conversely community property of the spouses in a community property domicile of the spouses remains the property of both although removed to a noncommunity property state and although the title appears in the name of one of the spouses only.[49] Even if the form of the property is changed after its removal, by conversion to some other type of property, the nature of the ownership rights is not affected thereby.[50]

New York, a noncommunity property state, and subsequently the wife died. A claim was made by her heirs to proceeds of the sale of sugar from the plantation, on the ground that the proceeds were community property. The court announced that after the change of domicile acquisitions of property are governed by the law of the new domicile, but incorrectly decided the particular proceeds here were the separate property of the husband, failing to distinguish between acquisitions by the husband through his own labor and industry and acquisitions which merely represent a changed form of property in which both spouses have an ownership. It admitted that if the sugar itself were involved it was community property, being the product of community property, but insisted that since the sugar had been sold and the proceeds placed in a bank to the husband's credit, such proceeds were then his separate property, under the law of his domicile, New York. It is extremely unreasonable to suppose that New York would have failed to recognize the wife's half ownership in proceeds of the sale of property in which she had a half ownership. Incidentally, the case was decided prior to the enactment of the statute as to acquisitions of property in the state by nonresident spouses. Equally erroneous decisions, see In re Hunter's Estate, 125 Mont. 315, 236 P.2d 94; Commonwealth v. Terjen, 197 Va. 596, 90 S. E. 2d 801, criticized by de Funiak, 43 Va. L. Rev. 49.

[48]Slocomb v. Breedlove, 8 La. 143,

28 Am. Dec. 135; Trapp v. U.S., 177 F.2d 1, cert. den. 339 U.S. 313.

[49] See Rozan v. Rosen (Mont.) 431 P.2d 870. And see preceding section as to property removed to another state when spouses change their domicile to that state.

[50] Estate of Warner, 167 Cal. 686, 140 P. 583; Noble v. Com'r of Int. Rev. (10 C. C. A.), 138 F.2d 444, where credit was advanced to husband in Oklahoma by his business partner with which to acquire oil and gas leases in Texas; Stephen v. Stephen, 36 Ariz. 235, 284 P. 158. See Tomaier v. Tomaier, 23 Cal. 2d 754, 146 P.2d 905. See also ante, § 91, as to change of form of property taken to new domicile.

An obviously erroneous decision is presented in the case of Morgan v. Bell, 3 Wash. 554, 28 P. 925, 16 L. R. A. 614. A husband domiciled in Ohio purchased realty in Washington. The purchase seems to have been made with his own earnings which, according to the law of Ohio, must have been his separate property, but because it was not money owned by him at the time of his marriage or acquired after marriage by gift, devise, bequest or descent, the Washington court assumed without apparent question that when he converted it into realty in Washington, such realty constituted community property.

The Louisiana court does not always seem to inquire into the nature of funds as separate property or not when used by a nonresident to purchase realty in Louisiana. Thus, in Rawlings v. Stokes,

This brings us to the matter of property acquired in another state than that in which the spouses are domiciled, which may, instead of being acquired by purchase or exchange through the use of property in which the spouses' interest has already been fixed, be acquired by industry or labor, by rise of some cause of action, or by gift, devise, bequest or inheritance. Courts and legal writers are prone to a failure to distinguish among the various methods by means of which the acquisition is made. They too frequently fall into the error of saying that one case holds that the law of the domicile governs property acquired and that another case holds that the law of the situs governs property acquired, without attempting to analyze the cases to see how and by what means the property was acquired.[51] If the property

194 La. 206, 193 So. 589, where husband and wife were domiciled in Mississippi, a noncommunity property state, and the husband during the marriage, purchased realty in Louisiana, the court assumed that just because it was purchased during the marriage it was community property and, on dissolution of the marriage by divorce in Mississippi, belonged to them both in equal proportions. If the funds used were his separate property, the realty purchased should also have been thus separate property.

[51] Thus, writers frequently cite Gooding Milling & Elevator Co. v. Lincoln County State Bank, 22 Idaho 468, 126 P. 772, as a case holding that the law of the situs of movables at the time of their acquisition governed the marital interests in the movables. In that case the spouses were domiciled in Idaho, and the wife individually and in her own name purchased movables in Illinois. It is true that the Idaho court said that "title passed to her in that state, and that under the laws of that state such property became her separate property" and that if that were true "it would still remain her separate property when brought to this state." But where did the wife get the money with which she purchased such movables? She borrowed it from a bank, primarily upon the basis of recommendations of her as "an honest, reliable and straightforward woman who was desirous of entering into business in the town of Gooding." The money was evidently lent to her upon the basis of her personal credit, and was used by her as if it were her own, as it undoubtedly was. If it constituted her separate property, anything she purchased with it was her separate property (acquisitions on personal credit, see ante, § 78). While it is stated that "she and her husband procured" the money, it is evident that the husband was associated to that extent as a matter of form, for the recommendation referred to was the deciding factor in the obtaining of the money and she engaged in business dealings with the money without any knowledge or control by the husband. Furthermore, the evidence shows that the husband at all times disclaimed any interest in the movables or the business, etc. It is clear that the movables were acquired with her separate property and thus were also her separate property, and that should be so regardless of whether she acquired them in Illinois or in Idaho.

In 1852, the Louisiana legislature enacted that property acquired in the state by either or both of nonresident spouses was to be governed by the statutes relating to the community of acquests and gains between citizens of the state. See La. Civ. Code, art. 2400. This is assumed by some writers (see Horowitz, 11 Wash. Law Rev. 216, n. 70) to mean that any property acquired by nonresidents is community property, and the same view is to be gleaned from two Louisiana decisions (Williams v. Pope Manufacturing Co., 52 La. Ann. 1417, 27 So. 851, 78 Am. St. Rep. 390, 50 L.R.A. 816; Succession of Dill, 155 La.

acquired by labor or industry is immovable property the usual rule is to apply the law of its situs to determine the nature of the marital rights therein,[52] and the same rule may with propriety be applied in the case of movables which are intended to have a permanent situs at the place of their acquisition.[53] However, where movables are acquired by a spouse through labor and industry in another jurisdiction than that of his matrimonial domicile with the intention to take such property to the matrimonial domicile, it is to be considered by the courts of the matrimonial domicile to be controlled as to its nature by the laws of the matrimonial domicile,[54] and by all principles of justice it should be so regarded by the courts of the place of its acquisition.[55] For example, if property has been acquired by labor and industry of one or both spouses in a community property state which is their domicile and thus acquires the status of community

---

47, 98 So. 752). However, such a view fails to distinguish as to how and by what means such property is acquired, that is, whether by labor and industry, by the use of the spouse's own separate property, by gift or otherwise. In other words, the property acquired in Louisiana by nonresident spouses should be community property in a similar situation if acquired by citizens of the state. If property acquired by a citizen of the state by gift is by the law of Louisiana his or her separate property, the same should be true of property acquired by gift by a nonresident spouse; if property acquired by a citizen through the use of his or her separate funds also retains the character of separate property, the same should be true in the case of a nonresident spouse in a similar case.

[52] Steven v. Steven, 36 Ariz. 235, 284 P. 158; Fuchs v. Lloyd, 80 Idaho 114, 326 P.2d 381; Bryan v. Moore, 11 Mart. (La.) 26; Burlingham v. Burlingham, 72 N.M. 433, 384 P.2d 699; Hammonds v. Com'r of Int. Rev., 106 F.2d 420; Tirado v. Tirado (Tex.), 357 S. W. 2d 468; Morgan v. Bell, 3 Wash. 554, 28 P. 925.

Where spouses were domiciled in Texas and husband owned separate realty in California, the income therefrom was his separate property under the law of California and not community property as would be the case under law of Texas. Com'r. of Int. Rev. v. Skaggs (5 C.C.A.), 122 F.2d 721,

certiorari denied 315 U.S. 811, 86 L. Ed. 1210, 62 Sup. Ct. 796; Hammonds v. Com'r. of Int. Rev., 10 C.C.A., 106 F.2d 420.

[53] Sometimes by statute in community property states provision is made as to nonresident wives filing for record an inventory of their separate property in the state. See Nev. Rev. Stat. 1957, §§ 123.150, 123.160.

[54] Gallagher v. U.S. (D.C., Cal.) 66 F. Supp. 743; Sampson v. U.S. (D.C., Wash.) 63 Supp. 624; King v. Bruce, 145 Tex. 647, 201 S. W. 2d 803, 171 A.L.R. 1328; Snyder v. Stringer, 116 Wash. 131, 198 P. 733 (a frequent illustration of rule).

In New Mexico, the Attorney General has expressed the opinion that earnings of the wife outside the state become community property where the marital domicile remains in New Mexico. Op. Atty. Gen. 1943-44, No. 4478. See also Colpe v. Lindblom, 57 Wash. 106, 106 P. 634.

In Edrington v. Mayfield, 5 Tex. 363, husband and wife were domiciled in Texas and the law of that state governed as to the husband's interest in movables given to the wife while on a visit in Tennessee.

[55] The Restatement of Conflict of Laws, §§ 289, 290, is of the opinion that the law of the domicile of the husband at the time of the acquisition of movables should determine the interests of the spouses therein.

property by the law of that state, and the property is then removed to a noncommunity property state, the courts of the latter state recognize it as community property belonging equally to both spouses. There appears to be no reason why, if the labor and industry is immediately translated into earnings or property in the noncommunity property state with the intention to take it back to the community property state, the courts of the noncommunity property state should hesitate to recognize such property as community property.

Some differences of view may now arise as to acquisitions through labor and industry while domiciled in a noncommunity property state. If this is considered the separate property of the acquiring spouse by the law of the domicile, upon its being taken or sent into a community property state, most community property states will consider that it continues to be separate property of the acquiring spouse.[56] But in Arizona and California, in dealing with such property, its disposition or treatment by the courts differs from that of separate property which would also have been separate property if acquired while domiciled in Arizona or California. If it would have been community property if acquired while domiciled in Arizona or California, the governing domiciliary law that it is separate property is ignored and it is dealt with as if it were community property. In California it is called by statute "quasi-community property."[57] A similar result has been reached in Arizona by judicial decision.[58]

If separate property, as so determined at its acquisition by the governing law of the noncommunity property domicile, is movables or is converted into movables and then taken or sent into a community property domicile and there used to acquire immovables, naturally the law of the immovables should govern to determine the nature of the immovables as separate or community property.[59] While presumably community property, the presumption may be rebutted by clear evidence of the nature of the funds used,[60] assuming that a distinction is not to be made, as in Arizona and California.[61] But notice that such jurisdictions as Idaho, Louisiana and Texas, while considering the immovables as separate property, by their law treat the income or profits therefrom as community property.[62] This has not always been realized by state and federal courts sitting in noncommunity property jurisdictions.[63]

In the case of property acquired in another state than that of the domicile by reason of gift, bequest, devise or inheritance, such property both by the present laws of the community and noncommunity

---

[56] See supra, this section, and ante, § 91.

[57] See post, § 92.1.

[58] See Rau v. Rau (Ariz. App.) 432 P.2d 910, 914, citing de Funiak, 7 Ariz. L. Rev. 50.

[59] See ante, § 91, and supra, this section.

[60] See ante, § 60 et seq.

[61] See supra, this section, and post, § 92.1.

[62] See ante, § 71.

[63] See, e.g., Trapp v. U.S. (10 C.A.) 177 F.2d 1, cert. den. 309 U.S. 913.

property states is the separate property of the person to whom given or left, so that aside from any local laws as to succession, distribution and the like, the actual nature of the title, right or interest obtained would seem to present no question of conflict as between community and noncommunity property states.

Another problem as to which there has been variation in views concerns a chose in action. That is, a cause of action for a tort or breach arising in one state in favor of a spouse domiciled in another state. Many cases have concerned spouses domiciled in one state who are making an automobile journey in another state wherein they become involved in a collision or other such accident and one or both spouses suffer personal injury.[64] The cause of action, if any, is property and since it cannot be classed as real property or an immovable, it must be in the nature of personal property. By the usual conflict of laws principle the nature of the interest in or nature of the property is to be governed by the law of the domicile.[65] But here another difficulty arises in that the existence of a right of action and its extent is to be determined by the law of the place of the tort.[66] To what extent does this qualify or change the rule that the law of the domicile is governing? Also, where do we distinguish between the governing substantive law and the governing procedural law when the action is not brought in the domicile?[67]

As can be realized, where one of the states is a noncommunity property state recognizing that a tort cause of action is the property of the injured person and the other state is a community property state which considers the causes of action to be wholly or even partly community property, a definite conflict exists. Even between community property states there can be conflict where one considers the cause wholly community property and the other community property state does not.[68] Where the cause of action is considered community property or some part of it is, the contributory negligence of the other spouse can become an important factor.[69]

In the situation where the domicile was a noncommunity property state and the wife was injured in and brought suit in a community property state, cases in California[70] have held that the law of the domicile governed and determined that the property right was that of the wife. In a federal case arising in Texas the same view has

---

[64] Generally, see annotations 97 A.L.R. 2d 725, 127 A.L.R. 803; notes, 30 So. Cal. L. Rev. 92, 43 Marquette L. Rev. 127; 28 Cal. L. Rev. 211; Marsh, Marital Property in Conflict of Laws, pp. 171–179, 193–194.

[65] See, e.g., Rest. Conflict of Laws, §§ 208, 290.

[66] See, e.g., Rest. Conflict of Laws, § 383 et seq.

[67] Prosecution of action, see also post, § 127.

[68] See ante, § 82.

[69] See ante, § 83.

[70] Schecter v. Superior Court, 49 Cal. 2d 3, 314 P.2d 10, 14 (whether Kentucky was domicile); Bruton v. Villoria, 138 Cal. App. 2d 642, 292 P.2d 638, noted 30 So. Cal. L. Rev. 92 (domicile in Ontario, Canada).

been upheld by the Court of Appeals[71] having the effect of overruling a prior federal district court case to the contrary, which applied the law of the forum, Texas.[72] The latter case has been followed by a federal court in Idaho.[73] A view similar to that expressed in California has been followed in Nevada,[74] although both states involved were community property states. The domicile was Idaho, which considers the whole cause of action to be community property. The tort and the action took place in Nevada, where the wife's pain and suffering give rise to a cause of action which is her separate property.[75] In applying the law of the domicile, Idaho, the contributory negligence of the husband had the effect of defeating the wife's action.[76] An opposite result seems to have been reached in Louisiana. There the domicile was Texas, by which law the cause of action for injury to the wife was entirely community property, and the tort to and the action by the wife were in Louisiana. The Louisiana court applied the law of Louisiana, as giving her a right of action.[77] Of course, it may be argued that this is recognizing the law of the forum as applying procedurally.[78] And there is nothing to prevent the Texas court, upon later litigation in that state involving the amount of the recovery, from deciding that it is community property under their law and awarding or dividing it accordingly.[79] In two other Louisiana cases where the wife, domiciled in Mississippi, was injured in and sued in Louisiana, the court appears to be applying the law of the domiciles substantively.[80] But in effect, substantively and procedurally would the law of the two states be essentially the same?[81]

In actions brought in some of the noncommunity property states by a wife domiciled there but injured in a community property state where the cause of action was community property, the courts of the

---

[71] Reeves v. Schulmeier (5 C.A.) 303 F.2d 802, 97 A.L.R. 2d 718 (domicile in Oklahoma).

[72] Redfern v. Collins, 113 F. Supp. 892 (domicile in Colorado).

[73] Miller v. Ashton, 155 F. Supp. 417 (domicile in Nebraska). Generally as to Idaho conflicts of laws, see Brockelbank, The Community Property Law of Idaho, p. 180 et seq.

[74] Choate v. Ranson, 74 Nev. 100, 323 P.2d 700.

[75] See ante, § 82.

[76] Contributory negligence of spouse, see ante, § 83.

[77] Matney v. Blue Ribbon, Inc., 202 La. 505, 12 So.2d 253, noted 5 La. L. Rev. 467.

[78] See discussion, Marsh, Marital Property in Conflict of Laws, pp. 173–179.

[79] And see supra, Marsh, ibid.

[80] Lewis v. American Brewing Co. (La. App.) 32 So.2d 109; Williams v. Pope Mfg. Co., 152 La. Ann. 1417, 27 So. 851, 78 Am. St. Rep. 390, 50 L.R.A. 816.

[81] By statute in Louisiana, property acquired therein by nonresident spouses is governed by the same provisions regulating community of acquests and gains between citizens of the state. La. Civ. Code, art. 2400. But in Williams v. Pope Manufacturing Co., supra, it was held that right of action accruing to a nonresident married woman, domiciled in Mississippi, by reason of personal injury inflicted on her in Louisiana was not property acquired in Louisiana within the above statute but an intangible thing accompanying her wherever she might go.

forum — and the domicile — have applied their own laws.[82] This, of course, is in accord with the usual principle, referred to above. However, there have been decisions where the action by the injured wife was brought in the state where she was injured and the court has applied the law of the place of injury, and not the law of the domicile which was elsewhere.[83]

§ 92.1.   — Quasi-community property.

At the present time, quasi-community property is a statutory development in California.[84] It may be defined as property acquired while domiciled in a noncommunity property state which would have been community property if acquired while domiciled in California.[85] The purpose of the statutes is to have this property governed in California, to the extent legally possible, by the law relating to actual community property.[86] This relates to such situations as its disposal during marriage,[87] its division on divorce,[88] and its descent and distribution,[89] as in the case of community property itself.[90]

Of course, by the law of the noncommunity property domicile, this property then acquired is usually the separate property of the spouse acquiring it, subject to whatever curtesy or dower right that law conferred.[91] Upon being brought into California upon a change of domicile to that state, it then was no longer subject to dower or curtesy since these do not exist in California,[92] or in any community property state for that matter.[93] Since it has usually been the husband who acquired and brought the property into California, the wife who may well have contributed to the success of the marital partnership, had no share whatever in this property upon the death of the husband domiciled in California. California might well have legislated for the surviving spouse to take the same share in such property as she would have had in the other state,[94] but the device actually adopted was that of calling it quasi-community property and regulating especially as to its division upon dissolution of the marital partnership.[95] Any

[82] Hammschild v. Continental Gas Co., 7 Wis. 2d 95, 95 N. W. 2d 814, noted 43 Marqu. L. Rev. 127, where injury occurred in California.

[83] See Texas & V. P. R. Co. v. Humble, 181 U.S. 57, 45 L. Ed. 747, 21 S. Ct. 526.

[84] See ante, § 68.3.

[85] See, e.g., Cal. Civ. Code § 4803.

[86] See discussion, Addison v. Addison, 62 Cal. 2d 558, 43 Cal. Rptr. 97, 399 P.2d 897 (1965).

[87] See post, Chap. VII, B.

[88] See post, § 227.1.

[89] See post, § 201.

[90] See appropriate sections. As subject to inheritance tax, see Rogers v. Cranston, 53 Cal. Rptr. 572.

[91] See ante, §§ 91, 92; Marsh, Marital Property in Conflict of Laws, 1951.

[92] Cal. Civ. Code § 5129.

[93] See post, § 201.

[94] In Cal. Prob. Code § 201.6, as to real property left in state on death of a nondomiciliary, same interest may be claimed by surviving spouse as given by the state of actual domicile.

[95] Generally, see de Funiak, Conflict of Laws in the Community Property Field, 7 Ariz. L. Rev. 50.

belief that the policy enunciated in the past in the Thornton case[96] would make this legislation invalid has been met, in 1965, by the decision of the California Supreme Court that the legislation is valid and that the Thornton case is to be distinguished.[97]

It should be noted that separate property acquired by a spouse while domiciled in the noncommunity property state that would equally have been considered separate property by California standards, continues to be treated as separate property when brought into California.[98]

Some similarity to the California view as to property earned while domiciled elsewhere and then brought into the state upon a change of domicile may be noted in Arizona, stemming from judicial views. Thus the Arizona court has refused to treat such property the same as separate property coming from gift or the like.[99]

[96] In re Thornton's Estate, 1 Cal. 2d 1, 38 P.2d 1, 92 A.L.R. 1343.

[97] Addison v. Addison, footnote, supra.

[98] See especially interesting comparisons by Professor Marsh in Chapter 2 of his Marital Property in Conflict of Laws.

[99] See Rau v. Rau (Ariz. App.) 432 P.2d 410, citing de Funiak, 7 Ariz. L. Rev. 50.

CHAPTER VII

OWNERSHIP AND MANAGEMENT

A. Ownership

B. Management

A.   OWNERSHIP

§ 93.   In general.

We come now to a consideration of the ownership and administration of the community property, a matter which certainly so far as it concerns the nature of the wife's interest in the community has been the subject of continued controversy for many years.[1] The chief argument has revolved around the question whether the wife's half interest in the community is an immediate, present ownership of half of the community or whether she has merely a sort of inchoate or expectant interest in half of the community during the marriage which vests in her fully upon the dissolution of the marriage. In recent years this question of the nature or extent of her interest became particularly important in view of the federal income tax law, in respect to the question whether husband and wife might file separate returns, each for his or her half of the marital income, or whether the husband had to file a return on the basis that all his earnings or income were entirely his property.[2]

The Spanish law of community very plainly provided that "Everything the husband or wife may earn during union, let them both have it by halves."[3] The administration of the community property, as has been customary in most community systems, was placed in the hands of the husband,[4] who had the power of alienation during the marriage without the necessity of consent or conveyance of the wife, and the contract of alienation was valid unless it was proven that the wife was defrauded or injured by such alienation.[5] The extent to which this exercise of administrative duty has been continued or limited in our community property states is dealt with subsequently in this chapter.[6]

§ 94.   Factors generally in determining nature of wife's interest.

In the effort to determine whether in our several states the wife has an immediate, present half interest or merely something in the nature of an expectancy, much stress has been laid not only on the extent of the husband's right of control or management but also on

[1] See Daggett, Community Property System of Louisiana with Comparative Studies, p. 158 et seq.; Holmes, J., in Arnett v. Reade, 220 U.S. 311, 55 L. Ed. 477, 31 S. Ct. 425. See also, Comment, The Juridical Nature of the Marital Community, 25 La. L. Rev. 721.

[2] Income taxes, see post, Chap. XI, B.

[3] Novísima Recopilación, Book 10, Title 4, Law 1.

See also ibid., Law 4, that "the property which husband and wife have belong to both by halves, except that which each one may prove to be his separately; and so we order that it be observed as law."

[4] Administration generally, see post, § 106 et seq.

[5] Novísima Recopilación, Book 10, Title 4, Law 5; Laws of Estilo, Law 205.

[6] See post, § 106 et seq.

the wife's right of expenditure, her liability to creditors, her right of action respecting the community, her right of testamentary disposition, etc.[7] But curiously enough, when the Spanish law and commentaries have been investigated by our courts for light on the subject to determine what was considered by that law the nature and extent of the wife's interest, the investigation has been confined mainly to the extent of the husband's control and management as to whether it was to be considered as making him the actual owner or not, and thus the wife's interest merely expectant or not. Little or no effort has been made to consider matters equally important in determining the answer, such as resort to the question of the wife's liability for debt, her testamentary rights, her right to sue or liability to be sued, and other matters of like nature. As we shall see subsequently, not only was the wife liable for and suable for debts of the community but she had possessory remedies where the husband fraudulently disposed of the community property.[8]

§ 95. Nature of community of property and standard of determination.

Community of property has been variously described as being in the nature of a partnership, a trust, single ownership by the husband with the expectancy of an heir on the part of the wife, an estate in entirety, an interest sui generis, and so on.[9] But since the community system in effect in our American states is that which was developed

[7] William D. Mitchell, when acting Attorney General of the United States, after a hearing given to representatives of taxpayers in community property states, by letter to them of date of March 12, 1926, said in part that "we would like to have it pointed out what management, possession, and control the wife and husband, respectively, exercise; whether the husband has power to spend community income as he pleases, what restrictions there are on his disposition of it; whether the wife has a right to expend it, and whether her creditors have a right to resort to it in payment of her debts; whether the husband's obligation to support the wife is based on the notion that she has an ownership in the community or is a general marital obligation, and whether obligations contracted for her support are payable out of her share of the community, on the theory that she owns it, or whether such debts for necessaries are collectible out of the husband's share of the community or his separate estate; whether the wife may maintain any action respecting the community property during the existence of the community or is a proper party to a suit involving community property; whether on dissolution of the community the wife has any right of testamentary disposition."

[8] See post, this chapter, subd. B.

[9] See Daggett, Community Property System of Louisiana with Comparative Studies, p. 166; McKay, Community Property, 2nd Ed., § 1179 et seq.; Fields v. Michael, 91 Cal. App. 2d 443, 205 P.2d 402, citing first edition; Comment, 25 La. L. Rev. 159.

Dean Evans has described four theories regarding the nature of the the ownership of community property: California or single ownership theory, Washington or entity theory, Idaho or double ownership theory, and Texas or trust theory. Evans, Ownership of Community Property, 35 Harv. Law Rev.

in Spain,[10] the way in which it was viewed there is entitled to great weight.[11] And there is no escape from the fact, however much some may cavil at it, that it was viewed there as being in the nature of a partnership between the spouses. The continued description of the community by the Spanish jurisconsults as a form of partnership and their explanation of it in terms of partnership law leave no doubt of that fact.[12] Their partnership was usually described as in the nature of a general partnership, as distinguished from the universal partnership or special partnership.[13] It is difficult to see how it can be considered in any other light, for it represents the right to share equally in the acquests and gains of the spouses during the marriage as well as liability for the obligations incurred on behalf of the community, usual

---

47. Since the date of that article, however, in California by statute the situation has been clarified to make it plain that there is not single ownership. See post, § 107. And Washington now denies an entity theory. See post, this section.

These various theories have been justly declared to be so much judicial hocus-pocus and based too much on common law premises. Nicholas, California Community Property, 14 Calif. State Bar Jour. 9.

[10] See ante, Chap. IV.

[11] The Washington court has said that while the Spanish statutes are not binding on it, they may aid the court in resolving the legislative intent. In re Salvini's Estate, 65 Wash. 2d 442, 397 P.2d 811.

When Hawaii temporarily had community property, the court recognized that the system was borrowed from the Spanish law "and we must look to this source for . . . the rules and principles, which govern its operation and effect." Bulgo v. Bulgo, 41 Haw. 578, 581.

[12] See Nov. Rec. Book 10, Title 4, Law 1, commentaries thereto of Matienzo, Glosses I-III; Azevedo, No. 20 et seq.; Gutiérrez, Quaestio CXVIII, No. 5 et seq.; Nov. Rec. Law 8, Commentaries of Llamas y Molina thereto.

"In the Philippines the marital community is called the 'conjugal partnership.' " Com'r of Int. Rev. v. Cadwallader, 9 C.C.A., 127 F.2d 547, per Healey, J.

[13] After describing partnerships as

of three kinds, universal, general, and special or singular, Llamas y Molina declared: "To the second class of these partnerships corresponds the one contracted by husband and wife during their marriage by virtue of our laws; it is not a universal partnership because it does not comprise the present property or all of the future property, but only that which is acquired by work, industry or negotiation, which is the property acquired during marriage which civil law says precedes *ex questu* (from industry), without including that which is acquired by lucrative title, such as a legacy, inheritance or donation; nor is it a special partnership because it is not limited to one sole kind of property or industry or negotiation; but extends in a general manner to whatever the consorts may acquire by any kind of negotiation or industry; and in consequence the partnership contracted during marriage is general, covering all the property acquired by industry or negotiation, but exempting that which proceeds from lucrative title, as amongst others Matienzo declares on the basis of Law 3, Title 9, Book 5, of the [Nueva] Recopilación, Gloss I (Law 2, Book 10, Title 4, Novísima Recopilación)." Llamas y Molina, No. 37, to Nov. Rec. Law 8, Book 10, Title 4.

For what it is worth, it may be noticed that Febrero refers to their right to participate equally in the profits because "they are partners in a universal partnership." Febrero, Librería de Escribanos, Cinco Juicios I, Book I, Cap. IV, § 4.

attributes of partnership. Moreover, while this marital community of property is naturally coincident with the marriage, it can usually be dissolved by agreement or contract during the marriage without affecting the subsistence of the marriage itself,[14] or by agreement or contract before the marriage, community of property will never come into existence and this without affecting all the subsistence of the subsequent marriage. These latter matters are apparently not always understood by opponents of the community property system, who seem to think that it attempts to substitute some sort of cold-blooded partnership for what they view as a sacrament. But actually there is attached to the marriage a marital partnership based on the view that two individuals are equally devoting their lives and energies to furthering the material as well as the spiritual success of the marriage. The wife usually remains the home maker, the husband the bread winner, and because his share thus has to do with the earnings and properties acquired, their management remains in his hands.[15] The view most correctly expressed by our American courts, then, is that it is a form of partnership with the husband as the managing partner.[16]

Other descriptive terms, such as the "trust" theory at one time

[14] Not unqualifiedly true in some of our states. See § 136 et seq.

[15] "With regard to community of goods the law has regard to the industry and common labor of each spouse and to the burdens of partnership and community. . . . And so for these just and logical reasons there is by royal law an implied contract of partnership between husband and wife . . . the principle in accordance with which it was enacted by royal law that profits should be shared between husband and wife . . . being the fact that while the one spouse supplies work and labor the other supplies money or other property, the fact of their undivided habit of life ordained by both natural and divine law, the fact of the mutual love between husband and wife which should be encouraged." Matienzo, Gloss I, Nos. 6, 13, to Nov. Rec. Law 1, Book 10, Title 4.

[16] See, e.g., Succession of Wiener, 203 La. 649, 14 So.2d 475; Nace v. Nace, (Ariz. App.) 432 P.2d 896, 902; Bulgo v. Bulgo, 41 Haw. 578, 581. Agency of the husband is neither a contract nor a property right; he is merely by law created the agent of the community to manage and control the property. See Warburton v. White, 176 U.S. 494, 44 L. Ed. 555, 20 S. Ct. 404.

See also In re Monaghan's Estate, 65 Ariz. 9, 173 P.2d 107; Vai v. Bank of America, 15 Cal. Rptr. 71, 364 P.2d 247, citing 1 de Funiak, § 95; Fields v. Michael, 91 Cal. App. 2d 443, 205 P.2d 402, citing and following 1 de Funiak, § 95.

"In the Civil Law of Spain and Mexico, which furnishes the historical background for our community property system, the comparison was generally to a partnership. That was the idea favored in Beals v. Ares (25 N.M. 499, 185 P. 780), where it was said the wife is 'an equal partner with the husband in the matrimonial gains.' It was there said, also, that the power of the court to divide the property does not extend further than to set apart to each of the spouses 'their undivided half interest in the property.' To my mind, this expression is entirely inconsistent with any theory that the interest of the husband and wife in community property is comparable to estates by the entirety or in joint tenancy." Estate of Chavez, 34 N.M. 258, 280 P. 241, 69 A.L.R. 769.

"The reason is that the one spouse is deemed to be appointed business

employed by the Texas courts and the "entity" theory of the Washington courts, so often instanced by writers as examples of separate and even conflicting theories,[17] it develops upon analysis, are not so conflicting with the idea of a form of partnership as might at first appear. Thus the "trust" theory of the Texas courts represents only the application of the principle that where two persons have interests in property but the legal title is in one, that one must also be considered to be holding the title for the benefit of, i.e., in trust for, the other owner. The Texas courts unequivocally recognized equal and present vested interests in both spouses in the community property and apply the so-called "trust" theory equally as well where the wife has the legal title in her name[18] as where the husband has it in his.[19] In other words, there is nothing in such a "theory" that conflicts with the view of a marital partnership, a term frequently used by the Texas courts, since it is merely designed to make clear that fiduciary obligations are imposed upon the one holding the legal title, the same fiduciary obligations which are imposed on any partner who has control and management of partnership assets.[20] And the so-called "entity" theory of the Washington courts, so often cited by writers, represents actually only a form of convenient phraseology, according to the Washington Supreme Court, which has declared that it no more considers the marital community as a legal person separate and apart from the members composing the marital community than it does in the similar case of an ordinary partnership.[21] The frequent description, by the Washington courts, of the husband as the managing agent of this "entity" by virtue of the statutes is also misleading, since the statutes

agent by the other, just as two partners carrying on different businesses are deemed to be mutual agents of each other, so that what one does benefits or hurts the other." Matienzo, Gloss II, No. 2, to Nov. Rec. Law 1, Book 10, Title 4.

[17] See Daggett, Community Property System of Louisiana, p. 166; McKay, Community Property, 2nd Ed., § 1179 et seq.; Evans, 35 Harv. Law Rev. 47.

[18] See Mitchell v. Schofield, 106 Tex. 512, 171 S. W. 1121; Houston Oil Co. v. Choate (Tex. Com. App.), 232 S. W. 285.

[19] See Burnham v. Hardy Oil Co., 108 Tex. 555, 195 S. W. 1139.

[20] "The relation of husband and wife toward the community property is that of a partnership." Simpson v. Brotherton, 62 Tex. 170, 3 Tex. Law Rep. 240. See also Brownson v. New, (Tex. Civ. App.) 259 S. W. 2d 277, writ dism.; Leyva v. Rodriguez (Tex. Civ. App.) 195 S. W. 704, W/e ref., n.r.e.

"These conclusions harmonize with the conceptions underlying the Texas decisions that the wife's capacity to own and hold property is as complete as that of the husband; *that each marital partner owns an estate in the community property equal to that of the other partner;* and that statutes empowering the husband to manage the wife's separate lands and community assets make the husband essentially a trustee, accountable as such to the separate estate of the wife, or to the community." Arnold v. Leonard, 114 Tex. 535, 273 S. W. 799. (Italics ours.)

[21] "By the community property law of this state . . . the legislature did not create an entity or a juristic person separate and apart from the spouses composing the marital community. . . . We have for convenience of expression employed the terms 'entity' and 'legal

do not use any such terminology and merely describe in much the same language as the statutes of other community property states that the husband shall have the management and control of the community property.[22] In other words, he may much more accurately be termed the managing partner of the marital partnership, which in fact is what he is. One obtains a clearer idea of the so-called "marital entity" if one looks at it rather as a conjugal partnership. The word "entity" is a convenient term but one must not think of it as meaning something in the nature of a corporate body which owns property apart from the members. The conjugal society is a partnership in which certain property owned by both conjugal partners is devoted to the furtherance of the success and well-being of the conjugal partnership. In an ordinary partnership the property used for partnership purposes is not owned by the partnership as a separate entity apart from the partners. The partners themselves continue to own a certain share of the property used in the partnership, and the dissolution of the partnership does not suddenly vest title to his share in each partner. He already owned his share even when it was devoted to partnership purposes. If care is taken to view the conjugal society as a form of partnership, which is the way it was viewed in the Spanish law, many of the difficulties of comprehension will vanish.[23]

Apart then, from phraseology employed at one time as matter of convenience by the Washington courts, there is at bottom no difference between the ownership of the spouses in Washington and that of the spouses in Idaho, Arizona, Nevada, New Mexico, Texas, and now in California, under the so-called "double ownership" theory according to which each spouse owns an undivided half of the community property;[24] a "theory" which is in accord with the principles of community property law developed in Spain.[25] If there is to be any genuine recog-

---

entity' in referring to a partnership and to a marital community. However, we have never held that a partnership or a marital community is a legal person separate and apart from the members composing the partnership or the marital community, or that either the partnership or the marital community has the status of a corporation." Bortle v. Osborne, 155 Wash. 585, 285 P. 425, 67 A.L.R. 1152.

[22] See Wash. Rev. Code, §§ 26.16.-030 and 26.16.040.

[23] "The Washington theory of legal entity is perhaps the most accurate common law analogy of the four theories to which the courts of the community property states are committed, but even using the term 'legal entity' in this connection, we should try to examine legal entities from the view-

point of a jurist of a civil law nation rather than a common law country." Nicholas, California Community Property, 14 Cal. State Bar Jour. 9, 11, n. 12. And see In re Wegley's Estate, (Wash.) 399 P.2d 326; In re Heringer's Estate (Wash.) 230 P.2d 297.

The community is not a legal fiction or civil person but a partnership in the sense of a partnership in which each partner acquires the same share in the properties as his co-partners. Laurent, Principes de Droit Civil, vol. 21, p. 250.

[24] That in Texas, also, each marital partner owns an estate in the community property equal to that of the other partner, see Arnold v. Leonard, 114 Tex. 535, 273 S. W. 799.

[25] See post, § 96 et seq.

nition in these states of a community of property in which both husband and wife have an equal, present and existing ownership, it must follow, whether the courts of those states like or do not like so to describe it, that there is what may be termed a conjugal partnership, differing in many respects, it is true, from an ordinary partnership, but also having many of the attributes of the latter.

§ 96.   Community property law of Spain as determinative of wife's interest.

Since our community property system is that which was developed in Spain and continued there, a fact early recognized by the courts of our community property states,[26] it must be interpreted by the rules and principles governing the Spanish community system, a fact also early recognized by our courts.[27] It thus becomes of prime importance to ascertain what was the nature of the wife's interest in the community property in the community system in Spain. This, in short, is to be ascertained from the Spanish laws and commentaries. And the importance of the latter is extremely great and is not to be underestimated.[28] It has been stated that the opinions of the Spanish jurisconsults upon this point, as expressed in their commentaries, are in extreme conflict and that anything and nothing can be proved by them.[29] Such statements have little foundation to support them and can only arise from lack of comprehensive study of the commentaries. Arguments that in the Spanish law of community property the wife did not have an equal and present ownership of half of the community property apparently rest upon several misconceptions. One of these probably is a misunderstanding of some of the remarks of earlier commentators as to the "common law"; another probably results from an unfortunate reliance on Febrero's writings as well as upon misunderstanding of his meaning; others probably result from lack of knowledge of such things as revocable and irrevocable ownership, the true meaning of the administrative control rested in the husband, and a general failure to comprehend the various shades of ownership in the civil law. When it is attempted to understand the civil law by applying common law property concepts, any confusion or misconception is multiplied a thousandfold.

§ 97.   Equal, present and existing ownership of husband and wife.

That disagreements and arguments among the commentators and jurisconsults are frequently discoverable is undoubtedly true in one

[26] See ante, §§ 4, 37 et seq.
[27] See ante, § 4.
[28] See ante, § 4.

[29] See Daggett, Community Property System of Louisiana with Comparative Studies, p. 164.

sense. Like terrier pups getting their teeth into an old slipper, the commentators shake and worry innumerable points. They frequently disagreed over whether remuneratory gifts to the husband constituted his separate property or community property. They argued the point of whether and to what extent the husband, in his management of the community property, could make gifts from it to dependents or relatives, whether dowries promised by a spouse to children of the marriage were payable from the common property, and so on.[30]

Although many of these differences of opinion were surface differences as to the matters involved, on one point they were definitely and certainly agreed. That was that husband and wife, during the marriage itself, were equal and present owners of the common property.[31] "Above all things," said Juan Sala, "it must be kept in mind that the property owned by the husband and wife belongs to them by halves, except that which each proves belongs to him or her separately." And again he said: "The ownership of the property acquired during marriage which we customarily call the common property is common equally to husband and wife. . . . And Matienzo showed plainly that this community of property is understood in regard to ownership and to possession."[32] Joaquin Escriche in his highly regarded and authoritative *Diccionario* stated that "The husband and the wife have the ownership of the ganancial properties."[33] This was, he pointed out, because there was a partnership between the spouses whereby their acquisitions during marriage were reciprocally shared between

[30] It is also to be noticed that frequently the jurisconsults, before stating the prevailing view, in fairness marshalled all the arguments that might be presented for an adverse view. Thus, one should not read a paragraph or two of their commentaries and then desist, for the wrong impression might be gained thereby.

[31] These surface differences frequently revolved around points of terminology. For example, Matienzo, in discussing the fact that the deceased spouse's share of the common property passed to his or her heirs, objected to calling this share "profits" and said it should be termed more properly a "mutual sharing." But whatever the difference of opinion as to terminology, it will be seen that the commentators reached the same conclusions as to the law relating to the property passing to the heirs. Similarly, the commentators agree that a legacy from the husband to the wife is not to be set off against

her share of the common property, but must be in addition thereto, since she was already owner of her share of the common property and thus the husband's legacy cannot dispose of property not his but the wife's and must therefore be a disposition to the wife from his own property. But in discussing the matter, Azevedo and Llamas y Molina speak of the husband's management of the common property during the marriage and state that to the extent that he has property of the wife in his hands he is her debtor to that amount; Gutiérrez on the other hand objects to describing him by that term. Yet none of them fails to agree that during the marriage the wife owns her share of the common property. These differences present merely problems in semantics and nothing more.

[32] Sala, Mexican edition of 1807, pp. 72, 78.

[33] Escriche, Diccionario, "Ganancial Properties."

them.[34] And in his *Elements of the Spanish Law* he states: "The ownership in this property is common to both during the partnership."[35] Matienzo, Gutiérrez, and Llamas y Molina, among many others discussing the meaning of the Spanish law, "Everything that the husband and the wife may earn or purchase during marriage, let them both have it by halves,"[36] point out that the word "have" (*"ayan"* in the Spanish law and equivalent to the Latin *"habere"*) is a general word including ownership, possession, detention, and even rights of action, and also that the word "have" is in the present tense and can mean only that the ownership of the wife is a present ownership, and was always so interpreted.[37] Matienzo flatly puts it "that ownership and possession of a moiety of the property acquired during marriage passes automatically (*ipso jure*) to the wife without delivery and the wife is owner even during marriage of the share which belongs to her."[38] In the words of Gutiérrez, "Therefore, just as the husband is owner

[34] "The ganancial properties are in common of the husband and wife, and belong to each of them by halves, even though the husband has more separate property than the wife, or the wife more than the husband; even though one earns more afterwards than the other; and finally, even though one only may acquire them, trafficking or working. Because, by virtue of the marriage, there is established between the spouses a legal partnership, different from the others, whereby their acquisitions are reciprocally shared between them." Escriche, Diccionario, "Ganancial Properties."

[35] Escriche, Elements of Spanish Law (Coopwood's translation), Title IV.

[36] Novísima Recopilación, Book 10, Title 4, Law 1.

[37] Matienzo, Gloss III, to Nov. Rec. Law 1, Book 10, Title 4; Gutiérrez, Quaestio CXVIII, to Nov. Rec. Law 1; Llamas y Molina, commentaries to Nov. Rec. Law 8, Book 10, Title 4.

". . . and therefore the words in this law *'ayanlo ambos'* are explained by the subsequent addition *'de por medio,'* i.e., equally. And if the husband were to have the ownership of property acquired while the wife were only to have the use during marriage of the property, the division would not be equal and they would not each have an equal but an unequal share. And that would be clearly contrary to the words and intent of this law. The wife is therefore owner of her half share, as the husband is of his." Matienzo, Gloss III, No. 4, to Nov. Rec. Law 1.

[38] "In the second place, you should note from the words *'ayanlo ambos de por medio'* that ownership and possession of moiety of the property acquired during marriage passes automatically to the wife without delivery and the wife is owner even during marriage of the share which belongs to her. . . . If this law, which gives to the husband and wife the property acquired during marriage, were to be understood as meaning that the wife is only entitled to the use thereof while the husband acquires the ownership, its provisions would be defective." Matienzo, Gloss III, No. 2, to Nov. Rec. Law 1. See also same Gloss, No. 3; and Gloss I to Law 8.

"And so when Law 1 above [i.e., Nov. Rec. Law 4] derived from the above mentioned law *Styli* [Laws of Estilo No. 203), uses the words 'are common property' which are in the present tense, it should not be referred to a future date, viz. the time of the dissolution of the marriage. It applies to the duration of the marriage when such goods are acquired and says that at such time they are common to husband and wife in respect of both ownership and possession [citing authorities]." Matienzo, Gloss III, No. 15, to Nov. Rec. Law 1.

and possessor of his half share, so is the wife too."[39] Pointing to the law that provided that the property of the wife was subject to confiscation or penalties for her delicts and that her half share of the community was expressly included in that category,[40] Matienzo asks how the Treasury could confiscate as her property half of the community property if she did not own it during the marriage; for if she had nothing but a mere right of action, an expectant right, to such half share after dissolution of the marriage, she would have no ownership in the community property during marriage which could warrant its seizure.[41] Other pronouncements in similar vein could be quoted from these same jurisconsults as well as from the writings of many others. Additional references to these matters are made in the subsequent sections analyzing the nature of the ownership and the effect of the husband's duty of management of the community property.[42] It is sufficient to conclude with the positive and unanswerable remark of Llamas y Molina that "It is evident according to law that what is gained by husband and wife while they are together is the common property of both and they must divide it in two, and there is no one amongst the authors who dares to doubt it."[43]

[39] Gutiérrez, Quaestio CXVIII, No. 4, to Nov. Rec. Law. 1. See also Azevedo, No. 21, to Nov. Rec. Law 1.

[40] See Novísima Recopilación, Book 10, Title 4, Law 11.

[41] Matienzo, Gloss III, No. 2, to Nov. Rec. Law 11, cited preceding note.

[42] Perusal of the foregoing commentaries will supply a complete picture.

[43] Llamas y Molina, No. 46, to Nov. Rec. Law 8, Book 10, Title 4. He recognizes, however, in another number the partial dissent of an early commentator, Tello, as to whom see post. this note.

Gutiérrez listed, with appropriate citations to their works, the array of Spanish jurisconsults and commentators who upheld the view that ownership and possession of half the goods acquired during marriage passed straight to the wife, automatically, without formal delivery, so that she was owner during marriage of that part, viz. Palatius Rubeus, Roderic Suarez, Antonio Gomez, Covarruvias, "and better than all" Gregorio Lopez, Gaspar Baeza, Quemada, who "attests this as the common view of Spaniards," Matienzo, Burgos de Paz, and Velásquez. See Gutiérrez, Quaestio CXVIII, No. 12, to Nov. Rec. Law 1, Book 10,

Title 4. To the foregoing we may add, of course, Azevedo and Llamas y Molina, and others cited throughout this section.

The equality of ownership of the spouses during the marriage in the marital acquests and gains as confirmed by recurring language in Laws 1 to 11 of Book 10, Title 4 of Novísima Recopilación (previously Book 5, Title 9 of of Nueva Recopilación), is analyzed by Burnett in his Community Property Law according to Sala, Chap. 4, who points out that such phrases as *ambos por medio, communal de ambos, communes de ambos a dos,* and *de consuno* (meaning variously "to both by halves," "common to both," etc.) appear half a dozen times, that reference to the wife's share of the community property as her *mitad* (i.e., half or moiety) appears twice, and that *durante el matrimonio* occurs ten times, and the equivalent phrase *estando de consuno* once.

"The decision which affirms that the wife obtains during matrimony the ownership and possession of half of the property acquired during marriage, is generally accepted by our national authors, as will be seen in Covarrubias Lib. 3, Variarum, Chap. 19, No. 2, and Matienzo in Gloss 3 to Law of Toro,

This ownership of the wife accrued not by reason of liberality of the other spouse or by reason of contract between them but by operation of law,[44] and the ownership and possession of her share was transferred to her *ipso jure* the moment the property was acquired.[45] This present, existing and immediate ownership during marriage was recognized so that the wife's half share of the common property was not liable for the husband's delict,[46] so that on the husband's death the wife did not "inherit" it but already owned it,[47] so that if her husband left her anything by testamentary disposition, whatever was so left was in addition to her half share in the common property which was already hers,[48] so that if the husband gave away or transferred the wife's half share in fraud of or in prejudice to her rights, she might enforce her rights by immediate action,[49] and so on, as exemplified in numerous other situations.[50]

That the foregoing statements of the jurisconsults, that the husband and the wife owned the ganancial property by halves, represented the correct view of the Spanish law as it existed prior to the adoption of the Spanish Civil Code in 1889 is well recognized in

No. 9, Book 5 of the Recopilación, and Azevedo in his commentaries of the law in question, in which other authors are quoted, although with the compromise introduced by Covarrubias in the previous quoted text No. 2, that the ownership vested in the wife is *'in habitu et credito'* until the matrimony is dissolved . . . only Tello differs from it. . . ." Llamas y Molina, No. 29 to Nov. Rec. Law 8, Book 10, Title 4.

However, one of the earliest of the commentators, Tellus or Tellius (Tello Fernandez), seems to have constituted a rare exception, but he was most uniformly dismissed by the other jurisconsults, as, in the language of one of them, "most singular in departing from our principle by trying to prove, in opposition to the generally accepted view, that a wife does not acquire ownership and possession of her half-share of the profits during her husband's life." Azevedo, No. 2 to Nov. Rec. Law 8, Book 10, Title 4. Similarly see Gutiérrez, Quaestio CXVIII to Nov. Rec. Law 1; Llamas y Molina, No. 29 et seq. to Nov. Rec. Law 8. Llamas y Molina, No. 54, to Nov. Rec. Law 8, points out that Tello did not deny absolutely this ownership between husband and wife during marriage, but contended that under a strict interpretation of the law it existed only as to property acquired by them "conjointly."

[44] Matienzo, Gloss III, No. 1, to Nov. Rec. Law 1, Book 10, Title 4.

[45] Azevedo, No. 19, to Nov. Rec. Law 1; Matienzo, Gloss III, No. 2, to the same.

[46] See post, § 181 et seq.

[47] See post, §§ 202, 203.

[48] See post, §§ 193, 198.

[49] See post, this chapter, subd. B; also post, Chap. VIII.

"But if it be proven that the alienation is made with fraudulent intent to damage the wife, her interest in them will continue, since she has a right of action to demand her half, upon proof, of the fraud practiced by the husband." Alvarez, Institutes of Royal Law of Spain, 2nd Ed., vol. 2, p. 111.

[50] As to gifts, it has been said: "Since, therefore, in cases where the acquisition or gift is not shared, one spouse is sole owner of the entire gift, so when the gift is shared, e.g., if it is made to both spouses, they each acquire ownership in respect of their own share. Hence the wife is owner of her share during marriage." Matienzo, Gloss IV, No. 1, to Nov. Rec. Law 1, Book 10, Title 4.

Spain today.[51] Indeed, the adoption of the Civil Code has made no change in the principle that husband and wife own the common property equally during the marriage.[52]

§ 98. Febrero.

Of these several bases of misunderstanding, let us take up first that concerning Febrero, and the effect of certain words such as *dueño* and *dominio,* culled from his writings. It is undoubtedly unfortunate that of all the commentators upon the Spanish law Febrero should have been relied upon in an early case and the consideration of his views, however mistakenly interpreted, given an undue prominence and carried down the years through successive cases. There are innumerable eminent jurisconsults whose treatises are preferable for an understanding of the Spanish law. Matienzo, for example, eminent as a distinguished judge, who wrote more thoroughly and at greater length upon the subject than most, who examines exhaustively all the preceding commentaries, whose analyses, reasoning and conclusions are the result of sound thinking and scholarship, whose commentaries abound with practical illustrations, and whose work has been cited and referred to with respect by succeeding commentators. Or Juan Sala, whose work on the civil law became established as the accepted civil law of Spain and was first reproduced in Mexico in 1807 and republished there in subsequent editions and relied on in that country also as a highly authoritative exposition of the law. Or Gutiérrez, whose scholarship and keen and logical perception cut through quickly to the core of every problem and who reconciled many seeming differences of view. Or Llamas y Molina, whose work represents literally some forty years of study and thought, whose learning was immense, and who at the same time was an eminent public figure and jurist of his day. All of these men and many others of similar stamp and caliber were marked by a combination of scholarship, capability in the legal

---

[51] See decision of the Supreme Court of Madrid (Sentencia, 28 Enero, 1898; Gac. 26, Febrero, p. 135) declaring: "Considerando, por ultimo, que no prevalaciendo el recurso por los fundamentos relativos a la prueba, no pueda resultar violada por el fallo la ley 4, tit. 4, lib. 10 de la Novísima Recop., en la que se establece que los bienes que han marido y mujer son de ambos por medio, salvo los que probase cada uno que son suyos apartamente." Thereby the Court recognizes that the Novísima Recopilación established that the property which husband and wife had belonged to both equally except that which each one could prove belonged to him or her separately.

[52] "The ganancial properties belong to the husband and the wife during marriage and the proprietorship of the wife is not nominal or theoretical, but real and effective, and as proof of that are all the limitations placed upon the husband." Manresa, Commentaries on Spanish Civil Code, vol. 9, p. 655, who remarks, quoting Fiore, that although the wife is reduced to inaction while the husband administers wisely, her rights are revealed with energy when the husband compromises her interest by fraudulent or unwise acts.

profession and eminence in the life of their day. Not only jurisconsults whose commentaries mirrored the law of their country as well as establishing it authoritatively, they were also important figures as jurists, high governmental administrators, and teachers of law.[53] Febrero is not comparable to these men. He did not and could not equal them in scholarship, ability and eminence. In fact he was not a lawyer, but a notary. Praiseworthy though his effort was to prepare a desk book for notaries, he himself in his introduction to his *Librería de Escribanos* acknowledged that it was an arduous and difficult task "for one ignorant of the elementary principles of jurisprudence."[54] His work represents only a pedestrian effort to reproduce the conclusions of his more eminent predecessors and displays no scholarship or original thought, other than an occasionally amusing diatribe against the extravagance of women, in itself an illuminating fact. As the work of one not a lawyer, a jurisconsult or a jurist, his work necessarily lacks authoritativeness, except insofar as it accurately restates the principles established by reputable and authoritative commentators.

In short, his work is really worthy of only passing notice, but so great has been the unfortunate effect of early reliance upon him, coupled with misconception as to what he was driving at, that it is necessary to give him some attention. Indeed, we have even quoted from his work with some frequency in our footnotes. It would be wiser to devote that space to others, but because of the undue prominence his name has achieved, it seemed advisable to demonstrate that in the main he correctly reflects, and frequently in simpler language designed for the benefit of the notaries for whom he wrote, briefly sets forth the true principles of the community property laws as expounded by more capable and more scholarly men.

No doubt the reliance upon him in some of the earlier cases resulted from the fact that his work was more readily available, by reason of having been published at a later date than some of the jurisconsults' works, and because it was written in Spanish rather than in Latin, customarily the universal language of scholarship. True, the work of Llamas y Molina, published not long before that of Febrero, was also written in Spanish, a departure from the usual custom for which Llamas y Molina makes some apology in his preface, but its more confined scope, to the Laws of Toro only, and its weightier content, probably militated against its wide appearance on the desk of the average practitioner.[55]

[53] Brief biographical matter concerning these various jurisconsults, see vol. 2 of first edition, de Funiak.

[54] In the Spanish: "sumamente ardua, y difícil para quien carece de los principios elementales de la jurisprudencia."

[55] "It being therefore evident that laws to be observed by nations should be written in the language of their people, and as the Commentaries on such laws have the purpose of facilitating the knowledge and intelligence of such laws, it is manifest that the language in which such Commentaries should be written must be the same as that of the law." Llamas y Molina, Prologue, Commentaries on Laws of Toro.

The undue reliance upon Febrero and the misconception as to his meaning seems to have arisen first in an early case in Louisiana,[56] which was followed by an early California case,[57] and even relied upon to some extent by the United States Supreme Court,[58] wherein much weight seems to have been placed on one section of his work. This section, which we reproduce in the footnotes below,[59] actually dealt with the question of the management of the community property by the husband, a matter to be disassociated from the question of ownership and possession but a matter which common-law lawyers have apparently not always been able to view in its proper perspective in the Spanish law. This articular section comprises in brief content many of the matters requiring explanation for the common-law lawyer and the exposition of these matters will be found in the sections immediately following.

§ 99.   — "Dueño" and "dominio."

While the importance of the subject matter of this section probably does not approach that of some of the other sections, it is probably wise to clear away, at this point, any misunderstanding that may result from the use of certain words in some of the Spanish language commentaries on community property. The word *dueño,* particularly, seems to have been a cause of confusion, and this has been particularly true of its use by Febrero where not only the meaning of the word but of the whole context of the paragraph in which it appears was misunderstood by the Louisiana court in the case of *Guice v. Law-*

---

[56] Guice v. Lawrence, 2 La. Ann. 226. Further as to this case, see post, § 106 et seq.

Likewise does this erroneous reliance upon a mistranslation of Febrero seem to have been true of an early Missouri case. Moreau v. Detchemendy, 18 Mo. 522.

[57] Van Maren v. Johnson, 15 Cal. 311. See also post, § 107.

[58] Garrozi v. Dastas, 204 U. S. 64, 51 L. Ed. 369, 27 S. Ct. 224 (Puerto Rico); Ballester-Ripoll v. Court of Tax Appeals of Puerto Rico, 142 F.2d 11.

[59] "To the married woman is given and transferred *en hábito* (that is, the right of 'having' as opposed to the right of 'holding' and managing, in the meaning of the civil law, see post, § 100) and *potencia* the ownership, and the revocable and constructive possession, of half of the goods earned and acquired with the husband during the marriage; and after the latter dies it is transferred to her irrevocably and effectively, since his death constitutes her complete *dueña* [that is, mistress or one having right of control] in possession and *propriedad* [in loose translation, property] of half of that left, in the manner that as to conventional partnerships is provided by Law 47, at the end of Title 28, Partida 3, thus: We declare likewise that all gains that any of them make that the *señorío* [right, ownership or the like] of it passes to others as if each of them had made it himself. But the husband does not need the dissolution of the marriage to constitute him the real and true *dueño de todos,* since during the marriage he holds [as opposed to the right of 'having,' in the civil law, see post, § 100] his ownership irrevocably; and thus can administer, exchange, sell," etc. Febrero, Librería de Escribanos, Cinco Juicios I, Book I, Cap. IV, § 1, Nos. 29, 30. For the concluding sentences of No. 30, see post, § 100.

rence.[60] Febrero, in discussing the fact that the husband "holds" the property for purposes of management and that the wife cannot interfere with his management by reason of her ownership of half the property,[61] declares that he is *"dueño de todos"* during the marriage, unlike the wife who becomes *"dueña"* of her half only upon dissolution of the marriage.[62] This expression *dueño de todos* the Louisiana court apparently thought meant "owner of everything" and that the wife only became owner of her half upon dissolution of the marriage. However, the word *dueño,* while it may carry the implication of ownership, means primarily the master or head, that is, the one having the control and management. One who is *dueño* may also have some form of *dominio,* that is, ownership, as is the case of the husband who has ownership of half the community property and management of all of it, but the description of one as *dueño* relates primarily to management, not ownership.[63] The wife, however, although having ownership of half the community property during marriage, as we have already seen,[64] does not become mistress of her half, that is, does not obtain the administration of her half, until the dissolution of the marriage.[65] It may be remarked, in passing, that at the same point Febrero then goes on to say that while the husband is alive and the marriage undissolved the wife, merely by reason of her ownership, cannot interfere with his right to manage the community property.[66]

The use of the word *dominio* by several writers, including Febrero, seems to have been the subject of some discussion and disagreement. Its meaning has been so thoroughly discussed by Justice Abbott of the New Mexico Supreme Court[67] that little more need be added thereto. It is sufficient to point out that *dominio* means ownership, but an ownership that does not exclude rights of ownership in others. *Dominio,* indeed, may be of many kinds which is usually expressed by adjectives accompanying it. The kind of *dominio* which would mean full and absolute ownership is expressed by the words *dominio pleno y absoluto.* Another expression which may be mentioned is

[60] 2 La. Ann. 226, ante, § 98.

[61] As to this, see particularly post, § 100.

[62] Text of Febrero's statement, see ante, § 98, in the footnotes.

[63] Juan Sala in stating flatly that the wife had *"dominio y posesión"* in *"la mitad"* of the community property (i. e., ownership and possession of one-half the community property), adds that the husband is *"dueño in actu en razon a la administración,"* in other words, that the husband is the manager *"in actu"* or active manager with respect to the administration. Sala, Digestum Romano-Hispanum, Book 17, Appendix No. 11.

[64] See ante, § 97; also post, § 100.

[65] Notice the Spanish word *dueña* (duenna) with which we are familiar, as indicating an older and more discreet woman who has the care of and responsibility for a young girl. It will be apparent that it cannot mean the "owner" of the young girl.

[66] See ante, § 98.

[67] See dissenting opinion of Abbott, J. in Reade v. De Lea, 14 N.M. 442, 95 P. 131, which was reversed and Justice Abbott's opinion approved in Arnett v. Reade, 220 U. S. 311, 55 L. Ed. 477, 31 S. Ct. 425, 36 L. R. A. (N. S.) 1040, per Holmes, J.

dominio directo y util, which indicates the power to control the disposition of a thing and to receive all the fruits of the thing.[68] It will thus be grasped that the word *dominio* by itself has no such meaning as exclusive ownership.[69] The word comes, of course, from the Latin word *dominium* which as used in the Roman law is roughly translatable as "ownership" and means "a minimal residual right" subject to rights vested in others.[70] The point to be noticed is that *dominio* does not imply an ownership that is sole and exclusive of other rights. It does not necessarily carry with it a right of control, which must be added by other words. To say that a husband had *dominio* of property would not in itself exclude the wife from having *dominio* also. As a matter of fact the jurisconsults uniformly describe the *dominio* of the marital gains, in other words, the ownership thereof, as being in both the husband and wife. This is moreover described as an equal ownership. That is, the ownership of one was equal to that of the other. However, the husband in addition had the power of administration.[71]

To recapitulate, notice that the *dominio* or ownership of the marital acquests and gains is equally in the husband and wife. Both are owners by halves. The ownership of the wife is not affected by the fact that the administration of the common property is placed in the husband, and her ownership continues to be the equal of his. If it had been intended to give the husband the exclusive ownership of the property to do with as he wished, his ownership would have been described as *dominio pleno y absoluto* or some equivalent expression and no *dominio* would have been attributed to the wife.[72]

---

[68] See, e. g., Alavárez, Institutes of Royal Law of Spain, vol. 1, p. 142.

[69] It is also necessary to distinguish fine shades of meaning among several such words as *dominio, propriedad,* and *señorío.*

[70] Buckland and McNair, Roman Law and Common Law, pp. 60, 61.

[71] See Escriche, Elements of Spanish Law, as follows: "Q. Who has the *dominio* in the ganancial property? A. The *dominio* in this property is common to both during the union, but only the husband can alienate it while both are living, even without the consent of the wife, provided he does not do it with intent to injure her." (See Coopwood's translation wherein "dominio" is translated as "dominion.")
And see the Novísimo Sala Mexicano, Sec. 2a, Title 4, No. 5, wherein it is said: "El dominio de los gananciales es comun por mitad al marido y la mujer (citing Laws 1 and 4, Book 10, Title 4 of the Novísima Recopilación), sin consideración a si alguno llevo mas bienes que el otro al matrimonio." [The ownership of the ganancial properties is common equally by halves to the husband and wife, without consideration as to whether one brought more properties than the other into the marriage.]

[72] "If this law, which gives to the husband and wife the property acquired during marriage, were to be understood as meaning that the wife is only entitled to the use thereof while the husband acquires the ownership, its provisions would be defective. And this must not be, see Dig. 4.8.11.5 and Dig. 18.5.1 and 2. And so we must understand this law as meaning that both the husband and the wife acquire ownership of property acquired during marriage." Matienzo, Gloss III, No. 2, to Nov. Rec. Law 1, Book 10, Title 4.

§ 100.   — Ownership and possession "in habitu" and "in actu."

While it was unquestioned, as we have already seen, that husband and wife both equally had ownership and possession of the common property,[73] a difference in their positions was recognized, in that the husband had in addition to his ownership and possession the power and duty of administering the common property while the wife had ownership and possession without administration. Putting aside common-law concepts of ownership and possession, as one must to understand this civil law ownership, it must be remembered that the Spanish law was influenced by the Roman law and the result was that the Spanish law recognized certain shades of distinction not always recognized today by the common-law lawyer. Thus, in the Roman and Spanish law "to have" (*habere*) was distinguishable from "to hold" (*tenere*) and "to possess" (*possidere*). The first refers to the right, the second to the fact, and the third to both the preceding ones. One might own property without having possession of it, since the two attributes were distinct.[74] And one might both own and possess property without "holding" the property in the sense of exercising administration over it.[75] Although with us any former distinction between the words has now disappeared and become meaningless, it will be recalled that as creatures of habit we lawyers still are inclined in this country to use in deeds of conveyance the words "to have and to hold." Undoubtedly, we would now assume that if one "has" property he also "holds" it. But in the Spanish law the wife "had," that is, owned the property — and also "possessed" it — but did not "hold" it. It was the husband who "held" it (the *tenere* of the Latin or *tiene* of the Spanish) in order to administer it, as well as owning and possessing it equally with the wife. That is, the husband's ownership was one of "having," as well as "holding" for purposes of administration, while

---

[73] See ante, § 97.

[74] Distinction in the Roman law between property or ownership on the one hand and possession on the other, as indicated by Dig. 41.2.12.1.: "Nihil commune habet proprietas cum possessione" [Ownership has nothing in common with possession], see Buckland and McNair, Roman Law and Common Law, p. 58 et seq.

"Ownership and the possession of a thing are entirely distinct," declares La. Civ. Code, art. 496, in part.

See also Matienzo, Gloss III to Nov. Rec. Law 1, Book 10, Title 4, who discusses ownership and possession, including the civil law possession, etc.

[75] "The word to 'have' is general and includes ownership, possession, detention, and even rights of action." Matienzo, Gloss III, No. 5, to Nov. Rec. Law 1. To same effect, Gutiérrez, Quaestio CXVIII, No. 4, to Nov. Rec. Law 1.

After declaring that ownership and possession of a thing are entirely distinct, La. Civ. Code, art. 496, goes on to point out that the right of ownership exists independently of the exercise of it and that an owner is no less an owner because he performs no act of ownership or because he is disabled from performing any such acts.

the wife's ownership was one of "having," without "holding" for purposes of administration. The ownership and possession of the community property by both husband and wife was described as *habitus*, from the Latin word *habere*, and meaning the act of "having" or "owning." The wife had ownership and possession *in habitu* and the husband had ownership and possession *in habitu*, because they both "had" or "owned" the property and, moreover, had or owned it equally. But because the husband was empowered to administer the community property, he necessarily "held" it in order to exercise this administration. The husband thus had what was called the *actus*, which meant the right to do or perform a thing, in other words, to administer. Accordingly, the wife's ownership and possession was frequently described as *in habitu* and the husband's as *in habitu* and *in actu*.[76] Since it was well understood that the husband's ownership was *in habitu* as in the case of the wife, since he "had" or "owned" the property as did the wife, since the important distinction was that the husband had the *actus*, that is, the administration, it was generally considered sufficient to describe the wife's ownership as *in habitu* and the husband's only as *in actu*, the *habitus* in his case being understood, since his *actus* depended necessarily upon his *habitus*.[77] Incidentally, the "possession" of the wife, which has been referred to, was, under

---

[76] "The husband and the wife have the ownership of the ganancial properties (Nov. Rec., Book 10, Title 4, Laws 1 and 4), with the difference that the husband has it *in habitu* and *in actu*, as the commentators explain, and the wife only *in habitu*, the *actu* passing to her when the marriage is dissolved. For that reason the wife cannot give or convey such properties during the marriage, but the husband can without the consent of the wife make their *inter vivos* conveyances moderately and for just causes; but excessive or capricious gifts will be void, and the conveyances made with intent to defraud the wife, who will have action in all these cases against the properties of the husband and against the possessor of the things conveyed." Escriche, Diccionario, vol. 2, "Ganancial Properties."

The wife had a right of ownership (*"dominio en hábito"*) and the husband had a right of ownership (*"dominio en hábito"*) and in addition a right of management (*"dominio en acto"*) as was said by Burnett, Community Property Law according to Professor Juan Sala, Chap. 11,

in an interesting discussion of this matter.

[77] "The decision which affirms that the wife obtains during matrimony the ownership and possession of half of the property acquired during marriage is generally accepted by our national authors, as will be seen in Covarrubias Lib. 3, Variarum, Chap. 19, No. 2, and Matienzo in Gloss 3 to Law of Toro No. 9, Book 5 of the Recopilación, and Azevedo in his commentaries of the Law in question, in which other authors are quoted, although with the compromise introduced by Covarrubias in the previous cited text, No. 2, that the ownership vested in the wife is 'in habitu et credito' until the matrimony is dissolved." Llamas y Molina, No. 29 of commentaries to Nov. Rec. Law 8, Book 10, Title 4.

"The property of the conjugal community belongs, while it exists, and afterwards individually 'to each of the spouses by halves' . . . from which the ancient experts deduce that the distinction of ownership *in habitu* which the wife has and the ownership *in actu* which the husband has in the

the civil law, a real and not a constructive possession, and carried with it the right to all possessory remedies (interdicts) to acquire, retain, and to recover possession of her half of the community property. For under the civil law, possession whether transferred to one actually or constructively was as real a possession in one case as in the other.[78]

No doubt it has been the failure to understand these distinctions that has caused misinterpretations of Febrero's statement "that while the husband is alive, and the marriage has not been dissolved, and there has been no divorce, the wife ought not to say that she *tiene gananciales,* nor interfere with him in his lawful administration of those acquired on the ground that the law grants her half thereof, because that grant is intended for the situation mentioned, and no other, whatever some ignorant wives may believe."[79] The statement does not mean, as has sometimes been mistakenly assumed, that she must not say that she "owns (or has) the community property." What it does mean is that the wife must not say that she "holds" the community property, i.e., for purposes of administration; nor must she interfere with the husband's lawful administration by advancing the fact of her "having" ownership of half of the property. For her ownership, although an existing ownership by halves, did not have attached thereto the administration of the property. Obviously, it would be of no avail for the law to place the administration of the community property in the husband's hands and then allow the wife, on the ground of her ownership of half the property, to hinder and impede him when, in entire good faith and for the purpose of benefiting the conjugal partnership, he attempts to enter into some transaction concerning the community property. Accordingly, all that Febrero is saying is that the wife must

ganancial property, is because one was owner without administration and the other owner with it." Felipe Sanchez Roman, Estudios de Derecho Civil, 1899 Ed., vol. 1, p. 820.

"A la mujer casada se communica, y transfiere *en habito,* y potencia el dominio," etc. See Febrero, translated ante, § 98, n. 59. Incidentally, the Spanish for *in habitu* and *in actu* was *en hábito* and *en acto.*

"One can say with regard to her, as with regard to a person in a partnership which has an appointed manager, that her right is 'potius in habitu quam in actu'" (better in having than in administering). Brissaud, History of French Private Law, § 560.

[78] Matienzo, Gloss III, No. 20, to Nov. Rec. Law 1, Book 10, Title 4.

"Civil law possession which is transferred without any act, actual or constructive, is called real and not constructive possession (citing authorities). From which it may be inferred that the wife is entitled to all the possessory interdicts in respect of her moiety of the property acquired during marriage, viz. to acquire, retain, and to recover possession." Matienzo, Gloss III, No. 21, to Nov. Rec. Law 1.

[79] "Por lo que mientras el marido vive, y no se disuelve su matrimonio, o no hay divorcio, no debe decir la muger que tiene gananciales, ni impedirle el uso licito de los que adquiera a pretexto de que la ley la concede su mitad, porque esta concesión se entiende para los casos expresados, y no en otro, como algunas necias creen." Febrero, Librería de Escribanos, Cinco Juicios I, Lib. I. Cap. IV, § 1, No. 30.

not interfere with the husband's right to administer the property by claiming such a right in herself.[80] Indeed, what Febrero is discussing in the entire paragraph is the husband's right of administration, and not any question of ownership.[81]

Returning again, however, to the matter of the wife's ownership and possession, it might, in short, be described as "inactive," and the husband's as "active." Frequently in translations of discussions of the wife's ownership *in habitu* and the husband's ownership *in actu,* the terms have been inaccurately translated as "constructive ownership" and "actual ownership," thus giving the erroneous impression that the husband's ownership was a real ownership and the wife's was not. The wife's ownership was no less a real ownership, as clearly shown by the codes and commentaries, and a correct translation of the wife's ownership is that it was an inactive ownership and the husband's an active ownership, i.e., ownership with the administration. Since the husband's ownership was *in habitu,* just as the wife's, since he "had" or "owned" the property just as she did, it can be seen that translating *dominio in habitu* to mean "constructive ownership" is reducing the matter to an absurdity, because it amounts to saying that both husband and wife had "constructive ownership" and that the husband in addition to having constructive ownership also had actual ownership. Comprehension of the true meanings of *habitus* and *actus* is necessary to an understanding of the commentaries of the Spanish jurisconsults.

It must not be assumed, then, that the wife's ownership was any less an equal ownership just because the husband administered the property for both. As head of the family he had the administration but the ownership belonged to both alike.[82] Thus where Azevedo

---

[80] In Guice v. Lawrence, 2 La. Ann. 226, the word *tiene* in this statement of Febrero was mistakenly translated as "has" instead of "holds," and the whole force of the Spanish law distinctions between ownership and administration lost. See also ante, § 98; post, § 107.

The somewhat general terms and the brevity of Febrero's statement need supplementation to the extent of pointing out that the wife is not to interfere in the husband's management only so long as he is managing capably and for the benefit of them both. So soon as he acts in regard to the property in a manner prejudicial or detrimental to the wife's interests, she may interfere. See post, §§ 119, 126.

[81] The expression in the beginning

of this same paragraph that the husband was *"dueño de todos"* is discussed previously, § 99.

[82] "But if the husband alone acquired ownership and possession of goods acquired during marriage, and not the wife, there would be no equal division, nor would an equal share belong to each, but an unequal one, contrary to the intention and the language of our laws. And so the wife too will be the owner of her half share during marriage, no less than the husband, since the law has not contradicted this, though the husband alone has the administration of these goods during marriage and not the wife, as we see in Law 5 *infra eodem,* because that law lays it down so, and rightly, seeing that the husband is head over the wife. It is not then

remarks that "And it is quite true that immediately upon any goods being acquired by the husband, ownership and possession of a moiety of them passes to the wife, *in habitu et potentia* though not *in actu,* without any delivery, but revocably not irrevocably,"[83] this means nothing more, as is illustrated by the language of Juan Sala, than that "Azevedo to Law 1, Nov. Rec., No. 17, says that half of the community property of which the wife has ownership and possession is hers *in habitu* and not *in actu;* because the husband must be understood to be the manager (*dueño in actu*) as to the administration and power of alienation that he holds (*tiene*) in the community property."[84] As a matter of fact there were many situations, instanced by the commentators (and with which we deal in this work), in which the wife might acquire administration even during marriage or might impose a check upon the husband's management. But in ordinary circumstances of proper administration, not requiring his displacement or the questioning of his course of administration, there was ordinarily no occasion for the wife to assume the administration of her share of the community property until dissolution of the marriage. This fact made her ownership and possession during marriage no less a legal reality and no less than that of the husband. "The ganancial properties belong to the husband and the wife during marriage and the proprietorship of the wife is not nominal or theoretical, but real and effective, and as proof of that are all the limitations placed upon the husband," said Manresa, who adds, quoting Fiore, that although the wife is reduced to inaction while the husband administers wisely, her rights are revealed with energy when the husband compromises her interest by fraudulent or unwise actions.[85] The wife's rights of ownership must be gauged by the Spanish law of community and not by principles of English-derived common law relating to a wife's inchoate right of dower or similar principles. The situation in the Spanish law has been most properly translated into English legal terminology by most of the courts of our community property states as meaning a present and equal ownership during the marriage between the spouses in the common property, with the power of administration of the common prop-

---

surprising if he alone has the administration of these goods, whereas the ownership belongs to both parties alike, as is clearly shown by the said laws regarded in the said way." Gutiérrez, Quaestio CXVIII, No. 4, to Nov. Rec. Law 1, Book 10, Title 4.

[83] Azevedo, No. 17 to Nov. Rec. Law 1, Book 10, Title 4.
Revocable and irrevocable ownership, see post, § 101.

[84] Sala, Digestum Romano-Hispanum, Book 17, Appendix, No. 11.

[85] Manresa, Commentaries on Spanish Civil Code, vol. 9, p. 655.
The right of the wife to obtain the administration in her hands, where circumstances warranted it, must be kept in mind. See Subdivision B of this chapter. Certainly we have never seen the argument advanced that where community property was under the management of the wife the husband had no ownership therein. There is a homely but expressive phrase, "What is sauce for the goose is sauce for the gander."

erty placed in the husband's hands, that he is the managing partner of the partnership property or managing agent of the conjugal partnership. This, in effect, is what the Spanish law of community property amounts to in our terminology.[86]

What has undoubtedly proved another source of confusion to those referring to the Spanish jurisconsults for information is the fact that the latter frequently referred to the *acquisition* of ownership and possession by the wife during marriage as being *de jure* or *ipso jure* or as *potentia* (in the Spanish, *potencia*).[87] This, coupled with Febrero's use of the word *fieta* in relation to the acquisition of ownership by the wife — and it must be kept in mind that the reference is to the manner of acquisition, not to the existing ownership after acquisition[88] — has led to the advancement of the argument that the wife did not have any real but only a constructive or technical ownership under the Spanish law. But a study of the entire commentaries of these various writers, including those of Febrero likewise, will disclose the fact that these identical commentators state time after time that the wife had a full and complete ownership during the marriage equal to that of the husband and that her ownership was not open to question.[89] Much of the difficulty has arisen from confusing with the fact of the wife's ownership, the fact of the creation or acquisition of her ownership. Her ownership and possession as an existing fact during the marriage, equal to the ownership and possession of the husband, was asserted numerous times by the jurisconsults, as has been seen.[90] As to its creation, it will be noticed that they repeatedly described it as created by operation of law. Thus, they sometimes referred to the ownership and possession as passing or transferred to her *de jure* or *ipso jure;* occasionally, as by Matienzo on one or two occasions, the jurisconsults described it in the Latin of their text as created or made, using some

---

[86] The spouses' "rights of property in the effects of the community are perfectly equivalent to each other. The difference is this, that, during coverture, her rights are passive; his are active. . . . So long as he discharges his duty as a husband, his superior rights remain unquestionably in full vigor. But when he abandons the administration of the common property . . . do not his rights over the effects of the community, from the nature of things, cease? And are not the passive rights of the wife quickened into vigorous activity? She is necessarily compelled to assume the position of the husband; to discharge his duties and incur his responsibilities. . . . Her right in the property is equal to that of the husband. During his presence he has the administration, subject to the trusts incumbent upon the property. This right of control must necessarily cease where he can and will no longer exercise it; and the wife, the other joint owner, must be vested with the authority, or it cannot exist anywhere." Wright v. Hays, 10 Tex. 130, 60 Am. Dec. 200.

[87] See Matienzo, Gloss III, No. 17, to Nov. Rec. Law 1, Book 10, Title 4. Gutiérrez, Quaestio CXVIII, Nos. 13, 14, to same; Azevedo, No. 17, to the same.

[88] See ante, § 98.

[89] See ante, § 97.

[90] See ante, § 97.

form of the Latin verb *fingo, fingere, finxi, fictum,* or some derivation thereof, which word in its classical meaning meant to form, shape, fashion or make.[91] Thereby, they meant, of course, that it was made or created by law, and not, as was specifically pointed out, by result of the liberality of the other spouse or by reason of contract.[92] Merely that we have derived our present word "fictitious" from a form of this verb *fingo* (*fictum*) does not justify confusing our meaning with that of the jurisconsults' meaning in describing the acquisition as "created" or "made," i.e., by operation of law, nor justify confusing the manner of the creation of the ownership with the actually existing ownership itself. Her acquisition of ownership, and for that matter the husband's acquisition of ownership in earnings or gains of the wife, was "made" by law (*fingo, fictum*), but the acquisition once effected by law (*ipso jure*) was as complete and as equal as that of the other spouse.[93] It is extremely important, therefore, to keep in mind that any such terms as *de jure, ipso jure,* or the like, including forms of or derivations from the word *fingo* (the latter little used, incidentally), were used in relation to the acquiring of ownership and possession and not to the existence of the ownership and possession once acquired.

The occasional use of the Latin word *potentia,* or in the Spanish, *potencia,* it will be found when it was used, was in connection with the acquisition of ownership by the wife as being *in habitu et potentia* (in the Spanish, *en habito y potencia*).[94] It was thereby merely meant that her ownership, although acquired *in habitu* was acquired with potency or potentiality, that is, the capability of developing into ownership *in actu* at the proper time.

§ 101.   —Ownership and possession as revocable or irrevocable.

Additional terminology with respect to the ownership and possession of the spouses, which has given rise to misconception as to the equality of the wife's ownership and possession, are the commentators' references to the husband's ownership and possession as irrevocable and the wife's as revocable.[95] It has been assumed that the wife's ownership and possession of her share of the community property could be taken away from her at any moment, for example, by the husband's alienation of the community property, and hence that the wife had no real ownership. But this matter of revocability is only another matter revolving around the question of the husband's admin-

---

91 See Matienzo, Gloss I, No. 3, to Nov. Rec. Law 8, Gloss I, No. 3, to Nov. Rec. Law 9, both Book 10, Title 4.

92 Matienzo, Gloss III, No. 1, to Nov. Rec. Law 1, Book 10, Title 4.

93 See ante, § 97.

94 See Azevedo, No. 17, to Nov. Rec. Law 1, Book 10, Title 4. Febrero, ante, § 98.

95 Febrero's description of the wife's possession as revocable, coupled with his other descriptions relating to her ownership and possession, has probably been the one attracting the most attention. See ante, § 98.

istration of the community property. As the spouse exercising the administration, he might, so long as he was not acting in fraud or prejudice of the wife's interests, alienate the community property without the necessity of having her consent. When he did alienate some particular piece of community property, obviously the ownership and possession of the wife in such partnership no longer existed. In other words, it could be said to have been "revoked." No one could "revoke" the husband's ownership and possession in the community property, so that his ownership and possession might be described as "irrevocable"; although he himself might, of course, elect to transfer the property.

But what seems not to be understood is the fact that the wife's position did not actually change by reason of the husband's alienation of the community property. She immediately acquired, equally with the husband, ownership and possession in the money, goods or property received in exchange upon such alienation. In other words, she always had a full, immediate half ownership in the community property, although the nature or character of the property might change from time to time, as the husband in the exercise of his right of administration transacted such business matters concerning the property as he in his judgment believed necessary. He had no power of disposition, however, which could ever defeat his wife's equal and half ownership in the community property, whatever its changes and mutations.[96] His powers to give away the community property were definitely limited and he could not alienate in fraud or injury of the wife's rights. In fact, if he did so, the wife had rights of action which she could prosecute; certainly proof enough of her present and existing half ownership, as was the fact that where circumstances warranted she could have the administration of the community shifted into her hands.[97] He was thus subject to the obligations and duties of any agent or fiduciary in the administration of property entrusted to his care.[98] So, while her ownership and possession in half of presently existing community property was "revocable" in the sense that that particular property might be alienated or exchanged for some other property in the course of management, her ownership and possession of half

[96] "The only difference or distinction whatever [that] the law has made between the husband and wife with reference to community property is that during the continuance of the community the husband is the managing agent, vested with absolute disposition of the property, and that the wife cannot sell or incumber such property, except in specified instances. The receipts, however, from any disposition that may be made of the property, still remain community property, and the wife's interests in the receipts from any sale of community property are just as great as they were in the original community property which was thus sold or transferred." Kohny v. Dunbar, 21 Idaho 258, 121 P. 544, 39 L. R. A. (N. S.) 1107.

[97] See post, §§ 124–129.

For example, the husband could not by will and last wish make a disposition that would alienate profits after his death. See Azevedo, No. 15, to Nov. Rec. Law 5, Book 10, Title 4.

[98] See post, Chap. VIII.

of all community property, in whatever form it existed, was never "revoked" or lost, any more than was the husband's. Indeed, the use of the word "revocable" has been criticized by later Spanish writers for the very reason that it was inaccurate if considered as pertaining to ownership and possession, for equal and existing ownership and possession between the spouses remains constant during the marriage, and administration by the husband can result only in changes in form or character of property.[99]

In another connection, as concerns "revocable," it was explained that although ownership of earnings and gains passed automatically to the wife by force of law, her ownership was "revocable" in that she could renounce her share of the earnings and gains, if she desired. Thus Gutiérrez explains that "though the wife during marriage *ipso jure* acquires ownership and possession of these goods, yet this must be understood to be revocable, i.e., the wife may, if she wishes, renounce the aforesaid share of the profits."[1] However, the force of this explanation is considerably weakened by the fact that the husband also could renounce his share of the earnings and gains if he wished, so that his interest therein was equally as "revocable" as the wife's, if the term is to be applied to renunciation.[2]

§ 102.   Misconception due to management.

What seems to confuse legal minds trained in the English common law are the discussions by the commentators that the wife might not obtain actual possession of her half of the community property so as to "control" or manage it until the death of her husband. Applying principles of property law with which they are familiar, they are unable to understand how, by their principles, there can be "ownership" without a "control." Many lawyers trained in the common law, and viewing the matter in the light of common-law concepts, seem to feel that if the husband, under the Spanish community property system, had "control," i.e., the administration of the community property, he must have been the virtual owner of the property; that the wife,

---

[99] In the 1918 edition of Febrero, prepared by Don Josef Marcos Gutiérrez, vol. 3, p. 164, the latter says: "The distinction which is here made between the *dominio* of the wife and that of the husband in the ganancials,—designated for the one revocable, and for the other irrevocable,—is confused and even false; since that of one consort is just as irrevocable as that of the other. By force of the law, the ganancials belong equally and undividedly to the husband and to the wife. But he has also the administration, which she lacks, until at the death of the husband, the property which belongs to her is delivered to her, and she becomes able to administer for herself. Likewise, the possession of the husband and of the wife in the ganancials is the same, although the former holds the management."

[1] See Gutiérrez, Quaestio CXVIII, No. 13, to Nov. Rec. Law 1, Book 10, Title 4.

[2] See as to renunciation, post, § 135 et seq.

accordingly, was not an owner in any real sense. What they seem to fail to comprehend is that the management of the common property placed in the husband was an administrative duty only, in other words, administration of the common property, and not in any sense the equivalent of the common law "control" by the husband of the wife's property which made him virtual owner and gave him the right to appropriate its use to his own enjoyment and benefit.[3] To enter now upon a discussion of administration of the community property would merely be duplicative of the treatment of that subject in the latter half of this chapter. It must suffice to stress here that husband and wife both had an ownership, each one to a half of the acquests and gains of the marriage, an ownership that was immediate and present. The husband's ownership, however, had as incident thereto the administration of the community. Immediately upon dissolution of the marriage, the wife's ownership in her half of the community acquired the same incident of administration which the husband's ownership had formerly had an incident thereto.[4] However, even during the marriage her ownership was so full and complete that she might vigorously oppose and seek to correct any administration by the husband that was in fraud of or prejudicial to her interest, and upon occasion the administration of the entire community property might be shifted to her. And any acts of administration were fraudulent or prejudicial as to her which deprived or tended to deprive her of the benefit and enjoyment of half the community property or to deprive her of such half without adequate consideration.[5]

§ 103.   — Misconception due to question of who earned or acquired property.

Since by usual common-law concepts, where a husband or wife earns or acquires money or property through his or her own industry or labor, such earnings or acquisitions constitute the separate property of the one earning or acquiring it, it is not easy for lawyers trained in the common law to comprehend a property concept alien thereto. Indeed, some of them obstinately refuse to concede that there can be any other logical result, especially when it appears to them that the one earning or acquiring the property apparently continues in the management or "control" of it.[6] But to insist that all other systems of law must be interpreted only in terms of and by concepts of that law with which one is familiar and which is preferable to one is abysmally stupid. The intelligent lawyer tries to comprehend a system

[3] See post, this chapter, subd. B. An understanding view is well expressed in People v. Bejarano (Colo.) 358 P.2d 366, approving remarks by de Funiak in 43 Va. L. Rev. 49.

[4] See also ante, § 100.

[5] See post, §§ 126, 128, 129.

[6] Husband's "control" was not, however, the kind of "control" that a husband had at common law. See ante, § 102.

of law by its own concepts. Accordingly, it is necessary to understand that under the community property system, earnings and gains by either or both spouses during marriage through their labor and industry become by operation of law the common property of both spouses from the moment of acquisition, in fact from the very inception of the right to the property.[7] The ownership is acquired by operation of law and not by reason of contract or by reason of liberality of the other spouse.[8] Both spouses immediately own the property equally. If the common-law lawyer must or needs to apply a parallel from his own system of law, let him consider the ordinary commercial partnership. What is gained by the partnership belongs fully and equally to all partners in proportion to the interests in the partnership. So in the conjugal partnership under the community property system, what is acquired during its existence belongs fully and equally to the spouses by halves. It is not a question of which spouse earned it, whether one earned more than another, or whether one has more separate property than another. Whatever is earned or gained belongs to both. This is a basic principle, a fundamental property concept of the community property system.[9]

In a noncommunity property jurisdiction the fact that earnings or gains by a person are owned by the person who earned or gained them is itself true because made so by operation of law. At least it is true so long as the person in question is twenty-one years of age or older. If the person is under that age and not emancipated, the earnings belong not to the person but to his or her parents, and that again is by operation of law. There is no instant at which they are owned by the minor and then transferred by the minor to the parents. The earnings belong immediately to the parents by operation of law. This principle which has existed in the common law for centuries, is parallel to the principle that has existed in the community property system for centuries — that earnings by either spouse during marriage are owned equally by both from the moment of acquisition.

---

[7] Acquisition as including the inception of the right to the property, see ante, § 64.

[8] Matienzo, Gloss III, No. 1, to Nov. Rec. Law 1, Book 10, Title 4.

[9] "Ownership of property howsoever acquired during marriage by the husband passes to the wife in respect of her half-share without delivery even before the marriage is dissolved. This may be compared with a contract of partnership, see law 47, title 28, part. 3. And the same rule applies to the passing of possession." Matienzo, Gloss III, No. 13, to Nov. Rec. Law 1, Book 10, Title 4. Likewise, see Gutiérrez, Quaestio CXVIII, to the same; Azevedo, No. 19, to the same.

"In the second place, you should note from the words 'ayanlo ambos de por medio' (let them both have it by halves) that ownership and possession of a moiety of the property acquired during marriage passes automatically to the wife without delivery and the wife is owner even during marriage of the share which belongs to her." Matienzo, Gloss III, No. 2, to Nov. Rec. Law 1. And see the succeeding numbers in which the analogy of partnership is discussed.

§ 104. — Misconception arising from consideration of non-Visigothic law.

Neither at common law (i.e., the civil law or law derived from Roman law implanted in Spain prior to the Visigothic conquest) nor at canon law was property acquired during marriage shared or divided between the spouses.[10] Property acquired by the husband was presumed his unless it could be proved that it was acquired with property of both spouses so as to make them both owners of it.[11] Under this common or Roman law, property acquired by a wife during marriage was presumed to have been acquired from the husband's property.[12] It was the statutory or "royal law," beginning with the Fuero Juzgo in 693 A.D., based on the Visigothic law that definitely established, for all, the Visigothic law of community.[13] Consequently, as to those commentators on the "common" or "imperial" or Roman or canonical laws it must be borne in mind that they are discussing something entirely different from the community property system established by the "royal law." Thus, when one reads the commentaries on the community laws themselves and finds those commentators referring to earlier commentators who appear to be arguing that the wife does not have an ownership in property acquired during the marriage, it must frequently be differentiated that those earlier writers are commentators on the common or canonical laws.

Incidentally, it was frequently common practice for the commentators to present all the adverse arguments that might be adduced, before stating how a law was to be interpreted. Unless one follows through to the very end the commentator's discussion of a certain problem or point, there is possibility of coming away with a wrong impression of the commentary.

§ 105. Recognition by American courts of wife's ownership.

At the present time in all of our American community property states it is recognized, by virtue of statute or judicial decision, that the

---

[10] See Matienzo, Gloss I, No. 2, to Nov. Rec. Law 1, Book 10, Title 4. Llamas y Molina, Nos. 4, 5 to Law 6, No. 15 to Law 8.

Under the "old" law, "all the properties were presumed to belong to the husband, and the wife had only those which she proved to be hers, to avoid the suspicion that she had acquired them by illicit means." Febrero, Librería de Escribanos, Cinco Juicios I, Book I, Cap. IV, § 1.

[11] See Azevedo, Summary No. 1, to Nov. Rec. Law 4, Book 10, Title 4. Llamas y Molina, No. 5 to Nov. Rec. Law 6, Book 10, Title 4.

[12] See Rec. Law 4, Book 10, Title 4, and Matienzo, Gloss 1, No. 1, thereto.

[13] "Note that by the general custom of this realm, now confirmed by this law, all movable and immovable property, and all rights and actions and all other things whatsoever are presumed to be the common property of husband and wife, except such things as either of them proves to be his or her own property." Matienzo, Gloss II, No. 1, to Nov. Rec. Law 4, Book 10, Title 4.

interests of the husband and the wife in the community property are present, equal and existing interests during the marriage itself, that the wife, in other words, has an ownership of half of the community property, equal to that of the husband, from the moment of the acquisition of, or from the inception of the right to, such property.[14] This is quite in accord with the usual interpretation in community property jurisdictions of the present day,[15] and with the interpretation in the Spanish community property system itself, as has already been seen.[16] So far, however, as concerns California the qualification would seem to exist that such an interpretation relates only to community property acquired since 1927.[17]

It is to be understood, also, that possession is equally in the wife as in the husband just as ownership is equally in her as in her husband. The community property is owned and possessed by both, no matter in the hands of which spouse it may be for purposes of administration. Even though the one holding the property for purposes of administration may be said to have actual possession, there is a constructive possession in the other spouse, a right of possession as well as of ownership enforceable against the other spouse and anyone to whom he or she wrongfully transfers the property.[18]

[14] Poe v. Seaborn, 282 U. S. 101, 75 L. Ed. 239, 51 Sup. Ct. 58 (Washington); Goodell v. Koch, 282 U. S. 118, 75 L. Ed. 247, 51 Sup. Ct. 62 (Arizona); Hopkins v. Bacon, 282 U. S. 122, 75 L. Ed. 249, 51 Sup. Ct. 62 (Texas); Bender v. Pfaff, 128 U. S. 127, 75 L. Ed. 252, 51 Sup. Ct. 64 (Louisiana); La Tourette v. La Tourette, 15 Ariz. 200, 137 P. 426, Ann. Cas. 1915 B 70; Cal. Civ. Code, § 5105; Kohny v. Dunbar, 21 Idaho 258, 121 P. 544, Ann. Cas. 1913 D 492, 39 L. R. A. (N. S.) 1107; In re Williams' Estate, 40 Nev. 241, 161 P. 741, L. R. A. 1917 C 602; Beals v. Ares, 25 N.M. 459, 185 P. 780; Arnold v. Leonard, 114 Tex. 535, 273 S. W. 799; Schramm v. Steele, 97 Wash. 309, 166 P. 634.

And see Kirkwood, Equality of Property Interests Between Husband and Wife, 8 Minn. Law Rev. 579.

"The titles of the husband and wife to the community property are equal, the only difference being, that during the continuation of the married relation, the husband, as the head of the family, has the management, control, and disposition of this property for their joint benefit." Zimpleman v. Robb, 53 Tex. 274.

Wife by virtue of ownership of half the community property, upon which taxes had been paid by husband as agent of the marital community, was a property owner entitled to vote in a bond election. Baca v. Village of Belen, 30 N.M. 546, 240 P. 803.

[15] "The Supreme Court of the [Philippine] Islands has characterized the wife's interest in the conjugal property as 'vested' and 'equal to' that of the husband. Gibbs v. Government (1933), 59 Phil. 293." Com'r of Int. Rev. v. Cadwallader, 9 C. C. A., 127 F.2d 547, per Healey, J. See also Helvering v. Campbell, 139 F.2d 865. But see erroneous view in Puerto Rico, as expressed in Ballaster-Ripoll v. Puerto Rico Court of Tax Appeals, 142 F.2d 11.

Both in France and in the Province of Quebec, the wife's interest in the community is a "real proprietary right" and not a mere "hope of a certain distribution." See De Nicols v. Curlier, [1900] App. Cas. 21; Beaudoin v. Trudel, [1937] 1 D. L. R. 216. See also ante, §§ 14, 18, 38, 39.

[16] See preceding sections.

[17] See post, § 107.

[18] See post, § 124 et seq.

The recognition and understanding of the correct principles governing the matter of the wife's ownership was not arrived at in some of our states without considerable fumbling on the part of the courts. In California, it was only arrived at through positive action by the state legislature. But since the situation is now more or less uniform in all our states and represents an accomplished fact, there is little need for any extended discussion of the previous judicial history in those states where misconceptions existed at one time or another. Reference is made, more or less briefly, in the sections following to some of the particular states. These states are considered in the order in which the misconception took its course, rather than in alphabetical order by states.

§ 106.   — Louisiana.

In Louisiana where a more accurate understanding of the principles of the community property law might well be expected than in many of the other states, an unfortunate misconception, in an early case, of the principles arising chiefly from mistranslation and misunderstanding of a passage from Febrero, lead to the continuance of an erroneous view not only in that state but in California,[19] and momentarily to confusion in New Mexico.[20] Originally, in considering the wife's ownership the Louisiana court indicated adherence to the correct principle that the wife has a present right of ownership during the marriage in the community property, originating from the marriage itself rather than arising from the dissolution of the marriage.[21] But shortly thereafter, in *Guice v. Lawrence,* relying on the law of Spain as to the nature of the wife's ownership during the marriage, it mistakenly conceived that under that law the wife had no ownership during the marriage and only obtained ownership upon dissolution of the marriage.[22] This misconception resulted largely from the court's

[19] California, see post, § 107. In turn, the error continued in California momentarily influenced the Idaho court, see post, § 109.

[20] See post, § 108.

[21] See Dixon v. Dixon's Ex'rs, 4 La. 188, 23 Am. Dec. 478; Theall v. Theall, 7 La. 226, 26 Am. Dec. 501.

[22] Guice v. Lawrence, 2 La. Ann. 226, which held, under the mistaken impression that under the Spanish law that the wife had no ownership in acquests during the marriage, that the husband's alienation of all the community property to his debtors was valid, and that the wife's only remedy would be in case she was defrauded by the alienation, and even then would be against the heirs of the husband. The court relied very heavily on discussion of the wife's interest under the French customs prior to the Code Napoleon, a criticism that also may be made of the United States Supreme Court in Garrozi v. Dastas, 204 U. S. 64, 51 L. Ed. 369, 27 Sup. Ct. 224, in relation to the law of Puerto Rico. Principles of the Spanish law of community can be sufficiently ascertained from its own source material. The view that the wife, defrauded by a wrongful alienation by the husband, had no remedy until the dissolution of the marriage and then only against the heirs of the

reliance upon a quotation from Febrero dealing with the husband's power of management and stating that the wife should not interfere therewith by claiming that she *tiene,* that is, "holds," ganancial property, and which the court mistranslated to mean that she must not claim that she "has" ganancial property. In this, the court missed entirely the difference in the Spanish law between "having" in the sense of "owning," and "holding" in the sense of having the right to administer the property. It thus confused the fact that the wife does not "hold" the property, in the sense of managing it, until the dissolution of the marriage, with ownership, and arrived at the conclusion that the wife did not "own" the property until dissolution of the marriage. This complete ignorance of the distinctions in the Spanish law of community property with relation to having, holding and possessing, which have already been discussed,[23] continued to affect the views of the Louisiana courts for many years, leading them to describe the wife's interest as inchoate during the existence of the community,[24] or as residuary.[25] On the other hand, several decisions were consistent with a recognition of an existing and equal ownership in the wife and in 1926, the Louisiana court expressly disavowed *Guice v. Lawrence,* declaring that it had been based on a mistranslation of Febrero, and that the correct principle had always been in Louisiana that the wife's ownership of half of the community property was vested in her from the moment of its acquisition by the community or by the spouses, even though acquired in the name of only one of them.[26] This latter view has been accepted by the United States Supreme Court as representing the principle applicable in Louisiana.[27]

§ 107.   — California.

In California, it has turned out most unfortunately that in the first case before it concerning a question relating to the community property, it relied upon the Louisiana case of *Guice v. Lawrence,* and the mistranslation and misinterpretation therein of the quotation

husband, was entirely erroneous. She not only had a right of action against the husband and those to whom he alienated, but might be barred by limitations if not enforcing her right of action within the time prescribed. See post, subd. B. of this chapter, and Chap. VIII.

[23] See ante, § 100.

[24] Jacob v. Falgoust, 150 La. 22, 90 So. 427.

[25] Peck v. Board of Directors, 137 La. 334, 68 So. 629.

[26] Phillips v. Phillips, 160 La. 813, 107 So. 584. See likewise, Succession of Wiener, 203 La. 649, 14 So.2d 475; Succession of Helis, 226 La. 133, 73 So.2d 221; Thigpen v. Thigpen (La.) 91 So.2d 12. It is interesting to note, however, that while the court recognized that there had been confusion between the idea of ownership and that of management, it traced such confusion to a mistranslation of the word *dominio,* and failed to see the mistranslation as to *tiene.* See ante, §§ 99, 100.

[27] Bender v. Pfaff, 282 U. S. 127, 75 L. Ed. 242, 51 Sup. Ct. 64. And see Henderson's Estate, 155 F.2d 310, 164 A. L. R. 1030.

from Febrero.[28] Although the California decisions, in the period from 1851 to 1926, were in such frequent conflict over the question of the wife's ownership as to cause comment thereon by the courts of other states,[29] and sometimes described the wife's interest as an equal and present interest or ownership in the community property during the marriage,[30] at other times referring to it as a mere expectancy, and even as the expectancy of an heir,[31] the view that it is only an expectant interest during marriage, influenced by the first case of *Panaud v. Jones,* was reiterated and adverted to with more emphasis, so that it came to be the prevailing view of the California courts. This view the court has frequently attempted to justify on the ground that it represents the true view of the Spanish and Mexican community

[28] See Panaud v. Jones, 1 Cal. 488.

[29] See, c. g., Kohny v. Dunbar, 21 Idaho 258, 121 P. 544, Ann. Cas. 1913 D 492, 39 L. R. A. (N. S.) 1107; In re Williams' Estate, 40 Nev. 241, 161 P. 741, L. R. A. 1917 C 602.

[30] See Beard v. Knox, 5 Cal. 252, 63 Am. Dec. 125; Buchanan Estate, 8 Cal. 507; Smith v. Smith, 12 Cal. 216, 73 Am. Dec. 533; Meyer v. Kinzer, 12 Cal. 247, 73 Am. Dec. 538; Scott v. Ward, 13 Cal. 458; Ord v. De La Guerra, 18 Cal. 67; Payne v. Payne, 18 Cal. 291; Hart v. Robinson, 21 Cal. 348; Fuller v. Ferguson, 26 Cal. 546; Morrison v. Bowman, 29 Cal. 337; Peck v. Brummagim, 31 Cal. 440, 81 Am. Dec. 195; Dow v. Gould and Curry, etc., 31 Cal. 629; Galland v. Galland, 38 Cal. 265; DeGodey v. DeGodey, 39 Cal. 157; Broad v. Broad, 40 Cal. 493; Estate of Silvey, 42 Cal. 210; Broad v. Murray, 40 Cal. 228; Johnson v. Bush, 49 Cal. 198; King v. LaGrange, 50 Cal. 328; Estate of Frey, 52 Cal. 658; Estate of Gwin, 77 Cal. 313, 19 P. 527; Estate of Gilmore, 81 Cal. 240, 22 P. 655; Directors v. Abila, 106 Cal. 355, 39 P. 794; Estate of Smith, 108 Cal. 115, 40 P. 1037; Cunha v. Hughes, 122 Cal. 111, 54 P. 535, 68 Am. St. Rep. 27; Estate of Wickersham, 138 Cal. 355, 70 P. 1076, 71 P. 437; Estate of Vogt, 154 Cal. 508, 98 P. 265; Estate of Prager, 166 Cal. 450, 137 P. 37; Estate of Rossi, 169 Cal. 148, 146 P. 430; Estate of Brix, 181 Cal. 667, 186 P. 135; Schneider v. Schneider, 183 Cal. 335, 191 P. 533, 11 A. L. R. 1386; Taylor v. Taylor, 192 Cal. 71, 218 P. 756, 51 A. L. R. 1074; Estate of Jolly, 196 Cal. 547, 238 P. 353; Bone v. Dwyer, 48 Cal. App. 137, 240 P. 769.

[31] See Panaud v. Jones, 1 Cal. 488; Van Maren v. Johnson, 15 Cal. 308; Packard v. Arrellanes, 17 Cal. 525; Greiner v. Greiner, 58 Cal. 115; Estate of Rowland, 74 Cal. 523, 16 P. 315, 5 Am. St. Rep. 464; Estate of Burdick, 112 Cal. 387, 44 P. 734; Spreckels v. Spreckels, 116 Cal. 339, 48 P. 228, 58 Am. St. Rep. 170, 36 L. R. A. 497; Sharp v. Loupe, 120 Cal. 89, 52 P. 134, 586; Estate of Moffitt, 153 Cal. 359, 363, 95 P. 653, 1025, 20 L. R. A. N. S. 207, aff'd 218 U. S. 400, 54 L. Ed. 1086, 31 Sup. Ct. 79; Spreckels v. Spreckels, 172 Cal. 775, 158 P. 537; Dargie v. Patterson, 176 Cal. 715, 169 P. 360; Roberts v. Wehmeyer, 191 Cal. 601, 218 P. 22; Blethen v. Pacific Mutual Life Ins. Co., 198 Cal. 91, 243 P. 431; Stewart v. Stewart, 199 Cal. 318, 249 P. 197, id., 204 Cal. 546, 269 P. 439.

"Nowhere has the confusion thus engendered been more keenly felt than in California. In the teeth of constant legislative enactment ever more carefully protecting the interest of the wife, and in effect reversing contrary decisions, the courts have stubbornly continued to speak of her interest as a mere 'expectancy' like dower." 39 Harv. Law. Rev. 762, 763.

property law, although its misconceptions and reliance on erroneous translations have been pointed out by courts of other community property states.[32] It is difficult to see how it could justify itself on the ground that it was following the Spanish and Mexican community property law in holding that the wife's interest in the community property is only the expectant interest of an heir, when that very law most plainly considered that the wife, upon the husband's death, did not take over the administrative control of her half of the community property as an heir but as one already owning it.[33]

These conflicting decisions, of course, fail to interpret properly the matters of ownership under Spanish community laws, the wife's liability for debts, her possessory remedies, and other similar matters indicating her ownership. The courts have tended to interpret community of property by common law concepts, especially by the control of property that the husband has under the common law. This control by the husband at common law which makes him virtual if not actual owner of the property under his control and gives him the exclusive enjoyment and benefit of such property is the most misleading concept that one can apply to interpret the "control" of the husband under the community property system, which is nothing but the administration of property owned by halves by both spouses, and which the husband can administer only for the benefit of both. The minute he tries to use the community property for his own enjoyment and benefit he violates his position and lays himself open to action against him by the wife; indeed if his use or appropriation of the community property for his own enjoyment and benefit is flagrant it should warrant his removal from the administration of the community property and the substitution of the wife.[34]

So far as California is concerned, however, the state legislature attempted to put the matter at rest in 1927 by enacting a statute expressly providing that the respective interests of husband and wife in the community during the marriage are "present, existing and equal interests under the management and control of the husband."[35] But it would seem that the statute is not retroactive, so it may therefore be considered that there are at the least two kinds of community property in California, that acquired prior to 1927 in which the wife has only an expectant interest, and that acquired after 1927 in which

[32] See, e. g., Thompson v. Cragg, 24 Tex. 582.

[33] See Novísima Recopilación, Book 10, Title 4, Law 8, and commentaries thereto, in vol. 2 of first edition.

"Moreover a wife receives a moiety of the profits as her own by virtue of our law and similar enactments, and as to this she is not called an heir." Azevedo, No. 8, to Nov. Rec. Law 8, Book 10, Title 4.

Dissolution of community by death of one spouse, see post, Chap. X, B.

[34] See post, Chap. VIII.

[35] Cal. Civ. Code, § 5105. And see United States v. Malcolm, 282 U. S. 792, 75 L. Ed. 714, 51 Sup. Ct. 184. Present California cases recognizing present vested interest of wife, see de Funiak, 43 Va. L. Rev. 47; California Jurisprudence, 2d Ed., article "Community Property."

the wife has a complete and existing half share. At least such must be the assumption if the line of California cases is regarded which held that the wife's interest was expectant only.[36] In the authors' opinion the enactment of this statute in 1927 should have been entirely unnecessary. Since 1872, at least, it has been provided by statute that "The ownership of property by several persons together is either: 1. Of joint interests; 2. Of partnership interests; 3. Of interests in common; 4. Of community interest of husband and wife."[37] This certainly recognizes between husband and wife just as much an equality of present interests in community property as there is between partners in partnership property, joint tenants in joint estates, etc., for otherwise this grouping would not have been made. And, certainly, we have never heard it advanced that just because one joint tenant undertakes the collection of rents and the payment of taxes the other loses any present ownership in his own half and merely has an expectant interest therein during the life of the former. And the code commissioners, upon the enactment of the code in 1872, in recommending a section authorizing a right of action in the wife in case of fraudulent transfers, waste or mismanagement by the husband, pointed out as to property acquired during marriage that "the property is made common between the husband and wife. They have a common interest in it."[38]

§ 108.   — New Mexico.

The New Mexico court at one time momentarily allowed itself to be led astray through reliance on the Louisiana case of *Guice v. Lawrence*,[39] and on the California cases,[40] among others. An excellent and forceful dissenting opinion in the New Mexico case in question pointed out that actually the wife had an ownership existing during the marriage, subject only to the management placed in the husband's hands, and this view of the dissenting opinion was approved by the United States Supreme Court.[41] In a subsequent opinion the New Mexico court determined that the proper view was that the wife

---

[36] See Hooker, Nature of Wife's Interest in Community Property in California, 15 Calif. Law Rev. 302; Kirkwood, Ownership of Community Property in California, 7 So. Calif. Law Rev. 1; Simmons, Interest of Wife in California Community Property, 22 Calif. Law Rev. 404.

The difficulties inherent in the view that community property legislation in California can have no retroactive effect is interestingly discussed in Comment, 27 Calif. Law Rev. 49.

[37] Cal. Civ. Code, § 682.

[38] "Common," according to Webster's Dict.: "shared equally or similarly by two or more individuals." And "in common" is defined "equally with another."

[39] As to which, see ante, § 106.

[40] California, see ante, § 107.

[41] Reade v. De Lea, 14 N.M. 442, 95 P. 131, rev'd in Arnett v. Reade, 220 U. S. 311, 55 L. Ed. 477, 31 Sup. Ct. 424, 36 L. R. A. (N. S.) 1040.

does have a present and existing ownership during the marriage,[42] and there seems since to have been no variation from recognition of that principle.[43]

§ 109. — Idaho.

The Idaho court, at one period, seems to have been influenced by the views of the California court that the wife's interest in the community property was a mere expectancy during the marriage. It recognized correctly that the husband's interest during marriage was active and the wife's passive, but was unaware that such terms relate only to the matter of administration or management of the property and do not affect the actual matter of ownership itself. It seemed unaware of the community property principle that the husband and the wife both own the community property by halves during the marriage, and relied unduly on the common law principle that title is all important.[44] Shortly thereafter, the Idaho court corrected itself and announced that husband and wife are equal partners in the community property with no distinction between them except so far as the husband is by law made the managing agent of the conjugal partnership.[45] This correct view it has consistently continued to maintain.[46]

§ 110. — Nevada.

Nevada can hardly be described as one of the states in which the courts have fallen into error as to the nature of the wife's ownership during marriage in the community property. Although the Nevada constitutional provision establishing the community property system and the Nevada community property statutes were modeled after those of California,[47] and although it was said by the Nevada court that it was the Spanish-Mexican community property law as administered in Mexico and under the early California statutes that was adopted and that it was from those sources that solutions should be sought,[48] that court has definitely and positively refused to follow the mistaken view of former California decisions that the wife's

[42] See Beals v. Ares, 25 N.M. 459, 185 P. 780.

[43] Present, vested interest of wife, see McDonald v. Senn, 53 N.M. 198, 204 P.2d 990; Dillard v. New Mexico State Tax Commission, 53 N.M. 12, 201 P.2d 345.

[44] See Hall v. Johns, 17 Idaho 224, 105 P. 71.

[45] Kohny v. Dunbar, 21 Idaho 258, 121 P. 544, Ann. Cas. 1913 D 492, 39 L. R. A. (N. S.) 1107.

[46] See Davenport v. Simons, 68 Idaho 21, 189 P.2d 90, citing the first edition; Hansen v. Blevins (Ida.) 367 P.2d 758; Peterson v. Peterson, 35 Idaho 470, 207 P. 425; Ewald v. Hufton, 31 Idaho 373, 173 P. 247.

[47] See ante, § 52.

[48] See Nixon v. Brown, 46 Nev. 439, 214 P. 524.

interest in the community property during marriage is only an expectant interest in the nature of dower. On the contrary, it insisted that the wife owns one-half of the community property during the marriage as completely as does the husband and that this is in no wise detracted from because the administrative control of the community property has been placed in the husband. It declared itself unable to arrive at any other conclusion than that which was the intention of the framers of the state constitution and of the legislature in establishing the community property system.[49]

B. MANAGEMENT

§ 111. In general.

We come now to the matter of the exercise of management and the power of disposition over the community property, to which reference has already been made at the beginning of this chapter.[50] Because these matters are regulated in the several community property states by statutes which frequently vary in their provisions and because these statutes have been frequently modified or amended during the passing years, caution should be exercised in approaching problems concerning these matters. Too great a reliance should not be placed on the older texts or even on the older decisions of the courts; statements based on the decisions of one state may not be true of other states or even any longer true of the state in which such decisions were

---

[49] In re Wiliams' Estate, 40 Nev. 241, 161 P. 741, L. R. A. 1917 C 602; In re Condos' Estate (Nev.) 266 P.2d 404.

In Crow v. Van Sickle, 6 Nev. 149, relating to the right of the husband to prosecute a right of action pertaining to the community, it was said: "The power of management and absolute disposition of the common property thus conferred by the statute clothes the husband with such ownership and authority as to warrant the allegation, in a complaint of this kind, that he is the owner of the chose in action. Certainly the wife has no interest which will justify any interference on her part, nor has the defendant in such case any ground of complaint; for the plaintiff is the owner of the moiety, and, so far as the right of prosecuting the action is concerned, he is, in effect, the absolute owner of the entirety." Here the court

seems confused as to how to describe the distinction between ownership and management and seems to have difficulty in describing the husband's right to prosecute an action pursuant to his power of management otherwise than in words descriptive of ownership so far as the right of action is concerned. But it will be noticed that the court describes him as the owner of a moiety of the property, so far as ownership of the property itself is concerned. What it is evidently trying to do is to explain that he is the owner of half of the property with the duty to prosecute actions concerning the property by reason of his duty of management. There is actually no denial of the wife's ownership of half of the property but only the denial of any right on her part to take part in the management.

[50] See ante, § 93.

made. Instead, careful consideration should be given the existing statutes and the basic principles of community property law.[51]

It is to be remarked that under the Spanish law the husband was the head of the family, with the duty to provide for its wants, and had the right of choosing the place of residence.[52] The laws of our community property states are in consonance with such principles.[53]

§ 112. Management of separate property.

Our concern is chiefly with the question of the management of the community property but we may digress momentarily to refer to the management of the spouses' separate property.[54] The legislatures of our community property states have been careful to specify, in varying phraseology, that the wife shall have the exclusive control, management and disposition of her separate property, or that she may, without the consent of her husband, convey her separate property.[55] This includes the rents and profits of her separate property in states where such rents and profits also remain separate property.[56] In Texas, however, both spouses must join in any conveyance or encumbrance of homestead realty, although otherwise each has the sole management, control and disposition of his or her separate property, both real and personal.[57] Similarly, it was formerly true in Louisiana that the wife, even though having the right to manage her separate property, had to obtain the consent or concurrence of her husband to alienation, etc., of her separate property, but this

---

[51] See Ariz. Rev. St. 1956, §§ 25-211, 33-451, 33-452; Cal. Civ. Code, §§ 5124, 5125, 5127, 5128; Ida. Code 1948; § 32-912; La. Civ. Code, art. 2404; Nev. Rev. St. 1956, § 123.230; N.M. St. 1953, § 57-4-3; Tex. Family Code 1969, § 5.22; Wash. Rev. Code 1961, § 26.16.040.

[52] See Schmidt, Civil Law of Spain and Mexico, p. 11, citing Las Siete Partidas, Part. 3, Title 2, Law 5. And see post, § 132.

[53] See, e. g., Cal. Civ. Code, § 5101: "The husband is the head of the family. He may choose any reasonable place or mode of living, and the wife must conform thereto."

Rights, duties, agreements and transactions between spouses, see post, Chapter VIII.

[54] We may have fallen into the error of assuming that it is well known that under the community property system the right of a woman to own separate property is equal to that of a man

and that she continues to own such property as her own during marriage. Such definitely is the case. As to her exercise of management over such property during marriage, see post, this section.

[55] Ariz. Rev. Stat. 1956, §§ 25-214, 33-451, 33-452; Cal. Civ. Code, § 5107; Ida. Code 1948, § 31-1104; La. Acts 1928, No. 283; La. Civ. Code, art. 2384; Nev. Rev. Stat. 1956, § 123.170; N.M. St. 1953, § 57-3-4; Wash. Rev. Code 1961, § 26.16.020. And see the interesting case of Christiansen v. Department of Social Security, 15 Wash. 2d 465, 131 P.2d 189.

As to necessity of joining husband in actions against wife on her separate obligations, see post, § 167.

[56] Management of profits and income of separate estate where such profits and income are community property, see post, § 115.

[57] Tex. Family Code 1969, §§ 5.81, 5.21.

disability has now been removed.[58] In some jurisdictions, a spouse under the age of twenty-one years has to be joined by the other spouse.[59]

Some legislatures have felt it necessary, apparently, to add similar provisions as to the husband, that is, that he shall have the sole management, control and disposition of his separate property, both real and personal.[60]

The wife may, of course, desire to have her husband administer her separate property for her,[61] but her rights of complete ownership and control enable her to withdraw its administrative control from his hands whenever she wishes.[62] Similarly, the husband may desire the wife to manage his separate property, as where he has to be absent for compelling reasons, as in the armed forces.[63]

In regard to the wife, this legislation has undoubtedly been

---

[58] Louisiana Acts 1928, No. 283, has had the effect of repealing Art. 122 of the La. Civ. Code which required consent or concurrence of husband to wife's alienation, etc., of her separate property. See First Nat. Bank v. Coreil (La. App.), 145 So. 395. See also Effect of Recent Acts on Disabilities of Married Women in Louisiana, 8 Tulane Law Rev. 106.

In Louisiana, formerly under Civ. Code, art. 1480, a married woman could not make a donation inter vivos without the consent of her husband or of the court, but this disability was removed by Act 283 of 1928.

Specific performance would not lie to compel conveyance of wife's separate property under contract signed only by husband and not by wife. Bland v. Conner (La. App.), 25 So.2d 815.

[59] See Ariz. Rev. St. 1956, §§ 33-451, 33-452.

[60] See, e.g., Ariz. Rev. St. 1956, §§ 33-451, 33-452; Nev. Rev. St. 1956, § 123.230; Tex. Family Code 1969, § 5.21; Wash. Rev. Code 1961, § 26.16.010.

Husband's mortgage of his separate property as not requiring signature of wife, see Priddel v. Shankie, 69 Cal. App. 2d 319, 159 P.2d 438, holding also that in partition suit involving husband's separate property wife not necessary party.

[61] Agreements between spouses to such effect, see also post, § 146.

Husband has no authority to convey realty of wife without written power of attorney from her in form required by law. Miera v. Miera, 25 N.M. 299, 181 P. 583. Likewise, as to contract to sell wife's separate realty, see Bland v. Conner (La. App.), 25 So.2d 815.

Effect on nature of income from wife's separate property, depending on whether husband manages property as her agent or as head of the community, see Trorlicht, v. Collector of Revenue (La. App.), 25 So.2d 547, wherein appeal transferred from supreme court, 209 La. 167, 24 So.2d 366.

[62] See La. Civ. Code, art. 2387.

See Dority v. Dority, 96 Tex. 215, 71 S. W. 950, 60 L.R.A. 941, deciding that a wife, without suing for divorce, could maintain suit to enjoin her husband from continuing to exercise control over her separate property, in order to prevent its diversion and mismanagement.

[63] Bassi v. Bassi, 89 Cal. App. 2d 886, 202 P.2d 96 (in military service); Svetinich v. Svetinich, 124 Cal. 216, 56 P. 1028, 71 Am. St. Rep. 50 (in naval service), where husband transferred title to himself and his wife in order that she might manage it more easily during his absence. He successfully rebutted evidence of a gift to the wife so as to defeat its sale under execution against the wife individually by one of her creditors.

influenced by consideration of the fact that under the English common law and our common law as derived therefrom, the husband had the control and management of the wife's separate property; and by the apparent belief that the same situation existed under the Spanish community property system and would continue to exist in a Spanish-derived community property system, unless definite provision was made to the contrary. As a matter of fact, the exercise of management by the husband of the wife's separate property did not exist under the Spanish law of community property, except as to her dowry, or as to her *paraphernalia* where she gave its management to her husband expressly in writing. The right of a woman to own separate property and to continue to own it after marriage, subject to her own managerial control of it, was one of the oldest features of the community property system introduced into Spain by the Visigoths and is found among Visigothic laws and customs in other parts of Europe. Any weakening of this right in some parts of Europe — but definitely not in Spain — was due to the influence of concepts alien to those of the community property system, as in England and Normandy.[64]

In the Spanish community property system, the wife's separate property at the time of the marriage taking place was of three kinds: her dowry,[65] her *paraphernalia,* and her other private, i.e., separate, property *(bienes proprios)*. Since the dowry was the consideration, or one of the considerations, for the husband entering into the marriage, its management was placed in his hands that he might have the advantage of its use. It remained in effect the separate property of the wife, however, and neither the husband nor his heirs had any interest therein after the dissolution of the marriage.[66] But since dowry is a matter of a special nature in itself which has not become a part of our customary law and is not an integral part of the community property system in any event, we may dispense with any further discussion of it.[67] The wife's *paraphernalia* was the property the wife was accustomed to bring to the marriage also, but for her own separate use.[68] Its control remained in her, unless as has been

[64] See ante, Chap. II.

In some of the community property systems, the control of the wife as under the control of the husband, see Calisse, History of Italian Law, § 350; Huebner, History of Germanic Private Law, § 95.

[65] As to dowry, see post, this section, and ante, § 12.

[66] On the dissolution of the marriage it ought to return to the wife or to whomsoever it may belong." Asso and Mañuel, Institutes of the Civil Law of Spain, Book I, Title VII, Cap. 1, § 5.

"When the marriage is dissolved, in what manner does the division of the property take place? The answer is as follows. The wife or her heir must first of all take out the dowry and the marriage deposit and the other private property known as the wife's separate estate. . . ." Matienzo, Gloss II, No. 3, to Nov. Rec. Law 4, Book 10, Title 4.

[67] See ante, § 12.

[68] The modern tendency is to use the term *paraphernalia* to designate all separate property of the wife not embraced in the dotal properties. This is true of the Louisiana statutes. While

mentioned she placed the control in the husband by express writing.[69] Her other separate property *(bienes proprios)* was that which was not brought in any way to the marriage for use therein and the husband had no right of management over it. This was also true of property which the wife acquired during the marriage by gift, inheritance and the like.[70] Although the matter is also dealt with elsewhere, it may be well to remark here that as to paraphernal property of the wife placed by her under her husband's management, the wife had a tacit lien or mortgage on the husband's property to the extent of the value of such paraphernal property which took priority over the claims of

such interpretation might be made from the Greek and Roman law, it seems a more accurate interpretation that the term applied to personal effects brought by the wife to the husband's house and which remained her separate property under her control although such effects as used by her were to the common benefit. See Dig. 23.3.9; Cod. 5.14.9. Accordingly, in addition thereto, and this seems to have been the case formerly under the Spanish law, she might have other separate properties, such as estates, which would not fall under the designation of *paraphernalia* in the sense of personal effects brought to the husband's house for her to use during the marriage. Such distinctions as to her various kinds of separate property were made by some of the jurisconsults in describing her properties, and one of the earlier codes, Las Siete Partidas, Part. 4, Title 11, Law 17, described all property and possessions, real and personal, which women brought to the marriage but kept separately for themselves as constituting the paraphernal property.

[69] "The woman is accustomed to bring, beside her dowry, other property which is called *paraphernalia,* and which is or are the property and things whether personal or real which wives retain for their separate use, and which are not accounted part of the dowry. From this definition it follows, 1st, That if the wife gives to the husband this property, with the intention that he may have the control of it, he shall possess it during marriage; and if she should not do this expressly in writing, the control of such property will always be in the wife. . . . 3rd, That if it be sold without the assent of the wife, she will have her action or remedy against the purchaser, and if not, she shall take the value from the fund of property before partition be made. 4th, That the property of the husband is always bound or liable for the prejudices and injury which he shall cause to the *paraphernalia* of the wife." Asso and Mañuel, Institutes of the Civil Law of Spain, Book I, Title VII, Cap. 2, citing Las Siete Partidas, Part. 4, Title 11, Law 17. Palacios Rubios, however, observed that this law did not specify that a written instrument was necessary to transfer dominion to the husband. The actual language of the Partidas was, as a matter of fact, "specifically given." Writing would certainly be the best evidence of this.

Notice also that under the Louisiana statutes, the dowry is given to the husband to enjoy but the paraphernal property remains under the control of the wife unless she does not undertake to administer it, in which case it is deemed under the control of the husband. See La. Civ. Code, arts. 2384, 2385, 2387.

[70] "A wife can have property of three kinds, dowry, *paraphernalia* and private property of which the husband has not the right of administration, as is shown by Antonius Gómez on law 50 *Tauri* no. 20 at the words '*item adde,*' to whom you should refer. To this you should add a fourth kind, viz. property acquired during marriage." Matienzo, Gloss IIII, to Nov. Rec. Law 11, Book 10, Title 4.

The *arras,* that is, the dowry as-

purchasers from the husband as well as over the claims of subsequent creditors of the husband. Moreover, she had a right of action against a purchaser to whom the husband sold such paraphernal property without her consent.[71]

In brief then, in the Spanish law, the wife managed her own separate property, other than the dowry or any separate property she requested the husband to manage for her. This was continued in effect in Mexico under the Spanish system.[72] A requirement that the husband consent to contracts by the wife seems to have been a formality, for the wife could apply to the court for any necessary authorization in the case of the husband's refusal.[73] And in fact if the contract made by the wife without her husband's consent benefited or profited her, it was a valid contract.[74] Moreover, if she occupied a public office or exercised a trade, she could make contracts relating to either, without the necessity of such consent.[75] It should be clearly evident that the Spanish community property system which we have continued in this

---

signed to or settled upon the wife by the husband (which could not exceed the tenth part of his property or fortune), was placed under the administration of the wife by the Fuero Real, Book 3, Title 2, Law 1, and later by the Novísima Recopilación, Book 10, Title 3, Law 2, so that she might dispose of it by alienation or testamentary disposition, although the husband still enjoyed the usufruct while the *arras* was retained by her. However, if she died intestate and childless, the *arras* reverted to the husband.

[71] See, e.g., Asso and Mañuel, Institutes of Civil Law of Spain, Book I, Title VII, Cap. 2.

Lien or right of wife, both under Spanish law and law of community property states, as against claims of husband's creditors, see post, § 175.

[72] "The administration of this (paraphernal) property belongs to the wife, unless she has expressly conferred the power of administration on her husband, and in all cases of doubt the wife is presumed to have preserved the administration." Schmidt, Civil Law of Spain and Mexico, p. 81.

Recognition of Mexican law as allowing wife to contract with respect to her separate estate, real or personal, see Racouillat v. Sansevain, 32 Cal. 376.

[73] See Leyes de Toro, Laws 54–59.

Where the husband refused consent "the present law provides that the judge should be informed in regard to the wishes of the wife and the refusal of the husband and if he considers the reason valid or necessary he can proceed to compel the husband to give his consent, and if the husband refuses to do so the judge can then grant it himself." Llamas y Molina, Commentaries to Law 57 of Leyes de Toro.

"The other civil effects of the marriage are: . . . III. That the husband can give permission to the wife to contract. . . . And if the husband does not give it, he may be compelled to by the judge upon hearing or legal and necessary cause; and if even being ordered, he does not give it, it shall be given by the judge, who may give the same also upon hearing of cause, the husband being absent and his return not soon expected, or there being danger in the delay. . . ." Novísimo Sala Mexicano, Sec. 2a, Title IV, No. 9.

[74] Llamas y Molina, Nos. 6 and 7, to Law 55 of Leyes de Toro, citing Antonio Gómez and Matienzo to the same effect.

[75] Schmidt, Civil Law of Spain and Mexico, p. 109, citing Fuero Real, Book 3, Title 20, Law 13. See also post, § 116.

country gives as much consideration to the wife as to the husband as concerns the matter of the separate property. Our statutes do nothing more than make a pronouncement of what was already true of the community property system existing in this country prior to the enactment of such statutes.

It is perhaps appropriate to notice one more feature of the Spanish law. Under that law the age of majority was twenty-five years. In the case of orphans, by which was understood those having no father,[76] a guardian, primarily of the person, was appointed for a male orphan until he was fourteen years of age and for the female orphan until she was twelve years of age.[77] The guardianship then ended, and in turn a curator was appointed,[78] primarily to have charge of the orphan's property until the orphan reached the age of twenty-five, that is, the age of majority.[79] But it appears that the minor orphan of sound mind could not be compelled to receive a curator against his or her will.[80] Thus, in the case of a young woman under the age of twenty-five who married, she could control and manage her own private property if she objected to the appointment of a curator or to the continuance in office of an already appointed curator. But if she did have a curator of her property it was decreed, above all, that the husband should not be appointed to that position and it was incumbent upon the husband to petition the judge to appoint some one other than himself.[81] This seems to have been a matter of delicacy or strict honesty, that all suspicion might be avoided,[82] for it was recognized that the wife might be inclined to excuse the husband, by reason of her love for him, of any loss that he might cause her property and not to demand reparation.[83] Incidentally, a husband who had attained the age of eighteen years could administer his own property as well as the dowry

[76] "By orphan is understood one who has no father, with the difference that formerly this appellation was given only to those who were without father or mother, until they reached the age of fourteen, as was laid down in Law 1, Title 3, Book 4, Fuero Juzgo." Asso & Mañuel, Book I, Title II, Cap. 1.

[77] "From this definition of guardianship it follows, 1st, That the guardian appointed principally for the protection or care of the person of the orphan, and consequently for that of his property, Law 1, Tit. 16, Part. 6. 2nd, That the guardian is only given to the male minor under fourteen years, and the female under twelve, same law." Asso & Mañuel, Institutes of Civil Law of Spain, Book I, Title

II, Cap. 1, § 3.

[78] Las Siete Partidas, Part. 6, Title 16, Law 13.

[79] "The curator is appointed in the first place for the care of the property, and consequently of the person of the minor." Asso & Mañuel, Institutes of Civil Law of Spain, Book I, Title II, Cap. 3.

[80] Las Siete Partidas, Part. 6, Title 16, Law 13; Asso & Mañuel, Institutes of Civil Law of Spain, Book I, Title II, Cap. 3.

[81] Las Siete Partidas, Part. 6, Title 17, Law 3.

[82] Asso & Mañuel, Institutes of Civil Law of Spain, Book I, Title IV, Cap. 1, § 1.

[83] Las Siete Partidas, Part. 6, Title 17, Law 3.

of the wife or any of her *paraphernalia* which she wished to place under his control.[84]

§ 113.   Management of community property — By husband.

One of the attributes common to all community property systems has been that the management of the community property has been, to a greater or lesser degree, placed in the hands of the husband. This has resulted from the consideration of the husband as the head of the family, as the one who due to economic and biological factors has been the member of the marital partnership more practiced and experienced in the acquisition and management of property.[85] In the Spanish system of community we find that this management and control of the community property was definitely placed in the hands of the husband,[86] as the business agent of a form of partnership,[87] to the extent that he had the power of alienation of it during marriage without the necessity of the consent or conveyance of the wife, subject to the condition that his alienation was not valid if it was proven to be in fraud or injury of the wife's rights.[88] His right to manage and dispose

[84] See Novísima Recopilación, Book 10, Title 2, Law 7.

[85] See Brissaud, History of French Private Law, § 560; Huebner, History of Germanic Private Law, § 95; Calisse, History of Italian Law, § 350.

"The law, in giving this power to the husband during coverture to dispose of the personal property, does not do this in recognition of any higher or superior right that he has therein, but because the law considers it expedient and necessary in business transactions affecting the personalty to have an agent of the community with power to act. So it has clothed the husband with this agency, deeming him the best qualified for the purpose, but limiting such agency to the personalty and during the period of coverture." La Tourette v. La Tourette, 15 Ariz. 200, 137 P. 426, Ann. Cas. 1915 B 70.

See Daggett, Is Joint Control of Community Property Possible? 10 Tulane Law Rev. 589.

[86] See Schmidt, Civil Law of Spain and Mexico, p. 11.

The husband is the lawful administrator of the conjugal partnership, where there is no agreement of the spouses or judgment of the court to the contrary in case of absence or impediment of the husband, or when the latter has unjustifiably abandoned the conjugal domicile. Hall, Mexican Law, § 2626.

[87] "The reason is that the one spouse is deemed to be appointed business agent by the other, just as two partners carrying on different businesses are deemed to be mutual agents of each other, so that what one does benefits or hurts the other." Matienzo, Gloss II, No. 2, to Nov. Rec. Law 1, Book 10, Title 4.

[88] Novísima Recopilación, Book 10, Title 4, Law 5, Laws of Estilo, Law 205.

"Note then from this law that the husband can sell and alienate property acquired during marriage, as being the lawful administrator thereof. The same custom is in force in Burgundy and in nearly the whole of the kingdom of France, as Cassaneus testifies in his *Consuetudines Burgundiae* rub. 4 at the beginning of § 3." Matienzo, Gloss VI, No. 2, to Nov. Rec. Law 5, Book 10, Title 4.

The husband "can convey the properties of the partnership without necessity of the consent of the wife, and the conveyance is valid unless it is

of the community property could only be exercised, however, in endeavors to preserve or use it for their common benefit. He could not dispose of it for his own exclusive benefit, dispose of it for inadequate consideration, or otherwise deal with it in a manner indicative by its very nature of an express or implied intent to prejudice the rights of the wife.[89] While the wife's interest was described as *in habitu* or passive, it was passive only so long as the husband administered wisely and not in prejudice of her rights. Immediately that he violated his managerial duties, her interest might be most vigorously enforced and protected.[90] But even when the husband was managing wisely, it must not be thought that the wife was wholly without voice. She might object to a proposed plan of action by the husband and agree that she was not to have any part therein, either as to sharing the profits or bearing the burdens.[91]

In our community property states the management and control of the community property has generally been left in the hands of the husband as the business head or managing agent of the marital partnership,[92] but the statutes of the several states, in providing as to the management and control, frequently differ in extent and frequently add qualifications, limitations or exceptions to the right of control and management on the part of the husband.[93] The statutes should at all times be examined, but it may be remarked generally that in the main they give the husband the managerial control of the community personal property, with the like power of disposition (other than testamentary) as he has of his separate estate;[94] and give him the

---

[89] See more particularly post, §§ 119–123.

made with the intention to defraud or injure her." Novísimo Sala Mexicano, Sec. 2a, Title IV, No. 5.

See Civil Code, art. 1412, in force in Cuba, Puerto Rico and the Philippines: "The husband is the administrator of the conjugal partnership, with the exception of what is prescribed in article 59." And art. 1413: "Besides the powers the husband has as administrator, he may alienate and encumber for a valuable consideration the property of the conjugal partnership without the consent of the wife. Nevertheless, every alienation or agreement which the husband may make with regard to said property in contravention of this code or in fraud of the wife shall not prejudice her or her heirs." As to Puerto Rico, see also Garrozi v. Dastas, 204 U.S. 64, 51 L. Ed. 369, 27 Sup Ct. 224.

Right of wife to dispose of community property, see post, § 121.

[90] See ante, §§ 100, 102; post, § 119 et seq.

[91] See Matienzo, Gloss I, No. 60, to Nov. Rec. Law 1, Book 10, Title 4: "If, for example, the husband wishes to buy a house or to take a lease of state revenues and the wife opposes and says that she is unwilling to bear a share in such purchase or lease and makes an agreement to that effect with her husband, such a renunciation and agreement is valid." And see post, Chap. VIII, as to agreements between spouses.

As to management by spouses jointly, see post, § 115.1.

[92] See, e.g., Shreeve v. Greer, 65 Ariz. 35, 173 P.2d 641, citing and following 1 de Funiak, § 113.

[93] Effect of insanity or incapacity of husband, see post, § 128.

[94] See Ariz. Rev. St. 1956, § 25-211; Cal. Civ. Code § 5125 (with certain

managerial control of the community real property, but with the condition that the husband and wife must both join in the execution and acknowledgment of any instrument by which it is sought to convey, transfer or encumber it.[95] In some of the states, however, the husband has the same power to dispose of the community realty as he does of the community personalty without the joinder of the wife, except where homestead property is involved.[96] In Louisiana the husband has this power even where the community realty stands in the names of himself and his wife;[97] but if the community realty stands in the name of the wife alone, it is necessary to obtain her written consent or authority before the husband may sell or mortgage it.[98] In many of the states, an exception exists in the matter of the community personalty so far as concerns the earnings of the wife, in that the management, control and sometimes the disposition thereof is placed in the hands of the wife.[99] And sometimes exception has been made of all community property, the title to which stands in the wife's name, in that the wife has the right of management thereof.[1]

It has been well recognized in the community property states, as it was in Spain, that the husband's administration and disposition of the community property must be for the spouses' joint benefit,[2] and that any violation of his duties in this respect give rise to remedial relief in favor of the wife.[3]

---

important limitations); N.M. St. 1953, §57-4-3; Wash. Rev. Code 1961, § 26.16.030.

As illustrative, see Cummings v. Weast, 72 Ariz. 93, 231 P.2d 459, as to power of husband to invest community personalty in business partnership without necessity of wife's consent.

Effect of divorce proceedings as suspending husband's power of alienation, see post, § 225.

[95] See post, §§ 115.1, 117, 118.

[96] See La. Civ. Code, art. 2404; Nev. Rev. St. 1956, § 123.230.

It should be noted here that prior to the changes made by the 1967 Texas legislature, this same rule obtained in Texas also. Prior to 1967 changes, see Tex. Rev. Civ. St. 1925, arts. 4618, 4619. And as to Texas, see also post, § 115.2.

[97] See Young v. Louisiana-Arkansas Gas Co., 184 La. 460, 166 So. 139; Otwell v. Vaughan, 186 La. 911, 173 So. 527.

Contract to sell community property which constitutes family homestead must be signed by both spouses. Watson v. Bethany, 209 La. 989, 26 So.2d 12.

[98] La. Civ. Code, art. 2334; Ohio Oil Co. v. Ferguson, 213 La. 233, 34 So.2d 746.

Illustration of exception, see Robinson v. Marks (La.) 30 So.2d 200.

[99] See post, § 114.

[1] True in some of the former temporary community property states, discussed ante, § 53.1. In Texas, as adopted in 1969, Tex. Family Code 1969, §§ 5.22, 5.24, accomplish virtually this. These statutes divide the community into several sections and provide for management of these different sections exclusively by the husband, or by the wife, or by them both jointly. And see post, § 115.2.

[2] See, e.g., Greer v. Goesling, 54 Ariz. 488, 97 P.2d 218; Zimpelman v. Robb, 53 Tex. 274; Hanley v. Most, 9 Wash. 2d 429, 115 P.2d 933.

[3] See post, § 119 et seq.

§ 114.   — By wife — Earnings.

Management of all or of part of the community property by the wife is possible and may come about in a number of ways.[4] It may result from an agreement between the spouses that the wife shall manage all or part of such property,[5] as where the husband delegates authority to her,[6] so that, in effect, she is an agent.[7] It may result from statutory authorization;[8] it may result from necessity or emergency[9] (which may or may not be recognized expressly by statute).[10] It has been recognized in the Spanish law and in our American community property states that where the husband fails to act and it is necesssary to protect or preserve the community property, the wife as the other owner is fully justified in acting and is legally authorized to act.[11]

The managerial authorization of the wife by the husband must be in the form required by law.[12] Thus authority to her to sell, encumber or lease for more than one year may be required to be in certain written form.[13] Indeed, authorization to act as agent in acquiring realty may have to be in writing in some jurisdictions,[14] although not in others as where the wife is merely in the management of personalty in paying out community funds for an acquisition.[15]

Where the husband has effectively delegated authority to the wife,[16] her contracts are binding on the marital community, that is on herself and the husband,[17] until such time as the authority is revoked or otherwise terminated.[18] Since the wife is not in the usual sense the

---

[4] And see succeeding sections of this chapter.

Must not act in fraud or prejudice of husband's rights, see post, § 120.1.

[5] See, e.g., Munger v. Boardman, 53 Ariz. 271, 88 P.2d 536; Hulsman v. Ireland, 205 Cal. 345, 270 P. 948; Travers v. Barrett, 30 Nev. 402, 97 P. 126; Lucci v. Lucci, 2 Wash. 2d 64, P.2d 393.

[6] See, e.g., Travers v. Barrett, supra.

[7] Delegation by husband of authority to wife to contract concerning community, see post, § 116.

[8] See infra, this section and post, succeeding sections of this chapter.

[9] See post, §§ 128, 129.

[10] See post, § 128.

[11] See, e.g., Wright v. Hays, 10 Tex. 130, 60 Am. Dec. 200. And see especially post, § 128.

[12] This is within the realm of delegation of authority to an agent.

[13] In Noble v. Glenns Ferry Bank, Ltd. (Ida.), 421 P.2d 444, it was said that a statutory provision for one spouse to create the other an agent by a power of attorney did not prevent the use of other methods of delegating authority to sell or mortgage.

[14] See La. Civ. Code, art. 1787; Parham v. Gaspard (La. App.), 26 So.2d 300.

[15] Evidentiary requirements make a writing important, of course.

[16] In Lacaze v. City Bank & Trust Co., 207 La. App. 735, 21 So.2d 891, husband who entrusted community funds to management by wife could not compel bank in which she had deposited the funds to pay them to him.

[17] See, e.g., Hulsman v. Ireland, 205 Cal. 345, 270 P. 948; Lucci v. Lucci, 2 Wash. 2d 64, 99 P.2d 393.

[18] As in Travers v. Barrett, 30 Nev. 402, 97 P. 126.

manager, it should be incumbent on the person dealing with her to ascertain the existence and extent of her authority.[19] Of course, where the husband has accepted the benefits of her management, he is not in a position to deny her authority. He cannot at the same time accept the benefits and the gains of her management and escape the obligations arising therefrom.[20] In short, besides being estopped he may also affirmatively ratify her acts so as to bind himself.[21]

The earnings of the wife for her personal services, although constituting community property, are frequently placed by statutory enactment under the management and control of the wife.[22] Other enactments do not confine this right of management and control to her earnings "for personal services," but are apparently broader in their implication by specifying "earnings" without any qualifying clause.[23] And broader enactments have given the wife not only the entire management and control of her earnings and accumulations, with power of disposition, but also of those of her minor children living with her, when such earnings and accumulations are used for the care and maintenance of the family.[24] This latter type of enactment is to be distinguished from that which makes the earnings of the wife and of the minor children while they are living separate from the husband the separate property of the wife, which has been discussed previously.[25]

[19] Marston v. Rue, 92 Wash. 129, 159 P. 111.

No authority in wife to sell grape crop. La Rosa v. Glaze, 18 Cal. App. 2d 354, 63 P.2d 1181.

Husband did not authorize wife in writing to act as agent and sell realty and husband did not sign exclusive listing agreement. Tamini v. Bettencourt, 52 Cal. Rptr. 273, as to liability of wife and non-liability of husband for broker's commission.

Bill of sale executed by wife ineffective to transfer personal property. Newell v. Brawner, (Cal. App.) 295 P.2d 460.

No authority in wife, after interlocutory divorce decree to make binding contract to assign community interest under contract to purchase realty. Eckley v. Bonded Adjustment Co., 30 Wash. 2d 96, 190 P.2d 918.

Cf. Svetina v. Burelli, 87 Cal. App. 2d 707, 197 P.2d 562, where court erroneously puts no obligation on third person to investigate extent or lack of wife's authority but in effect allows freedom to accept her contract.

[20] See, e.g., Munger v. Boardman, 53 Ariz. 271, 88 P.2d 536; Hulsman v. Ireland, 205 Cal. 345, 270 P. 948; Holbrook v. Flynn, 68 Ida. 396, 198 P.2d 355; Hartman v. Anderson (Wash.), 298 P.2d 1103.

[21] Leyva v. Rodriguez (Tex. Civ. App.) 195 S. W. 2d 704.

[22] Ida. Code 1948, § 32-912; Wash. Rev. Code 1961, § 26.16.130.

[23] Cal. Civ. Code, § 5124; Tex. Rev. Civ. St. 1925, art. 4621.

The California statute also now covers damages recovered by the wife for her personal injuries.

[24] Nev. Rev. St. 1956, § 123.230; Tex. Family Code 1969, § 5.22.

Notice the provision that when the husband has allowed the wife to appropriate to her own use her earnings, the same, with the issues and profits thereof, is deemed a gift to her from the husband and is, with such issues and profits, her separate property. Nev. Rev. St. 1956, § 123.190. See also post, § 142.

As to gifts, see post, § 140 et seq.

[25] See ante, § 66.

§ 115. — By wife — Income of her separate property.

As we have already seen, in some of our community property states, the rents, issues and profits of the separate property of a spouse are community property.[26] As such they are under the managerial control of the husband to the same extent as other community property, unless it is otherwise provided by statute.[27] In states where the rents, issues and profits of separate property are also separate property they remain under the control and management of the spouse owning them.[28]

§ 115.1. — By spouses jointly.

As has already been indicated, in some areas the management of community property or affairs is placed by some states in both spouses jointly.[29] This is particularly so as to the execution and acknowledgment of a transfer, conveyance or encumbrance of community real property,[30] including leases thereof for more than one year.[31] While some of the statutes do not make an express reference to "leases," the use of such words as "convey," "conveyance," and "encumbrance," and requiring joinder of the spouses therein, are held to include within their meaning leases which are required to be in writing.[32]

This requirement that both spouses join has been described by

[26] See ante, § 71.

[27] See Ida. Code 1948, § 32-193; Tex. Family Code 1969, § 5.22.

In Texas, under previous statutes, see Hawkins v. Britton, 122 Tex. 69, 52 S. W. 2d 243; Chandler v. Alamo Mfg. Co. (Tex. Civ. App.), 140 S. W. 2d 918.

[28] See ante, § 107.

[29] See ante, § 113. Consider Daggett, Is Joint Control Possible? 9 Tulane L. Rev. 589.

[30] See Cal. Civ. Code, § 5127; N.M. St. 1953, § 57-4-3; Wash. Rev. Code 1961, § 26.16.040.

Similarly in Arizona, excepting unpatented mining claims by one having the title or right of possession. Ariz. Rev. St. 1956, §§ 33-451, 33-452.

Conveyances, leases or mortgages of community realty in which wife under age of 21 years joins with husband in excuting have like full force and effect as if such minor had attained her majority at time of execution thereof. N.M. Stats. 1953, § 57-4-4. And see Tex Family Code 1969, § 4.03.

Petition for improvement of street on which community property abut-ted was properly signed by husband as manager of community; wife's signature was unnecessary. Fry v. O'Leary, 141 Wash. 465, 252 P. 111, 49 A.L.R. 1249.

[31] See Cal. Civ. Code § 5127 (except as to interest leased for less than one year). More fully, see post, § 118.

[32] See Maricopa Laundry Co. v. Levandowski, 40 Ariz. 91, 9 P. 2d 1014; Intermountain Realty Co. v. Allen, 60 Ida. 228, 90 P.2d 704, 122 A.L.R. 647; Goddard v. Morgan, 193 Wash. 83, 74 P.2d 894. And see post, § 118.

In New Mexico, the statute requiring wife's joinder in deeds and encumbrances did not include lease of community realty for three years. Fidel v. Venner, 35 N.M. 45, 289 P. 289 P. 803, Cf. Terry v. Humphreys, 27 N.M. 564, 203 P. 539, where oil and gas lease for five years was held a conveyance of realty requiring wife's signature.

Leasehold estate of five years with option to purchase required wife's joinder. Coppidge v. Leiser, 71 Ida. 248, 229 P.2d 977.

Where husband and wife have con-

the California court as a "veto power" in the wife,[33] but the New Mexico Supreme Court describes it as a form of "dual management" by the spouses.[34]

In California, such joinder by the wife with the husband must exist as to the transfer or encumbrance of certain community personal property, such as household furniture, furnishings and clothing.[35] And each must join in the other's wage assignments.[36]

The nature, effect and consequences of such transactions are discussed more fully in a later section in this subdivision.[37]

In conclusion and as a note of caution, it must be remembered that while a situation may be one in which legally the wife has no voice in the management, from a practical standpoint she may exercise a great deal of influence. The wise husband who wants a happy marriage will always remember to consult his wife.[38]

§ 115.2.   — Texas.

In 1967 the legislature of Texas adopted two statutes radically changing the usual rules with respect to management of the community property. The basic approach of the legislature was to divide the community into sections and to provide for management of these different sections exclusively by the husband, or by the wife, or by their joint management.[39] Basically this statute gives each spouse the sole management, control and disposition of that community property which he or she would have owned if a single person, including (but not limited to) his or her personal earnings, the revenues from his or her separate property, the recoveries for personal injuries awarded to him or her, and the increase, mutations and revenues of all property subject to his or her sole management, control and disposition. If community subject to the management of one spouse is commingled with community property subject to the management of the other spouse, the mixed or combined community property is subject to the joint management of the spouses unless they have agreed otherwise. Any other community property is subject to the sole management, control and disposition of the husband.

tracted to sell community realty, wife having joined in execution of written contract, oral waiver by husband alone of strictness of time requirements as to purchaser was sufficient. Stringer v. Swanstrum, 66 Idaho 752, 168 P.2d 826.

[33] Estate of Risse, 156 Cal. App. 2d 412, 319 P.2d 789.

[34] See Frkovich v. Petranovich, 48 N.M. 382, 151 P.2d 337, 155 A.L.R. 295.

[35] Cal. Civ. Code, § 5127; Matthews v. Hamburger, 36 Cal. App. 2d 182, 97 P.2d 465 (sale of furniture); Dynan v. Gallinatti, 87 Cal. App. 2d 533, 197 P.2d 391 (chattel mortgage of furniture).

[36] Cal. Labor Code, § 300.

[37] See post, § 117. Joinder in civil actions, see post, § 124 et seq.

[38] See pertinent remark in Chapman v. Tarentola, 8 Cal. Rptr. 228.

[39] Tex. Family Code 1969, § 5.22.

These statutes, it should be noted, do not make any change in the ownership of the community property; rather they relate solely to management. These provisions with regard to management are reasonably clear if the person dealing with the husband or wife can determine the class of the property involved in his particular transaction. To assist in this determination, the legislature further provided that during marriage property held in a spouse's name or property possessed by a spouse is presumed to be property subject to his or her sole management, and any person dealing with the spouse during marriage without notice to the contrary or being a party to a fraud upon the other spouse or another, is entitled to rely, as against the other spouse, upon the authority of that spouse to deal with the property.[40]

§ 116.   Contracts concerning community affairs or property.

Subject to any existing statutory limitations[41] and such principles as that prohibiting the husband from acting in fraud of or to the injury of the wife's rights,[42] the husband's right as managing partner of the marital partnership to manage the community property ordinarily carries with it the right to make contracts on behalf of the community or with relation to the community property.[43] The liabilities and obligations on the part of the spouses created by these contracts are dealt with in a subsequent chapter.[44]

Necessarily and by implication the power of the husband to contract, arising from his duty to manage the community property, leaves the wife with no power to contract on behalf of the community. Sometimes this prohibition against the right of the wife to contract is expressly provided by statute.[45] Nevertheless, it was a basic principle

[40] Tex. Family Code 1969, § 5.24. See also McSwain, A Survey of the New Marital Property Statutes, 2 Newsletter of the Family Section of the State Bar of Texas 3.

[41] Requirements as to consent of wife to disposition of community property (which would necessarily affect the right of the husband to contract for its disposition), see ante, § 113; post, § 117.

[42] See post, § 119.

[43] See, e.g., Shreeve v. Greer, 65 Ariz. 35, 173 P.2d 641, citing first edition; Tindall v. Bryan, 54 N.M. 114, 215 P.2d 355; Dipuccio v. Hanson (Tex.), 233 S. W. 2d 863; Kupka v. Dickson (Wash.), 432 P.2d 657.

The empowering of the husband to contract as the managing head of the marriage is very jealously preserved in some jurisdictions, perhaps to an extreme. Thus, in Louisiana, where a gas and oil lease on community property was executed by the husband with provision for extension of the lease upon payment or tender of a certain sum by the lessee to the "lessor," or to the latter's credit in a certain bank, it has been held that a deposit by the lessee to the credit of the husband and the wife was not in accord with the lease. Clingman v. Devonian Oil Co., 188 La. 310, 177 So. 59; Rosen v. North Central Texas Oil Co., 169 La. 973, 126 So. 442. [This seems over-technical. Whether placed to the credit of the husband or husband and wife, as community property it would be subject to the husband's control.]

[44] See post, Chap. IX.

[45] That married women 21 years of age or older have the same legal rights as men except the right to make contracts binding the common property, see Ariz. Rev. St. 1956, § 25-214.

of Spanish community property law that the husband might consent to the wife acting or contracting,[46] and the same has been true with us. Our cases have been consistent in holding that the contracts of the wife, relative to the community property or affairs, made with the permission of the husband, are valid on a theory of agency or estoppel.[47] And, under the Spanish law, where the husband improperly withheld his consent, for example, so as to deprive the wife of necessaries, or had disappeared or was absent, the wife might apply to the court for power to act or contract.[48] The statutes of our community property states frequently confer upon the wife the right of contracting in certain cases of necessity, as where the husband has failed to provide necessaries for her and the minor children,[49] or where he has become incompetent or incapacitated or has disappeared.[50] Even in the absence of statute conferring authority upon the wife to contract in cases of disappearance of the husband, his refusal to supply necessaries, etc., common sense would indicate that the wife should be recognized to have the power to enter into necessary contracts.[51]

Under the Spanish community property law, if the wife held or exercised some public office or trade, she could make contracts relating thereto without the consent of the husband.[52]

---

[46] See Laws of Toro, Nos. 54–56; Matienzo, Gloss II, No. 2, to Nov. Rec. Law 1, Book 10, Title 4.

See Cahn, The Contractual and Proprietary Status of Married Women at Civil Law (1927); Noble v. Glenns Ferry Bank, Ltd. (Ida.) 421 P.2d 444, 447, quoting and following 1 de Funiak, § 116.

"The other civil effects of marriage are: . . . III. That the husband can give license to his wife to contract and do all that which otherwise she could not do, and that the same being given to her, all that she may do by virtue thereof is valid." Escriche, Diccionario, "Ganancial Properties."

[47] See, e.g., Cato v. Bynum (La.), 98 So.2d 257; La. Civ. Code, art. 1787; Travers v. Barrett, 30 Nev. 402, 97 P. 126; Lockhart v. Garner (Tex.), 298 S. W. 2d 108.

See also ante, § 114.

Right to contract in management of business as sole trader, see post, § 149.

[48] "The judge has the power to grant the wife authority to do all the foregoing acts (i.e., make contracts, etc.), when the husband improperly withholds his consent; and in cases of the absence of the husband, when delay may be attended with danger." Schmidt, Civil Law of Spain and Mexico, p. 12, citing Laws 57 and 59 of Toro.

"And if the husband does not give it (i.e., permission to the wife to contract), he may be compelled thereto by the judge upon hearing of legal and necessary cause; and if even being ordered he does not give it, it shall be given by the judge, who may give the same also upon hearing of cause, the husband being absent and his return not soon expected, or there being danger in the delay, and all that is done under the license of the judge shall be valid, the same as if the husband had given it." Escriche, Diccionario, "Ganancial Properties."

[49] See, e.g., Ariz. Rev. St. 1956, § 25-215.

See also post, § 162.

[50] See post, § 128.

[51] See Sassaman v. Root, 37 Idaho 588, 218 P. 374.

[52] Schmidt, Civil Law of Spain and Mexico, p. 109, citing Fuero Real, Book 3, Title 20, Law 13.

Likewise, in Louisiana as to wife who is "public merchant," see La. Civ. Code, art. 131.

Reference has already been made to the right of the husband to dispose of community property and the statutory provisions of our community property states in respect thereto.[53] In those states which require the joinder of the wife in conveyances or encumberances of community realty, in some the failure to join the wife renders the conveyance or encumbrance void and of no effect,[54] in others it would seem to be voidable at the instance of the wife.[55]

If the transaction is void, of no valid effect whatever, this can certainly be pointed out by anyone properly before the court,[56] but in jurisdictions where the transaction is voidable, it remains effective until questioned within the time permitted therefor.[57] In some of the latter jurisdictions it has been said that the right to avoid the transaction is personal to the wife and cannot be enforced by someone else in her place,[58] as by a repentant husband.[59] But this personal right of the wife to avoid the transaction does exist in favor of her guardian where she is incompetent or in favor of her personal representative after her death.[60]

§ 117. Transfers, conveyances and encumbrances of community property.

Some transactions are not classified as conveyances or encumbrances within the statutory requirement that the wife join with the husband. Thus, the husband has been entitled to enter into a boundary agreement concerning the community realty without the wife's express consent, by reason of his managerial authority and because a sale,

[53] See ante, § 113.

Right of husband, after death of wife, to control and dispose of property, see post, § 206.

[54] Ariz. Rev. St. 1956, §§ 33-451, 33-452; Robinson v. Merchants Packing Co., 66 Ariz. 22, 182 P.2d 97; Maricopa Laundry Co. v. Levandowski, 40 Ariz. 91, 9 P.2d 1014; N.M. St. 1953, § 57-4-3; McGrail v. Fields, (N.M.) 203 P.2d 1000; Jenkins v. Huntzinger, 46 N.M. 168, 125 P.2d 327. See also Thomas v. Stevens, 69 Ida. 100, 203 P.2d 597; Hart v. Turner, 39 Ida. 50, 226 P.282.

In Nevada and Texas the conveyance is void if it is of homestead property. Nev. Rev. St. 1956, § 123.030; Tex. Family Code 1969, § 5.81. Otherwise as to Texas, see ante, § 115.2.

[55] Cal. Civ. Code, § 5127; Trimble v. Trimble, 219 Cal. 240, 26 P.2d 477; Waldeck v. Hedden, 89 Cal. App. 485, 265 P. 340 (contract to exchange

realty); Tombari v. Grieppe (Wash.) 350 P.2d 452.

See also post, § 122.

Spouse guilty of felony in falsely representing self to be competent to sell or mortgage real estate, where assent of other spouse necessary, and selling or mortgaging such realty, see Cal. Penal Code, § 534.

[56] Equitable estoppel of wife to raise invalidity, see infra, this section.

See also post, § 122.

[57] See, e.g., Cal. Civ. Code, § 5127 that voidability of transaction must be raised within one year from the date of its recordation. If not recorded, then other limitation statutes must be looked to.

[58] Jack v. Wong She, 33 Cal. App. 2d 402, 92 P.2d 449.

[59] Brandt v. Brandt, 32 Cal. App. 2d 99, 89 P.2d 171.

[60] Harris v. Harris, 57 Cal. 2d 387, 19 Cal. Rptr. 793, 369 P.2d 481.

conveyance or encumbrance of the property was not involved.[61] And if an agreement to abandon a contract for the purchase of realty need not be in writing, the authorization by the purchaser's wife and the vendor's wife to their husbands to cancel the agreement need not be in writing to be valid.[62] There is also authority that listing community realty with a broker for sale does not require a joinder of the wife with the husband,[63] but it has also been considered that such a listing with a broker does require joinder to make it binding.[64] But even if it is not enforceable against the spouses, the spouse listing the property with the broker may be liable to him in damages.[65]

There may be situations, of course, in which the wife did not join in the execution and acknowledgement but is estopped by her conduct to deny that the transaction is void[66] or voidable,[67] as the case may be.

Whether the failure of the wife to join in execution of a deed or mortgage affects the validity of the instrument may be seriously influenced by the fact that record title to the realty stands in the husband's name and by the fact that the grantee or mortgagee is one in good faith without knowledge of the marriage relation. In California, it is provided by statute that where the record title to community realty stands in the name of the husband alone, the husband's sole lease,

---

[61] James v. Le Deit, (Cal. App.) 39 Cal. Rptr. 559.

[62] Martin v. Butter, 93 Cal. App. 2d 562, 209 P.2d 636.

[63] See McDonald v. Bernard, 87 Cal. App. 717, 262 P. 430.

Where husband and wife owned community real property in Idaho and husband executed contract in Utah giving Utah broker exclusive listing of the realty for sale for six months, such contract was not void because not signed by the wife, since it was a contract of employment and not one purporting to convey an interest in land. Johnson v. Allen, 108 Utah 148, 158 P.2d 134, 159 A. L. R. 256.

[64] See, e. g., Geoghegan v. Dever, 130 Wash. 2d 877, 194 P.2d 397, that commission contract to broker amounted to placing encumbrance on community realty without joinder of wife and was not an obligation binding the community.

[65] Where wife alone signed broker's commission contract and husband did not authorize her in writing to act as agent and to sell the community

realty, the husband was not liable to the broker for a commission, although the wife was. Tamini v. Bettencourt, 52 Cal. Rptr. 273.

[66] Treadwell v. Henderson, 58 N.M. 230, 269 P.2d 1108, noted 27 Rocky Mt. L. Rev. 1109, holding wife precluded by equitable estoppel.

In Viramontes v. Fox, 65 N.M. 275, 335 P.2d 1071, wife's name was signed by husband with notation that he signed for her and wife ratified this; held a sufficient joinder by wife. See also Pickett v. Miller, (N.M.) 412 P.2d 400, where wife ratified act of husband sending telegram on their joint behalf, accepting purchase offer.

In Arizona it seems that to estop the denial of the validity of the conveyance or encumbrance, both spouses must have indulged in the conduct giving rise to the theory of estoppel. See Heckman v. Harris, 66 Ariz. 360, 188 P.2d 991.

[67] Harger v. Haldeman (Cal. App.) 16 Cal. Rptr. 557; Stephens v. Nelson, 37 Wash. 2d 28, 221 P.2d 520; Tombari v. Grieppe (Wash.) 350 P.2d 452.

contract, mortgage or deed to a lessee, purchaser or encumbrancer in good faith without knowledge of the marriage relation is presumed to be valid, and action to avoid the instrument must be brought within one year from its filing of record.[68] In Texas, one purchasing in good faith for value from the husband in whose name legal title stands would take good title; only the purchaser's actual knowledge of the true facts, shown by direct or circumstantial evidence, defeats a claim of purchase in good faith.[69] While a Washington statute provides that any bona fide purchaser of realty from the spouse in whose name the legal title stands of record receives the full legal and equitable title free of all claim of the other spouse,[70] the courts have construed the statute to mean such persons as purchase without knowledge of the marriage relation or who could not with reasonable diligence have obtained such knowledge. In a number of cases the wife was denied the right to challenge a deed or mortgage executed by the husband when the marriage relation had never been established or maintained in the state. The opposite was held, however, where although separated for some years without divorce, both spouses had lived as husband and wife in the state and both were still within the state so that reasonable diligence could have established that fact.[71]

It is provided in some jurisdictions where the wife must join in the conveyance or encumbrance of the community realty, that she may do so by duly authorized agent,[72] or may by duly executed power of attorney authorize the husband to execute the conveyance or encumbrance.[73]

In respect of the husband's right to dispose of the community personalty without the consent of the wife, it must be borne in mind that this right is usually restricted to disposition *inter vivos* and does not include the right to make testamentary disposition of it, or at most only of his half of it,[74] and does not include the power to make dis-

---

[68] Cal. Civ. Code, § 5127.

The presumption is not conclusive and may be controverted. Mark v. Title Guarantee & Trust Co., 122 Cal. App. 301, 9 P.2d 839.

[69] See Oakes, Speer's Marital Rights in Texas, 4th Ed., §§ 368, 369, 370. See also post, § 206.

[70] Wash. Rev. Code 1961, §§ 26.16.095, 26.16.100.

[71] Campbell v. Sandy, 190 Wash. 528, 69 P.2d 808, citing numerous authorities.

[72] Cal. Civ. Code, § 5127.

[73] Ariz. Rev. St. 1956, §§ 33-451, 33-452; Ida. Code 1948, § 32-912.

[74] See ante, § 113.

Testamentary disposition, etc., see post, Chap. X, B.

"And consequently a husband cannot by will and last wish make a disposition which will alienate profits after his death, as that will not be during marriage." Azevedo, Nos. 15, 16, to Nov. Rec. Law 5, Book 10, Title 4.

"And further, this power of the husband to dispose of the personal property of the community is limited to the period of the coverture, and does not extend to his disposal thereof by will, but he is restricted in the disposal by will to his one-half thereof." La Tourette v. La Tourette, 15 Ariz. 200, 137 P. 426, Ann. Cas.

positions, which are wrongfully in fraud or injury of the wife's rights.[75] And sometimes the husband's apparently untrammeled right to dispose of the personalty is considerably limited, as in California where it is provided that he cannot make a gift of it or dispose of it without valuable consideration, or sell, convey or encumber the furniture, etc., or the clothing of the wife and minor children, without the wife's consent.[76] Where the husband has full power of administration over the community personalty, he may of course, convey or encumber it without the necessity of the wife's joinder therein, and her signature is unnecessary to an encumbrance of such personalty, at least so long as the encumbrance is to secure a community obligation.[77]

Although the title to the community property is usually in the name of the husband or in the names of the husband and wife, it sometimes is in the name of the wife alone. What are the rights as between the husband or his heirs and one who, for value and without notice of the marriage relation takes a conveyance or encumbrance executed to him by the wife? It might be inferred that one taking conveyance of such property from the wife, especially in good faith without knowledge of the marriage relation, would acquire a title good as against the husband or the husband's heirs. However, such an inference would overlook the possibility of fraud or injury to the husband's rights by such a conveyance, for just as the wife is entitled to protection against fraudulent or injurious alienations by the husband, even when he has power to alienate without her consent,[78] so should the husband or his heirs be entitled to protection from alienations in fraud or injury of the husband. In California and New Mexico the statute is more explicit, providing that whenever any real or personal property or any interest therein or encumbrance thereon is acquired by a married woman by written instrument the presumption is that it is her separate property, and such presumption is declared to be conclusive in favor of any person dealing in good faith and for a valuable consideration with such married woman (or with her legal representative or successors in interest, according to the California

---

1195 B 70. See also Davenport v. Simons, 68 Ida. 21, 189 P.2d 90, citing first edition.

[75] See post, § 119.

[76] Cal. Civ. Code, § 5125.
Thus, as to household furniture and furnishings husband cannot transfer it without wife's written consent, even for valuable consideration. Matthews v. Hamburger, 36 Cal. App. 2d 182, 97 P.2d 465.

And he cannot subject it to chattel mortgage even for valuable consideration. Dynan v. Gallinatti, 87 Cal. App. 2d 533, 197 P.2d 191, noted in 22

Sou. Cal. L. Rev. 291.

[77] See Greer v. Goesling, 54 Ariz. 488, 97 P.2d 218; Porter v. Porter, 67 Ariz. 273, 195 P.2d 132; Azar v. Azar (La.) 120 So. 2d 485; Tindall v. Bryan, 54 N.M. 114, 215 P.2d 355; Kane v. Klos (Wash.) 314 P.2d 672. See also, accord, N.M. St. 1953, § 57-4-3; Shermack, Nevada Community Property Law, 15 La. L. Rev. 559.

But cf. Idaho position, seeming to ignore Ida. Code 1948, § 45-1102. See Brockelbank, The Community Property Law of Idaho, § 6.6.

[78] See post, § 119.

statute).[79] A statute very similar in effect is in force in Washington.[80] In states without such a statute as those referred to, in situations where the wife has without the husband's knowledge alienated or encumbered community realty, title to which was in her name, the alienee or encumbrancer, even when taking in good faith without knowledge of the marriage relation, has not been protected as against the husband or his heirs. This has been dependent, however, on the fact that the wife had no authority so to convey or encumber the particular property involved, such power being vested in the husband.[81] Where the community property, title to which stands in her name, is property over which she is given power of management and disposition, one taking from her in good faith for value and in ignorance of any rights of the husband should undoubtedly occupy the same position of a purchaser from the husband in a like situation.[82]

Of course, where the wife alone has executed the contract or transfer, the invalidity or voidability that might otherwise result from the failure of the husband to join may be cured by a showing that the husband has ratified the wife's act or is otherwise estopped by his conduct to object, or in fact that both spouses are estopped.[83]

We have been considering chiefly the disposition of property, particularly community realty, but it may be noticed briefly that usually a husband can purchase realty without the wife's joinder or legal consent, if he is using community personalty for its acquisition, since he is authorized to manage community personalty without the wife's joinder.[84] This has been so held even where the realty is acquired

[79] Cal. Civ. Code, § 5110; N.M. St. 1953, § 57-4-1. Notice that such "good faith" is very difficult to establish.

Where the community property is in the names of the husband and the wife, can one spouse purport to transfer only his or her interest, so as to create some such relationship as that of tenancy in common between other spouse and the purchaser? Not without the proper consent of the other spouse. The community property is not divisible by the act of one spouse. (Cf. situation in California and Louisiana presented in § 129.)

At the period when the California courts were holding the community property to be the husband's property with only an expectant interest as an heir in the wife, the wife's conveyance of her interest was said not to be wholly void but to operate on her interest after the husband's death, under Cal. Civ. Code, § 1106, that where one purports to grant realty in fee and subsequently acquires any title or claim the same passes by operation of law to the grantee or his successors. See Lynch v. Lynch, 207 Cal. 582, 279 P. 653. Since the wife's interest is not now that of an heir or expectant but is fully equal to that of the husband, Civ. Code, § 1106, could not now be applicable to the wife any more than to the husband.

[80] Wash. Rev. Code 1961, § 26.16.095.

[81] See Richards v. Warnekros, 14 Ariz. 488, 131 P. 154; Thomas v. Stevens, 69 Ida. 100, 203 P.2d 597; Thomas v. Winsey (La.), 76 So. 2d 33.

[82] See Tex. Family Code 1969, § 5.24; Oakes, Speer's Marital Rights in Texas, 4th Ed., § 368.

[83] See, e. g., Holbrook v. Flynn (Ida.), 195 P.2d 355. See also post, § 162.

[84] See ante, §§ 113, 116.

subject to leases, reservations or exceptions.[85] In some jurisdictions he can even execute a purchase money mortgage back to the vendor without the necessity of the wife's joinder.[86] But in other jurisdictions, he would need the wife's joinder in such a situation.[87]

Of course, once property is acquired, the spouse holding it holds as trustee for the benefit of the other spouse as to that spouse's interest or for the benefit of marital community, if this latter method of expression is preferred.[88]

§ 118.   — Leases and leasehold interests.

Among those community property states which give the husband absolute power of disposition of community personalty but require the joinder of the wife in instruments transferring, conveying or encumbering the community realty, some apparent conflict exists as to whether or not the wife must join in the execution by the husband of a lease of the community realty.[89] We say "apparent" because the determination of the matter is frequently dependent upon the wording of the particular statute, although one must also consider the conflicts of opinion among our courts as to whether a leasehold interest is real or personal property. For example, in California the statute clearly provides that the wife must join with the husband in executing any instrument by which the "community real property or any interest therein is leased for a longer period than one year, or is sold, conveyed, or encumbered."[90] Accordingly, the execution by the husband without the joinder of the wife of a lease for longer than a year rendered the lease, under the California view, voidable at the option of the wife, if she sues within one year of the date of any recordation of such lease.[91] But even under a statute, as in Idaho and Washington, which has contained no specific reference to leases but has provided that the husband cannot sell, convey or encumber community realty without the wife joining in the execution and acknowledgment of the deed or other instrument, the view has been taken that a lease comes within the meaning of the words "conveyance" and "encum-

---

[85] Munger v. Boardman, 53 Ariz. 271, 88 P.2d 536; Morgan v. Firestone Tire & Rubber Co., 68 Ida. 506, 201 P.2d 976.

[86] Morgan v. Firestone Tire & Rubber Co. (Ida.), preceding note; Davidson v. Click, 31 N.M. 543, 249 P. 100, 47 A. L. R. 1016.

[87] See annotation, 47 A. L. R. 1025.

[88] Jorgensen v. Jorgensen, 32 Cal. 2d 13, 193 P.2d 728; Sande v. Sande, 83 Ida. 233, 360 P.2d 998; Brownson v. Neal (Tex. Civ. App.), 259 S. W. 2d 277.

[89] And see ante, § 115.1.

[90] Cal. Civ. Code, § 5127.

[91] Maxwell v. Carlon, 30 Cal. App. 2d 356, 86 P.2d 666.

Husband as agent of wife in making lease with option to purchase and wife knowing facts and confirming his actions. Moreno v. Blinn (Cal. App.), 185 P.2d 332.

brance" so as to require joinder of the wife in its execution,[92] and in its acknowledgment where acknowledgment is required.[93]

Arizona requires the joinder of the wife to lease community realty, unless she is estopped,[94] under a statute that requires her joinder in conveyances or encumbrances of community realty.[95] This same statute does not require the wife's joinder in an agreement to buy realty for the community.[96]

On the other hand, a New Mexico statute using similar language has been so construed as to render a lease for years of community realty valid where executed by the husband alone.[97] But even here the New Mexico court has made a distinction between a mere lease for years of community realty, as exemplified by its view set out in the preceding sentence, and an oil lease for an indefinite, indeterminable period. The latter situation it has declared represents a conveyance and sale of part of the realty itself — the oil thereon which was to be

---

[92] See Hancock v. Elkington, 67 Ida. 542, 186 P.2d 494; Coppedge v. Leiser, 71 Ida. 248, 229 P.2d 977; Morgan v. Firestone Tire & Rubber Co., 68 Ida. 506, 201 P.2d 976; Whiting v. Johnson (Wash.), 390 P.2d 985. And see cases cited ante, § 115.1.

Similarly as to agreement of husband to extend lease, see Kaufman v. Perkins, 114 Wash. 40, 194 P. 802.

As to oral leases, see Spreitzer v. Miller, 98 Wash. 601, 168 P. 179.

[93] In Washington, lease for more than year must be acknowledged. Wash. Rev. Code 1961, § 59.04.010. See also Durant v. Snider, 65 Ida. 678, 151 P.2d 776; Stabbert v. Atlas, etc., Co., 39 Wash. 2d 789, 238 P.2d 1212.

As to unacknowledged lease, with element of estoppel present, see Little v. Bergdahl Oil Co., 60 Idaho 662, 95 P.2d 833; Matzger v. Arcade Building & Realty Co., 80 Wash. 401, 141 P. 900, L. R. A. 1915 A 288. Wife not estopped to contest validity of three years lease of community property executed and acknowledged by husband alone merely by reason of fact that she had always been satisfied to have her husband handle community affairs, including the leasing of community realty. To constitute estoppel of the wife, there must be some ratification of the husband's leasing and this must be more than mere knowledge of leasing. Benedict v. Hendrickson, 19 Wash. 2d 452, 143 P.2d 326.

[94] See Wilson v. Metheny, 72 Ariz. 339, 236 P.2d 34; Maricopa Laundry Co. v. Levandoski, 40 Ariz. 91, 9 P.2d 1014.

Where spouses as plaintiffs sought to recover from defendant damages for breach of lease and for rentals past due prior to breach of lease, and lease had been signed only by husband, recovery of past due rentals allowed but not recovery for breach of lease, since no valid lease was in existence. Robinson v. Merchants' Packing Co., 66 Ariz. 22, 182 P.2d 97.

[95] Ariz. Rev. St. 1956, §§ 33-451, 33-452. And see ante, § 115.1.

[96] See King v. Uhlmann (Ariz.), 437 P.2d 928.

[97] See Fidel v. Venner, 35 N.M. 45, 289 P. 803. And see ante, § 115.1.

Lease of community realty in which married woman under age of 21 years joins with husband has like full force and effect as if minor had attained her majority at time of execution thereof. N.M. Stats. 1953, § 57-4-4.

extracted — and that in such situation the joinder of the wife in the execution of the oil lease was absolutely requisite.[98]

The question of a leasehold interest as personalty or realty has arisen in some instances where the husband is the lessee and the lease represents an asset of the marital community and he has, without joinder of the wife, entered into a modification of the lease or has assigned the interest therein. The Idaho court has considered such a lease as community realty and, consistent also with its view that the wife must join with the husband in leasing community realty on the ground that such a lease is a "conveyance" and an "encumbrance" within its statute, has held that the wife must join with the husband in an instrument modifying the terms of a lease executed to the husband.[99] But the Washington courts which have held, under a statute similar to that of Idaho, that the wife must join with the husband in the execution of a lease of the community realty on the ground that the lease is an "encumbrance" within the terms of the statute, have held that where a lease is executed to the husband it constitutes community personalty and that he can assign it as he would other community personalty, that is, without the necessity of joinder by the wife.[1] Formerly in California, a leasehold interest which constituted community property amounted merely to a chattel real with which the husband had full power to deal. Its transfer or surrender was said not to be within the statute requiring the joinder of the wife.[2] But statutory amendments in 1961 provided expressly that a leasehold interest is realty and not personalty.[3] Logical interpretation of such a provision would bring the leasehold interest within the area of the necessary joinder by the wife with the husband.

§ 119.   Alienation, disposition or the like in fraud or injury of the wife.[4]

It is clear from the terms of the Spanish code provisions that the husband's alienation, without the wife's consent, of property acquired during the marriage was invalid if it was proven to have been wrong-

[98] Terry v. Humphreys, 27 N.M. 564, 203 P. 539, explained and distinguished in Fidel v. Venner, ante, preceding note; Attaway v. Stanolind Oil & Gas Co., 232 F.2d 790.

[99] Intermountain Realty Co. v. Allen, 60 Idaho 228, 90 P.2d 704, 122 A. L. R. 647.

Lease of property obtained by husband was an asset of the community and the wife could be considered as a co-lessee so as to make the landlord liable to her for injuries from defects in the premises. Crawford v. Magnolia (La. App.), 4 So.2d 48.

[1] Tibbals v. Iffland, 10 Wash. 451, 39 P. 102. See also American Sav. Bank & Trust Co. v. Mafridge, 60 Wash. 180, 110 P. 1015; Anderson v. National Bank of Tacoma, 146 Wash. 520, 264 P. 8.

[2] See First Nat. Bank v. Brashear, 200 Cal. 389, 253 P. 143.

[3] See Cal. Civ. Code, § 5110. Similarly as to quasi-community property, see Cal. Civ. Code, § 4803.

[4] Where wife manages community property, see post, § 120.1.

fully made, that is, made with wrongful intent, so as to defraud or injure the wife.[5] While this placed the burden upon the wife or her heirs of proving that the alienation was wrongfully made so as to defraud or injure her,[6] this did not mean that in each individual case inquiry had to be made into the motive of the husband in making the alienation and an express wrongful intent proved. The alienation was by presumption or implication wrongfully made or made with wrongful intent so as to defraud or injure the wife when it was an alienation of property for an inadequate consideration,[7] or was a large gift made for no good reason,[8] or an excessive gift in proportion to the total amount of the community property, or the like; and a showing of one of those facts was sufficient to establish a wrongful alienation.[9] To give was to lose, said the jurisconsults, and aside from the moderate gifts in certain circumstances permitted to the husband to make,[10] any alienation by the husband which deliberately and unjustifiably caused loss or depreciation of the community property was wrongful as to the wife.[11] "For this is not allowed and no one is permitted to be guided by wrongful intent. Nor is anyone who has full and general power of administration allowed to do anything with wrongful intent; if he does so, he will not bind the owner."[12]

One of the things which the husband could not do, as being in fraud of the wife's rights, was to go surety for another, binding the moiety of the profits belonging to the wife. One charged with the management of the property of another had no right, it was said, to risk the substance in that way, for if the one for whom the husband

[5] See ante, § 113.

[6] See post, § 126.

[7] "The law invalidates fraudulent alienations, such as a sale by the husband of property which is of great value for a small price, since such sale appears to be more in the nature of a gift than a sale, Dig. 18.1.38." Matienzo, Gloss VI, No. 13, to Nov. Rec. Law 5, Book 10, Title 4.

[8] "Understand by this ('save it be proven') that anyone who alleges fraud or wrongful intent — unless wrongful intent or fraud is obvious, e. g. in a large gift made for no good reason — is bound to prove such fraud or wrongful intent." Azevedo, No. 17, to Nov. Rec. Law 5.

[9] "In cases where by the nature of the title or of the contract fraud is presumed in the alienor, e. g., in the gift of the whole of the property and the like, such gifts are not allowed to prejudice the wife, as is stated by Antonius Gómez on law 53 *Tauri* no. 73 at the words 'quod limita'." Matienzo, Gloss VI, No. 9, to Nov. Rec. Law 5. This statement attributed to Gómez is worthy of notice because he was one of those who argued that the power of alienation conferred on the husband included the right to make gifts, although he qualified his argument to the effect that the gifts must not be of such nature as worked a fraud on the wife. As to this, see post, § 121 et seq.

[10] See post, §§ 121, 122.

[11] Some specific citations have been made to foregoing statements, but the entire discussions of the jurisconsults on this subject should be considered as a whole. See, e. g., Matienzo, Gloss VI; Azevedo, No. 8 et seq.; Gutiérrez, Quaestio CXXI; all to Nov. Rec. Law 5. See also post, § 150.

[12] Azevedo, No. 18, to Nov. Rec. Law 5.

went surety was insolvent so that the husband could not recover from him if the husband was called on to pay, the husband was clearly losing that amount to the prejudice of the wife.[13]

That in our community property states the husband's power of disposition is also limited by the principle that he must not act in fraud of the wife's rights in the community property is well recognized.[14] The criticism has been made that the cases are frequently vague as to what conduct will constitute such fraud, and it has been questioned as to what yardstick should be employed in determining the intent to defraud.[15] But enough has already been said in this section to indicate that, while the principle itself is stated and preserved in only a broad general outline, there is not always a necessity of proving an actual intent to defraud or an improper motive on the part of the husband,[16] since it may be obvious from the very nature of the alienation, that is, an implied intent or improper motive may necessarily exist because of the nature and effect of the alienation or conduct of the husband,[17] as where he alienates for an inadequate consideration.[18]

§ 120.   — Debauchery and dissolute living.

It is not to be assumed from the foregoing that the husband had to make good from his share of the community or from his separate property the losses resulting to the community from his management or from misfortune or the like, there being no bad faith, for the wife shared the burden of losses as well as the benefit of gains accruing to

---

[13] Azevedo, Nos. 20, 21, to Nov. Rec. Law 5. See also post, § 163.

[14] Citation of authority to this point is unnecessary, but see cases post, §§ 122, 123.

See also Weinberg v. Weinberg, 63 Cal. Rptr. 13, 432 P.2d 709.

In Louisiana, as to disposal by husband by fraud, to injure the wife, see La. Civ. Code, art. 2404.

Discussion of Louisiana law on donations of community property in fraud of wife, see note, 22 Tulane L. Rev. 650, to Succession of Geagan, 212 La. 574, 33 So.2d 118, also noted, 4 Loyola L. Rev. 195.

Since encumbering the property, equally as well as transferring it outright, may be in fraud of the wife's rights, reference is recommended at all times to Chap. IX, dealing with rights of creditors, etc.

[15] See Huie, Community Property Laws as Applied to Life Insurance, 18 Tex. Law Rev. 121, 126.

[16] See, e. g., Berniker v. Berniker, 30 Cal. 2d 439, 182 P.2d 557; McElroy v. McElroy, 32 Cal. 2d 828, 198 P.2d 683.

In Estate of Smith, 86 Cal. App. 2d 456, 195 P.2d 842, court indicates somewhat startling view that husband can take funds belonging to both spouses and purchase property with intent that it shall be his separate property.

[17] Oakes, Speer's Law of Marital Rights in Texas, 4th Ed., Chap. 11.

Relief available to wife, see post, § 126.

[18] Consideration so inadequate as to support conclusion that alienation purposely made to defraud wife of her rights, see Vanasek v. Pokorny, 73 Cal. App. 312, 238 P. 798.

the marital partnership.[19] But could the husband use up the profits, accruing during the marriage, in "gambling and harlotry," as the jurisconsults expressed it. Some of the jurisconsults, including Gutiérrez, declared that although a husband did wrong in gambling he had no intent to defraud his wife but, indeed, thought to gain by it; that though by the letter of the law such losses might be debitable against the share of the husband, that in practice such a rule was not observed.[20] Others, including Azevedo, declared that it was a mode of wasting and losing but that it must be presumed that the spending of the profits in that manner was not done with intent to defraud the wife and that in the absence of proof of fraud and wrongful intent such conduct was permitted to a husband. *If wrongful intent and fraud were provable, however, as in the case of excessive gifts, the husband's share of the community was chargeable with waste and loss.*[21] It will be perceived that the sum and substance of the Spanish view was that the wasting of the community property in dissolute living was wrong in theory but that in practice no account was taken of such losses in the partition of the community property, unless the losses were so excessive as to be undeniably a fraud on the wife. In other words, the jurisconsults took the practical view that man not being a perfect creature, a husband might perhaps stray from the straight and narrow path or make a fool of himself upon occasion, and some loss from that fact was a risk that a wife took just as she shared the benefit of good management by a sober and efficient spouse; and to make allowance for loss on that ground might induce endless litigation over every loss resulting in the ordinary course of the husband's management of the property. But, and this is important to notice, if the waste was of a nature to be in fraud of the wife, or involved gifts, as to a mistress or to dissolute women, that was another matter.[22]

So far as concerns the statements sometimes made by our courts and writers that the husband can waste the community property in debauchery and that the wife has no redress, professedly made on the authority of the Spanish law,[23] such statements are too frequently made without adequate investigation and analysis of the Spanish authorities. For the husband had no such right, in any unlimited sense, as has been pointed out. Immoderate or excessive wasting, or expenditures on dissolute women, gave rise to remedial rights in the

---

[19] Matienzo discusses the nature of the marital partnership as similar to the business partnership in its sharing of profits and losses, in Gloss I to Nov. Rec. Law 1, Book 10, Title 4.

Debts, obligations and liabilities, see post, Chap. IX.

[20] Gutiérrez, Quaestio CXXI, Nos. 7, 8, to Nov. Rec. Law 5.

[21] Azevedo, No. 19, to Nov. Rec. Law 5.

[22] See Matienzo, Gloss VI, No. 12; Azevedo, No. 19; to Nov. Rec. Law 5.

[23] As was remarked by Holmes, J., in United States v. Robbins, 269 U. S. 315, 70 L. Ed. 285, 46 Sup. Ct. 148.

wife's favor.[24] So far as we are concerned in this country, if the waste is so excessive as to prejudice the wife's rights or if it involves excessive donations of the community property, she can proceed for the usual relief in such cases.[25] And in addition, it may be pointed out that the wife has redress in the divorce courts, wherein she may obtain a division of the community property, and if the husband's conduct is of an aggravated nature she may in many states obtain all or a larger share of the community property in redress of such wrongdoing.[26]

§ 120.1.   — In fraud of husband where wife manages.

Where the management of any part of the community property rests in the wife, whether by authorization of law or by authorization of or by agreement with the husband, it must logically follow that she is subject to the same obligations and duties as the husband is when he manages[27] and the husband has the same rights as the wife has when the husband's management is in fraud of or prejudicial to her rights.[28] In other words, the wife while managing must do nothing in fraud of or prejudicial to the husband's rights.[29] She cannot make gifts to herself from the community property in her control[30] nor can she make gifts from such property to third persons without the husband's consent.[31] In jurisdictions where the husband may not even validly

---

[24] Wife's right to take control of automobile which husband gave to his mistress, see Marston v. Rue, 92 Wash. 129, 159 P. 111. Similarly, see Lynn v. Herman, 72 Cal. App. 2d 614, 165 P.2d 54.

Where husband gambled and paid losses with community personalty, wife sued to recover from payee. Trial court held for defendant on ground of transfer of personalty for valuable consideration but appellate court reversed on ground transfer was unlawful and without consideration. Novo v. Hotel Del Rio, 141 Cal. App. 2d 304, 295 P.2d 596, noted in 30 Sou. Cal. L. Rev. 95, 9 Stanf. L. Rev. 400.

The attempted interpretation of the husband's power, made in Garrozi v. Dastas, 204 U. S. 64, 51 L. Ed. 369, 27 Sup. Ct. 224, arising in Puerto Rico, relies almost entirely on the views of French authorities as to the French law, and is entirely undependable in considering the Spanish law, which gave no such unlimited and unchecked authority to the husband.

[25] See post, § 126.

[26] Dissolution of marriage by divorce, see post, Chap. X, C.

Obtaining division of community property without obtaining divorce, in California and Louisiana, see § 129.

[27] See, e. g., Odone v. Marzocchi, 34 Cal. 2d 431, 211 P.2d 297.

[28] See cases cited infra and see also post, § 126.

[29] Sometimes the statutes authorizing her to manage specify the same obligation on her as do statutes relating to the husband. See, e. g., Cal. Civ. Code, § 5124.

[30] See Estate of Baer, 81 Cal. App. 2d 830, 185 P.2d 412; Milisich v. Hillhouse, 48 Nev. 166, 228 P. 307; Sullivan v. Albuquerque Nat. Trust & Sav. Bank, 51 N.M. 456, 188 P.2d 169; Abbott v. Weatherby, 6 Wash. 507, 33 P. 1070, 36 Am. St. Rep. 176.

[31] See Odone v. Marzocchi, 34 Cal. 2d 431, 211 P.2d 297; Munson v. Haye, 29 Wash. 2d 733, 189 P.2d 464. See also Estate of Rouse, 149 Cal. App. 2d 674, 309 P.2d 34; Henry v. Hibernia Sav. & Loan Soc., 5 Cal.

transfer or encumber community property for valuable consideration without the wife's joinder or consent, so the wife may not transfer or encumber even for valuable consideration without the husband's joinder or consent.[32]

§ 121.   Gifts of community property — Spanish and Mexican views.

Since the husband, under the Spanish law of community property, had the power to alienate, without the wife's consent, the property acquired during the marriage, and such alienation was valid save it be proved in fraud or injury of the wife,[33] did this power of alienation include the power to give away such property or were such gifts in fraud or injury of the wife's rights?

The Spanish jurisconsults were uniformly of the view that the husband could not make a gift of such property which would be in fraud or injury of the wife, but they were not uniform, or so one would assume from a first glance, in considering that all gifts of such property were prohibited or were necessarily in fraud or injury of the wife. Actually, analysis shows little difference between the views of many of those jurisconsults whose language, at first examination seems to be so in conflict. Azevedo, in an excellent discussion, was quick to see this.[34] But let us briefly examine some of these apparently diverse views. We find Matienzo, Gutiérrez, and many other jurisconsults to whom they refer, flatly expressing the view that the power of the husband to alienate property acquired during the marriage did not include any power to give it away. They considered that "alienation" necessarily meant for value and that the chief concern and duty of the husband in the administration of the marital community was in the acquisition of property and that the power of alienation was given as an incident thereof to further the husband in dealings and management which would increase the marital property.[35] Indeed, Matienzo succinctly points out that since a sale by the husband of property of great value for a small price is clearly in fraud of the wife's rights, an alienation of property for no consideration, that is, by way of gift, is even more so to be deemed fraudulent. It would be ridiculous, he added, to provide that the wife should have half of the property acquired during the marriage and at the same time allow

App. 2d 141, 42 P.2d 395 (dictum).

In Frymire v. Brown, 94 Cal. App. 2d 334, 210 P.2d 707, wife's transfers to her business agent were induced by latter's fraud and husband recovered from such agent.

[32] Cal. Civ. Code, § 5124; Odone v. Marzocchi (Cal.), supra.

[33] See ante, §§ 113, 119, 120.

[34] Azevedo, No. 7 et seq., to Nov. Rec. Law 5, Book 10, Title 4. And see post, this section.

[35] Matienzo, Gloss VI, No. 3 et seq.; Gutiérrez, Quaestio CXXI; both to Nov. Rec. Law 5.

the husband to give away such property.[36] Gutiérrez expressed the same view, remarking further that the laws relating to community of property would be easily evaded and that wives could be defrauded of their labors at the husband's will.[37] Nevertheless, after giving vent in the strongest language, to the upholding of his view, we find Matienzo concluding by announcing approvingly that there are generally accepted limitations; thus, that gifts might be made to daughters by way of dowry or support or other necessary reasons, or to a son, a mother, or other relatives where the motive is proper, as to relieve from poverty or to help them in financial difficulties.[38] Likewise, Gutiérrez declared that the view should be modified as being understood to apply to extravagant gifts and to those made without good cause, and not to moderate gifts with good cause, such as dowry to a child, or sustenance to a daughter, or moderate presents to kindred, friends and servants, or other similar things wherein fraud and squandering could not be supposed.[39] Thus, we see that the qualifications and modifications added to their strongly expressed views in reality bring them into conformity with those authors, such as Escriche, Febrero and Llamas y Molina, who proceed first to argue that the power of alienation includes unquestionably the power to give away the property acquired during marriage and who then qualified or modified this stand by adding that capricious gifts could not be made, or those which gave away too large a proportion of the community property although given without actual intent to defraud or injure the wife.[40] In other words, these jurisconsults whose points of depart-

[36] Matienzo, Gloss VI, No. 13, to Nov. Rec. Law 5.

One of the early commentators, Baldus, "says that if the statute provides that the husband can at his pleasure and without the wife's leave and consent sell and alienate property acquired during marriage, this must be understood to refer to the husband's own share of such property and not to the wife's. And if, says Baldus, that right does apply to the wife's share, the husband is not permitted to alienate by way of gift, since gift is a species of waste and is clearly not permitted to prejudice the wife." Matienzo, Gloss VI, No. 12, to Nov. Rec. Law 5.

[37] Gutiérrez, Quaestio CXXI, No. 2, to Nov. Rec. Law 5.

[38] Matienzo, Gloss VI, Nos. 14, 15, to Nov. Rec. Law 5.

[39] Gutiérrez, Quaestio CXXI, No. 4, to Nov. Rec. Law 5.

[40] See Llamas y Molina's Commentaries on the Laws of Toro, Laws 46 and 53. The latter law, continued in the Novísima Recopilación, Book 10, Title 3, Law 4, expressly provided that if the father alone endowed, or made a donation on account of marriage, to one of the children, payment might be made from the marital property.

"For that reason (i. e., that the administration is in the husband), the wife cannot give or convey said properties during the marriage, but the husband can without the consent of the wife make *inter vivos* conveyances moderately for just causes; but excessive or capricious gifts will be null, and the conveyances made with intent to defraud the wife, who will have action in all these cases against the properties of the husband and against the possessor of the thing conveyed." Escriche, Diccionario, "Ganancial Properties."

Some of these views are discussed

ure are from opposite poles reached what was in effect a common ground of agreement. Indeed, Gutiérrez, whose initial language would stamp him as strongly opposed to recognizing the right of the husband to make gifts has been considered, probably because of his concluding qualifications and modifications, as an exponent of a moderate view.[41]

Brief mention has already been made of the perception of Azevedo in respect to the apparently conflicting views. He remarks: "Can a husband give away goods acquired by way of profit during marriage, even to the extent of alienating and giving away the half-share of the wife? Antonius Gómez . . . says that the husband can do so, in the absence of fraud. . . . But the contrary view was held . . . by Palatius Rubeus . . . Matienzo, gloss 6, no. 6, attests this (latter view) as being the truer and more popular view. . . . I agree both with Antonius Gómez and his followers and also with Palatius and the others cited in the second view. They are not contrary. Antonius Gómez holds a view conformable to this law viz. that a gift of profits by a husband is valid, provided that the gift is not made with wrongful intent or in fraud of the wife. This is approved by the present law. Palatius Rubeus and his school who hold the second view say that such a gift is invalid on the ground that wrongful intent and fraud are presumed. And so where there is wrongful intent and fraud, Antonius Gómez agrees with them that the gift is invalid, while in the absence of fraud and wrongful intent, gifts and contracts made without consideration are valid. Thus they are not contrary to each other. And so I am amazed at all these very learned Doctors so anxiously creating contradictions of opinion where no contradiction exists. And so the point depends entirely on investigating whether such a gift is tainted with fraud or wrongful intent. If fraud and wrongful intent are present, all agree, that the gift is invalid; in the absence of fraud all agree that the gift is valid. . . . And so there is absolutely no difference between the learned Doctors above cited; on the contrary they are in harmony. . . . Thus we must say that a husband can from the multiplied goods make gifts in moderation and for good cause, e.g., he can dower a daughter of the marriage without his wife's consent, provide main-

by Professor Huie, one of the few American writers on community property to investigate the Spanish source material, in his article Community Property Laws as Applied to Life Insurance, 18 Tex. Law Rev. 121 et seq., and who quotes briefly from Febrero to the effect that the better rule was that "if the gift is small and made for just cause to relatives, servants or friends, it is valid; but if it is immoderate, or without legitimate cause for making it, or if it is such as would ruin the patrimony, or would reduce it considerably, to the contrary." Further as to Febrero, see post, this section.

[41] "It is also disputed among the authors, if in the power to convey is included that of giving or donating, Gómez with others taking the affirmative, and Matienzo with others taking the negative. Molina and Gutiérrez take a middle course, which appears to be the most correct, and is that the husband can make moderate donations, not excessive and without cause." Novísimo Sala Mexicano, Sec. 2a, Title IV, No. 5.

tenance for a daughter of the marriage, or make the customary moderate gift to kinsmen, friends and members of the household, and do similar things in which no presumption of fraud or prodigality can arise. But gifts which are excessive or are made for no legitimate reason or waste the common patrimony cannot be validly made; for such cases reek of fraud and wrongful intent, and prejudice the wife."[42]

It seems that a line must be drawn, however, between this approval of gifts of a moderate nature to relatives and the principle that the community property was not liable for obligations or debts of a spouse contracted before the marriage, under which some of the jurisconsults classed the act of supporting a child of a former marriage, or the giving of a dowry to a daughter of a former marriage, or the purchase of property for a son of a former marriage, or the like. To make payments from the community for such purposes as these was said to be imposing upon it obligations arising prior to the marriage.[43] Even here the objection seems to have rested on the belief that a continuous support or the gift of a dowry or property made too large a drain on the community property to the prejudice of the other spouse, for one of the jurisconsults qualified his stand in the matter of giving a dowry to a daughter of a former marriage by saying that if the dowry was small it was permissible, for small gifts might be made.[44] Thus, we only approach from another direction the conclusion that gifts of any kind had to be moderate and not too excessive so as to be disproportionate in value to the entire amount of the community property.

It appears that the view followed in Mexico was that the husband could make moderate donations, if not excessive and not without cause, especially if made to relatives.[45]

---

[42] Azevedo, Nos. 8–10, to Nov. Rec. Law 5.

"As regards whether or not he (the husband) may donate them (the common properties), there is a difference of opinion among the authors, and I, agreeing with what Azevedo affirms in Law 5, title 9, book 5, Recop. Nos. 9-18, reconciling the opinions, say that he can, provided the donation or gift be to kindred, or moderate, in such manner that in any event he does not defraud the wife to the extent of one-half, or more of the part which falls to her," etc. Febrero, Librería de Escribanos, Testamentos y Contratos I, Cap. I, § XXII, No. 245. (The remainder of this statement of Febrero, which is omitted here, consists of a somewhat amusing misogynistic railing at the expenses to which women put their husbands.)

[43] See Azevedo, Nos. 20-25; Gutiérrez, Quaestio CXXIX; to Nov. Rec. Law 9.

As to whether a child by a former marriage of one of the spouses or a mother or father of one of the spouses should be supported from the common property or the cost debited to that spouse whose was the child or parent, Matienzo held the former view; Gutiérrez the latter. Gutiérrez, Quaestio CXXIX, to Nov. Rec. Law 9; Matienzo, Gloss VII, No. 10, to Nov. Rec. Law 2.

Obligations and debts in general, see post, Chap. IX.

[44] See Azevedo, No. 24, to Nov. Rec. Law 9.

[45] See Novísimo Sala Mexicano, quoted ante, in a preceding note; Schmidt, Civil Law of Spain and Mexico, p. 14.

But while the Spanish community property law placed in the hands of the husband the management of the property acquired during the marriage, with the power to dispose of it without the consent or conveyance of the wife, an important fact which seems little known, if known at all by most, and deserves to be borne in mind, is that under the Spanish law the wife could, from the common property, make gifts for the support of a needy person or for pious objects without leave of the husband.[46] This, however, did not give her the right to alienate property without the husband's consent and was confined to gifts of money in limited amounts.[47]

§ 122. — American views.

In our community property states, the question has also arisen and will continue to arise as to whether and to what extent the husband can make gifts of the community property where the wife has not consented, although to a more limited extent, since as we have seen in many of our states the wife must join with the husband in conveyances or encumbrances of the community realty,[48] and in California she must join in transfers and encumbrances as to household furniture, and furnishings and family clothing.[49] But even in most of those states the husband retains the absolute power of disposition of the community personalty, and in some few other states he has that power both as to the realty and personalty. To what extent, in respect to such community property, can he make gifts thereof? In California, although the husband has power to dispose of much of the community personalty, the statute attaches the provision that he can not make a gift of such property without the written consent of the wife.[50] If he does so the wife may set it aside in its entirety during the lifetime of her husband, and after his death may set it aside as to one-half thereof.[51] In Washington, even in the absence of any express statutory limitation, the courts follow the view that the husband has no power to give away community property even to a relative without

[46] Matienzo, Gloss VI, Nos. 8, 12 to Nov. Rec. Law 5.

[47] See Azevedo, No. 11 to Nov. Rec. Law 5.

[48] See ante, §§ 113, 117.

[49] See ante, §§ 115.1, 116, 117.

[50] Cal. Civ. Code, § 5125 (providing that he cannot dispose of it except for valuable consideration without the wife's written consent).

And see Schwartz, Gifts of Community Property: Need for Wife's Consent, 11 UCLA Law Rev. 26.

Prior to statute, the earliest cases favored the view that the husband might make gifts not unreasonably out of proportion to the entire amount of the community property if not made with any intent to defeat the wife's claims. See Smith v. Smith, 12 Cal. 216, 73 Am. Dec. 533; Lord v. Hough, 43 Cal. 581. Compare Peck v. Brummagim, 31 Cal. 440, 81 Am. Dec. 195; De Godey v. De Godey, 39 Cal. 157, to the effect that the gifts must not be with intent to defeat the claims of the wife.

[51] See Ballinger v. Ballinger, 9 Cal. 2d 330, 70 P.2d 629, and cases cited.

Whom she may sue, see post, § 126.

the wife's consent, except as to the veriest trifles, and this without regard to the neediness of the recipient or the fact that the amount attempted to be given is not unreasonably disproportionate to the entire amount of the community property.[52] The entire gift is invalid and may be set aside by the wife in its entirety even after the death of the husband.[53] Indeed, the right of the wife to retake and dispose of community personalty given by the husband to his mistress has been recognized.[54]

In others of the community property states, however, the principles of the Spanish and Mexican community property law have been followed in allowing moderate gifts of the community property where there is no intent to injure or defraud the wife and the amounts of the gifts are not unreasonable in any way so as to be in prejudice of her rights. Among this group may be listed Arizona,[55] Nevada,[56] and

[52] Marston v. Rue, 92 Wash. 129, 159 P. 111, an unusual case; Munson v. Haye, 29 Wash. 2d 733, 189 P.2d 464; Hamlin v. Merlino (Wash.), 272 P.2d 125; Occidental Life Ins. Co. v. Powers, 192 Wash. 475, 74 P.2d 27, 114 A. L. R. 531, where the recipient of the attempted gift was the indigent mother of the husband to whom he owed a statutory duty of support. There was a strong dissent, however, by four justices who argued as to the need of the mother and that the amount was reasonable when viewed in relation to the whole value of the community property. The Washington court would seem to find some support, however, in remarks of Gutiérrez, in Quaestio CXXIX, No. 1, to Nov. Rec. Law 9, Book 10, Title 4. On the other hand, compare the Spanish law that the wife was required to support her mother and the view of Matienzo that she could not escape her responsibility by saying she had no means to do so, for she had her half of the community property which was liable therefor. See Matienzo, Gloss VII, No. 10, to Nov. Rec. Law 2, Book 10, Title 4.

To the effect that the wife may be estopped from asserting the invalidity of the husband's gift of community property, see Yiatchos v. Yiatchos, 376 U. S. 306, 84 S. Ct. 742.

However, it was not considered a gift where the husband formed a partnership with his son, contributing community property to the partnership in which he gave the son a one-half interest in consideration of the son's contribution of labor to the partnership. See Fields v. Andrus, 20 Wash. 2d 452, 148 P.2d 313.

[53] Occidental Life Ins. Co. v. Powers, 192 Wash. 475, 74 P.2d 27, 114 A. L. R. 531.

Consent of the wife to the husband's giving away community personalty to children of the marriage cannot be implied where she had no knowledge of his acts. In re McCoy's Estate, 189 Wash. 103, 63 P.2d 522.

[54] Marston v. Rue, 92 Wash. 192, 159 P. 111.

[55] See Gristy v. Hudgens, 23 Ariz. 339, 203 P. 569.

[56] Nixon v. Brown, 46 Nev. 439, 214 P. 524.

"The systems are not exactly alike, as the statutes differ in several respects in the various states, the state of Nevada adopting the law almost as it was administered in Mexico, known as the Spanish-Mexican civil law, and as it was administered in California under the early statutes. These statutes have been judicially construed in California with reference to the question under consideration [husband's gift of community property without wife's consent], and it is therefore to those early California cases and the

Texas,[57] although as to Texas it must be noticed that the statutory enactments of 1967 have now limited this power.[58] Louisiana may be listed with the foregoing states, for although the matter is governed by statute in that state, the statute is somewhat broad in its terms and in the construction of it the Louisiana courts seem to have arrived at a result similar to the principles of the Spanish community property law followed in most of our states. The statute provides that the husband "can make no conveyance *inter vivos,* by a gratuitous title, of the immovables of the community, nor of the whole, or of a quota of the movables, unless it be for the establishment of the children of the marriage. A gratuitous title within the contemplation of this article embraces all titles wherein there is no direct, material advantages to the donor. Nevertheless he may dispose of the movable effects by a gratuitous and particular title, to the benefit of all persons. But if it should be proved that the husband has sold the common property, or otherwise disposed of the same by fraud, to injure his wife, she may have her action against the heirs of her husband, in support of her claim in one-half of the property, on her satisfactory proving the fraud."[59] Under that statute, a husband has been allowed to use community funds of a second marriage to maintain an adult daughter who was issue of his first marriage.[60] But, of course, in the foregoing jurisdictions, if the gift is designedly intended to defraud the wife or if it constitutes an unreasonably large proportion of the community property the wife may either void the whole gift or that much of it that represents her half, dependent upon the view of the

original law we must look for a solution, rather than to those of Washington, Arizona, Idaho, and Texas, because the statutes are in many respects different, and because the question has never been directly passed on by the Supreme Court of this State." Nixon v. Brown, ante.

[57] See Stramler v. Coe, 15 Tex. 211 (dictum); Moody v. Smoot, 78 Tex. 119, 14 S. W. 285; Davis v. Prudential Ins. Co., 331 F.2d 346. And see cases cited post, § 123.

[58] See Tex. Family Code 1969, § 5.22. having effect of giving wife exclusive power to make gifts of her special community and requiring her joinder in gifts of commingled community.

[59] La. Civ. Code, art. 2404. See also Oliphint v. Oliphint, 219 La. 781, 54 So. 2d 18, holding "quota" is synonymous with fraction or percentage and does not refer to specific movables.

Good discussion of Louisiana Law, see note, 22 Tulane L. Rev. 650.

Compare interpretation of conveyance to religious society as not being one by gratuitous title, Thompson v. Société Catholique, 157 La. 875, 103 So. 247.

"This limitation on the right of the husband, as head and master of the community, to do as he pleased with the effects of the community, was first introduced into our law by the Code of 1825 and is taken verbatim from the Code of Napoleon, art. 1422." Snowden v. Cruse, 152 La. 144, 92 So. 764. The statement of the court is not entirely accurate, for the same limitation must have existed under the Spanish law in force in Louisiana.

[60] Succession of Boyer, 36 La. Ann. 506.

particular jurisdiction, and that regardless of the fact that it has been made to relatives of the husband.[61]

It should be unnecessary to dwell at length upon the fact that the wife by her consent may sanction the gifts by the husband, provided, of course, that her consent is not obtained by wrongful means.[62]

§ 123.   — Insurance policies.

What is the result as concerns the wife where the husband takes out insurance on his own life, names some third person as beneficiary and pays the premiums with community funds?[63] In California the view seems to be that naming a third person as beneficiary in such circumstances amounts to a gift of the community property which the husband by virtue of statute cannot make without the wife's consent. Such gifts are not void, however, but merely voidable as to the wife's half; she can assail such gifts after the husband's death and recover one-half of the proceeds of the policy as community property. This has been true even in situations where the beneficiary has been a relative, even a dependent relative, of the husband.[64] However, this recovery can be sought from the insurer only if it has been properly notified of the claim. Until it receives such notice it is justified in making payment to the named beneficiary.[65] Recovery can always be sought from the beneficiary, of course, after the proceeds have been received by the beneficiary, unless some bar arises as to this.[66]

Virtually the same view has been taken in Washington, except that the wife can set aside this gift in its entirety even after dissolution of the marriage.[67]

---

[61] See cases cited in this section and in §§ 117, 123, 126.

Effect of divorce proceedings as suspending husband's power of alienation, see post, § 225.

[62] Consent obtained by fraud or mistake may be nullified under usual equitable principles. See, e. g., Field v. Bank of America, 100 Cal. App. 2d 311, 223 P.2d 514.

[63] For excellent discussion, see Huie, Community Property Laws as Applied to Life Insurance, 18 Tex. Law Rev. 121. See also 114 A. L. R. 545.

Rights of creditors, see post, § 171.

Generally as to life insurance policies and their proceeds as community or separate property, see ante, § 79.

[64] Beemer v. Roher, 137 Cal. App. 293, 30 P.2d 547 (brother of insured as beneficiary); Modern Woodmen v.

Gray, 113 Cal. App. 729, 299 P. 754 (children of insured as beneficiaries); New York Life Ins. Co. v. Bank of Italy, 60 Cal. App. 602, 214 P. 61 (brother of insured as beneficiary, after several changes).

But where husband named as beneficiary a sister who had lent him money, it was said not to come under the head of a gift. Union Mut. Life Ins. Co. v. Broderick, 196 Cal. 497, 238 P. 1034.

[65] Cal. Ins. Code, § 10172; Cal. Civ. Code, § 5105. See Blethen v. Pacific Mut. Life Ins. Co., 198 Cal. 91, 243 P. 431.

[66] Dismissal of action, see Blethen case, supra; consent to change of beneficiary, see Ettlinger v. Conn. Gen. L. Ins. Co., 175 F.2d 870.

[67] Occidental Life Ins. Co. v. Powers, 192 Wash. 475, 74 P.2d 27,

Unlike the foregoing view, in states such as Texas, which recognize the right of the husband to make moderate gifts or donations from the community property, not excessive and not in fraud or injury to the wife's rights, it appears that a husband may, during marriage, insure his life in favor of his parents or of children by a former marriage, and pay the premiums with community funds, and that so long as he is fulfilling a duty, even though it be only a moral one, to provide for such relatives, and so long as the community funds so expended are not unreasonably out of proportion to the other community assets remaining, there is no fraud upon the wife and she cannot recover any of the premiums so paid or any of the proceeds of such policies for the benefit of the community.[68] But if the course of conduct of the insured husband clearly shows a course of action designed to defraud the wife, the latter can recover the proceeds of a policy made payable to a relative of the husband.[69] We may compare with such a view that of the Washington court already referred to that even a statutory duty upon a husband to care for an indigent mother does not warrant his right to charge such liability against the community, although the amount so expended was not disproportionate or unreasonable as compared with the total amount of the community property.[70]

In Louisiana, apparently the provisions of the statute quoted in the preceding section have not been applied in any way so as to

114 A. L. R. 531 (indigent mother of insured, upon whom statute imposed a duty of support, as beneficiary). And see In re Towey's Estate, 22 Wash. 2d 212, 155 P.2d 273, noted in 20 Wash. L. Rev. 167.

[68] Jones v. Jones (Tex. Civ. App.), 146 S. W. 265; Rowlett v. Mitchell, 52 Tex. Civ. App. 589, 114 S. W. 845. And see The Community Life Insurance Policy, 18 Baylor L. Rev. 627; Huie, Texas Marital Property Rights, p. 246 et seq.

Nor where the wife predeceased the husband could her sole heir recover half of the proceeds of a policy made payable to the husband's sisters. Nor was the community estate entitled to reimbursement for the community funds used in paying the premiums. Volunteer State Life Ins. Co. v. Hardin, 145 Tex. 245, 197 S. W. 2d 105, 168 A. L. R. 337, noted 25 Tex. Law Rev. 676, continuing to follow the rule stated in the text and distinguishing Womack v. Womack, 141 Tex. 299, 172 S. W.

2d 307.

[69] Kemp v. Mut. L. Ins. Co. (5 C. A.), 205 F.2d 857, quoting 1 de Funiak, § 123; Moore v. California-Western States Life Ins. Co. (Tex. Civ. App.), 67 S. W. 2d 932 (husband's mother as beneficiary).

In Gristy v. Hudgens, 23 Ariz. 339, 203 P. 569, wherein the husband named as beneficiary of a mutual benefit certificate one who was not a member of his family or in any way related to him, there was apparently a lack of evidence as to payment of the premiums from community funds, but the court declared that even if premiums were so paid from community funds there was no showing that such funds were paid in fraud of the wife's rights and no showing that she had not received her share of the community.

[70] Occidental Life Ins. Co. v. Powers, 192 Wash. 475, 74 P.2d 27, 114 A. L. R. 531.

restrict the husband in using community funds to pay premiums on insurance on his life in favor of third persons.[71] So, in a situation where the husband, during marriage, insured his own life and named his mother as beneficiary, his surviving wife was denied the right to claim the proceeds as community property. While it is not actually stated in the case that community funds were used to pay the premiums on the policy, that fact was presumably the basis of the wife's claim that the proceeds were community, and indeed she claimed that taking out the policy for the benefit of the mother amounted to a donation to her. The court argued that under the Louisiana law a man had a right to take out a policy of insurance on his life in favor of any one he wished, that it was not a donation either *inter vivos* or *mortis causa,* that the fact that he had reserved the right to change the beneficiary resulted in the beneficiary acquiring no vested right until the insured's death, and that the proceeds of a life insurance policy form no part of the estate of the insured at his death. Unless there are facts not shown on its face, the case represents the situation that in Louisiana a husband can insure his life in favor of another, at the expense of the community, without having to make any accounting therefor, and without regard to how the amount of community funds spent on premiums compares with the total amount of the community property.[72]

Where the husband has insured his own life in favor of his wife but, having reserved the right to do so, changes the beneficiary and makes some third person, such as a relative, the new beneficiary, it will be found that the courts of the various jurisdictions in the main follow the same principles that they apply when such third person has originally been named the beneficiary.[73]

To the contention frequently made by the beneficiary that the wife's right of recovery should be measured by the amount of the community funds used to pay the premiums and not by the proceeds of the policy, the courts have usually rejected that contention[74] and held either that the entire proceeds of the policy should be restored

[71] Criticism, see Nabors, Civil Law Influences Upon Law of Insurance in Louisiana, 6 Tulane Law Rev. 515.

[72] Pearce v. National Life & Accident Ins. Co., 12 La. App. 608, 125 So. 776, relying heavily upon Sherwood v. New York Life Ins. Co., 166 La. 829, 118 So. 35.

[73] See cases cited ante; see also cases cited, 114 A. L. R. 555; 168 A. L. R. 342.

[74] "Neither can it be said that the wife should be restricted to her interest in the premiums paid for the policies, because she has as much interest in the profits made by the husband's trades as she has in the consideration paid. She is required to share the losses he makes [sic], and as part compensation is given the right to participate in the gains." Martin v. Moran, 11 Tex. Civ. App. 509, 32 S. W. 904.

Discussion of whether there should be a distinction between policies in which the insured husband reserves right to change beneficiary and those in which he does not, see Huie, Community Property Laws as Applied to Life Insurance, 18 Tex. Law Rev. 121.

to the community[75] or that the wife should recover one-half of the proceeds as her share of the community, the beneficiary keeping the rest.[76]

An insurance situation differing from those already referred to is that wherein two business partners are married men and have made contributions to the partnership from the marital community of each. They contract that each shall insure his own life in favor of his own wife or heirs, that the premiums on both policies shall be paid by the partnership, and that upon the death of one partner the surviving partner shall receive the deceased partner's interest in the partnership business. Does the wife of the deceased partner have the right, despite this contract, to claim a portion of the partnership assets as community property of herself and her deceased husband? The Arizona court, in denying the right of the widow to an accounting of the partnership assets in such a situation, instanced the right of the husband to dispose of the community personalty with the exception that he cannot make a testamentary disposition of the wife's interest or dispose of it in fraud of her rights and declared that the present situation did not come within either of the exceptions, that the contract with the other partner was made in good faith and with no intent to defraud the wife and did not prejudice her rights in any way. It is to be noticed, however, that the amount of the policy proceeds was virtually the equivalent of the partnership interest of the deceased partner.[77]

We have been considering primarily the situation of the husband as manager of the community who pays premiums on a life insurance policy with community funds and names some third person as a beneficiary. Cases are naturally much less frequent in which the wife insures her own life, pays premiums with community funds and names some third person as a beneficiary. In at least one California case, the husband was able to recover one half the proceeds of the policy after the wife's death[78] but in two others the husband was considered to have relinquished his interest in the wife's earnings with which she paid the premiums as well as having relinquished his interest in the policies and their proceeds.[79]

Some attention must be called, of course, to the matter of National Service Life Insurance policies and the effect of the amazing decision by the United States Supreme Court in the Wissner case. On the basis of the well-established principles in the California law that the wife has a vested one-half interest in the proceeds of a policy paid for with

---

[75] As in Washington.

[76] As in California.

[77] Coe v. Winchester, 43 Ariz. 500, 33 P.2d 286.

Partnership interest of partner who is married as community property, see ante, § 80.

[78] Estate of Rouse, 149 Cal. App. 2d 674, 309 P.2d 34. See Shields v. Barton, 60 F.2d 351, under Washington law.

[79] Pac. Mut. L. Ins. Co. v. Cleverdon, 16 Cal. 2d 788, 108 P.2d 405; O'Connor v. Travelers Ins. Co., 169 Cal. App. 2d 763, 307 P.2d 893.

community funds and can recover that amount from a beneficiary who has not paid consideration for being named and where the wife has not consented to such naming, a California court held that a wife could recover one-half from a beneficiary of a National Service Life Insurance policy *after* receipt of the proceeds by such beneficiary, on the basis that to deprive her of such vested right would be in violation of the 5th and 14th amendments of the Federal Constitution.[80] However, in a decision which has been subjected to frequent and bitter criticism,[81] the United States Supreme Court reversed the California court,[82] on the ground that the federal statute authorizes the insured to designate the beneficiary and provides that no one else shall have a vested right in the proceeds. It was considered the federal law must be paramount to the state law; just how the vested property rights given by the state law can be ignored was not adequately explained.[83] The state courts have been trying to live with this decision ever since.[84] It is the hope of the authors and of many others that the Supreme Court decisions with respect to United States savings bonds can be adapted to modify its decision in the Wissner case.[85]

§ 124. Prosecution of civil actions.

Under most community property systems, the husband, as the one empowered to manage and control the community property, is the proper person to prosecute actions on behalf of or in protection and preservation of the marital community. In doing so, he is the representative of the wife and appears on her behalf as well as his own.[86] This was true under the Spanish community property system[87] and

[80] Wissner v. Wissner, 89 Cal. App. 2d 759, 201 P.2d 837.

[81] See, e. g., Harvey L. Davis, The Case of the Missing Community Property, 85 S. W. L. Jour. 1.

[82] Wissner v. Wissner, 338 U. S. 655, 70 S. Ct. 398, 14 L. Ed. 424.

[83] A minority opinion contended that Congress did not intend to sanction the taking of the wife's property by what would amount to lack of due process of law.

[84] See successful effort in Estate of Allie, 50 Cal. 2d 794, 329 P.2d 903.

[85] See Yiatchos v. Yiatchos, 376 U. S. 306, 84 S. Ct. 742; Free v. Bland, 369 U. S. 663, 82 S. Ct. 1089, 8 L. Ed. 2d 180.

[86] "The relation of husband and wife toward the community property is that of a partnership. The business of the firm is transacted in the name of the husband, and he prosecutes and defends its suits with the same effect as if his partner were named in the case. Judgments in such suits bind both partners, or accrue to their joint benefit if in their favor. . . . In fact, the wife is as much a party as if the record recited that the husband instituted or defended the suit for the use and benefit of himself and wife. Having all the attributes of a partner, she must be treated as such, and must be excluded from testifying whenever her husband and partner could not be admitted to the witness stand." Simpson v. Brotherton, 62 Tex. 170, 3 Tex. Law Rep. 240.

Execution of appeal bond by husband, see Fisher v. Hagstrom, 35 Wash. 2d 662, 214 P.2d 654.

[87] Schmidt, Civil Law of Spain and Mexico, p. 11.

for the most part is true of the United States today.[88] In Washington, both spouses must join in the action if it concerns community realty, otherwise the husband is the only necessary party.[89] Under the Texas management statutes the wife would have exclusive right to sue for her special community property, the husband for his special community property, and both spouses would have to join in a suit for commingled community property.[90]

Just as the husband is the one who usually sues on behalf of the community, so where actions are brought by others in regard to community property or transactions on behalf of the marital community, the husband usually should be named defendant. Whether, or in what situations, the wife should also be joined as a defendant or even sued alone is discussed in a subsequent chapter.[91]

It must be most definitely and clearly understood that the prosecution of the action by the husband is not on the basis of his being sole owner of the right of action, for he owns only a moiety of it, but on the basis of the fact that he has the administrative duty of managing the community property and is performing a managerial function. The fact that he brings the action in his name alone or that the judgment is in his favor alone in no way lessens the fact that the wife owns half of the recovery as completely as does the husband. Common-law concepts as to title which give primary importance to the question of in whose name title is, should not becloud one's understanding that ownership and not merely title is the important consideration in marital community of property. The provision of the Spanish community property law that everything that the husband and wife gain during marriage "let them both have it by halves," and regardless of which one gained it, is the very basis of our community property system and is true today as it was a hundred years ago.[92]

In some of the states provision has been made for the wife to prosecute or defend actions at law for the preservation and protection of her rights and property as if unmarried,[93] or concerning her right

---

[88] See, e. g., Coker v. Harper, 8 La. App. 402.

[89] See Erhardt v. Havens (Wash.), 330 P.2d 1010; Hansen v. Hansen, 110 Wash. 276, 188 P. 460; Gustin v. Crockett, 44 Wash. 536, 87 P. 839. See also Howell v. Harris (La. App.), 18 So.2d 668.

[90] See Tex. Family Code 1969, §§ 5.22, 4.03.

[91] See Chap. IX.

[92] See Simpson v. Brotherton, 62 Tex. 170, 3 Tex. Law Rep. 240; and ante, Chap. VI.

[93] Cal. Code of Civ. Proc., § 370; Wash. Rev. Code 1961, § 26.16.130;

Royer v. Carter, 37 Cal. 2d 544, 233 P.2d 539.

Where husband and wife sued to recover for labor and materials furnished to defendants while the plaintiffs were conducting a business owned by them and managed by the wife with the full knowledge and consent of the husband, and to foreclose a lien filed in the wife's name, the wife was entitled to foreclose such lien if the allegation was established that she was the manager of the business with the consent and approval of her husband. Neill v. Bennett, 34 Wash. 2d 128, 208 P.2d 137. In another case to recover for

and claim to the homestead property,[94] or, especially where the power of managing and controlling her own earnings is given her, to maintain an action therefor in her own name,[95] or to bring actions in her own name for personal injuries, libel, slander, and malicious prosecution,[96] or to bring actions where the husband is mentally incompetent or has abandoned her, and so on.[97] In other states she may sue or be sued alone only when she is living separate and apart from her husband.[98] In the Spanish law, although the wife retained control of and administered her separate property, if she so desired, it was provided, similarly to the case of her contracts,[99] that she might not appear in a suit without the permission of her husband. This was a formality, however, for the judge with cognizance of the cause could compel the husband to give this permission or else grant the wife the necessary permission if the husband refused or failed to do so.[1] And if she proceeded to sue without the husband's consent, nevertheless the judgement obtained was a valid and subsistent one.[2] Even where the formality of the husband's permission was requisite, such formality pertained only to suits of a contractual nature, and not to suits for injury to her property, for the wife did not need the husband's consent to sue in a delictual proceeding.[3]

It is not purposed to refer other than briefly to the effect of joining the wife as a party plaintiff in an action which the husband as managing partner or agent of the marital partnership should prosecute. Despite the view of some few of the older cases that such joinder was demurrable, it is difficult to see how such joinder can in any way be prejudicial to the defendant and the most sensible thing is to consider it as mere surplusage.[4] Certainly the more modern cases consider the wife a proper party but not a necessary or indispensable party.[5] The

labor and materials furnished by a business owned by the spouses and managed by the wife, the wife was said not to be a necessary party plaintiff. Golmis v. Vlachos, 34 Wash. 2d 627, 208 P.2d 1204.

[94] Cal. Code of Civ. Proc., § 370.

[95] Cal. Code of Civ. Proc., § 370; Wash. Rev. Code 1961, § 26.16.130.

[96] See post, § 125.

[97] See post, § 128.

[98] Nev. Rev. St. 1956, § 123.120.

[99] See ante, § 112.

[1] Asso and Mañuel, Institutes of the Civil Law of Spain, Book III, Title III, Cap. 1, citing Novísima Recopilación, Book 10, Title 1, Laws 12 and 13; Febrero, Novísimo, No. 27.

A similar provision of the La. Civ. Code, art. 124, has been designated a useless formality which may be dispensed with. Ring v. Schilkoffsky, 158 La. 361, 104 So. 115. In any event, Louisiana Acts 1928, No. 283, has had the effect of repealing art. 124.

[2] Llamas y Molina, No. 16, to Law 55 of Leyes de Toro.

[3] See ante, § 81.

[4] See Brown v. Penn, 1 McGloin (La.) 265; Mahlstrom v. People's Drain Ditch Co., 32 Nev. 246, 107 P. 98.

Dismissal of wife on timely exception, see Gentry v. McCarty (Tex. Civ. App.), 141 S. W. 152.

[5] See, e. g., Shreeve v. Greer, 65 Ariz. 35, 173 P.2d 641; Erhardt v. Havens, Inc. (Wash.), 330 P.2d 1010.

same should be true where the husband is joined as a party plaintiff in an action brought by the wife under some statutory authorization, such as that to maintain an action to recover her own earnings.[6]

Where one spouse fails to join in or consent to the contract to sell or encumber the community realty, the contract purchaser cannot compel specific performance of the contract,[7] even as to the share owned by the spouse who did contract with him,[8] although the latter may, of course, be liable in damages.[9] Nor can the non-consenting spouse, by some change of mind, now join with the other spouse in seeking to compel a specific performance against the contracting third person, for there is a lack of mutuality of obligation between the contracting parties.[10] Such lack can be fatal under equitable principles.[11]

§ 125.   — Wrongs to the person or reputation of the wife.

Since the husband is the one to bring actions on behalf of the marital community, in those community property states which consider the wife's right of action for injuries to her person or reputation and the damages recovered therefor as community property, the husband is the necessary party plaintiff to bring the action to recover for the injuries to the wife, just as he is the necessary party plaintiff to sue for the damages for expenses or losses imposed upon the marital community by such injury. These states allow the wife to be joined as a proper party plaintiff.[12] Where the spouses have joined in filing the action and the husband dies while the action is pending and the wife is executrix or administratrix of his estate, she is properly sub-

---

[6] See Garver v. Thoman, 15 Ariz. 38, 135 P. 724.

[7] See, e. g., Wilson v. Bidwell, 88 Cal. App. 2d 832, 199 P.2d 439; Ellwood v. Wiedermeyer, 12 Cal. App. 2d 699, 56 P.2d 279.

[8] See, e. g., Waldeck v. Hedden, 89 Cal. App. 485, 265 P. 340.

Of course, if spouses own realty in joint tenancy, a spouse's contract would be enforceable as to such spouse's share, since the interest of each spouse is separate property of that spouse. Anderson v. Brady, 151 Cal. App. 2d 579, 312 P.2d 35.

[9] Wilson v. Bidwell (Cal.), supra.

[10] Thomas v. Stevens, 69 Ida. 100, 203 P.2d 597.

[11] See de Funiak, Handbook of Modern Equity, 2nd Ed., chap. 11.

[12] See Labonte v. Davidson, 31 Idaho 644, 175 P. 588; Erhardt v. Havens, Inc. (Wash.), 330 P. 2d 1010; Magnuson v. O'Dea, 75 Wash. 574, 135 P. 640, Ann. Cas. 1915 B 1230, 48 L. R. A. (N. S.) 327; Schneider v. Biberger, 76 Wash. 504, 136 P. 701, 6 A. L. R. 1056; Ostheller v. Spokane & I. E. R. Co., 107 Wash. 678, 182 P. 630. In the Ostheller Case it was declared, apparently as dictum, that the wife need not be joined. Apparently, if the husband in the exercise of his honest judgment and without wilfully intending abandonment, waste or dissipation of community property refuses to institute the action the wife cannot do so, even though joining the husband as a party defendant. Hynes v. Colman, 108 Wash. 942, 185 P. 617.

This rule obtained in Texas prior to 1967 statutory changes. See Ellis v. City of San Antonio (Tex. Civ. App.) 341 S. W. 2d 508, w/e ref'd, n.r.e.

stituted as party plaintiff for the deceased husband.[13] Of course, where the wife is injured while living separate and apart from the husband, those states recognize that the cause of actions is her separate property and that she is the necessary party plaintiff.[14]

In those community property states which recognize an injury to the person or reputation of the wife,[15] we have the following situations. The husband is the necessary party plaintiff to bring the action to recover for the expenses or losses to the marital community from such injury,[16] although it would be perfectly proper to join the wife in the action for such damages alone.[17] Indeed, there is recognition in some states that the husband can authorize the wife as his agent to bring such action, whereupon she would be the only necessary party.[18]

Where the action is to recover for the wife's pain and suffering, the invasion of her right of personal security, she is the necessary party plaintiff.[19] The husband would not be a proper party where this is the only purpose of the action and his joinder should be dismissed as surplusage and without prejudice to the wife.[20] Since the two causes of action are based on the same occurrence, it is perfectly proper for both spouses to join as parties plaintiff, the husband asking for the damages to repair the losses to the community and the wife asking for the damages to which she is entitled, and the damages must then be segregated.[21] In this matter of joinder, notice that though the contributory negligence of the husband might defeat his right to recover for the community,[22] such contributory negligence is not applicable to defeat the wife's separate property action.[23]

---

[13] Fox Tucson Theatres Corp. v. Lindsay, 47 Ariz. 388, 56 P.2d 183.

Similarly, under former but now revised California view, see Gomez v. Scanlan, 2 Cal. App. 579, 84 P. 50.

Formerly in Texas, see Fordyce v. Dixon, 70 Tex. 694, 8 S. W. 504.

[14] Lorang v. Hays, 69 Ida. 440, 209 P.2d 733; Good v. Martinis (Wash.), 361 P.2d 941. See also Christiana v. Rose, 100 Cal. App. 2d 46, 222 P.2d 891.

[15] See ante, § 82.

[16] See ante, § 124. And see Soto v. Vandeventer, 56 N.M. 483, 245 P.2d 826, 35 A. L. R. 2d 1190, and other cases, infra.

[17] See ante, § 124.

[18] See La. Code Civ. Proc., art. 695 (enacted 1961).

In California, under the view that all the recovery was community property, husband could delegate to wife authority to sue for the damages to the marital community, the so-called "consequential damages." Louie v. Hagstrom's Food Stores, Inc., 81 Cal. App. 2d 601, 184 P.2d 708.

[19] See Cal. Civ. Code, § 5109; Cal. Code Civ. Proc., § 370; La. Civ. Code, arts. 2334, 2402; Sanders v. P. & S. Ins. Co. (La.), 125 So.2d 24; Frederickson & Watson Const. Co. v. Boyd, 60 Nev. 117, 102 P.2d 627; Soto v. Vandeventer, 56 N.M. 483, 245 P.2d 826, 35 A. L. R. 2d 1190, Tex. Family Code 1969, §§ 5.01, 4.03.

[20] Especially if he has been contributorily negligent, it would seem wise to remove him.

[21] Nev. Rev. St. 1956, § 41.170; Meagher v. Garvin (Nev.), 391 P.2d 507. And see Cal. Code Civ. Proc., § 427, subd. 9.

[22] See ante, § 83.

[23] See, e. g., Vitale, Checker Cab Co., 166 La. 527, 117 So. 579, 59 A. L. R. 148. And see ante, § 83.

Where the husband and wife may join their claims, as mentioned, they may also join them in the federal courts in the same jurisdictions,[24] but the respective amounts of their claims may not be added together in order to create the federal jurisdictional amount.[25]

In the Spanish law, as we have seen, the injury to the person or property of a wife was considered an injury to her, for which she could bring action without the necessity of any consent by the husband.[26] And if her action was against the husband as defendant or as one of the defendants, no such assent or permission was necessary.[27]

§ 126.   — Transfers and the like in fraud or injury of other spouse.

Although it is usually incumbent upon the husband to prosecute actions in preservation and protection of the community property, where he has made alienations in fraud or injury of the wife it is readily apparent that he will usually fail or refuse to seek to avoid the consequences of his own acts voluntarily committed. Thus, it becomes necessary for the wife to take or to be able to take the necessary steps to ensure the protection of her interest in the community property so alienated. Similarly, where the wife is managing any part of the community property, it may become necessary for the husband to protect his interest in the community property.[28]

Whether alienation or disposition of community property in fraud of the wife's rights is void or voidable depends upon the provisions of the statute. Under the Spanish codes it was termed invalid,[29] by which it appears that it was voidable at the suit of the wife or her heirs. The wife had a right of action in all such cases against the properties of the husband and against the possessor of the things transferred.[30] However, if the property alienated were fungibles or intangibles, her first recourse was apparently to seek reimbursement from the husband's estate or from his heirs, because it was considered that the husband had alienated his own property and not hers, for lack of power to do so. In other words, it was her share which remained. If resort to the husband's estate was unavailing, as by reason of his being poor, the wife might demand the property from the person possessing it. In the case of things other than fungibles or intangibles, she could make demand of possessor without first resorting to the husband's estate.[31]

---

[24] Hollinquest v. Kansas City Sou. Ry. Co., 86 F. Supp. 905 (in Louisiana).

[25] Muse v. U. S. Cas. Co., 306 F.2d 30. And see Cyc. Fed. Proc., 3rd Ed., § 2.220.

[26] See ante, § 81.

[27] See post, § 151.

[28] Cases in this area are much less frequent, naturally. See end of this section.

[29] See ante, § 113.

As void under the code of Puerto Rico, see Garrozi v. Dastas, 204 U. S. 64, 51 L. Ed. 369, 27 Sup. Ct. 224.

[30] Escriche, Diccionario, Vol. 2, "Ganancial Properties." See also Stramler v. Coe, 15 Tex. 211.

Actions against the husband himself, see post, § 151.

[31] See Febrero, Librería de Escribanos, Testamentos y Contratos I, Cap. I, § XXII, No. 246.

Such actions by the wife, or by her heirs, were usually brought at the time of the partition and division of the community property upon dissolution of the marital community,[32] although there was no question as to the right of the wife to take legal steps during the marriage.[33] Indeed, it was provided that prescription of causes (i.e., limitation of actions) ran against her when she knew that her husband was dissipating her property and yet remained silent.[34] It is also to be noticed that where the wife had placed any of her separate property in the husband's hands to manage for her and he sold it without her consent, she had her action or remedy against the purchaser or to take its value from the community property.[35]

In some of our community property states, such as California, Texas and Washington, the statutes giving the wife a right to sue in her own name in protection or preservation of her own rights should naturally allow the wife to proceed against the alienee.[36] The institu-

---

[32] See Matienzo, Gloss III, Nos. 21–25, to Nov. Rec. Law 1, Book 10, Title 4, in relation to the wife being entitled to all "possessory interdicts" in respect of her half of the property for the purpose of acquiring, retaining or recovering possession.

[33] Thus, in Chavez v. McKnight, 1 N.M. 147, under the Spanish civil law in force, the right of the wife was unquestioned to enjoin a sale on execution of her husband's separate property and of community property by a creditor of the husband where she had a superior lien on the husband's property to protect her dotal property under his management and which he had improvidently managed. See also Stramler v. Coe, 15 Tex. 211. "But if it be proven that the alienation is made with fraudulent intent to damage the wife, her interest in them will continue, since she has a right of action to demand her half, upon proof of the fraud practiced by the husband." Alvarez, Institutes of Royal Law of Spain, 2nd Ed., vol. 2, p. 111.

[34] Schmidt, Civil Law of Spain and Mexico, p. 298; Las Siete Partidas, Part. 3, Title 29, Law 8.

[35] Asso & Mañuel, Institutes of Civil Law of Spain, Book I, Title VII, Cap. 2.

"Prescription does not run . . . against a married woman to recover her dowry, except that knowing that her husband is dissipating it, she is dilatory in exercising her right; but it does for her *paraphernalia,* because in order to sue for them she may cause the judges to compel her husband to give her license." Febrero, Novísimo, "Prescription," No. 27.

[36] See, e. g., Cal. Code of Civ. Proc., § 370; Tex. Family Code 1969, § 4.03; Wash. Rev. Code 1961, §§ 26.16.130, 26.16.160. And see Marston v. Rue, 92 Wash. 129, 159 P. 111.

Despite the provisions of the California code, provision just cited that the wife may sue in all actions without joining the husband, the California courts require the husband's joinder where community realty is involved. Gallagher v. Gallagher, 98 Cal. App. 180, 276 P. 634 (wherein she sued alone); Vanasek v. Pokorny, 73 Cal. App. 312, 238 P. 798. Wife may sue alone to recover personalty or its value. Matthews v. Hamburger, 36 Cal. App. 2d 182, 97 P.2d 465.

Wife establishing trust of community personalty transferred by husband to his father. Berniker v. Berniker, 30 Cal. 2d 439, 182 P.2d 557.

Washington rules the same, see ante, § 124.

tion of such an action may be during marriage upon learning of the alienation,[37] although frequently these actions are not brought until after the dissolution of the marital community because the extent and effect of the husband's alienation may not be learned until then.[38] If the dissolution results from the husband's death, the wife is entitled to sue. In California, where her right of recovery is for her half only,[39] she may sue either the transferee[40] or her husband's estate.[41] In Washington, where the recovery is of the whole amount or value, to be returned to the estate, the wife and the husband's personal representative may join.[42] If the dissolution has resulted from the wife's death, her personal representative is entitled to sue in her behalf.[43] If the dissolution results from divorce, the wife's recovery from her ex-husband or from the transferee is based on the proportionate division of property upon the divorce.[44] In all of these varying situations the effect of existing statutes of limitations must naturally be considered.[45]

Even in the absence of such statutes enabling the wife to sue in her own name in relation to her community property rights, she (or her heirs, of course) may upon dissolution of the community and upon the partition and division of the community property seek reparation from the husband's estate or proceed in her own name against the alienee.[46] Even if she seeks during marriage to bring action against

[37] In California her action to avoid an instrument executed by the husband holding the record title must be brought within one year from the filing of such instrument for record. Cal. Civ. Code, § 5127; Strong v. Strong, 22 Cal. 2d 540, 140 P.2d 386.

"The gift of community property by the husband without the consent of the wife may be set aside in its entirety by the wife during the lifetime of her husband, Britton v. Hammell, 4 Cal. 2d 690, 52 P.2d 221, and after his death may be set aside as to one-half thereof, Trimble v. Trimble, 219 Cal. 340, 26 P.2d 477." Ballinger v. Ballinger, 9 Cal. 2d 330, 70 P.2d 629.

[38] This may be particularly true in the case of life insurance policies. See ante, § 123.

In Louisiana it has been said that where the husband disposes of the community immovables by onerous title, that is, for value, the wife's right upon dissolution of the community by the husband's death to proceed against the husband's heirs depends upon the question whether the alienation was made in fraud of her rights. If he has disposed of them by gratuitous title, the wife has no right of recourse against the heirs of the husband and must recover directly from the parties in possession of her share. Bister v. Menge, 21 La. Ann. 216.

[39] After dissolution by death. See ante, §§ 113–119.

[40] See cases supra.

[41] Fields v. Michael, 91 Cal. App. 2d 443, 205 P.2d 402, noted 23 So. Cal. L. Rev. 84.

[42] See Benedict v. Hendrickson, 19 Wash. 2d 452, 143 P.2d 326.

[43] Harris v. Harris, 57 Cal. 2d 367, 19 Cal. Rptr. 793, 367 P.2d 481.

[44] See post, § 224 et seq.

[45] Note the Spanish statute and the California statute, in the footnotes ante, this section.

[46] Division and partition upon dissolution of marital community, see post, Chap. X.

the alienee she is entitled to do so,[47] or even to join the alienee and her husband as parties defendant.[48] There seem to be few cases in this country on the question of the wife's maintaining alone an action against the alienee where the husband has acted in fraud or injury of her rights. Cases exist in which the wife has maintained an action against the alienee without her right to do so being questioned[49] and there are cases in which there is dictum as to her right to do so.[50] In other cases she has been required to join her husband as a necessary party plaintiff.[51] However, the question whether she should as a formality, at least, join her husband as a party plaintiff or defendant is not so important as the consideration that she is entitled to institute the action against the alienee. Unless she is permitted to do so [and she certainly should be] she is left without the means of protecting and preserving her interest in the community property, an interest which is the equal of that of the husband.

Suits by one spouse against the other are discussed in a subsequent chapter.[52] But we may notice here that where the husband has trans-

[47] Since the same principles govern where the husband has encumbered the property, reference should be made at all times to Chap. IX, post.

In Louisiana, Civ. Code, art. 2404, and the judicial decisions seem to relate to the wife bringing action only after the conjugal partnership has been dissolved. There should be no reason, however, why she should not be entitled to bring the action during marriage upon discovery of the wrong, especially as delay might be damaging to her, and a recent case recognizes her rights in this regard. See In re F. H. Koretke Brass & Mfg. Co., 195 La. 415, 196 So. 917.

[48] Action for declaratory relief by wife against husband and others to establish mining claims as community property, see Cutting v. Bryan, 206 Cal. 254, 274 P. 326.

Right of wife to sue husband, see post, § 151.

[49] In fact, it is unquestionably affirmed on authority of Chavez v. McKnight, 1 N.M. 147, decided under Spanish law of community property in force in the Territory of New Mexico.

[50] See Holt v. Empey, 32 Idaho 106, 178 P. 703, indicating that upon allegation of fraud and collusion on the part of the husband the right of the wife to maintain a suit alone to quiet title to community realty would be recognized. And in Hynes v. Colman, 108 Wash. .642, 185 P. 617, it is intimated that the wife might sue alone if alleging the husband's wilful abandonment or dissipation or waste of community personalty and his failure to exercise his honest judgment in refusing to institute the action.

[51] See Vanasek v. Pokorny, 73 Cal. App. 312, 238 P. 798, despite provisions of Cal. Code Civ. Proc., § 370.

Where the husband is absent from the state so that he can be served only by publication, it is immaterial that no personal judgment can be obtained against him, where wife seeks to recover community property or her interest therein from those having it in their possession. A personal judgment against them relative to the property or its value is warranted upon the court's finding that the property is community property of husband and wife and properly recoverable by wife. See Murray v. Murray, 115 Cal. 266, 47 P. 37, 37 L. R. A. 626, 56 Am. St. Rep. 97; Nichols v. Nichols, 135 Cal. App. 488, 27 P.2d 414; McElroy v. McElroy, 32 Cal. 2d 828, 198 P.2d 683.

[52] See post, § 151.

ferred community property in fraud or prejudice of the wife's rights, besides her rights to sue the alienee, she also has a cause of action against her husband or against his estate when he is deceased.[53] Undoubtedly difficulties can be presented if she sues the husband while the marriage is still existent, but nevertheless, she does have the legal right.[54]

Under the provision of the Spanish codes that a transfer by the husband of property acquired during the marriage without the consent of the wife was valid "save it be proven that it was done wrongfully so as to defraud or injure the wife,"[55] the burden of proving the wrongful intent of fraud was upon the wife or her heirs.[56] Proof of actual fraud or wrongful intent was not required, however, if fraud or injury to the wife was obvious from the nature and effect of the alienation, that is, was to be implied therefrom.[57] Little more need be said about this matter for it has been the subject of comment in some of the preceding sections.[58] It need only be added that, of course, in our community property states the wife who is questioning the husband's alienation has the onus of establishing fraudulent intent on the part of the husband, either by proving an express intent to act in fraud or injury of her or by showing that the circumstances of the alienation and its nature and effect obviously work to her injury.[59]

Where the wife, having by virtue of statute control of any of the community property, alienates or otherwise deals with such property in fraud of the husband's rights, the latter is naturally entitled to the same remedies to which the wife, in his place, would be entitled.[60]

§ 127. — Conflicts of laws.

Conflict of laws with respect to property as community or separate property has been dealt with in the preceding chapter.[61] The application of its doctrine to the prosecution of civil actions with

---

[53] Fields v. Michael, 91 Cal. App. 2d 443, 205 P.2d 402, noted in 23 So. Cal. L. Rev. 84 and citing 1 de Funiak, 1st Ed.; Swisher v. Swisher, (Tex. Civ. App.), 190 S. W. 2d 382; Kemp v. Metropolitan L. Ins. Co. (5 C. A.), 205 F.2d 857, 866, citing and following 1 de Funiak.

[54] See Fields v. Michael, in preceding note.

[55] See ante, §§ 113, 117.

[56] Matienzo, Gloss VII, No. 2, to Nov. Rec. Law 5, Book 10, Title 4.

[57] "Understand by this ('save it be proven') that anyone who alleges fraud or wrongful intent — unless wrongful intent or fraud is obvious, e. g., in a large gift made for no good reason—is bound to prove such fraud or wrongful intent." Azevedo, No. 17 to Nov. Rec. Law 5.

[58] See particularly ante, §§ 120, 121.

[59] Consideration so inadequate as to support conclusion that alienation purposely made to defraud wife of her rights, see Vanasek v. Pokorny, 73 Cal. App. 312, 238 P. 798.

[60] See ante, § 120.1 and cases there cited. And see People v. Swalm, 80 Cal. 46, 22 P. 67, 13 Am. St. Rep. 96.

[61] See ante, §§ 87—92, and especially § 92.

respect to community property is discussed briefly here. The chief difficulty in the past seems to have arisen with regard to the right of action for injury to the person or reputation of the wife. The prosecution of civil actions has also been the subject of numerous and extended discussions as to the application of conflict of laws doctrines, especially in relation to actions to recover for injuries to the person or reputation of the wife. The existence and nature of a cause of action for tort, by the usual conflict of laws doctrine, is governed by the law of the place where the wrongful act occurs and this despite the fact that both parties may be domiciled elsewhere.[62] Thus, if husband and wife are domiciled in a community property state in which the right of action for injury to the person or reputation of the wife pertains to the community and must be prosecuted by the husband, nevertheless if she sustains such injury in a state in which the right of action pertains to her and for which she can bring the action, the law of the latter state should govern in establishing the right of action in her. This should be true whether she brings the action in the state where the injury was sustained,[63] or in the state of her domicile,[64] or in some other state. [65] If the husband and wife are domiciled in a community property state in which the right of action is considered to belong to the community with the right to sue therefor in the husband, and the wife sustains the injury in that state but seeks to bring the action herself in another state, what should be the result? If the action is brought in a state, whether common law or community property state, which recognizes the right of action as being the separate property of the wife, nonetheless such state, if literally following the conflict of laws doctrine, would consider the right of action as community

[62] See Beale, Conflict of Laws, § 378.2.

In Horowitz, Conflict of Laws: Problems in Community Property, 11 Wash. Law Rev. 212, 229–230, the author seems to take the view that the law of the husband's domicile should govern the nature of the right of action for injuries to the wife as community or separate property, under the rule that spouses' interests in "postnuptial movables" are determined by the law of the husband's domicile. Contrary views, see ante, § 92, as in Wisconsin.

[63] See Texas & P. Ry. Co. v. Humble, 181 U. S. 57, 45 L. Ed. 747, 21 Sup. Ct. 526, where wife domiciled in Louisiana sustained personal injuries in Arkansas and sued there in her own name. This was at a period when the Louisiana law gave the right of action therefor to the husband and the damages recovered apparently fell under his control as part of the community. Presently, in Louisiana, see ante, § 92.

[64] For, after all, such right of action or the compensation recovered is not something earned or gained by onerous title as is the case of money or movables acquired outside the domicile by labor and industry and intended to be returned to the domicile. See ante, §§ 82, 91.

[65] Even if such other state were itself a community property state recognizing the right of action and damages recovered as community property in case of such injury occurring within its own territorial borders it should apply the law of the state where the injury is sustained.

property. Even so, however, there is no reason why it should not allow the wife alone to bring the action, if it recognizes the right of one having an ownership to bring an action in regard thereto, since by the law of the place of injury the wife has a one-half ownership in the cause of action. The provision of the state of the domicile that the right of action for the injury to the wife is to be prosecuted by the husband may conceivably be considered by the court of the forum as procedural law which it is not bound to give effect to.[66] But is the court of the forum literally bound, even, to give effect to the law of the place of injury that the right of action for personal injuries to the wife is community property? We have pointed out previously the fallacies in such a view and that the damages for the actual injuries and the pain and suffering should belong to the wife, although the loss of any of her earnings or of her services, as well as medical expenses, etc., paid with community funds, are properly injuries to the community.[67] If the husband and wife are domiciled in a state which recognized the right of action for personal injury to the wife and the damages recovered therefor as the separate property of the wife, but the wife is injured in a community property state which considers such matters as belonging to the community, with the right of action in the husband, and the wife attempted to bring the action in the latter state, strict application of the local law would bar her right to bring the action, although in one much-cited case involving such a situation the court found an excuse for letting the wife prosecute the action.[68] However, the local court should, in logic and common sense, consider the necessity of the wife suing because of the inability, failure or refusal of an absent husband to bring the action himself and give the wife the same right to bring action that it would in the event her husband had disappeared or was mentally incompetent.

§ 128. Incompetency, incapacity, failure or absence of spouse.

The absence, incapacity or mental incompetency of the husband will naturally affect his ability to manage and control the community property. Similarly, the absence, incapacity or mental incompetency

---

[66] It is interesting to note that actions in the federal courts would be governed by Rule 17 (b) of Federal Rules of Civil Procedure, providing that "the capacity of an individual, other than one acting in a representative capacity, to sue or be sued shall be determined by the law of his domicile."

[67] See ante, § 82.

Undoubtedly, though, once the wife returned the proceeds to the place of her domicile, where the injury also occurred, that state would treat the proceeds as community property, however fallacious that theory may in part be.

[68] See Williams v. Pope Manufacturing Co., 52 La. Ann. 1417, 27 So. 851, 78 Am. St. Rep. 390, 50 L. R. A. 816, wherein the injury was sustained in Louisiana, which at that time empowered the husband only to bring the action. Since that time in Louisiana, see ante, § 92.

of the wife naturally affects her ability to join in the execution of conveyance or other instruments relating to the community property where such joinder is prescribed by law.[69] The difficulties brought about by these situations are dealt with, in varying degrees, by statutory enactments in most of the community property states. Because of the variance among the provisions of these several enactments it is not possible to do more here than briefly summarize the position that each state takes; reference to the precise statute is recommended as advisable at all times.

The failure of the husband to act, whether by reason of any of the foregoing matters or by reason of bad faith or the like, may raise an emergency situation. If protection of the marital property from loss, depreciation or danger generally becomes necessary because of the husband's failure to act, the wife, as the other owner, is uniformly recognized as the one naturally entitled to take the appropriate steps.[70] This may be recognized or provided for by statute, but in the absence of applicable statutes, judicial decisions have uniformly recognized this right of the wife.[71]

Arizona requires the appointment of a guardian to deal with the property of any incompetent, and no person has any power as guardian of property except as provided in the statutes.[72]

In California, the management of community property where either or both spouses are incompetent has been the subject of statutory provisions of varying terminology over the years. The most recent amendments and enactments, at this writing, are those of 1959. Incompetency relates to physical as well as mental disability. The appointment of a guardian for incompetent spouses is provided for, and this guardian may be the other spouse, if competent. The guardian joins in the execution of instruments in the place of the incompetent spouse. Where the wife is the incompetent, the joinder of her guardian in any disposition of the property must be approved by the court.[73]

---

[69] Suits between spouses, including questioning of husband's competency to manage, see also post, §§ 151, 152. And see annotation, 155 A. L. R. 306.

[70] See Wright v. Hays, 10 Tex. 130, 60 Am. Dec. 200.

[71] See, e. g., Vides v. Vides (Cal. App.), 30 Cal. Rptr. 447; Kenney v. Kenney, 97 Cal. App. 2d 60, 217 P.2d 151; Lynn v. Herman, 72 Cal. App. 2d 614, 165 P.2d 64; Zimpelman v. Robb, 53 Tex. 274; Wright v. Hays (Tex.), preceding note; Reed v. Beheler (Tex. Civ. App.), 198 S. W. 2d 695; Marston v. Rue, 92 Wash. 129, 159 P. 111. And see Reich v. Reich (La. App.), 23 So. 2d 567;

Merrill, 2 Ida. L. Jour. 120; Johnston v. Pike, 14 La. Ann. 731.

See also Lynch v. American Motorists' Insurance Co., 101 F. Supp. 946, holding that although the husband primarily has the exclusive right to conduct litigation respecting community property, such right is not absolute, and the wife may act if the husband shirks his responsibility.

[72] Ariz. Rev. St. 1956, §§ 14-806, 14-861—14-864.

[73] Cal. Prob. Code, §§ 1435.1— 1435.18.

Where wife was the incompetent and the husband was the guardian, husband had to obtain consent of

In Idaho, the adjudicated insanity of either spouse allows the other to petition the Probate Court of the county if he or she desires, to sell, lease or mortgage real property located in that county.[74] However, the only ground for making the conveyance is to discharge a lien on community property or to provide for the support of the family.[75] If the husband has been adjudged insane, the wife shall have the management and control of all community property.[76]

Louisiana statutes provide for the "interdiction" of an incompetent spouse and the appointment of a curator to deal with his or her property. The married woman who is interdicted is under the curatorship of her husband without any court appointment. On the other hand, a wife may be appointed curatrix of her husband if she qualifies.[77]

Nevada requires the appointment of a guardian to deal with the property of incompetent persons, but gives the spouse a preferential right of appointment as the guardian.[78]

When the husband is incompetent or has abandoned his wife in New Mexico, the wife may petition for authority to manage the community property and, upon such petition being granted, she is thereafter the head of the family with the same power that the husband had while competent.[79] But the New Mexico court points out that so far as community realty is concerned, both spouses have equal interests and equal voice in its alienation and that as to such realty there is no head of the community; consequently, even though the wife is appointed head of the community in lieu of a mentally incompetent husband, she cannot alienate or encumber the community realty by her act and signature alone, any more than the husband could while he was managing.[80] Evidently she would require the joinder of the husband's guardian.

Texas makes a graphic distinction between adjudicated incompetency and other factors affecting management. Whenever a husband or wife is judicially declared to be incompetent, the other spouse acquires full power to manage, control, and dispose of the entire

court as consent of the wife. Estate of Risse, 156 Cal. App. 2d 412, 319 P.2d 789 (under prior form of statute). In Ellwood v. Niedermeyer, 12 Cal. App. 2d 699, 56 P.2d 279, the defendant, who was his wife's guardian, made a contract to convey realty owned by himself and his wife in joint tenancy and deposited in escrow a deed signed only by himself, although he had knowledge that the court's approval was necessary for consummation of the contract, and he was liable in damages for breach of contract.

[74] Ida. Code 1948, § 15-2001.

[75] Ida. Code 1948, § 15-2002.

[76] Ida. Code 1948, § 15-2011.

[77] La. Civ. Code, arts. 389–413; La. Rev. St. 1950, arts. 9:1001–9:1021.

Suit to interdict husband as insane and for appointment of curator, see, e. g., In re Leech, 45 La. Ann. 197, 12 So. 126.

[78] Nev. Rev. St. 1956, § 159.120.

[79] N.M. St. 1953, §§ 57-4-5, 57-4-6.

[80] Frkovich v. Petranovich, 48 N.M. 382, 151 P.2d 337, 155 A. L. R. 295.

community estate, including the part which the incompetent spouse would legally have power to manage in the absence of such incompetency, and no administration shall be necessary.[81] On the other hand, if a spouse is insane but there has been no adjudication of incompetency, or if a spouse disappears and his or her whereabouts remain unknown to the other spouse, or if one spouse permanently abandons the other, or if the spouses are permanently separated, then sixty days thereafter the capable spouse or the remaining spouse or the abandoned spouse or either spouse in the case of permanent separation may file a sworn petition stating the facts that make it desirable for the petitioning spouse to manage the community property which would otherwise be subject to the sole management, control, and disposition of the other.[82] The effect of this statutory provision is to allow the capable spouse to become head of the community. It does not, however, allow that spouse to deal with the homestead property. A separate statute deals with conveyance of the homestead in these exceptional circumstances.[83]

Washington generally requires the appointment of a guardian to deal with the property of an incompetent, but a special provision is made whereby one spouse may petition for authority to sell the homestead if the other spouse is insane, without a full guardianship.[84]

These matters were also features of the Spanish law, which recognized the necessity of appointing a curator of the property and person of one who was insane or deprived of sense and even of one who was

[81] Tex. Prob. Code, § 157. Power in wife to change life insurance policy beneficiary, see Salvato v. Volunteer State L. Ins. Co. (Tex. Civ. App.), 424 S. W. 2d 1.

[82] Tex. Family Code 1969, § 5.25.
As to disappearance of husband, see Tex. Family Code 1969, § 5.25; Wright v. Hays, 10 Tex. 130, 60 Am. Dec. 200. Compare, as to separation through fault of husband, Masterson v. Bouldin (Tex. Civ. App.), 151 S. W. 2d 301, error refused; commented on, 20 Tex. Law Rev. 97.
Where the husband had abandoned the wife, leaving her without means of support, and the only community property was wages due the husband from his employer, part of which the employer had paid the husband and part of which it still had in its possession, the wife was held entitled to collect and use for necessities the part of the wages still in the employer's possession. However, she was denied the right to recover from the husband any part of the wages already paid to him by his employer. Irwin v. Irwin (Tex. Civ. App.), 110 S. W. 1011, where wife joined husband and husband's employer as defendants.

[83] Tex. Family Code 1969, §§ 5.81 –5.85.

[84] Wash. Rev. Code 1961, §§ 6.12.300, 11.88.040.
Petition by husband to court for appointment of guardian of wife to join in execution of instrument, see Merriman v. Patrick, 103 Wash. 442, 174 P. 641.
Right of wife, where husband had abandoned and deserted her, to bring action to recover damages for personal injuries to her sustained at a time when she was living with her husband, see Wampler v. Beinert, 125 Wash. 494, 216 P. 855.
And see Marston v. Rue (Wash.), supra, this section.

a prodigal or a spendthrift,[85] and recognized the wife as the proper person in whom to place the administration of the community property when the husband became incapacitated or incompetent.[86] The wife could apply to the court, which was empowered to authorize her to make contracts, alienate property, appear in suits as plaintiff or defendant and do other acts which had become necessary and as to which the husband was failing or refusing to act and as to which he was failing or refusing to consent to the wife taking the necessary action; likewise, the wife might so apply to the court where the husband was absent and any delay in acting might be attended with danger.[87]

§ 129.   — Complete dissolution of conjugal partnership but not of marriage.

In one of the states, Louisiana, seemingly due to a statutory provision adopted from the French Code Napoleon,[88] the wife whose dowry is in danger may petition the court to obtain a dissolution of the marital community and for separation of the community property upon showing that the husband is an unfit manager of the prop-

---

[85] Las Siete Partidas, Part. 6, Title 16, Law 13.

"A curator is he who is appointed as guardian of those above fourteen and under twenty-five years of age, being of sound mind, and of those above twenty-five, who are insane or deprived of sense, Law 13, Tit. 16, Part. 6, which definition should be extended to prodigals or spendthrifts, who are considered insane or foolish by reason of their bad conduct." Asso & Mañuel, Institutes of Civil Law of Spain, Book I, Title II, Cap. 3.

[86] Ordinarily, women were not favored by the law as guardians or curators but this objection would not seem to exist where it was presumed that their great affection for the ward, as a mother for a child or a wife for her husband, offset any question of sex. See Asso & Mañuel, Institutes of Civil Law of Spain, Book I, Title II, Cap. 1, § 4.

Under the Spanish Civil Code, arts. 1436, 1441, the administration of the community property may be transferred to the wife where she has been appointed guardian of the husband.

[87] See Leyes de Toro, Laws 54–59,

and Commentaries of Llamas y Molina thereon.

"The Judge has the power to grant the wife authority to do all the foregoing acts (i. e., make contracts, alienate the property, etc.), when the husband improperly withholds his consent; and in cases in the absence of the husband, when delay may be attended with danger." Schmidt, Civil Law of Spain and Mexico, p. 12, citing Laws 57 and 59 of Toro.

In Aragon, if the husband absented himself without appointing an agent, the wife had the administration of the properties. Gómez and Montalbán, Elementos del Derecho Civil y Penal de España, Cuarto Edición, Vol. 1, p. 260, n. 3.

In Mexico, the wife was the lawful administrator of the conjugal partnership, where there was no agreement or judgment of the court to the contrary, in case of absence or impediment of the husband or when the latter had unjustifiedly abandoned the conjugal domicile. Hall, Mexican Law, § 2626.

[88] Now French Civ. Code, art. 1443 et seq.

erty.[89] The statute is given broader application than its language would lead one to suppose and seems to cover the case of maladministration of the community property as well as any of the wife's separate property under the husband's management.[90] Although this Louisiana statute is, as we have said, seemingly adopted from the French Code Napoleon, it is to be remarked that in innumerable civil law countries both in Europe and the Americas, present day codes, whether derived from French, Spanish or Portuguese law, contain similar provisions.[91] Somewhat similarly in California, either the husband or wife, upon the same grounds for which a divorce would be obtainable but without obtaining a divorce, upon petition for separate maintenance or support, may obtain the same disposition of the community property as would be made if the marriage were dissolved by decree of court.[92] In Texas, on the other hand, it was formerly flatly stated that as concerns living spouses there is no authority warranting a partition of the community property except in a divorce proceeding.[93] But since that judicial decision, a statutory enactment in 1948 has provided that the spouses may partition between themselves in severalty or in equal undivided interests all or any part of their existing community property without prejudice to pre-existing creditors.[94]

In these instances, it will be remarked that the matter goes beyond removal of the administration from the husband and involves an actual dissolution of the marital partnership in the earnings and gains during marriage, although not a dissolution of the marriage itself.[95]

---

[89] La. Civ. Code, art. 2425 et seq. And see La. Civ. Code art. 64, as to right to dissolve community or marital partnership of matrimonial gains upon absence of other spouse for five years.

[90] "It has long been settled that the wife may obtain the separation of property provided for by article 2425, Civ. Code, for causes other than those specified in that article (citing authorities); and we are not prepared to say that, on proof that the husband was of a speculative disposition and that he was 'daily incurring heavy indebtedness,' a case might not be made out of danger to the dotal and paraphernal rights of the wife and to her future acquisitions, which would entitle her to such separation." Jones v. Jones, 119 La. 677, 44 So. 429. And see language of Succession of Wiener, 203 La. 649, 14 So.2d 475, "The wife may, without obtaining a divorce, and even in the absence of fraud, sue for a dissolution and liquidation of the community partnership and secure the delivery into her own exclusive management and control of her half of the community property whenever her husband proves to be incompetent, a bad manager, of a reckless or speculative disposition, or whenever her affairs are in such disorder that her property rights are jeopardized."

[91] See Lobingier, "Modern Civil Law," 40 Corpus Juris 1271. Mexico is among these countries.

As to contracts or agreements between spouses during marriage by which the conjugal partnership in acquests and gains is terminated although the marriage continues to subsist, see post, Chap. VIII.

[92] Cal. Civ. Code, § 137.

[93] Martin v. Martin (Tex. Com. App.), 17 S. W. 2d 789.

[94] Tex. Family Code 1969, § 5.42.

[95] Dissolution in general, see post, Chap. X.

§ 130.   Criminal proceedings.

It is usual, in the case of theft or the like of community property, to allege, in the indictment, ownership and possession of the property in the husband, rather than in the wife or in the husband and the wife.[96] This customary practice does not deny the equal ownership and possession of the wife but merely results from the fact that in the criminal law in theft cases the test of the ownership or at least the special property right, which must exist in the person from whom the property is stolen, is the exclusive care, control and management of the property.[97] In other words, the essential element regarding the ownership is that the property must be that of someone other than the one taking it, and a special ownership or possession in the one from whom the property is taken has always been considered sufficient.[98] Thus, alleging the ownership and possession in the husband is no more than an allegation that the exclusive care, control and management of the property taken was in him. Since it is usually the husband who has the exclusive care, control and management of the community property it is in him that the ownership and possession is therefore usually alleged, but it is perfectly proper and correct to allege the ownership and possession in the wife when the community property taken has been under her care and control. This may result where the community property has been placed under the wife's control and management by act or agreement of the husband,[99] or where

[96] See cases cited, 2 A. L. R. 354.

[97] Miles v. State, 51 Tex. Crim. Rep. 587, 103 S. W. 854. But cf. Bundage v. State (Tex. Cr.), 215 S. W. 2d 339, in which conviction reversed because of fatal variance where indictment alleged ownership in wife and at trial proof showed property to be community. However, Tex. Code Crim. Proc., § 21.08, now permits alleging ownership in either or both of joint or common owners.

[98] See Clark & Marshall, Criminal Law, 6th Ed., § 12.03.

[99] Miles v. State, 51 Tex. Crim. Rep. 587, 103 S. W. 854; Lane v. State, 69 Tex. Crim. Rep. 68, 152 S. W. 897. See also State v. Cook, 113 Wash. 391, 194 P. 401, where community funds were placed in bank account in names of husband and wife with right of both to check against it and wife drew checks in favor of accused who made false representations.

"The proof on this point clearly shows that the stolen money was community property of the said husband and wife; but it also clearly shows that the husband had turned it over to his wife and put it in her custody, and that she so had it for their benefit. Under our law community property belongs to both the husband and the wife, and article 457, C. C. P., expressly provides: 'Where one person owns the property, and another person has the possession, charge, or control of the same, the ownership thereof may be alleged in either. Where property is owned in common, or jointly, by two or more persons, the ownership may be alleged to be in all or either of them.' In this case it was proper to have alleged the ownership in either the husband or the wife; but as she had possession, charge, and control of the same at the time, there is no variation between the proof and the allegation in any respect." Lane v. State, 69 Tex. Crim. Rep. 68, 152 S. W. 897.

it is placed under her control and management by statute or by judicial order upon establishment of the incompetency of the husband,[1] or where it is under her control and management by reason of absence or abandonment on the part of the husband,[2] or as to the wife's share of the community property received upon division of the property.[3] It must be borne in mind that the wife is as equally the owner of the community property as the husband and when she couples with her ownership the control and management of the property in question she must necessarily come with the terms of the usual statute relating to allegations of ownership and possession.

[1] Generally, as to these matters, see ante, §§ 113–115, 128.

[2] Ware v. State, 2 Tex. App. 547. See also Nugent v. State, 89 Tex. Crim. Rep. 168, 229 S. W. 855.

[3] Generally, see ante, § 129; post, Chap. X.

CHAPTER VIII

RIGHTS, DUTIES, AGREEMENTS AND
TRANSACTIONS BETWEEN SPOUSES

§ 131.   In general.

Rights, duties, agreements and transactions between the spouses cover a variety of situations, as may be expected. The more important of these are discussed in this chapter but it is not possible in all of these situations to make a clean-cut cleavage, since the rights and obligations of third persons will frequently be involved. For example, gifts or other transactions between the spouses may affect the rights of creditors.[1] Accordingly, it is necessary to keep in mind the scope of other chapters. So far as concerns the separate property of each spouse and the other spouse's rights or interests or lack of rights or interests therein, the matter has been dealt with in preceding chapters.[2]

[1] Creditors generally, see post, Chap. IX.

[2] See ante, Chaps. VI, VII.

§ 132.   Husband as head of family.

It has already been seen that under the community property system the husband is the member of the marital partnership entrusted with the administration of the community property, subject sometimes to qualification as to certain types of community property, and that is so because he is usually considered the one best fitted by experience and by economic and biological factors to exercise such administration.[3] In respect to his position as the managing agent or partner or head of the marital partnership in respect of its property he may be termed, on that ground alone, the head of the family.[4] The fact that he is considered, as in English common-law jurisdictions, the head of the family in more respects than that pertaining to the marital property alone, is unnecessary to discuss. It is not particularly pertinent to this work to attempt a monograph on male dominance as resulting from religious, economic, biological or other considerations. We may confine ourselves to remarking that under the Spanish law the husband was denominated the head of the family, with certain duties and authorities growing therefrom, which included the right of choosing the place of residence.[5] Likewise, in our community property states the husband is denominated the head of the family with the right to choose any reasonable place or mode of living.[6] This right to choose the dwelling place may be said to include the right of the husband, as head of the family, to select and designate a homestead for the family, a right usually fixed by statute, of course.[7] But if it is attempted to select the homestead from the separate property of the wife, her consent must usually be shown by her making or joining in making the homestead declaration.[8]

§ 133.   Duties of support.

The Spanish law imposed a duty of support upon the husband[9] and this is also true of the law of our community property states.[10]

[3] See ante, §§ 111, 113.

[4] Fontenot v. Central Louisiana Elec. Co. (La.), 147 So.2d 773, relying on La. Civ. Code, arts. 691 and 2404, supports this view. But cf. Frkovich v. Petranovich, 48 N.M. 382, 151 P.2d 337, 155 A. L. R. 295, in which the New Mexico court declared that since the interest of the spouses in the community realty is equal and since they have an equal voice in the matter of its alienation, as to such property there is no head of the community. This may be subjected to the criticism that, aside from the actual alienation, the management of the community realty continues to rest with the husband, including initiation of consideration of the wisdom and advisability of alienation.

[5] See Schmidt, Civil Law of Spain and Mexico, p. 11, citing Las Siete Partidas, Part. 3, Title 2, Law 5.

[6] See, e. g., Cal. Civ. Code, § 5101.

[7] No detailed discussion of homestead laws is included in this work. As to acquisition of homesteads from public lands, see ante, § 75. Cases on selection of homestead from community property, see 89 A. L. R. 554.

[8] See Cal. Civ. Code, § 1239.

[9] See Schmidt, Civil Law of Spain and Mexico, p. 11, citing Las Siete Partidas, Part. 3, Title 2, Law 5.

[10] See cases collected, 41 C. J. S.,

It is sometimes provided that he may be excused from this liability of support if the wife has abandoned him, until she offers to return, unless she was justified by his misconduct in abandoning him.[11] In respect to this continuing liability to support her where she has been compelled to leave him and live apart because of his misconduct, it is to be remarked that in the Spanish law, also, the same was true. "Similarly, a wife who is wrongfully and without good cause expelled by her husband is entitled to be supported by her husband, even if she has no dowry."[12] Or he may also be excused from liability for her support when she is living separate from him by agreement, unless such support is stipulated by the agreement.[13]

The criticism is sometimes made that the custom of the community property jurisdictions in imposing the duty of support upon the husband is not consistent with the declaration that the wife is an equal and present half owner of the marital earnings and gains, that if she owns half of such property anyway there is no reason to impose on the husband a duty of support. Such arguments overlook too many important matters. First, the Spanish law of community property continued in our community property states is only a community of property in the earnings and gains during marriage. If there are no earnings or gains there is nothing to share equally between the spouses, and so probably nothing to provide them and their children with food, clothing and shelter. The Spanish law recognized, and the law of our community property states recognizes as a matter of common sense, that the husband is customarily the wage earner, the breadwinner, and the wife the homemaker. The wife's services in that respect are considered to counterbalance the husband's contribution of earnings.[14] If he fails or refuses to make his contribution to the marital partnership, not only does his marital partner suffer but so do any children of the spouses. It is unthinkable in any civilized society, whether a community property jurisdiction or not, that such a situation should be allowed to exist. Therefore, the laws of the community property jurisdictions quite properly insist that the husband fulfill his customary duty and contribution to the success, safety and well-being of the marital partnership.[15] Lastly, it is to be observed that as a matter of

---

Husband and Wife, § 15. Civil and criminal liability of husband differs little in community property states from that in common-law states. Generally as to duty of husband to support the wife, see Brown, 18 Va. Law Rev. 823.

[11] Cal. Civ. Code, § 5131; Nev. Rev. St. 1956, § 123.100.

[12] Matienzo, Gloss I, No. 50, to Nov. Rec. Law 1, Book 10, Title 4. See also post, Chap. X, A and C.

[13] Cal. Civ. Code, § 5131; D. H. Holmes Co. v. Morris, 188 La. 431,

177 So. 417.

Resumption of marital relations, following reconciliation subsequent to interlocutory decree of divorce, cancelled executory obligations of separation agreement and restored husband's obligation to support wife. Lloyd Corp. v. Industrial Accident Commission, 61 Cal. App. 2d 275, 142 P.2d 754.

[14] See ante, § 67.

[15] Debts and obligations contracted during marriage for purposes of support, see post, §§ 159—164.

fact a majority of the community property states impose mutual obligations of support on both husband and wife. Traditionally, California, Idaho, Nevada and New Mexico have imposed mutual obligations of support on both husband and wife.[16] Texas adopted such a position in 1967.[17] In Washington the expenses of the family and the education of the children are chargeable upon the property of both husband and wife.[18] This seems entirely in accord with the Spanish law of community property that the paraphernal property of the wife which she had placed under his management might be sold by the husband where he was so poor that its sale was necessary to maintain himself,[19] or that if the husband had no property and was compelled to borrow money to support the wife, the creditor could look to the wife to repay such sum from her separate property.[20]

§ 134. Holding property together other than in community.

In some of the community property states it is provided by statute that husband and wife may hold property as joint tenants or tenants in common, as well as holding it in community. In Arizona, the statute provides that, except as to husband and wife, all conveyances to two or more persons create tenancies in common and not joint tenancies.[21] While the Arizona courts have felt that the spouses may hold property as joint tenants or as tenants in common if a clear intention to that effect appears,[22] the presumption favors its nature as community property even though the instrument by which it is

---

[16] Cal. Civ. Code, §§ 5100, 5132; Ida. Code 1948, § 32-915; Nev. Rev. St. 1956, § 123.110; N.M. St. 1953, § 57-2-5.

Fact that wife was earning money and devoting it to needs of family as affecting right of husband to receive old age support from state, see Kelley v. State Board of Social Welfare (Cal. App.), 186 P.2d 429.

[17] Tex. Family Code 1969, § 4.02. Wording of statute suggested by Dean Angus McSwain of the Baylor Law School that expression of general liability for support and concomitant necessaries in terms of personal duty was far preferable to a statement of law in terms of property liability which had previously been the Texas position.

[18] Wash. Rev. Code 1961, § 26.16.205.

See In re De Nisson, 197 Wash. 265, 84 P.2d 1024, as to allowance from wife's separate estate for support of destitute husband; and compare therewith, Christiansen v. Department of Social Security, 15 Wash. 2d 465, 13 P.2d 189, to effect that destitute husband not disqualified to receive social security by fact that wife had separate property, on ground that husband had no enforcible right of action against wife to compel her to support him.

[19] See Asso and Mañuel, Institutes of Civil Law of Spain, Book I, Title VII, Cap. 2.

Many codes of modern civil law jurisdictions impose the obligation of mutual support. See Lobingier, "Modern Civil Law," 40 Corpus Juris 1266.

[20] Matienzo, Gloss VII, No. 5, to Nov. Rec. Law 2, Book 10, Title 4.

[21] Ariz. Rev. St. 1956, § 33-431.

[22] Collier v. Collier, 72 Ariz. 405, 242 P.2d 537.

transferred to them states that they take as tenants.[23] The mere language of the conveyance is not binding. It must appear that both spouses knew of this language, realized its meaning and agreed thereto.[24]

Apparently Idaho permits the spouses to hold property in joint tenancy or tenancy in common if they have so agreed by a matrimonial property settlement.[25] Nevada allows the spouses to hold property as joint tenants, tenants in common or as community property; the presumption is for community status and for the property to be held in some other form a clear intention to that effect must appear.[26] And even though on its face an instrument describes the property as joint tenancy, it can be shown that the spouses intended it to be community property,[27] following the California view.

In New Mexico, the spouses may also hold property as joint tenants, tenants in common or as community property.[28] It is further provided by statute that when a conveyance is to a married woman and another the interest she receives is as a tenant in common, except when the conveyance is to a husband and wife, describing them as such, whereupon the presumption is that the property is community unless a contrary intention is expressed.[29] It has been said that where property is conveyed to husband and wife as tenants in common, under the statute, that the wife owns her half as separate property and that she has a one-half interest in the husband's share because he holds his share as community property.[30] In the authors' opinion this is obviously a most ridiculous interpretation of the statute — property must be held by both entirely as community property or each must hold his or her share as a separate property interest, which is the rule applied to them where they hold as joint tenants.[31]

Texas is more restrictive in regards to spouses holding property together other than in community. When property is acquired by an individual while he is married, it immediately takes on the character of community property or separate property.[32] If the interest of each spouse in a particular item of property is as his or her separate prop-

[23] Estate of Baldwin, 50 Ariz. 265, 71 P.2d 791. See Blackman v. Blackman, 45 Ariz. 374, 43 P.2d 1011.

[24] Estate of Baldwin (Ariz.), preceding note.

[25] Brockelbank, The Community Property Law of Idaho, § 3.10.

[26] Nev. Rev. St. 1956, § 123.303; In re Condos' Estate (Nev.), 266 P.2d 404.

[27] Millikin v. Jones, 71 Nev. 14, 278 P.2d 876.

[28] N.M. St. 1953, §§ 57-3-2, 57-4-1; Chavez v. Chavez, 56 N.M.

393, 244 P.2d 781; Hugh K. Gale Post, V.F.W. v. Norris, 53 N.M. 58, 201 P.2d 777.

[29] N.M. St. 1953, §§ 57-3-2, 57-4-1; Chavez v. Chavez (N.M.), preceding note.

[30] In re Trimble's Estate, 57 N.M. 51, 253 P.2d 805. Notice infra, this section, that there has been California authority to this effect in the past.

[31] In re Trimble's Estate (N.M.), preceding note. This view has also been expressed in California.

[32] See cases collected, Oakes, Speer's Marital Rights in Texas, 4th Ed., § 355.

erty, the relationship of the spouses is that of tenants in common. This would occur if someone made a gift to both spouses during the marriage. The property could not be community property, and the interest of each spouse in that property would be separate — hence their relationship would be that of tenants in common. Furthermore, Texas permits the spouses by written agreement to create joint tenancies out of their property. However, the Supreme Court has ruled that statute unconstitutional insofar as it permits the spouses to create a joint tenancy out of their community property prior to a partition of it.[33]

In Washington, there have been some shifts back and forth, insofar as whether joint tenancies between spouses are permissible or, at least, favored. Ordinarily, they have not been favored and spouses have held property either in community or as separate property. There have been instances of deposits of community funds in a joint bank account which have been considered to have created a joint tenancy therein,[34] but the presumption in favor of such a form of deposit has been considered rebutted by proof that the funds deposited were community funds; clear and convincing proof has been required to establish an intention to change the nature of the community property in the funds.[35] And, while there has been agitation to change the matter, at this writing, by statute in Washington,[36] joint tenancies have been abolished. But this is not applicable to nonresidents owning corporate stock in Washington under a joint tenancy agreement.[37]

The somewhat peculiar situation has existed in California that when the husband and wife take property as tenants in common, the interest conveyed to the wife is presumptively her separate property, while that conveyed to the husband is community property,[38] but the modern view is that where the spouses own property as tenants in common, the interest of each is the separate property of that spouse and each owns his or her interest in full.[39] And they own equal interests where holding as joint tenants. The interest of each is then separate property, and this is true even though the property in question was acquired with community funds, for this is considered tantamount to an agreement between them that the property shall not any longer

---

[33] See Tex. Prob. Code, § 46 and Williams v. McKnight, 9 Tex. Sup. Ct. Jour. 376, 402 S. W. 2d 505.

[34] Iver's Estate, 4 Wash. 2d 477, 104 P.2d 467.

[35] Munson v. Haye, 29 Wash. 2d 733, 189 P.2d 464. And see Douglas' Estate (Wash.), 398 P.2d 7; Wash. Rev. Code 1961, §§ 64.28.010, 64.28.030.

[36] See Wash. Rev. Code 1961, § 11.04.070.

[37] Bellinger v. West Coast Tel. Co., 54 Wash. 2d 574, 343 P.2d 189.

[38] See Dunn v. Mullan, 211 Cal. 583, 296 P. 604, 77 A. L. R. 1015.

[39] Estate of Adams, 39 Cal. Rptr. 522, citing Estate of Maxwell, 7 Cal. App. 2d 641, 46 P.2d 777, which in turn cites as its authority Cal. Civ. Code, §§ 682, 685, 686 and Siberell v. Siberell, 214 Cal. 767, 7 P.2d 1003.

constitute community property.[40] However, in Tomaier v. Tomaier,[41] where community funds were used to purchase realty to which husband and wife took title as joint tenants, it is the view of the court that spouses can acquire property as joint tenants ostensibly but with the intention that the property is to be community property and that evidence is admissible to show this intent. Indeed, the court indicates that even if the property is taken in joint tenancy it may be converted into community property at any time by oral agreement. Further, where the spouses hold the family residence in joint tenancy, it is presumed to be community property.[42]

It will be recalled that in the case of a joint tenancy, upon the death of one the survivor takes the fee, as opposed to the usual principle of community property law that each owner may dispose of his half.[43] Thus, it will be seen from the foregoing that certainly so far as the husband is concerned, joint tenancies are far more disadvantageous than holding property in community. And in sober truth, this grafting by statute of tenancies of common-law origin upon the community property system is entirely inconsistent with the community property system.[44]

It has been recognized that the common-law tenancy by the entireties is inconsistent with the community property system.[45]

§ 135. Agreements between spouses as to earnings and gains — Spanish authorities.

From the earliest inception of the Spanish statutory law governing marital community property, it was permitted to the spouses to

---

[40] Siberell v. Siberell, 214 Cal. 767, 7 P.2d 1003.

[41] 23 Cal. 2d 754, 146 P.2d 905, distinguishing the Siberell case above. And notice the provisions of some statutes that money placed on deposit in the name of husband or wife alone shall be presumed to be the separate property of that spouse. Tex. Rev. Civ. Stats. 1925, art. 4622; and see Deering's Cal. Gen. Laws, Act 652, § 15a.

[42] Baker v. Baker, 66 Cal. Rptr. 905.

[43] See Swan v. Walden, 156 Cal. 195, 103 P. 931, 134 Am. St. Rep. 118, 20 Ann. Cas. 194.

In many of the community property states, upon the death of a spouse, that spouse's interest in the community goes to the spouse's descendants if not disposed of by will; in California, the spouse may dispose of his or her half by will but if this is not done, such spouse's interest goes to the surviving spouse. Other variations exist in other states. See post, Chap. X.

[44] "From these statutory provisions it is clear that in California we have a modified form of certain estates known to the common law and have them operating alongside of the community property system, an importation from the Spanish law. Naturally, therefore, at times there will appear to be difficulty in harmonizing these systems. But our statutes have been amended from time to time, so altering the original provisions of each of the systems as to allow them both a place in our jurisprudence." Siberell v. Siberell, 214 Cal. 767, 7 P.2d 1003.

Curtesy and dower as nonexistent in community property system, see post, § 201.

[45] See Swan v. Walden, 156 Cal.

contract, agree or stipulate as between themselves, either before, at the time of or even during marriage, as to the manner in which they wished to share the property earned or gained during the marriage. That is, if they did not wish to be governed by the statutory provisions regulating the division of such earned or gained property, they might elect by virtue of agreement, contract or stipulations to divide it upon some other basis or to allow each spouse to keep as his or her own separate property that which he or she earned or gained during the marriage.[46] This was true of the Fuero Juzgo in the year 693, providing that: "And as to earned property as to which they shall make written contract, each shall have such share as the written contract stipulates";[47] and of Las Siete Partidas in 1263, providing that: "It often happens that when a husband and wife marry, that . . . they jointly agree in what manner they shall hold the property which they jointly earn. . . . And we say that the agreement they had made before or at the time of their marriage ought to have its effect in the manner they may have stipulated";[48] and this continued to exist as a recognized principle of the Spanish community property law.[49]

In other words, the Spanish law so far regarded the husband and the wife as separate persons that they could validly enter into onerous contracts between themselves, and the wife needed no authorization or license to do so.[50] This matter is so thoroughly and completely established, developed and recognized by the Spanish codes and the commentaries of the Spanish jurisconsults that it is inconceivable how denial of it can be made in the face of such clear-cut authorities.[51]

195, 103 P. 931, 134 Am. St. Rep. 118,' 20 Ann. Cas. 194; McDonald v. Senn, 33 N.M. 198, 204 P.2d 990, 995.

[46] In the absence of any contract, agreement or stipulation the rights of the spouses were governed, of course, by the community property statutes. See ante, § 54.

[47] Fuero Juzgo, Book 4, Title 2, Law 17 (in part), according to the Castilian version of the thirteenth century. According to the version translated by Samuel Parsons Scott from the original Latin of that code: "The distribution and possession of other property concerning which an agreement in writing has been entered into by both parties, shall be held and enjoyed by them according to the terms of that written agreement." Scott, The Visigothic Code.

[48] Las Siete Partidas, Part. 4, Title 11, Law 24 (in part).

[49] Llamas y Molina, No. 8 et seq. to Law 55 of the Leyes de Toro. See also the citations, post, this section, to other jurisconsults.

Although the legal community also exists in France under the French Civil Code, the parties are permitted to contract for some other arrangement. French Civ. Code (Cachard, Rev. Ed.), §§ 1400 et seq., 1497 et seq.

[50] See Llamas y Molina, No. 8 et seq. to Law 55 of Leyes de Toro. See also Fuller v. Ferguson, 26 Cal. 546; L'Abbe's Heirs v. Abat, 2 La. 553, 22 Am. Dec. 151.

Wife relinquishing control of paraphernal property to husband, see ante, § 112.

[51] It is astonishing to find such statements as those of McKay, Community Property, 2nd Ed., § 856, that dealings between spouses are not contemplated by the community prop-

The agreement had to be one clearly entered into by the wife with full intent and not subject to pressure.[52] For example, such an agreement entered into before marriage could not be made for her by anyone else. She herself had freely to assent.[53] If the contract was attempted to be made for her where she was below the age of majority — twenty-five years — her rights were most carefully safeguarded and usually the sanction of the court was necessary rather than the agreement of any curator of her person and property; this was equally true where she herself attempted to make the contract.[54]

Such an agreement between spouses or intending spouses could validly be, and frequently was, one whereby there was to be no community of property, in that the wife renounced her right to share equally in the profits to be gained during the marriage,[55] either in

erty system and that as influenced by the civil law that system forbade dealings between spouses except in an extremely restricted way. Such observations cannot accurately be made of the Spanish community property system, and it is to be noticed that the author does not venture to attempt the citation of any authorities to such observations.

[52] See post, § 138, as to undue influence by husband.

[53] Notice that under the Spanish law that if renunciation of community of property was made by the woman's father on her behalf, before marriage, she was not bound thereby, even though she was present and silent. Gutiérrez, Quaestio CXXVI, No. 2, to Nov. Rec. Law 9, Book 10, Title 4.

[54] See Las Siete Partidas, Part. 4, Title 11, Law 14; Part. 6, Title 16, Laws 17, 18.

A woman under the age of majority who desired to give to her husband a dowry consisting of realty could not herself determine to do so, and whether or not she had a curator of her person and property she had to apply to the court for permission; in the case, however, of giving a dowry from her personal property she could do so with the consent of the curator of her person and property without application to the court. Las Siete Partidas, Part. 4, Title 11, Law 14.

Right of minor to disaffirm a pre-judicial contract on reaching age of majority, see Asso & Mañuel, Institutes of Civil Law of Spain, Book I, Title III, Cap 1, § 4.

Illustration under modern Mexican law of spouses who then made their home in California. Fernandez v. Fernandez, 36 Cal. Rptr. 352.

[55] "When the wife renounces the profits, let her not be obliged to pay any part of the debts which the husband made during the marriage." Novísima Recopilación, Book 10, Title 4, Law 9. As to liability for debts generally, see post, Chap. IX.

"Here is a law (i. e., Law 9) validating in general terms the woman's renunciation of these profits. Therefore, it must be understood to apply generally and at whatever time that pact or renunciation took place, either before marriage (during the proposals for a marriage), or during marriage, or after." Gutiérrez, Quaestio CXXVI, No. 1, to Nov. Rec. Law 9.

"This renunciation by the wife can be made at one of these three times: when the marriage is contracted, after it has been contracted and ganancials are known to exist, and when the marriage is dissolved. . . . In the first case it does not appear that there should be any difficulty in the renunciation being valid, for by it the wife gives up the property in which she was to benefit or which she was to acquire, before it existed, in the same manner as an

whole or in part.[56] The husband, of course, could renounce his right to share equally in such profits but this was naturally more uncommon than renunciation by the wife. In his case, renunciation seems to have occurred usually during marriage and was not considered to be a gift between the spouses so as to be prohibited under the Spanish law.[57] The renunciation by the husband could not, of course, relieve him from liability for debts incurred in the maintenance and support of the family.[58] No registration of the agreement renouncing the right to share in matrimonial gains was necessary except where an already acquired right was renounced.[59]

Where the conjugal sharing of gains was dissolved or never entered into at all by reason of such an agreement, then the fruits of each spouse's separate property were not shared. "It should be carefully noted however that just as the fruits of the property of a husband are not shared as profits by the wife if she renounces her right to profits acquired during marriage, so the fruits of the property of the wife who renounces are not shared and go to the wife alone. For as it is by reason of the partnership which is entered into between husband

inheritance, a legacy or a trust can be resigned." Llamas y Molina, Nos. 2 and 3 to Nov. Rec. Law 9, who in the subsequent numbers also discusses the other two situations, concluding renunciations at those times are also valid.

"Profits are not shared if before the marriage is contracted the parties agree that the wife shall not enjoy this right given to her by law and shall not have a moiety of property acquired during marriage and shall not be liable for debts incurred during that period. Such an agreement is valid." Matienzo, Gloss I, No. 58, to Nov. Rec. Law 1.

"But this sharing of ganancial properties ceases in the following cases: . . . When the wife renounces the ganancial properties, in which case she is not responsible for the debts of the marriage, Law 9, Tit. 4, Book 10, Nov. Rec.; it being understood that she can make this renunciation before contracting the marriage, after contracted, and after it is dissolved." Escriche, Diccionario, "Ganancial Properties."

Renunciation made after dissolution of marriage, see post, Chap. X.

[56] "And you should, in the first place, extend this limitation to apply even if the wife during marriage makes a general or special renuncia-

tion of profits. If, for example, the husband wishes to buy a house or to take a lease of state revenues and the wife opposes and says that she is unwilling to bear a share in such purchase or lease and makes an agreement to that effect with her husband, such a renunciation and agreement is valid." Matienzo, Gloss I, No. 60, to Nov. Rec. Law 1.

"Such renunciation can be made at the outset when they are discussing the contract of marriage, if the parties so agree; for such a decree is valid. . . . This rule may be understood to apply also even in cases where the wife during marriage renounces her right to profits either generally or specially . . . ; and agreement to that effect is valid." Matienzo, Gloss I, Nos. 1, 2, to Nov. Rec. Law 9.

As not within prohibition against gifts between spouses, see post, § 140.

[57] See Matienzo, Gloss I, Nos. 4–7, to Nov. Rec. Law 9.

Gifts between spouses distinguished, see post, § 140.

[58] See Llamas y Molina, No. 16, to Nov. Rec. Law 9.

As to husband's renunciation when affecting rights of creditors, see post, Chap. IX.

[59] Azevedo, No. 2, to Nov. Rec. Law 9.

and wife that the fruits are shared (citing the laws), if the partnership is dissolved or not entered into at all, by reason of the wife's renunciation, the fruits are not shared. For the effect of a partnership ceases when the partnership, which is the cause, ceases."[60]

Where the spouse, during marriage, made a complete renunciation of all profits, in the view of the Spanish law of community property there was just as effective a dissolution of the marital community as in the case of death or divorce. The marriage itself still subsisted, of course, but the community or marital partnership no longer existed.[61]

§ 136. — American authorities.

In consonance with the Spanish community property law, we find statutory provisions in our community property states authorizing the parties to a marriage to make marriage settlements, but it is usually provided that such contracts must be in writing, acknowledged and recorded.[62] Some of the states have been quite strict in holding oral marriage settlements invalid,[63] even though performed during marriage.[64] But others consider the oral agreement valid if it has been performed[65] or ratified during the marriage.[66] Usually, these statutes permit agreements or stipulations as to the marital property which are contrary to the provisions of the legal community,[67] but this view does not obtain in all states, certainly not in all particulars.[68] Certainly, the agreement cannot be one in violation of public policy.[69]

[60] Azevedo, Nos. 13, 14 to Nov. Rec. Law 9.

"It should be carefully noted however that just as the fruits of the property of the husband are not shared as profits by the wife if she renounces her right to profits acquired during marriage, so the fruits of the property of the wife who renounces are not shared and go to the wife alone." Azevedo, No. 13, to Nov. Rec. Law 9.

[61] Dissolution, see post, Chap. X.

[62] Ariz. Rev. St. 1956, 25-211; Cal. Civ. Code, § 5133; Ida. Code 1948, §§ 32-905, 32-916—32-920; La. Civ. Code, art. 2325 et seq.; Nev. Rev. St. 1956, § 123.010 et seq.; N.M. St. 1953, § 57-2-6 et seq.; Tex. Family Code 1969, § 5.41; Wash. Rev. Code 1961, § 26.16.120.

[63] McDonald v. Lambert, 43 N.M. 27, 85 P.2d 78, 120 A. L. R. 250, overruled in Chavez v. Chavez, 56 N.M. 393, 244 P.2d 741, in so far as it states that no contract can be made; Leroux v. Knoll, 28 Wash. 2d 964, 184 P.2d 564. And see Lieber

v. Mercantile Nat. Bank (Tex. Civ. App.), 331 S. W. 2d 463, writ ref'd, n.r.e.

[64] Rogers v. Joughlin, 152 Wash. 448, 277 P. 988.

[65] Kenney v. Kenney, 220 Cal. 134, 30 P.2d 398.

[66] Estate of Piatt, 81 Cal. App. 2d 348, 183 P.2d 919.

[67] E. g., La. Civ. Code, arts. 2332, 2424.

[68] It now appears that Texas alone refuses to allow spouses to enter into contracts, either before or during marriage, whereby the community property system will not govern their marital property acquisitions. See Vaughn, The Policy of Community Property and Interspousal Transactions, 19 Baylor L. Rev. 20; McSwain, A Survey of the New Marital Property Statutes, 2 Newsletter Family Law Section Texas Bar 3.

[69] La. Civ. Code, art. 2325.

Agreements to pay a wife a salary for her services as housekeeper are void. See Brooks v. Brooks, 48 Cal.

A minor capable of contracting matrimony may make a valid marriage settlement, according to the statutes of many of the community property states,[70] although some of the statutes add a proviso that the written consent of parents or guardian is a prerequisite.[71]

But in authorizing these marriage settlements, the statutes relate to settlements or contracts made before or at the time of the marriage. As concerns agreements or contracts during the marriage, there is a lack of uniformity. In some of the states, as under the Spanish community property law, the husband and the wife during the marriage may by contract with each other alter their legal relations as to their property.[72] The mutual consent of the spouses is a sufficient consideration for such an agreement.[73] In others of the states, however, there may be no alteration of the matrimonial agreement after solemnization of the marriage.[74] These latter statutes would seem to prevent any agreements during marriage that altered the character of com-

App. 2d 347, 119 P.2d 970; Frame v. Frame, 120 Tex. 61, 36 S. W. 2d 152, 73 A. L. R. 1512.

But Judge Hutcheson while on the United States District Court in Texas held, after reviewing decisions in Texas and other jurisdictions, that husband and wife could validly enter into a contract whereby the husband was to pay the wife a weekly wage for working as a clerk in his business, and upon the husband becoming bankrupt he approved the wife's claim for arrears of wages, although without priority. In re Gutiérrez, 33 F.2d 987.

Altering order of descent, as prohibited, see post, § 137.

[70] Ariz. Rev. St. 1956, § 25-201; Cal. Civ. Code, § 5137; Ida. Code 1948, § 32-920; La. Civ. Code, art. 2330; Nev. Rev. St. 1956, § 123.310; N.M. St. 1953, § 57-2-11; Tex. Family Code 1969, § 5.41.

[71] Ariz. Rev. St. 1956, § 25-201; Tex. Family Code 1969, § 5.41.

[72] Cal. Civ. Code, § 5103; Brockelbank, The Community Property Law of Idaho, § 2.2.2.; Nev. Rev. St. 1956, § 123.070; N.M. St. 1953, § 57-2-6; Wash. Rev. Code 1961, § 26.16.120; O'Bryan v. Commissioner of Internal Revenue (9 C. C. A.), 148 F.2d 456, where spouses' separation agreement had effect of extinguishing community character of

husband's earnings while he was domiciled in California. See Estate of Brimhall, 62 Cal. App. 2d 30, 143 P.2d 981.

As to Washington, see especially Volz v. Zang, 113 Wash. 378, 194 P. 409; In re Brown's Estate, 29 Wash. 2d 20, 185 P.2d 125; Union Securities Co. v. Smith, 93 Wash. 115, 160 P. 304, Ann. Cas. 1918 E 710.

Declaration in a will is a unilateral statement. See Plummer v. U. S., 89 F. Supp. 911.

Property settlements upon separation, see post, § 231.

[73] Cal. Civ. Code, § 4802; Nev. Rev. St. 1956, § 123.080; N.M. St. 1953, § 57-2-13.

[74] Ariz. Rev. St. 1956, § 25-201; La. Civ. Code, art. 2329.

Prior to 1967, Texas allowed antenuptial or postnuptial contracts, although they could not operate to negate the community property system. See Weidner v. Crowther, 157 Tex. 240, 301 S. W. 2d 621 and Vaughn, "The Joint and Mutual Will," 16 Baylor L. Rev. 167 (1964). However, the language of Tex. Rev. Civ. St. 1925, art. 4610, as amended in 1967, specifically relates to contracts before marriage but would not operate to permit the spouses to contract away the community.

338

munity property to separate property,[75] but it is evident that they do not prevent the alteration of the character of community property to separate property when accomplished by means of gift or donation from one spouse to the other.[76]

§ 137.   — Agreement as affecting legal order of descent.

Under the Spanish law, in the case of profits to be made, the wife could, even at the outset of the marriage, validly renounce such profits,[77] even though it was to the hurt of her parents or sons to whom a statutory portion might be owed.[78] In some of our community property states, however, agreements by way of marriage settlements, it is sometimes specified, cannot be made if altering the legal order of descent either as to themselves or in what concerns the inheritance of their children or posterity, whether children that either spouse has had by another person or their common children.[79] But under the Spanish law, the wife during marriage could not renounce ganancial properties in fraud of or to the prejudice of legitimate rights of inheritance of her ascendants or descendants as established by law.[80]

---

[75] As to invalidity of agreements between spouses altering character of community property to separate property, see Cox v. Miller, 54 Tex. 16; Green v. Ferguson, 62 Tex. 525; Arnold v. Leonard, 114 Tex. 535, 273 S. W. 799; Hilley v. Hilley, 161 Tex. 569, 342 S. W. 2d 565.

In Louisiana, spouses can enter into prenuptial agreement but cannot alter that agreement after the marriage is solemnized. The Louisiana statutes defining community and separate property are of mandatory application only in the absence of prenuptial agreement stipulating what is to be community and separate property. Clay v. United States (5 C. C. A.), 161 F.2d 607.

[76] See Arizona, Louisiana and Texas cases cited post, § 141.

[77] See ante, § 135.

[78] Gutiérrez, Quaestio CXXVII, No. 4, to Nov. Rec. Law 9, Book 10, Title 4.

It is to be noticed, however, that so far as children of the marriage were concerned they would receive from their father so much of his property as was provided by law and of which he could not deprive them

even by testamentary disposition. See post, § 193.

[79] Ariz. Rev. St. 1956, § 25-201; La. Civ. Code, art. 2326. And see Tex. Rev. Civ. St. 1925, art. 4610, prior to 1967 amendment.

Unenforceability of agreement between spouses that upon death of either, all property of deceased should vest in survivor, as contrary to statute relating to contracts concerning community property, see Bartlett v. Bartlett, 185 Wash. 278, 48 P.2d 560, because further clause provided that on death of survivor their children should take, thus defeating survivor's alienability. Notice Washington statute, referred to in § 136, providing that spouses may jointly agree concerning the status or disposition of community property to take effect upon the death of either. Such an agreement as not restricting alienation of community realty by joint deed of the spouses, see Hesseltine v. First Methodist Church of Vancouver, 23 Wash. 2d 315, 161 P.2d 157.

[80] "Another very important doubt in this matter is whether 'constante matrimonio' the wife can renounce

Similarly, the husband could not renounce goods and profits already acquired, to the hurt of the treasury to which the goods might afterwards devolve (as by reason of forfeitures, claims for taxes, etc.).[81]

§ 138.   — Undue influence of husband.

In the case of renunciation of profits already made, a few of the Spanish jurisconsults, headed by Gregorio López, held such a renunciation of that already acquired to be invalid. But the great majority of the jurisconsults considered that in ordinary circumstances and in the absence of certain complicating factors, such as the rights of creditors, or of heirs, such a renunciation was valid.[82] They pointed out that as concerned the wife, while her ownership vested upon the acquisition of the profits, it was an ownership different from that of the husband in that it was *in habitu* and not *in actu* and thus more easily renounced, especially since by the renunciation there was a return to the common law (i.e., Roman or nonstatutory law) under which goods acquired by the husband were not shared with the wife.[83] But it was commonly considered that a renunciation by the wife of profits already made was voidable where it had been induced by the husband through threats, or even through entreaty or importunity.[84] We find a somewhat similar principle declared in the statutes of some of our community property states that while husband and wife may be authorized to enter into any engagement or transaction with each

the ganancial properties to the prejudice of the legitimate portion of the estate to be inherited by her ascendants or descendants, and it seems that she cannot do so, according to the opinion of Sr. Olea in Tit. 2, Question 3, No. 22, and the following numbers in which he quotes various authors who should be consulted in order to corroborate this opinion." Llamas y Molina, No. 18 to Nov. Rec. Law 9.

"Whence it is to be inferred that a daughter without descendants may not renounce goods acquired between her and her husband during marriage, or otherwise fraudulently give them away, or sell them, to the hurt of her father who has acquired a right." Gutiérrez, Quaestio CXXVII, No. 4, to Nov. Rec. Law 9.

[81] Gutiérrez, Quaestio CXXVII, No. 4, to Nov. Rec. Law 9.

Renunciation by either spouse defeating rights of creditors, see post, Chap. IX.

[82] Matienzo, Gloss I, to Nov. Rec. Law 9, Bk. 10, Tit. 4. Gutiérrez, Quaestio CXXVI, to the same.

Creditors, see post, Chap. IX.

Heirs, see ante, § 137; post, § 193.

[83] Matienzo, Gloss I, No. 2, to Nov. Rec. Law 1, and Gloss I, No. 5, to Nov. Rec. Law 9; Gutiérrez, Quaestio CXXVI, Nos. 1, 5, to Nov. Rec. Law 9.

Nature of wife's ownership as *in habitu*, see ante, § 100.

Roman or common law, see also ante, § 104.

[84] Gutiérrez, Quaestio CXXVI, No. 5, par. 2, to Nov. Rec. Law 9.

If the renunciation is brought about by wrongful inducement, threats or other deceit it should be voided or revoked but if there is nothing of that sort it should be considered valid. Novísimo Sala Mexicano, Sec. 2a, Title IV, No. 7.

As to undue pressure, etc., upon the wife, see also ante, § 135.

other respecting property, as if unmarried, when they do so they are subject to the general rules controlling the actions of persons occupying confidential relations with each other.[85] And whether or not this principle is declared in the statutes, the courts uniformly apply it to transactions between the spouses.[86] The husband bears a heavier burden, in that if he obtains any advantage from the transaction, a constructive fraud is presumed and the husband has the burden of establishing that he made a full and fair disclosure or explanation to the wife and that she understood fully the effect upon her.[87]

Said the California court: "It is an established rule in an action involving a transaction between a husband and his wife that if there is a finding, supported by substantial evidence, that a just and fair disclosure of all that the wife should know for her benefit and protection concerning the nature and effect of the transaction has been made to her, such finding dispels the presumptions of undue influence which arises when the husband gains an advantage in a transaction with his wife. It is likewise established that if it is a fact that the transaction between the spouses is fair and just and there has been a full and fair disclosure to the wife of all facts essential to her protection, it is not essential, in order to overcome the presumption that the husband has exercised undue influence over his wife, that there be evidence that she had received independent advice."[88]

It is not to be supposed that it is the wife alone who may be subjected to undue influence, pressure, fraud or the like by the husband; the husband likewise may very well be the one subjected thereto on the part of the wife.[89]

§ 139.   — Conflict of laws.

The effect, where spouses who have agreed or contracted with respect to marital property move to another domicile with different laws as to marital property, has already been discussed.[90] Where they

---

[85] Cal. Civ. Code, § 5103; N.M. St. 1953, § 57-2-6.

[86] See, e.g., Estate of Newman, 36 Cal. Rptr. 352; Sande v. Sande, 83 Ida. 233, 360 P.2d 998; Curtis v. Curtis, 56 N.M. 695, 248 P.2d 683.

[87] See, e.g., Estate of Marsh (Cal. App.), 311 P.2d 599;. Peardon v. Peardon, 65 Nev. 717, 201 P.2d 309. And see post, § 141.

[88] Estate of Brimhall, 62 Cal. App. 2d 30, 143 P.2d 981.

[89] See Buchmayer v. Buchmayer, 68 Cal. App. 2d 462, 157 P.2d 9; Smith v. Smith (La.), 119 So.2d 827; Martinez v. Martinez (N.M.), 307 P.2d 1117.

Importunities, nagging, threats, and unfulfilled promises, as those of the wife inducing conveyance of property by husband from which equity relieved him, see Trigg v. Trigg, 32 N.M. 296, 22 P.2d 119. See also Crawford v. Crawford, 24 Nev. 410, 56 P. 94, as to husband's charge of fraud and undue influence against wife in inducing him to convey property to wife if she returned to live with him and she left him again thereafter; in denying relief in this case the court referred to the spouses as persons occupying fiduciary and confidential relations to each other.

[90] See ante, § 90.

remain domiciled in one state and enter into an agreement concerning realty located in another state, the law of the state where the realty is located governs in determining the effect of their marital contract respecting such realty.[91] On the other hand, agreements with respect to personalty are generally held to be governed by the law of the spouses' domicile;[92] this same law is generally held to control the spouses' right to contract with each other.[93]

§ 140.   Gifts between spouses — Spanish law and distinctions therein.

It has been frequently declared by American courts and legal writers that under the Spanish law, while husband and wife could enter into onerous contracts with each other, gifts or donations between them were prohibited; some of them state that such a gift or donation was not void but voidable and could be revoked by the giver at any time during his or her life, but that it became irrevocable on the giver's death, others state that it was prohibited outright in Spain but was revocable as voidable in the Spanish law as it was in force in Mexico and Louisiana.[94] Reference to the Spanish codes and to the commentaries thereon shows that the law, as established as far back as the year 1263 and which continued unabatedly in force, was that donations between spouses made by reason of affection were not valid. But the declaration that they were not valid meant that they were voidable rather than void, because if the one making the gift did not revoke it during his or her life, the donation was validated by the death of the donor. It is to be noticed that the power to avoid the donation lay only with the donor.[95] It may also be remarked that if the donee died before the donor the donation was inoperative.[96]

---

[91] See Black v. Commissioner of Internal Revenue, 9 C. C. A., 114 F.2d 355; Colden v. Alexander, 141 Tex. 134, 171 S. W. 2d 328.

[92] Where spouses remained domiciled in Texas but transferred bank account containing community funds to New York and in New York entered into a contract dividing such funds into equal parts to be separate property of each, such contract was held to be governed by Texas and not by New York law. Upon wife bringing her share back to Texas, it was held subject to garnishment by a judgment creditor of the husband since contract was invalid in attempting to defeat rights of creditors. King v. Bruce, 145 Tex. 647, 201 S. W. 2d 803, 171 A.L.R. 1328, cert. den. 332 U.S. 769.

[93] Marks v. Loewenburg, 143 La. 196, 78 So. 444.

[94] See Fuller v. Ferguson, 26 Cal. 546; L'Abbe's Heirs v. Abat, 2 La. 553, 22 Am. Dec. 151; 11 Am. Jur. 215; McKay, Community Property, 2nd Ed., § 994; Ballinger, Community Property, § 58.

[95] Las Siete Partidas, Part. 4, Title 11, Law 4; Asso and Mañuel, Institutes of Civil Law of Spain, Book II, Title IX, § 1; Matienzo, Gloss I, No. 60, to Nov. Rec. Law 1, Gloss I, No. 2, to Nov. Rec. Law 9; Gutiérrez, Quaestio CXX, No. 11, to Nov. Rec. Law 2.

[96] See Schmidt, Civil Law of Spain and Mexico, p. 256. To same effect, Gutiérrez, Quaestio CXX, No. 11, to Nov. Rec. Law 2: "When marriage is

There were two exceptions to the prohibition against such donations. A donation was valid which increased the wealth of the donee if it did not diminish the estate of the donor, although it might prevent the donor from receiving an increase in wealth. For example, a spouse might renounce an inheritance, a legacy, or a trust in order that it might pass to the other spouse as substituted or joint intestate successor.[97] Likewise, a donation was permitted which, though diminishing the estate of the donor, did not make the donee any wealthier. At first sight this appears an impossible situation but it applied in this respect, admittedly a very limited one. That is, one spouse might donate funds to be used for a tombstone or other burial purposes for the benefit of the other spouse, or for some other purpose of similar nature which brought no increase of usable wealth to the donee during the donee's life.[98]

It must especially be observed that the prohibition against donations related to the separate estates of the spouses and not to the community interests, for they might enter into agreements as to those which would amount to a renunciation by one in whole or in part of interests in the community property and thus effectively make what we would term a gift thereof to the other.[99] These permissible agreements or transactions with relation to the spouses' interests in the community property were specifically distinguished from the question of donations which were made from the separate property of a spouse,[1] a distinction not usually comprehended by our courts and legal writers.[2]

---

dissolved by the woman's death . . . then a gift from the husband is revoked, and so also would be a gift from a third party in contemplation of the husband."

[97] Las Siete Partidas, Part. 4, Title 11, Law 5; Matienzo, Gloss I, No. 60, to Nov. Rec. Law 1, Gloss I, No. 2, to Nov. Rec. Law 9.

It will be seen also that small gifts by one spouse to the other, in the nature of those customarily made on anniversaries, holidays or like occasions, would not appreciably diminish the estate of a spouse. See Schmidt, Civil Law of Spain and Mexico, p. 255.

[98] Las Siete Partidas, Part. 4, Title 11, Law 6.

[99] See ante, § 135.
Of course, transactions between the spouses might take place in relation to their separate estates which would not fall under the head of gifts, as where the wife authorized the husband to manage her paraphernal property.

See ante, § 112.

[1] See Llamas y Molina, No. 11, to Nov. Rec. Law 9. See also ante, § 135, that renunciation by husband of his right to share in gains during marriage was not a "gift" to the wife.

"And Didacus Covarruvias there lays down another rule, viz. that either spouse can during marriage renounce profits already acquired during marriage in the same way as future acquisitions can be renounced. . . . It should not be thought that such an act is a gift between husband and wife and so prohibited, since a person who remits a share of profits, it is clear, repudiates profits but does not lose anything of the property which he previously possessed. The person to whom the gift is offered acquires nothing to make him richer but merely acts thus in order that what he has earned perhaps by very great labor may not be shared by his idle spouse." Matienzo, Gloss I, No. 5, to Nov. Rec. Law 9.

[2] See post, § 141.

While the agreements relating to the community interests were permissible, it was believed necessary to throw safeguards around the matter of the separate estates because mutual affection between the spouses might lead one to strip himself or herself of his or her property in favor of the other, and this might be brought about by the other with more or less ease.[3] This is not to say that safeguards were not also thrown around the matter of agreements or renunciations by the wife in respect to the ganancial properties, for as we have seen such agreements or renunciations were voidable if induced by the husband through threats, or even through entreaty or importunity.[4]

§ 141.   — American views.

While the Spanish community property law distinguished between agreements and transactions relating to the community property and gifts to one spouse made from the separate estate of the other, in our community property states it is difficult, if not impossible, to find any such distinction. The situation seems undoubtedly to be that the spouses may usually enter into agreements and contracts of an onerous nature with each other concerning either the community property or other separate property,[5] or may make gifts to each other from their separate estates or from their interests in the community property. In the latter respect, renunciation of rights or interests in the community property which the Spanish law did not class under the head of donations but as permissible transactions relative to community interests, our courts and writers usually term gifts.[6] We do not wish to be understood to be contending that it is erroneous that we term these to be gifts, but rather to point out that our courts do not make the distinction that the Spanish law did. Accordingly, we should be chary of citing the Spanish views as to gifts when we call things gifts which the Spanish law did not.[7] In any event, spouses in our community property states may, as we understand the term, make gifts

[3] See Asso and Mañuel, Institutes of Civil Law of Spain, Book II, Title IX, § 1.

This was also true of the ancient Roman law and the early French customary law, for much the same reason. See Kopecky, Spousal Donations in Louisiana, 1 Loyola Law Rev. 194, and authorities cited.

[4] See ante, § 135.

[5] See Fuller v. Ferguson, 26 Cal. 546; L'Abbe's Heirs v. Abat, 2 La. 553, 22 Am. Dec. 151. And see cases collected in 41 C.J.S., Husband and Wife, § 515.

[6] However, in Wren v. Wren, 100 Cal. 276, 34 P. 775, 38 Am. St. Rep. 287, where the court upheld the right

of the wife to sue and recover for earnings for personal services as her separate property, it stated that her right to these earnings as her separate property rested not on a gift of them to her by her husband but on an agreement or contract between them pursuant to Cal. Civ. Code, §§ 158–160 (after January 1970, §§ 4802, 5103).

[7] In Fuller v. Ferguson, 26 Cal. 546, where the husband, while California was part of Mexico, had taken some of the community funds for his personal use and reimbursed the wife by turning over to her some of his separate property, the court discussed the transaction as one which husband and wife might validly make, then

one to the other, either of their separate property or of their interest in the community property, in whole or in part,[8] and these are valid if not induced through fraud, duress, undue influence or the like,[9] or are not in fraud of creditors.[10]

§ 142. — Wife's earnings and improvements upon wife's separate property, etc.

In community property states where the wife does not manage her own earnings, the fact that the husband turns over the management of such earnings to her should not in itself amount to a gift to

said that if that were not true then the transfer to the wife might constitute a donation under the Spanish law, which became irrevocable upon the husband's death.

"And it would seem that under the Spanish and Mexican law, a more comprehensive meaning was attached to the term donation than that usually given it in our jurisprudence. Conditions are sometimes attached to donations which would be regarded at common law as changing the character of the transaction from one of gift to one of purchase." Scott v. Ward, 13 Cal. 458.

[8] See Schofield v. Gold, 26 Ariz. 296, 225 P. 71, 37 A. L. R. 275; Sanguinetti v. Sanguinetti, 51 Cal. App. 347, 196 P. 799; Hobbs v. Hobbs, 69 Ida. 201, 204 P.2d 1034; Ouilliber v. Solis (La.), 204 So.2d 625; Succession of Byrnes, 206 La. 1026, 20 So.2d 301; Goldsworthy v. Johnson, 45 Nev. 355, 204 P. 505; McElyea v. McElyea, 49 N.M. 322, 163 P.2d 636; Hamilton v. Charles Maund Oldsmobile-Cadillac Co. (Tex. Civ. App.), 347 S. W. 2d 944, writ. ref., n.r.e.; State v. Miller, 32 Wash. 2d 149, 201 P.2d 136.

In California, a spouse who uses his or her separate property for community purposes is not entitled to reimbursement from the community property or from the other spouse's separate property unless and only if there is an agreement between them to that effect. See v. See, 64 Cal. 2d 778, 51 Cal. Rptr. 888, 415 P.2d 776; Weinberg v. Weinberg, 63 Cal. Rptr. 13, 432 P.2d 709.

The Louisiana statute providing

that the husband can make no gifts without the consent of the wife does not prevent him making a gift to the wife herself. Snowden v. Cruse, 152 La. 144, 92 So. 964. And it is now established by statute that donations between spouses are irrevocable unless there is express reservation of the right to revoke. See La. Civ. Code, art. 1749.

Apparently the situation in Texas must be viewed with caution. That gifts to the wife of the rents of her separate property cannot be made before they accrue, see Chandler v. Alamo Mfg. Co. (Tex. Civ. App.), 140 S. W. 2d 918, and cases cited therein. Early cases sanctioned gifts by husband to wife, either of community or separate property. See Hartwell v. Jackson, 7 Tex. 576; Stafford v. Stafford, 41 Tex. 115; Fisk v. Flores, 43 Tex. 340. Judge Speer, in discussing the permissibility of gifts of community interests between spouses, seems to have in mind property already acquired. See Speer, Law of Marital Rights in Texas, 3rd Ed., § 132.

[9] See Beals v. Ares, 25 N.M. 459, 185 P. 780; Trigg v. Trigg, 32 N.M. 296, 22 P.2d 119; Crawford v. Crawford, 24 Nev. 410, 56 P. 94. And see ante, § 138.

[10] Nicholls v. Mitchell, 32 Cal. 2d 598, 197 P.2d 550; Hobbs v. Hobbs (Ida.), 204 P.2d 1034; Gooding Milling & Elevator Co. v. Lincoln County State Bank, 22 Ida. 468, 126 P. 772; Kolmorgan v. Schaller (Wash.), 316 P.2d 111.

Creditors generally, see post, Chap. IX.

her or waiver by the husband of his community property interest. It must be coupled with permitting her to use these earnings for her own separate purposes as opposed to family or community purposes, in order to be indicative of a gift or waiver.[11]

Where the state is one wherein by statute the wife is authorized to manage her earnings,[12] this in itself does not affect the nature of the earnings which continue to be community property.[13] Where the husband allows her to appropriate her earnings to her own use, for other than family purposes or use, it may be deemed that he has waived his interest in them in her favor.[14]

The foregoing is true whether the earnings are wages or the like for personal services or are profits resulting from the conduct of a business.[15] Indeed, it must be borne in mind that merely turning over property to the wife does not and should not raise a presumption of a gift, in itself, but merely indicates a transfer for managerial purposes,[16] unless it is transferred by an instrument in writing to the name of the wife under a statute which raises therefrom a presumption that this is the wife's separate property.[17]

In California, and in some other jurisdictions influenced by the California decisions, when community funds are used by the husband to improve the wife's separate property, in the absence of any specific agreement to the contrary it is presumed that it was the intention of the husband that such funds so used were to accrue to her interest,

---

[11] As in California, prior to 1951. See Pacific Mut. L. Ins. Co. v. Cleverdon, 16 Cal. 2d 788, 108 P.2d 405; Rayburn v. Rayburn, 54 Cal. App. 69, 300 P. 1054.

In Makeig v. United Security Bank & Trust Co., 112 Cal. App. 138, 296 P. 673, mere keeping of her earnings in a bank account of her own, with husband's consent or knowledge, was not in itself any relinquishment by the husband.

[12] As in California, Idaho, Nevada, Texas and Washington. See ante, § 114.

[13] See Cal. Civ. Code, § 5124; McMillan v. United States Fire Ins. Co., 48 Ida. 163, 280 P. 220.

In Texas, however, where it was said that the husband cannot make a gift of community property to the wife until such property has actually come into existence, the view has been taken that although the husband followed a course of conduct of allowing the wife to take her monthly earnings and deposit them in a bank and exercise control over them, it would be necessary for him each month as the salary was earned to make a gift of it to the wife. See Davis v. Davis (Tex. Civ. App.), 108 S. W. 2d 681.

[14] See Nev. Rev. St. 1956, § 123.190.

Statements and conduct of the husband may often be looked to, as in Rayburn v. Rayburn, 54 Cal. App. 69, 200 P. 1064.

[15] See Diefendorff v. Hopkins, 95 Cal. 343, 28 P. 265, 30 P. 549.

Wife as sole trader, see post, §149.

Again, Texas prohibits a gift of the community property unless it is in existence, even if it is income resulting from the conduct of a business. See Moss v. Gibbs (Tex.), 370 S. W. 2d 452; Johnson v. First Nat. Bank of Ft. Worth (Tex. Civ. App.), 306 S. W. 2d 927.

[16] See ante, § 114.

[17] See ante, § 60.

in other words were a gift to her.[18] The liberality of the California court in presuming gifts to the wife from the husband is generally recognized as having its origin in the frequently expressed view of the California courts, prior to 1927,[19] that the wife's interest in the community property was only an expectancy which did not become vested until dissolution of the marriage; to counterbalance this view the courts were prone to adopt constructions giving the wife property as her separate property. Actually, although the improvements affixed to separate property of the spouse also partake of the separate nature of the property to which affixed,[20] the right to reimbursement to the extent of the enhancement in value of the property by the improvements should exist on the part of the community, in the absence of clear intent that the improvements were intended as a gift.[21] In other words, a presumption of gift should not obtain, and the burden of proving a gift should be on the one alleging the gift.[22] As to whether or not the use of community funds in that manner is in fraud of creditors is dealt with in a subsequent chapter.[23]

It is necessary, also, to notice that there are many cases to the effect that property purchased by the husband with community funds and directed by the husband to be conveyed or transferred to the wife is deemed to be a gift by the husband to the wife.[24] These cases are sometimes based on a statute, of course, where the transfer is to the wife by a written instrument, but where this is not the case, the presumption should always be that such property is community property and only upon adequate proof should it be deemed the wife's separate property.[25] One of the oldest principles of community property has always been the presumption that property acquired during the

---

[18] This view, as followed in California, Idaho and Nevada is discussed ante, § 73, which refers also to the disparate view taken by Arizona, Louisiana, New Mexico, Texas and Washington.

And see de Funiak, Improving Separate Property, Retiring Liens or Paying Taxes on Separate Property with Community Funds, 9 Hastings L. Jour. 36; annotation, 54 A.L.R. 2d 429.

[19] Statutory change in 1927, see ante, § 51.

[20] See discussion, ante, § 73.

[21] See discussion ante, § 73, with reference also to opposing view.

[22] See ante, § 73. And see Oakes, Speer's Marital Rights in Texas, 4th Ed., § 414.

[23] See post, § 174.

[24] See cases cited, 37 A.L.R. 289, 305.

Subsequent transfer to wife after purchase in husband's name, see § 147.

Where husband intended that his wife be named as grantee and upon delivery to him of the deed with his name alone as grantee he erased his name and substituted his wife's name and also apparently altered the date of acknowledgment of the grantors, it was held that no gift to the wife was thereby effectuated. Stroope v. Potter, 48 N.M. 404, 151 P.2d 748.

[25] See particularly, Higgins v. Higgins, 46 Cal. 259; In re Wilson's Estate, 56 Nev. 353, 53 P.2d 359. And see ante, § 60.

marriage is community property, no matter by which spouse acquired or in the name of which spouse acquired.[26]

§ 143.   — Life insurance.

In a previous chapter, gifts through the medium of life insurance policies have already been discussed. It may be briefly repeated here that the view is usually taken that where the husband insures his own life in favor of his wife, paying the premiums with community funds, the policy and the proceeds thereof are the separate property of the wife, it being presumed that the husband has made the wife a gift of his interest in the community funds.[27] On the other hand, it is said that where he insures his own life making the proceeds payable to his estate or to his executors, administrators or assigns, and the premiums have been paid with community funds, the proceeds belong to the community; this is frequently explained on the ground that he cannot exercise his position to make a gift to himself from the community property. This latter principle should also apply where the husband insures the wife's life in his favor and pays the premiums from the community funds, since otherwise he is actually using the community funds to benefit himself or make a gift to himself.[28]

§ 144.   Transfer of separate property to the community.

In the sections immediately preceding, we have been considering as from one spouse to the other the gift or transfer of separate property or of the donor's interest in the community property, and where the gift or transfer is the interest in the community, the change in the character of the community property to separate property. The situation may also arise that one spouse, either as a gift to the community or for consideration advanced by the community, may wish to transfer his or her separate property to the community and thus alter its character to community property. Our community property system, as established by the law, is essentially a community of property in the earnings, gains and acquisitions during marriage, but since most of our community property states permit antenuptial agreements or marriage settlements containing stipulations contrary to provisions of our legal community,[29] there is no reason why an antenuptial agreement cannot be made providing that all or certain separate property of one or of both the parties shall fall into the community so as to

---

[26] See ante, § 60.

[27] Where no right has been reserved to change the beneficiary, the gift is complete, but if there is a right reserved to change the beneficiary, the gift to the wife of the husband's interest is conditional upon his dying without having made the change. Where the right was reserved, see In re Towey's Estate, 22 Wash. 2d 212, 155 P.2d 273.

[28] That the contrary was held in Texas, see ante, § 79.

[29] See ante, § 136.

become a part of it, as do the earnings and gains during the marriage.[30] This would create a modification of the legal community, that is, a modified legal community.[31] The intending spouses are unquestionably as free, under these laws of our community property states, to choose a modified legal community as they are to choose not to have their marital property rights governed at all by the community property system. This was undeniably true of the Spanish community property system, with its permission to the spouses to contract between themselves as they saw fit as to how their property was to be held.[32]

Additionally, in those community property states which permit the spouses during marriage to enter into agreements between themselves in relation to their property, the separate property of a spouse can, by agreement of the spouses, be transferred to the community.[33] This, likewise, was also true under the principles of the Spanish community property system. A spouse might, during the marriage, contribute or devote to the community his or her separate property, thereby to further the interests of the community. Thus, the wife might consent to the sale of her paraphernal property for the benefit of the community, in which case upon ultimate division of the ganancial profits, its price or value was not deducted, for her benefit, from the ganancial profits before their division, but was included in the division since it had been devoted to the community.[34] It is necessary to distinguish, of course, those situations in which the separate property has been used to benefit or advance the interests of the community to the extent of making whatever is purchased or obtained through use of the separate property constitute community property, but the spouse is entitled to reimbursement upon partition to the extent of the value of the separate property so used.[35] In such case, the use

---

[30] California, New Mexico and Washington cases in support of this principle, see 120 A.L.R. 264.

See also Chavez v. Chavez, 56 N.M. 393, 244 P.2d 781, expressly overruling McDonald v. Lambert, 43 N.M. 27, 85 P.2d 78, 120 A.L.R. 250; In re Shea's Estate (Wash.), 376 P.2d 147.

[31] See ante, § 54.

Compare community of property under the Roman-Dutch law whereby all property owned as separate property by the spouses at the time of the marriage falls into the community. See ante, §§ 1, 16.

[32] See ante, § 135.

[33] Estate of Watkins, 16 Cal. 2d 793, 108 P.2d 417, 109 P.2d 1 (joint and mutual wills constituting agreement that property held in joint tenancy was to be community prop-

erty); Volz v. Zang, 113 Wash. 378, 194 P. 409.

As to Idaho, see Black v. Com'r of Int. Rev., 9 C. C. A., 114 F.2d 355.

Purchase by husband of realty with his separate funds, taking title thereto jointly in his name and that of his wife, and payment of taxes thereon from community funds. Blaine v. Blaine, 63 Ariz. 100, 159 P.2d 786.

Evidence of intent to make gift to wife of community interest in husband's separate property, see Wilson v. Wilson, 76 Cal. App. 2d 119, 172 P.2d 568.

[34] Asso and Mañuel, Institutes of Civil Law of Spain, Book I, Title VII, Cap. 2.

[35] See, e.g., Searles v. Searles, 99 Cal. App. 2d 869, 222 P.2d 938; Nichols v. Nichols (Ida.), 372 P.2d 758.

of the separate property is in the nature of a loan for the benefit of the community rather than in the nature of a gift. Where no consideration was given the spouse for the use or contribution of the spouse's separate property, it is to be presumed that reimbursement is in order.[36]

The situation as to transferring separate property to the community is otherwise, of course, in those states which do not sanction agreements or transactions during the marriage in respect to property of the spouses which change the nature of the property as fixed by law,[37] and this is not affected by the fact that even in those states gifts or donations between the spouses may be permitted, for a distinction seems to be made between gifts from one spouse to the other and a gift by one spouse to the community.[38] Such a distinction seems to be one of degree rather than kind. If one spouse owns Blackacre as his or her separate property, it may be given or donated to the other spouse as the latter's separate property; if it were given to the community the result would be to give half of Blackacre to the other spouse, but that is prohibited, although it would be all right to give half of Blackacre directly to the other spouse as that spouse's separate property.[39] But note the indication that if consideration is given to the wife for her separate property, her property may become community property.[40]

In respect to agreements or transactions to transfer separate property to the community, statutory requisites that such an agreement or contract must be in writing must be complied with. Some courts have held a parol agreement invalid even though the spouses have per-

---

[36] Reference may be made to the view of many of the Spanish jurisconsults that the spouse's use of money of his own was in contemplation of its return upon partition of the community property, although what was purchased with it was for the benefit of the community and was community property. See ante, § 77.

In Texas, as to improvement of marital property with funds from another estate, see Comment, 4 S. W. L. Jour. 100.

[37] Kellett v. Trice, 95 Tex. 160, 66 S. W. 51, which has sometimes been cited in support of this, involved an attempted conveyance by a wife of her separate property to the community in consideration of $1, and which the court held to be in effect a gift. It added: "It may be that a purchase may be made of such property by the husband with community funds, so that the consideration will belong to the wife separately, and the

property taking its place will belong to the community estate. If this is true, it is because the law, and not the mere agreement, would give such effect to the transaction. No such case is presented here."

[38] See Oakes, Speer's Marital Rights in Texas, 4th Ed., § 364.

[39] The wife apparently can pledge or mortgage her property to secure a debt of the husband. See Rogers v. Bryan (Tex. Civ. App.), 270 S. W. 1066.

[40] In Taylor v. Hollingsworth, 142 Tex. 158, 176 S. W. 2d 733, the case of Kellett v. Trice is distinguished on ground that wife received no consideration for transferring her separate property to the community and it is denied that in that case any general rule was laid down preventing wife from making such a conversion, if accomplished by a conveyance recognized by law. (As to forms of conveyances required in Texas, see § 147.)

formed the agreement,[41] but others declare that an agreement is not invalid by reason of being oral if it has been fully performed.[42]

Such agreements or transactions discussed above should always be subject to the same close scrutiny as those converting the property or interest of one spouse into the separate property of the other, in order that there may be no fraud, overreaching, undue influence or the like accomplishing detriment to one spouse.[43]

§ 145.   — Conflict of laws.

Where spouses who are domiciled in a noncommunity property state agree and contract between themselves that all the separate real property each owns or shall thereafter acquire, which is located in a community property state, shall henceforward be converted to and held as community property, the law of the state where the realty is located governs the effectiveness of such agreement. Where such law permits agreements between spouses altering the character of separate property to community property, such agreement is effective.[44] It is to be presumed that the same would be true where the agreement related to personal property having a fixed location, as for business purposes, in a community property jurisdiction.

§ 146.   Agreements or arrangements as to separate property.

Although the wife, under the Spanish community property system, retained the control and management of her separate property other than the dotal property, and continues in our community property states to control and manage her separate property, she could under the Spanish law, if she wished, and as she may also do in our community property states, place the administration of her separate property in her husband's hands.[45] The husband administered such

---

[41] See Rogers v. Joughlin, 152 Wash. 448, 277 P. 988; Leroux v. Knoll, 28 Wash. 2d 964, 184 P.2d 564.

[42] Tomaier v. Tomaier, 23 Cal. 2d 754, 146 P.2d 905; Estate of Sears, 6 Cal. Rptr. 148.

[43] See also ante, § 113 et seq.

Statutes permitting agreements between spouses with respect to property frequently specify that rules are applicable which govern actions of persons occupying confidential relations. See Cal. Civ. Code, § 5103; N. M. Stats. 1953, § 57-2-6.

[44] See Black v. Com'r of Int. Rev., 9 C. C. A., 114 F.2d 355 (realty located in Idaho and Washington and spouses domiciled in Oregon).

Similarly, where spouses resident in California orally agreed that all separate property held by them should be converted into community, the effectiveness of this agreement as to separate realty of the husband in Texas was governed by Texas law. Under the law of Texas an oral contract was ineffective to convey any interest in realty. Colden v. Alexander, 141 Tex. 134, 171 S. W. 2d 328.

Spouse by labor and industry acquiring realty in state in which not domiciled, see ante, § 92.

[45] See ante, § 112.

property at his own risk and his own property was impliedly pledged as security in respect of his administration.[46]

In Louisiana, this act of allowing the husband to manage her separate property or to join with her in managing it results in making its fruits and profits community property.[47]

§ 147. Form and effect of conveyance or transfer between spouses.

To the lawyer accustomed to the restrictions of the common law on contracts and dealings between husband and wife, it may be difficult to conceive of the freedom of husband and wife under the community system to make conveyances or transfers one to the other. However, being free to contract and deal with each other as separate individuals, they are entitled to convey or transfer one to the other, just as any other two persons convey or transfer one to the other. No devious or roundabout methods are or should be necessary to accomplish such transfers and conveyances between the spouses. In some of our community property states, it is sometimes expressly provided by statute that the husband may convey community property to the wife or the wife to the husband without the other joining in the conveyance.[48] So a conveyance of community realty by the husband to the wife is sufficient and effective to convert it into her separate property.[49] Even if it is not so expressly provided, it is obvious that where they have the right during marriage to enter into transactions with each other, such conveyances are permissible,[50] without such roundabout methods as both jointly conveying the property to a third person, such as a trustee, who then makes conveyance to the spouse intended to have the property.[51] The spouses could make such trans-

---

[46] See, more fully, post, § 150.

Superiority of wife's implied or tacit lien over rights of creditors of or purchasers from husband, see post, § 175.

[47] See ante, § 71.

[48] Cal. Civ. Code, § 5127; Ida. Code 1948, § 32-906; N.M. St. 1953, § 57-4-3; Wash. Rev. Code 1961, § 26.16.120. See Texas Family Code 1969, § 5.22. See also Shorett v. Signor, 58 Wash. 89, 107 P. 1033.

[49] Johnson v. Wheeler, 41 Wash. 2d 246, 248 P.2d 558 (deed recorded by husband and no evidence that wife failed to accept deed); Shorett v. Signor, 58 Wash. 89, 107 P. 1033 (deed reciting consideration).

[50] See Schofield v. Gold, 26 Ariz. 296, 225 P. 71, 37 A.L.R. 275, point-ing out that the statutory requirement that husband and wife join in conveyances of the community property does not mean that one cannot alone execute a conveyance of his or her share to the other; in joining in the conveyance to a third person, each is acting for himself or herself and each holds the same interest in the property conveyed, so there is no reason why one, even the wife, may not convey his or her interest to the other without both having to join as the grantors; Hartman v. Hartman (Tex. Civ. App.), 217 S. W. 2d 872, writ ref'd, n.r.e.

[51] As seems to have been done in Houston Oil Co. v. Choate (Tex. Com. App.), 232 S. W. 285. The intervention of trustees apparently

fers, one to the other, in the Spanish law of community property without the use of devious methods, for they were considered separate persons who might deal with each other in a straightforward fashion. That being so, they could convey or transfer one to the other, as was the case with those whose transactions were not affected by circumstances of marriage.[52] This should be kept firmly and clearly in mind, for we are too much influenced, even in our community property states, by notions of the English common law. The rights of the spouses to deal with each other and to make transfers directly to each other should be considered in the light of community property principles and not common-law principles.[53]

Where one spouse transfers his or her entire interest in the community property or in a component part of the community to the other spouse, it is sometimes presumed in this country, frequently due to statutory provisions,[54] that the intention was to change the character of such community property to separate property, so that the entire property involved is then the separate property of the transferee.[55] The wisdom of such a presumption is open to question. It runs contrary to the basic principle that the presumption to be indulged is that property acquired and possessed during the marriage is community property. Rather than indulging any presumption as to property being separate property, proof should always be required by the spouse making the allegation or claim that the property is not community property. Certainly, if any presumption that an interest in community property transferred to one spouse has its character changed

was not considered necessary in the earlier Texas cases. See Reynolds v. Lansford, 16 Tex. 286; Fitts v. Fitts, 14 Tex. 443; Story v. Marshall, 24 Tex. 305; Smith v. Boquet, 27 Tex. 507; Hall v. Hall, 52 Tex. 299. And this should not be necessary under later statutory changes. See Tex. Family Code 1969, § 5.22.

Cases involving conveyance of interest in community property between spouses, see 37 A.L.R. 282.

[52] See Llamas y Molina, No. 8 et seq. to Law 55 of Leyes de Toro.

"According to these [Spanish] laws it is clear that husband and wife were considered so far separate persons that they could validly enter into any onerous contracts between themselves. A sale is the example given to illustrate this doctrine. They seem to have been prohibited only from making donations to each other, during the marriage, of property actually in possession. By the same laws the wife was permitted to renounce her rights to the matrimonial acquests and gains, at any time before, during, or after the dissolution of the marriage." L'Abbe's Heirs v. Abat, 2 La. 553, 22 Am. Dec. 151.

[53] Their dealings with each other are subject, of course, to the fact that fraud, undue influence or the like on the part of one spouse should be nonexistent. See ante, §§ 119, 120.1, 138.

[54] Presumptions generally, see ante, § 60.

[55] See Petition of Fuller, 63 Nev. 26, 159 P.2d 579, citing de Funiak, 1st edition; Tittle v. Tittle, 148 Tex. 102, 220 S. W. 2d 637; Shorett v. Signor, 58 Wash. 89, 107 P. 1033; Johnson v. Wheeler, 41 Wash. 2d 246, 248 P.2d 558. And see Estate of Walsh, 66 Cal. App. 2d 704, 152 P.2d 750, pointing out distinction between transfer by written instrument and transfer by manual delivery.

to separate property is to be indulged, such presumption should be indulged only where it is clear that it is an entire interest in the community property or an entire interest in a component part of the community property that is transferred.[56] To the extent that such a presumption is warranted it is, or certainly should be, as true of transfers by the wife to the husband[57] as it is of transfers by the husband to the wife.[58]

In the matter of agreement between the spouses to convey or transfer or to alter the character of community property to separate property, the validity or invalidity of such an agreement in a particular jurisdiction depends, of course, upon the extent to which the spouses are there authorized to deal with each other in respect to their property. That is, there may be restrictions, for example, on the right to effect changes in the character of property during marriage.[59] Even in the cases of agreements that may validly and freely be made, whether before or during marriage, the possible effect of other statutes, such as the Statute of Frauds, must be considered.[60]

In the case of a transfer or conveyance of the separate property of a spouse to the community, the effect naturally is to alter its character to community property.[61]

§ 148.   Spouses as business partners.

Whether husband and wife can join as partners in a business partnership and hold property together as business partners presents a difficult question. The conflicts that would arise between their rights and obligations as business partners and their rights and obligations as marital partners under the community property system would involve many problems. It has been said that the two relationships are so inconsistent that they cannot exist together and that the community partnership must supersede the commercial partnership.[62] Other

---

[56] Rebuttability of presumption, see ante, § 60.

[57] Schofield v. Gold, 26 Ariz. 296, 225 P. 71, 37 A. L. R. 275.

Effect of quitclaim deed, see Hayden v. Zerbst, 49 Wash. 103, 94 P. 909.

[58] Main v. Main, 7 Ariz. 149, 60 P. 888; Taylor v. Opperman, 79 Cal. 468, 21 P. 869; Story v. Marshall, 24 Tex. 305, 76 Am. Dec. 106.

[59] See ante, § 136. And see cases cited, 37 A. L. R. 298.

[60] See Hill v. Du Pratt, 51 Nev. 242, 274 P. 2; Franzetti v. Franzetti (Tex. Civ. App.), 124 S. W. 2d 195, err. ref'd; Union Savings & Trust Co.

v. Smith, 93 Wash. 115, 160 P. 304, Ann. Cas. 1918 E 710.

[61] It must be remembered, though, that it may be a question of evidence as to whether there was an agreement or intention to alter the character of the separate property to community property. See Title Insurance & Trust Co. v. Ingersoll, 153 Cal. 1, 94 P. 94; Scott v. Currie, 7 Wash. 2d 301, 109 P.2d 526.

[62] Squire v. Belden, 2 La. 268.

It is observable that in Louisiana spouses have engaged in business as commercial partners (see Monroe Grocery Co. v. Davis, 165 La. 1027, 116 So. 546), although it has been

decisions, although not many in number, also have denied the right of the wife to engage as a partner with her husband in a business or commercial partnership, upon various other grounds. Chiefly, the reasoning has seemed to have been influenced by common-law concepts that a married woman's individuality is merged into that of her husband and that she cannot contract with him or engage, even as his partner, in conduct of a business as could a *feme sole*.[63] The older cases in Texas followed similar rules to the foregoing, refusing to permit the wife to be a partner in any partnership, including one with the husband.[64] This disability may have been removed by changes in the Texas statutes relating to the contractual powers of married women,[65] but there is some question as to this.[66]

There would seem to be no reason, however, why the spouses might not by antenuptial contract or by contract during marriage, in those states permitting it,[67] provide that the legal community should not govern their property and that they should proceed on the basis of commercial partners,[68] if the jurisdiction is one giving a married woman the necessary powers as a *feme sole* which would be requisite to her exercising the ordinary powers of a commercial partner.

Even without any express arrangement, husband and wife as marital partners, in the light of community property principles, could proceed in the joint operation of a business or commercial partnership, for there is no reason why they should not concentrate their joint labor and industry in that way as well as any other in order to further the success of the marital partnership. Both may separately exercise labor and industry to advance the marital community, and earnings, gains and acquisitions so separately made fall into the community and benefit it. Accordingly, there is no sensible reason why they cannot join their labor and industry into one common source

held prior to 1921, at least, that a wife could not be a partner with her husband (Thompson-Ritchie Grocery Co. v. Graham, 15 La App. 534, 132 So. 394).

[63] Fairbanks, Morse & Co. v. Bordelon (La.), 198 So. 391; Board of Trade v. Hayden, 4 Wash. 263, 30 P. 87, 32 P. 224, 16 L. R. A. 530, 31 Am. St. Rep. 919; Elliott v. Hawley, 34 Wash. 585, 76 P. 93, 101 Am. St. Rep. 1016. And see Morreau Gas Fixture Co. v. Cox, 161 F. 381 (Wash.).

Validity of partnership agreement between spouses, see 20 A. L. R. 1304; 157 A. L. R. 652.

[64] See Miller v. Marx and Kempner, 65 Tex. 131; Purdom v. Boyd, 82 Tex. 130, 17 S. W. 606; Cash v. Com'r of Int. Rev., 63 F.2d 466, cert. den. 290 U.S. 644.

[65] See Tex. Family Code 1969, § 4.03.

[66] See Amsler, The New Married Woman's Statutes: Meaning and Effect, 15 Baylor L. Rev. 145, at 155–158; Amsler, The Status of Married Women in the Texas Business Association, 43 Tex. L. Rev. 669, at 674–678.

[67] See ante, § 136.

[68] See Squire v. Belden, 2 La. 268.

In California, it is indicated that spouses can hold property together as business partners. See Estate of Inman, 148 Cal. App. 2d 952, 307 P.2d 953.

Legal and conventional community, see ante, § 54.

of earnings and gains.[69] The chief difficulty in this situation would rest on the limitations on the wife's powers to contract or to alienate property and so to act equally with the husband so far as concerned the affairs of the commercial venture. But those dealing with the partnership could not in the ordinary course of events be unaware that the partners were husband and wife and thus could govern themselves accordingly in always obtaining the sanction of the husband or of both husband and wife, as the circumstances warranted, when engaging in transactions with the partnership. Indeed, the husband's authorization to the wife to bind him would undoubtedly be implied.[70]

§ 149. Wife as sole trader or as business partner of another.

In ordinary circumstances, of course, where a wife engages in the conduct of a business of her own, her earnings and gains therefrom are community property just as are her earnings for her personal services.[71] If the husband, without objection, allows the wife to conduct a separate business, manage it without his interference, and keep the gains and profits therefrom for her own use as she sees fit, it may be described as a gift of such gains and profits to the wife by the husband,[72] or it may be described as an implied agreement or contract between them to that effect. (The evidence, of course, should be clear that such was the intent of the spouses, for the presumption always should be that acquests and gifts during marriage by either spouse are community property, not that they are separate property of the individual spouse. That is one of the very bases of the community property system.)[73] Whichever way it is described, the result is the same, of course, in that the gains and profits from the business constitute the wife's separate property. The result is the same, likewise, where the husband and wife expressly agree that she may conduct a separate business and keep the gains and profits as her separate property.[74] Such an agreement could be made in all the community

---

[69] The fact that spouses have so been partners with each other, even in jurisdictions questioning the right at the time, is shown by the Louisiana cases, cited ante, this section.

In Barnes v. Thompson, 154 La. 1036, 98 So. 657, wherein it appeared the spouses jointly conducted a mercantile business, the court said: "As to the stock of merchandise, it is clear that the same was acquired under like conditions, that is, by the joint industry of the two spouses. It is conceded that the wife was the better business 'man' of the two, and that she probably contributed more of time and energy to its earnings; but, nevertheless, the business was conducted by both, and was undoubtedly a community asset."

Recognition of business partnership between spouses, that returns therefrom are community property, and that commingling of separate funds in the business was such as to convert them to community property, see Estate of Kane (Cal. App.), 181 P.2d 751.

[70] See Lobingier, "Modern Civil Law," 40 Corpus Juris 1268, n. 82.

[71] See ante, § 66.

[72] See ante, § 142.

[73] Presumptions, see ante, § 60.

[74] Agreements between spouses, see ante, § 136.

property states in the antenuptial marriage contract or marriage settlement, and during the marriage in those states permitting agreements between spouses during marriage in relation to their property. But in those states which do not permit alteration of the legal community after solemnization of the marriage, such an agreement or arrangement could not, strictly speaking, be made. It might be sanctioned in those states as a gift, however, from husband to wife, if gifts are permissible. Otherwise, the right of the wife to act as a sole trader would have to depend upon special statutory authorization. As a matter of fact, in many of the community property states, without regard to whether they are states in which postnuptial agreements may or may not be made, statutes exist respecting the right of the wife to act as a sole trader.[75] In the main, these statutes may be divided into two groups, those that enable the wife to petition a court for the removal of her disabilities of coverture with the consent of her husband,[76] and those designed to protect the wife against an improvident husband, in that she may obtain authorization from the court to act as a sole trader, without the necessity of consent by the husband, upon showing insufficiency of his support.[77] Such statutes are not to be used to cloak any fraudulent intent or purpose, such as the defrauding of creditors.[78]

Besides the matter of the gains and profits from a business conducted by the wife, we may note that as an incident of such right to conduct a separate business, whether conducted by consent of the husband or by statutory authorization, that the wife is necessarily empowered to make contracts relative to its conduct.[79]

When the wife conducts a business as a sole trader she may

---

[75] Wife as "public merchant" in Louisiana, see La. Civ. Code, art. 131, authorizing her, without husband's consent, to obligate herself in anything relating to her trade; husband is bound also if there exists a community of property between them.

In Louisiana, however, the nature of property to be acquired in the future cannot be changed by a postnuptial agreement; and in Texas the nature of property to be acquired in the future cannot be changed by antenuptial or postnuptial agreement.

[76] As was true in Texas prior to 1963. See Tex. Rev. Civ. St. 1925, art. 4626, as enacted in 1911 and amended in 1937. In 1963, art. 4626 was amended to give married women general power of contract with the proviso that her contracts could not bind the community property. In 1967, further amendments of the statutes

leave art. 4626 giving complete power to contract. This article is § 4.04 of the 1969 Texas Family Code.

[77] Nev. Rev. St. 1956, 124.010–124.050; Youngworth v. Jewell, 15 Nev. 45.

In California, for the wife to qualify as a "sole trader," she must show "justification for the application." Cal. Code Civ. Proc., § 1813.

[78] See Gray v. Perlis, 76 Cal. App. 511, 245 P. 221; Youngworth v. Jewell, 15 Nev. 45.

[79] Right generally of wife to contract, see ante, § 112.

"A married woman cannot enter into any contract without the express consent of her husband. Nevertheless, if she exercises publicly some office or trade, she may make contracts relating to either." Schmidt, Civil Law of Spain and Mexico, p. 109, citing Fuero Real, Book 3, Title 20, Law 13.

employ her husband therein in a subordinate capacity, although it might possibly constitute a circumstance tending to establish fraud.[80]

Just as a wife may work or engage in business, so she may engage in business in partnership with another person. In the latter event, her earnings and profits from such a partnership constitute, of course, community property,[81] unless by agreement with or by gift from her husband such earnings and gains are to be her separate property.[82] Where the earnings and gains inure to the benefit of the community or where community funds or property are invested in such partnership, the consent of the husband would seem necessary to permit the wife to deal and contract with reference thereto, as in other situations. But here, too, one must consider the effect of any statute permitting a wife to manage her own earnings. It is much more common, of course, for a husband to be engaged in a business partnership with another than it is for a wife, and cases of the latter sort are not numerous.[83]

§ 150. Property losses.

Just as the spouses, in the Spanish community property system, equally shared the earnings and gains acquired during the marriage, so they equally bore the burden of losses incurred by the marital partnership during the marriage,[84] where the loss was not due to fault by either spouse.[85] So, in ordinary circumstances of administration of the community property the husband was not charged with loss sustained, where he acted with due care and without fraudulent or wrongful intent. However, if the husband in his administration of the community property caused loss to it through fraudulent alienation or wrongful waste, his share of the community was chargeable therewith so as to make the wife whole.[86] Indeed, any poor manage-

---

[80] Gray v. Perlis, 76 Cal. App. 511, 245 P. 221; Youngworth v. Jewell, 15 Nev. 45.

[81] See Hulsman v. Ireland, 205 Cal. 345, 270 P. 948, where burdens as well as benefits were shared by spouses.

[82] Gains from commercial partnership as community property, see ante, § 80.

[83] Liability of community property to creditors as predicated on wife's membership in commercial partnership, see post, § 172.

[84] "Note from this law that just as profit is shared between husband and wife, so are losses and expenses incurred by reason of the partnership, e.g., doctor's fees, the price of medicines, travelling expenses. . . . For you cannot speak of profit unless losses are first deducted." Matienzo, Gloss VII, No. 1, to Nov. Rec. Law 2, Book 10, Title 4.

Debts and obligations of community generally, see post, Chap. IX.

[85] "Consequently, if common property is lost or destroyed without fault by either spouse, the loss is at common risk." Matienzo, Gloss VII, No. 6, to Nov. Rec. Law 2. The word "fault" as here used implies, of course, negligence or carelessness.

[86] See ante, § 119.

ment by the husband classifiable as in fraud of or to the prejudice of the rights of the wife might come under that head.[87]

It was the practice if loss occurred to the separate property of either spouse to make it good from the community property acquired during marriage.[88] This resulted from the fact that the fruits and profits of the separate property constituted community property; accordingly, since the community property was benefited by the separate property it was considered only fair that the community property should restore any loss suffered by the separate property, where such loss was not due to the fault of the spouse who owned the separate property.[89] But if the loss occurred through the fault of the spouse who owned the property, the loss was the owner's sole risk.[90] In the case of separate property of the wife which was administered by the husband, such as the dotal property or the wife's paraphernal property placed by her under his management, the husband managed such property at his own risk and his own property was impliedly pledged as security in respect of his administration. In other words, the wife had a tacit lien or mortgage upon the husband's property to the amount of her property under his administration, and if loss occurred to her property through his negligence, such loss had to be made good from his separate property rather than from the community property, although his interest in the community property was also subject to such lien or mortgage of the wife.[91]

[87] Thus, it was said, "That the loss or injury caused to the real estate (*hacienda*) by reason of the husband having rented it out at a low rate or price, or having paid annuities (*censos*) or debts for an illicit cause ought not to prejudice the wife; and therefore in these cases the amount of the loss or injury must be deducted from the mass of property and given to the wife before dividing the property." Asso and Mañuel, Institutes of Civil Law of Spain, Book I, Title VII, Cap. 5, § 2.

[88] Azevedo, Nos. 16, 17, to Nov. Rec. Law 9; Matienzo, Gloss VII, No. 6, to Nov. Rec. Law 2, Gloss II, Nos. 2, 3, to Nov. Rec. Law 3.

[89] Matienzo, Gloss VII, No. 6, to Nov. Rec. Law 2, stating that it was so decided in the Royal Chancery.

[90] Matienzo, Gloss VII, No. 6, to Nov. Rec. Law 2, Gloss II, No. 2, to Nov. Rec. Law 3.

[91] Las Siete Partidas, Part. 4, Title 11, Law 17; Azevedo, Nos. 22–24 to Nov. Rec. Laws 2 and 3, and Nos.

16, 17, to Nov. Rec. Law 9; Matienzo, Gloss VII, No. 6, to Nov. Rec. Law 2, and Gloss II, No. 2, to Nov. Rec. Law 3.

"By the civil law, which is recognized and established by legislative enactment as the rule of practice in this territory, in all civil cases the wife acquires a tacit lien or mortgage upon the property of her husband to the amount of the dotal property of which he became possessed through her: Febrero, vol. 3, p. 366, sec. 10; White Recopilación, vol. 1, pp. 139, 140. The recognition of this principle and the maintenance of the right of married women to such an *hipotecación* runs through all the elementary authorities of the civil law. According to the provision of the Spanish law, Partidas 4, 11, 1, 17, the wife had a tacit mortgage on the property of her husband for the restitution of both her dotal and paraphernal effects: Gasquet et al. v. Dimitry, 9 La. 588; Benj. & S. Dig. 437." Chavez v. McKnight, 1 N.M. 147, 153–154.

"Where a husband has alienated

The application of these and similar principles in our own community property states should be obvious. Indeed, their application has been clearly recognized in the case of separate property of the wife which has been placed under the husband's administration.[92] Their application is equally as applicable to the administration of the community property. Where negligent conduct, fraudulent conduct or the like of the husband has prejudiced the wife's interest in or share of the community property, the husband must be responsible therefor. Distinction must be made between such matters and loss occurring in the course of careful and honest administration by the husband. As pointed out by Judge Speer, the husband is not a guarantor to the wife that all his ventures will prove advantageous; and loss may well result from an honest administration and for which he should not be held responsible.[93] The foregoing is equally applicable in cases where the wife is administering the community property or any part of it.[94] So far as claims of the wife conflict with those of other creditors of the husband, such matter is discussed in the following chapter.[95]

§ 151.   Suits by one spouse against the other.

Since it is fundamental in the community property system that husband and wife are separate persons with equal interests in the

parapharnal property of his wife and receives the proceeds, she has a lien and privilege therefor on his estate, nor is it necessary that any evidence of her claim be registered: Dreux v. Dreux's Syndics, 3 Mart. N. S. (La.) 239; Benj. & S. Dig. 436. And in this respect there is no difference between her dotal and her paraphernal rights." Chavez v. McKnight, 1 N.M. 147, 154–155, adding that such mortgage extends to the community property as well as to the husband's separate property.

"For the capital of the wife and the capital of the husband must first be deducted, and what is then left is called profits, as Ayora says, . . . he remarks that, if there are no profits, the husband is not allowed to deduct his capital which has been used up, since he is personally liable for the wife's dowry while she is not liable for her husband's capital." Azevedo, No. 12, to Nov. Rec. Law 1.

[92] The right of the wife to a lien upon the property of the husband for the amount of the dotal property of which he became possessed through her was recognized in several cases in New Mexico. See Chavez v. Mc-Knight, 1 N.M. 147; Ilfeld v. De Baca, 13 N.M. 32, 79 P. 725; In re Chavez, 149 Fed. 73. "We think that she also has a tacit lien or mortgage on the property of her husband for all of her separate property which came into his possession during coverture and which was used by him." Ilfeld v. De Baca, ante.

In Louisiana the Civil Code gives the wife a legal mortgage on the immovables of the husband and a privilege (i. e., a lien) on his movables for the restitution of her dotal effects in his hands. See La. Civ. Code, arts. 2376–2378. And as to her paraphernal property, see La. Civ. Code, art. 2390. And see Gasquet v. Dimitry, 9 La. 588.

[93] See Speer, Law of Marital Rights in Texas, 3rd Ed., § 153; Oakes, Speer's Marital Rights in Texas, 4th Ed., § 184.

[94] See Hulsman v. Ireland, 205 Cal. 345, 270 P. 948, as somewhat illustrative.

[95] See post, §§ 173–175.

common property, with rights to hold separate property, and with the right to enter into transactions with each other,[96] it must follow as a logical result that each is entitled to protect or enforce against the other his or her rights in the common property or to enforce or protect as against the other his or her rights in separate property, even by civil action. This right of action by one spouse against the other was a thoroughly established principle of the Spanish community property law,[97] dating back hundreds of years,[98] and equally recognized under the modern civil codes of Spain.[99] The common-law fiction that husband and wife are one person, so that one cannot

[96] See ante, §§ 112, 135 et seq.

[97] "According to the civil law, a woman, on marrying, parts with many of her civil rights, and amongst the rights alienated by the conjugal association is that of appearing generally in court as plaintiff or defendant, alone or without the consent of her husband. But she does not part with the right of prosecuting suits against her husband when causes of action against him arise. Escriche, under the head of Mujer Casada, 451, says: '. . . But the wife does not require the express permission of her husband in order to proceed against him for his civil or criminal action.' Such are the well established principles of the civil law. Although a wife is thereby prohibited from entering alone into litigation with other persons without the consent of her husband, she is not prohibited from instituting and maintaining suits against him whenever she may have a legal or equitable cause of action." Chavez v. McKnight, 1 N.M. 147, 150–151, wherein wife charged husband with improvidently dealing with her dotal property. As mentioned previously in this work (ante, § 112), the dotal property brought by the wife to the marriage was placed under the husband's administration but remained the separate property of the wife, being returned to her upon dissolution of the marriage. At the time of this action, New Mexico had enacted no specific community property statutes but was proceeding under the original Spanish community property law; notice that the wife could proceed against the husband during the exis-

tence of the marriage.

[98] Possibly the earliest authorization in the Spanish law of the right of one spouse to sue the other appears in the thirteenth century in Las Siete Partidas, Part. 3, Title 2, Law 5, where it was said that they should not be parties to an action by one against the other but that one might sue the other when unjustly deprived of any property by the other and its return or reparation therefor was sought. And "property," as Azevedo pointed out in his commentaries to Nueva Recopilación, Book 5, Title 3, Law 7, denotes, at law, ownership, and the wife had ownership of property earned during the marriage just as she did of her separate properties.

[99] "Although it is certain that, until the dissolution of the marriage and the previous liquidation of the statutory society, one can neither know nor determine if there are gains or losses, such a doctrine, determined by numerous decisions of the Supreme Court, only holds efficacy when one treats of making effective the rights asserted by the participants in the gains which are supposed to be realized; but not when during the marriage, controversies come up concerning the nature of certain properties in which event in order to settle the controversies it is necessary to observe the rules which establish the economic regimen of the marriage and define the common properties and the separate properties of each spouse." Supreme Court of Spain, decision of Jan. 28, 1898, vol. 83, p. 218, Jurisprudencia Civil.

sue the other during coverture, is alien to the community property system's view of the spouses as individuals in their own right, and this common-law principle can have no more value or applicability than other common-law principles in interpreting and deciding matters relating to community property.[1] Accordingly, courts of community property states should not allow themselves to be hampered by common-law considerations in respect of suits between spouses in relation to the marital property. If the courts feel that they must have some precedent or authority to proceed upon, other than the clear principles inherent in the community property system, they can assume to permit such suits by virtue of their equity powers and jurisdiction.[2]

If this right to sue did not exist, one spouse, especially if the title to the property were in his or her name, might be enabled to appropriate community to his or her own use or otherwise deny or injure the rights therein of the other spouse, without the other spouse having any remedy whereby to defeat such conduct. This right of one spouse to proceed by civil action against the other to enforce and establish the respective rights in the common property or the complainant's right in separate property should be recognized even in the absence of express statutory authorization of such suits or actions. Since the right existed under the Spanish community property system and since that system was continued or adopted in our community property states, the right must continue with us as a necessary incident of the system.[3] The very policy of the law, by virtue of the community property system in force in these states, is to recognize the separate legal and civil existence of the wife, her separate rights of property, and her present and equal half ownership in the acquests and gains during the marriage.[4] Accordingly, the very constitutional provisions

[1] See ante, §§ 3, 4.

[2] Generally, see de Funiak, Handbook of Modern Equity, 2nd Ed., Boston, 1956.

[3] See Chavez v. McKnight, 1 N.M. 147, quoted ante, this section.

[4] "The present policy of the law is to recognize the separate legal and civil existence of the wife, and . . . involves a necessity for opening the doors of the judicial tribunals to her, in order that the rights guaranteed to her may be protected and enforced. . . . We find the right of the wife to sue the husband expressly recognized, and the right is not limited to any particular action, or class of actions." Wilson v. Wilson, 36 Cal. 447, 95 Am. Dec. 194 (action to recover on promissory note executed to wife by husband before marriage).

[5] In Arizona, the wife's right to sue her husband to redress wrongs to her separate property seems to be considered as based on the statute giving her the right to manage and control her separate property. See Eshom v. Eshom, 18 Ariz. 170, 157 P. 974. Similarly, in California, in an early case it was said that the policy of the law recognizing the separate legal and civil existence of the wife and her separate rights of property authorized her to bring action against the husband during marriage to recover on a promissory note executed by him to her before marriage. Wilson v. Wilson, 36 Cal. 447, 95 Am. Dec. 194.

Other cases relating to wife's right to sue husband in respect of her separate property, see McDuff v. McDuff, 45 Cal. App. 53, 187 P. 37;

and statutes which continue and establish this policy, even if not providing in so many express words, must be authority for the right of the wife to bring action against the husband in relation to her separate property,[5] and as well in relation to her interest and rights in the common property. There is no point in trying to make the distinction, as some courts have, that the wife is entitled to sue the husband to enforce her rights in or to protect her separate property from injury but not to sue him to enforce her rights in or to protect her interest in the community property. What makes her interest in the community property any less valuable or important to her than her interest in her separate property? She is as much entitled to establish and protect her rights in one as in the other.[6] Indeed, it is now recognized that she has a course of action against the husband or against his estate if he is deceased, as well as against one to whom he has wrongfully transferred community property. Her rights are the same as those of anyone against a fiduciary.[7] Any statute, such as that of California, which authorizes a wife to sue in all actions without her husband being joined must necessarily be express authority for the wife to sue her husband on any cause of action against him.[8]

However, in some of the states express statutory provisions do exist.[9] In Washington, it is provided that an agreement between the

Airhart v. Airhart (La.), 152 So.2d 140; Wilkinson v. Wilkinson, 147 La. 315, 84 So. 794; Jenkins v. Maier, 118 La. 130, 42 So. 722; Bouligny v. Fortier, 16 La. Ann. 209; Ryan v. Ryan, 61 Tex. 473; Vercelli v. Provenzano (Tex. Civ. App.), 28 S. W. 2d 216; Borton v. Borton (Tex. Civ. App.), 190 S. W. 192; Heintz v. Heintz, 56 Tex. Civ. App. 403, 120 S. W. 941. And see Clark, Community of Property and the Family in New Mexico, p. 27.

[6] See Azevedo, Commentaries to Nueva Recopilación, Book 5, Title 3, Law 7.

[7] Fields v. Michael, 91 Cal. App. 2d 443, 205 P.2d 402, citing de Funiak, 1st ed., and noted in 23 So. Cal. L. Rev. 84; Swisher v. Swisher (Tex. Civ. App.), 190 S. W. 2d 382, and authorities cited therein. See also Oakes, Speer's Marital Rights in Texas, 4th Ed., §§ 185–187.

[8] See Cal. Code Civ. Proc., § 370. Indeed, this section has been cited as authority for the wife to sue her husband to recover possession of her separate property representing a gift

to her by her husband from the community property. McDuff v. McDuff, 45 Cal. App. 53, 187 P. 37. Consider Kashaw v. Kashaw, 3 Cal. 312; Cutting v. Bryan, 206 Cal. 254, 274 P. 326; Mann v. Mann, 76 Cal. App. 2d 32, 172 P.2d 369.

To any argument that such a statute must be strictly construed as in derogation of the common law, it may be replied that the community property system has nothing to do with the common law. This fact is expressly recognized by statute in Washington, providing that the rule of common law which provides that statutes in derogation thereof are to be strictly construed has no application to the community property laws. See Remington's Wash. Rev. Stats., § 6989. The principle expressed by this Washington statute holds good without statutory sanction.

[9] See La. Civ. Code, art. 2391; La. Rev. St. 1950, art. 9:291; Slater v. Culpepper, 233 La. 1071, 99 So.2d 348; Boyd v. Boyd (La.), 142 So.2d 43.

Actions for divorce, see post, Chap. X, C.

spouses concerning the status or disposition of the community property may be set aside or cancelled for fraud, at the suit of either spouse.[10] And should either spouse obtain possession or control of property of the other, either before or after marriage, the owner may maintain an action therefor in the same manner as if unmarried.[11]

Unquestionably, however, the right of the wife to sue the husband in relation to her rights in the community property should be subject to the husband's right of management and control of the community property. In ordinary circumstances, she cannot demand an accounting or a division of the community property during the marriage, since the power of management is placed in the husband and he is entitled to exercise the management free from interference so long as he is conducting a careful and honest management.[12] But she is entitled to proceed against him when extraordinary circumstances warrant, as where he is denying her interest in the community property,[13] or he is threatening to dispose of community property to her prejudice (in which case injunction is the proper remedy),[14] or he is incompetent to manage the community property,[15] or he has abandoned her, leaving her without adequate support. In this latter situation, justice requires that she be entitled to proceed against him to enforce either her right to support or her right to have so much of the community property turned over to her as is necessary for her maintenance and that of any children of the union.[16] Yet curiously enough there is authority denying her right to do so, particularly in Texas. Basis for the denial is sometimes put on the ground that she

---

[10] Wash. Rev. Code 1961, § 26.16.120.

[11] Wash. Rev. Code 1961, §§ 26.16.150, 26.16.160.

[12] Management of community property generally, including right of wife to a voice therein or to object thereto, see ante, Chap. VII, B. See also Daniel v. Daniel, 106 Wash. 659, 181 P. 215.

Accounting and partition after dissolution of marital community, see post, Chap. X.

[13] See Kashaw v. Kashaw, 3 Cal. 312.

Action for declaratory relief or to quiet title or other appropriate remedy as the circumstances call for should be warranted.

[14] See Mahl v. E. A. Portal Co., 81 Cal. App. 2d 494, 254 P.2d 278; In re F. H. Koretke Brass & Manufacturing Co., 195 La. 415, 196 So. 917; In re Coffey's Estate, 195 Wash. 379, 81 P.2d 283.

Cf. Greiner v. Greiner, 58 Cal. 115,

saying that probably the wife might file suit to restrain the husband from transferring community property which would result in a loss to her but stating that she could not during the marriage maintain an action to set aside such a fraudulent transfer once accomplished. Under such a view, if the husband is able to conceal his intention from her until he successfully accomplishes it she is without remedy until his death.

If the property has already been disposed of, an action against the husband and his grantee or mortgagee to quiet title or for other appropriate relief may be warranted. See ante, § 126.

Suits to quiet title by one spouse against the other, see comment, 1 So. Calif. Law Rev. 161.

[15] Incompetency, see post, § 152.

[16] Recognition of this right seems to find support in Kashaw v. Kashaw, 3 Cal. 312, cited ante, this section.

is authorized to contract for necessaries on the husband's credit or on the credit of the community (which is, of course under the husband's management), and that that is the remedy she should pursue instead of proceeding directly against the husband. This overlooks the fact that merchants may deny her necessaries on the husband's credit, or that other equally important factors may make it not a feasible course to pursue.[17]

It may be added that since the husband is usually the one having the management of the community property, and this was particularly true in Spain and Mexico, the wrongful use or misdealings with respect to the property usually will be by his act, resulting in the wife being the complainant against the husband. But under such statutes of our community property states as place the management of certain kinds of the community in the wife,[18] it may very well result that the husband will be the aggrieved party and as such entitled to bring action against the wife.[19]

---

[17] Denial of right of wife, abandoned without cause, who used her separate property to obtain necessaries, to maintain action against husband for reimbursement from the community property or from his separate property, see Gonzales v. Gonzales, 117 Tex. 183, 300 S. W. 20. The court argued that the statute made the wife the husband's agent, duly authorized to contract for necessaries and made the community property and the husband's separate property liable therefor and that she should have exercised that power instead of pursuing the course that she did. What happens if merchants refuse her necessaries on the husband's credit is not explained. It is clear that in such case she would have to use her own credit and certainly should be entitled to reimbursement if she can obtain it from available community property or separate property of the husband.

In Irwin v. Irwin (Tex. Civ. App.), 110 S. W. 1011, where the husband abandoned the wife, leaving her without means of support, and she had no separate property, and the only community property was wages earned by the husband, the wife was allowed to recover the unpaid wages still in the employer's hands but was denied the right to recover from the husband any part of such wages already paid to him by his employer, on the ground that he had the disposal of it and could do so as he saw fit.

See also Cohen v. Cohen (Tex. Civ. App.), 181 S. W. 2d 915.

[18] See ante, §§ 113–115.

[19] Where the wife had assumed the management of the community property after the husband's desertion, it was said that her discretion in its disposition would not be reviewed "unless, perhaps, in a case where it has been used as a fraud upon the rights of the husband." Zimpelman v. Robb, 53 Tex. 274.

Right of husband or one claiming under him to maintain action to quiet title against wife or one claiming under her, where title to community property has been taken in her name, see Mitchell v. Moses, 16 Cal. App. 594, 117 P. 685.

As to husband's right to maintain action against wife to settle property rights in relation to property of his, see Newman v. Newman (Tex. Civ. App.), 86 S. W. 635; Kelly v. Gross (Tex. Civ. App.), 4 S. W. 2d 296, writ ref'd, n.r.e.

See, as to action for accounting as to community property by husband against wife after divorce, Salveter v. Salveter, 135 Cal. App. 238, 26 P.2d 836.

§ 152.   — Questioning husband's competency to manage common property.

In the preceding section has been considered the situation where one spouse, usually the wife, proceeds against the other to establish or protect some property right. So far as the wife is concerned, her entire interest in the community property, or her entire separate property which has been placed for any reason under the husband's management, may be threatened by the husband's course of conduct, particularly by his mismanagement. This mismanagement may result from his incompetency in business affairs or even by his mental incompetency or insanity. In such a situation, the wife is justified in seeking to have him removed from the management and control of the property. Where the husband has become mentally incompetent or insane, as we have already seen in a previous chapter, the wife is usually authorized by statute to have herself substituted in the management of the community property or to have a guardian of the estate appointed. Some of the statutes expressly go further than that and provide for the removal of the husband where he is an habitual drunkard or is for any other reason incapacitated to manage the community property.[20] Indeed, the incompetency or lack of capacity in business affairs may present as serious a situation as the mental incompetency of the husband and warrant the wife seeking and receiving relief therefor. In either case the welfare of the wife and any children of the marriage is endangered, not to mention the welfare of the husband who should be protected against his own incompetency of whatever kind. In Louisiana, the mismanagement of the husband in certain circumstances entitles the wife to seek a dissolution of the marital community and the separation of the property. Somewhat similarly, in California the wife, upon the same grounds for which she may procure a divorce, may without seeking a divorce obtain a division of the community property.[21]

§ 153.   — Personal injuries and other torts.

If the husband causes personal injury to the wife or joins, intentionally or negligently, with another in injuring the wife, can the wife sue the husband? Two difficulties have presented themselves. First, the influence of the English common law that the wife cannot sue the husband, except as abrogated by statute; second, the fact that in some of the community property states, damages recovered by the wife for injury to her are community property and frequently in such an action the husband is a necessary party plaintiff and he cannot,

---

[20] See ante, § 128.

[21] See ante, § 129. It must be understood that dissolution of the marital community does not necessarily mean dissolution of the marriage itself. See post, § 187.

of course, be on both sides of the case at once.[22] As relates to the first difficulty, notice that we say "the influence of the English common law." For even in those community property states where the common law is not and never has been in force as to marital property rights, the courts in denying the right of the wife to sue the husband for his torts against her must have necessarily been influenced, if perhaps unconsciously, by their common-law training or by common-law considerations. In Texas, Judge Speer has pointed out that the denial of the wife's right to sue her husband in this regard cannot be placed on common-law grounds, and is tenable, if at all, only upon grounds of public policy. And on what basis, he asks, does public policy proceed to grant the wife the right to sue the husband as to her property but not when he has committed some atrocious assault or the like upon her?[23] As respects the second difficulty, even if the husband were not a necessary party plaintiff and could be sued, in some community property states the compensation recovered from him would merely revert to his hands as manager of the community property.[24]

The situation should be as follows. Actually, since any pain and suffering of the wife is to her individually, and her right of action therefor and the compensation recovered should be her separate property,[25] she should be entitled to sue the husband for compensation to that extent. But in those states which now recognize that a wife does have a separate property cause of action against one who commits a tort against her person,[26] it has been held in Nevada[27] and in New Mexico[28] that she has no cause of action against and cannot sue her husband, in the absence of statutory authorization.[29] However, in Nevada, the wife has been allowed to recover from her husband's employer for personal injury to her as a result of her husband's negligence while in the scope of his employment.[30] On the other hand

---

[22] See cases collected at 43 A. L. R. 2d 626. And see McCurdy, Personal Injury Torts Between Spouses, 4 Villanova L. R. 303. Common-law states, see 29 A. L. R. 1482; 33 A. L. R. 1406; 44 A. L. R. 794; 48 A. L. R. 293; 89 A. L. R. 118.

[23] Speer, Law of Marital Rights in Texas, 3rd Ed., § 307.

In Crim v. Austin (Tex. Com. App.), 6 S. W. 2d 348, Judge Speer, speaking for the court, said: "The common law is not, and never has been, in force with respect to the marital rights in Texas."

[24] Damages or compensation for injuries to a spouse as property of the community has been fully discussed ante, §§ 81–84, 125.

[25] See ante, § 82.

[26] See ante, § 82 et seq.

[27] Kennedy v. Kennedy (Nev.), 352 P.2d 833; Morrissett v. Morrissett (Nev.), 397 P.2d 184.

[28] Rodgers v. Galindo (N.M.), 360 P.2d 400 (where wife sued a third person, latter could not bring in husband and obtain contribution from him as a joint tortfeasor); Romero v. Romero, 58 N.M. 201, 269 P.2d 748.

[29] Morrissett v. Morrissett (Nev.), supra.

[30] Frederickson & Watson Const. Co. v. Boyd, 60 Nev. 117, 102 P.2d 627; King v. Yancey, 147 F.2d 379. Contra, see Doremus v. Root, 23 Wash. 710, 63 P. 572, 54 L. R. A. 649.

it has been said in California[31] and in Louisiana that the wife does have a cause of action against her husband where he inflicts a tort upon her person, with the exception that in Louisiana she cannot sue her husband, but rather she can sue and recover from her husband's insurer.[32] Indeed, since the well-being of the community is as important to the wife as to the husband, if his tort deprives the marital community of her services or earnings, she should be entitled on behalf of the community to recover from the husband therefor. The husband, by his tort, should have removed himself as the proper person to protect the community and enforce its rights, in this case at least. This should apply to his control and management of these particular funds recovered from him for his wrong. Moreover, since his wrong has caused a loss to the marital community by depriving it wholly or in part of the wife's services, his separate property should be liable to make good that loss, as well as making good any loss to the community from hospital and medical bills, and also compensating the wife for her pain and suffering and any monetary loss she may have incurred.[33]

Even in those states which consider that a wife's cause of action for the tort against her is in its entirety community property, it is coming to be recognized that if the wife is living separate and apart from the husband, although not divorced, that her cause of action is her separate property.[34] In these circumstances her right to sue her husband for his tort against her has been recognized in Idaho[35] and in Washington.[36] Indeed, in Washington, where the husband killed the wife and then committed suicide, the wife's personal repre-

[31] Self v. Self, 58 Cal. 2d 683, 26 Cal. Rptr. 97, 376 P.2d 65 (intentional tort), expressly overruling Peters v. Peters, 156 Cal. 32, 103 P. 219; Klein v. Klein, 58 Cal. 2d 692, 26 Cal. Rptr. 102, 376 P.2d 70 (negligent tort).

And see present wording of Cal. Civ. Code, § 5108, that recovery by one spouse from other is separate property; and new statute, Cal. Civ. Code, § 5113, as to property subject to judgment.

And see de Funiak, Personal Injuries Under the California Community Property Law, 3 Cal. West. L. Rev. 69.

[32] Burke v. Mass. Bonding & Ins. Co. (La. App.), 19 So.2d 647.

Husband permitted to recover from wife's insurer where wife injured husband, see McHenry v. American Employers' Ins. Co. (La. App.), 18 So.2d 840, conforming with answer to certified question in 206 La. 70, 18 So.2d 856, noted 19 Tulane L. Rev. 456.

In California, recovery from insurer, see Cal. Civ. Code, § 5113.

[33] We are much indebted to Professor Jacob who is also dissatisfied over the question of torts by the husband against the wife and who discusses many aspects of the situation very ably in his article, Community Property Law in Idaho, 1 Idaho Law Jour. 1, 42 et seq. Judge Speer of Texas has been equally dissatisfied. See Speer, Law of Marital Rights in Texas, 3rd Ed., § 307.

[34] See ante, § 82.

[35] See Lorang v. Hays, 69 Ida. 440, 209 P.2d 733.

[36] Goode v. Martinis (Wash.), 361 P.2d 941. Cf. opposing view in older Texas case, Nickerson v. Nickerson, 65 Tex. 281.

sentative has been allowed to sue the husband's estate on the theory that the wife's inability to sue the husband was personal and not inherent in the tort and was not passed to her personal representative.[37]

In the case of torts by one spouse to the property or property interests of the other, action between the spouses should lie on the basis of the principles discussed in the preceding section.[38]

In the Spanish civil law, it may be remarked, the wife could proceed against the husband, and that without requiring his permission, either for his civil or delictual act.[39]

§ 154.   Criminal proceedings.

Whether or to what extent one spouse is criminally responsible for injuries to the person or property or for theft or the like of property of the other spouse are matters more properly left to general treatises on criminal law. So far as concerns theft, larceny, embezzlement or the like by one spouse of separate property of the other spouse, the development of modern legislation is to make such conduct punishable in criminal proceedings against the guilty spouse, whether husband or wife.[39a] It will undoubtedly be a long time, however, before the influence of the common law is overcome, in all jurisdictions. Even in many of the states which have enacted Married Women's Property Acts, giving the wife control of her separate property, the tendency is still to cling to the common-law principle that because of the unity of husband and wife neither could commit theft or the like against the separate property of the other.[40] In respect of the theft or embezzlement of community property by one spouse, it is probable that in most jurisdictions the principle of the common law is still influential, that one cannot steal or embezzle that of which he is part owner. Only where statutes expressly impose criminal responsibility upon a joint owner wrongfully taking property that is partly owned by another, is it likely that a spouse would be criminally liable for the theft or embezzlement of the share of the community property belonging to the other spouse.[41]

In the Spanish system, the wife could proceed of her own volition and without the necessity of any consent against the husband for his delict against her.[42] This included, it may be instanced, theft by the husband from the wife, although the wife was specifically freed from

[37] Johnson v. Ottoemeier, 45 Wash. 2d 419, 275 P.2d 723.

[38] And see ante, § 86.

[39] Escriche, Diccionario, "Married Woman."

[39a] In Arizona, husband liable, see Whitson v. State, 65 Ariz. 395, 181 P.2d 182.

[40] See Clark & Marshall, Criminal Law, 6th Ed., § 12.03; Vernier, American Family Laws, vol. 3, p. 162 et seq.; 55 A. L. R. 558.

[41] Generally as to joint owners, see Clark & Marshall, Criminal Law, 4th Ed., §§ 312, 344.

[42] Escriche, Diccionario, "Married Woman."

Delict of the Spanish law, see ante, § 81.

penal responsibility for theft from the husband.[43] This distinction, in imposing criminal liability upon the husband, resulted because in his fiduciary capacity as manager of the common property he should be subject to strong check in the performance of his fiduciary obligation.

[43] Las Siete Partidas, Part. 7, Title 14, Law 4.

CHAPTER IX

DEBTS, OBLIGATIONS AND LIABILITIES OF SPOUSES

§ 155.   In general.

The liability of the spouses and of their property for their debts, obligations and liabilities is one of the most clearly defined features of the Spanish community property system. Unfortunately, the clear and well-defined principles thereof have not been adequately grasped, recognized and followed in most of our community property states.[1] This must be attributed primarily to the failure to investigate properly the source materials on the subject, coupled with the attempt to supply deficiencies of knowledge by superimposing upon the community property system many of the common-law concepts and rules.[2] In the sections following a succinct exposition of these community property principles is essayed, with comparative comment upon the situation, so far as the confusion permits it be disentangled, in our American community property states.

§ 156.   Antenuptial debts and obligations.

The antenuptial debts and obligations of one spouse should only be chargeable against the property of that spouse and not against the property of the other spouse. This was established by statute as a basic principle of Spanish community property law as far back as the year 1255, the statute declaring, in part, that if one of the spouses contracted a debt before marriage, "let that one pay it who contracted it, and the other shall not be liable to pay it from his or her properties."[3] This continued, without change, as a basic principle of the Spanish community property law through the centuries, as can be seen by the consistently uniform statements on the subject by the writers and commentators of successive periods. Moreover, in providing that the spouse who had not contracted the debt should not be liable to pay it from his or her properties, the word "properties" meant not only the separate property of that spouse but also that spouse's share of the community property. For, as was pointed out, the word "properties" denotes, in law, that which is owned, and each spouse, the wife as well as the husband, during marriage owned half of the community property just as much as he or she owned his or her separate property.[4] Thus it was said that "In respect of debts contracted before marriage (by the husband) the wife will not be liable to pay anything out of her share of the profits acquired during marriage. And the converse of this proposition is by these words of this law most clearly laid down. For a partner is only liable for debts when such debts were contracted during the partnership; he is not liable for debts contracted before the formation of the partnership."[5] As a matter of fact not even the share of the community property of

---

[1] Arizona and Washington appear to be the only community property states in which the courts have had, in large part, an accurate recognition of the principles and to have applied them correctly. Curiously enough, the Louisiana courts have frequently seemed to stray from the interpretation and application that might be reasonably expected from those courts.

[2] Generally as to these faults, see ante, Chap. I.

[3] Fuero Real, Book 3, Title 20, Law 14.

[4] See discussion by Azevedo, post, § 160, as to this matter.

[5] Azevedo, No. 20, to Nov. Rec. Law 9, Book 10, Title 4.

The community property during marriage is not liable "for those (debts) of either spouse prior to the

the spouse who had contracted the debt could be reached during the marriage, for the community property during the marriage was a fund available only for the payment of community debts and obligations, and it was only after dissolution of the marriage and partition of the community property that the definitely ascertained share of the community property of the one who had contracted the debt became subject to liability for such debt. It was well established, in other words, that the community property was liable only for debts contracted during the marriage which concerned the actual marriage and the conjugal partnership, and which accrued and were contracted on its account.[6]

It might well result, on occasion, that the husband having the community property under his administration used such property to discharge his antenuptial debts. But if, in discharging during marriage debts contracted by him before marriage, he used community property, he had to make good and pay to the wife or to her heirs, upon partition of community assets, half of the amount so paid out, even to the extent of doing so from his separate property.[7] However, the wife was not required to wait until dissolution of the marital community for remedy or relief but could, as in other situations where his actions were in detriment or to the prejudice of her interest in the community property, take appropriate action against the husband to prevent his wrongful use of the community property, or against the one having it in his possession.[8]

§ 157.   — Liability of separate property.

In our community property states, the statutes are usually explicit in declaring that the separate property of one spouse shall not be liable for debts or obligations contracted or incurred by the other spouse before the marriage. Sometimes, they are in a form declaring that the separate property of the husband or the wife is not liable for debts of the other contracted before the marriage.[9] Sometimes, it

marriage because only their separate properties are obligated for them." Gómez y Montalbán, Elementos del Derecho Civil y Penal de España, 4th Ed., vol. 1, p. 260.

[6] Since the principles are more appropriately discussed, post, § 160, in relation to separate debts contracted by a spouse during marriage, they are not repeated at length at this point.

[7] Azevedo, No. 21, to Nov. Rec. Law 9. To the same effect, Gutiérrez, Quaestio CXXIX, to Nov. Rec. Law 9.

[8] See ante, Chaps. VII, VIII.

[9] Ariz. Rev. St. 1956, § 25-216.
In Louisiana it is provided that

"the debts of both husband and wife, anterior to the marriage, must be acquitted out of their own personal and individual effects." La. Civ. Code, art. 2403.

In Nevada a statute, among others, provides that neither husband nor wife shall be liable for debts or liabilities of the other incurred before marriage. Nev. Rev. St. 1956, § 123.050; Slack v. Schwartz, 63 Nev. 47, 161 P.2d 345, citing and following de Funiak, first edition. In Washington there is a similar statute with the additional statement that rent or income from separate property of either is not liable for separate debts of the other. Wash.

is apparently thought necessary to phrase the statutes to specify expressly that the separate property of the husband shall not be subject to debts contracted by the wife before marriage,[10] and that the separate property of the wife shall be liable for her own debts contracted before marriage but not for the debts of the husband.[11] The latter form of phraseology probably results from common-law considerations influencing the minds of the legislators. They seem to forget that they are dealing with community property rather than trying to negative common-law doctrines.

§ 158.   — Liability of community property.

When we come to the matter of the liability of the community property for antenuptial debts and obligations, there is little accord, and frequently a great deal of silence, in the statutes of the community property states. For that reason, the statutes of each state should be considered carefully in solving a problem arising in that state. At this juncture a brief summary of the law of each state is all that is practicable. Properly, one spouse's half share in the community property is just as much the spouse's property as is the spouse's separate property, and should not therefore be liable for the other spouse's antenuptial debts and obligations. Indeed, it is a primary principle of the community property system that community property is subject to the payment of only those debts contracted during marriage which concern the actual marriage and the conjugal partnership and were contracted on its account. Views which are not in accord with the foregoing are in direct conflict with and a denial of governing principles of the community property system.

Arizona law is well settled that community property is liable for community debts contracted by the husband during marriage.[12] Similarly, it is not liable for the obligations of either spouse incurred before marriage.[13] After the community is dissolved, the creditor of a spouse may enforce a separate claim against that spouse's share of the property that had been community.[14] In a decision not in consonance with other expressions, it was held that the community property was liable for a joint and several judgment for damages against two persons who later married, arising out of a tort committed

---

Rev. Code 1961, §§ 26.16.010, 26.16.020, 26.16.200.

Tex. Family Code 1969, § 5.61 provides that the separate property of a spouse is not subject to liabilities of the other unless both spouses are liable by other rules of law.

[10] See Cal. Civ. Code, § 5120; Idaho Code 1948, § 32-910; Nev. Rev. Stat. 1956, § 123.200; N.M. Stat. 1953, § 57-3-8.

[11] Cal. Civ. Code, § 5121; Idaho Code 1948, § 32-911; Nev. Rev. Stat. 1956, § 123.210; N.M. Stat. 1953, § 57-3-9.

[12] Ariz. Rev. Stat. 1956, § 25-216.

[13] Morgan v. Bruce, 76 Ariz. 121, 259 P.2d 558; Hirales v. Boegen, 61 Ariz. 210, 146 P.2d 352.

[14] Tway v. Payne, 55 Ariz. 343, 101 P.2d 455.

before coverture.[15] The court seemed to be persuaded by the notion that the community property was not being taken for the debt of one spouse or the other, overlooking the obvious fact that the obligation of each spouse was separate in character as to the community and the marriage did not transform the two separate obligations into one community debt. And on the ground of public policy, the Arizona court has held that the community property is liable for an alimony debt imposed by a divorce decree dissolving a prior marriage of the husband.[16] Again, as a public obligation, the wife's half of the community property has been subjected to payment of her property tax, even though it was her separate obligation.[17]

In California, while formerly the view was that the community property in its entirety was subject to liability for the antenuptial debts of the husband but was not liable for antenuptial debts of the wife,[18] the present statutes exempt the husband's earnings from liability for the wife's antenuptial debts[19] and provide that the wife's earnings "are not liable for the debts of the husband."[20] This exemption of the wife's earnings from liability for debts of the husband is lost when they are mingled with other community property so as to lose their identity.[21] And any exemption that the husband's earnings might have for an antenuptial debt of the wife may conceivably be lost, similarly, where mingled beyond identification with earnings of the wife,[22] which are liable for her antenuptial debts.[23]

In Idaho the community property is liable for the antenuptial obligations of the husband arising from tort or contract.[24] This is a part of the general position that the community property is liable for separate obligations of the husband, but not for separate obligations of the wife.[25] The cases to that effect involve postnuptial separate obligations of the wife, but the principle seems applicable to antenuptial obligations also.[26]

When we consider Louisiana, we find that it is provided by statute that debts of either spouse contracted before marriage must be paid from that spouse's own personal and individual property.[27] The

[15] Hirales v. Boegen, 61 Ariz. 210, 146 P.2d 352.

[16] Gardner v. Gardner, 95 Ariz. 202, 388 P.2d 417.

Liability of the community for alimony from a prior marriage, see Comment, 7 Ariz. L. Rev. 87.

[17] Oglesby v. Poage, 45 Ariz. 23, 40 P.2d 90.

[18] See Van Maren v. Johnson, 15 Cal. 308. Public policy prefers premarital creditors of husband. Weinberg v. Weinberg, 63 Cal. Rptr. 13, 432 P.2d 709.

[19] Cal. Civ. Code, § 5120.

[20] Cal. Civ. Code, § 5117.

[21] Porter (Truelsen) v. Nelson, 42 Cal. App. 2d 750, 109 P.2d 996.

[22] Consider Tinsley v. Bauer, 125 Cal. App. 2d 714, 271 P.2d 110.

[23] Cal. Civ. Code, § 5116.

[24] Holt v. Empey, 32 Idaho 106, 178 P. 703.

[25] Hall v. Johns, 17 Idaho 224, 105 P. 71.

[26] Brockelbank, The Community Property Law of Idaho, §§ 4.3, 4.4, 4.5.

[27] La. Civ. Code 1932, Art. 2403.

situation is not so clear as it might appear, however. At an early date the view of the courts was that the real ownership of the community property was in the husband, with merely an expectant future interest in the wife. Accordingly, the community property was held subject to payment of the husband's antenuptial debts, but not of the wife's.[28] However, in one case where the husband paid an antenuptial debt of his from community funds under his management and control, the community had to be credited with that amount, and the same was true where community property was used to pay the wife's antenuptial debt.[29] Although the Louisiana position is firmly established that the wife has an equal and present ownership with the husband of the community property, the courts have continued to rely on the older cases and hold that the antenuptial debts of the husband may be satisfied from community property.[30]

The general position of Nevada is that neither the husband nor the wife is liable for the antenuptial obligations of the other.[31] Specifically, the community property may not be used to satisfy the antenuptial obligation of husband or wife, with the one exception that the community property, to the extent of the husband's earnings, is subject to the husband's contractual obligation to pay specified sums for the support of a former wife and the issue of a former marriage.[32]

New Mexico is clouded in this area.[33] Statutorily, the community property is not liable for the postnuptial contracts of the wife.[34] The cases appear to hold that the community property is liable for all debts of the husband, including antenuptial obligations.[35] Of course,

---

[28] See Davis v. Compton, 13 La. Ann. 396, cited with approval in Hawley v. Crescent City Bank, 26 La. Ann. 230.

[29] Glenn v. Elam, 3 La. Ann. 611; Childers v. Johnson, 6 La. Ann. 634.

[30] See Stafford v. Sumrall (La. App.), 21 So.2d 83, relying on Davis v. Compton, supra. In Fazzio v. Krieger, 226 La. 511, 76 So.2d 713, it was recognized that the holding of the Davis case related to the theory of the wife's right as an expectancy, but the court held that the repudiation of that theory did not affect the Davis holding that the husband's antenuptial debts could be satisfied out of the community property. The case cites de Funiak, Principles of Community Property (1st Ed.), but distinguishes it. It does allow recovery out of the husband's one-half of the community property only. But cf. Jefferson Lake Sulphur Co. v. Walet, 104 F. Supp. 20, affirmed 202 F.2d 433, cert. den.

346 U. S. 820, 74 S. Ct. 35, which appears to allow recovery for the husband's antenuptial debts from the entire community.

See also Succession of Ratcliff, 209 La. 224, 24 So.2d 456; 20 Tulane L. Rev. 136; 21 Tulane L. Rev. 125.

[31] Nev. Rev. Stat. 1956, § 123.050.

[32] See Slack v. Schwartz, 63 Nev. 47, 161 P.2d 345, citing and following de Funiak, Principles of Community Property (1st Ed.), for the general rule. And see Greear v. Greear, 303 F.2d 893, citing de Funiak, Principles of Community Property (1st Ed.), p. 441, and relying on the rationale therein for the exception.

[33] See Clark, Community of Property and the Family in New Mexico, p. 28.

[34] N.M. Stat. 1953, § 57-4-2.

[35] In re Chavez, 149 Fed. 73; Denton v. Firemen's Fund Insurance Co., 357 F.2d 747.

the personal earnings of the wife, even though community property, would not be liable.[36] There are no cases considering the liability of the community property for antenuptial obligations of the wife. One major case, McDonald v. Senn, allowed execution against the wife's half of the community realty to satisfy a judgment arising from a separate tort committed by her during coverture.[37] The court said that the statute related only to what the community property was not liable for, and did not specifically exempt it from liability for separate torts of the wife. Furthermore, the court stressed the present, vested nature of the wife's interest in the community property. The language of the cases may be interpreted as allowing execution against the wife's half interest in community realty of judgments arising from antenuptial torts also. There is no relevant decision on antenuptial contract obligations, but should the question arise, a careful study of controlling principles should lead to a decision that the community property is not liable for antenuptial contractual obligations of the wife.

Texas compounded and continued its previous case law errors by statutory enactments in the 1960s. The test of liability is tied to the question of which spouse has control of the particular community property upon which execution is sought.[38] The community property under the sole management of the wife is liable for all her antenuptial obligations, but not those of the husband. Similarly, the community property under the sole management of the husband is liable for all his antenuptial obligations but not those of the wife. The community property subject to the joint management of the husband and wife is subject to all their antenuptial obligations.[39]

In Washington, the general view is that only community debts may be satisfied from community property.[40] The necessary corollary then is that community property is not liable for the antenuptial debts of the husband or wife.[41] There are two exceptions to that corollary: the husband's earnings during a later marriage can be subject to liability for an award made in a divorce decree terminating a previous marriage,[42] and the liability of a spouse for income taxes accruing on antenuptial earnings may be satisfied from the community property.[43]

[36] N.M. Stat. 1953, § 57-3-6.

[37] 53 N.M. 198, 204 P.2d 990, 10 A. L. R. 2d 966.
A federal court has interpreted the McDonald case as recognizing the principle that each spouse's half of the community property may be segregated and subjected to liability for any separate liability of the owning spouse. U. S. Fidelity & Guaranty Co. v. Chaves, 126 F. Supp. 227, where bonding company's judgment against husband subjected husband's duly segregated half of community property to liability.

[38] See supra, § 113.

[39] Tex. Family Code 1969, § 5.61.

[40] Achilles v. Hoopes (Wash.), 245 P.2d 1005; Escrow Service v. Cressler (Wash.), 365 P.2d 760.

[41] Kinman v. Roberts, 151 Wash. 35, 274 P. 719; Streck v. Taylor, 173 Wash. 367, 23 P.2d 415; Katz v. Judd, 108 Wash. 557, 185 P. 613.

[42] Fisch v. Marler, 1 Wash. 2d 698, 97 P.2d 147.

[43] Draper v. United States, 243 F. Supp. 563.

It should be noted that community realty is not subject to the award in the divorce decree; only the earnings of the husband are liable.[44] It has been indicated that after dissolution of the marital community the share of either spouse in the common property may be subject to that spouse's separate debts.[45]

§ 159. Debts and obligations contracted during marriage — Community debts.

It was fundamental in the Spanish community property system, as would naturally be supposed in any community property system, that just as the gains and profits during marriage were shared between husband and wife, so were the losses and expenses incurred by reason of the conjugal partnership. For, as we said earlier, it is not possible to speak of profit unless losses and expenses are first deducted.[46] It naturally followed from this, and indeed was so provided by statute as early as 1255, that every debt that the husband and wife contracted in common was likewise dischargeable by them in common.[47] The uniform construction given the statute was that debts contracted during marriage by the spouses or by either of them for the common benefit were payable from the common property,[48] and this included

---

[44] Stafford v. Stafford, 10 Wash. 2d 649, 117 P.2d 753.

[45] "The only reason for exempting community property from the separate debts of either spouse is for the benefit of the community, and when this is dissolved the reason no longer exists." Columbia National Bank v. Embree, 2 Wash. 331, 26 P. 257.

[46] Matienzo, Gloss VII, No. 1, to Nov. Rec. Law 2, Book 10, Title 4, saying in part: "Note from this law that just as profit is shared between husband and wife, so are losses and expenses incurred by reason of the partnership, e.g., doctor's fees, the price of medicines, travelling expenses. This applies to all losses and expenses."

"... and by profit should be understood the part of the property acquired during marriage remaining after all the losses have been indemnified." Llamas y Molina, No. 47, to Nov. Rec. Law 8.

"Until the common debts are paid, there are no 'ganancias' or gains to divide." Commodores Point Terminal Co. v. Hudnall, 283 Fed. 150, in reference to Spanish law formerly in force in Florida.

"The intent of the law is that, as it gives the wife a share of profits automatically, similarly she may be liable for debts." Matienzo, Gloss III, No. 16, to Nov. Rec. Law 1.

[47] Fuero Real, Book 3, Title 20, Law 14.

The words of that statute were repeated again in an enactment of 1310, with the addition of the express provision that the wife was obligated for half the debt contracted by the husband even though she had not authorized it and was not a party to the evidence of the debt; and if she bound herself jointly with the husband, she was obligated for the whole debt if demand therefor was made upon her. Leyes del Estilo, Law 207.

[48] "From which it may be inferred debts contracted during marriage by spouses or by either of them should be discharged out of the common property, law 14, tit. 20, book 3 (of the Fuero Real). That law is so construed by Episcopus and Alphonso à Montalvo." Matienzo, Gloss VII, No. 2, to Nov. Rec. Law 2.

Where the debt is common to both,

the wife's share of the common property,[49] even though the debt was contracted by the husband alone; however, even so, she was liable only to the extent of her half share of the community property and no more.[50] If the wife bound herself jointly and severally with her husband for the community debt, she was, upon demand upon her, obligated to pay the whole debt.[51]

What if the common property was insufficient to pay the debts contracted during marriage for the benefit of the marital community? They were then payable from the separate property of the contracting spouse, i. e., usually the husband. If he had no property and had contracted the debt in order to support and care for the wife, it was suggested that then her separate property was liable for the payment thereof. But this suggestion must be considered in the light of the statements in the preceding paragraph.[52] Of course, where by agree-

---

execution must be levied only on property common to both. Asso and Mañuel, Institutes of Civil Law of Spain, Book III, Title X, Sec. 6, Par. 12.

[49] "Conversely, if the wife does not renounce her right to profits, she is liable for the payment of debts out of the share of profits which accrues to her. It is in this sense that you must understand 1.14 tit. 20 lib. 3 Fori (Fuero Real, Book 3, Title 20, Law 14), as the last gloss thereon says. Advantages and disadvantages must be shared by both partners, according to Covarruvias . . . and as Palatius Rubeus excellently says. . . ." Azevedo, Nos. 15, 16, to Nov. Rec. Law 9.

[50] "Every debt that husband and wife have contracted in common, let them likewise pay it in common. And that is to say, that a debt that the husband contracts, although the wife does not authorize it and is not a party to the evidence of debt, she is obligated for half of the debt." Leyes del Estilo, Law 207 (in part).

"And so even in respect of a debt (i.e., community debt) contracted by the husband alone the wife is liable to pay a half share." Matienzo, Gloss VII, No. 2, to Nov. Rec. Law 2.

"The view to be adopted is that she is liable only in respect of her own half-share and no more." Azevedo, No. 18 to Nov. Rec. Law 9.

The wife was liable to pay a moiety of taxes and mortgage interest on the community property. Azevedo, No. 19, to Nov. Rec. Law 9. As to taxes, see also post, Chap. XI.

"The burdens of the legal society of gananciales are: 1. The payment of the obligations which rest on the husband as head of the family while the marriage lasts. 2. The debts contracted during the marriage, although contracted by the husband alone, in order to pay the obligations of the conjugal partnership; but not those of either spouse prior to the marriage because only their separate properties are obligated for them." Gómez y Montalbán, Elementos del Derecho Civil y Penal de España, 4th Ed., vol. 1, p. 260. (A third burden or obligation, relating to dowries of children is omitted.)

[51] Leyes del Estilo, Law 207; Matienzo, Gloss VII, No. 2, to Nov. Rec. Law 2.

As to wife binding herself jointly and severally with the husband upon his separate obligations and undertakings, see post, the section following.

[52] Matienzo, Gloss VII, No. 5, to Nov. Rec. Law 2.

In Louisiana, as to liability of husband's separate property for community debt where community property insufficient to pay, see Succession of Lamm, 40 La. Ann. 312, 4 So. 53.

"But if both spouses promise a dowry to their daughter or a gift on

ment between the spouses there was to be no community of property and the wife relinquished or renounced her right to share in the profits to be acquired during marriage, she was not liable to pay any debts contracted for the common benefit by the husband during marriage.[53]

§ 160.   — Separate debts.

In the Spanish community property system, "only those debts contracted during marriage were common and therefore payable from goods multiplied and acquired during the same marriage, which concern the actual marriage of man and wife and their partnership, and which accrue and were contracted on its account by both or one of them."[54] It followed that debts contracted by a spouse in a matter not concerning the actual marriage and the conjugal partnership and not for its benefit were not payable from the community property.[55] Thus neither the wife nor her share of the common property was bound in any way for the debts or undertakings of the husband or for a security or pledge that he contracted where he was not acting for the benefit of the marital community.[56] In discussing the law that neither the wife nor her property (ni sus bienes) was obligated or bound in any way for the separate debts and undertakings of the husband, the jurisconsult Azevedo pointed out that the word "property (bienes) is one which, in law, denotes ownership" and, since the wife has ownership in the ganancial property acquired during marriage, her "property" included that in which by law ownership, and pos-

account of marriage to their son and the common property is insufficient to pay the whole or any part thereof, each spouse is bound in respect of a half-share to pay the balance out of his or her private property, even out of dowry; if, however, the father alone made the promise in such a case, he will be bound to pay the whole out of his private property." Matienzo, Gloss VII, No. 7, to Nov. Rec. Law 2. That is to say, in the latter instance, that the father pays from his private property alone, if the community property is insufficient. Nov. Rec. Book 10, Title 3, Law 4.

[53] Novísima Recopilación, Book 10, Title 4, Law 9. And see commentaries thereto.

Effect of spouses' agreements as affecting rights of creditors, see post, § 173.

[54] Gutiérrez, Quaestio CXXIX, No. 1, to Nov. Rec. Law 9.

[55] Asso and Mañuel, Institutes of Civil Law of Spain, Book III, Title X, Sec. 6, Par. 12, which describes the extent to which dotal and paraphernal property or the fruits thereof are subject to execution for separate debts of the spouses. That only charge to which community property was subject, after death of one of the spouses, and before partition, was debts contracted by either or both spouses for partnership benefit and not in the private business of one of the spouses, see post, § 210.

But compare the view where the obligation of one spouse was imposed by law. See post, § 165.

[56] See Novísima Recopilación, Book 10, Title 11, Law 2.

For a suretyship obligation undertaken by the husband, the wife was not bound to pay anything in whole or in part from her share of the goods acquired during marriage. Gutiérrez, Quaestio CXXVIII, No. 3, to Nov. Rec. Law 9. See also post, § 163.

session as well, was transferred to her automatically in the property acquired during the marriage by the husband. Moreover, he pointed out, it cannot be determined before the dissolution of marriage, as by the death of the husband *(ante mortem mariti),* what exact amount she will be entitled to from the acquisitions earned during marriage. Therefore, if it were permitted to subject the community property, during marriage, to the separate debts of the husband, it would result in subjecting some part of the half belonging to the wife to the husband's debts. His right to alienate community property did not, it was said, entitle him to charge such property with his own debts, since that was taking the wife's share of such property without consideration and thus in fraud and injury of her rights. Finally, while debts contracted on behalf of a partnership are properly chargeable against the property of the partnership, the personal debts of one partner were said not to be properly chargeable against the partnership property.[57]

The situation might exist, of course, that one spouse or the other, although usually it would be the husband, used the common property for his or her own personal uses or in discharge of separate debts. Where that happened, such spouse's share of the community property was charged or debited with half the amount so used.[58] But this matter of separate debts contracted during the marriage occupied much less prominence in the Spanish law than it does with us. In all but three of our community property states the income, profits, etc., from separate property are also separate property. Even in two of the other three states certain situations result in the income, profits, etc., of separate property also constituting separate property. Thus transactions in connection with separate property which raise obligations on the part of the spouse owning such property will usually relate almost entirely to the separate interests of that spouse. In the Spanish law, on the other hand, the income, etc., from the separate property or business interest of either spouse was community property. Hence, contracts or transactions in connection with such separate property or separate interests of the spouse which raised obligations on the part of the spouse would usually be transactions to assure or further

---

[57] Azevedo, Commentaries to Nueva Recopilación, Book 5, Title 3, Law 7, which was continued as part of Novísima Recopilación, Book 10, Title 11, Law 2.

In declaring that the wife's share of the common property was not liable for an obligation incurred by the husband in going surety for another, Gutiérrez points out that the act of the husband is not one that can benefit the conjugal partnership but is a transaction of the husband alone. See Gutiérrez, Quaestio CXXVIII, No. 3,

"Secondly," to Nov. Rec. Law 9.

[58] As to obligations imposed by law, see post, § 165.

Dowry or donation on account of marriage promised by husband and wife to one of their children, see Novísima Recopilación, Book 10, Title 3, Law 4.

Money given from common property to support of or to provide dowry for children of prior marriage or to other relatives as unauthorized gift unless moderate in amount, see ante, § 121.

interests or property rights, the returns from which would belong to the community. Even though the debts or obligations might arise from transactions relating to interests or property belonging individually to the spouse, it would be highly probable that the community had been or would be benefited in some way. And any debt or obligation relating to the community affairs and the success of the conjugal partnership would come under the head of a community debt.[59]

It has already been remarked that if the wife bound herself jointly and severally with the husband for a debt or obligation incurred on behalf of the marital community, she was obligated, upon demand upon her, to pay the whole debt.[60] But she could not bind herself as surety for her husband upon his own obligations and undertakings. Even if she and the husband bound themselves jointly and severally upon his obligations and undertakings, she was not liable for anything, unless it was proved that the proceeds or consideration of the debt were converted to her benefit and then she was liable only *pro rata* to the extent of such benefit; even then she was not liable if the things used for her benefit were such things as food, clothing or necessaries which the husband was bound to supply her anyway. But if she bound herself jointly with her husband to obtain money to pay claims of the Crown against her, such as its rents or taxes, she was liable accordingly.[61]

§ 161.   — Confusion in community property states.

To attempt the formulation of brief and concise statements of the situation prevailing in our community property states is exceedingly difficult, for the statutes of the different states are all at sixes and sevens. The ease and brevity of treatment with which the writers of many articles and treatises on community property dispose of this particular feature of community property compel our admiration but we find ourselves unable to follow them. While they turn the corner to pass on to the consideration of some other aspect of community property, we are left behind gazing with dismay at the statutory confusion enveloping this question of liability of property for debts and obligations contracted during marriage.

But before entering upon any survey of these various statutes let us evaluate and consider the particular situation with which these statutes attempt to deal. We must recognize that upon espousal the husband and the wife thereafter direct their best efforts, or should

---

[59] Income from separate property, see ante, § 71.

[60] See preceding section.

[61] Novísima Recopilación, Book 10, Title 11, Law 3.

That a wife who had contracted a debt jointly with her husband could recover from her husband's property any sums she had been compelled to pay in respect to such a contract, if the husband had received the entire benefit of the contract, see Azevedo, No. 16, to Nov. Rec. Book 10, Title 3, Law 4.

do so at any rate, to further the success of the conjugal partnership, and to maintain, preserve and protect the family thus established. There are obligations and responsibilities imposed upon them by reason of the marriage. Their successful shouldering of these obligations and responsibilities, their accomplishments, their earnings, their gains, all these go to further and benefit the marital community by which the family is maintained, preserved and protected, in other words to further and benefit the family itself, not only as a unit but as an institution. Therefore, in the main the debts contracted during the marriage are contracted because they are intended to and because it is believed that in the long run they will further the interests of the marital community. They are intended to result in common benefit or to preserve the common interests and should accordingly be borne or shouldered in common, that is, they should be obligations of the common property. While it happens at times, it is not usual for one spouse to be engaged in a course of dealing and contracting, of assuming obligations, for the selfish purpose of advancing only his or her own interests. This is not to say that there are not genuine instances where one spouse has separate property or perhaps a separate business interest with relation to which such spouse contracts debts and obligations. Where that happens the debt or obligation should be chargeable only against such separate property or separate interest of that spouse. But it should not be so difficult to determine the nature of a debt or obligation as incurred on behalf of such separate property or interest. Usually, however, the debts and obligations are actually incurred on behalf of the community and the community property should be liable therefor. Indeed, the presumption is that debts contracted during the marriage are community debts,[62] and to rebut this presumption it must usually be alleged and proved that the debt did not arise from a transaction in the furtherance of community interests.[63]

Nothing that has been said should incline us to fail to distinguish carefully the matter of debts which are wrongfully incurred or contracted. One spouse's share in the common property should never be subjected to liability for any debt or obligation incurred or contracted by the other spouse where the latter is, in effect, violating the fiduciary duty he or she has by reason of a power of management. A spouse cannot wrongfully or negligently enter into a contract or engage in dealings which risk the substance of the other spouse

[62] Cosper v. Valley Bank, 28 Ariz. 373, 237 P. 175; Keplinger v. Boyett (Ariz.), 433 P.2d 1006; Shaw v. Hill, 20 La. Ann. 531, 96 Am. Dec. 420; Strong v. Eakin, 11 N.M. 107, 66 P. 539; Davidson v. Click, 31 N.M. 543, 249 P. 100, 47 A. L. R. 1016; Foster v. Hackworth (Tex. Civ. App.), 164 S. W. 2d 796; Dizard and Getty v. Damson (Wash.), 387 P.2d 964; Bryant v. Stetson & Post Mill Co., 13 Wash. 692, 43 P. 931.

[63] LaSelle v. Woolery, 14 Wash. 70, 44 P. 115, 53 Am. St. Rep. 855, 32 L. R. A. 75.

without prospect of gain, or act fraudulently or injuriously to the detriment of the other spouse's interests. If absence of notice of some other equity on the part of the creditor enables him, nevertheless, to resort to the common property, the injured spouse is entitled to look to the other spouse's share in the common property or the other spouse's separate property to make good the inroad on the share of the injured spouse.[64]

§ 162.   — Statutes of the community property states.

As already remarked, the differences between the statutes of the various states make it difficult to evolve any general statements, and the statutes of any state in question should always be carefully considered.[65] There is usually an expressed indication that the community property shall be liable for debts contracted during the marriage,[66] which is correct if thereby is meant debts contracted on behalf of and for the benefit of the marital community.[67] It should not be liable for debts contracted by a spouse for that spouse's individual or separate benefit. Some courts, pursuant to governing principles, have refused to allow it to be touched at all by creditors on the individual or separate obligation of a spouse contracted during marriage, at least during the subsistence of the marriage.[68] To any argument that the half share of the community property belonging to the spouse contracting the separate debt should be liable for that debt, on the ground that such half share constitutes property of the spouse just as much as does the spouse's separate property, it may be pointed out that the exact amount of that share is not definitely ascertainable until the payment of community debts and the partition of the residue of the community property after such payment, upon

[64] See especially ante, § 150.

[65] Ariz. Rev. Stat. 1956, §§ 25-216, 25-215; Cal. Civ. Code, §§ 5116, 5117; La. Civ. Code, art. 2403; Nev. Rev. Stat. 1956, §§ 123.040, 123.210, 123.050; N.M. Stat. 1953, §§ 57-3-6, 57-3-9, 57-4-2; Tex. Family Code 1969, § 5.61; Wash. Rev. Code 1961, §§ 26.16.170, 26.16.200, 26.20.010.

[66] See Ariz. Rev. Stat. 1956, § 25-216; La. Civ. Code, art. 2403; Tex. Probate Code 1955, § 156; Tex. Family Code 1969, § 5.61.

Descent of community property charged with debts against it, see post, § 209 et seq.

Power of husband after dissolution to contract debts on account of community property, see post, § 206.

In Louisiana, the husband is bound for the wife's debts incurred in business as a public merchant. See La. Civ. Code, art. 131; Lob's Sons v. Karnofsky, 177 La. 237, 148 So. 34. It is to be noted that the profits of such business are community property. See Houghton v. Hall, 177 La. 237, 148 So. 37.

[67] Fact that community property stands in wife's name should not make it any less subject to liability for community debts. See Carlton v. Durr, 9 La. App. 269, 120 So. 124.

[68] Cosper v. Valley Bank, 28 Ariz. 373, 237 P. 175; Tway v. Payne, 55 Ariz. 343, 101 P.2d 455; Schramm v. Steele, 97 Wash. 309, 166 P. 634; Snyder v. Stringer, 116 Wash. 131, 198 P. 733; LaSelle v. Woolery, 14 Wash. 70, 44 P. 115, 53 Am. St. Rep. 855, 32 L. R. A. 75; Olive Co. v. Meek, 103 Wash. 467, 175 P. 33.

dissolution of the conjugal partnership. Moreover, those courts which have not permitted the community property, or even the debtor's half share thereof, to be reached during marriage, have reasoned that the welfare of the family requires that the common property should be left intact for the support and maintenance of the family and that it should not be subject, during marriage, to inroads for obligations not incurred for the benefit of the family.[69]

In other states the community in its entirety has been subjected to liability for the husband's own debts contracted in his separate interest (as well as, of course, for those contracted by him for the benefit of the marital community). This has been true in California,[70] (subject to a statutory qualification),[70a] in Idaho,[71] and at one time in Texas.[72] It would also seem to be true in Nevada and New Mexico.[73]

[69] See Columbia Nat. Bank v. Embree, 2 Wash. 331, 26 P. 257. And see Forsythe v. Paschal, 34 Ariz. 380, 271 P. 865. Such public policy has even outweighed public policy as to support of the aged. Maricopa County v. Douglas, 69 Ariz. 35, 208 P.2d 646.

When community status is dissolved by death, the community estate becomes ipso facto two separate estates, except as to rights of community creditors; surviving spouse and heirs of deceased spouse each take half of community estate, each half being subject to its ratable share of community debts and half taken by heirs being subject to separate debts of deceased spouse. Greer v. Goesling, 54 Ariz. 288, 97 P.2d 218. See also Tway v. Payne, 55 Ariz. 343, 101 P.2d 455. It is necessary to consider, however, that the claim may be barred by the statute of limitations long before the marital community is dissolved.

Nevertheless, where the property of an honorably discharged soldier was exempted from taxation by constitutional provision, and this exemption included his half of the community property, but not the wife's half, her share was assessable for taxes and could be separated and sold under tax lien upon her failure to pay such taxes. Oglesby v. Poage, 45 Ariz. 23, 40 P.2d 90. Taxation generally, see post, Chap. XI.

[70] Prior to 1927, it was insisted in many California decisions that title to the community property was entirely in the husband, with the wife having only an expectant interest, and that logically such property should be liable for the husband's debts. The enactment in 1927 of Civ. Code, § 161a (after January 1, 1970, § 5105), providing that the interests and ownership of both spouses are present, equal and existing should have altered this situation but the California Supreme Court has continued to insist that the community property is subject to the husband's individual debts and obligations as if it were still all his property. See Grolemund v. Cafferata, 17 Cal. 2d 679, 111 P.2d 641.

[70a] That earnings of wife are not liable for debts of husband, see Cal. Civ. Code, § 5117.

[71] Holt v. Empey, 32 Idaho 106, 178 P. 703. See also Brockelbank, The Community Property Law of Idaho, pp. 270–272.

[72] See, e.g., Cleveland v. Cole, 65 Tex. 402. However, presently, all the community property is liable for torts of a spouse during marriage but the community property subject to wife's sole management is not liable for nontortious liability of husband incurred during marriage. That under sole management of husband or joint management of spouses is subject to nontortious liabilities of husband incurred during marriage. See Tex. Family Code 1969, §§ 5.22, 5.61.

[73] This may be inferred from the fact that part of the community prop-

This amounts to an absolute denial of the basic principles of community property since it is equivalent to the assertion that the property is not community property but is entirely the property of the husband. If any liability is to be imposed, at most only the husband's half share should be liable for his individual debts, and on any division or partition of the community the amount paid on his debt should be debited against his share of the community. In these states, with some qualification in California,[74] as might be supposed the community property is not liable for the separate debts of the wife. This would be subject to commendation if it were not obvious that it results merely as a correlative of the attitude that the community property is so much the husband's that it is subject only to his creditors.[75]

A statute, such as that of Washington, which provides that expenses of the family and education of the children are chargeable upon the property of both or either spouse and in relation thereto they may be sued jointly or separately, is not out of accord with community property principles, although properly the community property should bear the primary liability and the separate property should be liable only where the community property is insufficient. Even then the separate property of the husband should be first liable, since the duty of support is imposed upon him.[76]

---

erty represented by the wife's earnings is expressly excepted from liability for the husband's debts. Nev. Rev. St. 1956, § 123.040; N.M. St. 1953, § 56-3-6.

See Strong v. Eakin, 11 N.M. 107, 66 P. 539; Carron v. Abounador, 28 N.M. 491, 214 P. 772; In re Winston's Will, 40 N.M. 348, 59 P.2d 904; Ginn v. McAluson (N.M.), 310 P.2d 1034.

[74] Earnings of wife are liable for her contracts. Cal. Civ. Code, § 5116.

[75] See Cal. Civ. Code, § 5116; Peterson v. Wiesner, 62 Nev. 184, 146 P.2d 789.

In Idaho it would seem that wife cannot by her contracts bind the community property but only her separate property. See Jacob, Community Property Law of Idaho, 1 Idaho Law Jour. 118 et seq.; Hall v. Johns, 17 Ida. 224, 105 P. 71.

This was also true in Texas at one time but now under Tex. Family Code 1969, § 5.61, all community property is liable for torts of wife committed during marriage and community property under sole management of wife

and that under joint management of spouses is liable for all debts of wife incurred during marriage.

[76] See Wash. Rev. Code 1956, § 26.20.010. What are "family expenses," see Jones-Rosquist-Killen Co. v. Nelson, 98 Wash. 539, 167 P. 1130.

Compare Ariz. Rev. St. 1956, § 25-215, which, in relation to debts contracted by the wife for necessaries for herself and the children, provides that execution be levied first on the community property, secondly on the husband's separate property and thirdly on the wife's separate property.

Under an early form of the Texas statutes providing that upon debts contracted by the wife for necessaries execution might be levied upon the community property or upon the wife's separate property, at the creditor's option, it was held that the provision was unconstitutional on the ground that her separate property was liable only where there was no community property. See Christmas v. Smith, 10 Tex. 123. This decision was ignored in Grant v. Whittlesey, 42 Tex. 320, al-

In Louisiana the community property is clearly liable for all community debts,[77] but it is also liable for separate debts of the husband.[78] It appears that only the husband's half of the community property is liable.[79] The community property is not liable for separate debts of the wife.[80]

The California Supreme Court has declared that there are no such things in that state as "community debts" and "separate debts," but only "debts of the husband" and "debts of the wife," although it states that the first two terms are sometimes used for purposes of convenience.[81] Be this as it may, it is to be noticed that the trial courts and the intermediate appellate courts make frequent use of the terms "community debts" and "separate debts" in settling the affairs of spouses.[82] And the California legislature has made provision as to debts for "necessities of life" and for "necessaries of life" contracted for by either of them and furnished to them or either of them while they are living together.[83] This would clearly seem to be a recognition of what are community debts and not only is all of the community property liable for such debts[84] but also all the husband's separate property[85] and much of the wife's separate property.[86]

Since the management of the community property is largely in the husband's hands it is considered that it should be his contracts which should bind the community property, with the result that it is sometimes expressly provided that the wife's contracts during marriage shall not bind the community property, unless in some specified manner the husband joins with her,[87] except in instances where the debt is contracted by the wife for necessaries supplied for herself

lowing execution upon either at the creditor's option. In Milburn v. Walker, 11 Tex. 329, where there was no common property or separate property of the husband the wife's separate property was held liable for the payment of debts contracted by the husband for necessaries for the support of the family; it is to be noted under the law then in force in Texas the husband had the administration of the wife's separate property.

[77] See Washington v. Palmer, 213 La. 79, 28 So.2d 509, 34 So.2d 382.

[78] See Jefferson Lake Sulphur Co. v. Walet, 104 F. Supp. 20, affirmed 202 F.2d 433, cert. den. 346 U. S. 820, 74 S. Ct. 35.

[79] See Fazzio v. Krieger, 226 La. 511, 76 So.2d 713.

[80] See Jones v. Read, 1 La. 201.

[81] See, e.g., Wilson v. Wilson, 33 Cal. 2d 107, 199 P.2d 671.

[82] See, e.g., Hill v. Hill, 82 Cal. App. 2d 682, 187 P.2d 28.

[83] Cal. Civ. Code, §§ 5117, 5121.

[84] Including the earnings of the wife, Cal. Civ. Code, § 5117.

For the community property acquired by husband to be liable, the action and judgment must be against him as well as against the wife. See Sellman v. Sellman, 82 Cal. App. 2d 192, 185 P.2d 846.

[85] See Grolemund v. Cafferata, 17 Cal. 2d 679, 111 P.2d 641; Heaton v. Justice Court, 19 Cal. App. 2d 118, 64 P.2d 1004.

[86] Cal. Civ. Code, § 5121.

[87] Community property not liable for contracts of wife made during marriage unless secured by pledge or mortgage thereof executed by husband, see Cal. Civ. Code, § 5116; N.M. St. 1956, § 57-4-2.

and the children.[88] It is probable, however, that these provisions that the community property shall not be liable for debts contracted by the wife during marriage frequently are designed to cover the situation of contracts of the wife made in pursuance of her own interests rather than the community interests.

The statutes relating to liability and nonliability of separate property of a spouse on contracts executed by either spouse during marriage are so varied as almost to defeat description. Some of the states provide with perfect equality that the separate property of either spouse shall not be liable for the debts contracted by the other.[89] Others exempt the separate property of the wife from debts contracted by the husband.[90] In some of those exempting the wife's separate property from liability on contracts made by the husband during marriage it is difficult to ascertain whether they refer to contracts for the husband's own separate ends, contracts for the community benefit, or both.[91] Not infrequently the separate property or some part of the separate property of a spouse is made liable for debts or obligations contracted on behalf of the community.[92]

[88] Ariz. Rev. St. 1956, § 25-215; Cal. Civ. Code, § 5130; Nev. Rev. St. 1956, § 123.090.

Liability of husband and wife for support of each other, see ante, § 133.

Husband not liable for non-necessaries purchased by wife on charge account in her own name, see Harrah v. Specialty Shops, Inc., 67 Nev. 493, 221 P.2d 398.

[89] Property or pecuniary rights owned by either spouse before marriage or acquired by either after marriage by gift, descent, bequest or devise, with rents, issues and profits thereof, shall not be subject to debts or contracts of other spouse. Wash. Rev. Code 1961, §§ 26.16.010, 26.16.021, 26.16.200.

In Texas, separate property of spouse is not subject to debts of other spouse unless both liable by other rules of law. See Tex. Family Code 1969, § 5.61.

[90] See Ariz. Rev. St., § 25-214; Ida. Code 1948, § 32-911; Nev. Rev. St. 1956, § 123.210; N.M. St. 1953, § 57-3-9.

[91] Separate property of wife liable for her own debts contracted after marriage, see Idaho Code 1948, § 32-911; Nev. Rev. St. 1956, § 123.210; N.M. St. 1953, § 57-3-9; see also

Wash. Rev. Code 1961, §26.16.170.

Separate property of wife liable for her debts but not for husband's, with certain provisions as to its liability for necessaries, see Cal. Civ. Code, § 5121.

Generally, see 41 C.J.S., Husband and Wife, § 528, for cases dealing with liability or nonliability of separate property for community debts. Bear in mind that some cases may be under prior forms of statutes.

In California it is clear that "debts of the husband" unless otherwise qualified includes debts incurred by the husband for the benefit of the community as well as his own separate debts. Street v. Bertolone, 193 Cal. 751, 226 P. 913, quoted with approval in Grolemund v. Cafferata, 17 Cal. 2d 679, 111 P.2d 641.

In Louisiana, "under the provisions of Article 2403 of the Civil Code and the jurisprudence bearing on said article, it is well established that debts contracted during marriage are community obligations for which the wife is not personally liable." Ward v. Trimble (La. App.), 20 So.2d 765, wherein merchant joined spouses as defendants in suit on open account for household goods purchased by them.

[92] Liability of community property, then of husband's separate property, and lastly of wife's separate property

Finally, the statutes relating to the wife's earnings, apart from their connection with various of the foregoing situations, when considered together add further to the confusion.[93] Their provisions usually run contra to community property principles in that their tendency, although this has been denied,[94] is in effect to create in the wife a separate estate of such earnings. These earnings, properly, should be as liable to the payment of community obligations as is other community property. Undoubtedly, the reason, in part if not in whole, for these statutes is that in the states where they have been enacted the community property has usually been held liable for the husband's own separate debts and it was probably considered unfair to subject these earnings to such liability. Why it should be any fairer to subject the wife's share in the other community property to the separate creditors of the husband is difficult to comprehend. Nor is there any particular justice in denying creditors of obligations contracted for the benefit of the community the right to resort to the part of the community property represented by the wife's earnings. She should share the burdens as well as the gains of the conjugal partnership. The remedy is to go to the root of the situation and remove all the community property from the burden of being liable for the separate debts of the husband.

to levy of execution for debts for herself and the children. Ariz. Rev. St. 1956, § 25-215.

Wife's separate property liable for debts for necessaries contracted by her or by her husband. Cal. Civ. Code, § 5121.

Separate property of wife not liable for any debt or obligation secured by mortgage, deed of trust or other hypothecation of community property unless wife expressly assents in writing to the liability of her separate property therefore. Cal. Civ. Code, § 5123.

Liability of husband's separate property for community debts, see Succession of Lamm, 40 La. Ann. 312, 4 So. 53; Drs. Levy and Culichia v. Lomm (La.), 193 So. 2d 383.

Expenses of family and education of children chargeable upon property of both or of either of the spouses. Wash. Rev. Code 1961, § 26.20.010.

Community obligation, upon dissolution of community, as enforceable either against community property or against separate property of husband, see First Nat. Bank of Ritzville v. Cunningham, 72 Wash. 532, 130 P.

1148. Under Cal. Civ. Code, § 5121, that certain of the wife's separate property would be liable for debt contracted for operation on husband necessary to save his life, see Credit Bureau of San Diego, Inc. v. Johnson (Cal. Super.), 142 P.2d 963.

[93] Earnings of wife not liable for debts of husband. Cal. Civ. Code, § 5117; Nev. Rev. St. 1956, § 123.040; N.M. St. 1953, § 56-3-6; but are liable for debts contracted by either spouse for necessities of life. Cal. Civ. Code, § 5117. Exemption lost after wife's earnings mingled with other community funds. Porter (Truelsen) v. Nelson, 42 Cal. App. 2d 750, 109 P.2d 996.

Earnings of wife liable on her contracts made before or after marriage. Cal. Civ. Code, § 5116.

[94] Statute exempting earnings of wife from liability for debts of husband as not constituting such earnings the separate property of the wife, see Albright v. Albright, 21 N.M. 606, 157 P. 662, Ann. Cas. 1918E 542; Arnold v. Leonard, 114 Tex. 535, 273 S. W. 799; Street v. Bertolone, 193 Cal. 751, 226 P. 913.

§ 163.   — Husband going surety for another.

While, under the Spanish law, debts contracted during the marriage by the spouses or either of them for the common benefit were dischargeable out of the common property, that rule did not apply where the husband went surety for another. The wife was not liable to pay such a debt or her proportion thereof out of the property acquired during marriage. The act of the husband in going surety was not considered one from which any profit could accrue to the community, so that the wife was no more liable therefor than for his debts contracted before marriage.[95] The argument that profit might be said to accrue to the marital community where the husband received some consideration for going surety was considered far outweighed by the risk assumed and the fact that any such consideration was rarely the equivalent in amount to that which might be lost and "it is usually loss instead, as experience shows."[96] To permit the husband so to bind the wife's half of the community property by going surety for another was considered in fraud of the wife's rights. One charged with the administration of the property of another had no right to abuse the substance in that way and to risk the loss of the wife's share of the common property to her prejudice.[97]

The logic of this is so plain that it is astonishing to find the Washington court, in a case where the husband was a lawyer who agreed to indemnify a surety on his client's bail bond, holding that the community property was liable on this indemnity agreement, although it was recognized that no profit resulted to the community from the transaction. The basis for this decision seems to be that the indemnity agreement was made in the exercise of his profession and that such exercise of his profession was "community business."[98] The court distinguished other decisions in which it held the community

[95] Matienzo, Gloss VII, No. 3, to Nov. Rev. Law 2, Book 10, Title 4.

"And we order, that for the debts that the husband shall owe, or for the security or pledge that he shall contract, the wife shall not be charged, even though the debts are for our (i.e., the Crown's) rents, taxes, or legal claims." Novísima Recopilación, Book 10, Title 11, Law 2 (in part). And according to Palacios Ruvios this debt arising from the husband going security for another affected neither the wife's individual property nor her half of the ganancial property.

[96] Arguments both for and against are fully presented by Gutiérrez who concludes that the law was against holding the wife's share of the community property liable where the hus-

band went surety for another. Gutiérrez, Quaestio CXXVIII, to Nov. Rec. Law 9.

[97] Azevedo, Nos. 20, 21, to Nov. Rec. Law 5.

[98] O'Malley v. Lewis, 176 Wash. 194, 28 P.2d 283.

An equally far-fetched case is Fidelity Nat. Bank v. Fox, 144 Wash. 494, 258 P. 335, where the husband was a stockholder and trustee of a bank which posted surety bonds in order to become a depositary of public funds; the husband joined with others in executing indemnity bonds to the surety companies as well as joining in other indemnity agreements for the benefit of the bank. The court said that these indemnity agreements were executed "to protect" the community

not liable, as where the husband gratuitously signed as surety on a bond,[99] or as accommodation indorser of a promissory note,[1] on the ground that such acts were not community enterprises but were outside the regular course of the husband's business. This is merely a technical splitting of hairs, for it is difficult to comprehend how any act done in prejudice of and to the risk of the wife's share of the common property and without any return of profit to the common property, an act done in abuse of the trust imposed on the husband from his power of administration, can on any ground be said to bind the property of the wife.[2] What the husband is really doing is pledging the security of his individual credit and he has no right to risk the wife's property without her definite assent, and even this is questionable for, as she will often be without business experience and influenced by considerations of affection, she may be induced to join with the husband without realizing the threatened detriment to her interests.[3] In those jurisdictions where the community property is

property and were obligations of the community.

In Floding v. Denholm, 40 Wash. 463, 82 P. 738, wherein the husband went surety on the debt of a corporation in which he had purchased stock for the community, not only was the corporation insolvent at the time but the wife had opposed the purchase of the stock. Nevertheless, the community property was held liable. Compare this fruitless opposition of the wife with the view of the Spanish community property law that "where she says she does not wish to share a house purchased by the husband or a lease of state revenue taken by him" they might agree that the venture should be his separate venture and not a community venture and her share of the common property was not subjected to any liability therefor. See Matienzo, Gloss I, No. 2, to Nov. Rec. Law 9.

[99] Kanters v. Kotick, 102 Wash. 523, 173 P. 329.

[1] Harry L. Olive Co. v. Meek, 103 Wash. 467, 175 P. 33. In this regard, see also Payne v. Williams, 47 Ariz. 396, 56 P.2d 186.

[2] "Ever since the case of Horton v. Donahoe Kelly Banking Co. (15 Wash. 399, 46 P. 409), decided in 1896, it has been well settled law (in Washington) that community property is liable for such a suretyship debt only if the community has been 'benefited' by the suretyship obligation. The writer does not know exactly what is meant by the requirement that the community be benefited by the suretyship obligation. . . . Whatever that requirement turns out to be, creditors of the husband must take account of the general proposition of which it is a part in determining whether or not to extend credit in reliance upon a husband's signature as surety." Mechem, Creditors' Rights in Community Property, 11 Wash. Law Rev. 80, 87. As to a more recent case that the community must be "benefited," see Zarvell v. Mantas (Wash.), 204 P.2d 203.

[3] This necessity of guarding the wife from being induced to strip herself of her property through considerations of affection was well recognized by the Spanish law. See Asso and Mañuel, Institutes of Civil Law of Spain, Book II, Title IX, § 1, who remark that donations between man and wife were not valid because their mutual affection might induce them to strip themselves of their property.

Cases involving the husband going as surety for another seem mostly to have arisen in Washington, where the courts attempt a distinction between the husband's suretyship in furtherance or protection of community interests and his suretyship entered

liable for separate obligations and debts of the husband contracted or incurred during marriage, the community property is subject, of course, to liability on contracts of suretyship of the husband without any question as to whether the community is or is not benefited.[4]

The matter of the wife going surety for the husband or joining with him upon his own obligations is to be distinguished from the above, and is dealt with in the succeeding section.

§ 164.   — Wife going surety for husband or another.

To repeat what was said in a previous section, under the Spanish law the wife could not bind herself as surety for her husband upon his own obligations and undertakings, nor could she bind herself with him jointly and severally for his obligations, although she might in the latter case be liable *pro rata* for such benefit as she could be shown to have received therefrom. However, she might join with the husband to obtain money to pay claims of the Crown against her for taxes or the like.[5] For that matter, a woman, whether married or unmarried, could not go surety for another except in certain specified instances.[6] There is no particular uniformity among our community property states, as the following illustrations will serve to demonstrate.[7] In Idaho, that the wife cannot be personal surety for her husband or for one other than her husband seems to be discernible from the cases. But she can mortgage or pledge some specific piece of her separate property to secure the husband's debts or the debts of another, although no personal deficiency decree can be rendered against her.[8]

into without the scope of community business. For a large collection of these cases, see Evans, Community Obligations, 10 Calif. Law Rev. 120. To somewhat the same effect in Arizona, see Perkins v. First Nat. Bank, 47 Ariz. 376, 56 P.2d 639; Keplinger v. Boyett (Ariz.), 433 P.2d 1006; Payne v. Williams, 47 Ariz. 396, 56 P.2d 186. One case has arisen in Texas, which may be noted, in which the act of the husband in going surety for another was held to bind the community property, evidently on the ground that any debt or obligation contracted by the husband during marriage bound the community property. See Hinzie v. Robinson, 21 Tex. Civ. App. 9, 50 S. W. 635.

[4] See, e.g., Holt v. Empey, 32 Ida. 106, 178 P. 703.

In New Mexico, see U.S. Fidelity & Guaranty Co. v. Chavez, 126 F. Supp. 227, that only the husband's half of the community liable.

[5] Novísima Recopilación, Book 10, Title 11, Law 3.

[6] Las Siete Partidas, Part. 5, Title 12, Laws 2 and 3. None of the exceptions could relate to the wife going surety for her husband for to that extent they were repealed by the later law of the Novísima Recopilación cited in the preceding note. See Asso and Mañuel, Institutes of Civil Law of Spain, Book II, Title XVIII (Johnson's translation, nn. 6, 7).

[7] Wife who becomes surety for husband must renounce laws in her favor, see Beauregard v. Piernas, 1 Mart. O. S. (La.) 281.

[8] See Jacob, Community Property Law of Idaho, 1 Idaho Law Jour. 118, 125. And see Dernham & Kaufmann v. Pawley, 4 Idaho 753, 44 P. 643, that wife can contract debts for benefit of her separate property but

In Texas the wife can be a surety in the same manner as if she were a *feme sole*.[9] The California code provision may also be noticed which provides that the separate property of the wife is not liable for any debt or obligation secured by mortgage, deed of trust or other hypothecation of the community property unless she expressly assents in writing to liability of her separate property therefor.[10]

§ 165.   Obligations imposed by law.

Under the Spanish law of community property, as previously stated, in case of debts contracted during marriage by either spouse for that spouse's own benefit or interest, such debts were dischargeable from the separate property of the contracting spouse.[11] The same would seem to have been true as to an obligation imposed by law, as for the support of a parent or of children of a former marriage. In respect of the liability of such spouse's share of the community, it was stated by Matienzo that so far as concerned the obligation imposed by law to support a parent, if the private property of the spouse was insufficient then that spouse's share of the community property could be subjected to the obligation. Thus, where there was a legal obligation upon a wife to support her mother, liability upon this obligation could not be escaped on the ground that the wife had no separate property available, since her share of the common property was liable therefor. It was no answer, observed Matienzo, to say that the husband and not the wife had the management of such property, seeing that in spite of that the wife herself was the owner of half of that property acquired during the marriage.[12] It was pointed out by Gutiérrez, however, that only those debts contracted during marriage and which concerned the actual marriage of husband and

debts contracted by husband for his own or the family's benefit could not expose the separate property of the wife to levy and sale even though she voluntarily became surety therefor.

[9] Tex. Rev. Civ. Stats. 1925, art. 4625. See also Oakes, Speer's Marital Rights in Texas, 4th Ed., § 266.

In Westbrook v. Belton Nat. Bank, 97 Tex. 246, 77 S. W. 942, wherein husband's note was secured by deed of trust lien given by wife on her separate property, it was held that extension of husband's note without wife's consent released the lien.

[10] Cal. Civ. Code, § 5123.

It would seem that the wife cannot render her separate property liable by signing a note and deed of trust with her husband to secure a debt of the husband or of the community where no new consideration is received therefor. Hamaker v. Heffron, 148 F.2d 981, construing California law and following Chaffee v. Browne, 109 Cal. 211, 41 P. 1028.

Although a wife joining with husband in execution of promissory note is personally liable, her oral promise after husband's death to assume personally such obligation was not valid novation, since no additional consideration was received therefor and it was not between all the original parties. Garthofner v. Edmonds, 74 Cal. App. 2d 15, 167 P.2d 789.

[11] See ante, § 160.

[12] Matienzo, Gloss VII, No. 10, to Nov. Rec. Law 2, Book 10, Title 4.

wife and their partnership and which accrued and were contracted on its account by both or one of them were common debts and therefore payable from goods acquired during the marriage. An obligation to support a parent or children of a former marriage was, on the other hand, an obligation apart from and even antecedent to the marriage and thus fell rather into the class of separate prenuptial debts of a spouse which could under no circumstances be charged against the community property. In support of this he cited other commentators who remarked that where a husband supported a child of a former marriage from profits of a second marriage, the second wife or her heirs could demand back a half part of the cost of such support.[13] Actually, as so often happened where the commentators were in apparent disagreement, they are actually in agreement although approaching the matter from opposite directions. Matienzo never stated, as Gutiérrez' objections thereto would lead one to assume, that the entire common property should be liable to the legal obligation, but only that share belonging to the spouse concerned. This, in effect, is exactly what Gutiérrez says, for he points out that if a husband did support a child of a former marriage from common property of a second marriage, he should account to the second wife or her heirs for half of the amount so expended. Thus, each was agreed that no more of the community property than the half share belonging to the spouse under the legal obligation should be used to meet that obligation. It is undoubted that the conclusion to be drawn is that where a spouse having a duty or obligation imposed by law had insufficient separate funds at the moment to meet such duty or obligation, it might be met from the spouse's share in the community property, provided that the other spouse suffered no detriment therefrom and that expenditures by one spouse from the common fund were properly charged against that spouse's share. It will be seen, then, that when the law itself imposed an obligation on a spouse, as for support of a parent, or for taxes, or for a penal sum upon sentence for a criminal delict, or the like, the spouse's half share of the community property might be reached, unlike the case of the ordinary separate creditor of the spouse. In the case of the ordinary separate creditor, his rights to reach his debtor's properties were subordinated to the well-being and interests of the family which required that the community property be kept intact for its benefit during the marriage. But obligations imposed by the state itself took priority over everything else.[14] A comparable view will be found in Arizona whose public policy follows closely that of the Spanish community property principles in refusing

---

[13] Gutiérrez, Quaestio CXXIX, to Nov. Rec. Law 9.

[14] Termination of conjugal partnership in acquests and gains and subjecting guilty spouse's half share of community property to penalty or confiscation upon sentence for criminal delict, see post, § 188.

The mistake should not be made of assuming that a judgment obtained by a creditor against the debtor spouse was, by reason of being a judgment, an obligation imposed by law. It did not come within the meaning of that term.

to allow any part of the community property to be reached during marriage for separate debts incurred by a spouse during marriage, on the ground that the safety of the family requires that the community property be preserved intact during marriage. Nevertheless, the right of the state to subject the wife's half of the community property to liability for taxes thereon was said to be superior to any public policy as to preserving the community property intact during marriage.[15]

In our community property states, where an obligation of a separate nature, such as for the support of a parent, is imposed by law upon a spouse, the extent to which separate or community property is liable usually follows the pattern applied in the particular state in the case of contractual obligations.[16] This is illustrated by the cases discussed immediately hereafter.[17] In Washington, where the community property, during the marriage, is not liable for the separate debts and obligations of either spouse, and where the husband has no power to give away community property without the wife's consent, except as to the veriest trifles, the wife has been allowed to recover as community property the proceeds of a life insurance policy which the husband had taken on his life for the benefit of his mother. It was so held, although the amount attempted to be given to the mother was not unreasonably disproportionate to the entire amount of community property and the mother was indigent and a statutory duty to support her was imposed upon the husband.[18] A more pertinent case, perhaps, is one arising in California where a mother obtained, in the lower court, a judgment against her married daughter for the payment of a specified monthly sum for support, upon authority of a statute imposing a duty of support. Upon appeal, however, the appellate court reversed on the ground that the married daughter had no separate property available and that her interest in the community property was not subject to liability therefor.[19] Analysis of the case reveals the underlying tendency of the California courts to regard the community property as actually the husband's property, regardless of lip service rendered to community property principles. Thus, the court remarks that there was no statutory duty upon the husband to support his wife's mother, as if all the community property in his hands was his property and therefore subject only to

---

[15] See post, § 235.

[16] Liens arising by operation of law, see § 169.

Obligations imposed by divorce decree as enforceable against property of second marriage, see ante, § 158; post, § 191.

Liability for taxes, see post, Chap. XI.

Support of illegitimate children, see Peterson v. Eritsland (Wash.), 419 P.2d 332.

[17] The extent to which a husband may devote community property under his control to aiding or supporting relatives is discussed ante, Chap. VII, B.

[18] Occidental Life Ins. Co. v. Powers, 192 Wash. 475, 74 P.2d 27, 114 A. L. R. 531, in which there was a strong dissent by four justices.

[19] Grace v. Carpenter, 42 Cal. App. 2d 301, 108 P.2d 701, noted in 14 So. Calif. Law Rev. 481, as to duties of support.

obligations imposed upon him. As further reasons why the wife's share of the community property was not reachable, the court states that the management and control of the property is placed by law in his hands and that, moreover, it cannot be segregated or divided, so as to make the wife's share subject to her obligations. Of course, the mere fact that its management is placed in the husband's hands does not defeat the fact that the wife owns half of it, or make it any more the husband's property. The fact of management must be distinguished from ownership. When we consider the court's argument that the property cannot be segregated so as to make the wife's share subject to her statutory liability, we may well ask what would be the court's decision if it had been the husband's mother who was involved instead of the wife's mother. Would the court have advanced its nonsegregation argument then, and declared that the community property could not be reached? Reasoning from other California cases, it may be fairly concluded that the court would have forgotten its nonsegregation argument and held the community property liable solely on the basis of the fact that the husband had the management of it.[20] To be consistent, of course, and render equality between the spouses as to their equal and existing half ownership, the community property should either be exempt from liability upon the separate obligations of both spouses, or each spouse's half share of the community property should equally be subject to the separate obligations of that spouse.[21]

In Arizona, where a county obtained a judgment against a wife for support rendered to the wife's mother, under the state old age assistance act imposing responsibility on relatives for support of the aged, such judgment could not be satisfied from the community property. Public policy was said to favor the maintenance of the community and the protection of the family over support of the aged.[22] The Arizona court has found, however, that community money spent by a father ". . . for the support and education of the daughter (by prior marriage) was a legal obligation of the husband," but he was required to account to the community for excess amounts so spent.[23]

§ 166.   — Stockholders' liability.

When we consider the added or double liability imposed by constitutional or statutory provisions upon bank stockholders, we are faced with a liability that in some situations is penal rather than contractual.[24] Even where it is termed contractual, as it frequently is

[20] As seems to have been done in Grolemund v. Cafferata, 17 Cal. 2d 679, 111 P.2d 641.

[21] General language in Smedberg v. Bevilockway, 7 Cal. App. 2d 578, 46 P.2d 820, would indicate an adherence to the first alternative, if given full effect.

[22] Maricopa County v. Douglas, 69 Ariz. 35, 208 P.2d 646.

[23] Spector v. Spector, 94 Ariz. 175, 382 P.2d 659.

[24] See Fletcher Cyc. Corp., Perm. Ed., §§ 6271, 6272.

by the courts,[25] it is actually inserted into the contract between the corporation and the stockholder by operation of law. But although the law operates to fix liability of the stockholder, the liability, being usually considered contractual, is enforced as to a married woman who is a stockholder accordingly as the law of the place of enforcement provides for liability in relation to her contracts. This is true even where the liability is sought to be enforced as to national bank stock.[26] Thus, in jurisdictions where community property is not liable, or only part of it is liable, for separate debts contracted by the wife, a judgment against the wife imposing added or double liability upon her as a bank stockholder cannot be enforced against the community property, or at least against that part of it not made liable.[27] When we consider the situation where bank stock is property of the marital community, although it may be in the name of one spouse only, the principle usually recognized that community property is liable for payment of community obligations is applicable. So, an assessment on stock which is community property is enforceable against other community property of the spouses.[28]

[25] See de Funiak, 28 Georgetown Law Jour. 320, at p. 334.

[26] Meek v. Stein, 5 F. Supp. 656; Best v. Turner, 1 F. Supp. 461, aff'd 67 F.2d 786, 90 A. L. R. 1293; both applying law of Texas.

[27] Best v. Turner, 67 F.2d 786, 90 A. L. R. 1293, aff'g 1 F. Supp. 461 (applying Texas law); Meek v. Stein, 5 F. Supp. 656 (applying Texas law); Shaw v. Finney (Tex. Civ. App.), 7 S. W. 2d 152.

Under the view in effect in Texas at that time, that the community property is liable for antenuptial debts of the wife contracted before marriage, the community property has been held liable for an assessment against the wife on stock in an insolvent bank owned by her before her marriage. Crim v. Austin (Tex. Com. App.), 6 S. W. 2d 348, aff'g. (Tex. Civ. App.), 299 S. W. 322. As might be supposed, the stock acquired by the wife in the two federal cases cited ante, this note, was acquired during the marriage. The matter is not entirely clear in the Shaw Case, but it may be assumed that the same was true in that case.

[28] See Shuey v. Adair, 24 Wash. 378, 64 P. 536.

In Austin v. Strong, 117 Tex. 263, 1 S. W. 2d 872, 3 S. W. 2d 425, 79 A. L. R. 1528, although the stock in question was community property, the assessment was not made until after the death of the husband and after the wife had disclaimed ownership. It was said that no liability could be enforced against the wife, on the ground that the relation of stockholder cannot be forced on one by the law of descent against his or her wish, and that she had disclaimed. It was contended by the Commissioner of Banking who sought to enforce the assessment that the wife could only disclaim the husband's half interest which passed to her by inheritance and that she was already owner of the other half by virtue of its being community property. The court refused to agree on the ground that the contract of purchase of the stock was made by the husband and was a charge only against his estate, and that no contractual relation was created between the bank and the wife. At first sight this decision has the effect of allowing a wife the option to accept the benefit of acquests and gains during the marriage but to escape any burdens or losses, but unknowingly the court is giving some effect to the principle of the Spanish law that on the husband's death the wife may renounce her rights under the community and thus escape any burdens. She could not, of course,

§ 167. Remedies and priorities in general of creditors.

Necessarily, much of what has been discussed in the preceding and following sections of this chapter must be considered in connection with such matters as are here dealt with. Since the husband is usually the one in whose hands the management of the community property and affairs relating thereto are placed, the husband is usually the proper party to sue or to be sued in regard thereto.[29] Accordingly, when any debt has been contracted on behalf of or for the benefit of the marital community, with the exception of Washington where the creditor must sometimes join the husband and the wife as parties defendant,[30] the husband ordinarily is the proper party against whom the creditor should proceed.[31] Indeed, in some cases the wife has been deemed outright an improper party even when joined with the husband,[32] although it would certainly seem that, even in situations where the husband is clearly the one against whom to proceed, there is no reason why the naming of the wife as a party defendant should constitute more than a harmless surplusage and be disregarded. Judgment obtained against him as the party defendant is then enforceable against the community property,[33] even against community property standing in the wife's name or in her possession and control,[34] unless it be some type of community property especially exempted by virtue

retain part of the community property and deny the burdens. It had to be a complete renunciation. See post, § 218. In the view of Judge Speer of Texas, the liability imposed was statutory and not contractual, however, and the wife should have been liable by reason of that fact. Speer, Law of Marital Rights in Texas, 3rd Ed., § 160.

[29] Actions by husband or wife on behalf of community, see ante, §§ 124–127.

[30] In actions to foreclose liens and mortgages on community property, the wife must be joined as party defendant. Dane v. Daniel, 23 Wash. 379, 63 P. 268. But where the relief sought by a creditor is only an ordinary judgment of liability of the defendant, the creditor has been allowed to name only the husband as defendant and thereafter is entitled to levy upon community property. The wife may intervene in the action or contest the execution to show that the debt was not a community debt. Of course, the plaintiff may choose to join the wife as a party defendant. See McKay, Community Property, 2d Ed., § 1089; Hendrickson v. Smith, 111 Wash. 82, 189 P. 550. And the creditor may sue either or both where the debt was incurred for expenses of the family or for the education of the children. Wash. Rev. Code 1961, § 26.20.010.

[31] This is true as a general rule in the community property states other than Washington.

[32] See Bienvenu v. Fournet, 28 La. Ann. 623; Brock Furniture Co. v. Carroll (La.), 86 So.2d 715; Wilson v. Dickey, 63 Tex. Civ. App. 155, 133 S. W. 437.

[33] The local statutes should always be examined carefully to ascertain the community property subject to execution.

[34] See Carlton v. Durr, 9 La. App. 269, 120 So. 124. Although not applicable in that case, such rule was stated in La Selle v. Woolery, 14 Wash. 70, 44 P. 115, 53 Am. St. Rep. 855, 32 L. R. A. 73.

of statute, such as the wife's earnings.[35] Even if the wife has power, either by virtue of statute or by virtue of her husband's authorization, to contract concerning the community, it may be required that the cause of action resulting from her contract be prosecuted against her and the husband, with the husband constituting an absolutely necessary party defendant.[36] So far, however, as statutory authorization to the wife to bind the community on her contracts, or statutory provision that community property placed under the wife's management is subject to seizure for community debts, is coupled with undoubted authorization to proceed against the wife alone, the creditor may naturally name her as sole party defendant.[37] Frequently, of course, there is authorization to sue the wife alone where she is living separate or apart from the husband,[38] and this is especially true where they have been separated by divorce,[39] or to sue the wife alone where she has been given management of the community property, with judicial approval, upon abandonment by or disappearance or incompetency

---

[35] For instance, in California, the wife's earnings would seem to be exempted from liability for community debts, unless the debts were incurred for necessities supplied to the spouses. See Cal. Civ. Code, § 5117; and see Credit Bureau of San Diego v. Johnson (Cal. Super.), 142 P.2d 963.

In Louisiana, see Personal Finance, Inc. v. Simms (La.), 148 So.2d 176.

And see ante, § 162.

[36] "The statute, however, requiring the husband to be made a party with the wife is imperative; the courts have no right to disregard the statute when the married woman sued is insisting, as the law permits her to do, that its terms be observed." Benson v. Hunter, 23 Ariz. 132, 202 P. 233.

In Louisiana, by virtue of La. Acts of 1926, No. 132, a married woman can by contract bind herself personally with her husband for the payment of a community debt. United Life & Accident Ins. Co. v. Haley, 178 La. 63, 150 So. 833.

Department store's action against husband and wife to recover for articles purchased on open charge account in wife's name by wife separated from husband, see D. H. Holmes Co. v. Van Ryper (La. App.), 173 So. 584.

[37] For example, where wife is given

power to administer her earnings, although they remain community property, and to sue and be sued in relation thereto. Many of these statutes are cited ante, §§ 114, 124.

And see Tex. Rev. Civ. St. 1925, arts. 4620, 4621, 4626.

[38] See, e. g., Nev. Rev. St. 1956, § 123.120.

[39] And see post, Chap. X.

In Ackley v. Maggi, 86 Cal. App. 631, 261 P. 311, where it appeared that during marriage the husband contracted for medical services to the wife and thereafter the spouses were divorced and the community property divided between them, the physician rendering the services was permitted to bring action therefor against the wife and recover judgment against her. Notice Cal. Civ. Code, § 5121, as to liability of her separate property for necessaries furnished her.

Compare Medical Finance Ass'n v. Allum, 22 Cal. App. 2d (Supp.) 747, 66 P.2d 761, noted 11 So. Cal. Law Rev. 359, where wife not held personally liable for medical services contracted for first husband so as to permit judgment against second husband. Obligation must be direct personal obligation of wife to subject husband to liability.

of the husband.[40] Even in the situation where the husband is the proper and necessary party defendant, it is or certainly should be recognized that the wife is entitled to intervene in order to establish that the property or certain of the property sought to be reached is actually her separate property, where her separate property is not subject to payment of the claims.[41]

Of course, where the community debt has been contracted by both husband and wife in their names, it would seem preferable to join them both as parties defendant, but actually the matter must be dependent upon the local statutes.[42] It may be required that both be joined as parties defendant,[43] or that the husband is the necessary party defendant, perhaps with the joinder of the wife permitted if the creditor elects but without altering the fact that the husband is the really requisite party defendant.[44] Whether or not both are required to be joined, the debt being a community debt, the separate property of the wife would not be liable therefor,[45] except as made so by statute.[46] If any of her separate property is made liable by statute, naturally she must be named a defendant in order that judgment be

[40] Generally as to administration by wife in these circumstances, see ante, § 128.

[41] This was the situation in Bank of Orofino v. Wellman, 26 Idaho 425, 143 P. 1169.

[42] Necessity that husband join in execution of contract with wife or that husband execute pledge or mortgage of community property in security of wife's contract, in order to bind community property, see Cal. Civ. Code, § 5116; N.M. Stats. 1953, § 57-4-2.

Where plaintiff sued husband and wife, on ground of false representations, to recover purchase price paid to them for alleged oil lands, the deed to which was executed by both spouses, in the circumstances a judgment against the wife as well as the husband was proper. Engle v. Farrell, 75 Cal. App. 2d 612, 171 P.2d 588, pointing out that to the extent wife profited from the fraud she was equally liable.

[43] Wife may be a proper, even a necessary, party where the contract has been entered into in relation to her separate estate or partly concerns her separate estate. See Silva v. Holland, 74 Cal. 530, 16 P. 385; Laws v. Ross, 44 Nev. 405, 194 P.

465; Brown v. Gurley, 58 N.M. 153, 267 P.2d 134.

[44] The courts frequently express it that the wife is a "proper party defendant" where she has joined in the execution of a contract or mortgage. See Anthony v. Nye, 30 Cal. 401; cf. Silva v. Holland, 74 Cal. 530, 16 P. 385.

In Arizona, if the wife is a party, the husband shall be joined with her except when the action concerns her separate party or is between the spouses. See Rule 17(e), Ariz. Rules Civ. Proc.; Pratt v. Daly, 55 Ariz. 535, 104 P.2d 147.

[45] Although husband and wife joined in securing the execution of a lease, and action thereon was brought against them jointly as defendants, a personal judgment against the wife and the subjection of her separate property to the payment thereof were not warranted where the evidence was insufficient to show that the purpose in procuring the leased premises was to protect and preserve the wife's separate property, the apparant purpose being to benefit a business carried on by the spouses for the common benefit. Borders v. Moran (Tex. Civ. App.), 51 S. W. 2d 434.

[46] See ante, § 161.

entered against her which will be enforceable against her separate property.[47] We have seen that under the Spanish law where husband and wife bound themselves jointly and severally upon a contract for the common benefit, both or either of them might be proceeded against.[48] Somewhat similarly, in Washington, either or both spouses may be sued upon debts incurred for family expenses or for the education of the children, and the community property and the separate property of each is liable for such debts.[49]

§ 168.　— Setting aside fraudulent conveyances.

The right of creditors to set aside conveyances which are fraudulent as to them is a subject of such magnitude in itself that any detailed discussion of it here is out of the question. Reference to specific works upon this subject is recommended.[50] Under the Spanish law, existing creditors could revoke or set aside transfers of property made with intent to defraud them. Likewise they could do so where the debtor made gifts *inter vivos* or bequeathed his property by will, for where these were concerned any actual fraudulent intent was immaterial since it was the result that had to be considered.[51] This, of course, applied in the case of community property so transferred by the husband in the exercise of his management thereof.[52] Any such right to set aside such fraudulent conveyances of the community property was a right resting, naturally, only in those creditors entitled to look to the community property for payment; in other words, creditors on community obligations or debts.

So far as concerns property transactions between the spouses themselves which are in fraud of creditors, the matter is dealt with in sections following.[53]

§ 169.　— Secured creditors.

Wherever community property is properly pledged or mortgaged to secure an obligation, naturally the creditor can resort to such

---

[47] In California, under Civ. Code, § 5121, providing that some of wife's separate property is liable for debts contracted by husband or wife for necessaries of life, it is necessary to join wife as party defendant with husband in order to subject her to liability under the statute. Credit Bureau of San Diego, Inc. v. Johnson (Cal. Super.), 142 P.2d 963.

[48] As to Spanish law, see ante, § 159.

Suit maintainable against husband alone where both husband and wife jointly and severally liable, see Payne v. Bentley, 21 Tex. 452.

[49] Wash. Rev. Code 1961, § 26.20.010.

[50] See, e. g., Glenn, Fraudulent Conveyances.

[51] Las Siete Partidas, Part. 5, Title 15, Laws 7, 11; Matienzo, Gloss VI, Nos. 5, 10, to Nov. Rec. Law 5, Book 10, Title 4.

[52] See Matienzo, Gloss VI, Nos. 5, 10, to Nov. Rec. Law 5.

[53] See post, § 173 et seq.

property in order to obtain payment of the debt. The power of the husband to pledge or mortgage the community property and the question whether the wife's joinder is required or not are matters that have been treated in a previous chapter.[54] It may be repeated here, very generally, that in most states the husband has such exercise of management over the community personalty that he can pledge it without the necessity of the wife's joinder, but that as to mortgages of the realty she is usually required to join in their execution in order to make them effective. In some situations, the community property may be subject to statutory liens, as where, for example, community realty is made subject to mechanics' liens for labor and material furnished in erecting structures and improvements thereon, or is made subject to liens of judgments recovered for community debts.[55] But even where a lien exists against community realty, either by virtue of the wife joining in execution of the lien or by virtue of operation of law, in an action against husband and wife no personal judgment can be entered against the wife so as to render her personally liable in the absence of any legal liability of her separate property for community debts.[56]

The rights of a creditor whose claim is secured by an encumbrance on the community realty are necessarily affected by the question of whether or not the encumbrance was executed by both husband and wife, since the joinder of the wife therein is now usually required by statute in most community property states. The necessity of this joinder by the wife and the effect of her failure to do so upon the validity of the encumbrance have been referred to in a preceding chapter. The view is definitely followed in some states, by virtue of statute and judicial decision, that one taking a deed or mortgage from a husband, in whose name legal title stands, thereby acquires a valid title or encumbrance as against any claims of the wife, provided it is shown that he took in good faith for value without notice of the marriage relation.[57] Undoubtedly, it should be shown that by

---

[54] See ante, Chap. VII, B.

[55] See, e. g., Wash. Rev. Code 1961, § 26.16.040.

Contract by husband alone for improvements on community property authorizes fixing of materialman's lien. Brick & Tile, Inc. v. Parker, 143 Tex. 383, 186 S. W. 2d 66.

Mechanic's lien as community obligation, see Willes v. Palmer, 78 Ida. 104, 298 P.2d 972.

[56] Where assessments were levied against community realty because of street improvements, personal judgment against the wife was a nullity. See Flynt v. City of Kingsville (Tex. Civ. App.), 50 S. W. 2d 414.

"The separate property of the wife is not liable for any debt or obligation secured by a mortgage, deed of trust, or other hypothecation of the community property, unless the wife expressly assents in writing to the liability of her separate property for such debt or obligation." Cal. Civ. Code, § 5123.

Realty held by spouses in joint tenancy and judgment lien against husband, see Solomon v. Phillips, 92 Cal. App. 2d 1, 206 P.2d 50.

[57] As to husband encumbering community realty of which he has record title, Cal. Civ. Code § 5127, provides that it "shall be presumed to be valid";

the most reasonable exercise of diligence he could not have known of the marriage relation. Incidentally, the same principle applies in those states where the wife conveys or encumbers community property, title to which is in her name and over which she has the exercise of administration and disposition. It has been denied, however, that a purchaser in good faith and without knowledge acquires any title against the claims of the husband or the wife's heirs, although title stood in her name, where the community property is that as to which she has no power or capacity of conveyance.[58]

In the absence, however, of good faith or reasonable diligence on the part of the mortgagee, the failure of the wife to join in the execution of the encumbrance will render it invalid not only as against the claim of the mortgagee but as against a subsequent lienor having a valid attachment lien.[59] In New Mexico it has been held that where a husband purchased property for the benefit of the community and gave back a purchase money mortgage without the wife joining therein, the mortgage was nevertheless valid and a subsequent judgment lien was subordinate thereto; it may be inferred, however, that the court was strongly influenced by the view that the purchase money mortgage was evidentiary of the grantor's vendor's lien and constituted at least constructive notice of such lien to subsequent lien creditors.[60] But aside from the rights of other creditors, the somewhat peculiar eventuality may come about that in security of a community obligation the husband alone executes a mortgage of community realty, which is invalid because of the failure of the wife to join in the execution, so that the creditor cannot resort to that security, yet if he obtains a judgment against the community upon the community obligation, the judgment then gives him a lien on such realty so that he can sell it under execution.[60a]

This situation affecting the right of the wife to assert her claim in community property as against such a bona fide purchaser is to be carefully distinguished from the right of the wife to assert claim to her separate property or its value in the hands of her husband as against creditors.[61]

§ 170. — Community and separate property.

Under the Spanish law a creditor on the separate debt of a spouse had to look for payment to that spouse's separate property, during

the wife has one year from date of recordation in which to bring action to avoid the encumbrance.

[58] See ante, § 117.
Criticism of bona fide purchaser doctrine as applied to community property, see post, § 206.

[59] See Campbell v. Sandy, 190 Wash. 528, 69 P.2d 808.

[60] Davidson v. Click, 31 N.M. 543, 249 P. 100, 47 A. L. R. 1016.

[60a] Doing indirectly what cannot be done directly is referred to in Holt v. Empey, 32 Ida. 106, 178 P. 703.

[61] See post, § 175.

the marriage,[62] for it was an established principle that the community property was primarily a fund for the payment of community obligations and that accordingly, claims of separate creditors were necessarily subordinated to those of community creditors so far as the community property was concerned. Indeed, it was only upon dissolution of the marriage and after community debts had been paid and the residue of the community property remaining was divided between one spouse and the heirs of the other, that separate creditors could then look to their debtor's share of the community property.[63] Even in our jurisdictions which have not recognized the principle that during marriage the community property should be liable only for community debts, and which have allowed the community property to be subjected, during marriage, to claims of creditors, priority has been given to claims of community creditors over the claims of separate creditors.[64] Thus, where both community property and the separate property of one of the spouses are pledged to secure one community debt, the creditor must first exhaust the community property before he can resort to the separate property.[65] In such a situation, a subsequent creditor who is able to reach only the community property and who faces the possibility that the community property may be exhausted by the claim of the prior creditor cannot for that reason insist that the prior creditor should resort first to the separate property which may be available to such prior creditor. The spouse owning the separate property cannot be deprived of the right to have the community property first resorted to by the prior creditor.[66]

The principle has been recognized as especially applicable where community debts exist at the time of the dissolution of the marital community by reason of the death of one of the spouses, since there must be satisfaction of such debts from the community property

---

[62] See ante, §§ 156, 160.

For debts contracted by husband before or during marriage, only fruits of dotal property left after satisfying charges of matrimony may be taken in execution, but if the wife has contracted the debt before marriage, the dotal property may be taken in execution in default of paraphernal property, and not the fruits which belong to the husband. If the wife contracted a lawful debt during marriage, execution cannot go against her dotal property, and much less if the debt were common to both because the execution must be levied on property common to both. Asso & Mañuel, Institutes of Civil Law of Spain, Book III, Title X, Sec. 6, Par. 12.

[63] See post, § 209 et seq.

[64] See In re Chavez. 149 Fed. 73 (in New Mexico), involving bankruptcy of husband having only community property; James v. Jacques, 26 Tex. 320, 82 Am. Dec. 613.

"The relation of husband and wife is regarded by the civil law as a species of partnership, the property of which, like that of any other partnership, is primarily liable for the payment of its debts." Packard v. Arellanes, 17 Cal. 525.

[65] James v. Jacques, 26 Tex. 320, 82 Am. Dec. 613.

[66] James v. Jacques, 26 Tex. 320, 82 Am. Dec. 613; H. O. Wooten Grocer Co. v. Smith (Tex. Civ. App.), 161 S. W. 945.

before a division is made of the community property between the surviving spouse and the heirs of the deceased spouse.[67]

§ 171.   — Insurance policies and their proceeds.

Elsewhere have been considered the questions of life insurance policies upon the life of a spouse and their proceeds as community or separate property,[68] and to what extent they constitute gifts by or between spouses.[69] Any right of community or separate creditors to reach the proceeds of such policies would depend upon the character of the proceeds as community or separate property, taken in connection, of course, with the usual rights of creditors under the local laws applicable.[70] Since the proceeds of a policy on the life of a spouse only become payable upon the death of the spouse, the character of and the rights in the proceeds are naturally questions determinable after dissolution of the marital community by such death, and any rights of creditors to reach such proceeds might better be left for discussion of payment of debts upon dissolution of the community.[71] However, the fact is that in many states the proceeds or avails of life insurance policies are by statute expressly exempted in whole or in part from liability for debts.[72] This may also include the cash surrender value of such policies, so that creditors during the existence of the conjugal partnership can not subject the policies to payment of their claims. However, it is not feasible to enter into a detailed discussion of this matter, since that is better left to treatises on insurance law or the law of exemptions. It is advisable that the reader examine the local statutes to determine the existence and extent of such laws, although it may be remarked in passing that in some form or other such statutes have existed in California, Louisiana, Texas and Washington.

Whether the proceeds of property insurance which are available are subject to the claims of the creditors should depend upon the nature of the property itself, and the insurance proceeds should partake of the same nature as the property.[73]

---

[67] See post, Chap. X, B.

[68] See ante, § 79.

[69] See ante, §§ 123, 143.

[70] For an excellent discussion of the general situation of community property laws as applied to life insurance, see Professor Huie's articles in 17 Tex. Law Rev. 121; 18 Tex. Law Rev. 121.

[71] See post, Chap. X.

[72] See, e. g., Holden v. Stratton, 198 U. S. 202, 49 L. Ed. 1018, 25

Sup. Ct. 656, in relation to a former Washington statute.

Accident insurance as life insurance within exemption law, see 111 A. L. R. 61.

[73] Insurance on property itself exempt, see 63 A. L. R. 1286; and property purchased with exempt proceeds of insurance, see 96 A. L. R. 410.

Proceeds of life insurance policy as community property subject to com-

§ 172.   — Debts and obligations of business partnership.

The business interests which the husband prosecutes to provide a livelihood for the family may consist in whole or in part of acting as a partner with third persons in a commercial partnership. In ordinary circumstances, his gains from his partnership interest, realized after the satisfaction of partnership obligations and demands, represent community property of himself and his wife, just as would his earnings and gains from any other business interest or employment.[74] It may also well be that property that he invests in the commercial partnership is community property of himself and his wife, so that she shares equally not only in the gains from the interest in the partnership but also equally in the value of such interest received by him upon dissolution of the partnership. But while such community property is employed by the husband in this commercial partnership it is under his management, since his right to invest and use it and to control it results from the power conferred on him by law to manage the community property, and ordinarily the wife cannot object to this use of the community property or interfere in any way in the partnership affairs.[75]

The husband having properly determined, by virtue of his exercise of management, to place the community property in the commercial partnership, it must be subject to all obligations and demands of the commercial partnership before any right of the wife is enforceable as to such property.[76] Similarly, her half share in profits from the commercial partnership take effect and are enforceable only in the actual profits to which the husband may be entitled after obligations and demands of the commercial partnership are satisfied. Just because community property is invested in the partnership, just because the wife has a half share in the profits realized by the husband from the commercial partnership, no more makes the wife herself a partner in the commercial partnership than would the husband's employment

---

munity debts, see In re Towey's Estate, 22 Wash. 2d 212, 155 P.2d 273.

[74] Discussion of possibility that partnership interest may have been owned before marriage and thus represent separate property and that his profits therefrom may also be separate property in some jurisdictions, see ante, § 80.

[75] See Coe v. Winchester, 43 Ariz. 500, 33 P.2d 286; McCall v. McCall, 2 Cal. App. 2d 92, 37 P.2d 496.

As manager of community personalty, the husband can invest in a partnership without the wife's consent,

see Cummings v. Weast, 72 Ariz. 93, 231 P.2d 439, pointing out that if community realty were to be transferred to a partnership, the wife's joinder would be required.

Acts of the husband generally which are in fraud or prejudice of the wife's rights, see ante, § 119.

Value of wife's interest in this property may be considered in division of property upon divorce. Generally as to divorce, see post, Chap. X, C.

[76] See Cummings v. Weast, 72 Ariz. 93, 231 P.2d 439, citing de Funiak, first edition; Attaway v. Stanolind Oil & Gas Co., 212 F.2d 790, quoting de Funiak, first edition.

by a corporation make the wife also an employee of such corporation. This fact must be kept clearly in mind. Therefore, just as her half ownership operates as to profits after the commercial partnership obligations and demands are met, when commercial partnership obligations and demands equal or outweigh earnings from such partnership the wife acquires nothing, for she must share losses resulting to the marital community just as she would share gains accruing to it. If the commercial partnership creditors, after exhausting its assets, proceed against partners' individual assets, then other community property of the spouses comes under the head of such "individual assets." For just as the marital community would profit from the husband's gains from the commercial partnership, so it must be ready to bear the burden of losses. Of course, ordinary rules applicable to commercial partnerships must be given effect. Thus, to the extent of the rule that individual creditors of a partner have priority over partnership creditors in his individual assets, individual community creditors, for example, those having claims for necessaries furnished to the spouses, would have priority in the spouses' community property not involved in the commercial partnership enterprise, as against any claims of commercial partnership creditors. Conversely, whether the claims of ordinary community creditors can be satisfied from the property or interest of the spouses in the commercial partnership must be subordinate to the claims of the creditors of the commercial partnership and the adjustment of equities between the members of the commercial partnership.[77]

While the courts seem to be able to take in stride the fact of the husband being a partner in a commercial partnership, they are frequently thrown into confusion when faced with the fact of the wife as member of a commercial partnership. Since the situation brought about by the wife's membership in a commercial partnership fairly approximates the situation where the husband is member of such a partnership, there is little reason for confusion; the same principles are usually applicable in either case. In most of our community property states, the wife has full control over her separate property and

---

[77] In Strong v. Eakin, 11 N.M. 107, 66 P. 539, the somewhat unusual situation was presented of the husband being a member of one business partnership and the wife being a member of another. The husband's partnership became bankrupt and several claims against it which had been reduced to judgments were then sought to be enforced against the wife's interest in her business partnership, on the ground that her interest therein represented property of the marital community. It was petitioned that a receiver be appointed of the assets of her firm, that such assets be sold, the debts of her firm paid, and her share thereafter remaining to the extent it constituted community property be made subject to the claims of the creditors of the husband's partnership. The petition was granted, there being no evidence to show that the property invested in the wife's business partnership was her separate property.

See also Cummings v. Weast (Ariz.), preceding note.

[78] See ante, § 112.

can contract in connection therewith.[78] Where that is true, she is quite free to invest or use her separate property in a business enterprise such as a commercial partnership of which she acts as a partner. The usual rules of liability or nonliability of a wife's separate property to claims of separate creditors of herself or her husband or of community creditors apply to her separate property used in the commercial partnership, so far, of course, as it is identifiable as her separate property. It must be remembered, however, that in jurisdictions where profits and gains from separate property constitute community property, the profits and gains from the wife's use of her separate property in a commercial partnership constitute community property and are subject to the payment of community debts incurred by the husband as manager of the marital community, or even to payment of his separate debts if the jurisdiction is one which (however erroneously) makes the entire community property liable for the husband's separate debts.[79] If the wife becomes a partner in a commercial partnership and invests or employs therein community property under her management or community property under the management of the husband and which he consents to her so using, or even if her contribution to the partnership consists of her services which is to entitle her to membership, the partnership earnings and gains to which she becomes entitled constitute community property. But it must be kept in mind that the marital ownership of such earnings and gains, or in other words the ownership therein of the wife and her husband by halves, exists only as they represent profits coming from the wife's partnership interest after the claims of the partnership creditors and the equities of the partners have been satisfied. Likewise, so far as community property is invested by the wife in the commercial partnership, any rights of the spouses therein, as a marital community, are not establishable until the satisfaction of the claims of the partnership creditors and the partners' equities. So far, then, as concerns the husband's half ownership in these profits, by reason of their being community property, he acquires it only when the profits accrue to the wife after satisfaction of the aforementioned claims. Until then he has no half ownership and he has no voice in the management of the commercial partnership. In short, he is not a partner in that commercial partnership just because his wife is, any more than he would be an employee of one for whom the wife was rendering services as a registered nurse although her earnings therefrom as they accrued would be half his as community property.[80] But since the

---

[79] But no longer in Texas, see Tex. Family Code 1969, §§ 5.22, 5.61.

[80] "If one partner admits a stranger into the partnership without the consent of his partners, such stranger is not a partner except only of the partner who admitted him. [Citing authorities.] They base this view on the fact that partnership arises by agreement, Dig. 17.2.31; and no one can be my partner whom I do not wish to be such, Dig. 17.2.19 and Baldus' note thereon; and my partner's partner is not my partner, Dig. 17.2.20." Matienzo, Gloss I, No. 17, to Nov. Rec. Law 1, Book 10, Title 4.

marital community, in other words the husband and wife, profit from the commercial partnership enterprise, the latter is a community enterprise for the community benefit just as would be a business enterprise prosecuted by the husband for the community benefit. Therefore, just as the marital community, in other words the husband and the wife, is entitled to share the profits from such commercial partnership enterprise, so the marital community, again the husband and the wife, must bear the burden of any loss resulting from the prosecution of such commercial partnership to the extent that such loss is apportioned to the community interest. Creditors of the commercial partnership, upon exhausting the partnership assets may proceed against the commercial partners' individual assets, which so far as the wife is concerned as such a partner means against the community assets of herself and her husband, since the marital community would have been entitled to profits if there were any. If there are none, it must bear the losses. And since the husband is ordinarily the manager of the community property, or certainly of the greater part of it, which is sought to be reached, he will necessarily be named as a party defendant to the attempt to reach such community assets. There should be nothing any more confusing in such a situation than in that where the husband is the member of a commercial partnership. Yet when the California court correctly allowed the creditors to reach, through the husband, community property, three of the seven judges dissented, chiefly upon the ground that this made the husband a partner against his will of whomsoever the wife associated herself with in any partnership business venture.[81] There would seem to have been a disability on the part of the dissenting judges to recognize the basic principle that just as husband and wife share the profits of any enterprise for the common benefit, so they must assume the burden of any loss therefrom, and that one does not calculate profits until expenses and losses have been deducted therefrom; plus their inability to distinguish the fact that an enterprise may be no less one for the community benefit just because it is managed by the wife instead of the husband, for it does not follow that an enterprise conducted by the wife is by that reason alone a separate venture of her own. This latter matter seems to have been the cause of confusion also in the minds of authors of notes in local law reviews discussing the case in question, for one writer describes the case as raising the question of liability of the husband "whose wife acquires property and incurs

[81] Hulsman v. Ireland, 205 Cal. 345, 270 P. 948.

In Miller v. Marx & Kempner, 65 Tex. 131, where a wife invested her separate property in a commercial partnership, the court held that the husband did actually become a member of such partnership; and that the husband was liable to the partnership creditors and that the wife's separate property was not liable, although her profits from the firm were community property, of course, under the Texas law. The decision, it must be noted, has been changed by the provisions of Tex. Family Code 1969, § 4.03.

409

liabilities in the course of an independent business career,"[82] and another describes it as imposing personal liability on the husband for the separate debts of the wife.[83] The property "acquired" by the wife was community property, used with the husband's consent, and the wife was not pursuing any separate business venture of her own, but was prosecuting a business venture for the common benefit. If the husband does not wish to share in any such venture, it is simple enough for him and the wife to enter into a valid agreement that she shall be entitled to prosecute whatever enterprise she has in mind as her separate business in which the husband is not to be concerned, either as to sharing profits or losses. If she wishes to use community property in her venture, the spouses can agree that it shall by gift to her become her separate property.

§ 173.   Effect of spouses' property agreements or transactions.

We have already considered the right of spouses to enter into agreements, contracts or transactions between themselves.[84] We have now to consider how the rights or claims of creditors may be affected thereby. The contract or transaction between the spouses may be in relation to the community property, whereby one spouse relinquishes or renounces in favor of or transfers to the other spouse the former's interest in all or part of the community property. If this is done gratuitously, it is usually termed a gift so far as our courts are concerned, and barring fraud or undue influence may be valid between the spouses and not to be set aside unless it be considered in fraud of existing creditors. While it was not called a gift under the Spanish law, which seems to have reserved that term for donations from the separate property of one spouse to the other spouse, we have seen that under the Spanish law of community property, one spouse might validly agree or contract with the other so as to renounce in favor of the latter the former's interest in part or all of the community property.[85] It was well settled, however, that since community debts contracted during marriage by either spouse were chargeable against community property already acquired, such a renunciation or transfer in favor of the other spouse, of community property already acquired, was not valid as to existing creditors.[86] It was explained that where the debts incurred during marriage exceeded the property acquired, there was actually no property to be shared until after the obligations of the marriage had been attended to,[87] hence the attempt to renounce or transfer the spouse's interest in the ganancial properties was an attempt to renounce or transfer an interest that did not exist as against the claims

[82] See note, 17 Calif. Law Rev. 265.

[83] See note, 2 So. Calif. Law Rev. 375.

[84] See ante, Chap. VIII.

[85] See ante, § 135.

[86] See Commentaries of Matienzo and Gutiérrez to Nov. Rec. Law 9, Book 10, Title 4.

[87] That until the common debts are paid there are no profits to divide, see ante, § 159.

of creditors. In other words, such a renunciation or transfer of an interest in existing community property was in fraud of existing creditors. Even if the debts did not exceed the ganancial property before such renunciation or transfer, if the transfer or renunciation left the remaining community property insufficient, or no community property, to meet the claims of the creditors, the effect was the same. In any event, in the case of the wife renouncing in favor of the husband, the latter had the obligation as manager of the community property to meet the obligations incurred during marriage, or if by agreement of the spouses there was to be no community of property the husband had the obligation of meeting from his separate property the obligations incurred during marriage, by reason of his duty of support and otherwise, so that whatever the spouses agreed to call the property could not defeat the claims of the existing creditors.[88] So far as concerned property to be acquired in the future, the wife could renounce or relinquish her right to share therein, and this relieved her from obligation to pay any debts thereafter contracted by the husband during the marriage.[89] Obviously, however, in view of the duties of support imposed on the husband his renunciation of the right to share in profits to be made did not relieve him from liability for debts incurred during the marriage for the family maintenance and support, etc.[90]

In our community property states it is also considered that any transaction between husband and wife whereby one renounces in favor of the other or transfers to the other his or her interest in the community property so as to make it the separate property of the other spouse is fraudulent as to existing community creditors, where the renunciation or transfer is voluntary or lucrative, in other words, without consideration, leaving insufficient community property to pay such creditors.[91] In states where the community property is also subject to the claims of the husband's separate creditors, the fore-

---

[88] See Commentaries of Llamas y Molina to Nov. Rec. Law 9.

[89] "When the wife renounces the profits let her not be obligated to pay any part of the debts which the husband made during marriage." Novísima Recopilación, Book 10, Title 4, Law 9; and see the commentaries thereto.

[90] See Llamas y Molina, No. 16 to Nov. Rec. Law 9, who warns against certain generality of language of Matienzo which should not be construed to mean that renunciation by the husband as well as by the wife would have the same result.

[91] Nichols v. Mitchell, 32 Cal. 2d 598, 197 P.2d 550; Succession of Trevino (La.), 180 So.2d 751; Ilfeld v. De Baca, 13 N.M. 32, 79 P. 723; Workman v. Bryce (Wash.), 310 P.2d 228.

Since a voluntary conveyance or transfer, in order to be fraudulent, must be of property to which creditors can resort for payment and they cannot complain of the transfer of property immune to their seizure, a separate judgment creditor of the wife who was not entitled to resort to community property could not complain of a voluntary conveyance by the husband and wife of community property, whatever the intention of the spouses. Citizens Nat. Bank v. Turner, 89 F.2d 600, aff'g 14 F. Supp. 495, arising in the district court in Texas.

going is true as to such transfers by him to the wife,[92] whereby the husband is left without property in his hands adequate to pay existing debts, whether community debts or his separate debts.[93] These matters are frequently declared by statute.[94] However, such a renunciation or transfer is good as against subsequent creditors unless made as a cover for future fraud.[95] It would seem necessary to bear in mind, at this point, that the various statutes authorizing antenuptial contracts and marriage settlements also provide that such contracts must be in writing, acknowledged and recorded.[96] Thus, if such a contract changes the status of the marital property in some way, it would seem that its recordation is necessary to give notice thereof to subsequent purchasers or creditors.[97]

§ 174. — Improvements or discharge of liens on separate property.

One of the situations of frequent occurrence is that in which the husband uses community property to improve, or discharge liens on, the separate property of the wife. Where this is a gratuitous or lucrative transaction for the wife's benefit, in other words what may be termed a gift to the wife of such community property, the question naturally arises whether it is not in fraud of the existing community creditors, or the husband's existing separate creditors where the community property is subject to their claims. Undoubtedly, it may be so intended, but the further question presents itself as to whether the creditors can then reach the wife's separate property to the extent of the value of such improvement. We have already seen that improvements to the separate property of one spouse originating from labor or industry or due to the use of community property become part of

---

[92] See Ilfeld v. De Baca, 13 N.M. 32, 79 P. 723.

[93] Van Bibber v. Mathis, 52 Tex. 407; Morrison v. Clark, 55 Tex. 444.

The burden is on the wife to show this fact. Braden v. Gose, 57 Tex. 41.

Spouses retaining domicile in Texas but going out of state to enter into contract dividing community funds and making each half the separate property of each spouse, see King v. Bruce, 145 Tex. 647, 201 S. W. 2d 803, 171 A. L. R. 1328, holding contract governed by Texas law and invalid and thus not preventing garnishment of wife's half by husband's judgment creditor. See also Marks v. Loewenburg, 143 La. 196, 78 So. 444.

[94] Agreements between husband and wife concerning the status or disposition of community property in whole or in part, then owned or to be afterward acquired, shall not derogate from the rights of creditors. Wash. Rev. Code 1961, § 26.16.120.

[95] See Bank of Orofino v. Wellman, 26 Idaho 425, 143 P. 1169; Ilfeld v. De Baca, 13 N.M. 32, 79 P. 723.

The effect of the Uniform Fraudulent Conveyance Act in force in many states must now be kept in mind, too.

[96] See ante, § 136.

[97] See, e.g., Tex. Family Code 1969, §§ 5.41 & 5.42; Tex. Rev. Civ. Stat. 1925, arts. 6632 & 6647. And see Reynolds v. Lansford, 16 Tex. 286; Raymond v. Cook, 31 Tex. 373; De Garca v. Glavan, 55 Tex. 56.

the separate property to which they were made and constitute part of such spouse's separate property in the sense that they are subject to that spouse's control and disposition but that the value of the improvement belongs to the community which is entitled to be reimbursed to the extent of such enhanced value, at least where the community property so used is not intended as a gift to the spouse owning the separate property improved.[98] The right of the creditors to subject the value of the improvements to their claims depends to a great extent upon what the right of the community is to reimbursement. The community may not be entitled to reimbursement until the adjustment of the rights of the spouses upon dissolution of the marital community. Where this is true, creditors would seem to have no greater rights. Moreover, the rights of the creditors may to some extent depend upon whether the community is said to have a lien itself or merely an equitable right to reimbursement. Nevertheless, where the expenditure of community funds upon one spouse's separate property is clearly a fraud on creditors, in some cases the creditors have not been required to wait until dissolution of the marital community to wait for enforcement of their claims against the value of the improvements. Much must depend, of course, upon the view of the courts of the various states, and reference to their decisions is naturally recommended.[99] It may, of course, be true that the community has no right of reimbursement because the use of the community property to make the improvements was intended as a gift to the wife, and if this is done when there are no existing creditors, there is certainly nothing to which subsequent creditors can object in the absence of any showing that it was designed to cover some plan of intended fraud in the future.[1]

§ 175.   — One spouse as creditor of the other.

In those community property states which recognize the right of the husband and the wife during marriage to contract or enter into

---

[98] See ante, § 73.

[99] See cases collected in 77 A. L. R. 1021; 133 A. L. R. 1097; notice especially Peck v. Brummagim, 31 Cal. 440, 89 Am. Dec. 195; Maddox v. Summerlin, 92 Tex. 482, 488, 49 S. W. 1033, 50 S. W. 567. For the most definitive treatment of this area see Bartke, "Yours, Mine and Ours: Separate Title and Community Funds," 21 Baylor L. Rev. 137 (1969).

Where it was sought to compel the specific performance of a contract by the wife for the sale of her separate real property, and the relief was granted, the decree should require the wife and not the marital community to execute the deed, although the spouses had been residing on the property for several years and community funds had gone into its improvement. The equitable lien in favor of the community for such improvements could be satisfied from the purchase price of the property, see Leroux v. Knoll, 28 Wash. 2d 964, 184 P.2d 564.

[1] See Bank of Orofino v. Wellman, 26 Idaho 425, 143 P. 1169.

transactions with each other,[2] the wife as a result of such a contract or transaction may validly become a creditor of her husband.[3]

Where the husband transfers community property to the wife for a valuable and adequate consideration out of her separate property,[4] or to repay her for loans she has made him from her separate property,[5] or to repay her for separate property of hers which has been under his administration and which he has misused, lost through negligence, or the like, or perhaps has converted into other forms in the course of his management,[6] his transfer is not in fraud of existing creditors, so long as the value of the property transferred to the wife does not so far exceed the value of what she is entitled to so as to raise a presumption of legal fraud. It may be incumbent upon the wife, however, to show that its value is not so excessive as to raise such presumption.[7] But if any such transfer is set aside as fraudulent then both subsequent as well as existing creditors may share *pro rata* in the property involved. Nevertheless, even where such transfer to the wife is set aside, in a jurisdiction which recognizes that the wife has a tacit lien or mortgage upon the husband's property to the extent of the value of separate property of hers placed under his control and management, the wife is entitled, from the property the transfer of which has been set aside, to payment of her claim against the husband before the creditors share in the proceeds.[8]

The Spanish and Mexican law gave the wife such a tacit lien or

---

[2] See ante, § 136.

[3] In a federal case in California, we have the situation where a partnership, of which the husband was a partner, was in bankruptcy, and a claim was presented by the wife for funds advanced by her to the partnership. The court seems to have considered that the funds advanced were community funds, as coming from earnings of the wife, and not separate funds of the wife, and thus that her claim should be subordinated to claims of general creditors. See In re McNair and Ryan, 95 F. Supp. 434. Compare In re Gutiérrez, 33 F.2d 987, in the District Court in Texas, where the wife seems to have been given equality of presentation of her claim with those of other creditors; the wife's claim was for wages due her for services rendered in the employment of the bankrupt business of the husband.

Indeed, many of the Spanish jurisconsults, including Llamas y Molina, declared that insofar as the husband had under his administration community property in half of which the wife had ownership, she was his creditor and he her debtor in respect thereof. See Llamas y Molina, Commentaries to Nov. Rec. Law 10, Book 10, Title 4. Gutiérrez, however, objected to such terminology on the ground it was not consonant with the fact of the wife's present and equal ownership during marriage. See Gutiérrez, Quaestio CXXIV, to Nov. Rec. Law 9, Book 10, Title 4. But as a matter of fact none of the authors using the debtor-creditor terminology differed with Gutiérrez as to the actual fact of the wife's ownership.

[4] Bank v. McClellan, 9 N.M. 643, 58 P. 347.

[5] See Gomila v. Wilcomb, 151 Fed. 470, arising in the District Court in Louisiana.

[6] Ilfeld v. De Baca, 13 N.M. 32, 79 P. 723.

[7] Ilfeld v. De Baca, 13 N.M. 32, 79 P. 723.

[8] See Ilfeld v. De Baca, 13 N.M. 32, 79 P. 723.

mortgage upon the husband's property to the amount of her dotal property or her other separate property which might be placed under his administration and care.[9] This principle has found application in some of our community property states, notably in Louisiana and New Mexico.[10] "So jealous and careful does the law seem to be in the protection of the rights of the wife," so it was said, "that no registration or record of her mortgage is required, but the marriage alone is left to give notice of her lien upon the property of her husband."[11] The lien or mortgage so acquired by the wife upon the husband's property took priority over claims of subsequent creditors and was not divested by the levying of process upon the mortgaged property by a creditor of the husband, or by sale under execution on the suit of such a creditor, or by sale thereof by the husband.[12] It was immaterial whether the property levied on or sold was ganancial property or the separate property of the husband, for the wife's lien or mortgage extended to both.[13]

While it would seem that the majority of our community property states do not go so far as to declare that the wife has a lien upon the husband's property to the value of her separate property placed in his care, or title to which is allowed by her to stand in his name, nevertheless she has frequently been allowed to claim her interest in such property even against creditors of the husband. Thus, it has been said that "We think, however, that it would be too harsh a rule to announce that under any circumstances the wife should be estopped from claiming her interest in realty which had been held in the name of the husband, as against the creditors of the husband, for credit obtained during the time such land was so held, notwithstanding the fact that the intimate relations existing between husband and wife render the perpetration of a fraud upon creditors, in this sort of a transaction, more probable than in cases where the parties did not sustain towards each other such relations. We think a better rule would be that the court should insist upon the most clear and convincing proof of the bona fides of the transaction, but that, when it did conclusively appear from the testimony that the property in dispute was actually the separate property of the wife, her interests ought to be protected by the court, notwithstanding the fact that the record

[9] Generally as to wife's administration of her separate property and effect of her placing it under husband's administration, see ante, § 112.

[10] See ante, § 150.

[11] Chavez v. McKnight, 1 N.M. 147, 154, citing Dreux v. Dreux's Syndics, 3 Mart. N. S. (La.) 239.

[12] Chavez v. McKnight, 1 N.M. 147, 155.

Sale of mortgaged property under execution, at suit of creditor of husband, did not extinguish wife's mortgage. Blanchard v. Blanchard, 6. La. 298.

Wife's mortgage given effect on such property in lands of husband's vendee. Eastin v. Eastin's Heirs, 10 La. 198.

[13] Chavez v. McKnight, 1 N.M. 147, 156, citing Cassou v. Blanque, 3 Mart. (La.) 392.

title was allowed to remain for a while in the husband."[14] In some instances the wife has been permitted to file her claim with those of creditors, but without priority.[15] Even if it is argued that the wife who has allowed her separate property to remain in the name of or under administration of the husband can enforce her right thereto as against a creditor or against a purchaser at an execution sale only when it is shown that the creditor or purchaser had notice of her right,[16] it must be remembered that knowledge by a creditor or a purchaser of the marriage relation should impose upon him an obligation to investigate with a reasonable degree of diligence before accepting any encumbrance or purchasing from the husband. But the wife's claim against the community property, based on the husband's receiving therefrom amounts in excess of his half share in the community property, is subordinate to a subsequent lien of judgment for a community debt, even though the wife's claim has achieved the dignity of a lien prior to the time of the judgment lien.[17]

§ 176.   Effect of limitation of actions and revival.

The effect of prescription or the operation of statutes of limitation to bar actions upon community debts presents of itself no situation differing from the usual.[18] The revival of barred debts is another matter, altogether. So far as concerns a community debt contracted by the husband and barred by limitation, such debt may be revived by the acts of the husband since his is the exercise of management of the community property and it is his acts which bind the community.[19] This has been said to be true even where the barred community debt revived by his acts was jointly contracted by husband and wife who both signed the evidence of indebtedness.[20] Conversely, no acts of the wife during the subsistence of the marriage could revive a barred

[14] Kemp v. Folsom, 14 Wash. 16, 43 P. 1100, holding that here the wife's interests were entitled to protection.

[15] See In re Gutiérrez (D.C., Tex.), 33 F.2d 987, per Hutcheson, J.

[16] See Raley v. Albright (Tex. Civ. App.), 43 S. W. 538.

[17] Ghent v. Boyd, 18 Tex. Civ. App. 88, 43 S. W. 891.

[18] That wife, learning of alienation by husband in fraud or injury of her rights, must bring action to establish her rights within certain period from time of discovering such wrongful alienation, according to Spanish codes and laws of some of our states, see ante, § 126.

[19] Catlin v. Mills, 140 Wash. 1, 247 P. 1013, 47 A.L.R. 545; Milroy v. Movic, 189 Wash. 17, 63 P.2d 496.

But cf. Gannon v. Robinson (Wash.), 371 P.2d 274, and Household Finance Corp. of Kelso v. Corby (Wash.), 377 P.2d 441, to the effect that when a community obligation has been discharged in bankruptcy a revival by the husband alone is ineffective.

[20] Bruce v. Thomas (Tex. Civ. App.), 106 S. W. 806.

If it is considered that the husband's acts, to bind the community, must be acts benefiting or designed to benefit the community, it may well be argued that acts reviving a barred debt are not beneficial to the community and should revive the debt only as to his half share in the community property.

community debt, even though she had joined the husband in contracting the debt, because only the acts of the husband, as the one having the management, can bind the community.[21] The situation may be otherwise, of course, where the debt was contracted by the wife in relation to community property over which the wife is given the exercise of administration. Here it is her acts which can revive the obligation against the community and the husband's acts cannot. Where the husband has died and there are community debts which are barred by limitations, whether acts of the wife toll the statute of limitations not only as to her half of the community property but as to the half of the deceased spouse, as well as the situation where the alleged acts reviving the debt occur after divorce, are discussed in the chapter on dissolution of the marital community.[22]

Where the spouses joined in mortgaging the community property to secure the separate debt of one of them, it has been said that the other spouse might be considered a surety for the separate debt so that acts of the spouse owing the separate debt which removed the bar of the statute of limitations were ineffective to subject to liability the half share in the community of the spouse going surety.[23]

§ 177. Effect of minority of spouses.

The liability in common of the spouses where they contracted debts in common, insofar as it was affected by the minority of one or both of the spouses, in the Spanish law was as follows: A husband who was a minor was bound for the whole debt incurred by him for the common benefit, although in other things where restitution to minors was authorized he could demand restitution. But a wife who was a minor was not obligated for a debt contracted by her husband where she did not bind herself with the husband on the note or evidence of the debt. However, if she bound herself with him on the evidence of the debt, she was obligated for half of the debt, and if the obligation was joint and several, she was obligated for the whole upon demand, even though a minor.[24] The community property laws

---

[21] See Winter v. Gani (La. App.), 199 So. 600.

[22] See post, Chap. X.

[23] See Stubblefield v. McAuliff, 20 Wash. 442, 55 P. 637.

In Haddad v. Chapin, 153 Wash. 163, 279 P. 538, where the debt was declared by the court to be a community debt, having been incurred for merchandise purchased for the benefit of the family on a running account, it was held on authority of the Stubblefield Case, ante, that payments by one spouse did not toll the statute as to the other. It would seem that this should be a situation in which the Stubblefield Case should not govern, but rather the Catlin Case, ante, which, however, is not referred to, although decided well before the date of this case. It may be that the distinction to be made here is that the spouses are made individually liable by statute, both as to the community property and the separate property of each, being suable jointly or separately, and on that basis liability of one which was barred by the statute should not be revived by acts of the other spouse.

[24] Leyes del Estilo, Law 207.

of our states only infrequently recognize the effect of the minority of a spouse as affecting the incurring of debts or obligations, although undoubtedly an examination of other statutes in those jurisdictions relating generally to marriage as emancipation of minors would provide an adequate answer to any questions arising.[25] Occasionally, however, the community property laws themselves take cognizance of the situation.[26]

§ 178. Insolvency and bankruptcy.

Insolvency and bankruptcy necessarily present some complicated issues because of the existence of two types of property, community and separate, as well as two types of creditors, community and separate. The possibility may well exist that the community property is insufficient to meet obligations to which it is subject, but can the spouses as a marital community or conjugal partnership be said to be insolvent if either or both owns considerable separate property? The converse of this question may exist where a spouse has insufficient separate property to meet the spouse's separate obligations but there is existent considerable community property. In a strict sense, insolvency should be determined in connection with separate property and separate obligations on the one hand or in connection with community property and community obligations on the other hand. Insolvency brought about by an excess of separate debts over separate property should not involve community property, any more than insolvency resulting from excess of community debts over community property should involve separate property. However, it is necessary to keep in mind the extent to which the law of a particular jurisdiction may make separate property liable to community debts or community property liable on separate debts. To that extent, the particular property must be considered on the question of insolvency, both as to determining whether there is insolvency or not and as to subjecting such property to liability. Whenever any such questions arise it is needful to study closely the statutes of the particular jurisdiction to determine what property is subject to what debts, keeping in mind at the same time the matter of priority between separate and community creditors who may be entitled to resort to the same type of property.[27]

---

[25] Right of minor capable of contracting marriage to enter into antenuptial agreement, see ante, §§ 135, 136.

[26] In Texas, all persons of whatever age who are married according to Texas laws have the power and capacity of a single person of full age, including the power to contract, except as to right to vote. Tex. Family Code 1969, § 4.03.

Notice the provision of the N.M. Stats. 1953, § 57-4-4, that any married woman under the age of 21 years may join with her husband in all conveyances, leases and mortgages of community property and that such instruments have same force and effect as if she had attained her majority at time of their execution.

[27] In Zeigler v. His Creditors, 49 La. Ann. 144, 21 So. 666, where the

It will be found that the sections immediately following deal more particularly with bankruptcy itself rather than with insolvency generally, but even so it is believed that the discussion will have considerable value on the question of insolvency. The Federal Bankruptcy Act has, of course, lessened resort to and application of state insolvency laws, although the latter, including those relating to assignments for the benefit of creditors, are not by any means obliterated.[28]

§ 179. — By reason of separate obligations and debts.

There is no reason why a spouse, whose debts incurred in furtherance of his or her own individual interests are greater in amount than the value of such spouse's separate property, cannot elect to avail himself or herself of insolvency or bankruptcy laws with relation to such separate property and individual obligations, and to do so without drawing in the community property.[29] This is certainly true in a jurisdiction where the community property, at least during the subsistence of the marriage, is not in any respect liable upon the separate

wife died and the husband was found to be insolvent, the community property had to be surrendered by him in its entirety, the community creditors classified separately, the community property sold separately, the proceeds accounted for according to the rights of the parties, which were that the deceased wife's heirs were entitled to one-half of the proceeds of the sale, after community creditors were paid, and the remaining half of the proceeds which represented the surviving husband's share of the community property then became available, along with his separate property, to the claims of his separate creditors.

In Lasswell v. Stein-Bloch Co., 93 F.2d 322, arising in the District Court in Texas, it was held that the value of the homestead, which was community property, was to be included in computing whether a husband was solvent or insolvent, on the ground that the word "property" used in the Bankruptcy Act, § 1 (15), was not limited to property available to pay the bankruptcy debts.

As to priorities, see particularly ante, §§ 167–172.

[28] Assignment for benefit of creditors in a somewhat unusual situation, see Purdom v. Boyd, 82 Tex. 130, 17 S. W. 606.

The Spanish code of the Partidas of 1263 contained provision as to one who was insolvent, authorizing him to surrender to the court the property which he had and which was then sold under order of court and the proceeds divided among the several creditors in the proportion their respective claims bore to the total of claims, subject to the existence of any priorities among such creditors, or the existence of liens, etc., in the debtor's property. The debtor was thereafter discharged, in a limited sense. Las Siete Partidas, Part. 5, Title 15, Laws 1–3.

[29] That a wife may be adjudicated a bankrupt where she has power to make contracts or engage in trade or business independently of her husband or where she is living separate and apart from her husband with authority to contract and manage her earnings and property, there should be no question. See In re Lyons (Dist. Ct. of Cal.), Fed. Cas. No. 8,649, and note thereto.

Community property which was transferred by the husband to the wife so as to become entirely her separate property was properly claimed by the wife's trustee in bankruptcy. Johnson v. Wheeler, 41 Wash. 2d 246, 248 P.2d 558.

obligations of one of the spouses, whether contracted before or during marriage.[30] This situation may be complicated, however, by the fact that there are community obligations which are permitted by law to be charged against separate property as well as against community property.[31] In such a case it would probably not be permissible to bar the community creditors from presenting their claims, since the Bankruptcy Act requires equality of treatment of creditors.[32] But undoubtedly such community creditors should be required to resort first to the community property and to show that they had done so without obtaining full satisfaction before being allowed to file their claims, to the extent that they are still unpaid, in the bankruptcy proceedings. Whether or not there is any specific statutory declaration that community obligations chargeable against separate property must first be charged against community property, such a requirement constitutes a fundamental principle of community property.[33]

We face a different problem in those states which hold that the entire community property is subject to liability for the separate debts of the husband but not in any respect subject to liability for the separate debts of the wife, and thus virtually adopt the view that the community property is not actually community property but in reality the separate property of the husband.[34] The wife, of course, might file a petition to be adjudicated a bankrupt where her separate obligations were greater than her separate property, without involving the community property or bringing in claims of community creditors. But the bankruptcy of the husband by reason of his separate obligations exceeding his separate property would involve the entire community property and possibly wipe it out entirely, to the great injury and detriment of the wife who yet is declared to have an immediate ownership of one-half of the community property.[35] There is no reason in

---

[30] E.g., in Arizona and Washington.

In In re Wallace, 22 F.2d 171, in the Eastern District of Washington, a husband filed a voluntary petition in bankruptcy "individually as to his own separate property and debts, and not as to the community property and debts of himself and Myrtle Wallace, his wife" and the adjudication was made accordingly. The separate debts scheduled were his own separate debts incurred before marriage. It was held that the community personalty should not be listed and vested in the trustee for the benefit of the separate creditors. See Moore, The Community in Bankruptcy, 11 Wash. Law Rev. 61, 67–68.

[31] This may be true as to debts contracted for family expenses or necessaries. See Ariz. Rev. St. 1956, § 25-215; Wash. Rev. Code 1961, § 26.16.-010.

[32] See Moore, The Community in Bankruptcy, 11 Wash. Law Rev. 61, 69.

[33] Recognition of such principle in the Spanish law of community property, see ante, § 159. And see the express requirement of Ariz. Rev. St. 1956, § 25-215.

[34] See ante, § 161.

[35] See Hornsby v. Hornsby (Tex. Com. App.), 93 S. W. 2d 379, rev'g (Tex. Civ. App.), 60 S. W. 2d 489, where husband filed voluntary petition in bankruptcy and listed community property among his assets and sale of such property by trustee in bankruptcy was not subject to collateral attack by wife. See also Phillips v. Vitemb, 235 F.2d 11.

justice why the property of one who has not joined in undertakings with another, who stands to share in no profits from such undertakings, should share the burdens of such undertakings or be liable therefor in any way, just because of the marital relationship. Those who have had no part in the undertakings of a blood-relative are not liable to have their property subjected to creditors of the relative just by reason of their relationship, and the same necessarily should be true of one joined by marital ties to a debtor.[36] It is true that generally speaking, title to property, the status of liens, the validity of claims and exemptions of property are, in bankruptcy proceedings, governed by the local law but the local law has been rejected by the United States Supreme Court where considered destructive of the purpose and spirit of the Bankruptcy Act.[37] Should it not, by the way, be just as destructive of the purpose and spirit of that Act to seize the property of an innocent wife to satisfy the claims of creditors of a husband arising from the transactions of the spouse for his own interests? At most only the indebted spouse's half share in the community should be subjected to liability,[38] and even this, as has been mentioned above, would not be permitted under the law of some states, at least during the subsistence of the marriage. However, the question might be solved by applying the principle of the Spanish law that an insolvent debtor who files a petition in bankruptcy is thereafter incapable of administering any of his property.[39] Applying this principle, the bankruptcy of a husband on account of his separate debts can be considered to render him unfit to manage further the community property—certainly a reasonable assumption—and the marital partnership thereupon dis-

[36] There are indications that in California, since 1927, the bankruptcy of one spouse because of such spouse's separate obligations will not involve the community property in the ruin. While Smedberg v. Bevilockway, 7 Cal. App. 2d 578, 46 P.2d 820, was a denial of the right of a trustee in bankruptcy of a wife adjudicated a bankrupt to subject community property in the hands of the husband to liability on a judgment against the bankrupt wife, the court seems to base its decision on the view that neither spouse can force a division of the community property except as a collateral issue in a divorce proceeding, and that the trustee in bankruptcy stood in no better position than the bankrupt spouse. This language would seem on its face to relate either to husband or wife who was adjudicated a separate bankrupt. And see Hannah v. Swift, 61 F.2d 307, arising in the District Court in California.

[37] See Local Loan Co. v. Hunt, 292 U. S. 234, 78 L. Ed. 1230, 54 Sup. Ct. 695 (in relation to an Illinois law).

[38] In this respect, see Van Allen v. Dorough, 15 F.2d 940, arising in the District Court in Texas. A husband, engaged in a mercantile business and possessed of a stock of goods which was community property, died leaving a widow and minor children. The administrator delivered the stock of goods to the wife as survivor of the community and as guardian of the children. She continued to operate the business but became bankrupt. In holding that there was a trust impressed on the goods and their proceeds in favor of the children the court said that their right "to reclaim their property is not affected by the bankruptcy of their mother, since the creditors are not entitled to the proceeds of any property except that of the bankrupt."

[39] See Civil Code de España, arts. 1913, 1914.

solved, the community affairs liquidated, the wife given management of her half of the community property and the husband's half added to his separate property for the satisfaction of his separate creditors in the bankruptcy proceedings.[40] In any event, whether the jurisdiction is one where the community property is or is not subject to be drawn in for the payment of separate obligations and debts of a bankrupt husband, the wife should be permitted the opportunity to establish a claim that certain of the property drawn in is community property, and certainly her half-share therein, at the least, should be saved to her. Common justice should require this.[41] It need hardly be said that, of course, the separate property of one spouse should not be subjected to the claims of the separate creditors of the other spouse upon the latter's bankruptcy.[42]

[40] Consider Zeigler v. His Creditors, 49 La. Ann. 144, 21 So. 666, set out in a footnote in the preceding section.

[41] See Gibbons v. Goldsmith, 222 Fed. 826, arising in the District Court in Washington, where it would seem that the obligations of a husband adjudged a bankrupt on petition of his creditors were community obligations; the wife, however, was given the opportunity to put in her claim that the property taken over by the trustee was community property.

[42] In Louisiana the husband is authorized by statute to replace any dotal or other property of the wife which he has alienated; consequently, where a husband, although insolvent and within four months of bankruptcy, transferred property to the wife which was not worth more than that which he owed her by reason of a loan of her separate property that she had made him, it was held that such transfer to the wife did not constitute a voidable preference. Gomila v. Wilcombe, 151 Fed. 470.

In Foster v. Christensen (Tex. Com. App.), 67 S. W. 2d 246, rev'g (Tex. Civ. App.), 42 S. W. 2d 460, it was said that the wife was entitled to prove that property conveyed jointly to her husband and herself was in fact her separate property, paid for with her separate funds, and to subject to collateral attack a sale of such land by her husband's trustee in bankruptcy. Not having been a party to the bankruptcy proceeding she was not bound by any orders of the bankruptcy court respecting her property or its sale.

In John v. Battle, 58 Tex. 593. where the bankruptcy of the husband was held to have no effect upon the separate estate of the wife held for her in trust by the husband under her father's will, and which he had scheduled as his property, the court said: "The assignment in bankruptcy by her husband did not have the effect to pass any greater interest in the land than was owned by him as his separate property, and that which he held in community with his wife. Her rights in the land in virtue of her separate estate were not affected by virtue merely of the bankrupt proceedings against her husband, and the purchasers under the bankrupt sale did not acquire her interest, unless they did so as purchasers without notice of the existence of that interest."

Right of wife to file claim for overdue wages agreed to be paid her by husband now become bankrupt for her services as a clerk in his business, see In re Gutiérrez, 33 F.2d 987, arising in District Court in Texas.

In Gray v. Perlis, 76 Cal. App. 511, 245 P. 221, the husband's trustee in bankruptcy was denied the right to reach separate property of the wife who was operating a business as a "sole trader" which she had started with separate property of her own. It is probable that in this case the husband's bankruptcy was brought about as much by community debts as by his separate debts. See also Phelps

§ 180.   — By reason of community obligations and debts.

Undoubtedly, the common property should be liable for debts and obligations contracted for the common benefit of the conjugal partnership. This we have already seen.[43] But what if these debts and obligations exceed the common property available? Should the separate property of the spouses also be subject to liability? Is the insolvency or bankruptcy, if it exists, that of the husband alone as the administrator of the common property, is it that of both spouses as individuals, or is it that of the marital partnership as a sort of entity in itself as would be the case of an association or business partnership? In the sense that the common property of both spouses is liable for their common obligations, its insufficiency, or if we consider any of their separate property in any way subject to such liability, then the insufficiency of the common and such separate property, to meet the common obligations renders both spouses insolvent in respect of such common obligations. But ordinarily, the husband as the one usually named the manager of the common property and the one who is therefore usually the one to sue and be sued in respect of the common property would be the only one of the spouses that the creditors would need to proceed against or to be named in a bankruptcy petition.[44] It is true that sometimes some of the common property is under the management of the wife who is authorized to sue or be sued in respect thereto. If such common property in her control is also subject to liability on the common obligations, then it would be necessary to join her with her husband in any proceeding by the creditors. Naming them in creditors' or bankruptcy proceedings as "John Doe, Husband and Jane Doe, Wife," should answer the difficulty.[45] In Washington, where husband and

v. Davies, 126 Cal. App. 419, 14 P.2d 922, to much the same effect, where the husband's trustee sought to reach what he claimed was community property but was defeated therein by proof that it was really separate property of the wife.

[43] See ante, § 159.

[44] In Strong v. Eakin, 11 N.M. 107, 66 P. 539, the husband's business was as member of a commercial partnership which became bankrupt. It was said that since he prosecuted this business interest for the benefit of the marital community and he and his wife would share any profits gained therefrom, the marital community must likewise bear the burden of losses resulting from the business enterprise. Consequently, other community property of the spouses was subjected to

the claims of judgment creditors of the husband's business partnership. As a matter of fact, the community property so subjected was community property employed by the wife in another business partnership of which she was a partner. Petition was granted for appointment of a receiver of the assets of the wife's firm, for determination of the interest of the marital community in such assets, the sale of such firm's assets, the payment of its creditors, and the subjection of the interest remaining which constituted community property of the spouses to the claims of the creditors of the husband's partnership.

[45] In Bankruptcy Act, § 75 (s), 11 U. S. C. § 203, allowing farmers to petition for composition and extension of their obligations, these benefits are

wife must frequently be joined in actions to enforce community obligations, Mr. Ben L. Moore, Referee in Bankruptcy at Seattle, has stated that it has been quite common for "John Doe and Jane Doe, his wife, as a marital community" to petition to be adjudged bankrupt and for the order of adjudication to conform with this language of the petition, and that to his knowledge no such petition or order in that form has ever been challenged.[46] He points out, however, that the Bankruptcy Act contemplates that only a juristic person or legal entity may be adjudicated, and concludes that whether the community can be adjudicated as a legal entity must depend upon whether it is such under the local law.[47] Whether or not the local law usually terms the marital union an entity or denies that it is an entity, it must be recognized that it has certain attributes of a form of partnership and in the Spanish law was described as a special kind of partnership.[48] Much of the confusion brought about by the discussions of or the objections to the spouses occupying dual positions as two separate entities owning separate property and as a common legal entity owning common property disappears in the matter of obligations and debts when we consider the situation in the Spanish law. There the spouses occupied no separate or dual positions where community obligations and debts were considered. The common property was liable, of course, but if it proved insufficient to pay debts contracted during marriage for the common benefit, then the separate property, first of the husband and then of the wife, was liable, if the debts were contracted for the support of the family.[49] According to those views, then, we do have a conjugal partnership which must subject the property of the members of the conjugal partnership, both common and separate, in certain orders of priority, to the claims of creditors upon

extended to "community ownerships." Thus, in In re Moser, 95 F.2d 944, which arose in the District Court in California, husband and wife petitioned together as "farmers" on the ground that they both personally engaged in farming and the principal part of their income was derived therefrom.

[46] Moore, The Community in Bankruptcy, 11 Wash. Law Rev. 61, 70–72.

"Early in the administration of the Bankruptcy Act, the district judge of this district stated from the bench that he would, for the purpose of the Act, consider the family relation as a partnership." In re Herbold (D.C., Wash.), 14 Am. Bkrcy. Rep. 118.

And notice that in Conley v. Moe, 7 Wash. 2d 355, 110 P.2d 172, 133

A.L.R. 1089, plaintiff is described as "trustee in bankruptcy of the marital community, consisting of defendants John Moe and Borghild J. Moe."

In Holden v. Stratton, 198 U.S. 202, 49 L. Ed. 1018, 25 Sup. Ct. 656, it appeared that separate proceedings in bankruptcy were begun in the district court in Washington against a husband and a wife and then consolidated and both parties adjudicated bankrupt. The case turned, however, upon the statutory exemption of life insurance proceeds or avails from liability for debts.

[47] Moore, The Community in Bankruptcy, 11 Wash. Law Rev. 61, 71–72.

[48] See ante, § 95.

[49] See ante, § 159.

common obligations of the conjugal partnership.[50] Thus, under such a view, where the insolvency or bankruptcy results from the weight of community obligations and debts we have the spouses occupying only one position. Admittedly, however, the dual position exists where the debts rest on contracts made by a spouse in his or her individual interest, for then the debts are not those of the community, which then stands as something apart. But there is nothing strange in that, from our viewpoint, for in our law a business partnership or each member thereof sustains no liability because of debts contracted by one partner in furtherance of his own individual interests apart from and unconnected with the partnership affairs. But returning to the principle of the Spanish law as to the spouses' separate property being liable for community debts, it may be remarked that any discussion of that principle is not entirely theoretical, for in many instances in our community property states the separate property of one spouse or the other is made liable for community debts.[51] There can be no doubt that in a bankruptcy proceeding the separate property so instanced would be brought in.[52] Indeed, we may notice that in the case of a business partnership, it has been held by the United States Supreme Court that involuntary adjudication against the partnership alone authorizes the administration of the separate estate of one of the partners by the firm's trustee in bankruptcy.[53] But separate property of a spouse which is definitely not subject to liability for community debts cannot be reached by the trustee in bankruptcy.[54]

Confining ourselves for the moment to a consideration of the community property, it is unquestioned that since it is subject to liability for community obligations it is subject to claims of community creditors in a bankruptcy adjudication and the trustee in bankruptcy is entitled to its possession for the benefit of the creditors of the com-

[50] In Benitez v. Bank of Nova Scotia, 110 F.2d 169, arising in the District Court in Puerto Rico, the court held that a Puerto Rican "Comunidad," an association of co-owners carrying on a joint enterprise for profit, was a "partnership" within the meaning of that term in the Bankruptcy Act. The "Comunidad" was composed of a widower and the heirs of his deceased wife. Would the situation be relatively different when the enterprise was carried on by husband and wife themselves prior to the wife's death?

It may be noted that the Uniform Partnership Act, adopted in many states, provides in Section 7(2) that common property does not establish a partnership even though the co-owners share any profits made from the use of the property. But this must be assumed to mean that such a situation does not establish the type of commercial partnership to which the act is designed to relate.

[51] See ante, § 162.

[52] See Moore, The Community in Bankruptcy, 11 Wash. Law Rev. 61,71.

[53] See Francis v. McNeal, 228 U.S. 695, 57 L. Ed. 1029, 33 Sup. Ct. 701, remarking that it would be impossible that a firm should be insolvent while the members of it remained able to pay its debts.

[54] See Phelps v. Davies, 126 Cal. App. 419, 14 P.2d 922.

munity. This right of the trustee cannot be defeated by the wife's claim to the community property.[55] Her right to share equally the gains and profits during the marriage carries with it the accompanying obligation to share the burden of the losses and expenses of the conjugal partnership during the marriage; for, as previously remarked, it is not possible to speak of profits unless losses and expenses are first deducted.[56] Consequently, if the losses and expenses exceed the profits and gains, the wife must bear these equally with the husband. She cannot claim for herself any or all of the common property as against creditors on community debts and obligations, unless there is some statutory exception in her favor as to some part of the community property.[57] This right of the trustee to reduce the community property to his possession has been extended to interests or equitable liens in favor of the community against separate property of one of the spouses on which community funds have been expended for its improvement or to discharge liens thereon.[58]

So far as any of the separate property of the spouses is liable to

[55] Hannah v. Swift, 61 F.2d 307, wherein involuntary petition in bankruptcy was filed against a husband in California; referee found that all debts were community debts and all property owned and in the possession of the bankrupt was community property.

In Louisiana, where the income from separate property is community property, certain revenues collected and administered by the husband which came from stocks and bonds owned separately by the wife constituted community property, to possession of which the trustee was entitled as against wife's claim of ownership. In re Lynch, 3 F.2d 82, rev'd on other grounds, 11 F.2d 931.

Where the husband, upon petition of creditors, was adjudged a bankrupt, the debts all having been incurred during the marriage, the presumption was that all such debts were community obligations, and the court having ordered the sale of what was admittedly community property to provide funds to pay such debts, and the wife having been given full opportunity to present her claim to the property, her petition that the District Court be adjudged to have no jurisdiction over the land or to make such sale or over the money realized therefrom was dismissed by the Circuit Court of Appeals. Gibbons v. Goldsmith, 222 Fed. 826, arising in the District Court in Washington.

[56] See ante, § 159.

[57] Formerly, Cal. Civ. Code, § 158, (after 1969, § 5117) provided that earnings of the wife were not liable for the debts of the husband. In holding that these earnings, which although part of the community property, were exempted from claims of creditors and thus could not be reached by the husband's trustee in bankruptcy, the California court said that it was immaterial whether the debts contracted by the husband were his separate debts or were contracted by him for the community benefit. Street v. Bertolone, 193 Cal. 751, 226 P. 913. But in 1937, the statute was amended to provide that these earnings should be liable for payment of debts contracted by the husband or the wife for the necessities of life furnished them or either of them while living together.

[58] See Conley v. Moe, 7 Wash. 2d 355, 110 P.2d 172, 133 A.L.R. 1089, and annotation 133 A.L.R. 1097.

But compare the situation in a jurisdiction such as California where it is presumed that the expenditure of community funds by the husband to improve the wife's separate property is a gift of such funds to the wife. And consider the effect of the view that no lien of any sort arises from the expenditure of community funds to improve separate property.

be charged for community debts and obligations it should also be drawn into the proceedings, and a trustee in bankruptcy should be entitled to possession of it for the benefit of the community creditors. At this point it may well be asked what are the rights as between creditors on community obligations and creditors on separate obligations of the spouses, in so much of the separate property as may be liable to community obligations. Since, as stated in the preceding section, the Bankruptcy Act requires equality of treatment of creditors, creditors upon separate obligations of the spouses should be permitted to come in and file their claims. The community creditors should be required to look first to the community property, after which the community creditors insofar as their claims are still unsatisfied should share with the separate creditors in the separate property which has been drawn in because it is subject to community obligations. Indeed, the very fact that certain of the separate property has been declared by statute to be subject to certain community obligations might well warrant the conclusion that the community creditors were designed to have priority over separate creditors in subjecting it to their claims.

In those states which subject community property to separate debts of a spouse,[59] separate creditors could undoubtedly file their claims, but the community creditors should always have priority over the separate creditors to payment from the community property, even though their claims may exhaust the community property.[60] Indeed, in allowing the separate creditors to file their claims, they should be required to show that they have resorted to the separate property of their debtor without obtaining full satisfaction.

The discharge of the husband in bankruptcy, from the obligation of a community debt, of necessity has also discharged the wife, even though she was not a party to the bankruptcy proceeding;[61] but this has not been a uniform view.[62] For, in the sense that the adjudication against the husband as administrator of the community is also an adjudication against the community, the discharge of the husband discharges the community.[63] Of course, the wife's separate property

---

[59] See ante, §§ 158, 162.

[60] This was recognized and applied in In re Chavez, 149 Fed. 73, arising in the District Court in New Mexico, where the claim of a creditor on an antenuptial debt of the husband was subordinated not only to claims of community creditors but to the wife's claim against the husband for squandering her property (in this case the dotal property) under his control. "The relation of husband and wife is regarded by the civil law as a species of partnership, the property of which, like that of any other partnership, is primarily liable for the payment of its

debts." Packard v. Arellanes, 17 Cal. 525.

[61] Bimrose v. Matthews, 78 Wash. 38, 138 P. 319. And see Gibbons v. Goldsmith, 222 Fed. 826, arising in District Court in Washington.

[62] See U. S. v. Miller (D.C., La.) 162 F. Supp. 726; General Ins. Co. v. Schian, 56 Cal. App. 2d 767, 56 Cal. Rptr. 767 (quoting de Funiak, 1st ed.).

[63] See Gibbons v. Goldsmith, 222 Fed. 826; Gibbons v. Dexter Horton Trust & Savings Bank, 225 Fed. 424; both arising in Washington.

may not in any event be liable upon community obligations, but to the extent that it is made so by local law, she would be discharged. And where the husband and the wife have both been adjudicated bankrupts as a marital community or conjugal partnership, they are both released from the community debts. The extent to which discharge from community debts and obligations affects a spouse's liability on his or her separate debts and obligations presents puzzling features and the answer would seem considerably dependent as to what extent separate property and separate claims were involved in the community bankruptcy proceedings. Undoubtedly, the rules applicable in the case of ordinary partnerships should be extremely helpful by way of analogy.[64]

§ 181.   Liability because of tort of spouse.

It was provided in the Spanish law by statute of long standing that neither spouse was liable to lose his or her separate property or his or her half of the community property on account of any delict which the other spouse might commit.[65] Since the term "delict" *(delito)* of that period of Spanish law was a general term applicable to both a criminal offense and a civil wrong,[66] the statute was applicable to save the property interests of the innocent spouse from liability for fine, penalty or confiscation imposed on the guilty spouse because of a criminal offense and from liability incurred by reason of the civil wrong committed by the guilty spouse. We are not concerned at the moment with the matter of criminal offenses but with civil wrongs or what we would describe as torts.[67] By reason of the statute mentioned, debts incurred through the delict of either spouse were not payable from that part of the common property which belonged to the innocent spouse.[68] In the case of the husband, while he might, by contract, alienate or bind the community property by

[64] See Moore, The Community in Bankruptcy, 11 Wash. Law Rev. 61, 74–79.

[65] Novísima Recopilación, Book 10, Title 4, Law 10, originally Law 77 of the Leyes de Toro of 1505.
"Before finishing this commentary, I cannot fail to remark that the decision of this law seems unnecessary, because it is a well known fact that neither by the delict of the husband, or by that of the wife, could an innocent person be deprived of his or her property either before or after a declaratory sentence, and Palacios Ruvios, who assisted in the drafting of the law, tells us that he was very insistent in the passage of it, without alleging any other reason for his

attitude than the common one and general one, familiar to everybody, that only the authors of a delict can suffer the penalty for it." Llamas y Molina, No. 43, to Nov. Rec. Law 10.

[66] Delict in the Spanish law, see ante, § 81.

[67] Liability of community property for fines, etc., imposed for criminal offense of spouse, see post, § 184.

[68] Matienzo, Gloss VII, No. 11, to Nov. Rec. Law 2. At this place Matienzo remarks, indeed, that such debts "are not payable out of the property acquired during marriage or out of that portion of it which belongs to the innocent spouse" and then refers for fuller treatment to his discussions under Laws 5 and 10. But

reason of his power of management, he could not by his delict cause the imposition of any obligation upon the common property which would cause the wife to lose her half share thereof, any more than he could by a wrongful or fraudulent alienation of common property deprive the wife of her half share in such common property.[69] Nor could he by his delict render liable therefor the separate property of the wife.[70] In other words, it was only the separate property and the half share of the common property belonging to the wrongdoer, even though the wrongdoer be the wife, that was liable because of such wrong.[71] The reason that the half share of the community property of the wrongdoing spouse could be reached was that the declaratory sentence making that spouse's property liable for the delict thereby terminated the community of property between the spouses. Upon division being made, that share of the wrongdoer was then subjected to the judgment against him or her.

It is at once apparent from the foregoing that the principles of the Spanish community property system are entirely at variance with the principles of the English common law which, instead of considering each spouse liable only for his or her own torts, imposed liability on the husband not only for his own torts but also for the tortious acts of the wife. In the English common law such principles are attributable to the fact that the wife's identity as a person merged into that of her husband so that any tortious acts of hers were his acts, and the fact that title and possession of all marital property from which recovery could be had were in the husband.[72] But in the Spanish community property system this situation did not exist, since not only was the wife viewed as a separate person in her own right but also she had, or could have, her own separate property and owned an existing half share in the community property.[73] Accordingly, she

---

so far as concerns his statement that the debts incurred by delict are not payable at all from property acquired during marriage, neither his discussion nor those of other jurisconsults contain such a broad interpretation. All agree that while the innocent spouse's half of the community is exempt from liability the half belonging to the wrongdoer is subject to liability.

[69] Azevedo, Commentaries to Nov. Rec. Law 10. See also Matienzo, Gloss II, No. 2, to the same.

"For although the husband can without his wife's consent alienate property acquired during marriage, see law 5 above and my gloss 6 thereon, and loss by delict is called alienation, yet administrators with full powers of alienation cannot alienate by delict the property of the person whose estate they are managing." Matienzo, Gloss II, No. 2, to Nov. Rec. Law 10.

[70] See commentaries of Matienzo, Azevedo, and Llamas y Molina to Nov. Rec. Law 10.

[71] See authorities cited ante.

That married woman might by her delict lose in whole or in part her share of marital profits, her dowry and everything else, see Novísima Recopilación, Book 10, Title 4, Law 11, and commentaries thereto of Matienzo, Azevedo, and Llamas y Molina.

[72] Common law, see ante, § 2.

[73] "The second part (of the statute) speaks of the profits acquired during marriage, and as this property is half the husband's and half the wife's in

could be held responsible for her own wrongful acts and compensation recovered therefor from her own property or property interests. No property of the husband, either his separate property or his share of the community property could be made liable for the wife's delict.[74]

§ 182.   — Community property states except Louisiana.

In view of the community property principles, it becomes the height of illogic for the court of one of our community property jurisdictions to apply common-law tort principles to an aspect of a system to which such common-law principles are so alien, although such action has been taken.[75]

Some effort has been made in the community property states to remove by statutory enactment the conflict between common law and community property principles but there are few of these states in which the statutes or the judicial interpretation of them are not subject to strong criticism. As we have seen, the fairness and equality of the principles of the Spanish community property law rendered liable for a spouse's civil wrong that spouse's separate property and half share in the community property, and no more. In no respect was the separate property or share in the community property of the innocent spouse subject to liability for the wrongful act committed by the other spouse. Moreover, a very careful distinction was made between obligations created by contract for which the entire community might be bound and obligations created by delicts which, it was pointed out, arose from wrongful acts and for which the half share of the innocent spouse in the community should not be liable.[76]

ownership and possession, as has been shown by Law of Toro 16, the present Law intends that neither of the consorts should lose his half owing to the delict of the other." Llamas y Molina, No. 17, to Nov. Rec. Law 10.

In stating the reason that the delict of the husband did not render the wife's half of the common property liable therefor, Azevedo says that as an elementary principle the ownership of half the common property was automatically transferred to the wife (upon its acquisition, of course), and that it was natural that it should not be confiscable for the delict of the husband, for one partner did not lose his share because of the delict of the other partner. See Azevedo, Nos. 16 and 17 to Nov. Rec. Law 10.

[74] "The wife, during marriage, may by reason of delict lose in part or in whole her dowry or ganancial prop-

erty or other property of whatever nature it may be." Novísima Recopilación, Book 10, Title 4, Law 11. See likewise, the same, Law 10.

[75] See Henley v. Wilson, 137 Cal. 273, 70 P. 21, 92 Am. St. Rep. 160, 58 L. R. A. 941, applying common law principle of husband being liable for wife's tort.

[76] The argument that if the husband is permitted by contract freely to alienate community property without the consent of the wife he can also do so by delict because by delicts a quasi-contract arises, so that in either case the wife's interest in the marital property is bound, is inapplicable, said Azevedo, adding "that it is by a fiction and not in truth and in fact that a man who commits a delict is deemed to have consented to the infliction of a penalty in respect of his offence. . . . Similarly the above mentioned

In Arizona, the community property may not be used to satisfy the separate tort liabilities of either spouse.[77] It is rather liable only for the torts committed with the intention of protecting the community property, and this regardless of whether the tort actually benefits the community,[78] or torts committed while transacting community business.[79]

In California, where both spouses join in the commission of a tort so as to be joint tort-feasors, the separate property of each, as well as all the community property, regardless of by which spouse acquired, becomes liable.[80] Certainly the same result would ensue where the husband directs or ratifies such a tort by the wife.[81] It is conceivable although not likely that the same might result as to the wife ratifying or even directing a commission of a tort by the husband.[82] In the case of civil injuries inflicted by the wife alone, neither the separate property of the husband nor community property acquired by him is liable.[83] However, the separate property of the wife, as well as the community property subject to her management, are liable.[84] It is always possible, of course, that exempt properties may be mingled beyond identification with properties that are liable, so as to lose their exemption.[85] In the case of a tort committed by the husband alone, all of his separate property is liable and the community property subject to his management,[86] but the community property represented by the wife's earnings and her community property personal injury damages are not liable,[87] unless commingled beyond identification with community property acquired by the husband.[88]

argument ceases to apply whenever the result would be absurd and contrary to the laws. In law no one should be punished for the delict of another nor should a wife be punished for her husband. . . . And so it is not surprising that a wife does not lose her half-share of profits by reason of the delict of her husband." Azevedo, commentaries to Nov. Rec. Law 10.

[77] Shaw v. Greer, 67 Ariz. 230, 194 P.2d 434.

[78] McFadden v. Watson, 51 Ariz. 110, 74 P.2d 1181.

[79] Babcock v. Tam (9 C.A.), 156 F.2d 116.

[80] See Bonneau v. Galeazi, 215 Cal. 27, 8 P.2d 133, where spouses jointly committed act of waste.

[81] See de Funiak, Personal Injuries Under the California Community Property Law, 3 Cal. West. L. Rev. 69.

[82] Under the Hawkins Act, which imposed liability for refusal to rent to one because of his race or color, where spouses owned apartment house which was managed by the husband, the wife was liable under the rule of the liability of a principal for the wrong by the agent in transacting the principal's business, even when not ratified or authorized by the principal, Hudson v. Nixon, 57 Cal. 2d 482, 20 Cal. Rptr. 620, 370 P.2d 324.

[83] Cal. Civ. Code, § 5122; McClain v. Tufts, 83 Cal. App. 2d 140, 187 P.2d 818, noted in 21 So. Cal. L. Rev. 388.

[84] Cal. Civ. Code, §§ 5116, 5122.

[85] Consider Tinsley v. Bauer, 125 Cal. App. 2d 714, 271 P.2d 110.

[86] Grolemund v. Cafferata, 17 Cal. 2d 679, 111 P.2d 641.

[87] Cal. Civ. Code, § 5117.

[88] See, e. g., Porter (Truelsen) v. Nelson, 42 Cal. App. 2d 750, 109 P.2d 996.

Separate property of the wife, there being no commingling, is not liable.[89]

Idaho law is very unsettled in this area. It would appear that the community property is liable for none of the wife's torts, whether community or separate; but that it is liable for all torts of the husband, regardless of character.[90]

New Mexico suffers from a marked lack of cases in this area.[91] Apparently the separate property of the wife is liable for all her torts, and the separate property of the husband is liable for all his torts; the separate property of one is not liable for the torts of the other.[92] The community property apparently is liable for community torts of either spouse, although there are no cases on this. It is clear, however, that the wife's half of the community property is liable for her postnuptial separate torts[93] and the husband's half is liable for his postnuptial separate torts.[94]

By recent statute, in Texas, all the community property is liable for all torts committed by either spouse during marriage. Also, the community property under the sole management of a spouse is liable for the antenuptial torts of that spouse; the community property jointly managed by both spouses is liable for the antenuptial torts of either spouse.[95] The separate property of either spouse is not liable for any of the torts of the other, but apparently is liable for the antenuptial torts of the owner spouse.[96] The code leaves unanswered the question of the liability of separate property for the owner's postnuptial torts, but, by implication, such property clearly would be.

In Washington, the community property is liable for all community torts committed by either spouse.[97] This liability is generally based on the theory of *respondeat superior*.[98]

Both spouses and their property may be liable, of course, if the tort is one for which both spouses would be jointly liable as if unmarried.[99] And in some jurisdictions it is held that the entire community property may be liable where the husband, in the course of his management of the community, commits a tortious act with the

[89] Cal. Civ. Code, § 5121.

[90] Brockelbank, The Community Property Law of Idaho, chap. 4.

[91] Clark, New Mexico Community Property Law: The Senate Interim Committee Report, 15 La. L. Rev. 571.

[92] N.M. Stat. 1953, §§ 57-3-8, 57-3-9.

[93] That the wife's share of the community property should be subject to liability for her separate tort, see McDonald v. Senn, 53 N.M. 198, 204 P.2d 990, 10 A. L. R. 2d 966, citing and quoting de Funiak, 1st ed., § 182.

[94] United States Fidelity and Guaranty Co. v. Chavez, 126 F. Supp. 227.

[95] Tex. Family Code 1969, § 5.61.

[96] Tex. Family Code 1969, §§ 5.01, 5.21, 5.61.

[97] Pruzan, Community Property and Tort Liability in Washington, 23 Wash. L. Rev. 259.

[98] See Sitarek v. Montgomery, 203 P.2d 1062.

[99] See Hirales v. Boegen, 61 Ariz. 210, 146 P.2d 352; Ruth v. Rhodes, 66 Ariz. 129, 185 P.2d 304; Cal. Civ. Code, § 5122; Bonneau v. Galeazi, 215 Cal. 27, 8 P.2d 133.

intention of benefiting the community thereby,[1] or where the community property receives some advantage or has some benefit added by reason of the tort of one of the spouses.[2] In speaking of the committing of a tortious act with intent to benefit the community thereby, it is meant that the very act itself was intended to benefit the community. Merely that a spouse, through negligence, commits a tort while on the way to do something for the benefit of the community, or while in conducting the community affairs but outside the scope of such affairs, is another thing.[3]

The doctrine of *respondeat superior* has sometimes been invoked

[1] See Hansen v. Blevins, 84 Ida. 49, 367 P.2d 758; McHenry v. Short, 29 Wash. 2d 263, 186 P.2d 900, noted 23 Notre Dame Lawyer 609; Milne v. Kane, 64 Wash. 254, 116 P. 659, Ann. Cas. 1913 A 318, 36 L. R. A. (N. S.) 88.

Where an assault was committed by the husband alone but was committed in taking possession of community property and with the purpose that the act should inure to the benefit of the community, a community liability was created. Geissler v. Geissler, 96 Wash. 150, 164 P. 746, 166 P. 1119.

Any tortious act intended for the benefit of the community renders the community liable for the unfortunate results of such act, even though the community has not actually benefited therefrom, according to McFadden v. Watson, 51 Ariz. 110, 74 P.2d 1181.

Where the tort is not one intended to and does not benefit the community and the community property would not be liable, a right of action for personal injuries or wrongful death against the wrongdoing spouse does not survive the death of such spouse, in the absence of a survival statute, and cannot be enforced against the community. Donn v. Kunze, 52 Ariz. 219, 79 P.2d 965; Bortle v. Osborne, 155 Wash. 585, 285 P. 425, 67 A. L. R. 1152. Right of action for wrongful death as separate or community property, see ante, § 84.

[2] Community considered to be engaged in calling or business of notary public so as to render community property liable for tort committed by husband while acting as notary public and which benefited

the community, see Kangley v. Rogers, 85 Wash. 250, 147 P. 898.

But compare principles relative to right of community to receive benefit of property unlawfully or wrongly acquired, ante, § 76.

[3] For example, the husband while driving to his work, negligently collides with another car. Undoubtedly, he is on his way to do something which will benefit the community, since his earnings from his work will accrue to the community, but the tortious act was not done with any intent to benefit the community. This distinction the court failed to make in Werker v. Knox, 197 Wash. 453, 85 P.2d 1041, where the wife, while driving an automobile on her way to get a sweater she had ordered, collided with the plaintiff, and the court held the purchase of the sweater was a community transaction and the community was liable for the wife's tort. But see De Phillips v. Neslin, 155 Wash. 147, 283 P. 691, where husband was said to have stepped outside his conduct of community business to commit an assault.

The Washington court carries the matter to an extreme, in King v. Williams, 188 Wash. 350, 62 P.2d 710, where husband was driving the family car on his way to a dance with some friends and injured the plaintiff. The wife was not present and it seems to have been one of those occasions when the husband "was out with the boys." The court declared that recreation is beneficial to the welfare of the community, so in seeking recreation the husband was benefiting the community so as to make it liable.

in an effort to fix liability on the husband for the tortious act of the wife, usually in cases where the tortious act results from the wife's driving of the family automobile or the husband's automobile by his authorization. On occasion it has been successfully invoked,[4] and at other times unsuccessfully.[5] It should be apparent under the principle of the community property system that each spouse is a separate person in his or her own right, that the wife is acting as an individual in driving the automobile just as much as the husband would be in driving it. He should no more be liable for her tort than she should be for his. The invocation of this doctrine is only another attempt to drag in by the heels the common-law principle that the wife is always subject to the husband's orders and that as her master he is responsible for her tortious acts. Even if the husband has requested or ordered her to proceed to do a certain thing, in the course of which she commits a tortious act, their relation is not one of master and servant. In the absence of any authorization of the tortious act itself, or ratification of it, so as to tar him with the same brush, there is no reason why his property should be liable. As an individual in her own right, she and her own property would bear the responsibility for her tort. Possibly, her share of the common property should also bear the responsibility. The entire community property should only be liable, if at all, upon a showing that she committed the tort with the intention to benefit the community or that it was benefited by her tort.[6] And this "intention to benefit the community" should not be carried to the extremes that it sometimes is.[7]

§ 183.   — Louisiana.

Turning to Louisiana, we find a somewhat different situation from that heretofore discussed in respect of other community property states. Because the common-law doctrine of the husband's liability for the wife's torts has never had any place in Louisiana, where the civil law is in effect, the situation in the past has been the reverse of

---

[4] Cohen v. Hill (Tex. Civ. App.), 286 S. W. 661. See also Mortensen v. Knight, 81 Ariz. 325, 305 P.2d 463, quoting de Funiak, 1st ed.; Selaster v. Simmons, 39 Ariz. 432, 7 P.2d 258.

[5] Hill v. Jacquemart, 55 Cal. App. 498, 203 P. 1021 under former Cal. Vehicle Code. Now see Cal. Vehicle Code, §§ 17150, 17151; Wilcox v. Berry, 32 Cal. 2d 189, 195 P.2d 414; de Funiak, Personal Injuries Under California Community Property Law, 3 Cal. West. L. Rev. 69.

See Louisiana cases post, § 183.

[6] In Washington, although husband and wife may jointly own automobile, one is not personally liable for the tort of the other committed while driving the automobile; judgment should be rendered only against the spouse driving the automobile. Hicks v. Baumgartner, 96 Wash. 71, 164 P. 743 (husband driving); Perren v. Press, 196 Wash. 14, 81 P.2d 867 (wife driving). In California, see materials in preceding note.

[7] As in Werker v. Knox, 197 Wash. 453, 85 P.2d 1041. And see King v. Williams (Wash.), supra.

that in other community property states. That is, the courts have continually announced that the husband is not personally liable for the wife's torts unless such liability should be imposed by statute. No statute, of course, imposes any such liability.[8] These cases contain somewhat questionable language, by way of dictum, which indicates that the situation would be otherwise if the husband were present at the time of the commission of the tort or knew of its commission at the time. Such dictum has too much of a common-law tinge to it. It implies subscription to the common-law theory that the mere presence of the husband, the lord and master, is a sanction or direction by him of the act, that he must be responsible for everything the wife does because she is his mere alter ego.

The Louisiana courts have gone further in the way of dictum, epecially in cases where the wife has committed a tort while driving the family automobile or the husband's automobile, declaring that the husband would be liable for the wife's tortious act while driving the automobile if it is affirmatively shown that while so driving it she is acting as the husband's agent and is authorized to attend and is attending to affairs or business of the community at the time of the tortious act. This view has been arrived at by interpreting article 2985 of the Civil Code as applicable, which article defines a mandate, the procuration of letter of attorney by which one person gives power to another to transact affairs for him, and by stating, in effect, that the husband as head and master of the community is making the wife his business agent pursuant to such code article. By so ingeniously converting the marital relationship into the equivalent of the relationship of master and servant or principal and agent, the Louisiana courts end up in the same position that the courts of our other states were, previous to statutes abrogating the common-law doctrine of liability of the husband for the wife's tortious acts. But after giving vent to such dictum most cases in the past have held the husband not personally liable for the wife's tort on the ground that in the particular case the wife was not attending to community affairs, etc.[9] But since then there has been the trend to hold that even social pursuits of the wife are within the scope of community obligations, so that the husband as head of the marital community has been held liable for her torts.[10]

[8] McClure v. McMartin, 104 La. 496, 29 So. 227; see also Adams v. Golson, 187 La. 363, 174 So. 876.

[9] See Bradford v. Brown (La.), 199 So. 2d 414; Aetna Casualty & Surety Co. v. Simms (La. App.), 200 So. 34; Wise v. Smith (La. App.), 186 So. 857; Tuck v. Harmon (La. App.), 151 So. 803; Paderas v. Stauffer, 10 La. App. 50, 119 So. 757, 120 So. 886;

Globe Indemnity Co. v. Quesenberry, 1 La. App. 364. And see Miller, 6 Loyo. L. Rev. 43.

Compare Selaster v. Simmons, 39 Ariz. 432, 7 P.2d 258, as to similarity of rule in Arizona.

[10] Brantley v. Clarkson, 217 La. 425, 46 So. 2d 614, noted in 11 La. L. Rev. 190, 5 S. W. L. Jour. 351, and overruling Adams v. Golson, 187 La. 363, 174 So. 876.

§ 184.   Liability because of crime of spouse.

We have already seen that it was thoroughly established in the Spanish community property law that neither spouse was liable to lose his or her separate property or his or her half of the community property on account of any delict committed by the other spouse, and that the term "delict" related both to a criminal offense or to a civil wrong.[11] Thus, any fine, penalty or confiscation of property imposed upon a spouse in punishment of a criminal offense committed by that spouse fell only upon the guilty spouse's separate property and half share in the community property. Neither the separate property nor the half share in the community property of the innocent spouse was subject to the fine, penalty or confiscation. It was immaterial whether the guilty spouse was the husband or the wife or whether the innocent spouse was the husband or the wife, the rule was the same.[12]

The reason for this can find no better expression than the succinct statement of the eminent jurisconsult, Azevedo, that "In law no one should be punished for the delict of another."[13] And Llamas y Molina adds that the Spanish statute relating to the matter was "unnecessary, because it is a well known fact that neither by the delict of the husband, nor by that of the wife, could an innocent person be deprived of his property either before or after a declaratory sentence, and Palacios Ruvios, who assisted in the drafting of the law, tells us that he was very insistent in the passage of it, without alleging any other reason for his attitude than the common and general one, familiar to everybody, that only the authors of a delict can suffer the penalty for it."[14]

While this principle has been repeatedly violated by our courts in tort cases,[15] at least there appears to have been no violation of it in regard to criminal offenses. Perhaps we should say, rather, that our attention has been called to no such violation. Certainly, in Arizona and Washington the courts have properly appreciated the principles of justice as well as the principles of community property and it is evident that in those states the property of an innocent wife is not subject to be sacrificed because of crimes committed by the husband.[16]

---

[11] See ante, § 181.

[12] See Novísima Recopilación, Book 10, Title 4, Laws 10 and 11; commentaries thereto of Matienzo, Azevedo and Llamas y Molina.

Confiscation of property as punishment under Spanish law, see post, § 188.

[13] Azevedo, No. 7 to Nov. Rec. Law 10; and he adds "nor should a wife be punished for her husband. . . . And so it is not surprising that a wife does not lose her half-share of profits by reason only of the delict of her husband."

[14] Llamas y Molina, No. 40 to Nov. Rec. Law 10, who also refers, in his commentaries, to other eminent authorities, stating the same principle, such as Grotius, De Jure Belli et Pacis, Vol. 2, Chap. 21, par. 12, and Puffendorf, De Jure Nat. et Gen., Vol. 8, Chap. 3, par. 30.

[15] See ante, § 182.

[16] In Bergman v. State, 187 Wash. 622, 60 P.2d 699, 106 A.L.R. 1007,

§ 185.   Liability for costs or the like.

In proceedings brought to remove the husband from the management and control of the community property because of his mental incompetency or the like, the proceeding has for its purpose the preservation and protection of the community property, so that costs and attorney's fees therein are properly chargeable against the community.[17] In suits between the spouses for divorce or separation from bed and board, whether the costs of the suit will be charged against the separate property of the loser or against such spouse's interest in the community property or just what property will be made responsible depends upon the view of the courts of the particular jurisdiction. The subject is not considered of sufficient importance to warrant any extended discussion.[18]

§ 186.   Conflict of laws.

The law of the place of acquisition of property acquired during marriage or the law of the place of domicile of the spouses as governing the nature of such property as community or separate property has been discussed at some length in Chapter VI.[19] The same principles are largely applicable in determining the nature of a debt as a community debt or as a separate debt of one spouse. Whether a separate debt incurred by a spouse in a noncommunity property state can be satisfied from the community property depends upon the principles applied in the particular community property state as to allowing or not allowing community property to be subjected to liability for separate debts of the spouses. Thus, the view taken in a

---

the court refused to hold the community property liable for a judgment for costs rendered in a criminal action against the husband in which he was convicted of arson. Although the arson was committed against community property it was said that it was not committed within the scope or conduct of the community business or for the benefit of the community but was in fact destructive of it. This case goes further than the Spanish community property law which would have permitted the husband's share of the community to be liable, but at least it protects the wife's share of the community.

The holding in Villescas v. Arizona Copper Co., 20 Ariz. 268, 179 P. 963, that community property was liable for the acts of the husband in the commission of a crime not committed in

the management of the community property was expressly disapproved in Cosper v. Valley Bank, 28 Ariz. 373, 237 P. 175, according to McFadden, v. Watson, 51 Ariz. 110, 74 P.2d 1181.

[17] Succession of Bothick, 52 La. Ann. 1863, 28 So. 458; In re Leech, 45 La. Ann. 197, 12 So. 126; Breaux v. Francke, 30 La. Ann. 336.

[18] See, e.g., Brenat v. Brenat, 102 Cal. 294, 36 P. 672; Gastauer v. Gastauer, 143 La. 749, 79 So. 326; Ghent v. Boyd, 18 Tex. Civ. App. 88, 43 S. W. 891.

Dissolution of marriage by divorce in general, see post, Chap. X, C.

Liability of wife for her share of fees of notaries and appraisers, see De Blanc v. De Blanc (La. App.), 18 So. 2d 619.

[19] See ante, §§ 87–92.

leading case in Washington has been that a debt incurred by the husband in connection with his business while the spouses were domiciled in a noncommunity property state was by the law of that state the separate debt of the husband. Accordingly, when suit on the debt was brought against the husband after the spouses had moved to a community property state, such debt, as well as the judgment obligation which replaced it, was considered the separate debt of the husband and was not enforceable against community property acquired in their new domicile. It was so held despite the admitted fact that if the same debt had been contracted by the husband in the community property state it would have been a community debt.[20] But where the spouses, in the noncommunity property state, jointly and severally subjected themselves and any and all of their property to liability, upon their change of domicile to Washington, their interest in community property in Washington was subject to such liability.[21] It may be added that in a community property state which allows the community property to be subjected to separate obligations of the husband, it would be probable that the separate obligation incurred by the husband in a noncommunity property state could be satisfied from community property.[22]

Of course, where spouses who have contracted community debts

[20] La Selle v. Woolery, 14 Wash. 70, 44 P. 115, 53 Am. St. Rep. 855, 32 L. R. A. 73; Huyvaerts v. Roedtz, 105 Wash. 657, 178 P. 801; Escrow Service Co. v. Cressler (Wash.), 365 P.2d 760, citing and following de Funiak, 1st ed.; Achilles v. Hooper, 40 Wash. 2d 664, 245 P.2d 1005, citing and following de Funiak, 1st ed.

See Cohen, Liability of Community for Separate Debts of Husband in Conflict of Laws, 11 Wash. Law Rev. 166.

More recently, see Meng v. Security State Bank (Wash.), 133 P.2d 293, wherein husband and wife executed a joint note, not for family expenses, in a noncommunity property state and then moved to Washington, where the husband alone executed a "renewal" note. The renewal note was said to have the same status as the original note insofar as the husband was concerned, and it and the judgment rendered thereon were said to be the separate obligation of the husband. It would seem that there was more a novation than a renewal, although even so it would be only the separate obligation of the husband.

Principle as applied to tort claim against husband acquired in noncommunity property state, see Mountain v. Price, 20 Wash. 2d 129, 146 P.2d 327; Moag v. Voukovich (Wash.), 280 P.2d 680.

[21] Household Finance Corp. v. Smith (Wash.), 423 P.2d 621.

[22] In Great American Indemnity Co. v. Garrison, 75 F. Supp. 811, surety company brought suit in federal court in Washington to recover for money paid by surety on official bond of husband in Idaho by reason of shortage in his accounts. In applying Washington conflict of laws rule, court stated liability of marital community for debt must be determined by law of place where debt arose and, as well, community liability for tort governed by law of place where tort committed. Although law of Idaho is very similar to that of California, and community property is liable for all debts contracted by husband, court decided community was not liable for torts of husband as a public officer from which community did not benefit.

See also Jones v. Weaver, 123 F.2d 403, where California spouses were

move to a noncommunity property state, such debts should be enforceable against whatever community property they have taken into the noncommunity property state. For although the latter state would not recognize "community property," it would recognize that the spouses have an equal ownership in such property and that it would be subject to debts for which the spouses were liable in common.

driving family automobile in Arizona; while wife was driving there was collision with plaintiff who sued in Arizona, claiming liability on husband under Arizona Family Car Doctrine. Of course, under California Vehicle Code, § 17151, husband could have limited liability.

CHAPTER X

DISSOLUTION OF MARITAL COMMUNITY

A. In General

B. Death of Spouse

C. Divorce and Separation

440

A. In General

§ 187. What is meant by "dissolution."

When we speak of "dissolution" we are referring primarily to dissolution of the marital community or, in other words, of the conjugal partnership in earnings and gains during the marriage, and not to dissolution of the marriage. Although the marriage is only the occasion for the partnership which the spouses have in the earnings and gains during its subsistence, and the cause of this conjugal partnership is the law which establishes it,[1] unquestionably, the dissolution of the marriage itself brings about the dissolution of the marital community because community of property is dependent for its continuance upon the subsistence of the marriage.[2] This partnership in such earnings and gains, this community of property, may upon occasion, where the law allows, be dissolved or cease to exist without the marriage itself ceasing.[3] Thus, in the Spanish law of community the marital community might be dissolved or cease to exist not only upon the death of one or both of the spouses or upon divorce, but upon confiscation of the property of one of them,[4] or upon agreement between the spouses during the marriage.[5] It might also be affected

[1] See Llamas y Molina, Nos. 13–15, to Nov. Rec. Law 8, Book 10, Title 4.

[2] Matienzo refers to the matter in the following language: "For then the marriage no longer subsists, and it was the marriage which was the cause of the sharing, by this and similar laws; and if the cause ceases, then the sharing must cease too." Matienzo, Gloss I, No. 56, to Nov. Rec. Law 1, Book 10, Title 4. American illustration, see Estate of Hansen, 91 Cal. App. 2d 610, 205 P.2d 686.

[3] Under the French Civ. Code (Cachard Rev. Ed.), Art. 1441, "A community is dissolved: 1, by natural death; 2, by civil death (now repealed); 3, by divorce; 4, by separation from bed and board; 5, by separation of property."

[4] See post, § 188.

[5] See ante, § 135 et seq.
After speaking of divorce, Sala remarks: "Besides this case there are two others in which the conjugal partnership is dissolved without marriage being dissolved, and they are, when the wife renounces the partnership, and the property of one of the two is confiscated." Novísimo Sala Mexicano, Sec. 2a, Title IV, No. 2.

in part by separation of the spouses brought about by the fault of one of them, whether the separation was a mere living apart or was legally sanctioned by divorce from cohabitation,[6] and there might also be a forfeiture by the wife, because of certain misconduct, to her right in the common property.[7]

In all of our community property states, divorce or death results in a dissolution of the marital community, and in the main these are the chief causes of dissolution. For that reason they are dealt with subsequently in separate subdivisions of this chapter, while in this subdivision we concern ourselves with other and miscellaneous matters. The dissolution of the marital community so far as concerned the sharing in the earnings and gains during marriage which might be accomplished by agreement of the spouses under the Spanish law may still be so accomplished in many of our community property states, although not in all of them. However, this matter has been previously considered, for the purposes of convenience, in the chapter dealing with agreements and transactions generally between spouses.[8] Also dealt with at another point is the question of the dissolution of the partnership in marital earnings and gains — although not of the marriage — because of mismanagement by the husband or the like.[9]

§ 188.   Confiscation for criminal delict as termination.

The dissolution of the marital community under the Spanish law by reason of confiscation, which was previously mentioned, may be briefly described as resulting from the confiscation by the Treasury of all the property of one of the spouses because of high treason, heresy or other criminal delict of certain designated nature committed by such spouse. So far as the innocent spouse was concerned he or she did not lose his or her half of the common property acquired up to the time of sentence because of the other spouse's delict. However, the conjugal partnership in marital gains thenceforth was effectively terminated by the sentence.[10] In Mexico such confiscation of property was abolished in 1843,[11] and thus was not in effect as part of the law of that portion of Mexico which came under American sovereignty a few years later. Nor for that matter is such confiscation of property within the public policy of any of our states. Indeed, in

---

[6] See ante, § 57; post, §§ 189, 190, 226.

[7] See post, §§ 189, 190.

[8] See ante, § 136.

[9] See ante, § 128.

[10] See Novísima Recopilación, Book 10, Title 4, Laws 10 and 11, commentaries of Matienzo, Azevedo and Llamas y Molina to such laws.

The conjugal partnership is dissolved "when the properties of one of the two are confiscated; it then continues only until the sentence of confiscation, leaving free to the innocent party the half of the properties gained up to that day." Novísimo Sala Mexicano, Sec. 2a, Title IV, No. 2.

[11] De las Bases de Organizacion Politica, Art. 179 (June 12, 1843); Schmidt, Civil Law of Spain and Mexico.

Spain itself, beginning with the Constitution of 1812, and culminating with the Penal Code of 1848, these penalties of confiscation seem to have been abolished.[12] But it will be observed that the principle of the Spanish law that the innocent spouse's half of the common property was not liable to confiscation is continued in effect with us in that we do not hold the innocent spouse's half of the common property subject to liability for payment of a penalty or fine imposed upon a guilty spouse.[13]

§ 189. Misconduct as forfeiting share of community property — Spanish law.

Moral views respecting the chastity of women have frequently taken shape in the form of legislation punishing wives for adultery or other misconduct by depriving them of their property rights and interests. This has been true of the law of England and of the law of our American states derived from English law as it has been of the Spanish law. The common-law lawyer will be familiar with the principle established in England by the Statute of Westminster in 1285, and recognized in many of our American states, that the wife by living in adultery forfeited her right of dower.[14] In the Spanish law, inspired both by moral views and consideration of the conjugal relation as a partnership requiring the utmost loyalty between the spouses, it was provided that the wife lost her share of the matrimonial acquests and gains acquired by the husband when she had been guilty of adultery,[15] or when she abandoned the husband without his consent

---

[12] In the language of Don Jose Vicente y Caravantes, in his annotation of 1853 of the Commentaries of Llamas y Molina: "For these reasons, these penalties have been abolished in the majority of countries as unjust, barbaric and antipolitical. In Spain it has been prescribed by article 305 of the Constitution of 1812, which is in force, that penalties are not transmissible from father to son, and as a more explicit and advanced declaration of this idea, it has been prescribed in art. 23 of the Penal Code of 1848, that the law does not recognize any defaming penalty. Lastly, it has been proclaimed by the Constitution of the Kingdom, Art. 10, that the penalty of confiscation of property will never be imposed on the crime of heresy by the law to which the present law of Toro (Law 77, later Novísima Recopilación, Book 10, Title 4, Law 10) refers, and which consequently has been abolished."

[13] See ante, § 184.

[14] Cases on misconduct as affecting spouse's rights in other's estate, see 71 A.L.R. 277, 139 A.L.R. 486.

[15] Las Siete Partidas, Part. 7, Title 17, Law 15. See also Part. 7, Title 25, Law 6.

The distinguished authors, Asso & Mañuel, in their Institutes of Civil Law of Spain, Book II, Title XX, "Adultery," state that the wife by her adultery lost only the dowry and marriage gifts and lost the property held in common only if the adultery was followed by flight from the husband's house. This interpretation is not borne out by the law of the Partida cited above. It mentions adultery without more and in specifying confinement in a convent for the guilty wife, adds that if the husband pardons the wife he can remove her from the convent and the dowry, marriage gifts and other property held in common shall

and without cause on his part.[16] This deprivation related not merely to community property acquired by the husband after her abandonment of her husband or her adultery but to all the community property acquired previous thereto.[17] Reconciliation with the husband regained for her, however, her share in this community property, although in the case of adultery it appears that the reconciliation and forgiveness by the husband had to be within two years of the adultery.[18]

It must be especially noticed that this deprivation or forfeiture related to her right to share equally with the husband in acquests and gains acquired by him. She did not lose or forfeit her communal right in those acquests and gains which she acquired, although she had to share them equally with the husband. In other words, the innocent husband was entitled to keep entirely for himself his own acquisitions and gains, but was entitled to share equally in acquisitions and gains of the wife. This was true as to all acquisitions and gains by either, whether acquired before or during any separation brought about by the adultery or abandonment on the wife's part.[19] The converse was also true, however, that if the separation was caused by act of the husband, such as his cruelty or adultery, the wife was entitled to her share of his acquisitions before and during the separation but was not

be restored to the same condition in which they were before the adultery was committed. The authors may have been momentarily misled by the provision about bringing her back to the husband's house as implying that she had fled from the house, as well as been confused by the further provision of that same law that if the wife left the husband's house and went to another's house with intent to commit adultery she lost the dowry, marriage gifts and property held in common.

[16] Fuero Real, Book 4, Title 5, Law 5. And see also Las Siete Partidas, Part. 7, Title 17, Law 15.

She lost not only the marriage gift from him but also all share of the community property acquired while they were living together. Fuero Real, Book 4, Title 5, Law 5.

As to these matters, see also post, this chapter, subd. C.

[17] "In such a case the wife is entitled to nothing from the property acquired by her husband, as is expressly noted by Joannes Lupi . . . and by Didacus Castelli . . . who cites the text of law 5 tit. 5 book 4 *fori* (i.e., Fuero Real), which enacts that a wife who leaves the home without her husband's consent shall be deprived of profits ac-

quired during marriage, and law 15 tit. 17 part. 7 (i.e., of Las Siete Partidas) which ordains that a wife by committing adultery loses both dowry and marriage deposit, see the last law of tit. 2 book 3 *fori*. The husband in such a case acquires the share of the property acquired during marriage which belonged to his wife; see law 1 tit. 7 book 4 *fori* which is observed in this kingdom and is confirmed by the text of law 5 tit. 20 *de adulteriis* in book 8 below which is taken from law 82 *Tauri* (i.e., Laws of Toro)." Matienzo, Gloss I, No. 55, to Nov. Rec. Law 1, Book 10, Title 4.

[18] Las Siete Partidas, Part. 7, Title 17, Law 15, providing that when the husband pardoned her offense, the dowry, the marriage gift and all the property which they held in common should be restored to the same condition as before the adultery was committed.

[19] Separation as here mentioned, does not mean a legal separation or divorce. As to them, see post, this chapter, subd. C.

As to rights of spouses in community property, when they had separated, see also ante, § 57.

required to share with him her acquisitions.[20] For it is to be especially noted that with perfect justice the "rules which apply to a wife apply to a husband and vice versa, since correlatives must be judged by one and the same standard."[21] This fact seems not generally understood.[22]

In addition, in Spain, because custom decreed the strict observance of a year of mourning by a widow after her husband's death and because decency demanded that the widow respect and honor the memory and name of her husband through whom she had acquired any rank and privileges and through whose industry she had acquired a share of profits, the Spanish law frowned upon misconduct by the wife after the husband's death.[23] It was provided by statute that if the wife having become and remaining a widow "live wantonly, she shall lose the property which she got by reason of her half of the property that was earned and improved by her husband and herself during the marriage between them, and that the said property be turned over to the heirs of the deceased husband in whose company it was earned."[24] The statute was construed to mean living dissolutely, wantonly, extravagantly, lustfully or the like, or in other words in a shameful, disgraceful or scandalous manner. It was not by any manner of means considered that the widow's share of the community property was forfeited by a single act of fornication, if such act in itself was not a notorious matter. So far as the living wantonly or dissolutely or the like was concerned, it was immaterial whether such course of life was during or after the year of mourning required. In either event, it was ground for forfeiture of her share of the community property which then, as the law provided, passed to her husband's heirs. Such misconduct also caused her to forfeit her right to any legacies bequeathed her by her husband, even where such conduct occurred after the year of mourning. An act of fornication did not deprive her of such legacies, however, unless the act took place within the year of mourning. No misconduct of the widow at any time affected her right to her own separate property, with the exception of her dotal property which had been under the husband's administration during the marriage. We forbear, however, to discuss the matter of dotal property since it is not a matter of primary concern to us.[25]

---

[20] "And in like manner if a wife is separated from her husband and ceases to cohabit with him owing to his fault, she does not acquire for him and need not share her acquisitions with him." Matienzo, Gloss I, No. 53, to Nov. Rec. Law 1, citing authorities.

[21] Matienzo, Gloss I, Nos. 53, 54, to Nov. Rec. Law 1.

[22] See also ante, § 57, as to separation; post, § 219 et seq., as to divorce.

[23] A law formerly in force imposing penalties upon widows who re-married within the first year of their widowhood was abolished by Nueva Recopilación, Book 5, Title 5, Law 3, in 1567.

[24] Novísima Recopilación, Book 10, Title 4, Law 5. See also Las Siete Partidas, Part. 4, Title 12, Law 3.

[25] More fully as to wife's loss of her share of community property, see Matienzo, Gloss VIII to Nov. Rec. Law 5; Azevedo, Nos. 22–24 to Nov. Rec. Law 5; Gutiérrez, Quaestio CXXII to Nov. Rec. Law 5.

Incidentally, Juan Sala stated that the share lost by the widow from living "dishonestly" went to benefit the heirs of the husband.[26]

The law of Mexico as to all the foregoing matters was, of course, the same.[27]

§ 190. — American jurisdictions.

So far as concerns adultery on the part of a widow after the husband's death as forfeiting her share in the community property, we have had no counterpart in our American jurisdictions. But our courts have not infrequently had occasion to consider the effect of adultery or other misconduct during marriage as affecting the guilty spouse's rights in the community property, as aside from any question of divorce.[28] These cases have seemed to deal principally with adultery or other misconduct on the part of the wife, and the impression to be gathered from some of these cases is that our courts have mistakenly conceived that the principles of the Spanish law were applicable only to the wife and not to the husband guilty of misconduct. No doubt this has been to some extent due to confusing with that situation the situation in the Spanish law in which a widow by adultery after dissolution of the marriage forfeited her share in the community property. In addition, the courts seem frequently unaware that the guilty spouse, in the Spanish law, forfeited only his or her rights to share in the acquisitions of the other spouse and did not forfeit rights in his or her own acquisitions although obliged to share them with the innocent spouse. Another source of confusion with our courts has been whether the misconduct affects rights in acquisitions prior to the misconduct or only as to acquisitions after the misconduct.[29] In some of

[26] Novísimo Sala Mexicano, Sec. 2a, Title IV, No. 2.

[27] See Schmidt, Civil Law of Spain and Mexico, p. 17; Novísimo Sala Mexicano, Sec. 2a, Title IV, No. 2.

[28] Consideration, upon divorce, of adultery as affecting guilty spouse's right to share in community property, see post, this chapter, subd. C.

[29] In Arizona, abandonment and adultery on the part of the wife was said to deprive her of all rights in gains made by the husband subsequent to her misconduct but not to an equal share of the community property prior to her misconduct. Although denying the application of the principles of the Spanish law in this latter matter, the court relied on principles of the Spanish community property system to argue that gains arising during marriage are subject to be shared. See Pendleton v. Brown, 25 Ariz. 604, 221 P. 213.

In Bedal v. Sake, 10 Idaho 270, 77 P. 638, 66 A.L.R. 60, and by implication in Keenan v. Keenan, 40 Nev. 351, 164 P. 351, abandonment of the husband by the wife seems to have influenced a decision that the wife had lost her right to share in the husband's acquisitions, both acquired before and after the abandonment. Although the Bedal Case was expressly overruled in Peterson v. Peterson, 35 Idaho 470, 207 P. 425, as to acquisitions before the abandonment, and which announced that who was at fault was not of controlling importance where the wife left the husband and went to another jurisdiction and obtained a divorce, it appears that in this latter case the wife was justified in leaving the husband. See also post, § 230.

the cases in which there may be sensed a reluctance on the part of the court to apply the principle of forfeiture or deprivation, it is difficult to say whether or not such reluctance stems from a feeling that such forfeiture or deprivation is a too severe and rigorous penalty of a system of law not in accord with principles of justice in the common law in which the judges have been chiefly trained.[30] There is no reason, however, why the flagrant misconduct and disloyalty of a spouse should be disregarded by our courts, whose moral conscience should be no less than those of the Spanish courts. Certainly many of our courts have not hesitated, in divorce suits brought on the ground of adultery or other flagrant misconduct, to penalize the guilty spouse when apportioning the marital property.[31] And the principle established by the Statute of Westminster already referred to shows that the views of the common law were no less strict than those of the Spanish law.

In regard to misconduct of the wife during the marriage, the community property principles applicable were considered in an early Texas case in which the wife not only wilfully abandoned the husband but thereafter lived in open adultery with another. The court, with insufficient source authorities before it, seemed uncertain whether the abandonment by the wife forfeited her share to all the property acquired by the husband or only to that part acquired after her abandonment, but it was aware that adultery of the wife definitely deprived her of all share in his acquisitions, and its decision accordingly was that she had no claim to any of such property.[32] This decision, shortly thereafter, was cited approvingly in a case which, however, was not concerned with precisely the same situation;[33] but at a somewhat later period the Texas court flatly denied the application of the civil law principles.[34] In this latter case it appeared that the deceased husband, after valid dissolution of a first marriage, of which there was issue, entered into a second marriage with the plaintiff from whom he separated by mutual agreement after flagrant misconduct on her part. Taking the children of his first marriage with him, he went to Texas and there, without first obtaining a divorce, married a third time. Upon his death he devised property to one of the children of his first

---

[30] The question, as arising under the laws of Puerto Rico, was considered in Garrozi v. Dastas, 204 U.S. 64, 51 L. Ed. 369, 27 Sup. Ct. 224. The case has little value from the standpoint of considering the principles developed in the Spanish law of community property, for it depends too much in its reasoning in discussions of French sources, and where it does touch upon the Spanish law it is permeated with error.

[31] Admittedly, doing so or refusing to do so in divorce actions has been greatly dependent upon whether the court deemed itself empowered to do so or not.

[32] Wheat v. Owens, 15 Tex. 241, 65 Am. Dec. 164.

[33] Carroll v. Carroll, 20 Tex. 731, 742.

[34] Routh v. Routh, 57 Tex. 589. See also Newland v. Holland, 45 Tex. 590.

marriage, and the second wife, the plaintiff, claimed an interest therein on the ground that it was community property. Although the dispute was entirely between this child and the second wife who had been guilty of misconduct and did not appear to concern the third wife, who was a putative wife, the court seems to have become somewhat confused as to the issue and considered that to some extent principles applicable to putative marriages were involved.[35] In any event, it denied that the second wife had forfeited her interest in the community property by her misconduct, under principles of community property, basing this upon the startling assertion that when the community property system was "adopted" the entire system of acquests and gains was not made part of the law, and that the marital rights of spouses in the community property was to be considered governed not by the community property principles but by common-law principles relating to marital property rights. The court even discussed at some length the rights at common law of husband and wife in property acquired during marriage. Of course, the existing community property system could not be continued without the continuation of the principles governing it; and it is an absurdity to say that "community of property" has been "adopted" but is to be governed by the principles of a system, viz. the common law, which knows no such thing as community of property and can thus have no principles which will govern and interpret it. However, the case in question can no longer be considered conclusive in any way, for the Texas court has frequently recognized the true situation, among others in the following language: "Texas, with just a few other states of the Union, has adopted as the basis of its laws relating to estates held by husband and wife the principles of the civil law, and our statutory enactments are in large measure declaratory of these principles. This is particularly true with reference to the laws relating to community property."[36]

In Arizona, the wife's abandonment of the husband and her living in adultery has been considered to defeat the right of the wife to claim

---

[35] As a matter of fact it is not entirely clear what the misconduct of the wife was. Cruelty to the children of the first marriage is instanced, as also were outrages and excesses making life with her insupportable. However, since the separation was by mutual agreement, certainly there should have been no right in the wife to share in property acquired after that time. Obviously, the realty in question was not acquired until after the separation, for the husband did not go to Texas until after the separation, and the fact that the action was brought in Texas indicates that Texas realty must have been involved.

Putative marriages, see ante, § 56.

[36] Lee v. Lee, 112 Tex. 392, 247 S. W. 828, concerning putative marriages.

However, the language of George v. Reynolds (Tex. Civ. App.), 53 S. W. 2d 490, indicates the view that so long as parties are husband and wife, whether separated pursuant to agreement or because of misconduct of one spouse, everything gained by either during such separation is community property.

half of the husband's gains acquired after her misconduct. While the court referred to the principles of the community property law and declared that by her abandonment the wife forfeited all right in such property, other factors were present, including laches in bringing the action. The evidence also indicated that she might still have been validly married to someone else at the time she intermarried with her husband.[37] While it is possible that the absence of laches and the other factors might have influenced the court to arrive at a different conclusion than it did, it is probable, judging from a consideration of the language of the decision and its evaluation of the justice of the principles that abandonment and adultery forfeit the guilty spouse's right to share in the husband's gains, that its decision would have been the same.

In New Mexico, on the other hand, an apparent unwillingness of the court to apply the pertinent principles led to an unusual and illogical denial of what had been well settled and confirmed for generations, that except where expressly modified by statute, Spanish community property principles controlled. However, we may note first that prior to the decision referred to, the New Mexico court, in a well-reasoned opinion following established principles of law, pointed out that the Spanish law of community property in force in New Mexico continued in force, under principles of international law, after the acquisition of that territory by this country, except for some later statutory enactments relating to descent of community property and which actually were suggested by the Spanish law. Accordingly, it reasoned, there was still in force and applicable there the principle that adultery by the wife deprived her of her share in the community property acquired during the marriage.[38] But this view that the Spanish community property system, except where modified by specific statute, continued in force in New Mexico, a view that was entirely consonant with other decisions of the court over a long period of time, was denied almost a quarter of a century later when the question of the effect of the wife's adultery again came before the court. Apparently, in order to avoid declaring that the wife's adultery deprived her of her share in the community property acquired during marriage, the court denied that the principles governing that matter were still law in New Mexico. Without sketching its arguments, which are considered in a previous chapter,[39] it suffices to say that the court held that community of property exists in New Mexico entirely by force of statute and that principles of the Spanish community property system which are not expressly enacted by statute are no longer in effect.

[37] Pendleton v. Brown, 25 Ariz. 604, 221 P. 213.

See also Armstrong v. Steeber, 3 La. Ann. 713, where abandonment of husband by wife and her living in concubinage affected her rights to claim a "marital fourth" given her by law. As to marital fourth, see post, §§ 193, 194.

[38] Barnett v. Barnett, 9 N.M. 205, 50 P. 337.

[39] See ante, § 49.

Accordingly, since there was no express statutory provision forfeiting the wife's share in the community property because of her adultery, the court held that she was, despite her adultery, entitled to one-half of the community property. Although the court had argued that the common law had supplanted the community property principles of the civil law relating to marital property rights, unless expressly retained by statute, it refused to apply the common-law principle established in 1285 by the Statute of Westminster II, on the ground of its inapplicability because the wife's rights under the community property system are "altogether different" from her common-law dower right.[40] One may well ask how questions relating to marital community of property are to be solved if the principles of the community property system are not continued in effect and are not to be looked to, and on the other hand common-law principles cannot be availed of because not applicable to fit the situation.

It may be noticed that in California where the wife unjustifiably abandons her husband, his acquisitions during the period are his separate property in which the wife does not share.[41]

In a preceding chapter, reference has already been made that in many of our community property states, statutes provide that earnings of the wife while living separate and apart from the husband are her own property. These statutes are extremely vague when compared with the explicitness of the Spanish law, but it is probable that they represent an attempt to reach the same result.[42] There is also recognition of the advisability of disposing of the community property upon legal separation in the same way that would be done upon divorce.[43]

In our states, there is no reason why, as under the Spanish law itself, reconciliation between the spouses and forgiveness of the guilty spouse's misconduct should not restore the community of property. Where the reconciliation takes place after there has been judicial decree of separation, difficulties resulting from statutory provisions or the absence of statutory provisions have been present.[44]

§ 191. Effect of remarriage.

The remarriage of a spouse after divorce from or after the death of the other spouse may have effects upon marital property rights which are much the same in one instance as in the other. While it

---

[40] Beals v. Ares, 25 N.M. 459, 185 P. 780.

[41] See Cal. Civ. Code, § 5131.

[42] See ante, § 57.

[43] See Cal. Civ. Code, § 4800.

[44] "In Ford v. Kittredge, 26 La. Ann. 190, it was held that the community once dissolved by a judgment of separation of bed and board cannot be re-established by the reconciliation of the parties. In that case the court pointed out that article 1451 of the Code Napoleon provided in express terms for the re-establishment of a dissolved community by consent of the parties evidenced by an act passed before a notary public, and

may not necessarily be true in every situation, the principles applicable are frequently the same whether the remarriage takes place after dissolution of the first marriage either from divorce or death. For that reason it is deemed advisable to refer to these matters at this place, so far as is practicable, rather than to divide their consideration between the ensuing subdivisions on death and divorce. This is not possible in entirety, as already intimated. In the subdivision following, relating to dissolution of the conjugal partnership by death, will be found reference to the Spanish principle governing in the case of the deceased spouse's share of the community property given to the survivor. That was that the surviving spouse who had been given the other spouse's share of the common property, whether by *inter vivos* gift, by will, or through descent, had absolute power of disposition over such property so long as he or she remained unmarried. But if the surviving spouse remarried he or she lost the absolute power of disposition over the property so received, retained only a usufructuary right in it, and had to reserve it for the benefit of descendants of the predeceased spouse.[45] And reference is also made in the same subdivision to usufructuary rights of a wife in certain of her husband's property which might be lost upon her remarriage.[46]

What may particularly be noticed is that debts contracted during the first marriage, although constituting community debts which were charges upon the community property of the first marriage, did not constitute an obligation chargeable against community property of a second marriage. This was well settled under the Spanish community property system. For example, an obligation imposed by law to support children of a first marriage was not a community obligation of the second marriage and was not chargeable against community property of the second marriage. Nor was community property of the second marriage to be used in dowering a daughter of a first marriage or in purchasing property for a son of a former marriage, or for any similar purposes. If any expenditures were made by a husband from community property of the second marriage for personal reasons of his own or to discharge obligations arising antecedent to the second marriage, the second wife or her heirs could demand back a half part of such expenditure or cost, on the ground that half of the community funds of the second marriage so expended or used belonged to the second wife. If property had been purchased with funds belonging to the second marriage the second wife was entitled to half the value

---

said: 'Here there is no such law, and we do not think that we can make one.' " Crochet v. Dugas, 126 La. 285, 52 So. 495. See also Reichert v. Lloveres, 188 La. 447, 177 So. 569.

Effect of wife's offer to return after unjustifiably abandoning husband, see Cal. Civ. Code, § 5131.

[45] See post, § 194.

[46] See post, §§ 196, 201.

A law formerly in force imposing penalties upon widows who remarried within the first year of their widowhood was abolished by the Nueva Recopilación, Book 5, Title 5, Law 3, in 1567.

of such property from property of her husband.[47] Other examples might be given, but these should suffice to illustrate the principle that only debts contracted during the second marriage which concerned that marriage and were contracted on its account were payable from the common property of that marriage. Debts and obligations arising before such marriage and concerning one of the spouses alone were not payable from the community property of that marriage.

Whatever the cause of the dissolution of the first marriage, if community obligations remain unpaid, the spouses, or the surviving spouse and heirs of the deceased spouse, are then respectively liable for one half of such debts. Upon remarriage by one of the spouses, the half of such community debts of the first marriage for which the spouse is liable has the standing, so far as the second marriage is concerned, of an antenuptial debt. In other words it should not be satisfiable from community property of the second marriage but from community property of the first marriage in the hands of such spouse and which would then have the character of separate property of such spouse. In the event of the insufficiency of that particular property, other separate property of such spouse might be resorted to. At any rate that would be the situation where community property principles are correctly regarded.[48] In states where the courts have become confused and have perverted the principles, that would not, of course, be the situation.[49]

---

[47] See, e.g., Azevedo, Nos. 22, 25 to Nov. Rec. Laws 9; Gutiérrez, Quaestio CXXIX, to the same.

[48] Surviving spouse's share of community property, after dissolution of community by death of other spouse, termed the separate property of the survivor, see Estate of Morgan, 203 Cal. 577, 265 P. 240; likewise as to share of community property assigned to spouse upon divorce, see People v. Croce, 208 Cal. 123, 280 P. 526.

Antenuptial debts, see ante, § 156 et seq., especially as to awards in decrees of divorce.

[49] In Medical Finance Ass'n. v. Allum, 22 Cal. App. 2d 747, 66 P.2d 761, a wife had been divorced from her husband and married a second time. She and her second husband were sued for medical services rendered to her during her first marriage. It was said that the duty to furnish and pay for such services rested upon the first husband and that he was personally obligated therefor, while there was no personal obligation therefor on the part of the wife. It was pointed out that under the California law if she had been personally obligated, in other words if it had been an antenuptial debt of hers, her second husband would have been liable. It will be noticed that there seems to be no thought of considering the wife liable for half of the amount due, as a community debt of the first marriage, as should properly be the case. The question presented was that either she was liable for the whole amount, in which case her second husband would have to pay the whole amount, or else she was liable for nothing, in which case her second husband was also liable for nothing. It would be difficult to imagine any more complete departure from community property principles than that illustrated by this case, but it seems to represent the California views. See also accord, Commiss'r of Int. Rev. v. Newcombe, 203 F.2d 128; Harrell v. Crow, 214 La. 543, 38 So.2d 226.

§ 192. Effect generally of death of spouse.

The death of one of the spouses necessarily not only terminates the marital relation but also dissolves the conjugal partnership existing between the spouses in acquests and gains during marriage. The very basis of the conjugal sharing of earnings and gains is "the fact that while the one spouse supplies work and labor the other supplies money or other property, the fact of their undivided habit of life ordained by both natural and divine law, the fact of the mutual love between husband and wife which should be encouraged, and other factors" such as "industry and common labor of each spouse" and the "burdens of partnership and community." All these factors cease to operate on dissolution of the marriage, and so it is natural that the law providing for the sharing of earnings and gains ceases to operate also.[50] This is recognized in our community property states.[51]

It is needless to add that the death of both spouses at the same time also terminates the conjugal partnership. The matter is mentioned only because of the presumption arising where both spouses die approximately at the same time and it was not known which died first. The presumption, in such case, was that the wife died first.[52] While this has been the presumption in some of our states, statutes in others establish a different rule.[53]

§ 193. Principles of the Spanish law — Testamentary disposition.

Under the Spanish law, both husband and wife were authorized to dispose of their respective properties by will, and each spouse could dispose by will of his or her share in the community property to the same extent as his or her separate property.[54]

Without going into an extensive discussion of the Spanish law of testamentary disposition and right of inheritance, it may be observed briefly that a spouse in disposing of his or her property by will had to institute his or her descendants as heirs, if having any, and could

---

[50] Matienzo, Gloss I, Nos. 6, 13, to Nov. Rec. Law 1, Book 10, Title 4.

[51] See cases collected, 25 Am. St. Rep. 227; 36 L.R.A. (N. S.) 1044. See also Jackson v. Griffin, 39 Ariz. 183, 4 P.2d 900; Clark v. Foster (Idaho), 391 P.2d 853; Succession of Butler (La.), 132 So.2d 85; In re Chavez, 34 N.M. 258, 280 P. 241, 69 A.L.R. 769; Waterman Lumber & Supply Co. v. Robbins (Tex.), 159 S. W. 360; Bortle v. Osborne, 155 Wash. 585, 285 P. 425; 67 A.L.R.

1152.

[52] Schmidt, Civil Law of Spain and Mexico, p. 260, citing Las Siete Partidas, Part. 7, Title 33, Law 12.

[53] See Cal. Prob. Code, § 296.4, that if there is no sufficient evidence of simultaneous death, halves of community property distributed as if each survived the other. In accord, Tex. Prob. Code, § 47.

[54] Asso and Mañuel, Institutes of Civil Law of Spain, Book II, Title III.

dispose of only one-fifth of the property to strangers or other persons. The other four-fifths had to be disposed of to such descendants but any one of them could be favored to the extent of giving him up to one-third of such four-fifths. In the absence of descendants, the spouse had to dispose of his or her property in favor of ascendants, if any, with the exception of one-third of the property which could be disposed of freely. In the absence of descendants or ascendants, the spouse might leave his or her property to strangers or relations not of the descending or ascending line.[55] And for certain of just causes, such as depraved conduct, unfilial conduct or the like, ascendants or descendants might be deprived of their heirship. The person to be deprived had to be clearly designated and the reason for the deprivation set forth.[56]

One spouse could devise or bequeath property to the other spouse, either from separate property or from the half-share in the community property, but subject to the limitations described in the preceding paragraph. That is, if the spouse disposing by will had descendants, only one-fifth of the disposing spouse's property could be left to the surviving spouse, or if having ascendants, then up to one-third. It has been said that in the absence of children, husband and wife could validly agree to inherit reciprocally the property of each,[57] but this obviously constitutes an incomplete exposition, for it is clear that there would have to be an absence of ascendants also.[58]

With respect to the community property, it will be recalled that the husband's power, during marriage, to alienate it resulted entirely from the administrative control imposed in him and that such power always had to be exercised with due respect and consideration for the fact of the wife's ownership of half of such property and never in a manner detrimental thereto. Similarly, this administrative right

---

[55] Asso and Mañuel, Institutes of Civil Law of Spain, Book II, Title III, Cap. 2, § 3; Matienzo, Gloss II to Nov. Rec. Law 8, Book 10, Title 4. See also Leyes de Toro, Law 6, and commentaries thereon of Llamas y Molina.

In the absence of lawful children or descendants, natural children might be favored to the exclusion of ascendants. Novísima Recopilación, Book 10, Title 21, Law 6.

In the civil law the word "descendants" included children and grandchildren, in fact all descendants in direct line.

We may here mention the *majoratus,* or in the Spanish, *mayorazgo,* which was certain property left upon

condition imposed that it pass perpetually and successively to the eldest son; in other words, an entailed estate. It was abolished in the year 1820, both in Spain and Mexico.

[56] Asso and Mañuel, Institutes of Civil Law of Spain, Book II, Title III, Cap. 3, § 1; Schmidt, Civil Law of Spain and Mexico, pp. 231, 232.

[57] Asso and Mañuel, Institutes of Civil Law of Spain, Book II, Title III, Cap. 2, § 3, citing Fuero Real, Book 3, Title 6, Law 9.

[58] See Novísima Recopilación, Book 10, Title 20, Law 1. See also Matienzo, Gloss II to Nov. Rec. Law 8, Book 10, Title 4.

of management and alienation during marriage included no right to dispose of the entire community property by will, for the entire community property did not belong to him so as to be disposable by him by will.[59] He could, then, dispose by will of only his own share of the common property,[60] for the wife's share already belonged to her.[61] To the extent, accordingly, that he could dispose of his property by will to his wife, any provision that he made in his will in her favor was necessarily a disposition of his own property.[62] Indeed, in order that there might be no confusion where the husband provided in his will a legacy for the wife, it was specifically provided by statute that such legacy was not comprised in her half of the community property, which she already owned, but was in addition thereto. The amount of any such legacy could not be set off against an equivalent part of her share of the community property.[63] It was superfluous for the law to mention a legacy of the wife to the husband, for since she did not have administration of the marital property, no confusion could arise from the case of a legacy by her to her husband.[64] Where the spouse attempted by will to leave community property to descendants or others, such a disposition was valid only as to the share of the testator. However, if it made no difference to the other spouse, and was not prejudicial, the latter might assent thereto, and accept reimbursement from other community property to the extent of half the value of the particular testamentary disposition.[65]

---

[59] See Azevedo, No. 15, to Nov. Rec. Law 5.

"The power of alienation which the laws concede to the husband only continues during the marriage. The husband is prohibited from disposing, by testament, of that portion of the ganancial property belonging to the wife." Febrero Reformado, Title 5, § xiii, No. 410, quoted in Thompson v. Cragg, 24 Tex. 582, 602.

[60] Subject, of course, to the restrictions upon him in favor of descendants and ascendants.

[61] See ante, Chap. VII, subd. A.

[62] "Therefore the husband cannot dispose by his will of the community property belonging to the wife, who rather enters by reason of her husband's death into the full administration of the half which belongs to her, without the necessity of reserving anything whatever in ownership or in usufruct for the children that she may have of another marriage that she may have previously contracted, and con-

sequently if the husband should leave her any legacy she will take it without deduction from her half." Novísimo Sala Mexicano, Sec. 2a, Title IV, No. 6.

[63] Novísima Recopilación, Book 10, Title 4, Law 8 (originally Law 16 of Toro). And see commentaries thereto, of Matienzo, Azevedo, Gutiérrez and Llamas y Molina.

"The reason for so deciding is because by operation of law the property is deemed to have been delivered (during marriage) to the wife, for otherwise she would not have the ownership and possession of that property. But because she is made the owner and possessor of that property — as I pointed out above in law 2 gloss 3 no. 2 et seq. and in gloss 4 — so there is no set-off." Matienzo, Gloss I, No. 3, to Nov. Rec. Law 8.

[64] Llamas y Molina, No. 81 to Nov. Rec. Law 8.

[65] See Gutiérrez, Quaestio CXXI, No. 6, to Nov. Rec. Law 5.

Advancements, see post, § 214.

§ 194.   — Obligation to reserve certain property for children.

Where either spouse by legacy left property to the other spouse, or for that matter by donation *inter vivos* or any other lucrative title gave property to the other spouse, there was a certain situation which might reduce the property right of the donee to a usufructuary right. If the donee remarried, and there were children of the donor-spouse living, it became the legal duty of the donee to reserve such property for those children, and the donee's right in the property became a right of usufruct only. But if there were no children of the donor-spouse, or if there were children but the donee-spouse remained unmarried, the latter retained ownership of the property and could dispose of it by will.[66] "Usufruct," in the civil law, it may be explained, is the right to enjoy a thing the property of which is vested in another, and to draw therefrom all the profit, advantage and utility which it may produce, provided it be without altering the substance of the thing itself.[67] The widow was, however, exempt from reserving this property for the children of the former marriage if the husband accompanied the property with permission to remarry without incurring such penalty, and the same result was accomplished by the consent of the children themselves.[68] It must be clearly understood, however, that the property which must be so reserved for the children was that acquired by the surviving spouse by lucrative title.[69] The survivor's own share of the community property, since it belonged to him or her absolutely, could be disposed of by him or her without any obligation to reserve it for the children.[70]

---

[66] Novísima Recopilación, Book 10, Title 4, Law 7; Llamas y Molina, commentaries to that law; Schmidt, Civil Law of Spain and Mexico, p. 257. See also Thompson v. Cragg, 24 Tex. 582, for an excellent discussion.

"The arras of the wife, or that property given to the woman by the man, in consideration of the marriage; the donations *propter nuptias,* or that property which either gave to the other, freely and without condition; the dower which the wife brought to the husband; and inheritances, under certain circumstances, by either the husband or wife, from the children of the marriage; constitute the property acquired by lucrative title, which was to be reserved for the children of the marriage, by and during which it was acquired." Thompson v. Cragg, 24 Tex. 582, 601.

[67] See Moore, Cyc. Law Dict. It has a similarity to the life estate of the common law.

[68] Llamas y Molina, No. 48, to Nov. Rec. Law 7, Book 10, Title 4.

[69] See Thompson v. Cragg, 24 Tex. 582, which contains an excellent discussion of the Spanish law. As to existence of this situation in Louisiana, see post, § 200.

[70] "Upon the dissolution of the marriage, the survivor may dispose of that part of the ganancial property which belongs to him or her, without being obliged, to reserve it for the children." Asso and Mañuel, Institutes of Civil Law of Spain, Book I, Title VII, Cap. 5, § 1, quoted in Thompson v. Cragg, 24 Tex. 582.

Through a most grievous and inexcusable error, the court in Panaud v. Jones, 1 Cal. 488, 515, construed the law to be that the survivor could dispose of the entire community property, rather than his or her own half. See criticism in Thompson v. Cragg, ante, also post, §§ 206–208.

§ 195.   — Intestate succession.

In the absence of testamentary disposition by a deceased spouse, his or her share of the community property, as well as his or her separate property, passed to his or her heirs according to the laws of succession or inheritance. These were, first, descendants. If there were no descendants, then ascendants. And if neither descendants nor ascendants, then collaterals.[71] In the case of the deceased spouse's share of the community property, such property passed to the heirs immediately without the necessity of any acceptance on their part. As we would say, title vested in them immediately. The property was at once theirs. They could, however, renounce their right thereto, if they so desired. If they did so they were under no liability for community debts; retention of the property, of course, rendered them liable for their share of community debts. No distinction existed in the case of the deceased spouse being the wife. Her equal share in the marital gains was immediately owned by her during marriage without the necessity of any formal acceptance by her, so that her share of the property passed to her heirs even though it had not been formally accepted by her.[72]

If there were no descendants, ascendants or collaterals, according to the law of the Fuero Juzgo and Partidas, husband and wife might succeed one another.[73] But according to the Nueva Recopilación and the Novísima Recopilación of later date, although containing no express repeal of these provisions, it was provided that in default of descendants, ascendants and collaterals the Crown succeeded to the property of an intestate.[74] That this later provision did not, however, abrogate or repeal the rights of husband and wife to succeed each other in the absence of descendants, ascendants and collaterals, provided for in the Fuero Juzgo and the Partidas, and thus with prior right to take before the Crown, was demonstrated by the jurist and commentator Llamas y Molina. That his demonstration was correct

---

[71] Asso and Mañuel, Institutes of Civil Law of Spain, Book II, Title IV, Cap. 3.

[72] Matienzo, Gloss IX, Nos. 2, 3, to Nov. Rec. Law 5; Gloss I, No. 8, to Nov. Rec. Law 9; Azevedo, No. 4, to Nov. Rec. Law 8; Gutiérrez, Quaestio CXXIII, No. 1, to Nov. Rec. Law 6.

In Louisiana, also, heirs of the deceased spouse become seised of the one-half share of their ancestor at the moment of his or her death. See Newman v. Cooper, 46 La. Ann. 1485, 16 So. 481.

Renunciation by wife, see post, § 218. Debts, see post, § 209 et seq.

[73] Las Siete Partidas, Part. 4, Title 11, Law 23; Part. 6, Title 13, Law 6. The latter law in prescribing that if there were no collateral relatives within the tenth degree, husband and wife inherited from each other, made only slight change from the previous law of the Fuero Juzgo, Book 4, Title 2, Law 11, that husband and wife succeeded each other mutually if there were no collateral relatives within the seventh degree. See Llamas y Molina, Nos. 41, 42, to Law 8 of Toro.

[74] Novísima Recopilación, Book 10, Title 22, Law 1 (Nueva Recopilación, Book 5, Title 8, Law 12).

457

is substantiated by an enactment of 1835 confirming his interpretation of the law.[75]

§ 196.   — Usufructuary and other rights of surviving spouse.

In the case where the intestate spouse was the husband, with children surviving, the foregoing would seem to leave the wife without any provision so that her situation might appear to have been unfortunate in the event the amount of community property was not great. However, it was provided by law that she had a usufructuary right in the property inherited by the children, a usufructuary right that she retained until she died or remarried.[76] Indeed, if either of the spouses died, the survivor acquired a usufruct in the inheritance of the children.[77] In addition, whether or not the husband died leaving children, if the wife was poor and did not possess sufficient means to live decently, in the comfort to which she had been accustomed, she was entitled to one-fourth of the husband's estate, not to exceed, however, a specified value. However, if the husband had left her sufficient property to live decently, she was not entitled to require anything more, even though such property was not equivalent to a fourth part of the estate.[78] Incidentally, this latter rule of law was said by some to extend in like case to the husband.[79] The wife lost this fourth part when she led a wanton or scandalous life or when she remarried.[80] The widow was entitled to support from the property of her husband until such time as her dowry was returned to her, according to Matienzo, so long as she continued to live chastely and so long as she herself was not the cause of the failure to repay the dowry. But the same author notes that other writers limited the widow's rights to support from the husband's property to one year from the time of his death.[81]

§ 197.   American laws — Statutory confusion.

In all of our American community property states, statutes have been enacted providing for the spouses' right or lack of right of testa-

---

[75] Llamas y Molina, Nos. 44, 45, to Law 8 of Toro, and note by his annotator, Caravantes, with reference to the Law of May 16, 1835.

Schmidt, in his Civil Law of Spain and Mexico, takes at their face value these latter enactments, and seems unaware of the continued right of husband and wife to succeed each other in the absence of descendants, ascendants and collaterals.

[76] Fuero Juzgo, Book 4, Title 2, Law 14; Llamas y Molina, No. 19 to Nov. Rec. Law 7, Book 10, Title 4.

[77] Fuero Juzgo, Book 4, Title 2, Law 13; Llamas y Molina, No. 20 to Nov. Rec. Law 7.

[78] Las Siete Partidas, Part. 6, Title 13, Law 7.

[79] Gregorio López, Gloss 1, to Las Siete Partidas, Part. 6, Title 13, Law 7.

[80] Fuero Juzgo, Book 4, Title 2, Law 15.

Loss of share of community property if leading wanton or scandalous life during widowhood, see ante, § 189.

[81] Matienzo, Gloss I, No. 10, to Nov. Rec. Law 1, Book 10, Title 4.

mentary disposition of their respective shares of the community property, and providing for succession or inheritance of such shares where no testamentary disposition is made or where it cannot be made, as the case may be.[82] The several statutes vary in their provisions to such an extent that each one is more or less *sui generis*.[83] Only in the most general way may any grouping or classification be attempted.

§ 198.　— Testamentary disposition.

In the majority of the community property states, each spouse has the right to dispose by will of his or her share of the community property. This is true in Arizona,[84] California,[85] Idaho,[86] Louisiana,[87] Nevada,[88] Texas,[89] and Washington.[90] In all of these states, except Idaho and Louisiana, this power of testamentary disposition appears to be an absolute one. But in those two states the situation is somewhat analogous to that of the Spanish law in limiting the extent to which the share of the community property may be left by will. In Idaho, the testamentary disposition can be in favor only of the surviving spouse, the children, grandchildren or parents of either spouse, or one or more of such persons, but provided that no more than one-half of the decedent's share of the community property may be left to parents unless limited to an estate for life or less, and provided that any part of the decedent's share in excess of the unincumbered appraised value of $25,000 may be disposed of as the testator sees fit.[91] And in Louisiana, the disposable portion to others cannot exceed

[82] Statutory prohibitions against agreements between spouses changing order of succession, etc., see ante, § 137.

[83] See Ariz. Rev. Stat. 1956, § 14-203; Cal. Prob. Code, § 201; Idaho Code 1948, § 14-113; La. Civ. Code 1932, art. 915; Nev. Rev. Stat. 1956, §§ 123.250, 123.260, 134.010, 134.020; N.M. Stat. 1953, §§ 29-1-8, 29-1-9; Texas Prob. Code 1955, §§ 45, 57, 58; Wash. Rev. Code 1961, § 11.04.015.

Discussion of the statutes of some of the states will be found in California Jurisprudence, "Community Property"; Daggett, Community Property Law of Louisiana; Oakes, Speer's Marital Rights in Texas, 4th Ed.; Brockelbank, Community Property Law of Idaho.

[84] Ariz. Rev. St. 1956, § 14-203.

If the homestead has been selected, during marriage, from the community property, upon the death of either spouse, the homestead vests absolutely in the survivor. Ariz. Rev. St. 1956, § 14-518.

[85] Cal. Prob. Code, §§ 21, 201.

Homestead selected from community property or quasi-community property goes to survivor. Cal. Prob. Code, § 663.

Community property acquired prior to 1923 cannot be willed by wife nor can she will her share of the income derived from such property since it has the same nature as the property itself. Boyd v. Oser, 23 Cal. 2d 613, 145 P.2d 312.

Quasi-community property, see ante, § 68.3.

[86] Ida. Code 1948, § 14-113.

[87] La. Civ. Code, arts. 1470, 1493 et seq.

[88] Nev. Laws 1957, ch. 264, § 1.

[89] Tex. Prob. Code, §§ 57, 58.

[90] Wash. Rev. Code 1961, § 11.04.-.015

[91] Ida. Code 1948, § 14-113.

two-thirds of the disposer's property, if he leaves a legitimate child, one-half if he leaves two children, and one-third if he leaves three or more children; and cannot exceed two-thirds if he leaves no children but leaves a parent or parents.[92]

In New Mexico the peculiar situation exists that the husband is empowered to dispose by will of his share of the community property, but the wife has no such right, her share going to the surviving husband. Certain exceptions exist, however, so far as the wife is concerned, in described cases of separation, which permit of testamentary disposition of the wife of her share of the community property.[93]

The correct view, following the principle established in Law 16 of Toro,[94] has been recognized in many of our cases that where the husband bequeaths or devises anything to his wife, such bequest or device is necessarily made from his own property, since he cannot devise or bequeath to her that which she already owns, and that, accordingly, she takes such bequest or devise in addition to her share of the community property. Consideration of this matter has usually arisen in connection with the question whether the wife must elect between taking under her husband's will or taking her share of the community property, and is discussed in a subsequent section relating to that point.[95]

§ 199.   — Intestate succession.

Whatever uniformity in a general way exists among the majority of states in allowing the spouses the testamentary right of disposition, such uniformity almost entirely disappears where the statutes provide for descent of the deceased spouse's share of the community property in the absence of testamentary disposition. In some of the states, in the absence of such testamentary disposition, the deceased spouse's share of the community property goes to the surviving spouse;[96] in

---

[92] La. Civ. Code, arts. 1493, 1494.

See Dainow, The Early Sources of Forced Heirship: Its History in Texas and Louisiana, 4 La. L. Rev. 42. Note that formerly, in Texas, a parent was forbidden to leave more than one-fourth of his estate to others than his children. See Paschal v. Acklin, 27 Tex. 173. See also Succession of Gurganus, 206 La. 1012, 20 So.2d 296, where testatrix had executed her will before marriage and died leaving neither descendants nor parents, it was held that it disposed only of property owned by her at the time of its execution and that the surviving husband inherited her share of the community property.

[93] N.M. St. 1953, §§ 29-1-8, 29-1-9.

This does not give husband greater interest in the community property. Dillard v. Tax Commission, 53 N.M. 12, 201 P.2d 345.

Somewhat similar provisions were once in force in California and Nevada. See Cal. Stats. 1961, ch. 323, p. 310; Nev. Rev. St. 1956, §§ 123.250, 123.260.

[94] See ante, § 193.

[95] See post, § 217, as to election by wife.

[96] Cal. Prob. Code, § 201; Ida. Code 1948, § 14-113.

Marriage as invalidating wife's prenuptial will, allowing husband to take wife's share of community property as if she had died intestate, see Estate of Piatt, 81 Cal. App. 2d 348, 183 P.2d 919.

others it goes to the descendants or issue of the deceased spouse and in the absence of such descendants or issue then to the surviving spouse,[97] and again provision may be made for parents in the absence of descendants,[98] and so on, as the peculiarities of local statutes provide.[99]

§ 200.   — Reservation of certain property for children.

The statutes of some of the states make provision for the descent of the share of the community property of a predeceased spouse which has come into the ownership and possession of the surviving spouse who then dies himself or herself. The purpose of these statutes seems to be to preserve such property for the descendants of the first spouse, or in absence of such descendants then for certain ascendants or collateral relatives of the first spouse or of both spouses, thus virtually giving the surviving spouse only the usufruct in such property, at least if he or she dies intestate.[1] They do not as a rule seem to deprive the surviving spouse of the power to dispose by will of that share of the

---

[97] Ariz. Rev. St. 1956, § 14-203; Wash. Rev. Code 1961, § 11.04.015.

In Texas, if there be no descendants the surviving spouse takes, but if there are descendants the surviving spouse takes only the one-half that he or she already owned and the descendants the other half. Tex. Prob. Code, § 45.

To what extent adopted children are included among such terms as "children" or "descendants" must depend upon the local statutes. Examination of local statutes must also be made for ascertainment of the rights of posthumous children.

Pretermitted heirs in California, need for clarification as to their rights in community property, see article by Sweet, 13 Stanf. L. Rev. 801; application of New Mexico statutes to pretermitted children, see Dunham v. Stitzberg, 53 N.M. 81, 201 P.2d 1000.

Escheat to state, see Estate of Roberts, 85 Cal. App. 2d 60, 194 P.2d 28.

[98] La. Civ. Code, art. 915, provides that, in absence of will, descendants take; in the absence of descendants but not of parent or parents of decedent, half shall go to such parent or parents and half to the surviving spouse; in the absence of descendants and parent or parents, all of the decedent's share goes to the surviving spouse.

See Oppenheim, Inheritance of Surviving Spouse — Article 915, Louisiana Civil Code 1870, 21 Tulane L. Rev. 54.

[99] See, e.g., N.M. St. 1953, §§ 29-1-8, 29-1-9, where, absent a will by husband, one-fourth goes to surviving wife, and rest to children of decedent.

[1] See Cal. Prob. Code, §§ 228, 229; Ida. Code 1948, § 14-103(8).

As to right of adopted child to succeed under such a statute, see Estate of Mercer, 205 Cal. 506, 271 P. 1067.

Formerly in Louisiana, however, where a surviving spouse had received property by gift or by will from the deceased spouse, there being children of that marriage, the surviving spouse lost all right to dispose of such property upon remarrying. Upon such remarriage, the property became that of the children of the preceding marriage and the surviving spouse who did so remarry had only the usufruct. La. Civ. Code, art. 1753 (now repealed); Zeigler v. His Creditors, 49 La. Ann. 144, 21 So. 666. The result was the spouse held such property by defeasible title, and any alienation he or she made would seem to have been subject to be defeated upon the spouse's remarrying. Certainly the spouse had to account to the children for such property. See Zeigler v. His Creditors, ante.

community property.[2] The effect of the statutes has been applied to community property of the predeceased spouse whether coming to the surviving spouse by gift, devise, bequest or descent.[3]

The provisions of these statutes are somewhat different in scope than the Spanish laws. The latter related to any property of the donor spouse, whether that spouse's separate property or share of the community property. Likewise, they related to donations *inter vivos* as well as donations by testamentary disposition. They had, however, no relation to intestate succession by the surviving spouse, for there was no intestate succession by such spouse where there were descendants.[4] But despite these differences, it is evident that the laws of both countries have a common basis.

As to what rights or interests are reserved to the children in homestead property should be determined by reference to local statutes.

§ 201.   — Usufructuary and other rights of surviving spouse.

In Louisiana, where the predeceased husband or wife leaves issue of the marriage with the survivor and has not disposed by will of his or her share of the community property, the survivor holds in "usufruct," during his or her natural life, so much of the share of the decedent in the community property as may be inherited by such issue, except that the usufruct ceases upon the survivor entering into a second marriage.[5] The purpose of this law, unless the deceased spouse has disposed by will, is to preserve intact the community property to be enjoyed by the surviving spouse during his or her natural life, or in the case of the wife, at least during her widowhood. If there are children of the marriage, they inherit, of course, the share of the deceased spouse in the community property, but they inherit it subject to the usufructuary rights of the surviving spouse.[6] It appears, however, that if the spouse leaves his or her share of the community

---

[2] Estate of McArthur, 210 Cal. 439, 292 P. 469, 72 A.L.R. 1318; In re Morrow's Will, 41 N.M. 723, 73 P.2d 1360.

[3] See Estate of Rattray, 13 Cal. 2d 702, 91 P.2d 1042.

A review of the California cases decided under Cal. Probate Code, §§ 228 and 229, as well as an interpretation of those code sections, is undertaken in Estate of Taitmeyer, 60 Cal. App. 2d 699, 141 P.2d 504; Estate of Nielsen, 65 Cal. App. 2d 60, 149 P.2d 737, which held that when the decedent died intestate, without issue or spouse, property which had come to such decedent as surviving joint tenant with her previously deceased spouse, and which had originally been acquired with community funds, should go wholly and entirely to the issue of the predeceased spouse, rather than to the decedent's next of kin. And see Estate of Allie, 50 Cal. 2d 794, 329 P.2d 903, noted 32 So. Cal. L. Rev. 199.

[4] See ante, § 194.

[5] La. Civ. Code, art. 916. And see Oppenheim, 18 Tulane L. Rev. 181.

[6] See Succession of Teller, 49 La. Ann. 282, 21 So. 265; Succession of Moore, 40 La. Ann. 531, 4 So. 460.

Necessity of usufructuary furnishing security in favor of heirs, see Waring v. Zunts, 16 La. Ann. 49.

property by will to his or her issue, the surviving spouse has no usufructuary right in the property, although the will leaves it to the very ones who would have gotten the property if there had been no testamentary disposition.[7] The husband may provide, however, in a will disposing of his share of the community property to his children, that the wife shall have the usufruct of such property, and he may provide that she shall not be deprived of it even though she marries again.[8]

Likewise in Louisiana, as under the Spanish law, if the wife has brought no dowry to the marriage or only an inconsiderable one, and if the surviving spouse is left in necessitous circumstances by the other's death, the survivor may take as a marital portion one-fourth of the succession in full property if there are no children, and one-fourth in usufruct if there are three or a lesser number of children, or if there are more than three children then a child's share in usufruct.[9] This is not a right of inheritance but a personal right in the nature of a charity or bounty in cases of need.[10]

In the community property states no estate is allowed the husband as tenant by curtesy upon the death of the wife, nor is any estate in dower allotted to the wife upon the death of the husband. This is frequently provided by statute, but is true even in the absence of statute because such common law marital property rights are not consistent with a system of marital community of property.[11] Numerous and varied statutory provisions do exist as to family allowances and the like; these are referred to briefly in a subsequent section.[12]

§ 201.1. — Conflict of laws.

We have already seen, under principles of private international law or conflict of laws, that when property is removed from one jurisdiction to another it retains the same character or nature that it had before its removal, and that this is true even where it is, after its removal, converted to some other form. Thus, property which has acquired the character or nature of separate or community property at the time of its acquisition, according to the law governing at that

[7] Succession of Schiller, 33 La. Ann. 1.

[8] See Succession of Carbajal, 154 La. 1060, 98 So. 666, 30 A. L. R. 1231; Succession of Lynch (La. App.), 145 So. 42.

[9] La. Civ. Code, art. 2382. See Facussé, The Marital Portion in Louisiana, 2 Loyola L. Rev. 58; Jackson, The Marital Fourth and the Widow's Homestead, 18 Tulane L. Rev. 290.

[10] Succession of Justus, 44 La. Ann. 721, 11 So. 95.

For capable and thorough discussion of this marital portion in Louisiana, and criticism of doctrinal departures by the Louisiana courts, see Facussé, Marital Portion in Louisiana, 2 Loyola Law Rev. 58.

[11] See Cal. Civ. Code, § 5129; Idaho Code 1948, § 32-914; Nev. Rev. St. 1956, § 123.020; N.M. St. 1953, § 29-1-23; Wash. Rev. Code 1961, § 11.04.060.

Neither husband nor wife has any interest in the property of the other. Cal. Civ. Code, § 5102.

[12] See post, § 215.

time, still retains its same character or nature as separate or community property when removed to another jurisdiction.[13] But suppose the owner of this property — or one of the owners, if it is community property — thereafter dies? What laws govern the succession to or distribution of the property? The British and American courts are usually agreed and uniform in applying the principles that in the case of realty, the law of its *situs* governs as to descent, and that in the case of personalty the law of the domicile of the owner governs as to its succession. This in no way denies the character or nature of the property or the ownership therein on the part of the deceased owner, or the ownership of anyone else in the property.

If a husband, in the course of his management of community property, transferred community funds from the community property state in which he and his wife were domiciled and invested the funds in realty in a noncommunity property state, taking title in his name, and then died, the courts of the latter state, while having no identically equivalent system to that of community of property, would recognize that the deceased husband had been the owner of only half of the realty. But as to that half, the law of the noncommunity property state which was the *situs* of the realty would be applied to determine how that half descended or was to be distributed. Similarly, if spouses changed their domicile from a community property·state to a noncommunity property state, removing community personalty with them, and retaining it in the latter state in the form of personalty, and one of the spouses died, the courts of the latter state would recognize that the deceased spouse had been the owner of only half of the personalty in question, but as to that half the laws of that state would govern the succession or distribution thereof.[14] The converse will, of course, be true in the case of removal of property from a noncommunity property state to a community property state.[15] In the latter case, for example, statutes enacted pursuant to principles of community of property may actually control descent of property fixed in its nature as separate property by the law of a noncommunity property state, such as those statutes relating to the descent of property of a spouse dying intestate leaving property received by gift or will from that spouse's predeceased spouse.[16]

[13] See ante, Chap. VI, subd. D.

[14] See Beaudoin v. Trudel, [1937] 1 Dom. Law Rep. 216, wherein the Ontario Court of Appeal, recognized that personalty owned by husband and wife domiciled in Ontario after removal from Quebec was owned equally by both spouses, so that half belonged to the surviving husband, and then held that the law of Ontario governed succession to the deceased wife's share of such personalty and by that law the husband was entitled to half of his deceased wife's share. See also Marsh, Marital Property and Conflict of Laws, p. 244.

[15] See Brookman v. Durkee, 46 Wash. 578, 90 P. 914, 123 Am. St. Rep. 944, 12 L. R. A. (N. S.) 921; Rustad v. Rustad (Wash.), 377 P.2d 414. See also Marsh, Marital Property and Conflict of Laws, p. 244.

[16] See ante, § 200; also Cal. Probate Code, §§ 201.5, 228, 229; Estate of Perkins, 21 Cal. 2d 561, 134 P.2d 231.

In other words, it is not primarily the law of the state which first fixed the nature of property as separate or community which governs its descent or succession, but the law of the state of the *situs* of realty and the law of the state of the domicile of the owner of personalty. It must be recognized, however, that it is quite possible that personalty may actually be at another place than the domicile of the owner, and statutes at the place where the personalty actually is may provide that it is to be subject to the law of actual location rather than of the owner's domicile. This is a statutory departure from the maxim *"Mobilia personam sequuntur"* so long followed.[17]

§ 202.   Surviving spouse's own share of community property — Basic principles.

Under the Spanish law, the ownership and possession of half of the community property continued in the surviving spouse just as it had during marriage, whether the surviving spouse was husband or wife. The only distinction between husband and wife related to the matter of management of the common property. If the surviving spouse was the husband, he continued in the exercise of management of his share of the community property just as he had had the management of the entire community property during the marriage. Where the wife was the surviving spouse, she acquired upon the dissolution of the marriage, the management of her share of the community property, a managerial right which she had not previously enjoyed.[18] But as to her share of the community property she received that as her own and not as an heir.[19] The surviving spouse, whether husband or wife, had complete power freely to dispose of his or her share of the community property.[20]

[17] In the case of personalty, it may actually be at a place other than that of the domicile of the owner, and even if the state where the personalty actually is recognizes the law of the owner's domicile as governing succession, etc., it may still make such property available to the claims of local creditors of the decedent before remitting the residue to the domiciliary administrator. This, however, is an aspect of the general law of administration of decedents' estates, and with which we are not immediately concerned.

[18] "Therefore the husband cannot dispose by his will of the community property belonging to the wife, who rather enters by reason of her husband's death into the full administration of the half which belongs to

her. . . ." Novísimo Sala Mexicano, Sec. 2a, Title IV, No. 6.

[19] "Moreover a wife receives a moiety of the profits as her own by virtue of our law and similar enactments, and as to this she is not called an heir." Azevedo, No. 8, to Nov. Rec. Law 8, Book 10, Title 4.

[20] "On the death of one of the spouses, the survivor can freely dispose of his or her share of the profits acquired during marriage, even if he or she marries a second time, and is not bound to keep such profits or the usufruct of them for the children of the marriage in which the profits were acquired." Azevedo, Summary to Nov. Rec. Law 6. To same effect, Escriche, Diccionario, "Bienes Gananciales."

"The Commentary of Llamas on this 15th law of Toro (i.e., Llamas y

We have already seen that under the Spanish law of community property the wife's ownership and possession of property acquired during marriage was equal to and complete as the ownership and possession of the husband. And that, furthermore, she acquired her ownership and possession during marriage automatically *ipso jure* without delivery.[21] The husband's death, therefore, added nothing to her ownership which was already full and complete as to her share of the community property. It merely had the effect of allowing her to enter into the management of the share which belonged to her. As to her possession, since, under the civil law, possession whether transferred actually or constructively was as real and true in one case as in the other, the husband's death added nothing to her possession which was already a real and true possession. Accordingly she was at once entitled to all possessory remedies in respect to her half of the community property to acquire, to retain and to recover possession, without the necessity of any formal act to place her in possession, control and management thereof.[22] The wife "can in all cases take action, without an assignment from the heirs, on behalf of her moiety against her husband's debtors," for the wife has had "transferred to her ownership and possession of goods which come as profit as soon as her husband acquires the profit, as we have seen under this heading. And therefore since she has ownership and possession, she can sue as owner, and no assignment is necessary."[23] She could sue, without more ado, in respect to her half share in any contracts or transactions entered into by the husband, even though they were entered into or made by the husband in his name alone. "Further in order to enforce a contract it suffices that the person who seeks enforcement should be by implication included in the deed. . . . By our laws a husband who purchases and makes profit acquires for himself and his wife." The wife as partner, owning an equal share in partnership assets, could sue without the necessity of any assignment to her by the husband's heirs, and that rule applied to debts and incorporated rights as well as to other property.[24]

Molina, Commentaries to Nov. Rec. Law 7), in which he quotes the opinions and expressions of many other commentators, shows in the clearest manner possible, the reasons and principles in which the 14th law of Toro had its origin; and the substance of the whole is, that inasmuch as the community or ganancial property is acquired by onerous title, as distinguished from lucrative title, the surviving husband or wife shall have the power freely to dispose of their portion of such ganancial property, without being under any obligation to reserve it for the children of the marriage during which it was acquired, . . ." Thompson v. Cragg, 24 Tex. 582.

[21] See ante, § 97 et seq.

[22] Matienzo, Gloss III, Nos. 20–25, to Nov. Rec. Law 1. See also Febrero, Librería de Escribanos, Cinco Juicios I, Book I, Cap. IV, § 1, No. 32.
Possession by heirs of deceased spouse of other half of community property, see post, § 206.

[23] Azevedo, No. 19 to Nov. Rec. Law 1.

[24] Azevedo, Nos. 19–22 to Nov. Rec. Law 1.
Gutiérrez presents the view that if

§ 203.— American recognition.

Since it is as well recognized now in our community property states, as it was in Spain, that the wife's ownership of half the community property is a present, equal and existing interest during the marriage,[25] it is equally well recognized that upon the death of the husband the wife does not take her half of the community property by inheritance, since she already owns it.[26] Such statutory provisions as those that upon the death of the husband one-half of the community property "goes" to or "vests" in the wife, cannot mean that the ownership thereof "goes" to or "vests" in the wife, for the wife already had such ownership from the moment of acquisition of the community property during the marriage. What does "go" to or "vest" in the wife is that which she did not have before, the managerial control of her one-half of the community property which prior to his death was in the husband's hands, and represents merely a managerial matter.[27] Apparently in an effort to distinguish the fact that the wife does not take by inheritance, some of the courts have declared that she "takes by survivorship."[28] This is a very questionable description for it might be inferred therefrom that it meant that her ownership is created by her survival of her husband, which is not at all the case. The only thing that she "takes by survivorship" is the management

an obligation had been made only in the name of and inured only in favor of the husband, though the benefit might be common to man and wife, the wife could not proceed against the debtors or enforce execution against them until probate administration surrendered the right into her hands to proceed on behalf of her share. Gutiérrez, Quaestio CXVIII, Nos. 15–17, to Nov. Rec. Law 1. Matienzo, Azevedo and others did not make that distinction.

[25] See ante, § 105 et seq.

[26] See cases cited post, the following notes.

That she does not take it by inheritance so as to be subject to state inheritance or succession tax thereon, see post, § 238.

In Arizona, this is well recognized. See Keddie, Community Property Law in Arizona, § 22, despite the wording of the applicable statute, as remarked by Smith and Tormey, Summary of Arizona Community Property Law, § 37.

In California, probably the wife's share of any community property acquired prior to 1927 would be said, on the husband's death, to go to her by inheritance or succession, pursuant to the view prior to 1927 that the wife had only the expectant interest of an heir in the community property. See ante, § 107.

[27] Quoted with approval, In re Condos' Estate, 70 Nev. 271, 266 P.2d 404. Accord, see In re Knight's Estate (Wash.), 199 P.2d 89; Com'r of Int. Rev. v. Chase Manhattan Bank, 259 F.2d 231.

[28] In Idaho, the statute recognizing the husband and wife as equal partners in the community estate and authorizing each to dispose of his or her half by will "clearly and unmistakably provides that the surviving spouse takes his or her half of the community property, not by succession, descent or inheritance, but as survivor of the marital community or partnership." Kohny v. Dunbar, 21 Idaho 258, 121 P. 544, Ann. Cas. 1913D 492, 39 L. R. A. (N. S.) 1107. See also Davenport v. Simons, 68 Ida. 21, 189 P.2d 90.

of her half of the community property which the husband formerly exercised. Her ownership of half of the community property was already a full and complete ownership during the marriage, so full and complete that nothing can be added thereto by the husband's death except that she then acquires the right to exercise management of her share of such property. Certainly she does not by "survivorship" acquire ownership of that which was already fully owned.[29] In succinct language: "No new right or interest is generated in the wife by the death of her husband; his death merely affords the occasion for the termination of the husband's interest in the community estate."[30] Undoubtedly, such terminology as "taking by survivorship" results from the mistake of applying to the explanation of community property law the common law terms used in relation to estates by entireties and joint estates.

---

[29] In In re Williams' Estate, 40 Nev. 241, 161 P. 741, L. R. A. 1917 C 602, under a statute providing that upon death of the husband "one half of the community property goes to the surviving wife, and the other half is subject to the testamentary disposition of the husband," the court concluded that the framers of the state constitution and the legislature, in establishing the community system and in promulgating the laws defining the spouses' rights as to such property, intended that the wife should have a present interest during the marriage of which she was at all times possessed and hence that "the community property goes to her, not by succession or inheritance, but rather by a right vested in her at all times during marriage" and that her interest was not subject to the state inheritance tax. (Incidentally, there is at the present writing no state inheritance tax in Nevada.)

"It is undisputed that all of the estate possessed by the testator was community property. As matter of law, the wife was the equal owner in her own right of one-half of that estate. To be sure, their estates existed in common, and during the marriage the common estate was indissoluble, but nevertheless her right, subject to certain statutory control, was the equal of the husband's. Upon the husband's death, the community estate passes, one-half to the widow and one-half

to the children (where there are children). But, while this provision of the law is found in our statutes of descent and distribution, nevertheless the wife's taking her one-half of the community is not the taking by an heir. She does not inherit such one-half, but she takes it as owner in her own separate right after the dissolution of the marriage. King v. Morris (Tex. Com. App.), 1 S. W. 2d 605. So that it is plain, if there had been no will, the surviving widow would not have been taxable for the one-half of the community which she would have taken, because the same would not have passed 'by the laws of descent or distribution.'" Jones v. State (Tex. Com. App.), 5 S. W. 2d 973.

"The old saying is not true that community is a partnership which begins only at its end. Upon the dissolution of the community by death, the wife does not inherit her share of the common property, but with the death of the husband the management and control of the statutory agent or trustee ceases. The wife acquires not her share for that was already hers, but in addition to her share she acquires the right of management, control, and disposition of that share." La Tourette v. La Tourette, 15 Ariz. 200, 137 P. 426, Ann. Cas. 1915 B 70.

Wife's ownership, see ante, Chap. VII, A.

[30] In re Coffey's Estate, 195 Wash. 379, 81 P.2d 283.

§ 204.   Relation between survivor and heirs prior to partition.

The surviving spouse and the heirs of the deceased spouse who succeeded to the latter's share of the community property did not — in the view of the Spanish law — become partners merely because they shared the ownership of the property which was formerly the common property of the two spouses. Although they had to see that any conjugal undertakings that were in course of transaction were properly completed, they were not bound to start new undertakings. They could, of course, agree among themselves to keep the property together and continue its management and operation in partnership; in fact, a partnership was to be presumed between them if they did so continue. But this was an entirely new partnership.[31] Or in case the heirs of the deceased spouse were minor children of the marriage, the surviving spouse might be impelled to keep the community property intact and manage it for the mutual benefit until such time as the children became entitled to receive or demand partition; indeed, there was a usufructuary right on the part of the surviving spouse in the children's share of the community property received from the deceased spouse.[32] But this did not constitute a partnership, in the absence of legal capacity of the minor children to enter into a contract of partnership, although it would be the duty of the surviving spouse to guard their interests and see that they obtained their share of the profits. Upon the minor children reaching majority they might consent to a continuation of the existing arrangement, which would then result in a partnership, or they might demand partition.[33] Division or partition of the property might be effected as soon as it was feasible, pursuant

---

[31] See Matienzo, Gloss 1, Nos. 9–40, to Nov. Rec. Law 1; Gutiérrez, Quaestio CXXX to Nov. Rec. Law 9.

"Therefore it appears more correct to say in this case the legal partnership does not continue, but that another new one is contracted between the surviving spouse and the heirs of the other." Novísimo Sala Mexicano, Sec. 2a, Title IV, No. 3.

"But this sharing of properties ceases in the following cases: . . . When either of the spouses dies, as is clear; because although the common properties remain undivided in the possession of the survivor, the partnership cannot be understood as continued with the heirs of the deceased spouse, but rather that a new one is tacitly contracted according to the general rules." Escriche, Diccionario, "Bienes Gananciales."

[32] See ante, § 196.

[33] In Puerto Rico, this would constitute a "comunidad," an association of co-owners carrying on a joint enterprise for profit. See Benitez v. Bank of Nova Scotia, 110 F.2d 169. And Schmidt, in his Civil Law of Spain and Mexico, p. 15, points out that the dissolution by death took effect from the moment of its occurrence although the heirs of the deceased spouse continued to live with the survivor; and though in such a case the community ceased to exist, a new one might be created between such heirs and the survivor, if they continued to keep their property in common; in such event gains and losses were apportioned among them, in proportion to the share of each, according to the principles governing ordinary partnerships.

Continuation of decedent's business by executor or administrator upon probate court's authorization, see Cal. Probate Code, § 572.

to the demands of those entitled thereto.[34] Any profits accumulating from the property during the period before division was made were shared equally by the surviving spouse and the heirs of the deceased spouse,[35] for even though the surviving spouse and the heirs did not occupy the status of copartners, in the absence of express or implied agreement, they did have the duty of carrying on and completing any current or unfinished transactions or businesses of the conjugal partnership, and the profits resulting therefrom were naturally divisible between them.[36] So far as concerned the sharing of the burdens and profits during the period before partition, it was immaterial whether the parties concerned continued the community property intact under a partnership arrangement of their own or whether they merely continued it intact for the period necessary to complete any unfinished business and pay off community debts. Thus, whether it was the local custom in any particular place to continue the community after the death of one spouse is not of importance in regard to these matters.[37]

This sharing of the ownership of the property in equal parts by the surviving spouse and the heirs of the deceased spouse until the division of the property between them has been described by some of our courts as a tenancy in common.[38] Apparently many of our courts do not feel sure of themselves or particularly happy until they have described in common law terms the various aspects of the community property system. The Louisiana court has spoken of the community as having a fictitious existence, after the death of one spouse, for the purpose of liquidation and settlement of community debts; and that in the absence of community debts the respective interests of the survivor and the heirs attach at once and the property is held in joint

---

Where husband has been a partner in a business partnership and he or his wife die, see discussion by Mullin, in Los Angeles Bar Bulletin, Aug. 1947; also Reprint No. 20, State Bar of California.

[34] Division, see post, § 205 et seq.

[35] "But what if, on the dissolution of the marriage by the death of the wife, the surviving husband retains all the property in common and then makes a considerable profit therefrom? If subsequently the emancipated sons apply for a division of the property, will there be assigned to the share of the wife and her heirs a moiety of the profits so acquired after the dissolution of the marriage by her death? We must answer this in the affirmative. . . ." Azevedo, No. 15, to Nov. Rec. Law 1, citing numerous authorities.

[36] Various illustrations, see Matienzo, Nos. 20–23, to Nov. Rec. Law 1. Incidentally, Matienzo's language in No. 13 must be read in the light of his entire discussion and is construable as meaning that division of profits after dissolution of the marriage is not on a basis of a partnership.

[37] See Pizerot v. Meuillon's Heirs, 3 Mart. O. S. (La.) 97, discussing on authority of Febrero the continuation of the community according to local custom.

[38] Surviving spouse termed tenant in common with heirs of deceased spouse, see Ewald v. Hufton, 31 Idaho 373, 173 P. 247; Heller v. Heller (Tex. Civ. App.), 269 S. W. 771; Lawson v. Ridgeway, 72 Ariz. 253, 233 P.2d 459.

ownership, until, of course, partition is accomplished.[39] But certainly there is no partnership between the surviving spouse and the heirs of the deceased spouse, in the absence of any express or tacit agreement to that effect.[40]

The right to partition should be enforceable in favor of anyone entitled thereto, that is, either in favor of the surviving spouse or any or all of the heirs of the deceased spouse. The right, however, is to a partition of the entire community property, not merely to some specific part of the entire community property. And, naturally, the right to have the partition is subject to the payment of the community debts.[41] Further partition may be necessary among the heirs of the share of the community property passing to them, but with this we are not here concerned. Nor is it intended to embark upon any discussion of rights in homestead property. It is recommended that the statutes as to homesteads be carefully examined, since the subject is entirely statutory and is frequently of some complexity.

§ 205. Probate administration or settlement of community estate — As to necessity and nature.

The probate administration or settlement of the estates of decedents under the Spanish law, as with us, was statutory.[42] Where a

[39] See Succession of Dumestre, 42 La. Ann 411, 7 So. 624; Newman v. Cooper, 46 La. Ann. 1485, 16 So. 481; Washington v. Palmer (La.), 28 So. 2d 509; McCullough v. U.S., 134 F. Supp. 173.

Minor children and surviving father owning community property in common, father's right of management, adjudication to him and liability to accounting, see Lasseigne v. Lasseigne, 205 La. 455, 17 So.2d 625.

[40] See Monroe Grocery Co. v. T. L. & M. Davis, 165 La. 1027, 116 So. 546.

The California court, in Johnston v. San Francisco Sav. Union, 75 Cal. 134, 16 P. 753, 7 Am. St. Rep. 129, seemed to think that under the Spanish law, during the period before division, a deceased wife's interest had not yet vested in her descendants, that the community continued, and that their interest did not vest in them until the division; it declared that such doctrine "did not obtain a foothold under our law. Under the act of 1850 the wife's interest vested in her

descendants." But it is patent from the Spanish authorities that not only did the wife's interest descend immediately to her heirs upon her death but also that the marital community did not continue, although a new partnership might be formed between the heirs and the surviving spouse.

[41] See Bartoli v. Huguenard, 39 La. Ann. 417.

Accounting sought from surviving spouse on behalf of minor child of deceased spouse, see Stroope v. Potter, 48 N.M. 404, 151 P.2d 748.

[42] Ordinarily, the correct way to describe the husband's duties toward the community property during marriage is by the words "administer" and "administration," since he exercises merely an administrative function with respect to such property, particularly as distinguished from the "control" of the marital property by the husband at common law, which signifies an entirely different situation. See especially ante, § 102. However, in this country we have tended to appropriate

decendent died intestate the court appointed *dativos,* i. e., dative executors, or what we would call administrators, to discharge the duties of administration. Since in the case of intestacy any right of a surviving spouse to succeed or inherit, aside from usufructuary rights already described, was dependent on the absence of descendants, ascendants and collaterals up to a certain degree, it can be seen that the interest of the surviving spouse was usually confined chiefly to obtaining division or partition of the community property which the spouses had equally owned. This would also be true where the spouse died testate, whether or not any legacy had been bequeathed to the surviving spouse. The legacy, in any event, as has been seen, was definitely limited in amount.[43] The importance and effectuation of this interest of the surviving spouse in the community property was a matter aside from administration of the estate of the deceased spouse. Indeed, in case of the wife being the deceased spouse the liquidation of the marital partnership took place in another proceeding than that of the administration of her estate. It was necessary that the husband, who had the management of the community property, charge community obligations against the community property, reduce rights of action to possession, etc., and deliver to the heirs of the wife her share of the community property.[44] Where the husband was the deceased spouse, the liquidation of the affairs of the marital partnership might be carried out during the administration of his own estate. But the administration of the community estate would have to be separate from, if not prior to, the administration of the separate estate of the deceased husband, and separate accountings made, etc.[45] It was quite true that immediately upon the death of a spouse, the heirs of that spouse immediately obtained title to that spouse's share of

such words as "administer" and "administration" almost exclusively to the estates of decedents. Accordingly, we have used the words in respect to a decedent's estate, and used the word "manage" to describe the administration exercised during marriage.

[43] See ante, § 193.

Duties of executors, see Asso and Mañuel, Institutes of Civil Law of Spain, Book II, Title V, Cap. 3, §§ 2, 3.

[44] This would seem to be the situation in Louisiana under the civil law. Likewise in the Philippines, see Enriquez v. Go-Tiongco, 220 U. S. 307, 55 L. Ed. 476, 31 Sup. Ct. 423.

Right to sell community property to pay debts, see post, § 208.

[45] Text quoted with approval, In re Condos' Estate, 70 Nev. 271, 266 P.2d 404. In Louisiana, see Elizaldi v. Kelly, 115 La. 712, 39 So. 851. The same principle was applied where the wife was the deceased spouse but the husband was insolvent; in such case he surrendered the community property in its entirety, its creditors were classified separately, it was sold separately, and the proceeds accounted for according to the rights of the heirs of the deceased wife to one half of the proceeds, and the rights of the husband's creditors in his half of the proceeds. His half of the proceeds could then be placed with his separate assets for the payment of his separate creditors. See Zeigler v. His Creditors, 49 La. Ann. 144, 21 So. 666. See also post, n. 54.

the community property; likewise, those heirs and the surviving spouse became entitled to have the community property partitioned between them.[46] Such rights were present and effective rights without the necessity of administration to confer them, in the sense that we think of the necessity of administration and of a decree of the proper court setting over to heirs their distributive shares.[47] But statements of some of our courts that under the Spanish or Mexican law the deceased spouse's share of the community property descended immediately to his heirs without the necessity of administration,[48] should not lead to the conclusion that there were no administrative details whatever to be settled. There necessarily had to be and was a settlement of the decedent's affairs. The point is that the title of the heirs was not dependent upon administration in order to vest title in them, and the right of partition existed without an administration to confer it. But it is to be recognized that community obligations had to be paid before it could be determined how much community property existed which could be partitioned. To that extent there had to be an "administration" of the community estate. It might also be necessary to separate the separate property from the community property.[49] Thus, even if the surviving spouse and the heirs of the deceased spouse took over the community property without what we would call an administration, there was the necessary termination of pending transactions, the satisfaction of community obligations, and the division of the residue of the community property to be accomplished. To the extent that they themselves might accomplish those matters there was in that sense an administration.[50]

The division of the property of the spouses was accomplished as follows: first the wife, or her heirs if she was the deceased spouse, took out the dowry and marriage deposit and any separate property of the wife, such as her *paraphernalia*, that property got by inheritance, and so on. Thereafter the husband or his heirs took out his separate property. The remainder, constituting the partnership profits acquired during the marriage was then divided between the husband and the wife's heirs or between the wife and the husband's heirs, as the case

[46] Text quoted with approval, In re Condos' Estate, 70 Nev. 271, 266 P.2d 404. Deceased spouse's share of community property passed to heirs without necessity of formal acceptance by them, see ante, § 195.

In Louisiana, also, the interests of the heirs of the decedent attach at the very moment of dissolution, subject of course to payment of community debts.

[47] In re Condos' Estate, 70 Nev. 271, 266 P.2d 404, quoting text with approval.

[48] See Lataillade v. Orena, 91 Cal. 565, 25 Am. St. Rep. 219; De La Guerra v. Packard, 17 Cal. 182.

[49] Deducting losses and expenses in order to determine marital gains, see ante, § 159.

[50] So taking over was probably the local custom in California under Mexican rule, according to McKay, Community Property, 2d Ed., chap. 83. The procedure would not conform with our notion of a formal statutory administration, of course, but did involve an administrative settlement.

might be.[51] The division of the community property was made, of course, after payment of the community debts and obligations.[52]

In our community property states whether and to what extent administration is necessary varies with the statutes of the respective states.[53] In some of the states administration of the community property takes place whether it is the husband or the wife who dies.[54] But even so the administration is not a necessity unless required by persons interested, as for example community creditors.[55] In others of the states administration of the community property is required where it is the husband who dies, but not where the wife is the deceased spouse and dies intestate as to her share of such property.[56] This is particularly true in New Mexico where the wife takes over control of her share of the community property on the death of the husband and the husband has the right of testamentary disposition of his share, but the wife has no testamentary right to dispose of her share which goes to the husband if she dies first. In the latter situation, the entire community property is already in the husband's hands for purposes of management, and he merely continues with it in his hands, except that he is then owner of all of it. The payment of the community obligations he can accomplish merely as they become due and payable.[57] In California, where each spouse has the right of testamentary disposition but in the absence of testamentary disposition the share of the deceased spouse goes to the survivor,[58] the community property

[51] Matienzo, Gloss II, No. 3, to Nov. Rec. Law 4, who declared that he himself could bear witness to such practice and that it was approved by the text of Novísima Recopilación, Book 10, Title 4, Law 3.

[52] See post, §§ 208, 210.

[53] Actual details of administration are not discussed herein.

[54] See Ariz. Rev. St. 1956, §§ 14-531, 14-533; Tex. Prob. Code 1955, §§ 155–175, 235, 385, 386; Wash. Rev. Code 1961, §§ 11.04.015, 11.28.030.
But in Texas, if husband or wife dies intestate, having no child or children, the common property all goes to the survivor, charged with the debts of the community, and no administration is necessary. Tex. Prob. Code 1955, § 155.
In Louisiana the community property must be liquidated and settled in proper judicial proceedings in order to ascertain the residue to be partitioned after payment of debts. Newman v. Cooper, 46 La. Ann. 1485, 16 So. 481. If the deceased spouse is the husband, two liquidations may be

necessary, one of his separate property and one in relation to the community property. See Succession of Bothick, 52 La. Ann. 863, 28 So. 458; Elizaldi v. Kelly, 115 La. 712, 39 So. 851. See also ante, n. 45.
Text quoted with approval, In re Condos' Estate, 70 Nev. 271, 266 P.2d 404.

[55] See Pauley v. Hadlock, 21 Ariz. 340, 188 P. 263; Burton v. Brugier, 30 La. Ann. 478; Hill v. Young, 7 Wash. 33, 34 P. 144; In re Hill's Estate, 6 Wash. 285, 33 P. 585.

[56] Idaho Code 1948, §§ 14-113, 14-114. See also as to Nevada in the note following; as to Texas in note 54.

[57] N.M. St. 1953, §§ 29-1-8, 29-1-9.
This was formerly the situation in California and Nevada. See Cal. Jur. "Community Property"; In re Condos' Estate, 70 Nev. 271, 266 P.2d 404, quoting text; Petition of Fuller, 63 Nev. 26, 159 P.2d 579.

[58] Cal. Probate Code, § 201. And see ante, § 198.
Petition by widow for partial distribution prior to final distribution as

passing from the husband's control, either by reason of his death or by virtue of testamentary disposition by the wife, is subject to administration as provided in the sections of the Probate Code relating to administration. In the event of testamentary disposition by the wife, the husband, pending administration, retains the same power to sell, manage and deal with the community personal property that he had during her lifetime. His possession and control of the community property is not transferred to the wife's personal representative except to the extent necessary to carry her will into effect.[59]

The fact that where the husband dies the administration of the community property should be separate and apart from, although inside, the administration of the husband's estate which is taking place, seems not always to be understood. It must also be remembered that, although such an administration of the community property is taking place in order to pay community debts and accomplish a partition, half of the community property so being administered belongs not to the deceased husband but to the surviving wife, and always belonged to her from the moment of its acquisition during the marriage.[60]

The determination, for purposes of administration, of the nature of particular property as community property or separate property would seem to present nothing that has not already been under discussion.[61]

§ 206. — Power of survivor generally over entire community property.

The absolute power of the surviving spouse, whether husband or wife, to manage and dispose of his or her share of the common property was, as already explained, well settled under the Spanish

customary means for having her community interests determined, see Estate of Stephenson, 65 Cal. App. 2d 120, 150 P.2d 222.

[59] Cal. Probate Code, § 202.

See Kasner, Administration of Deceased Wife's Interest in Community Assets, 4 Santa Clara Lawyer 30.

Husband's half of community not part of deceased wife's estate. Estate of Stone, 170 Cal. App. 2d 533, 339 P.2d 220.

[60] "Where the separate property of the deceased and the community property of the deceased and the surviving spouse is administered, the same should be kept separate, for the separate debts of the deceased would be primarily a charge upon the separate property, and the community

debts would be primarily a charge upon the community property." In re Hill's Estate, 6 Wash. 285, 33 P. 585. Similarly in Louisiana, see ante, this section.

Wife's half of community, being vested in her, does not become part of husband's estate in California, although subject to the administration. Com'r of Int. Rev. v. Siegel, 250 F.2d 339.

No power of sale conferred on executor by will of deceased husband can authorize him to sell and to pass title to the wife's share of the community property, except, of course, for the payment of debts to which it is subject. See Davenport v. Simons, 68 Idaho 21, 189 P.2d 90.

[61] Community and separate property, see ante, Chap. VI.

law.[62] This did not extend to or include, however, any right to control or dispose of the share of the deceased spouse in the community property. Thus, there was no right or power to dispose of the community property as a whole as if it were entirely the property of the surviving spouse.[63]

In most of our community property states in which the Spanish developed law of community property continued in unbroken force and effect, it was recognized by the courts from the earliest times that, upon the dissolution of the marriage by death, the surviving spouse, even though it be the husband, had no power or right to control or alienate the entire community property. The survivor's management and power of disposition existed only as to his or her own share of the community property.[64] This was definitely stated by the Texas court, with thorough discussion and understanding of the principles of the Spanish system of community property.[65] This was equally true of the Louisiana court which, in the approving language of the Texas court, "has, time and again, decided the question under consideration, and the principle has always been asserted and never questioned, that the community of acquests and gains, ceases to exist at the moment of the death of one of the partners, with all the legal effects resulting from it; that each party to the community is seized of one undivided half of the property composing the mass, and that the survivor cannot validly alienate the share not belonging to him."[66] But we may let the Louisiana court speak for itself, in these words, "That a community of acquests and gains, as such, continues after the death of one of the partners, with all the legal effects resulting from such a relation, with authority in the husband, if he should survive, to be still regarded as the head of the community, with power to bind the common property by new contracts, and to alienate it without restraint, is a proposition so repugnant to all our notions of a community, and so subversive of first principles, that it cannot be for a moment admitted."[67] Only the California court, in most evident

---

[62] See ante, § 202.

[63] "The 14th law of Toro means only, that upon the dissolution of the marriage, the surviving husband or wife may dispose of their portion of the ganancial property; but it does not mean that the surviving husband or wife could freely dispose of the whole of the ganancial property; and it was never so understood by any commentator, or by any judicial tribunal of the country in which it was promulgated." Thompson v. Cragg, 24 Tex. 582, 600.

[64] Morgan v. Bell, 3 Wash. 554, 28 P. 925, 16 L. R. A. 614, illustrates the recognition of this principle, although it seems undoubtedly to have been decided on a mistaken assumption that what was actually separate property was community property.

[65] Thompson v. Cragg, 24 Tex. 582. See also Clark v. Nolan & Campbell, 38 Tex. 416; Yancy v. Batte, 48 Tex. 46; Johnson v. Harrison, 48 Tex. 257.

[66] Thompson v. Cragg, 24 Tex. 582.

[67] Broussard v. Bernard, 7 La. 216.
Upon subsequent death of surviving husband, his executrix not entitled to collect any more than half of rents from former community property. Maybeno v. Battaglia (La. App.), 26 So.2d 415.

misunderstanding and misconstruction of the principles of the law of community property, has mistakenly sanctioned the right of a surviving spouse to exercise unquestioned control of the entire community property after dissolution of the marriage and to dispose of the whole of it. Only, said that court, when there was an intent to defraud the children of their legitimate inheritance from the deceased spouse could such alienation be restrained.[68] Although the California court spoke of that right as pertaining to either spouse if surviving, the fact that in the particular case the surviving spouse was the husband, and the mistaken language of the court as to the extent of his ownership, has undoubtedly been responsible for influencing later California judges to declare the husband the virtual owner of the entire common property, with right of disposal of it after marriage; as well as influencing the development of the mistaken idea that the common property is subject to liability not only for the community debts but also for the separate debts of the husband before it is partitioned.[69]

It is no excuse to the assumption of the right to sell the entire community property that the surviving spouse is poor and unable to support the children and that the sale of the property is necessary for the support of the children. Merely that one is the surviving spouse, without more, confers no ownership or authority over the deceased spouse's share of the community property. Accordingly, no title to that share of the community property would be conveyed to the grantee for there is no title to it which can be passed to the grantee.[70]

[68] Panaud v. Jones, 1 Cal. 488.

"I think it proper to notice the position assumed, and the case of Panaud v. Jones, not because the question involved is an open one, but because the sources of the learning by which the soundness of the propositions asserted in the case referred to must be tested, are not accessible to every member of the profession, and because, upon a question so fundamental in the Spanish jurisprudence in relation to community property, we are not willing that there should be any room for doubt, as to the correctness of the former decisions of this court. The judge who delivered the opinion in the case of Panaud v. Jones, was misled by detached passages of commentators, which doubtless came under his consideration, disconnected from the great body of Spanish law on the subject, with which the passages referred to are not at variance. He also misunderstood the scope and meaning of the 14th law of Toro." Thompson v. Cragg, 24 Tex. 582, 599.

[69] Debts, see post, § 209 et seq.

[70] See Bell v. Schwarz, 56 Tex. 353; Thompson v. Cragg, 24 Tex. 582; Robinson v. McDonald, 11 Tex. 385, 62 Am. Dec. 480.

[71] In California, where the wife's share of the community property goes to the husband upon her death, unless she has disposed of it by will, it is provided that "After forty days from the death of the wife the surviving husband shall have full power to sell, lease, mortgage or otherwise deal with and dispose of the community real property, unless a notice is recorded in the county in which the property is situated to the effect that an interest in the property, specifying it, is claimed by another under the wife's will." Cal. Probate Code, § 203 (in part). As to personal property, see ibid., § 202.

Earlier Texas decisions took the

Consideration has been given by some courts to the effect of rules or statutes protecting as a *bona fide* purchaser one who purchases in good faith for value and without notice from the one having the record title.[71] But it should be most questionable to consider that one can in any circumstances convey or transfer any title to that in which he has no interest whatever.[72] Certainly infant heirs of a deceased spouse, especially when under the guardianship of the surviving spouse, have little or no opportunity to insist that the record title be changed to show their ownership. And the very reason for protecting the so-called *bona fide* purchaser is based on the assumption that the one having the interest which does not appear on the records is negligent in not seeing that it does so appear, for which he ought to suffer rather than the *bona fide* purchaser.[73] It is difficult to see how such "negligence" can be imputed to minor children under the charge, control or guardianship of the surviving spouse. As a matter of fact, this rule relating to a *bona fide* purchaser has reference to his right against one having an "equitable" title not appearing of record. The wife's ownership of half the community property is as full and complete as that of the husband and, whatever some courts may call it to the contrary, is not an equitable title. And her heirs who succeed to her interest have as complete a title as she had.[74] To refer to or treat such title as "equitable" is mistakenly defining and interpreting it by common-law concepts instead of by community property principles. Certainly if any statute or rule is given effect to prefer the

view that a surviving husband's conveyance to a bona fide purchaser, unless made to pay community debts, passed no title as to the interest of the wife's heirs, since both the survivor and her heirs had legal title respectively to an undivided half. However, this view has been modified to hold that where the legal title shows only the husband's interest, the interest of the wife and those claiming under her is only an equitable interest and not enforceable against a bona fide purchaser from the husband. This actually has the effect of denying that the wife is an equal owner with the husband of community property. No great degree of inquiry seems to be imposed on the purchaser. See, e. g., Downing v. Jeffrey (Tex. Civ. App.), 195 S. W. 2d 696 and note 25 Tex. Law Rev. 170; Landry v. Williamson (Tex.), 335 S. W. 2d 400.

[72] The defense of bona fide purchaser can be maintained only in favor of a title, though defective, which a bona fide purchaser has. It is not available for the purpose of creating a title.

The surviving husband cannot convey or mortgage the half now belonging to the wife's heirs because he can convey or mortgage only that which he owns. Ewald v. Hufton, 31 Idaho 373, 173 P. 247.

[73] See Patty v. Middleton, 82 Tex. 586, 17 S. W. 909.

[74] See Johnston v. San Francisco Sav. Union, 75 Cal. 134, 16 P. 753, 7 Am. St. Rep. 129.

Where the wife dies her heirs succeed to her interest in the community property and any attempted conveyance or encumbrance of the property by the surviving husband is a nullity as to those heirs and can be set aside by them. The defense of bona fide purchaser is not available to the one to whom the conveyance or encumbrance was made. Bona fide purchase cannot create a title which does not exist in the grantor or encumbrancer. Ewald v. Hufton, 31 Idaho 373, 173 P. 247. See also Mabie v. Whittaker, 10 Wash. 656, 39 P. 172.

bona fide purchaser over heirs of the deceased spouse, constructive notice should be charged against the purchaser unless he can show the utmost in diligence and the making of the most thorough investigation possible into the background of the vendor.

The foregoing is not to say that if the surviving spouse is administering the entire community property according to the law of decedents' estates that he or she cannot alienate such property if circumstances or necessity warrant, but it should naturally be done only pursuant to the consent and subject to the supervision of the court. However, compliance with any such law must be shown before any alienation of the entire community property by the survivor is in any way justified.[75] Or if the deceased spouse is the wife, and the husband has in his control the community property, the husband must necessarily retire the community debts and obligations before he can divide the community property and turn the wife's share over to her executor or administrator. It may thus become necessary for him to sell the community property to pay the community debts prior to partition or division. To this extent he may be warranted in selling. This was true under the Spanish law of community property but is no longer uniformly true in our community property states.[76] If the transfer of the property is to be made pursuant to a contract made jointly by husband and wife or by the husband, before the wife's death, and the contract was validly made pursuant to the husband's right of management of the community property, the transfer may be completed after the wife's death.[77] Half of the proceeds of the transfer would belong, of course, to the wife's heirs. Such a situation merely corresponds to that discussed in a preceding section in relation to the surviving spouse and the heirs of the deceased spouse, under the Spanish law of community property, carrying to completion any unfinished transactions involving the community property.[78]

§ 207. — Statutory authorization of survivor to administer.

In some of the states the surviving spouse, whether husband or wife, is authorized to administer and settle the affairs of the conjugal partnership, sometimes after fulfilling some prerequisite to qualify as survivor of the marital community.[79]

In Texas, where a husband or wife dies intestate, leaving no child

[75] See Clark v. Nolan & Campbell, 38 Tex. 416; Patterson v. Twadill (Tex.), 301 S. W. 2d 680.

[76] See post, § 208.
Reviving barred debt, see post, § 216.

[77] See Brewer v. Wall, 23 Tex. 585, 76 Am. Dec. 76.

[78] See ante, § 204.

[79] See also post, § 208. Where husband and wife as tenants were wrongfully evicted by landlord, husband's death did not abate cause of action and upon his death his widow succeeded to his interest in the unexpired tenancy and was entitled to sue not only for herself but as administratrix of her husband's estate. Sanders v. Allen, 83 Cal. App. 2d 362, 188 P.2d 760.

or children or descendants of any child or children surviving, the total community property passes to the surviving spouse, charged with the debts of the community, and no administration is necessary.[80] On the other hand, if community property passes to one other than the surviving spouse, that survivor may file an inventory of the community property and a list of the community indebtedness, within a specified time, and qualify as survivor so as to administer the community property, pay the debts, and turn over half of the community property to those entitled thereto.[81] If letters testamentary or of administration have already been granted to the estate of the deceased spouse, the survivor would seem limited to making application to the court granting such letters for partition of the common property.[82]

And Washington provides by statute that the surviving spouse shall be entitled to administer the community property, notwithstanding any provisions of the will of the deceased spouse to the contrary. The court must, of course, find such surviving spouse to be otherwise qualified. The right to administer is considered waived if the surviving spouse does not make application within forty days from the death of the other spouse.[83]

§ 208. — Disposition of community property by survivor for purposes of liquidation or partition.

It will be noticed that where the wife was the deceased spouse, it was necessary for the husband to liquidate the community property and turn over the wife's share thereof. Obviously, such liquidation and division had to be prefaced by payment of the community debts from the community property. This conjoint right and duty thus rested upon the husband. If in order to accomplish the liquidation it was necessary for him to sell any or all of the community property, he could do so. But his right to sell the community property was only to permit of retirement of the community obligations and existed for no other purpose and was to be followed by division or partition of the community gains remaining after such retirement of the community debts and obligations.[83a] The right of the husband to that extent to sell the community property after the wife's death has been recognized in some jurisdictions in this country even where he has not qualified as administrator or as survivor of the community pursuant to statute. But his right to alienate went no further than that and could be

---

[80] Tex. Prob. Code 1955, § 155.

[81] See Tex. Prob. Code 1955, §§ 161–177.

Existence of community property is the important requisite; it is not necessary that there be existing community debts. And the qualified community survivor is not strictly speaking an administrator but a statutory trustee of very unique character. See Fidelity Union Ins. Co. v. Hutchins (Tex.), 133 S. W. 2d 105.

[82] See Tex. Prob. Code 1955, §§ 235,385,386.

[83] Wash. Rev. Code 1961, § 11.38.030.

[83a] See also ante, §§ 205, 206.

exercised for no other purpose.[84] Having paid any community debts existing, it then becomes his duty to turn over the wife's share of the residue of the community property left after such payment to the wife's administrator if there is one, or to her heirs if there are heirs and no administration, or to retain it himself if he has qualified as administrator or community survivor under statute, or retain it himself by right of succession, as the case may be. There are so many of these possibilities under our differing statutes, that the enumeration preceding is not necessarily a complete one.[85] However, in Louisiana, a surviving husband, although he may administer the community property and arrange to pay the community debts, cannot, without authority of court, alienate any part of it other than his own share.[86] In others of the states the right of a surviving husband to alienate the community property for the purpose of satisfying community debts before turning over the wife's share to her heirs was recognized at one time but later denied. In many of these states, since the share of a deceased wife goes to the husband, or the share of either spouse,

---

[84] See Johnson v. Harrison, 48 Tex. 257, discussing numerous Texas authorities. See also Bell v. Schwarz, 56 Tex. 353.

"Upon the death of the wife the marital partnership is dissolved, and the community estate immediately vests, one half in the husband and the other half in the heirs of the deceased wife. This property, however, thus descends burthened with the community debts. And after the death of the wife the husband may sell it for the purpose of paying these community debts. That is the full extent of his authority over it, without first qualifying as survivor in community." Rudd v. Johnson, 60 Tex. 91, 93.

Apparently, in Texas, the purchaser may safely assume that the surviving husband, in making the sale, is exercising his general power to sell in order to pay community debts. And the transfer or conveyance may be made in the name of the survivor alone or in his name alone as survivor, without joining the heirs. Griffin v. Stanolind Oil & Gas Co. (Tex. Com. App.), 125 S. W. 2d 545.

Compare the view in California that the surviving husband could alienate for any purpose not constituting a fraud on the rights of the heirs of the deceased spouse, a view

based on a misinterpretation of the extent of the husband's ownership. See Panaud v. Jones, 1 Cal. 488, and criticism thereof in Thompson v. Cragg, 24 Tex. 582.

That the surviving spouse, as well as having the right to alienate in order to pay community debts, can also in his or her name alone sue to set aside the conveyance as having been obtained by fraud, see Underwood v. Carter (Tex. Civ. App.), 51 S. W. 2d 1061.

[85] Difficulties presented where husband is member of a business partnership and husband dies first or wife dies first leaving a will, see Mullin, The Partner's Problems Augmented: His Wife Writes a Will, Los Angeles Bar Bulletin, Aug. 1947; also issued as Reprint No. 20 by State Bar of California, Committee on Continuing Education.

[86] See Rusk v. Warren, 25 La. Ann. 314; German v. Gay, 9 La. 580; Elizaldi v. Kelly, 115 La. 712, 39 So. 851; Washington v. Palmer, 213 La. 79, 34 So.2d 382.

Children reaching deceased mother's share of community property which father had previously transferred to a corporation which he liquidated after wife's death. Wainer v. Wainer, 210 La. 324, 26 So.2d 829.

in certain contingencies such as absence of testamentary disposition or of descendants, goes to the other spouse, without administration, the survivor as owner of the entire community naturally can alienate it in order to pay debts or for any other reason.[87]

§ 209.   — Debts and obligations generally.

Consideration has been given at some length, in a previous chapter, to the matter of debts and obligations of the spouses, and to the principles governing. The principles continue to be virtually the same where the marital community is dissolved and it becomes necessary to consider the satisfaction of debts and obligations in connection with the settlement of the community affairs and the partition of the community property.[88]

§ 210.   — Community debts and obligations — Basic principles.

Under the Spanish law of community, although death of one spouse terminated the partnership of acquests and gains, before there could be a division or partition of the community property representing such acquests and gains it was necessary to deduct the community obligations or debts. For, as was said, before there can be profits or gains, all expenses and losses must first be deducted.[89] The community property most definitely was subject to liability only for community debts or obligations. No separate obligations or debts of the deceased spouse, even though he were the husband, could be charged against the community property.[90] And, incidentally but no

---

[87] In New Mexico, the right of the surviving husband to alienate in order to pay community debts was recognized in Crary v. Field, 9 N.M. 222, 50 P. 342; but later denied in Mings v. Herring, 26 N.M. 425, 193 P. 497. The present provision of the New Mexico statutes that the wife has no power of testamentary disposition and that upon her death her share of the community property goes to the husband without administration (see ante, § 194), would necessarily leave the entire community property belonging to the husband with the right in him to alienate it to pay community debts.

Similarly, in Idaho, the right of the surviving husband seems to have been recognized in Von Rosenberg v. Perrault, 5 Idaho 719, 51 P. 774; but later denied in Ewald v. Hufton, 31

Idaho 373, 173 P. 247; it is to be noticed that if the wife dies intestate her share goes to the surviving husband without administration, so that as sole owner he could alienate.

[88] Chapter IX, relating to debts and obligations, should be considered in connection herewith.

[89] See ante, § 159.

[90] "The only charge to which the ganancial property is subject, after the death of one of the spouses, is the payment of the debts contracted during the matrimony, by either of them, provided they originated in the business of the partnership itself, and not in the private business of one of the partners." Febrero Reformado, Title 5, § xiii, No. 412, quoted in Thompson v. Cragg, 24 Tex. 582, 603.

"Febrero, in treating of the division

less importantly, the community property could not be subjected to liability for debts contracted after the dissolution of the marital community.[91] Although the title of the deceased spouse passed at once to his or her heirs, the latter received the property subject to the payment of community debts. Payment of community debts might be accomplished before partition and the giving of actual physical possession to them of half of the residue, or they might come into actual physical possession before such payment; in the latter event they were under liability for their share of the debts. Any transfer or encumbrance by the surviving spouse or by the heirs of the share of the community property belonging to such spouse or passing to such heirs on the dissolution of the marriage was necessarily made subject to liability of such share for half of the community debts. Community creditors could apply for an order of court to compel a surviving wife or the heirs to announce acceptance or repudiation of such property within a hundred days or such lesser period as the judge might set, for if they accepted the property they were subject to liability for debts.[92] The community creditors, it may be definitely stated, could sue the wife for debts contracted during the marriage.[93] This was so because she was an equal partner with the husband during the marriage, fully owned half of the profits of that partnership, and thus was liable for her share of the debts of the conjugal partnership.[94]

of inheritances, declares that there must be deducted all legitimate debts, which the husband, or the wife with his permission, or both jointly, may have contracted on account of the conjugal partnership, and which must be paid out of the ganancial property, and that the residue only is divisible, and is what is called the inheritance." Jones v. Jones, 15 Tex. 143.

Gutiérrez, in pointing out that expenditures by either spouse from the common property for personal reasons were to be charged or debited against the expending spouse's share of the common property, said that it was "for the same reasons as those on which it is held that on the dissolution of the marriage the debts of one of the spouses contracted before marriage should not be subtracted from the common heap of goods, but from the share of the spouse who contracted them" (which share was determined, of course, only after community debts were paid). Gutiérrez, Quaestio CXXIX, to Nov. Rec. Law 9, Book 10, Title 4.

[91] See Fuero Real, Book 3, Title

20, Law 14.

[92] Matienzo, Gloss I, No. 8, to Nov. Rec. Law 9.

[93] Fuero Real, Book 3, Title 14, Law 1; Novísima Recopilación, Book 10, Title 4, Law 9; Azevedo, No. 18, to Nov. Rec. Law 9; Gutiérrez, Quaestio CXVIII, No. 11, to Nov. Rec. Law 9.

[94] Gutiérrez, Quaestio CXVIII, No. 11, to Nov. Rec. Law 9.

"The third proof of this rule given by Gregorius Lupi is law 14 last title book 3 *fori* and law 9 below, which provide that a wife may be sued in respect of debts contracted during marriage by reason of the fact that she is by law entitled to share the profits, Dig. 50.17.10. The intent of the law is that, as it gives the wife a share of profits automatically, similarly she may be liable for debts." Matienzo, Gloss III, No. 16, to Nov. Rec. Law 1.

"If then she does not renounce, she *is* bound to pay debts contracted during marriage; and that the said debts must be paid from the said

§ 211.   — Community debts and obligations — American jurisdictions.

The principle is recognized and followed in many of our community property states that, upon the dissolution of the marriage by the death of one of the spouses, the community property is subject to the payment of the community debts charged against it.[95] Certain of the community property may be exempted by statute from liability for the payment of debts, as for example, life insurance proceeds[96] or homesteads constituted from community property.[97] Strictly speaking, the amount of the community property which is to be partitioned cannot be determined until the community debts have been discharged,[98] but if, before such discharge, half of the property denominated community property actually comes into the possession of the heirs entitled thereto, they take it subject to the payment of the community debts. At bottom, their half should be liable only for half of the community debts, so that if claims of community creditors are recovered from that half of the community property in the hands of the heirs, the heirs should be entitled to adjustment thereof from the other half of the community property. The surviving spouse, likewise, is liable for half of the community debts, by reason of the share of the community property in his or her hands. This is true of a surviving wife as of a surviving husband.[99] The statutes are usually rather vague, merely prescribing that the community property passes subject to liability for the community debts. The difficulties brought about by such a situation indicate the wisdom of the Spanish community property system in considering that the amount and extent of the marital gains were not determinable until expenses and losses had been deducted.[1] In Louisiana, proper appreciation of the matter

---

profits made during marriage is clear from *lex Styli 205, lex 14 tit. 20 lib. 3 Fori,* and thus does practice allow." Gutiérrez, Quaestio CXXVII, No. 3, to Nov. Rec. Law 9.

Liability only for her share of the community debts, see also ante, § 159.

[95] Ariz. Rev. St. 1956, § 14-203; Ida. Code 1948, § 14-113; Tex. Prob. Code 1955, §§ 45,155,156; Wash Rev. Code 1961, § 11.04.015; In re Schoenfeld's Estate (Wash.), 351, P.2d 935, quoting original ed.

Liability of community property for community debts, see also ante, Chap. IX.

[96] See ante, § 171.

[97] In re Schoenfeld's Estate (Wash.), 351 P.2d 935, quoting original edition. The law of homesteads, a statutory subject of some complexity, is not within the scope of this work. And see 36 A.L.R. 441; 97 A.L.R. 1099.

[98] In re Schoenfeld's Estate (Wash.), 351 P.2d 935, quoting original edition. Thus, a surviving wife took only half of the residue after administration of community property and payment of community debts. See Succession of Benton, 106 La. 494, 31 So. 123, 59 L. R. A. 135.

[99] Ellsworth v. Ellsworth, 5 Ariz. App. 89, 423 P.2d 364, 367, quoting original edition; In re Schoenfeld's Estate (Wash.), 351 P.2d 935, 937–938, quoting original edition. As to right of unpaid community creditors to resort to separate property of a spouse, see post, this section and ante, § 159.

[1] In re Schoenfeld's Estate (Wash.), 351 P.2d 935, quoting original edition.

is shown by the codal provision that "It is understood that, in the partition of the effects of the partnership or community of gains, both husband and wife are to be equally liable for their share of the debts contracted during the marriage, and not acquitted at the time of its dissolution."[2] It is otherwise, of course, if both spouses have bound themselves jointly and severally.[3] The same appreciation of the matter is shown in others of the states by judicial decision.[4] Incidentally, in accord with community property principles, any transfer or encumbrance by the surviving spouse of his share of the community property or by the heirs of their share of the community property should be effective to pass only such interest as the transferor or encumbrancer has, and if community debts have not at the time been paid, the interest is transferred or encumbered subject to the unpaid community debts, or, rather, to be more specific, to that interest's ratable share of the community debts.[5]

Although it has been remarked that heirs who succeed to a deceased spouse's share of the community property take it subject to liability for half of the community debts, this must be qualified by the understanding that their liability is limited to the extent of the value of their share of the community property. The same is true as to a surviving wife, in that her liability for her share of the community debts is a liability only to the extent of the value of her share of the community property.[6] An exception may exist in her case, however, to the extent that the law may impose liability on separate property of hers for community debts. In such case, community creditors may resort to the separate property as well as to the community property

---

[2] La. Civ. Code, art. 2409. See also Henderson v. Wadsworth, 115 U. S. 264, 29 L. Ed. 377, 6 Sup. Ct. 40 (Louisiana).

Taxes accruing after dissolution of community by death of spouse are not community obligations so as to be entitled to priority over right of heirs of deceased spouse to claim share of that spouse. Maybeno v. Battaglia (La. App.), 26 So.2d 315.

[3] See Henderson v. Wadsworth, 115 U. S. 264, 29 L. Ed. 377, 6 Sup. Ct. 40. See also ante, Chap. IX.

[4] Surviving spouse and heirs of deceased spouse each take half of the community estate, each half being subject to its ratable share of the community debts, and the half taken by the heirs being subject to the separate debts of the deceased spouse. Greer v. Goesling, 54 Ariz. 488, 97 P.2d 218.

Under Texas law, on dissolution of community, husband but not wife personally liable for community debts. Community property of wife is liable and husband can recover from it for advances made to pay community debts but no personal judgment can be obtained against wife. U. S. v. Stapf (5 C.A.), 309 F.2d 592.

[5] See Newman v. Cooper, 46 La. Ann. 1485, 16 So. 481; Webre v. Lorio, 42 La. Ann. 178, 7 So. 460.

[6] "The view to be adopted is that she (a surviving wife) is liable only in respect of her own half-share and no more. . . . And so, in respect of the share which comes to her, the wife can be proceeded against for debts contracted during marriage." Azevedo, No. 18, to Nov. Rec. Law 9.

No liability on separate estate of deceased wife, see Simpson v. Bulkley, 140 La. 589, 73 So. 691, L.R.A. 1917 C 494.

which she owns to recover her share of the community debts. Properly, her separate property, if liable at all, should be only secondarily liable.[7] Although a surviving husband, also, should be liable only for half of the community debts, there is more probability in his case than in the case of the wife, that statutes will subject his separate property to liability for such debts, in addition to the liability naturally existing upon his share of the community property. There is the likelihood, moreover, that in some states entire liability will be imposed on him for the entire community debts.[8] When a community creditor wishes to enforce his claim, he should proceed against whomsoever has actual possession of the community property, whether the surviving spouse alone, before partition, or the surviving spouse and the heirs, after partition.[9]

As under the Spanish system, in Louisiana the heirs of a deceased spouse have the privilege of renouncing the partnership or community of gains and thus exonerating themselves from liability for debts contracted during the marriage.[10]

In some of the community property states, the husband may provide in his will that the community debts are to be charged solely against his share of the community property.[11] This would allow of the division or partition of the community property between the surviving spouse and the heirs of the deceased spouse before debiting against such property the community debts, so that the share going to the surviving spouse would go free of any liability for the community debts. The debts would then be debited against the decedent's share of the community before its inheritance by those to whom it was disposed by will.

§ 212.   — Separate debts and obligations.

Under the Spanish community property system, once all community obligations and debts had been charged off, what remained was the common property subject to be divided equally between the sur-

---

[7] Liability of wife's separate property, see ante, § 159 et seq.

[8] See ante, Chap. IX. See also Guillory v. Desormeaux (La.), 179 So.2d 456.

Community obligations, upon dissolution of community, as enforceable against community property or against separate property of husband, see First Nat. Bank of Ritzville v. Cunningham, 72 Wash. 532, 130 P. 1148.

Liability of husband's separate property for community debt where community property insufficient to pay, see Succession of Lamm, 40 La. Ann. 312, 4 So. 53.

[9] See, e. g., Succession of Hooke, 46 La. Ann. 353, 15 So. 150, 23 L.R.A. 803.

[10] La. Civ. Code, art. 2410.

Title passes to them, however, immediately upon the death of their ancestor. Newman v. Cooper, 46 La. Ann. 1485, 16 So. 481.

Renunciation by heirs of deceased spouse and who takes, see Paline v. Heroman, 211 La. 64, 29 So.2d 473.

As to renunciation by surviving wife, see post, § 218.

[11] In California, see Estate of Chanquet, 184 Cal. 307, 193 P. 762; Estate of Marinos, 39 Cal. App. 2d 1, 102 P.2d 443.

In Washington, see In re Schoen-

viving spouse and the heirs of the deceased spouse. When the division or partition had been arrived at, or it could be determined what the amounts were which were to go equally to the surviving spouse and the heirs of the deceased spouse, then and only then were separate creditors of the deceased spouse entitled to enforce their claims against, and only against, that share of the community property allocated or partitioned to the heirs of the deceased spouse.[12] It has continued to be recognized in many of our states that it is inherent in the community property system that before partition of such property it should be charged only with community obligations, and that separate debts of the deceased spouse should not be charged against it. Only after it has been partitioned should there be any subjection of the halves of the partitioned property to separate debts, and even then the half belonging to one spouse should never be made subject to liability for separate debts of the other spouse.[13] In Arizona and Washington, which do not permit a spouse's share of the community property to be subjected to liability for a separate debt of the spouse during the existence of the marriage,[14] a surface view might lead to the conclusion that the community property is permitted to be subjected to the claims of separate creditors, after dissolution of the marriage by death. But examination will show that the deceased spouse's share of the common property is subject to liability for such separate debts of the deceased spouse only after the entire common property has been subjected to liability for the community debts and the residue then allocated or partitioned between the surviving spouse and the heirs of the deceased spouse.[15]

In others of our states, this basic principle has constituted one of

feld's Estate (Wash.), 351 P.2d 935; Redelsheimer v. Zepin, 105 Wash. 199, 177 P. 736; In re Hart's Estate, 150 Wash. 482, 273 P. 735; Lang's Estate v. Com'r of Int. Rev., 97 F.2d 867.

[12] See also ante, § 210.

That debts of one of the spouses contracted before marriage shall not be subtracted from the common heap of goods, but from the share of the spouse who contracted them (which share is determinable, of course, only after payment of community debts), see Gutiérrez, Quaestio CXXIX, No. 2, to Nov. Rec. Law 9, Book 10, Title 4.

And where a husband, during a second marriage, had supported a child of a former marriage from profits made during the second marriage, the wife or the heirs could demand back a half part of the cost

of such support. Gutiérrez, Quaestio CXXIX, No. 1, to Nov. Rec. Law 9.

[13] Discussion of preference of community creditors over separate creditors, see Newman v. Cooper, 46 La. Ann. 1485, 16 So. 481. See also Webre v. Lorio, 42 La. Ann. 178, 7 So. 460; Thompson v. Vance, 110 La. 26, 34 So. 112; Childs v. Locket, 107 La. 270, 31 So. 751; Jones v. Jones, 15 Tex. 143.

[14] See ante, §§ 158, 162.

[15] When community status is dissolved by death, the community estate becomes ipso facto two separate estates, except as to the rights of community creditors; the surviving spouse and the heirs of the deceased spouse each take half of the community estate, each half being subject to its ratable share of the community debts and the half taken by the heirs being subject to the separate debts of the deceased

the principles least understood and most often violated. In California, where the rule has long been followed that the community property, during the lifetime of the husband, is liable for his separate debts as well as for the community debts, the same rule is applied where the community property passes from his control, either by reason of his death or by virtue of testamentary disposition by the wife. Thus, upon the death of the husband or upon the death of the wife disposing of her share of the community property by will, the entire community property, even before division or partition, is subjected to liability not only for the community debts but for the separate debts of the husband. Only after the payment of all such debts is the community property then divided; the half which belongs to the wife is determined only after the payment of the husband's own debts from the community property.[16] Such a rule is a travesty on marital community of property. It dates, of course, from the time when the California courts held that the community property was virtually the property of the husband without any right in the wife except an expectant interest. Now that the legislature has, since 1927, recognized that the interests of both spouses are, during the marriage, present, equal and existing, it might be assumed that the property of the wife would not be taken from her to pay separate debts of the husband, but California has not yet returned to that principle.[17] The statutes in New Mexico also seem to subject the community property, on the husband's death, to liability for "his debts."[18]

§ 213.   — Claims on behalf of spouses.

In the preceding sections it has been pointed out that the community property is subject only to payment of community debts, and that only after such payment and the ascertainment of the extent of

spouse. Greer v. Goesling, 54 Ariz. 488, 97 P.2d 218. See also Tway v. Tway, 55 Ariz. 343, 101 P.2d 455; Columbia Nat. Bank v. Embree, 2 Wash. 331, 26 P. 257.

"In case there should not be enough of the separate property to pay the separate debts, the deficiency could be made good out of the decedent's interest in the community property, should there be anything remaining after the payment of the community debts, and the same would be true with regard to a deficiency of the community property, as, after the separate debts had been paid, the remainder of the separate property would be liable for the community debts so remaining unpaid." In re Hill's Estate,

6 Wash. 285, 33 P. 585.

[16] See Cal. Probate Code, §§ 201, 202; Estate of Coffee, 19 Cal. 2d 248, 120 P.2d 661.

[17] It would appear, in California, that a power of sale over community property given by a husband's will to an executor authorizes him to convey a good title only to the decedent's half of the community property, unless the sale is necessary for the purpose of paying debts. See Estate of Phillips, 203 Cal. 106, 263 P. 1017; Sharpe v. Loupe, 120 Cal. 89, 52 P. 134, 586. Debts, under the California view, would mean any debts, not just community debts.

[18] N.M. Sts. 1953, § 29-1-9.

the shares of the residue belonging to the surviving spouse and the heirs of the deceased spouse are such shares subject to the debts of the separate creditors of the spouses.[19] But there may well be claims of a surviving spouse or of the heirs arising in connection with the community property.[20] During the marriage, one of the spouses may have used community property for his or her own personal or private purposes which were not properly chargeable against the community property. Such use may have been without the consent of the other spouse or, even if with consent, not with any understanding that the community property so used should constitute a gift thereof to the spouse using it. Its amount or value should be replaced in the community fund, even if it must be taken from the separate property of the spouse who used the community property for his or her own personal purposes. If it was the deceased spouse who so used the community property, his or her separate property should be liable to replace the amount so taken, and the claim on behalf of the community against such separate property is a claim superior and prior to any rights of separate creditors in such separate property. If it was the surviving spouse who used community property for personal or private purposes, the heirs of the deceased spouse succeed to the latter's right to have such replacement. They have an enforceable claim therefor against the surviving spouse.[21]

In the event there are no community debts, it may be sufficient merely to require that half the value of the amount so taken be placed in the share of the other spouse or that spouse's heirs. It may be possible to accomplish this by merely debiting that amount, upon the partition, against the share of the spouse who used the community property for personal or private purposes. Even if there are community debts, it may be possible to accomplish the adjustment merely by debiting the share of the spouse who so used the community property, with any necessary accounting relative to community debts paid. The principles, as applicable in the foregoing and in analogous situations, were given full recognition and effect by the Spanish authorities[22]

---

[19] See ante, §§ 210–212.

[20] Wife as creditor of husband's estate by virtue of antenuptial agreement whereby she was to receive flat sum in place of any other interest. Estate of Schwartz (Cal. App.), 179 P.2d 863.

[21] See Langhurst v. Langhurst, 49 N.M. 329, 164 P.2d 204.

In Louisiana, where income from husband's separate property is community property, his ordinary expenditures from that income to preserve his separate estate created no debt against his separate estate in favor of the community upon his death. Succession of Brunies, 209 La. 629, 25 So. 2d 287. Acquisition of property generally through the use of community or separate property, see ante, § 77 et seq.

[22] These principles are illustrated by numerous statements and examples of the jurisconsults, some of which are reproduced below.

Where a husband, during a second marriage, supported a child of a former marriage from profits made during the second marriage, the wife or heirs could demand back a half part of the cost of such support, such bur-

and have received frequent recognition in our courts.[23] Indeed, the principles date from the very inception of the community property system among the Visigoths as they introduced it into Spain.[24]

As to the foregoing matters, reference is also recommended to discussions in preceding chapters relating to the use of community funds to benefit individual interests or separate property of one spouse as well as to the question of gifts to a spouse from the community, and also to the question as it arises where the marriage is dissolved by divorce.[25]

§ 214. — Advancements.

We have no concern here with advancements made from the separate property of the one making the advancement. By advancement is meant, of course, the gift by anticipation, from a parent to a child, of the whole or a part of what it is supposed the child would

den of support not being a part of the second marriage's particular partnership of profit and gain. "And I think that the same holds good if the husband spends anything else, or the wife, to recover the goods of a child of a former marriage, or for another personal reason, for the same reasons as those on which it is held that on the dissolution of marriage the debts of one of the spouses contracted before marriage should not be subtracted from the common heap of goods, but from the share of the spouse who contracted them." Gutiérrez, Quaestio CXXIX, to Nov. Rec. Law 9, Book 10, Title 4.

"From this it may be inferred that, if a husband during marriage discharges debts contracted by him before marriage, he must on dissolution of marriage make good and pay to the wife out of his private property a moiety of the debts so discharged during marriage. . . . And for these reasons Cassaneus, on the Customs of Burgundy, . . . very properly raises the question as to what happens if a father who has a son by his first wife buys land in the name of that son during his second marriage and delivers it to his son. Should the wife take a half-share thereof as of an acquisition during marriage? As to this Baldus draws a distinction, on Dig. 3.36.18, and eventually leaves it for consideration, after citing many writ-

ers who deal with this point. But I have no doubt that where the wife is not given a half of such land she is entitled to the value of such half out of her husband's property. The husband bought it during marriage; it is therefore profit and must be shared, since the husband has diminished the profits by an amount proportionate to the value of the land. Moreover he may not make gifts to the prejudice of his wife or enrich the sons of his first marriage to the prejudice of and in fraud of his second wife." Azevedo, Nos. 20, 21, 24, 25, to Nov. Rec. Law 9.

[23] Louisiana jurisprudence is an excellent example of this. See Whited v. U.S., 219 F. Supp. 947.

As to Texas, see Ghent v. Boyd, 18 Tex. Civ. App. 88, 43 S. W. 891; Lindsay v. Clayman, 151 Tex. 593. 254 S. W. 2d 777.

[24] The same principle is found among the laws of the Visigoths in Sweden, *circa* 1200 A.D., viz.: "A man buys with his land, gives anything to boot from their common property, as soon as the [common] property shall be divided, then shall so many *öre* be placed for division as were given to boot." Law of the West Goths, according to the Manuscript of Eskil [Bergin's Translation], p. 66.

[25] See ante, Chaps. VI, VIII; post, this chapter, subdivision C.

inherit on the death of the parent and which, upon the death of the parent, is charged against the amount the child is then to receive.[26] In the Spanish law, the right of one to make advancements to descendants was necessarily limited by the provision of the law that only one-fifth of one's property could be freely disposed of by will and that as to the other four-fifths one's descendants had to be instituted as heirs and none of such descendants could be favored by being given more than one-third of such four-fifths.[27] But, under the Spanish law, could an advancement be made from the community property, observing, of course, the limitations of the law just mentioned? It was said that "the husband alone cannot assign to one of their common children an advance of a 'third' or a 'fifth' in goods acquired during marriage and that an assignment made to him applies only in respect of a half, i.e., the husband's share." However, if it made no difference to the wife, and was not to her prejudice, she could assent to the advancement from the whole of the property in question, and reimburse herself to the amount of half the value of such advancement, from other community property acquired during the marriage.[28]

§ 215.　—— Family allowances, expenses of administration, funeral expenses, etc.

Provision is frequently made in the statutes of our community property states that the community property shall be subject not only to the community debts but also to the family allowance and the expenses of administration.[29] These allowances and expenses may naturally result in a reduction in the amount of community property to be partitioned between the surviving spouse and the heirs. In the Spanish law it will be noticed that while allowances for support of the widow were provided for until her dowry was returned to her, according to some commentators, or according to others for a period of one year after the husband's death, such allowances were made from the property of the husband and were not charged against the community property.[30]

[26] See Moore, Cyc. Law Dict.

[27] See ante, § 193.

[28] Gutiérrez, Quaestio CXXI, No. 6, to Nov. Rec. Law 5, Book 10, Title 4.

[29] See Ida. Code 1948, § 14-113; Nev. Rev. St. 1956, §§ 123.260, 134.-020; Wash. Rev. Code 1961, § 11.04.015.

In Arizona, widow's allowance is chargeable pro rata to the respective interests of the decedent and the survivor in the community property where there is no separate property being probated. If there's separate property it would bear its pro rata as a part of the estate being probated. In re Monaghan's Estate, 71 Ariz. 334, 173 P.2d 107.

In Texas, Prob. Code, § 287, provides for setting aside a widow's allowance to be taken from the property that is being probated if she does not have sufficient property of her own.

As to rights of surviving spouse and children in any homestead property, see the local statutes relative to homesteads.

[30] See ante, § 196.

While the allowances for family expenses are more or less dependent upon statutory authorization, it is clear that necessary expenses incurred in the course of administering or settling the affairs of the marital community, whether or not provided for by statute and whether or not incurred in a statutory administration or in a settling up of affairs by a surviving husband, are properly chargeable against the community property and each share of the community property is liable for half of such expenses. But there is no authority in the one so administering or settling up the community affairs to impose new burdens upon the community property in the prosecution of new enterprises or transactions. This would be permissible only if those owning the property agreed to its remaining undivided and continued in operation pursuant to some form of new partnership among themselves.[31]

The question has evidently at times puzzled our American courts as to whether funeral expenses of the deceased spouse are debts of the community property or of the separate estate of the deceased spouse. While funeral expenses are among those involved in administering and settling up the affairs of the decedent, they have no connection with the administration and settling up of the affairs of the conjugal partnership which is separate and distinct from the administration of the individual affairs of the decedent. Moreover, the funeral expenses relate to a time after the conjugal partnership has been dissolved. In the Spanish law, the funeral expenses were chargeable only against the separate estate of the decedent and, indeed, only against that fifth part of his estate which he was free to dispose of by will in any manner he saw fit. Even though the decedent had directed it, such expenses were not deductible from any other part of his estate.[32] The same view has been taken in Louisiana and New Mexico, that the funeral expenses are chargeable against the

[31] Langhurst v. Langhurst, 49 N.M. 329, 164 P.2d 204, noted 20 Tulane L. Rev. 604, and quoting de Funiak, 1st edition.

Ordinary expenses of administration of decedent's estate are chargeable only against decedent's share of the community property. Survivor's share of community is not included in probate unless there are community debts to be paid. In re Monaghan's Estate, 71 Ariz. 334, 173 P.2d 107.

In California, on death of husband, community interest of wife is chargeable with a proportionate share of debts and expenses of administration unless there is express intention to the contrary on decedent's part that his estate shall be liable. Estate of Mari-

nos, 39 Cal. App. 2d 1, 102 P.2d 443. Relation between survivor and heirs prior to partition, see ante, § 204.

[32] "The candles and masses and expenses of interment, with the other kindly bequests, are deducted from the fifth of the estate of the testator, and not from the bulk of the estate, even though the testator directs to the contrary." Law 30 of Leyes de Toro; Novísima Recopilación, Book 10, Title 20, Law 9. To the same effect, see Asso & Mañuel, Institutes of Civil Law of Spain, Book II, Title III, Cap. 2, § 3.

As to the fifth of his estate which he may freely dispose of, see ante, § 193.

separate estate of the decedent or his share in the community but certainly not in whole or in part against the survivor's share in the community property.[33] In Texas the opinion has been expressed that the separate estate of the deceased spouse and the community estate "are alike primarily liable for such expenses," with consideration given to the question upon the credit of which estate the expenses were incurred.[34] In California, the statute enacted in 1957 provides that funeral expenses and expenses of the last illness shall be deemed debts primarily payable from the estate of the deceased spouse, whether or not the surviving spouse is financially able to pay and whether or not the surviving spouse or any other person is liable therefor.[35]

So far as our community property jurisdictions are concerned, the matter must, of course, be largely dependent upon the language of the local statutes and these should be resorted to. Their examination here is not within the scope of this treatise. Without the strongest justification, from their interpretation, the community property should not be subjected to charges for funeral expenses. At most, only the decedent's share of the community property, after partition, should be so charged; or, naturally, if it is charged against the decedent's share before partition, his share should be debited with such amount.[36]

§ 216.— Limitation or prescription of action.

The situation has sometimes arisen that at the time of the death of one spouse, or perhaps shortly thereafter, a community debt has become barred by limitation or prescription. What is the effect if the surviving spouse renews or acknowledges the debt so as to remove

---

[33] See Lacour v. Lacour, 16 La. Ann. 103; Succession of Smith, 9 La. Ann. 107; Peyton v. Jones (La.), 38 So.2d 631; Succession of Pizzati, 141 La. 645, 75 So. 498; Maggio v. Papa, 206 La. 38, 18 So.2d 645; Langhurst v. Langhurst, 49 N.M. 329, 164 P. 2d 204, noted 20 Tulane L. Rev. 604, quoting de Funiak, 1st edition, with approval.

[34] See Goldberg v. Zellner (Tex. Com. App.), 235 S. W. 870. Compare Hocker v. Piper (Tex. Civ. App.), 2 S. W. 2d 997, as to community estate being liable. And see Goggans v. Simmons (Tex.), 2 S. W. 2d 997.

In Arizona, expense of tombstone not community debt chargeable against community interest of surviving wife. Nowland v. Vinyard, 43 Ariz. 27, 29 P.2d 139.

[35] Cal. Prob. Code, § 951.1. Wife's share of community property considered in charging fees and expenses of administration, see Estate of Manley, 169 Cal. App. 2d 649, 337 P.2d 487.

[36] Deductibility of funeral expenses in determining value for purposes of state inheritance tax, see Riley v. Robbins, 1 Cal. 2d 285, 34 P.2d 715 (where funeral expenses of deceased wife, although obligation of husband, were deducted from value of wife's estate); Wittwer v. Pemberton, 188 Wash. 72, 61 P.2d 993 (funeral expenses of deceased wife deducted from entire community rather than from decedent's share in determining tax, although indication that liability for expenses is secondary rather than primary obligation of surviving spouse).

it from the bar of the statute of limitation or prescription? Is this act binding on the heirs of the deceased spouse, so as to render them liable for half of the debt from their share of the community property? Or, so far as the surviving spouse is concerned, does it serve to render such spouse liable for all or for only his or her half share of the community debt? The problem is determinable with more ease where the husband is the surviving spouse who makes the renewal or acknowledgment. Having had the community property in his hands for purposes of management during the marriage, it is still in his hands after the wife's death, at least until such time as he can satisfy community debts and then turn over to the wife's executor or administrator her share of the community property. If during this period the surviving husband renews or acknowledges a community debt previously barred, it would undoubtedly subject the entire community property to payment of the debt before partition is made. Thus, in effect, the half share going to the wife's heirs is subject to liability for half the debt, although they themselves have not done anything to remove the bar of the statute. The foregoing is the answer to the problem, even in the face of the fact that upon the death of the deceased spouse, title to that spouse's share of the community property passes immediately to her heirs and they are immediately owners of that share.[37]

There may be more difficulty in the matter where the wife is the surviving spouse and makes some act of renewal or acknowledgment of the barred community debt. However, where she has, pursuant to statute, qualified as the husband's administratrix or as community survivor with the corresponding right and duty to pay community debts and bring about partition — assuming partition is desirable or demanded — her renewal or acknowledgement of a barred community debt would be equally as effective as in the case of the surviving husband, referred to above. Even if the wife has not actually qualified as the husband's administratrix or as community survivor, her position with respect to the community property may be such as to render her renewal or acknowledgement binding not only as to her but as to the husband's heirs. Thus, in Louisiana, where it may result that a surviving wife has, in addition to her own share of the common property, a usufruct in the share of the husband going to the children, she may be in a position and in authority, in her double capacity as owner and usufructuary, to make payments on a debt so as to interrupt prescription, even though she has not qualified in any official capacity as to the property or the children, and has received no authority from

---

[37] By way of illustration, reference may be made to Johnston v. San Francisco Sav. Bank, 75 Cal. 134, 16 P. 753, 7 Am. St. Rep. 129, although the current local peculiarities of view and some misconceptions in the case concerning the Spanish law have caused some hesitation on our part as to recommending it to the reader as an illustration.

Act of one spouse as surviving community debt, see also ante, § 176.

the children to act for them. Such payments interrupt prescription both as to her and the children.[38] And in Texas, where the homestead has been selected from community property, "it is well settled that the surviving wife, although she has not qualified as the community survivor, has authority to renew a lien on homestead property," so that her acknowledgement of the existence and justness of such a lien would serve to toll the statute of limitations.[39]

In brief then, whether it be the husband or wife, if the surviving spouse is in occupancy, possession and control of the community property prior to its partition or division, renewal or acknowledgment by that spouse of a community debt should be effective to toll the statute of limitations (or interrupt prescription, in the civil law phrase), so far as concerns the liability of the entire community property. But once the community property has been divided or partitioned between the surviving spouse and the heirs of the deceased, that principle is no longer effective. Acknowledgement or attempt at renewal of the community debt by the surviving spouse can have no effect to remove the bar of the statute so far as the heirs are concerned. The converse is also true, in that no act by the heirs can have the effect of removing the bar of the statute so far as the surviving spouse is concerned. There is no partnership or privity of any kind between them that authorizes one to perform acts binding the other.[40] But if the surviving spouse, for instance, after partition tolls or interrupts the running of the statute, is the surviving spouse and the community property in his or her possession liable for the whole of the debt or only for half of it? If the surviving spouse had, at the time of the creation of the debt, made himself or herself liable *in solido* for the entire debt, there is no question that the surviving spouse and the community property in his or her possession would be liable for the entire debt. But ordinarily, the creation of a community debt renders each spouse's share of the community property liable only for half of the debt. Strictly then, an acknowledgement of the debt by one spouse is an acknowledgement of liability for his or her half share of the debt, which was the extent of the original liability. This certainly would be true where the surviving spouse making the ac-

---

[38] Haight v. Johnson, 131 La. 781, 60 So. 248, where the debt was a mortgage debt upon the whole of the community property, and the husband's succession had never been opened and the surviving wife had never been judicially recognized as administratrix, usufructary or tutrix. See also Coreil v. Vidrine, 188 La. 343, 177 So. 233, where, after having occupancy and possession for seven years, she attempted to renounce her right to the community property so as to defeat the effect of her payments on a mortgage note.

[39] See Uvalde Rock Asphalt Co. v. Hightower (Tex. Civ. App.), 154 S. W. 2d 940.

[40] Although the dissolution was by divorce rather than by death, this principle is illustrated by Granjean v. Runke (Tex. Civ. App.), 39 S.W. 945. But compare Rutland Sav. Bank v. Seeger (Tex. Civ. App.), 125 S. W. 2d 1113.

knowledgement is the wife. It should also be true where the surviving spouse is the husband, but the matter may be affected by local law imposing complete responsibility on the husband for support of the family and the interpretation that, at least where the debt was contracted for necessaries, the husband should in any event be liable for the whole debt.

It is evident, of course, that no such problems arise where the surviving spouse has succeeded to the other spouse's share of the community property, so that all the community property belongs to the survivor.

§ 217. Election by wife.

The doctrine of election by the wife which has developed in some of the community property states, particularly in California and Texas, is an anomaly in the law of community property. That doctrine, briefly, is that when the husband assumes to himself the right to dispose by will of the entire community property as if it were his to dispose of, yet makes some provision therein for his wife, perhaps from his own properties, the wife can elect to take under the will, thereby assenting to his disposal of her share of the community property, or she can elect to take her share of the community property, thus denying any right in the husband to dispose of her share by his will and at the same time waiving the provision made for her in the will.[41] That this doctrine was borrowed from the common law as it relates to a widow's dower rights and engrafted onto the community property system is apparent and clear. For the rule at common law is that a widow may elect whether she will accept the provision made for her in her husband's will in lieu of her dower or statutory right in his property or whether she will refuse such testamentary provision and demand her dower right or its statutory substitute. At bottom, this common-law right of dower of the wife, or its statutory substitute, is a contingent or expectant interest in property of the husband. It is not unreasonable in such situation to allow the husband to offer the wife the choice of some other property of his or some other interest in property of his. But under the community property system as developed in Spain and brought to Mexico and our states, there is no question of the marital acquisitions and gains belonging to the husband, with a mere expectant interest therein in the wife. The wife owns half of such acquisitions and gains from the moment of the inception of the right thereto as equally and as completely as the husband.[42] The husband has no power of testamentary disposition over the wife's share of the community property, for one cannot dispose by will of that which belongs to another. Properly speaking,

[41] For collections of numerous cases involving this doctrine of election, see 22 A.L.R. 517; 68 A.L.R. 517; 171 A.L.R. 649; 60 A.L.R. 2d 730; 97 C.J.S., "Wills," § 1264.

[42] See ante, Chap. VII, A.

any such attempt to dispose by will of another's property should be completely ineffective. Insofar as a husband bequeaths anything to his wife, such bequest must belong to her in addition to her share of the community property. Indeed, that there might be no misunderstanding about that, the Spanish codes specifically stated that a legacy by a husband to the wife was not comprised in her half of the community property (which already belonged to her) but was in addition thereto.[43] It follows then that where the husband's will assumes or purports to dispose of any or all of the wife's share of the community property and at the same time makes some testamentary provision for the wife, the principles applicable should render entirely ineffective the husband's attempt to dispose of the wife's share of the community property but the testamentary provision in her favor should be given effect; for although the testator may have been mistaken as to his title to and right to dispose of the wife's share of the community property, it should be presumed that in any event he intended the wife to have that which he devised or bequeathed her.[44] It must be remembered that the common-law rule of election by the wife has its basis in the fact that she has a choice between one interest or another in the husband's property. That is not the situation where community property is concerned. Therefore, in the absence of a specific offer to the wife of certain property in return for her renunciation or surrender of her share of the community property, every intendment should be against the necessity of an election.[45] Our courts have sometimes been too prone to read into the husband's will the necessity of an election by the wife.[46]

While, under the Spanish law of community property, the husband had no power to dispose by will of the wife's share of the common property, he could, however, leave a legacy of his own property to the wife with intention that if it should be accepted it was to be set off against the dowry or against the wife's share of the common prop-

---

[43] See ante, § 193.

[44] La Tourette v. La Tourette, 15 Ariz. 200, 137 P. 426, Ann. Cas. 1915 B 70, is a good illustration of comprehension of some of these matters.

[45] It seems well recognized by our courts that where the husband disposes of property in his will in such terms as "all my property," "all my estate" or the like, that he must be presumed to have known the law and that he can dispose of only his own half of the common property, so that accordingly such disposition must relate to his own property and cannot affect the wife's share of the common property to which she remains entitled as well as to such property of the husband which he has devised or bequeathed her. See

La Tourette v. La Tourette, 15 Ariz. 200, 137 P. 426, Ann. Cas. 1915 B 70; Maxwell v. Harrell (Tex. Civ. App.), 183 S. W. 2d 577; Parker v. Parker, 10 Tex. 83; Farmer v. Zinn (Tex. Com. App.), 276 S. W. 191; Herrick v. Miller, 69 Wash. 456, 125 P. 974; Collins v. Collins, 152 Wash. 499, 278 P. 186.

[46] Parole or extrinsic evidence as admissible or inadmissible to show intent of testator to put wife to election, see La Tourette v. La Tourette, 15 Ariz. 200, 137 P. 426, Ann. Cas. 1915 B 70; Kreis v. Kreis (Tex. Civ. App.), 36 S. W. 2d 821; Herrick v. Miller, 69 Wash. 456, 125 P. 974, aff'd on rehearing 74 Wash. 699, 134 P. 189.

erty. But this seems to have been limited by the view that the legacy must be of the same nature as the property against which it was designed to be set off. It was doubted that a legacy of a quantity of property, for example, could be set off against a species of property.[47] The chief justification, under principles of community property, for a proffer by the husband of a choice by the wife would be that it represents a post-mortem offer of a contract or agreement changing their marital property rights. Under the Spanish system of community property, the spouses might either by antenuptial or postnuptial agreement or contract alter or modify the legal community.

It is true that under the Spanish community property system, as will be seen more at length in the next section, the wife could renounce, after the husband's death, her share of the marital acquests and gains. That is, she could declare the nonexistence of a conjugal partnership. But that renunciation was not made on the basis of her obtaining something else instead; rather it was an option which she had which might be exercised when the community debts exceeded the community acquisitions so that the conjugal partnership was a detriment to her rather than an advantage.

The development of the doctrine of election is more obvious in the case of California than in the case of Texas. In the former state, the frequent misinterpretation of the principles of community property, and the frequent attempt to explain them by the use of common-law concepts led to numerous decisions which declared that "community property" was actually owned by the husband and that the wife had merely an expectant interest in half of that property which vested in her at the husband's death. This torturing of the wife's rights under the community property system into something resembling the wife's common-law right of dower led logically to the belief that the husband had the right to proffer the wife some other property or property interest of his in place of her mere "expectant" interest in the marital acquisitions and gains, and that she had an election to take one or the other just as she chose. That the doctrine of election still exists in California and that it would apply to the husband as well as to the wife is the opinion of the standard encyclopedia of California law.[48] The cases substantiate this so far as concerns the wife.[49]

§ 218. Renunciation.

The right of the spouses, under the Spanish law of community property, to enter into antenuptial or post-nuptial agreements relating

[47] See Matienzo, Azevedo and Gutiérrez to Nov. Rec. Law 8, Book 10, Title 4.

[48] See Cal. Juris. 2d, "Community Property."

[49] See Estate of Chapin, 47 Cal. App. 2d 605, 118 P.2d 499; Security-First Nat. Bank v. Stack, 32 Cal. App. 2d 586, 90 P.2d 337.

As to election by agreement expressly made, see Brown and Sherman, Elections to Take by Will: Some Practical Considerations, 23 Cal. State Bar Jour. 11.

to the marital acquisitions and gains was well recognized. The wife (or the husband for that matter) might renounce the right to share equally in the marital acquisition and gains and thus there would not be any community of property between the spouses; whatever was acquired by either would be the separate property of the one acquiring it.[50] This right of renunciation extended to the wife even after dissolution of the marriage by the death of the husband.[51] In other words, she might at that time renounce her share in the gains and profits acquired during the marriage. If it be wondered what advantage there was to the wife in making such renunciation, the answer is that when a wife renounced her right to half of the common property, she was also relieved from liability for any part of the community debts contracted by the husband during marriage.[52] Thus the privilege was extended to her, where debts exceeded the amount of the property so as to make the conjugal partnership a liability to her, of renouncing that which was detrimental rather than beneficial. Since it may be rightly assumed in most cases that an excess of marital debts over marital acquisitions results from poor, wasteful or inefficient management by the husband who was the one exercising the control and management of community affairs, it would seem only fair that the spouse not responsible therefor and exercising no control in the matter should be allowed to repudiate and escape an injury or loss that would result through no fault of her own.[53] This right of the wife to renounce or repudiate must not be misconstrued as an indication that she had never owned and possessed her share, for that fact was not denied; but she did have, under the principles of community property, the right to revoke her ownership and possession.[54] If she showed no indication of whether she meant to accept or repudiate, community creditors might apply for a court order to compel her to indicate her acceptance or repudiation, and she had to do so within a hundred

---

[50] See ante, § 135.

[51] Matienzo, Gloss I, No. 8, to Nov. Rec. Law 9; Azevedo, No. 8 to the same; Gutiérrez, Quaestio CXXVI, Nos. 3, 4, to the same.

Renunciation under French customs, see Brissaud, History of French Private Law, p. 844 et seq.

[52] See Novísima Recopilación, Book 10, Title 4, Law 9.

Renunciation during marriage as affecting liability for debts, see ante, § 173.

[53] Moreover, she might have acquired or earned considerable property during the marriage which would constitute community property but which would disappear by reason of

the husband's poor management if subject to liability for community debts.

[54] "It is no answer to say that the renouncing wife had already acquired ownership and possession of the property acquired during marriage (as I fully demonstrated above in law 2 gloss 3 no. 2 et seq. and gloss 4) and therefore cannot renounce already acquired property. For we do not deny that the wife had acquired ownership and possession, but we say that this is not irrevocable as is ownership at international law (*jure gentium*) but revocable as I said above in law 2 gloss 3 no. 17." Matienzo, Gloss I, No. 5, to Nov. Rec. Law 9. See also Gutiérrez, Quaestio CXXVI, No. 5, to the same.

days or such lesser period thereof as the judge set.[55] Once having accepted or repudiated, she could not thereafter change her mind.[56]

In Louisiana, the right of the wife to renounce as an incident of dissolution of the marriage is established by statute.[57] The right exists regardless of whether the dissolution is accomplished by death, divorce, legal separation, or mere judicial separation of property.[58] While the statutory provisions were taken from the French Code Napoleon,[59] the principles established thereby closely resemble those of the Spanish community property law. Although a detailed discussion of the application of the statutory principles would not be hampered by lack of cases, of which there are many, such a detailed discussion is not within the contemplation of this work.[60] It is pertinent to notice, however, that the former interpretation that renunciation by the wife was presumed unless she formally accepted her share,[61] is no longer followed, and the presumption now seems to be that she accepts unless formally renouncing.[62] She cannot, however, continue to occupy and possess community property in her double capacity of owner of her share and usufructuary of the other share for a period of years and then renounce so as retroactively to relieve herself of liability for debts which she has acknowledged during her period of occupancy and possession.[63]

Some indication of the right of the wife to renounce after dissolution of the marriage is found in other states.[64]

C.   DIVORCE AND SEPARATION

§ 219.   Divorce and division of property under Spanish law.

Merely to state that in the Spanish and early Mexican law legal separation or divorce terminated the conjugal partnership in acquests and gains is insufficient. The matter is not subject to such brief dis-

---

[55] Matienzo, Gloss I, No. 8, to Nov. Rec. Law 9; Llamas y Molina, No. 17 to the same.

[56] Matienzo, Gloss I, No. 9, to Nov. Rec. Law 9; Gutiérrez, Quaestio CXXVI, No. 4, to the same; Llamas y Molina, No. 17, to the same.

[57] La. Civ. Code, arts. 2410–2419, 2421–2423, 2430.

[58] Divorce and legal separation, see post, § 231.

[59] See present French Civil Code, arts. 1453–1466.

[60] See collection of cases in Mr. Dart's annotated edition of the La. Civ. Code; also 41 C.J.S., Husband and Wife, § 560 et seq.

[61] See Hefner v. Parker, 47 La. Ann. 656, 17 So. 207.

[62] See Rawlings v. Stokes, 194 La. 206, 193 So. 589. But cf. Pelican Well Tool & Supply Co. v. Sebastian, 212 La. 217, 31 So.2d 745.

[63] See Coreil v. Vidrine, 188 La. 343, 177 So. 233.

[64] See Austin v. Strong, 117 Tex. 263, 1 S. W. 2d 872, 79 A.L.R. 1528, wherein it was said that the surviving wife had never accepted bank stock purchased by the husband during his life, so as to be liable for assessments.

Right of heirs of deceased spouse to renounce, see ante § 211.

position, for the nature of the legal separation or divorce and the conduct of the spouses must be considered.

Since we are concerned primarily with the effect of divorce upon the conjugal partnership in acquests and gains rather than with divorce itself, there is little necessity for a discussion of the history of divorce and the effect of religious and social forces on public views as to divorce.[65] But for purposes of understanding it is advisable to compare our definitions with those of the Spanish law. In considering the dissolution of marriage, we usually distinguish, at the present day, among the following: annulment of the marriage, that is, a sentence of nullity, which establishes that a supposed marriage never existed at all or at least was voidable at the election of one or both of the parties; divorce, that is, a dissolution of the tie or bond of marriage, which dissolves the marriage absolutely from the date of the decree so that the parties are usually free to remarry; and limited divorce or legal separation which effects merely a partial suspension of the marriage, or which may be said to dissolve the cohabitation but not the tie of marriage, or, in other words, which merely sanctions separation from bed and board. The last mentioned is not strictly a divorce as we would consider the term in this country, although it is true that the term "divorce" is frequently used loosely to cover both the absolute divorce and the limited divorce. But the Latin word *divortium* from which we obtain our word "divorce" and which long continued in the language of the law in those countries in which the law was influenced by the Roman law, did not have the more restricted meaning which we now give the word "divorce." Brissaud notes, in his discussion of the old French law, that the term *divortium* designated both separation of spouses upon annulment of the marriage and the judicial separation or separation of domicile.[66] Likewise, the Spanish code, Las Siete Partidas, promulgated in 1263, declared that *"Divortium* in Latin, means separation in Castilian."[67] And investigation of the Partidas as well as of the jurisconsults shows that such a separation, in the sense of legal separation, consisted of two kinds, an annulment of the marriage because of some impediment existing between the parties, as for example impotency; and a legal separation dissolving the marriage as to cohabitation only.[68] It must be remembered then that when the Spanish jurisconsults discuss divorce or legal separation they are referring both to what we would designate annulment of marriage or sentence of nullity and to what we would designate as limited divorce or separation from bed and board. For

---

[65] As to these matters, see such works as Bishop, Commentaries on Marriage and Divorce, 6th Ed., chap. II; Brissaud, History of French Private Law, pp. 141–151.

[66] Brissaud, History of French Private Law, p. 145.

[67] Las Siete Partidas, Part. 4, Title 10, Law 1.

[68] Las Siete Partidas, Part. 4, Titles 9 and 10; Matienzo, Gloss I, Nos. 44–57, to Nov. Rec. Law 1; Azevedo, No. 14, to Nov. Rec. Law 1, Book 10, Title 4.

there was no absolute divorce in the Spanish law in the sense of a divorce dissolving the tie or bond of marriage from the date of the decree.[69] In this respect, since Spain was pre-eminently a Catholic country, the Spanish law reflected the tenet of the Catholic Church that a marriage lawfully contracted, without any impediment existing between the parties, is indissoluble.[70]

§ 220.   — Grounds.

Since our primary concern, so far as relates to consideration of divorce, is the effect of divorce upon marital property rights, any discussion of the grounds of divorce may not be entirely relevant. It occurs to the authors, however, that a brief reference to the grounds in the Spanish law may be of value in showing their similarity to those in our local laws. The grounds or impediments which caused the annulment of a marriage, under the Spanish law, differed little from those which we recognize today, so far as concerned such matters as impotency or marrying within prohibited degrees of relationship. There were in addition, of course, a number having their basis in religious tenets, but these it is unnecessary to detail since they are not legal grounds for annulment in this country.[71]

The only ground of interest to us today which the Partidas provided as ground for the legal separation as to cohabitation was adultery and this was not alone adultery on the part of the wife, as some of our courts seem to think, but adultery on the part of either spouse.[72] But it also appears that, stemming from the Fuero Real promulgated

---

[69] See Las Siete Partidas, Part. 4, Titles 9 and 10.

"Marriage is the conjunction of man and woman, made with the intention to live always together, and not to separate; observing chastity one to the other and not cohabiting with any other woman or man, living both together. Upon this definition are founded the following principles, . . . 2nd, That this perpetual union cannot be dissolved, if marriage be lawfully contracted. . . . From the second principle it arises, . . . 3d, That the marriage consummated, but not that which is only duly solemnized, is indissoluble as to the tie or chain, but not with regard to cohabitation." Asso and Mañuel, Institutes of Civil Law of Spain, Book I, Title VI, § 2.

[70] Present day codes of many civil law countries, including Spain, still reflect this view; however, the majority of the civil law countries now

sanction absolute divorce, even though the predominant religion in most is Catholicism. See Lobingier, "Modern Civil Law," 40 Corpus Juris 1271; Ireland & Galindez, Divorce in the Americas, Dennis & Co., 1947.

[71] See Las Siete Partidas, Part. 4, Titles 9 and 10.

Impediments to marriage under French customs, see Brissaud, History of French Private Law, p. 111 et seq.

[72] "A husband and a wife can accuse each other in another way, in addition to those mentioned in the preceding law. This is on the ground of adultery, and where the accusation is brought for the purpose of separation, so that they should not live together or have carnal intercourse, no one else should make such accusation but themselves against one another." Las Siete Partidas, Part. 4, Title 9, Law 2.

in 1255, abandonment or desertion constituted a recognized ground.[73] Subsequently, other grounds were recognized, such as cruelty, dangerous insanity of one of the spouses which made living together dangerous, and continuous disputes endangering the life of either.[74]

§ 221.   — Dissolution or legal separation as to cohabitation.

Considering what constituted divorce in the Spanish law, we may first inquire whether the divorce in the sense of legal separation from cohabitation dissolved the conjugal partnership in acquests and gains. To attempt a correct answer in brief would merely warrant the statement that it might or might not, as the circumstances warranted, which would provide no explanation at all. It becomes necessary, therefore, to consider the matter somewhat more in detail. The first thing that is apparent is that the marriage itself was not dissolved by such a legal separation, since the separation itself was, in effect, only one from bed and board. The marriage bond still existed and in view of that fact it might be assumed by the reader that the partnership in acquests and gains still continued. On the other hand, it was a basic element for the existence of the conjugal partnership that there be cohabitation. To begin the conjugal partnership in the acquests and gains during marriage, it was not sufficient in the Spanish law that there merely be a duly solemnized ceremony of marriage. In addition to that, the wife had to go to live with the husband. In other words, only when the marriage had been duly solemnized and the spouses had begun to cohabit did the partnership in acquests and gains begin to function.[75] If there ceased to be cohabitation at any time, the partnership in the acquests and gains ceased, for that partnership was based upon mutual obligations of fidelity, loyalty and duty and the sharing together of the burdens of marriage. Nevertheless, this was subject to important qualifications, for it was well recognized that the circumstances of the spouses might compel them to live apart, as where the husband had to be absent for business reasons for a long period of time or where ill health of the wife compelled her to live in some more favorable locality than that in which the husband had

---

[73] See Fuero Real, Book 4, Title 5, Law 5.

Azevedo instanced the situation of a husband remaining away from home in an effort to deprive the wife of her share of his acquisitions, in other words an abandonment of the wife. See Azevedo, No. 14, to Nov. Rec. Law 1.

[74] See Schmidt, Civil Law of Spain and Mexico, pp. 9–11.

Another ground was where one spouse, with the necessary consent of the other, entered a religious order.

Apparently, the other spouse, besides giving this consent, also had to take a vow of chastity. See Las Siete Partidas, Part. 4, Title 1, Law 4; Part. 4, Title 10, Law 2. We have been informed that this is still recognized by the Catholic Church as a ground for separation but with the modification that both spouses must have entered religious orders.

[75] Necessity of cohabitation, see ante, § 57.

his business. In such cases, an absence of cohabitation did not affect the conjugal partnership because there was still a union of wills.[76]

It was also recognized that the husband merely by absenting himself from the wife could not claim that there was no cohabitation and thus no sharing in acquests and gains during marriage. That would have sanctioned fraud and permitted the wife to be cheated.[77] Likewise, if the husband expelled his wife from the home without just cause, he could not escape sharing the acquests and gains by contending that cohabitation had ceased. And by logical steps, it was considered that if she was compelled to leave the home because of his cruel treatment or by reason of his adultery and to live apart, it was the same as if he had forcibly expelled her. In such cases, then, in which the spouses lived apart due to the husband's fault, as by reason of his abandonment of the wife or his cruelty or his adultery, the wife was still entitled to share in all acquisitions and gains made by him both before and during the separation. Moreover, the husband, as the one at fault, forfeited his right to share in any acquisitions and gains made by the wife.[78]

Upon the granting of a legal separation from cohabitation, the wife was entitled to the return of her dowry and to a moiety of the

[76] Importance or necessity of cohabitation, see ante, § 57.

Agreements between spouses, see ante, § 135.

[77] "For the phrase '*De consumo*' should not be taken to refer to simultaneous and inseparable cohabitation but to the duration of the marriage, i.e., that at the time the husband made the profits the wife must have been taken to her husband's house and the marriage still existing. Otherwise, the wife might easily be cheated by her husband, remaining away. . . ." Azevedo, No. 14, to Nov. Rec. Law 1, Book 10, Title 4.

[78] "What happens if, after the husband has taken his wife to his house, he expels her from the house without fault on her part and without good cause and if meanwhile, while the marriage still subsists, he acquires something? Must he share this with his wife? Didacus Segura . . . says that such profits must be shared. . . . Otherwise the husband might profit by his wrongdoing and seize profits which the law takes from him. . . . The profits are given to the wife on condition that she cohabits with her husband, as we have seen; and this condition is taken as satisfied when it is not due to the wife that it has not been fulfilled. . . . I infer from this that a similar rule applies if on account of the husband's cruelty a separation takes place with regard to bed and cohabitation. . . . Similarly if the separation is due to the husband's adultery. . . . Not only must the wife be restored to her position . . . but she is entitled to a moiety of the profits acquired by her husband before the separation. . . . Not only property acquired before separation must be shared but also property acquired after the separation. For it would be most unjust that a wife expelled by her husband's fault and separated from him so far as concerns mutual cohabitation should be deprived of the profits given to her by law, i.e., of her moiety of the property acquired during marriage. . . . And in like manner if a wife is separated from her husband and ceases to cohabit with him owing to his fault, she does not acquire for him and need not share her acquisitions with him." Matienzo, Gloss I, Nos. 45, 47, 48, 53, to Nov. Rec. Law 1. (Several of the omissions in the quoted material are omissions of cited authorities.) And see Escriche, Diccionario, "Bienes Gananciales."

profits acquired by the husband before the separation — without, of course, having to share her acquisitions before that time — and the learned commentators cautioned lawyers to remember that upon petitioning on the wife's behalf for separation and divorce they should ask for a moiety of such profits as well as for the return of the dowry.[79] To the extent that acquisitions made by the husband up to that time were partitioned, it might be said that the legal separation terminated the conjugal partnership in acquests and gains, but even so it would be a somewhat misleading statement. For the principles applicable in the case of a mere living apart continued to be applicable thereafter. That is to say, the fact that the wife's right to live apart had been recognized by a "divorce" or legal separation as to cohabitation did not discontinue her right to share in the husband's acquisitions and not to share hers with him. So long as it was not due to fault of hers that she had to live apart, whether or not there had been entered a decree of dissolution of cohabitation, she continued to have the right to share in the acquisitions which the husband made meanwhile and the husband could not share in her acquisitions.[80] And if it was the wrong of the husband which compelled the wife to live separate and apart, the wife was entitled to be supported by the husband even if she had brought no dowry to the marriage.[81]

It is, perhaps, needless to point out that where she was forced

---

[79] See Matienzo, Gloss I, No. 47, to Nov. Rec. Law 1, citing Joannes Lupi, Antonius Gomez, Covarruvias and others.

That the husband was compelled to repay the dowry, and even according to some authors to give up the fruits or profits of the dowry which might have accrued to him by law or agreement, see Matienzo, Gloss I, Nos. 49, 51, to Nov. Rec. Law 1, citing other authorities.

Disposition of dowry upon dissolution of marriage, see also ante, § 112.

[80] "I infer from this that a similar rule applies if on account of the husband's cruelty a separation takes place with regard to bed and cohabitation." Matienzo, Gloss I, No. 47, to Nov. Rec. Law 1.

"Not only property acquired before separation must be shared but also property acquired after the separation. For it would be most unjust that a wife expelled by her husband's fault and separated from him so far as concerns mutual cohabitation should be deprived of the profits given to her by law, i.e., of her moiety of the property acquired during marriage [citing authorities]." Matienzo, Gloss I, No. 48, to Nov. Rec. Law 1.

The view that simultaneous cohabitation must exist "must be modified, however, if the absence of the husband is not due to the wife's fault but to the husband's . . . ; for example if the husband . . . has driven his wife from the home without cause, or if owing to the cruelty of the husband the wife has run away and lives apart by reason of divorce so far as concerns mutual cohabitation, due to no fault of the wife. For then the wife is not deprived of her moiety of the profits made meanwhile by her husband." Azevedo, No. 14, to Nov. Rec. Law 1.

[81] Matienzo, Gloss I, Nos. 50, 52, to Nov. Rec. Law 1.

"Escriche infers from the cedulas [i. e., royal orders] of the twenty-second of March, 1787, and eighteenth of March, 1804, that after divorce the husband must allow alimony to the wife, provided her necessities require it, although her conduct may have given occasion for the divorce." Wheat v. Owens, 15 Tex. 241, 65 Am. Dec. 164.

by the husband's fault to live apart or to separate from him, the wife obtained the independent management of her own acquisitions, as well as the share of the husband's acquisitions partitioned to her.

The foregoing principles were equally applicable where the divorce or living apart was due to the fault of the wife, for the principles which applied to one were equally applicable to the other. The husband was not required to share his acquisitions with the wife but was entitled to share in her acquisitions, whether the respective acquisitions were made before or during the separation.[82]

On the other hand, it might well happen that legal separation as to cohabitation was not caused by the fault of either spouse, in the sense of any wrongful conduct. For instance, where it became necessary to separate because one spouse became dangerously insane, so as to make living together a danger, or where one spouse with the other's consent entered a religious order.[83] In the situations where the legal separation from cohabitation was not due to the fault of one spouse, the conjugal partnership did cease upon the separation. But general statements, such as Schmidt makes, that the conjugal partnership in acquests and gains ceased upon legal separation "from bed and board," are inaccurate.[84] The Spanish commentators and jurisconsults are uniform in stating that the "divorce" or legal separation as to cohabitation terminated the conjugal partnership only if it resulted from no misconduct of one of the spouses; but if it did result from the misconduct of one of the spouses, it terminated the partnership only as to the guilty spouse who lost all right to share in the other's acquisitions, but did not terminate it as to the innocent spouse who

[82] "But if the divorce or living apart is due not to the husband's fault but to that of the wife, e.g., if the wife has committed adultery, the wife is bound to share with her husband anything which she has herself acquired. For rules which apply to a wife apply to a husband and *vice versa,* since correlatives must be judged by one and the same standard. . . . In such a case the wife is entitled to nothing from the property acquired or to be acquired by her husband. . . ." Matienzo, Gloss I, Nos. 54, 55, to Nov. Rec. Law 1.

"Nor likewise will the husband be deprived of his share if owing to his wife's fault, e.g., her adultery, they have been divorced and the wife has meanwhile acquired profits." Azevedo, No. 14, to Nov. Rec. Law 1.

The wife's adultery also caused her to lose dowry and marriage deposit. See ante, § 189.

[83] In relation to this latter situation, it was said: "Or it may be that by consent of both spouses a vow of chastity is taken and they live apart. . . . If so each one acquires for himself or herself and profits are not shared. . . ." Matienzo, Gloss I, No. 57, to Nov. Rec. Law 1. And as to this latter situation, see also ante, § 220, n. 74.

[84] Schmidt, Civil Law of Spain and Mexico, pp. 15, 16.

Cf. also the statement in 11 Am. Jur. "Community Property," § 73, that a decree of divorce against a wife for adultery, in the Spanish law, forfeited all her right to share in common property. Not only is this inaccurate in not specifying that she forfeited only her share in the husband's acquisitions, but it implies that this was true only of the wife and not also of the husband.

continued to be entitled to share in the acquisitions of the guilty spouse.[85] Of course, the death of one of the spouses brought to an end the sharing of the acquisitions of the guilty spouse and brought about the necessity of a partition of such acquisitions of the guilty spouse made subsequent to the separation.[86]

§ 222.   — Dissolution of marriage by annulment.

Heretofore we have considered only the *divortium* or "separation" in the Spanish law which involved dissolution as to cohabitation. In respect to the form of divorce or separation which was in reality an annulment of the marriage, the marriage itself no longer subsisted and since the conjugal partnership in acquests and gains depended upon the subsistence of the marriage for its own existence, the conjugal sharing ceased when the marriage did. Therefore, anything thereafter acquired by either party belonged entirely to the acquirer and was not shared with the other party.[87] It will probably be presumed

[85] See Matienzo and Azevedo, as quoted and cited in preceding notes, and see the quotations immediately following in this note.

"But this sharing of properties ceases in the following cases: . . . 4th. When the spouses separate with legal license, for then each makes his or her own separately whatever each may acquire after the separation; but if the husband expels the wife from the home without legal cause, or treats her cruelly so that she is compelled to separate from him, she will nevertheless acquire her half of the community property during the separation, in the same manner as before, according to the common opinion of the authors." Escriche, Diccionario, "Bienes Gananciales."

"Further in case that the separation should be by divorce, the same authors judge that the one who gave the cause therefor frees the other from the partnership, leaving himself or herself obligated, however, as happens in a wrongful renunciation of the common partnership." Novísimo Sala Mexicano, Sec. 2a, Title IV, No. 2.

"To this general rule, various cases are expected, in which the properties which they gained while married are not shared between them: . . . The second, when they are divorced for fault of one of them, in which case

the one at fault would take nothing." Febrero, Librería de Escribanos, Testamentos y Contratos I, Cap. I, § 22, No. 242. Febrero's brevity of expression which so frequently results in incomplete generalities is evident here. In stating that the one at fault takes nothing, he omits to add the important qualification that the one at fault would take nothing from the acquisitions of the other spouse.

[86] Dissolution of marital community by death, see ante, this chapter, subdivision B.

[87] "If however husband and wife are for some reason separated by papal dispensation (as to which see Decret. Greg. III. 32.7) and one of them subsequently acquires something, such acquisition belongs to the acquirer and is not shared with the other. For then the marriage no longer subsists, and it was the marriage which was the cause of the sharing, by this and similar laws; and if the cause ceases, then the sharing must cease too, Dig. 37.14.6.2." Matienzo, Gloss I, No. 56, to Nov. Rec. Law 1.

"And in no. 37 he [Segura] says that if for some reason the marriage has by dispensation been entirely dissolved and a separation has been made of the customary undivided life, then,

— and in making such presumption the reader will be correct — that the preceding statement implies that there was a sharing of the acquisitions and gains made prior to the sentence of annulment; and it may be wondered how there could be an equal sharing as between husband and wife when it turns out that the parties were never husband and wife by reason of annulment. The answer is that the attempted marriage was considered a putative marriage and in the civil law acquisitions of parties to a putative marriage were considered community property.[88] Thus, it will be seen that this form of "divorce" or "separation" in the Spanish law presents, in many particulars except possibly as to misconduct as the ground of dissolution, a situation somewhat analogous to that in our American states where an absolute divorce is granted.

§ 223.   — Claims of creditors.

So far as concerned the settlement and division of community property upon legal separation, the situation was much the same as that where dissolution of the marital community resulted through death. That is, the community property was subjected to the payment of community debts before any division or partition.[89] Where the wife was the guilty spouse, her acquisitions had to be shared with the husband and thus represented community property subject to the claims of community creditors. While the husband's acquisitions did not have to be shared with the wife, it was subject to the claims which were in the nature of community claims, for the husband's duty to support the family rendered him, in any event, liable for debts contracted in that respect, and his acquisitions were liable therefor. Where the husband was the guilty spouse, his acquisitions were subject to be shared and were liable to the claims of community creditors, but the wife's acquisitions were not subject to be shared and were not subject to community

since the parties are wholly separated and freed from the bond of matrimony, the first opinion would hold [i. e., that cohabitation by a husband and a wife are necessary to make profits divisible under this law]." Azevedo, No. 14, to Nov. Rec. Law 1.

Differing from the situation in which marriage was solemnized and consummated and then one spouse entered a religious order, with the consent of the other who also took a vow of chastity, in which case a legal separation was warranted, was the situation where one entered a religious order after solemnization of the marriage but before consummation of the marriage. In the latter

case the marriage was completely dissolved. See Matienzo, Gloss I, No. 56, to Nov. Rec. Law 1.

[88] A putative marriage as one forbidden or incapable of being contracted because of some legal impediment between the parties but contracted in good faith and in ignorance of the impediment on the part of one at least of the contracting parties, and the sharing of acquisitions as community property, see ante, § 56.

[89] See ante, this chapter, subdivision B. And see Ellsworth v. Ellsworth, 5 Ariz. App. 89, 423 P.2d 364, quoting de Funiak, 1st edition.

creditors, since her acquisitions were not community property and were not primarily liable for the support of the family, since that obligation was imposed upon the husband. An exception might exist as to the wife's acquisitions where she had entered into a joint obligation with the husband on account of marital expenses, or where the poverty of the husband had thrown the burden of supporting him upon her.[90]

As to partition brought about by the death of one of the spouses sometime after legal separation had taken place, or for that matter after a mere living apart resulting from the fault of one spouse, debts and claims by reason of marital obligations had to be first deducted. The property subject to such debts and claims would be governed by the same principles just enunciated.[91]

§ 224. American community property states.

In all of the community property states marriages may be annulled for impediments rendering them void or voidable. These impediments or grounds in such respects as impotency, the existence of a former husband or wife, marriage within prohibited degrees of relationship, and the like, are frequently similar to the canonical grounds; in other respects they may differ radically from canonical grounds. The problem is not one, however, that need be gone into here.[92]

In all of our community property states absolute divorce is provided for by legislative enactment. Most of these states seem to be uniform in listing adultery, cruelty, desertion and conviction or imprisonment for crime as grounds for absolute divorce. It is true that they are not altogether uniform in their definition of what constitutes these several grounds, for cruelty in some of the states may include mental cruelty, in others it may not; in some refusal of marital intercourse may constitute desertion, in others it may not. However, we are not here concerned with these distinctions. Other grounds occurring in varying degrees among these states include impotence, habitual intoxication, nonsupport, insanity, and others.[93] The effect of the absolute divorce is to dissolve the marriage entirely, leaving the former spouses in the status of single persons and usually with the right to marry again. The right to marry again is sometimes prohibited for a period immediately after the granting of the divorce, ranging in time from six months to a year,[94] or may be forbidden entirely to the

[90] Joint obligations of spouses and wife's duty of support, see ante, Chap. IX.

[91] See also ante, this chapter, subd. B.

[92] See Bishop, Commentaries on Marriage and Divorce; Vernier, American Family Laws.

[93] See Vernier, American Family Laws, vol. 2, § 62.

[94] Prohibition for limited periods against remarriage in Arizona, Idaho, Louisiana, Texas (divorce for cruelty), see Vernier, American Family Laws, vol. 2, § 92.

guilty party, as where the cause for divorce has been adultery.[95] There is also, as in California, the interlocutory decree of divorce, wherein the court, in determining that the divorce ought to be granted, enters an interlocutory decree which is not made final until several months thereafter. Only after this final decree is entered does the divorce become absolute with the parties having the status of single persons and the right to remarry.[96]

In California and Texas the policy is to make dissolution of the marriage possible upon what is in effect incompatibility of the spouses. Accordingly, former law, both statutory and judicial, must now be deemed largely inapplicable.[97]

So far as concerns the legal separation which dissolves the cohabitation but not the marriage, by whatever name it is called it is, in effect, provided for in the statutes of most of the community property states. In Arizona and Louisiana specific provision is made for "separation from bed and board,"[98] and in others of the states provision is made for suits for separate maintenance or for support and maintenance, or by similar names, which permit or sanction the dissolution of cohabitation although continuing to impose an obligation of support or maintenance or payment of alimony — by whatever term designated — upon the husband.[99] It is true, admittedly, that the legal separation from bed and board and the allowance of separate maintenance are distinguishable in that the former specifically authorizes the dissolution as to cohabitation or sanctions the refusal of the petitioning spouse to cohabit with the other, while the latter more directly involves property rights and may not expressly authorize the living apart of the spouses.[1] Nevertheless, the latter may authorize or sanction a dissolution of the cohabitation as well as making provision as to property rights, and where it is in fact so used it is similar in nature to the legal separation from bed and board in that they both then

---

[95] See La. Civ. Code, arts. 137, 139, 161; the provision also exists in Louisiana as to sentence to infamous punishment.

[96] See Cal. Civ. Code, §§ 4512–4514. Interlocutory decree as affecting rights in community property, see post, § 227.

Somewhat similarly, in Louisiana, the spouse must first obtain a decree of separation and wait one year for the decree of absolute divorce except in cases of adultery or sentence to infamous punishment. La. Civ. Code, art. 139.

[97] See, e.g., Cal. Civ. Code, § 4500 et seq., becoming effective January 1, 1970.

[98] Ariz. Rev. St. 1956, § 25-331;

La. Civ. Code, art. 138.

The Arizona court has described this legal separation from bed and board as being the ecclesiastical or common-law divorce from bed and board. Williams v. Williams, 33 Ariz. 367, 265 P. 87, 61 A. L. R. 1264.

[99] See Cal. Civ. Code, §§ 4516, 4700 et. seq.; Nev. Rev. St. 1956, § 125.190 et seq.; N.M. St. 1953, §§ 22-7-2, 22-7-6. See Radermacher v. Radermacher, 61 Idaho 261, 100 P.2d 955.

Cf. Martin v. Martin (Tex. Com. App.), 17 S. W. 2d 789.

Effect of prior decree of divorce, see Colbert v. Colbert (Cal. App.), 159 P.2d 668.

[1] Williams v. Williams, 33 Ariz. 367, 265 P. 87, 61 A. L. R. 1264.

have the effect of dissolving (or sanctioning an already existing dissolution of) cohabitation but do not dissolve the marriage itself.[2] The grounds for these legal separations may be, variously, the same grounds for which an absolute divorce is granted, or for such conduct on the part of the husband toward the wife that renders it unsafe or improper for her to cohabit with him,[3] or for desertion or nonsupport.[4]

§ 225. — Effect of institution and pendency of divorce proceedings.

The statutes of the several community property states are fairly uniform as to the manner in which the community property is affected by the institution and pendency of proceedings to dissolve the marriage or cohabitation. The text following touches briefly upon the salient matters with illustrative citations. The effect of the institution of the divorce proceeding is usually to suspend the husband's exercise of management of the community property in the sense that he shall not thereafter contract any debts on account of the community property or dispose of any of the community property.[5] Indeed, any alienation of community property after the institution of such proceedings may be declared null and void if proved to the satisfaction of the court that it was done with fraudulent view to injure the wife's rights.[6] The court is usually empowered to make whatever orders concerning the property shall be necessary,[7] restraining its use or disposition[8] or making provision for support and maintenance therefrom pending the divorce proceeding.[8a] The wife herself, in order to preserve her

[2] In the case of New Mexico, for instance, separate maintenance is granted where the husband and wife have permanently separated. See N.M. St. 1953, §§ 22-7-2, 22-7-6.

"It is true, Idaho does not recognize the right to a divorce from bed and board, but it does recognize the right to separate maintenance, as heretofore pointed out. The word 'separate', used in connection with 'maintenance' indicates that it is the right of the wife to be maintained by her husband while living apart from him. Our remedy of separate maintenance, while not identical with divorce *a mensa et thoro,* is similar to it in some respects and may be used in place of it." Radermacher v. Radermacher, 61 Idaho 261, 100 P.2d 955.

[3] See, for example, Ariz. Rev. St. 1956, § 25-331.

[4] See Vernier, American Family Laws, vol. 2.

[5] Ariz. Rev. St. 1956, §§ 25-314, 25-316; La. Civ. Code, art. 150; Tex. Family Code 1969, § 3.57.

[6] Ariz. Rev. St. 1956, §§ 25-315, 25-316; La. Civ. Code, art. 150; Tex. Rev. Civ. St. 1925, art. 4634.

Burden of proof upon spouse, see Sparks v. Taylor, 99 Tex. 411, 90 S. W. 485, 11 L. R. A. (N. S.) 381.

Wife's right to maintain action against husband and one to whom he had conveyed property pending divorce, see Fonner v. Martens, 186 Cal. 623, 200 P. 405. See also Kashaw v. Kashaw, 3 Cal. 312.

[7] N.M. St. 1953, § 22-7-6.

Jurisdiction of court over community real property, see Cal. Civ. Code, §§ 4502, 4518.

[8] N.M. St. 1953, § 22-7-6.

[8a] Cal. Civ. Code, §§ 4516, 4518; N.M. St. 1953, § 22-7-6; Tex. Family Code 1969, § 3.59.

rights, may be entitled to require an inventory and appraisement to be made of the property in the husband's control, and to have an injunction to restrain him from disposing of any part of the property in any manner.[9]

§ 226.   — Dissolution or termination of community of property.

Since the effect of an annulment of a marriage is not only to a dissolve the marriage but to dissolve it *ab initio,* there is most certainly no community of property between the parties in the acquisitions of either made after the decree of nullity. The marriage by virtue of such decree becomes nonexistent and there is then no basis for any conjugal partnership thereafter. In this respect, the situation with us is exactly the same as that in Spanish law with relation to the Spanish "divorce" that annulled the marriage.[10] Similarly, also, to the practice in Spain, our courts apply the principles of the Spanish putative marriage, or principles analogous to the Spanish putative marriage, in construing that prior to the decree of nullity the parties were making their acquisitions in community and it is usually determined that they shall share the acquisitions equally just as if a valid marriage and conjugal partnership existed between them.[11]

The absolute divorce, although not, of course, dissolving the marriage from its inception as does the decree of nullity, effectually and completely dissolves the marriage from the date of the decree of absolute divorce, and there is no longer any marriage subsisting upon which can be founded any community of property in acquests and gains thereafter made by either of the former spouses. The absolute divorce, in other words, dissolves and terminates the conjugal partnership in acquests and gains as completely as does the death of one spouse.[12] The effect of our absolute divorce is thus similar in effect to the divorce in the Spanish law which dissolved the marriage by annulling it.[13]

As we have seen, in the Spanish law the divorce which was a legal separation dissolving the cohabitation, although not the marriage, brought about a partition of the community property acquired up to the time of the legal separation, subject to the qualifications also noticed as to acquisitions while the spouses were living apart due

---

[9] Ariz. Rev. St. 1956, §§ 25-314, 25-316; La. Civ. Code, art. 149; Tex. Family Code 1969, § 3.56.

[10] Statutes in some states provide for partition of property in an annulment suit, where necessary. Absent such a statute, the courts may have jurisdiction to partition or divide, as in Wolford v. Wolford, 65 Nev. 710,

200 P.2d 988.

[11] Putative marriage, see ante, § 56 et seq.

[12] See Conrad v. Conrad, 170 La. 612, 127 So. 735; Byrne v. Byrne, 3 Tex. 336.

Effect of death of spouse, see ante, this chapter, subd. B.

[13] See ante, § 222.

to the fault of one of them prior to the legal separation. After the legal separation, however, community of property continued in that the innocent spouse was entitled to continue to share equally in the acquisitions of the guilty spouse, although the innocent spouse did not share his or her acquisitions with the guilty spouse. Moreover, the wife continued entitled to support from the husband, although it must be remembered that the acquests and gains of the husband which an innocent wife was entitled to continue to share might more than adequately suffice. Even a guilty wife was entitled to a measure of support.[14] The usual effect of our laws relating to legal separation from bed and board and even as to separate support and maintenance or the like is to accomplish, as in the case of absolute divorce, a termination of the conjugal partnership in acquests and gains and a partition of the community property so far acquired.[15] In some of the states, on the other hand, whether a termination of the sharing in acquests and gains and a division of community property is to result rests within the discretion of the court.[16] At first glance, the termination of conjugal sharing and the partition of the community property might seem dissimilar to the principles of the Spanish law, but closer examination will show that substantially the same principles are

[14] See ante, § 221.

[15] Separation from bed and board dissolves the community of acquests and gains, see La. Civ. Code, art. 123; and carries with it separation of goods and effects, see La. Civ. Code, art. 155. See also Dixon v. Dixon, 4 La. 188, 23 Am. Dec. 478.

In Louisiana, after this dissolution of the community by separation from bed and board, the community is not re-established by a reconciliation. De Blanc v. De Blanc (La. App.), 18 So.2d 619. However, amendment of La. Civ. Code, art. 155, by Acts 1944, No. 200, provides that spouses, upon reconciliation, may re-establish community from date of filing suit for separation by act before notary duly witnessed and recorded.

Effect of reconciliation upon property settlement agreement, see post, § 232.

According to the French Civil Code, art. 311, "A separation from bed and board always occasions a separation of property." And in the words of art. 1441, "A community is dissolved . . . 3rd, by divorce, 4th, by separation from bed and board. . . ."

[16] In Arizona, it would not seem

necessarily to follow that the legal separation from bed and board brings about partition of the community property unless the court should in its discretion decide upon such partition. The statute provides that, "The court may make such decree for the support of the wife and her children by the husband, or out of his property or earnings, as may be just and proper, and may make such further decree as the nature and circumstances of the case require. . . ." Ariz. Rev. St. 1956, § 25-333.

In Idaho, in granting separate maintenance with the right to live apart from the husband, the court did not actually partition the community property but made provision for the use of it by the wife. Radermacher v. Radermacher, 61 Idaho 261, 100 P.2d 955.

But in Washington, the court has no right or power to dispose of the community property when granting only a decree of separate maintenance. It may, however, impose a lien on such property to secure payment of any awards made. Cummings v. Cummings, 20 Wash. 2d 703, 149 P.2d 155.

followed. The legal separation of the Spanish law dissolving the cohabitation at least terminated any further mutual sharing where one spouse was guilty and partitioned the acquests and gains so far acquired. If legal separation occurred in circumstances where both spouses were innocent of misconduct, termination of the conjugal sharing was complete, and partition was of a final nature. As to the method of division of the property and as to the property provisions made between the spouses for the period of legal separation, the principles followed in our community property states differ in degree rather than in kind from those of the Spanish law. Support of the wife is provided, as under the Spanish principles, and the provisions as to the property are usually made in the light of who was innocent and who was guilty, which after all was the principle that governed in the Spanish law.[17]

§ 227.   — Division of community property upon divorce or legal separation.

The manner or basis of division of the community property upon the entry of a decree of divorce or of legal separation is usually dependent, in the view of our courts, upon the extent of the authority in that respect conferred upon the courts by the statutes.[18] The statutes, it need hardly be added, are not uniform upon the subject. In a considerable number of the states, the statutes authorize the court to divide the community property between the spouses in such proportions as it shall, from the facts of the case, deem just and right.[19] This allows the courts to take into consideration the respective situations of the spouses, as well as the situation of the children, and also allows the courts to consider the respective innocence and guilt of the spouses in deciding how to divide the community property.[20]

In another of the states the community property must be equally divided between the spouses, except in cases where the divorce is

---

[17] See also post, § 227.

[18] What is community property, see ante, Chap. VI.

[19] See Ariz. Rev. St. 1956, § 25-318; Tex. Family Code 1969, § 3.63.

See also Anderson v. Anderson (Wash.), 195 P.2d 986; Moss v. Moss (Wash.), 207 P.2d 901; Jensen v. Jensen, 20 Wash. 2d 380, 147 P.2d 512; Cummings v. Cummings, 20 Wash. 2d 703, 149 P.2d 155.

In Arizona, it would not seem necessarily to follow, as in the case of divorce, that upon legal separation from bed and board a division of the community property would be ordered, unless the court in its discretion, so

decides, see ante, § 226; and see the same section as to existence of legal separation in these several states.

[20] In McFadden v. McFadden, 22 Ariz. 246, 196 P. 452, the court took the view that the Arizona statute did not require that the innocent party be favored in dividing the community property, and that the court might consider the question of who contributed more labor or capital to the marriage and who would have the burden of the care and education of minor children. To the same effect, Laughlin v. Laughlin, 61 Ariz. 6, 143 P.2d 336; Markoff v. Markoff (Wash.), 180 P.2d 555. Effect of gifts or advancements, see post, § 232.

granted on the ground of adultery or extreme cruelty. In the excepted situations the court is authorized to divide the community property between the spouses in such proportions as it deems just, taking into consideration the facts of the particular case and the circumstances of the spouses.[21] This allows the court to consider the innocence and guilt of the respective spouses in making the division of the community property.[22]

In the remaining states, it is evident that the community property must be equally divided between the spouses, whatever the ground of divorce.[23] Thus, even the adultery of the wife as the ground for divorce has not been sufficient to defeat her right to half of the

---

[21] See Idaho Code 1948, § 32-712.

In Arizona, while a distribution of community property is justification for failing to order alimony, the converse is said not to be part of Arizona law. Nace v. Nace (Ariz. App.), 432 P.2d 896.

[22] The California court, prior to Jan. 1, 1970, said that, in cases of divorce on the ground of adultery or extreme cruelty, the innocent spouse was entitled to more of the community property than the guilty spouse. Tipton v. Tipton, 209 Cal. 443, 288 P. 65. However, where the divorce was awarded to both parties, the community property was divided equally, whatever the grounds of divorce. Weinberg v. Weinberg, 63 Cal. Rptr. 13, 432 P.2d 709.

Even in action for separate maintenance, court could exercise discretion where ground was extreme cruelty. Finnegan v. Finnegan (Cal. App.), 148 P.2d 37.

In Idaho, all of the community property can be awarded to the innocent spouse. Hobbs v. Hobbs (Ida.), 204 P.2d 1034.

[23] In Louisiana, as to divorce, see La. Civ. Code, arts. 155, 159, 2406; Rawlings v. Stokes, 194 La. 206, 193 So. 589; as to the same being true in case of legal separation from bed and board, see La. Civ. Code, arts. 155, 159; Dixon v. Dixon, 4 La. 188, 23 Am. Dec. 478. The wife has the right to renounce her share of the community property, but she is not presumed to have renounced by reason of failing to indicate an acceptance within the statutory period. See Phillips v. Phillips, 160 La. 813, 107 So. 584; Rawlings v. Stokes, 194 La. 206, 193 So. 594. Renunciation by wife upon dissolution by death of husband, see ante, § 218.

In New Mexico, the court has said: "In the absence of a statute conferring upon the court the power to apportion the community property between the spouses, giving the one a greater interest therein than such party had in the community, the court has no such power." Beals v. Ares, 25 N.M. 459, 185 P. 780. Consideration of the applicable statute — N.M. St. 1953, § 22-7-6 — shows that no such power is conferred upon the court. That statute authorizes the court, on final hearing, to allow the wife a reasonable portion of the husband's "separate property, or such a reasonable sum of money to be paid by the husband, either in a single sum, or in installments, as alimony"; and the only provision that would seem to affect the community property is that, on the final hearing, the court "may set apart out of the property of the respective parties, such portion thereof, for the maintenance and education of their minor children, as may seem just and proper" and if any of that property remains on hand, when the children come of age it "may be disposed of by the court as unto it may seem just and proper." Any discretionary power of disposition seems limited to the property just referred to; otherwise the community property has to be divided equally. The wording of the statute was in practically

community property acquired during the marriage, whether acquired before or after the adultery.[24]

Naturally, the community property should be charged with the community debts before it is partitioned, for it is only after the community debts are discharged that the amount of the community property remaining to be partitioned is ascertainable.[25] If the community property has been partitioned between the spouses without having been subjected to outstanding community obligations, some jurisdictions consider that each spouse takes his or her share subject to the same proportion of the obligations as represented by his or her share of the community property.[26] However, in other jurisdictions this view is subject to some qualification.[27] Or if there has been any use of community funds by one spouse for his or her own private benefit, the value thereof should be debited against his or her share of the community property, where there was no misunderstanding that such funds are to be a gift to the spouse from the community.[28] The situation is analogous to that in which the marriage has been dissolved by the death of a spouse, and reference should be had to that discussion.[29]

the same form when the court handed down its decision in Beals v. Ares, ante.

In New Mexico, court can make an award to the wife from the husband's share of the community property in lieu of alimony. Harper v. Harper (N.M.), 217 P.2d 857.

In New Mexico, in reference to incurable insanity as ground for divorce, it has been provided that "the court shall make such orders and decrees for the division and preservation of the community estate, if any . . . as shall seem necessary or advisable." N.M. St. Ann. 1941, § 25-714.

[24] See Beals v. Ares, 25 N.M. 459, 185 P. 780.

[25] See McKannay v. McKannay, 68 Cal. App. 701, 230 P. 214. See also ante, § 159.

Charges against community property, under California views, of payments made for family support, for income tax and for insurance premiums, see Van Camp v. Van Camp, 53 Cal. App. 17, 199 P. 885.

Charging off counsel's fees and costs, see Cal. Civ. Code, §§ 4525, 4526.

Wife's right to partition of community realty upheld as against judgment creditor who, after divorce, had purchased property at execution sale upon revival of judgment obtained by him during existence of marriage. Washington v. Palmer (La. App.), 28 So.2d 509.

[26] See Ellsworth v. Ellsworth, 5 Ariz. App. 89, 423 P.2d 364.

[27] In Mayberry v. Whittier, 144 Cal. 322, 78 P. 16, judgment creditor had obtained judgment against husband which had not been fully satisfied at the time husband and wife were divorced and community property divided between them. He then sought to levy on community property received by the wife under the decree. The general rule was stated that the spouses take the community property upon division subject to prior liens and that the part awarded to each is subject to community debts not reduced to liens. Under the doctrine of marshaling assets, wife was entitled to have the creditor resort first to the property awarded to the husband. Here he had done so, but his judgment was still unsatisfied. In Frankel v. Boyd, 106 Cal. 608, 39 P. 939, wife had been awarded all of community property. Cf. situation presented by Ackley v. Maggi, 86 Cal. App. 631, 261 P. 311.

[28] See post, § 232, as to effect of previous gifts or advances.

[29] See ante, this chapter, subdivision B.

Upon entering its final decree of divorce, the court should dispose of all the community property, either by partitioning it equally or in whatever proportions its authorized discretion allows or by ordering its sale and partitioning the proceeds where the property itself is not capable of partition.[30] However, the court may take steps to preserve the property, as for an indefinite period, where it is not subject to partitioning and a sale at the moment would be damaging.[31] Its disposition of the community property is subject to revision upon appeal in most of the community property states,[32] although there is little likelihood of the appellate court interfering in the trial court's disposition of the community property unless there has clearly been an abuse of discretion.[33]

To the extent that the amount, character and value of the community property is put in issue on the hearing and the community property is disposed of and partitioned between the spouses, the final decree of the court is *res judicata* as to those matters.[34] This is dependent, naturally, upon the fact of the court having jurisdiction over the community property in question. Conflict of laws principles must be kept in mind in this respect. The court which grants the divorce has no jurisdiction to effectuate the partition of community realty located in another state.[35] This does not mean that the spouse obtaining the

---

[30] See, e.g., Cauphen v. Cauphen (N.M.), 210 P.2d 942; Markoff v. Markoff (Wash.), 180 P.2d 555.

Awarding money to the wife in place of her interest in the community property, see Johnston v. Johnston, 33 Cal. App. 2d 90, 91 P.2d 142.

Disposition of homestead property, see homestead statutes of the several states.

[31] See, e.g., Ackel v. Ackel, 57 Ariz. 14, 110 P.2d 238, 111 P.2d 628, 133 A.L.R. 549. Somewhat similarly, see Rice v. Rice, 21 Tex. 58.

Creating trust of community property to provide for support and education of minor children, see Jones v. State (Ida.), 376 P.2d 371.

[32] See Ariz. Rev. St. 1953, § 25-351; Cal. Civ. Code, § 4810; Idaho Code 1948, § 32-714.

[33] See Malich v. Malich, 23 Ariz. 423, 204 P. 1020; Shapiro v. Shapiro, 127 Cal. App. 20, 14 P.2d 1058.

[34] See Tarien v. Katz, 216 Cal. 554, 15 P.2d 493, 85 A.L.R. 334, and numerous cases cited in 85 A.L.R. 339.

Where both parties voluntarily participated in a divorce proceeding in Nevada and both stated or admitted in their pleadings therein that there was no community property in which either was to share, the adjudication by the Nevada court, without introduction of proof, that there was no community property in which either was entitled to share was *res judicata* of that question on a subsequent suit by the former wife against the former husband in Kentucky to obtain a "just, fair and equitable division of all properties owned jointly." Kirkland v. Greer, 295 Ky. 535, 174 S. W. 2d 745.

Effect of failure to adjudicate as to community property, see post, § 229.

[35] See Taylor v. Taylor, 192 Cal. 71, 218 P. 756, 51 A.L.R. 1074.

But compare Tomaier v. Tomaier, 23 Cal. 2d 754, 146 P.2d 905, where court declared that its jurisdiction over the parties enabled it to require them to execute conveyances to the out-of-state land. And see Cal. Civ. Code, § 4800 et seq., effective Jan. 1, 1970.

This would undoubtedly be the case, also, as to personal property which had acquired a fixed situs somewhere through its use for business purposes. And notice also the effect of such a

divorce, even if obtaining it through service by publication, could not make a demand by appropriate action in the state where the community realty is located for his or her share of that community realty, when justly entitled to such a share. This would be equally true whether the court granting the divorce had purported to decree a partition of such community realty or had, more properly, made no effort to dispose of such realty. In the majority of cases, of course, the courts are fully aware of this lack of jurisdiction on their part in such a situation. However, it is believed more appropriate to discuss this situation in a succeeding section.[36]

It may be mentioned briefly as to California, in which an interlocutory decree of divorce must first be entered and remain in effect for a definite period before being made final, that the marriage is not dissolved by the interlocutory decree.[37] Thus, although it is proper, and indeed advisable, for the court at the hearing to determine what disposition shall be made of the community property and to provide therefor in the interlocutory decree, this disposition and the spouse's respective rights in such property as then determined do not become effective until the final decree is subsequently entered.[38] Under present day California statutes, earnings of the spouses during this interlocutory period are their respective separate property.[39] As to the Louisiana separation from bed and board which, except in the case of adultery or sentence to infamous punishment, must first be obtained before an absolute divorce can be obtained a year later, the separation from bed and board immediately dissolves the conjugal partnership in acquests and gains and entitles the parties to division of the community property.[40]

provision as Cal. Civ. Code, § 946, recognizing that the existence of a law to the contrary where personal property was situated would affect the rule that personal property follows the person of the owner.

[36] See post, §§ 229, 230.

[37] See ante, § 224.

[38] See Pereira v. Pereira, 156 Cal. 1, 103 P. 488, 134 Am. St. Rep. 107, 23 L.R.A. (N. S.) 180.
Generally as to interlocutory decree affecting marital property rights of spouses, see cases, 76 A.L.R. 284.

[39] Cal. Civ. Code, §§ 5118, 5119.

[40] See ante, § 226.
With regard to the California practice of entering an interlocutory decree and entering the final decree six months later (formerly a year later), it has been said that at the time of the interlocutory decree the court might make all proper inquiries into the subject of the community property and provide for its disposition, although the rights in such property as then determined did not become final until the final decree was entered. Pereira v. Pereira, 156 Cal. 1, 103 P. 488, 134 Am. St. Rep. 107, 23 L.R.A. (N. S.) 180. But since a court's decree, whether final or not, cannot affect property not within its jurisdiction, the Louisiana court was probably quite justified in deciding to treat a California interlocutory decree as similar to the Louisiana decree of separation from bed and board (which in Louisiana must precede by one year a decree of absolute divorce), and in deciding that the wife, after her husband had obtained an interlocutory decree in California, had the power to dispose of her undivided half interest in community realty in Louisiana. See Butler v. Bolinger (La. App.), 133 So. 778.

Insofar as the courts of some of our states can consider the innocence or guilt of the spouses as affecting the right to share in the community property, the principle in a general way approximates that of the Spanish community property system as applied in Spain and Mexico. But in that community property system it was considered that the reason for the mutual sharing in the gains was the mutual loyalty of the spouses, the mutual sharing of the burdens of the marriage, the joint industry and labor of the spouses in advancing the interests and well-being of the family, based of course upon cohabitation. If these ceased because cohabitation came to an end through the fault or misconduct of one spouse, there was no longer occasion or basis for the joint sharing of acquests and gains, except that it was justly considered that the innocent spouse should not suffer by reason of what was not his or her fault. There was, in other words, either community of property or no community of property, depending upon the innocence or guilt of the spouse.[41] There was no lumping of community property in one lot, to be carved in two pieces in such proportions as the court might decide, as a pie might be carved up. In this respect our present methods differ from the original principle. We do not criticize but merely state the fact. It may well be that our methods have more flexibility.

§ 227.1.   — Division of quasi-community property upon divorce or legal separation.

In California, in making provision for what it calls quasi-community property,[42] the legislature has declared that upon dissolution of a marriage by decree of court or upon decree of separate maintenance, such quasi-community property shall be divided upon the same basis as community property.[43] Since this type of property is usually separate property by the law governing its nature at the time of its acquisition, it was considered by many that to take any of it away from the owning spouse would violate the principles laid down by the California Supreme Court in the Thornton case,[44] plus the fact that in California separate property has never been considered subject to division upon divorce.[45] However, the validity of the statute has been upheld by the supreme court of the state,[46] buttressed by later legislation.[47]

§ 228.   — Disposition of separate property.

In many of the community property states, the courts upon entering final decree dissolving the marriage have no authority or power

41 See ante, §§ 219–223.

42 See Cal. Civ. Code, § 4803. And see ante, § 68.3.

43 Cal. Civ. Code, § 4803.

44 Estate of Thornton, 1 Cal. 2d 1, 33 P.2d 1, 92 A.L.R. 1343.

45 See post, § 228.

46 Addison v. Addison, 62 Cal. 2d 558, 43 Cal. Rptr. 97, 399 P.2d 899.

47 See Cal. Civ. Code, § 4804.

to divest a spouse of his or her title in separate property.[48] But even where this is so, the courts are frequently empowered to fix a lien upon the separate property of either spouse to secure the payment of any interest or equity that the other spouse may have in such property, or to secure any equity that may arise in favor of either party from his or her property during the existence of the marriage, or to secure the payment of allowances for support and maintenance of the wife or minor children;[49] or to subject separate property to charges for the support and maintenance of the children;[50] or like provisions. In others of the states, however, provision is made empowering the courts to apportion some of the husband's separate property to the wife or require setting apart property of either spouse for the maintenance and education of the children,[51] or provision of like nature. It is doubtful whether any actual distinction exists between the two situations, since the result is much the same in either case. Since the scope of discussion in this work is directed primarily to community property, it is suggested that for more detailed information upon separate property the statutes of the respective states be examined.

§ 229.   — Final decree not disposing of community property.

Where the final decree of divorce makes no disposition of community property, the usual view, either by virtue of statute or of judicial decision, has been that the former spouses equally own such property after the divorce as tenants in common.[52] This, it will be

---

[48] See Ariz. Rev. St. 1953, § 25-318.

Neither party shall be compelled to divest himself or herself of the title to real estate, see Tex. Family Code 1969, § 3.63.

Upon divorce, separate property of one spouse may not be assigned to the other. Fox v. Fox, 18 Cal. 2d 645, 117 P.2d 325.

"The court is without power to award the separate property of the husband to the wife, either permanently or temporarily." Radermacher v. Radermacher, 61 Idaho 261, 100 P.2d 955.

[49] See Ariz. Rev. St. 1953, § 25-318.

In California, no lien can be placed on husband's separate property to secure payment to wife of share of community property. Secondo v. Secondo, 218 Cal. 453, 23 P.2d 752.

[50] See Cal. Civ. Code, § 4803.

[51] See N.M. Stats. 1953, § 22-7-6.

[52] Ariz. Rev. St. 1956, § 25-318 A and G; Dempsey v. Oliver (Ariz.),

379 P.2d 908; Brown v. Brown, 170 Cal. 1, 147 P. 1168; Quinlan v. Pearson, 71 Ida. 26, 225 P.2d 455; Roux v. Jersey Ins. Co. (La.), 98 So.2d 906; First Nat. Bank v. Wolff (Nev.), 202 P. 2d 878; Jones v. Tate, 68 N.M. 258, 360 P.2d 920, citing and following de Funiak, first edition; Dillard v. Dillard (Tex.), 341 S. W. 2d 668; Ambrose v. Moore, 46 Wash. 463, 90 P. 588, 11 L.R.A. (N.S.) 103. See N.M. St. 1953, § 22-7-22, that failure to divide community property on divorce shall not affect the property rights of either party therein, and either may prosecute a suit for division. See also numerous cases cited, 85 A.L.R. 340.

Chose in action for death of minor child as property in question, see Hickson v. Herrmann, 77 N.M. 68, 427 P.2d 36.

Subsequent remarriage to each other as not restoring community nature of property, see McDaniel v. Thompson (Tex. Civ. App.), 195 S. W. 2d 202, noted 25 Tex. L. Rev. 177.

seen, corresponds to the view frequently expressed that, on the death of one spouse, the surviving spouse and the heirs of the deceased spouse hold the community property as tenants in common until it is partitioned.[53] Since the community of property does not owe its origin to the common law, it is not strictly accurate to define this ownership after divorce by common-law terms, such as tenancy in common, although it is understandable that applications of common-law terms makes this situation more easily understood by jurists trained in the common law. It is rather a form of joint ownership, peculiar to the civil law community property system.[54]

Either spouse has the right, of course, to demand and obtain a division of such undisposed of property. This right is sometimes specifically provided by statute[55] but is a right that must necessarily exist even in the absence of express statutory provision,[56] and is enforceable in an independent action rather than by application to the court granting the divorce, for the latter court by entering its final decree without having the question of the particular property put in issue has now no jurisdiction in the matter of such property, at least so far as the divorce proceeding is concerned. It might, of course, be the proper court in which to file the independent action by reason of the property being within its general jurisdiction.[57] Even if it be true, as the Washington court stated, that if a spouse prosecuting or defending a divorce suit fails to bring the property rights of the parties before the court such spouse waives any right in or to the *property of the other spouse,* and that the power to dispose of the property of husband and wife is a mere incident of the power to grant the divorce and ordinarily cannot be exercised by another court at another time or in an independent action (barring fraud or the fact that the property is within another court's jurisdiction), that court recognized that an ex-husband was still the owner of an undivided half interest in community property not disposed of in the divorce proceedings and had an independent cause of action therefor which was not subject to demurrer.[58]

The spouse, usually, of course, the husband, in whose hands the undisposed of community property rests, owns no more than his own share of such property and his mortgage or sale of the property can

---

[53] See ante, § 204.

[54] See Giglio v. Giglio, 159 La. 46, 105 So. 95; Phillips v. Phillips, 160 La. 813, 107 So. 584.

[55] See N.M. St. 1953, § 22-7-22.

[56] See Tarien v. Katz, 216 Cal. 554, 15 P.2d 493, 85 A.L.R. 334; Daigre v. Daigre (La.), 89 So.2d 41; Prophet v. Peterson, 77 Ida. 257, 291 P.2d 290; Gray v. Thomas, 83 Tex. 246, 18 S. W. 721; Nelson v. Geib (Tex.), 314 S. W. 2d 124; Olsen v. Roberts,

(Wash.), 259 P.2d 418.

Similarly in Puerto Rico, see Garrozi v. Dastas, 204 U. S. 64, 51 L. Ed. 369, 27 Sup. Ct. 224.

[57] See Tarien v. Katz, 216 Cal. 554, 15 P.2d 493, 85 A.L.R. 334; Conrad v. Conrad, 170 La. 312, 127 So. 735; Carpenter v. Brackett, 57 Wash. 460, 107 P. 359.

[58] Ambrose v. Moore, 46 Wash. 463, 90 P. 588, 11 L.R.A. (N. S.) 103.

convey no more than his undivided half interest therein.[59] This is complicated in some states by statutes or judicial decisions attempting to protect "bona fide purchasers." But it is difficult to see how one can acquire ownership of something of which his grantor had no ownership. It is not a question of the other spouse having a mere "equitable interest" which is subject to be defeated by a "bona fide purchaser's" rights. The other spouse has as full and complete an ownership as the one attempting to dispose of the property.[60]

Difficult questions may arise where the decree purports to dispose of all the community property and subsequently property which has not been disclosed upon the face of the record is claimed to be community property. It has frequently been held that the rights of the parties have been concluded by the decree and that questions concerning the property subsequently brought up should have been put in issue at the time of the divorce proceeding. But too strict a rule of interpretation should not be applied in such situations. Community property does not cease to be community property because not disclosed upon the face of the record at the time of the divorce proceeding. There is not any question of waiver or estoppel pursuant to equitable principles, because the ownership of either husband or wife is not an equitable ownership but an actual ownership which is entitled to be enforced by the owner.[61] A judgment, just because it purports to dispose of "all of the community property" cannot be *res judicata* as to community property not disclosed upon the face of the record and as to which no issues were raised as to its nature and its ownership. The judgment should not conclude questions as to community property not actually considered by the court.[62]

§ 230.   — Community property in another jurisdiction than that dissolving the marriage.

Since the court entering the decree of divorce has no jurisdiction over community property, for example realty situated in another state, and cannot adjudicate property rights therein, courts entering a decree of divorce will not usually attempt to effect any partition or division of such property without their jurisdiction. Even if they did purport to do so, such attempts would be of no effect in view of the

[59] See Rawlings v. Stokes, 194 La. 206, 193 So. 589; Jones v. Tate, 68 N.M. 258, 360 P.2d 920, following de Funiak, 1st edition.

[60] See discussion ante, § 206.

[61] Mere silence or inaction, without the running of prescription cannot serve as a basis of estoppel. Rawlings v. Stokes, 194 La. 206, 193 So. 589.

[62] Numerous cases upon this subject, see 85 A.L.R. 339.

Allegation and admission and judgment thereon in court of one state that there was no community property did not prevent party from claiming share of community property in another state. See Taylor v. Taylor, 192 Cal. 71, 218 P. 756, 51 A.L.R. 1074.

lack of jurisdiction over such property.[63] The spouse obtaining the divorce, even if obtaining it through substituted service on the other spouse, is not barred from demanding by appropriate action in the state where the community property has its *situs* his or her share of that property.[64] In itself, the obtaining of a divorce in another jurisdiction cannot deprive the spouse of his or her ownership of half of the community property, an ownership which is still in full force and existence.[65] There is no basis for any narrow interpretation, such as that once given by the Nevada court, that the court having jurisdiction of the community property can divide the property only if it also enters the decree of divorce.[66] One who has obtained a valid divorce in another jurisdiction should not by reason of that fact alone be denied the right to resort to the courts of the state in which the community property is located to recover the share of the property to which he or she is lawfully entitled.[67]

Of course, if the validity of the divorce can be questioned, as on the ground of lack of jurisdiction to decree it, the court having jurisdiction of the community property can refuse to recognize the

---

[63] See also ante, § 227.

As to property settlement agreements including property situated in other jurisdictions, see post, § 231.

Generally as to court's jurisdiction in divorce proceedings to dispose of realty in other states, see cases, 51 A.L.R. 1081.

[64] See Taylor v. Taylor, 192 Cal. 71, 218 P. 756, 51 A.L.R. 1074; Peterson v. Peterson, 35 Idaho 470, 207 P. 425.

[65] The frequently cited case to the contrary, Bedal v. Sake, 10 Idaho 270, 77 P. 638, 66 A.L.R. 60, was expressly overruled in Peterson v. Peterson, 35 Idaho 470, 207 P. 425. In the Bedal Case, the court held that a wife who abandoned her husband in Idaho, went to another state and obtained a divorce and there remarried, had formed a new community and had abandoned all her claim to the community property in Idaho under her first marriage. The Peterson Case, overruling the Bedal Case, held that a wife had a vested interest in the Idaho community property acquired at the time of the abandonment or leaving and was not divested of that interest by going to another state and obtaining a divorce there. The effect

of this later case is not always noticed by the writers. See, for example, 11 Am. Jur. "Community Property," §§ 75, 76. See also discussion of these cases, post, this section. See also Tomaier v. Tomaier, 23 Cal. 2d 754, 146 P.2d 905.

As to interest in insurance policy, see Cooke v. Cooke, 65 Cal. App. 2d 260, 150 P.2d 514.

State court assuming to hear divorce suit by wife and partitioning community property despite pendency of bankruptcy proceeding against husband in federal court and issuance of order by latter court restraining wife from prosecuting any action in any other court for purpose of fixing lien, etc., upon any property involved in bankruptcy proceeding, see Turman v. Turman (Tex. Civ. App.), 99 S. W. 2d 947.

[66] See Keenan v. Keenan, 40 Nev. 351, 164 P. 351.

[67] Virginia divorce decree on ground of adultery was *res judicata* of that issue and spouse obtaining such divorce was entitled, under former California law, to receive more than one-half the community property, in a suit for such division. Foley v. Foley (Cal. App.), 29 Cal. Rptr. 857.

divorce and on that basis refuse to sanction a partition, or can take cognizance of a divorce proceeding before it on the part of the other spouse and dispose of the community property on the basis of the latter spouse's divorce proceeding. Mr. McKay, in a criticism of the Nevada decision referred to above, remarked that if the Nevada court had placed its refusal on the ground that the divorce obtained by the plaintiff in another jurisdiction was void for lack of jurisdiction its position would have been "impregnable."[68] However, a consideration of the case indicates that according to present views it was not void for want of jurisdiction. The spouses would appear to have had their matrimonial domicile in California, and then separated, the wife going to Idaho, the husband to Nevada where he acquired the property in dispute. The wife obtained a divorce in Idaho and then filed action in Nevada to obtain half of the property acquired there by the husband. There is nothing to show that the wife did not have a valid domicile in Idaho, and it is well recognized at the present day that a wife may acquire a separate domicile for the purposes of bringing action for divorce.[69] Moreover, it seems established by the decision of the United States Supreme Court in *Williams v. North Carolina* that where the wife has acquired a separate domicile and obtained a divorce there, even though by constructive service only on the other spouse, the judgment of divorce must be given full faith and credit elsewhere, even in the last matrimonial domicile of the spouses.[70]

Presumably, what may have animated the Nevada court was the feeling that the wife, having left the husband and not having been living with him in Nevada at the time he acquired the property in question, was not in justice entitled thereafter to come forward and obtain half of that property. If this was the true situation, the court's conclusion was absolutely correct, although based on inappropriate reasoning. The very basis of the communal sharing in the marital acquests and gains is cohabitation between the spouses. It is their living together and mutually sharing the burdens of the marriage, their mutual loyalty one to another, their joint industry and labor in advancing and furthering the success of the marriage and the well-being of the family, that is the basis of their equal sharing of the gains of the marriage. When these things cease, and they do cease with the wilful cessation of cohabitation, there is no further basis for either spouse sharing in the acquisitions of the other.[71] Accordingly,

[68] McKay, Community Property, 2nd Ed., § 1352.

[69] See Beale, Conflict of Laws, § 113.1 et seq.

[70] Williams v. North Carolina, 317 U.S. 287, 87 L. Ed. 279, 63 Sup. Ct. 207. Whatever criticisms may be leveled at this decision, and there would appear to be many, need not be considered here; reference may be had to Burns, Two Nevada Divorces Get Full Faith and Credit, 29 Am. Bar Ass'n Jour. 125.

[71] In speaking of cessation of cohabitation, we do not have reference to any living apart which may have been caused by ill health of one spouse or separation brought about by exigencies of business or the like, where the will to union still exists. See ante, § 57, as to necessity of cohabitation.

where one spouse has abandoned or left the other without fault on the latter's part, there should be no right, certainly, to share in acquisitions made by the latter after such separation. This was well taken into account by the Arizona court, where a wife left her husband without cause, subsequently obtained a divorce in another jurisdiction, and thereafter sought to obtain half of his acquistions gained after she left him. The Arizona court most properly refused to allow her to share in such acquisitions.[72] Indeed, the Idaho court at one time took the view that where the wife abandoned the husband and went to another jurisdiction and there obtained a divorce and married again, she thereby abandoned all right to share even in the acquisitions of the first husband made during their cohabitation together.[73] Although it later expressly overruled that decision and said that the wife's share in the community property acquired during the marriage was vested in her and could not be divested by the fact that she later left her husband and went to another jurisdiction and obtained a divorce there, and further that it was not of controlling importance as to whose fault it was that the separation and divorce was brought about, it would appear in this latter case that she was justified by reason of her ill health and the husband's cruelty in leaving him.[74]

It is most definitely to be noted that in the foregoing situations there is no question of recognizing or refusing to recognize the validity of the foreign divorce. A divorce decree of another jurisdiction, even though validly dissolving the marriage, cannot affect the right of a court of a jurisdiction in which is located community property to decide the rights of the spouses in such property. So long as the latter court gives full faith and credit to the decree of divorce as to its dissolution of the marriage, there is no reason why it cannot inquire into the conduct of the parties, both of whom are before it and thus within its jurisdiction, in order to determine to what extent such conduct may affect their rights in the community property, which is also within the court's jurisdiction.

§ 231.   — Effect of property settlement agreements.

In a preceding chapter, reference has already been made to the right of spouses to enter into a postnuptial contract altering their marital property rights. In the majority of the community property states they may do so, in the others they may not.[75] In many of those

---

[72] Pendleton v. Brown, 25 Ariz. 604, 221 P. 213, wherein adulterous conduct on the wife's part after her act of desertion also influenced the court in its view.

See also ante, § 190, as to misconduct as effecting right to share in community property.

[73] Bedal v. Sake, 10 Idaho 270, 77 P. 638, 66 A.L.R. 60, but not overruling Peterson case as to property obtained by husband after the separation.

[74] Peterson v. Peterson, 35 Idaho 470, 207 P. 425.

[75] See ante, § 136.

states in which they can do so, they may, prior to separation or prior to the institution of divorce proceedings by one of the spouses, enter into a valid property settlement providing for the partition or disposition of the community property already acquired and providing as to what shall be the character or nature of property to be acquired by either spouse after they have separated or been divorced.[76] In fact, it is sometimes specifically provided by statute that a property settlement agreement made in contemplation of separation or divorce is valid.[77] In other jurisdictions, however, a property settlement agreement actually conditioned upon and made in contemplation of one spouse securing a divorce is against public policy.[78] When the agreement is presented for the court's approval in a divorce proceeding the court should examine it with the utmost care to determine that there has been no fraud or mistake. The court usually may approve, modify or reject it, in the exercise of the discretion conferred upon it.[79] Of course, since the husband is usually in a superior position, he is obligated not to conceal any of the community property but rather to make a full disclosure as to its existence and reveal material factors as to its value, otherwise the agreement may.be invalidated.[80]

Where the contract of property division and settlement between the spouses is passed upon and approved by the court at the instance of both parties, and the final decree of divorce declares that the community property interests of the spouses have been previously

---

[76] In California, see Hill v. Hill, 23 Cal. 2d 82, 142 P.2d 417; Comment, 35 So. Cal. L. Rev. 174; Judge Wilson, 14 So. Cal. L. Rev. 174. Tax aspects of agreement, see Hines, 12 So. Cal. L. Rev. 786.

In Washington, see Lee v. Lee (Wash.), 178 P.2d 296.

[77] See Nev. Rev. St. 1956, § 123.080. And see Cal. Civ. Code, § 4802; N.M. St. 1953, § 57-2-12; Estate of Brimhall, 62 Cal. App. 2d 30, 143 P.2d 941.

[78] In Texas, the cases are in conflict but more recent cases indicate that agreement that property to be acquired while living separate and apart shall be the property of the one acquiring would be violative of constitutional definition of separate property. See Chandler v. Chandler (Tex.), 32 S. W. 2d 377; Cox v. Mailander (Tex.), 178 S. W. 1012; George v. Reynolds (Tex. Civ. App.), 53 S.W. 2d 490.

As to Louisiana, see Nelson v. Walker (La.), 197 So.2d 619; Sciortino v. Sciortino (La.), 209 So.2d 355; Johnson v. Johnson (La.), 103 So.2d 263.

There is no authorization of wife, under La. Civ. Code, art. 2446, during marriage to enter into contract with husband relating to settlement or waiver of her right to alimony. Russo v. Russo, 205 La. 852, 18 So.2d 318. Quaere, as to full effect of this decision.

[79] See Lazar v. Superior Court, 16 Cal. 2d 617, 107 P.2d 249, also distinguishing between the effect of actually incorporating the agreement in its decree and the effect of merely approving it by reference.

Construction of property settlement agreement incorporated into divorce decree, see Murphy v. Murphy, 64 Nev. 440, 183 P.2d 632.

Enforceability of agreement even though not adopted or approved by court, see Green v. Green, 66 Cal. App. 2d 50, 151 P.2d 679.

[80] Flores v. Arroyo, 15 Cal. Rptr. 87, 364 P.2d 263; Vai v. Bank of America, 15 Cal. Rptr. 71, 346 P.2d 247; Lee v. Lee (Wash.), 178 P.2d 296.

adjusted and settled outside the court by their contract, the decree constitutes a final determination as to such community property interests and cannot with regard thereto be subjected to collateral attack by one of the spouses for any cause, including fraud, unless the decree is void on its face.[81] Suit may be brought, of course, in the court which entered the decree, to have the decree amended and reformed because of fraud by the other spouse in inducing the agreement to the property settlement.[82] What is the effect of such a property settlement agreement approved by the court so far as concerns property outside the jurisdiction of the court? If the property settlement agreement contains no reference at all, and indicates no intention to have it apply to property outside the court's jurisdiction, there is certainly nothing to prevent one of the spouses seeking a division of the property in the jurisdiction in which it is located.[83] But even if the property settlement agreement purports to relate to all community property, certainly if it does so only in general terms, on the basis of the fact that the court granting the divorce has no jurisdiction over property having its *situs* in another state, a court of the state in which the land is located can properly hold that the agreement and the decree confirming it can have no effect so far as such property is concerned and could not have been intended to relate to such property.[84] However, if the agreement confirmed by the divorce decree specifically includes property located in another state, a court of the latter state should, on the ground of comity and if convinced that there was no fraud or mistake in the making of the agreement, give it effect.

The effect upon the property settlement agreement of a reconciliation between the spouses has been the subject of many cases. It is not intended to enter into a discussion of the matter here, but some illustrative cases are cited in the note below.[84a]

---

[81] Berman v. Thomas, 41 Ariz. 457, 19 P.2d 685; Bullock v. Bullock, 131 Wash. 339, 230 P. 130.

Binding effect of community property settlement approved by court, see Herbert v. American Soc. of Composers, Authors & Publishers, 210 La. 240, 26 So.2d 732.

Fraud not extrinsic so as to entitle to relief, see Mazour v. Mazour, 64 Nev. 245, 180 P.2d 103.

[82] Senter v. Senter, 70 Cal. 619, 11 P. 782, wherein a defrauded wife was also enabled to have set aside a conveyance by the husband of community property which should have been divided between them and of which division she had been deprived by the husband's fraudulent representations.

[83] Rawlings v. Stokes, 194 La. 206, 193 So. 589.

[84] See Taylor v. Taylor, 192 Cal. 71, 218 P. 756, 51 A.L.R. 1074; Rawlings v. Stokes, 194 La. 206, 193 So. 589.

[84a] See, e.g., Tyson v. Tyson, 61 Ariz. 329, 149 P.2d 674; Luis v. Cavin, 88 Cal. App. 2d 107, 191 P.2d 527; Mundt v. Conn. Gen. Life Ins. Co., 35 Cal. App. 2d 416, 95 P.2d 966; Barham v. Barham (Cal. App.), 185 P.2d 420; Lundy v. Lundy, 79 Ida. 185, 312 P.2d 1028; La. Civ. Code, art. 155, as amended; Cox v. Mailander (Tex. Civ. App.), 178 S. W. 2d 1012, w/e ref'd.

Not only may court consider gifts from the community to the separate

§ 232.   — Effect of previous gifts or advances.

Ordinarily, the use by or advances to one spouse of community property for his or her private benefit or purposes should be considered in dividing the community property. Whatever amount has been received or taken by one spouse from the community property to be used for his or her own private benefit or purposes should be debited against that spouse's share of the community property.[85] If it is definitely clear that it was intended by the spouses that such amount was intended to be a gift from the community to that spouse, there is no reason why the remainder of the community property should not be equally divided between the spouses without charging the donee with the amount received by way of gift.[86] No undue presumptions should be indulged that a gift was intended. This has been overdone in some states.[87]

§ 233.   — Miscellaneous effects; insurance, pensions.

The division of the community property is not always easy of accomplishment, even allowing for such methods as selling the property and dividing the proceeds or evaluating the property and making an allowance of money to one spouse in lieu of his or her share in the property.[88] Developments of our complex way of life have introduced property interests, the division of which are accompanied by difficulties not previously contemplated.[89] Among these may be mentioned life

estate of a spouse, it may also take into consideration gift from spouse's separate estate to the community, according to Nace v. Nace (Ariz. App.), 432 P.2d 896.

[85] Using community funds to pay for improvements on a spouse's separate property is one example of this. See ante, Chaps. VI, VIII.

Effect of husband's commingling of his separate funds with community funds where in excess of community funds taken by him to pay taxes on his separate property and to make gifts to relatives. Blaine v. Blaine, 63 Ariz. 100, 159 P.2d 786, holding that commingling did not deprive spouse from taking credit for advancements to community.

Consideration of use for private purposes as arising upon dissolution of community by reason of death of spouse, see ante, § 214. See also Abunza v. Olivier (La.), 88 So.2d 815; Campbell v. Campbell (N.M.), 310 P.2d 266; Beeler v. Beeler (Tex.), 363 S. W. 2d 305; In re Hickman's Estate (Wash.), 250 P.2d 524.

[86] The Arizona court, however, which has a discretion to partition the community property as it considers that the circumstances warrant, has taken into account a gift or donation by the husband to the wife from the community property, in ordering a division of the remaining community property. Schwartz v. Schwartz, 52 Ariz. 105, 79 P.2d 501, 116 A.L.R. 633. And see cases cited in annotation following that case, 116 A.L.R. 638.

[87] See ante, Chaps. VI, VIII.

[88] See ante, § 227.

[89] Effect of awards of certain community property to one spouse as changing ownership so as to avoid insurance policy covering property, see Coffin v. Northwestern Mutual Fire Ass'n, 43 Idaho 1, 249 P. 89, 48 A.L.R. 1225.

Example of division of community property which included home, auto, bonds, insurance policies, bank accounts, pension rights, etc., see Fahnestock v. Fahnestock, 76 Cal. App. 2d 817, 174 P.2d 660.

Liability for costs of divorce proceeding, etc., see § 185.

insurance policies, pensions, old age benefits and other matters of a similar nature. It is particularly difficult to consider division where there are rights or interests in any of these which are community in character, as by reason of community funds or earnings having been paid on account of them, but as to which the right to payment in return has not yet come to maturity. Reference has already been made in preceding chapters to life insurance policies[90] and as to pensions and the like[91] as community or separate in character, and particularly as regards life insurance as to the right of the husband to use community funds to insure his own life for the benefit of some third person.[92]

In respect of a pension which has not yet become payable at the time of divorce but toward which deductions have been made from wages or salary of the husband which are community in character, it would appear that the amount of community funds which have gone toward the establishment of the pension right might be calculated and half that amount credited to the wife upon the division of the community property. It might, and perhaps more properly would be, considered that any allowance for support made to the wife would be sufficiently in lieu of any other adjustment, particularly as the support might ultimately and in fact be paid in whole or in part from the pension. Yet again, the court might evaluate the interest in the pension fund which the husband has acquired through the use of community funds and consider that value in dividing the community property, giving the wife community property equivalent thereto.[93] Similarly, where spouses are divorced at the time the husband is receiving a pension, even though the right to the pension has been acquired through deductions from wages or salary which are community in character, allowances for support of the wife might be considered in lieu of any community interest that she has therein, particularly as such support might come in whole or in part anyway from such pension. This might be especially true where the court has some discretion in dividing community property or in providing for allowances for support. If it is considered that community property should be divided equally, and all the wage deductions that went toward building up the right to the pension were community funds, half of the pension proceeds should be awarded to the wife. If the husband had begun to make contributions toward the pension, by

[90] See ante, §§ 79, 123, 143.

[91] See ante, §§ 62, 75.

[92] See ante, § 123.

[93] In Crossan v. Crossan, 35 Cal. App. 2d 39, 94 P.2d 609, where the husband was a state employee and had been contributing from his earnings— which were community property — to the State Employees' Retirement Fund from which he might receive a pension upon the happening of certain events provided for, the court declared that he had no property or contract right in such fund, but that nevertheless his interest was a valuable one, purchased with community funds. Accordingly, the court evaluated the right in the fund and considered this valuation in dividing the community property equally between the spouses.

wage deductions before he was married, the proportion of separate funds and community funds which went into building up the pension right might be considered, and the wife awarded half of that proportion of the pension built up by the wage deductions from community property.[94]

The question of life insurance is particularly difficult, and is complicated by questions of whether the policies were taken out before or during marriage, whether the beneficiary is the insured's estate, the other spouse or a third person, whether the right to change the beneficiary is reserved, and so on. Some of these matters have been previously discussed.[95] It is not feasible to go deeply into questions involving in themselves considerations of an independent branch of the law, i. e., the law of insurance.[96] It is extremely advisable, of course, that upon divorce especial consideration should be given to matters of insurance and the community interests of the spouses adjusted. Where the husband has insured his life in the wife's favor, paying premiums with community funds, it is usually considered that he has made a gift of community property to the wife.[97] Such a policy should be turned over to the wife, with the obligation thereafter upon her to continue the payment of premiums, in order that the gift to her may be effectively carried to a conclusion. Naturally, if the wife prefers the cash surrender value of the policy or wishes it to become a paid-up policy at whatever its value at the time of divorce would be, that should be her privilege.[98]

In the case of a policy upon the life of the wife, with the husband as beneficiary, and premiums paid from community funds, it should not be considered, in ordinary circumstances, a gift of community property to the husband, for this puts it into the power of the husband, by virtue of his management of the community property, to make gifts from the community property to himself.[99] It should, ordinarily, be considered as community property. Hence, though the policy might be turned over to the husband to keep and continue premium payments thereon, proper allowance of equal value should be made to the wife, based not merely upon the value of the community funds so far used to pay premiums but at least upon the cash surrender value of the policy. In this situation, as well as in the situation where the husband

---

[94] Wife's interest in old age benefits, upon dissolution of marriage by divorce, being received by husband under Social Security Act, see 15 So. Calif. Law Rev. 226.

[95] See ante, §§ 79, 123, 143.

[96] See Couch, Cyclopedia of Insurance Law; Vance, Insurance, 2nd Ed.; Huie, Community Property Law as Applied to Life Insurance, 17 Tex. Law Rev. 121, 18 Tex. Law Rev. 121.

[97] See ante, § 143.

[98] In Tompkins v. Tompkins (Cal. App.), 187 P.2d 840, where insurance policy on husband's life in favor of wife was taken out during marriage and premiums paid with community funds, it was proper for court to order husband to pay wife amounts necessary for premiums accruing after divorce, so as to protect continuance of her insurance interest in the husband.

[99] As to this, including the contrary view in Texas, see ante, § 143.

has insured his own life and made his estate the beneficiary, in which case the policy and its proceeds are community property, proper adjustments should be made in favor of the wife. Consideration may properly be given to the fact that the husband will thereafter pay premiums from his separate property, and the proportion of the premiums paid with community funds and with separate funds may be considered in arriving at what proportion of the proceeds would constitute community property. It would be fair to allow the wife, upon division at the time of divorce, an amount equal in value to half of the proceeds of the policy that would represent community property. But certainly, as we have already intimated, at the very least the cash surrender value of the policy at the time of divorce should be a basis of evaluation.[1] Consideration should also be given to the fact that the policy might have been taken out by the husband before marriage. Even though the policy be considered the husband's separate property, the subsequent use of community funds to pay premiums establishes a proportionate interest in the policy in the community.[2] Where the husband has insured his own life in favor of some third person and paid premiums with community funds, this ordinarily represents a gift of community funds which the husband has no authority to make and is detrimental to the wife's interests.[3] Where such a policy is in existence at the time of the divorce, proper allowances should be made to the wife on the basis of an interest in half the value of the proceeds to be derived from the policy.

Much of the litigation seems to have resulted from the fact that upon the divorce there was no adjustment of the respective rights in insurance policies.[4] Ordinarily, there is no reason why this cannot be avoided.[5]

[1] In Womack v. Womack, 141 Tex. 299, 172 S. W. 2d 307, life insurance policies were obtained during marriage, three on wife's life and one on husband's and, upon divorce, court held that cash surrender value constituted community property.

Increase in cash value of life-insurance policies by reason of premium payments during marriage were credited to community. Blaine v. Blaine, 63 Ariz. 100, 159 P.2d 786, wherein payments were from fund in which separate funds had been commingled with community funds.

Cash surrender value, see Arnold v. Arnold, 76 Cal. App. 2d 877, 174 P.2d 674.

[2] See ante, § 79.

[3] See ante, §§ 123, 143.

[4] In Metropolitan Life Ins. Co. v. Skov, 51 F. Supp. 470, decided under Washington law, notice that at the time the spouses had been divorced, the attorney for the plaintiff-wife stated that there were no property rights to be adjudicated, overlooking entirely policies taken out by the husband. This oversight was responsible for the expense and necessity of the litigation in this case. The case is well worthy of examination because of its discussion of the respective rights of spouses, upon divorce, in insurance policies. See note to case, 18 Tulane Law Rev. 487, discussing rules in several states. Divorce of insured and beneficiary as affecting latter's rights, see cases, 52 A.L.R. 386; 59 A. L. R. 172.

[5] In Berry v. Franklin State Bank & Trust Co., 186 La. 623, 173 So. 126, where policies on the life of the husband, payable to his estate, were taken out during the marriage, and the spouses subsequently divorced, the

court held that an attempted property settlement between them was void, and that upon the husband's death the proceeds were community property to half of which the divorced wife was entitled. The trial court seems to have deducted from the wife's half the amount of the premiums paid by the husband after the dissolution of the marriage by the divorce, and this seems not to have been disapproved by the appellate court.

CHAPTER XI

TAXATION

§ 234. In general.

Even in a work concerned primarily with the principles of the law of community property, one cannot ignore the subject of taxation which permeates the activities of civilized men. On the other hand, the vast expanse of this subject renders it impossible of treatment in any book not designed for that specific purpose. It would be a work of supererogation to attempt to expand this volume into a detailed treatment of tax law, in view of the many competent and excellent works available; accordingly, the existing situation is given only the most abbreviated treatment that good conscience will permit.

§ 235. Property taxes — In Spanish law.

Under the Spanish law, taxes assessed against community property were the obligation of both spouses as was any other debt or obligation of the community, and the half-interest of each spouse in the community property was liable for a moiety of such taxes. Thus, the wife was liable for a moiety of such taxes, but since the management of the community property was placed in the hands of the husband, it was incumbent upon him as such manager to see to the payment of those taxes, although they were charged equally against the interest of each spouse. The wife's liability for a moiety of such taxes might be enforceable against her, of course, where her share of the community property had come into her managerial control.[1] But the wife was never in any way liable for taxes which were separate obligations of the husband alone.[2] On the other hand, she was naturally liable

---

[1] See Azevedo, Nos. 18, 19, to Nov. Rec. Law 9, Book 10, Title 4.

[2] Novísima Recopilación, Book 10, Title 11, Law 2.

for taxes assessed against her own separate property, and the property itself was subject to liability therefor. Of course, if she had formally agreed that the husband should manage any of her separate property for her, it was incumbent on the husband as such manager to see to the payment of the taxes. Incidentally, while she was prohibited by statute from going surety for the husband or binding herself jointly or severally with him for his obligations, that prohibition did not apply to her joint undertaking and obligation with her husband to obtain money to pay taxes against her.[3]

§ 236.   — American jurisdictions.

In our community property states, taxes assessed against community property are an obligation of the community, although for purposes of convenience they may be assessed against the spouse in whose name the title stands.[4] It is incumbent upon the spouse having the management of the community property against which the tax is assessed to pay such tax.[5] If the tax is not paid, the property in question may be proceeded against to enforce payment of the tax.

Although ordinarily the community property may be liable as a whole for the tax assessed against it and the tax lien may be against the property as a whole,[6] this does not obviate the fact that the tax is, in actuality, assessed equally against the interests of husband and wife. The fact that all property of the husband may be exempt from taxation does not release the wife's share of the community property from liability for half of the tax imposed on the community property, and the tax has been held enforceable against her half of the community property so taxed, to the extent of selling her interest if necessary. This liability for taxes has been said to be superior to any public policy that the community property should be preserved intact during the marriage for the benefit of the family.[7]

[3] Novísima Recopilación, Book 10, Title 11, Law 3.

[4] See Oglesby v. Poage, 45 Ariz. 23, 40 P.2d 90.

"It is our opinion that it is immaterial whether such community property stands assessed on the tax records in the name of the husband or wife, or both, and that, if the husband pays the taxes on community property without any specific grant of power from the wife, the law will imply authority in him to do so by virtue of his family relation, particularly unless it is shown that it is done contrary to the expressed wishes of the wife." Baca v. Village of Belen, 30 N.M. 546, 240 P. 803.

[5] See Baca v. Village of Belen, 30 N.M. 546, 240 P. 803, "We think his position as head of the family warrants his payment of taxes levied upon community property out of the proceeds of community personal property of which he has the management and control, and during coverture the sole power of disposition other than testamentary."

[6] See Baca v. Village of Belen, 30 N.M. 546, 240 P. 803.

[7] See Oglesby v. Poage, 45 Ariz. 23, 40 P.2d 90. Notice that the exemption of all property of the spouse applied to the share of the community property as well as to the separate property of the spouse.

So far as concerns the separate property of husband and wife, each is liable for the taxes on his or her separate property, as in the case of any other natural persons owning property.[8] If the separate property of the wife has been placed by her under her husband's management, as such manager it is incumbent upon him to see to the payment of the taxes.[9]

§ 237.   Income tax.

At this writing residents of the community property states have little, if any, income tax advantages over citizens of noncommunity property states. The husband and wife are to be treated as separate taxpayers as to their respective portions of the community income, and each must report one-half of such income as his own.[10] This is merely a result of the principle that the husband and wife are present owners of the community property in equal shares. The question of what is community property and what is separate property is essentially one of local law.[11] Similarly, local law governs as to the validity of agreements changing the nature of property to be acquired, even though it may have tax consequences.[12]

Spouses may elect to file separate returns or a joint return. If separate returns are filed each spouse should report one-half the income, and is entitled to one-half of the total community deductions which would be available to both of them if they filed a joint return.[10] Separate losses or deductions are available, however, only to the spouse owning the property or incurring the expense.[14] With respect to the dividend exclusion and credit, this is available to both spouses, and the amount of the dividend taxable to each spouse is determined by applying local community property concepts.[15]

More difficult problems are to be encountered when the community is dissolved by divorce or death. With respect to divorce, all income earned prior to the divorce is taxed one-half to the husband and one-half to the wife, and each must report his half, even though

[8] See Spears v. San Antonio, 110 Tex. 618, 223 S. W. 166, as to personal liability of wife for assessments upon her property for special improvements.

[9] See Oakes, Speer's Marital Rights in Texas (4th ed.), § 199.

[10] Poe v. Seaborn, 282 U.S. 101, 75 L. Ed. 239, 51 S. Ct. 58.

As to problem where spouses have separated or live apart without any property agreement or settlement, including situation where one is in a community property state and one is not, see, e.g., Ritz, The Married Woman and the Federal Income Tax, 14 Tax Law Rev. 437.

[11] U.S. v. Stapf, 375 U.S. 118, 11 L. Ed. 2d 195, 84 S. Ct. 248.

[12] Helvering v. Hickman, 70 F.2d 985.

[13] Mellie E. Stewart, 35 BTA 406, aff'd 95 F.2d 821.

[14] Irma Jones Hunt, 47 BTA 829; W. O. Allen, 22 TC 70.

[15] Mertens, Law of Federal Income Taxation, § 19.08.

it is received subsequent to the divorce.[16] The income tax results of dissolution by death are much the same.[17] In either case each spouse is entitled to half the deductions properly chargeable against such income.[18]

§ 238.   Estate tax.

The basic relationship of the federal estate tax and community property is that the surviving spouse's one-half of the community property is not includable in the decedent's estate.[19] Similarly, only one-half of community debts may be charged to the decedent.[20] The marital deduction must be specifically considered, for if the decedent spouse owned no separate property, his estate is entitled to no marital deduction. On the other hand, if the estate is entitled to a marital deduction, it may be satisfied out of community property.[21]

A more complex problem deals with the practical aspect of assessing the estate tax and the statute of limitations, usually three years.[22] Certainly the return is required to list the property of the decedent and to categorize it as community or separate. If no return is filed[23] or if a return is fraudulent[24] the government is subject to no statute of limitations. If an item of property is completely omitted from the return, the Internal Revenue Service has six years within which to assess the tax.[25] This extended period does not apply "if such item is disclosed in the return . . . in a manner adequate to apprise the Secretary . . . of the nature and amount of such item."[26] On the other hand, what should be the result if an item that is actually separate property of the decedent is listed as community property? Should the usual three-year statute apply, should the government be allowed six years as in the case of an incomplete return, or should there be no statute of limitations as in the case where no return is filed? It seems clear that the latter would be inapplicable since a return was, in fact, filed. As to the six year period, this should also be inapplicable since the item was not omitted but rather affirmatively

[16] C.I.R. v. King, 69 F.2d 639.

[17] Mertens, Law of Federal Income Taxation, § 19.45.

[18] Mertens, Law of Federal Income Taxation, § 19.42.

[19] Duncan v. U.S., 247 F.2d 845.

To same effect, see In re Heringer's Estate, 38 Wash. 2d 399, 230 P.2d 297, 299, citing and following de Funiak, 1st edition, § 251.

Same application to Colorado state inheritance tax, see People v. Bejarano (Colo.), 358 P.2d 866, approving view by de Funiak in 43 Va. L. Rev. 49.

California quasi-community property, see Estate of Rogers, 53 Cal. Rptr. 572.

[20] U.S. v. Stapf, 375 U.S. 118, 11 L. Ed. 2d 195, 84 S. Ct. 248.

[21] Rabkin & Johnson, Federal Income, Gift and Estate Taxation, §§ 52.06, 53.04.

[22] IRC, § 6501 (a).

[23] IRC, § 6501 (c) (3).

[24] IRC, § 6501 (c) (1).

[25] IRC, § 6501 (e) (2).

[26] IRC, § 6501 (e) (2).

disclosed, and the error was as to the character of the property. The upshot of this could well be that on the death of one spouse, property, though in fact separate property, might be listed as community property and the tax paid accordingly. Then, on the death of the survivor, after the statute of limitations had run, the government would be precluded from asserting that the property was separate and more tax due, but the heirs of the first spouse could assert the separate status of the property to prevent its inclusion in the estate of the decedent spouse.

§ 239.   Gift tax.

Gifts made by spouses in community property jurisdictions to third persons are made one-half by each spouse. This arises by virtue of the principle that each spouse owns one-half of the community property. A partition of community property between husband and wife is not a taxable gift,[27] but the transmutation of separate property into community property is a gift to the extent of one-half the value of the separate property.[28] As to gifts from one spouse to another, the marital deduction is not applicable to property held by the spouses as community property at the time of the gift.[29]

---

[27] Rabkin & Johnson, Federal Income, Gift and Estate Taxation, § 51.07 (7).

[28] Herbert v. Damner, 3 TC 638.

[29] IRC, § 2523 (b) (1)

INDEX

References are to sections unless otherwise indicated. The addition of the letter "n" to a section number indicates that the matter referred to is in a footnote.